Man Is Not Enough

Why America's Morals Are Dying, and
Our Opportunity Is Now for God's Renewal

by
Carl W. Wilson

Andragathia, Inc., Books
Fayetteville, GA 30214-0642

Copyright 1998 by Carl W. Wilson

Charts by Beth Van Dyke

Most Scriptures are taken from NEW AMERICAN STANDARD BIBLE®,
Copyright © 1960, 1962, 1963, 1968, 1971, 1972, 1973, 1975, 1977, 1994
by The Lockman Foundation. There are exceptions where the NIV is used.
Copyright © 1973, 1978, 1984, 1988 by The Zondervon Corporation and are
indicated by an *. Used by permission according to their standards.

Published by Renewal Publishing Company & Andragathia, Inc., Atlanta 30214-0642
Website: .brave good men.org
Email address: cwilso@bellsouth.net

Library of Congress Cataloging-in-Publication Data
Carl W. Wilson
*Man Is Not Enough: Why America's Morals Are Dying and
Our Opportunity Is Now for God's Renewal*
ISBN 0-9668181-0-5

CONTENTS

CHARTS AND GRAPHS

Acknowledgements

The production of this book has occurred over three years, and a number of people have been invaluable in helping in the following ways: Melanie Duncan as librarian and part-time editor; Margaret Shuman as editor and designer according to New Chicago Style; Julie Turner for typesetting, and Charlotte Darnell in fixing corrections and setting type. Also, Mrs. Shuman and Mrs. Darnell composed the index; Sherry Baker, my secretary, spent hours of typing, editing, and attending to much other detail; Beth Van Dyke of Walker Printing did the art work; and most of all I thank my wife Sara Jo, whose detailed editing, patient suggestions, and corrections have been invaluable and her loving care kept me going.

There are over twenty-four pages of endnotes with hundreds of references to books and periodicals to which we have tried to give due credit for ideas and in many cases for useful quotations. It is unnecessary and counterproductive to try to thank all of these. Much effort has been made to try to comply with the publisher's and author's wishes in regard to their copyright privileges, especially where it may possibly exceed what is commonly regarded as the fair-use-rule.

Some books have been especially helpful and have been referred to often and quoted several times with permission. Details of these and all others are in the Endnotes. But I especially want to thank the following: A.M.S. Press for use of Otto Kieffer's old but invaluable work, *Sexual Life in Ancient Rome*; Simon & Schuster for the use of the renewed Will Durant's great work, *The Life of Greece*, for insights to the Greek democracy; to Christina Hoff Sommers', *Who Stole Feminism?* for her disclosure of perversions of "gender" feminists; Miriam Schneir, editor, *Feminism: The Essential Historical Writings*, by Vintage Books, gave firsthand information of documents; Random House's book by Peter G. Peterson, *Will American Grow Up Before It Grows Old?* furnished authoritative information and graphs which have been used to shed light on the economic future; Orlando Patterson's *The Ordeal of Integration*, produced by Counterpoint, was balanced and comprehensive in giving the picture of the Afro-American community; while Ellis Cose's books, *The Rage of a Privileged Class and A Man's World*, greatly helped look through the eyes of the African American man. The most important work on youth in past history was that edited by Stephen Bertman, *The Conflict of Generations in Ancient Greece and Rome*, published by Br. Gruner of Amsterdam and distributed by Benjamins North America, Inc. While I have done other extensive reading on the subject, Jeffrey Satinover's book, *Homosexuality and the Politics of Truth*, published by Baker Books, contained much on the subject and is given in an authoritative way. We are grateful to the University of Chicago Press for the use of their copyrighted book by James Davidson Hunter, *Evangelicalism: The Coming Generation*, for insights concerning evangelical church trends. John T. Noonan's *Contraception* (1965, 1986) helped in understanding the history of this matter, and we appreciate Harvard University Press for permission to quote from it. I could not have written this

Acknowledgements

book without the insights of some of my great teachers. Dr. Carl F. H. Henry's teachings on religious epistemology enabled me to understand the influence of the secular culture on Christian revelation and how to divide the truth of God from that of the many perversions of our time. The work under Dr. Everette F. Harrison on my Master of Theology Degree at Fuller Theological Seminary helped me encounter the idea of the main thesis of this book, and the study of Hellenistic Greek under Dr. George Eldon Ladd brought me into encounter with the Greek culture that launched me into further study that gave helpful understanding of trends.

I am grateful to Dr. Howard Hendricks of Dallas Theological Seminary who, because of the interest of his graduate assistant Barry Leventhal, allowed me to give an advanced presentation of the subject in the Christian Education lectures at Dallas Seminary many years ago. The ideas that crystallized there became the backbone of this work. My good friend Charles Dunahoo, coordinator of the Christian Education and Publications for the Presbyterian Church in America, was helpful by reading and criticizing this long manuscript, and he and members of my board encouraged me to persist in doing the work.

While it may seem a pious cliche, I have persisted for many years in examining the extensive data for this important book only because Jesus Christ called me to do it and His Spirit continued to motive me when I might have given up. I acknowledge His guidance, and I pray for blessing on you as you read this. I alone am responsible to Him for what is said here.

Preface

This book is a reporter's view of the historical journey of the United States: how its highly scientific and technical society has developed and grown in astonishing brilliance; at the same time, it is a view of the causes and the process of this country's spiritual and moral decline. The book's purpose is to show that the moral decline of America has occurred in a zigzag fashion for about two hundred years and that the nation is now probably in the last "zag" of improvement before progressing to moral meltdown, unless spiritual renewal soon occurs. To understand this, the biblical basis of human nature and the way it affects and is affected by culture has been studied and reported. In Paul's epistle to the Romans 1 - 2:3, he traces the path of degradation by man's bias to sin in the cultures of the Greek Democracy and the Roman Republic, and this path of sin has been examined and confirmed in history in some detail. Then the moral decline of the United States itself is examined in the light of Paul's description of this pattern of demise described in Romans.

Paul shows how the path of sin leads to a moral meltdown that results in anarchistic, judgmental attitudes of individuals and groups against each other. America's present moral crisis is presented in the first chapter of this book by descriptions given by leading historical analysts who say that group conflict in America and the world is nearing such conditions. These historians are those who in the past have been highly accurate in anticipating major trends. Such conditions have been the trap into which the Devil has led all past civilizations when he has brought about their demise.

The second chapter is the key to the book: if the reader understands the pattern of moral decline outlined by Paul there, he will see how America has arrived at its present situation and why it is in crisis. If the reader understands chapter two, the whole book will make much sense. By discerning this demonic path of sin from the history of Greece, Rome, and then America, the concluding solutions for renewal will be seen as a reasonable opportunity for God's power to bring renewal.

Since I see the major problem is theological, or caused by man's bias to intellectually reject God to be free from His control, I have sought to also focus on a correction in theology for churches in order to facilitate them to assist in stopping the moral decline. The most important Scripture in the Bible for influencing the change of religious teaching and practices in previous times, a passage which influenced Martin Luther in Germany, John Calvin in Geneva, Ulrich Zwingli of Zurich, the Anabaptists and later John Wesley in England, is Romans 1:16-17. This centers on the quote from the Old Testament, "The righteous shall live by faith." What Luther, Calvin, Wesley, and others saw in this passage was pivotal for understanding Christ in their day.

Examination of the context of this strategic passage shows that Paul never intended those verses to be interpreted only as salvation in the sense of justification from guilt of sin. His description of the path of human sin and the breakdown of society given in that chapter, salvation must also include overcoming the power of sin. He is also declaring the good news that God's power can save the believer *from the power of sin* that had progressively grown and brought tribulation to the Greco-Roman world. My analysis is that the solutions of the Reformers fit their age and were correct for them, but, because they focused mainly on their respective historic times, they spoke less about the context of salvation from the power of sin. In their world; the Reformers emphasized only the part of the truth of the gospel that was most applicable. Thus, my critical evaluation in this book is not only secular but theological.

In doing a second graduate degree at Fuller Theological Seminary, Pasadena, California many years ago, I became involved in Greek and Roman history. This led to seeing a pattern of moral decline in these nations that fit the Apostle Paul's descriptions about the inclinations of the weakness of human nature. The pattern of the decline of morals seemed to inevitably lead to the demise of the civilizations. Afterward, I expanded my studies to the history of other civilizations. In each of them it was interesting and yet frightening to see that the same pattern of increasingly rejecting one supreme God was the cause of the moral decline. I began to speak on this and in the 1970s I was invited to give the Christian Education Lectures at a leading evangelical seminary showing the implications for Christian Education. As I have watched the pattern of moral decline in America, I have felt the urgency to write this book.

I have divided what was once one long book into three books to present the whole picture. This book, *Man Is Not Enough*, presents and documents the pattern of the decline of civilizations, confirmed in Greek and Roman history but with special emphasis given to understanding America's path and opportunity for renewal. The second book, *Dark Shadows in the New Day of Science*, is concerned with the intellectual movement in the Western world which has led America's moral decline. While *Man Is Not Enough* covers the failure of the intellectual social theories, *Dark Shadows* reviews these briefly, but focuses primarily on the perversions of the scientific views that underlie the social theories and have been the source of the theological problem which is the root cause of the decline in America. The third book, *The Call*, is a review of the decline of the civilizations of the people of the Bible, again showing Paul's pattern. That book gives more detailed presentation of a biblical solution based on analysis given in the other two books.

Our nation's creative culture is now reaching its apex of brilliance from a material and technical point of view; but it is also now nearing the end of a long decline into spiritual poverty and the loss of moral control. Some historians view nations according to two outcomes: one is the accomplishment of the "vision of the anointed," as Thomas Sowell calls the plans of the educated elite, and the other is the "tragedy" in civilization's moral decline. From the optimistic one, "the vision" for America seems on the horizon of high development, but from the other, tragedy is much nearer than most intellectuals dare presume. This feeling that material progress is going forward forms the background for demonic deception which allows acceptance of further moral decay until there occurs a sudden meltdown to confusion and trouble.

I am not a prophet who can predict the exact moment the national Titanic of the United States will sink, but I am saying the time for renewal is urgent, or it will be very difficult to change course. Evidences are, trouble could begin about the year 2000, and hit hard later. I believe there can by God's grace be real spiritual renewal and Christian obedience, then He could intervene and give resolution to our great social problems. It is my view that America is now in a window of reaction to human sin and liberal humanistic ideas, and that this is an important and great opportunity that Christian believers must not let pass without proper and committed action. This book thus offers a solemn warning, but by seeing what has occurred, it points to the way of a positive solution.

At the demise of most great civilizations, the saddest part is the deception and denial of the intellectual elite leaders and their failure to see what is happening. As Jesus put it, "They are blind guides of the blind . . ." (Matthew 15:14; 23:16-26). In this book and the companion, *Dark Shadows,* I quote several prominent authors who show that America's intellectual elite refuse even to look at the facts of the failures in their vision. The worst part is they adamantly refuse to acknowledge that the moral problems are related to theological and spiritual issues. Unbelief in God (not lack of religion) is the most significant mark of a dying culture, because faith in man's ability and importance is so exaggerated. Most last-days religion is man-centered, designed to give therapeutic help, but does not really change the underlying problems. America today has a pluralism of religions and is intolerant of true faith in the one creator God. Most modern religion is centered in man and his needs even in many Christian churches.

There is a sense of growing disillusionment and urgent prayer by many American Christians. But there are millions of people who are looking for honesty in issues, even though the answers may not be popular. I hope you are one of those who believes the gospel of Jesus Christ is still the power of God for salvation and that "The righteous (in our time) will live by faith."

Carl W. Wilson, Fall, 1998

Part I:
The Biblical Pattern of
Decline of Civilizations

Chapter 1
America's Opportunity, or Pandaemonium?

A Story of Concern

Several years ago in a Colorado county there was a critical problem that developed that endangered the valley where the majority of the population lived. The sheriff who was responsible for informing the people and helping them to reach safety found himself in an excruciating situation where he was able to help only a small number of the people who were in serious danger. Rains had been coming down heavier than usual over an extended time, and people sensed that conditions were bad and growing much worse. The weather authorities and sheriff had sent preliminary warnings, but the people felt these were overdone. They had gone through some foreboding rainy times before, and they were unwilling to leave their possessions to get to a more safe area. Then the rains suddenly came in even greater downpours, and the flood waters rapidly built up in the Great River.

The sheriff started sending out warnings that the people in the valley must begin to leave. Then two things happened: Suddenly the rains stopped in the lower part of the valley and the sun began to shine, giving the residents and visitors hope the worst was over and things would be better. Secondly, about that time, the sheriff received emergency word that the control mechanism for the relief valves of the dam, which was holding a huge reservoir of water in the head-waters of the river, was unexpectedly not working. Unless there was some release for the force that was building up behind the dam, it would soon certainly give way. This would release a wall of water that would utterly destroy almost everyone in the valley.

The people did not grasp the urgency of the situation. For years, the people of the valley had been informed about the engineering superiority of that dam and had been told that it would never break. Added to the confidence in this engineering was a false optimism from the return of sunshine. The people had not been willing to move when early warnings had been given and had not taken seriously the warnings even as suddenly the rains got appreciably much worse. As the sheriff sought to move people, he found they were not responding. He knew the force about to be unleashed if the dam were to break would be unimaginably greater than the people would believe possible. All he could do was send out the final warning, and help the few people who did believe him to make it to safety. The realization that very few were responding left him, the dam authorities, and the weather people searching anxiously for a solution to relieve the force or to evacuate the people.[1]

4   *Opportunity, or Pandaemonium?*

Time for Anxiety in the United States

America has created the most amazing civilization of industry, technology, and communications that the world has ever known, and seemingly has even greater promise for tomorrow. But today America is facing the great danger that an enormous dam of hostility has been built up between various factions of American people and against controlling authorities. There is great danger that the moral control of the social walls which hold the hate in check will give way, thus flooding the land with barbaric violence such as has not before been experienced. Many like William Bennett identify the problem as a lack of virtue, or as Stephen L. Carter calls it, a loss of civility. Whatever one calls it, there is a sense that Americans have lost a sense of willingness to care for each other, to be patient with each other, and to work together to solve problems. Moreover, the teenage generation is expressing its anger in an irrational way. People seem to be increasingly committed to a selfish individualism that has accumulated anger in sympathetic groups—racial, class, ethnic, gender, sexual, gang, and the like. These feelings of hostility have grown through the years until the groups and individuals no longer care even to communicate in a reasonable way. Indeed, they have so deconstructed values to fit their own interpretations of right and wrong that it seems many *cannot* communicate any longer.

This book seeks to explain the origin of that accumulation of selfish individualistic hostility and its present intensity. The evidence is that it has grown out of distorted thinking derived from a human natural bias against God by people who want to be free to indulge in fulfilling their fleshly desires. *The root problem is this natural **bias against God for self**.* This has resulted in a deception and perversion of what the truth is about nature and about man, of what is right and wrong, and of what is best for mankind. This bias has been promoted by an educated elite who feel superior to others. They, because of their presumed intellectual superiority, feel they have a right to control education and government to promote everyone else's good. The distortions of this elite have developed this pent-up wall of explosive hostility by a multitude of groups that have grown out of these perverted views, and threatens to explode at any moment and flood our land with destruction against everyone, including those who are angry. This anti-God view has released most of the people from a sense of controlling accountability to divine standards and has allowed a takeover of pride, greed, and lust.

This wall of hate and suspicion is like a mighty wall of water about to be unleashed, or a huge accumulation of atomic power that is about to explode. A small error or misunderstanding causing fear from a number of factors could be a detonator that could go off at any moment, like a faulty valve causing the dam to overload and crack and break. It is vital that a solution to remove the force of the danger be found. Fortunately, there is a biblical answer of how God can enable His people to do this. But unfortunately most people who even see the problem have been motivated by such fear that accentuates their selfish desire to survive that they are not seeking a way to remove the threat. Moreover, there is skepticism that God or spiritual thinking has anything to do with the problem. This book seeks to show how to remove this destructive force.

American leaders are like the sheriff and the weathermen who can't get people to believe there is danger. While most Americans are alarmed at the moral disintegration, there is an unwillingness to sacrifice to do something about it. The American people are certainly facing an almost unimaginable flood of catastrophic evil, and very few believe there is a coming peril. If conditions continue, many will perish from the monstrous onslaught that is about to occur.

The story of what is occurring is that of the moral decline and possible breakdown of our civilization. But by understanding the source of the problem, it will also be seen that there is a great opportunity to begin to defuse the build-up and to begin to remove the powerful forces that threaten. Moreover, the data indicates that the story of the development of the conditions in America has occurred repeatedly to other people in history. In fact, most major civilizations have finally collapsed into tribulation under almost the same forces of evil that we face. The way this has occurred in two great civilizations other than America will be reviewed briefly.

A summary of the realization of the danger we are approaching in America is presented in this chapter by some of our most respected statesmen. The rest of the book will review the way our nation arrived at this point of peril. It will be evaluated by seeing the development of American thinking as well as by the statistical developments which together do not lie. In any society there are regularly losses of moral control and reigns of evil that are usually corrected. For over two hundred years, early American colonial civilization had some fluctuations of unbelief and evil without repudiating a standard of moral absolutes that allowed good development of a foundation.

But about the year 1800, there was a triumph of a small class of intellectually elite people that set in motion a zigzag trend of the nation's progressively rejecting faith in God. This unbelief has gradually freed men from a feeling of any accountability to God and caused moral deterioration. This rejection of God for selfish individualism reached its apex through secular educational control of American colleges, theological schools, and media about the year 1960, or at the time of the "Death of God" theologies and the demand by an elite corps of intellectuals to secularize and pluralize religion. Traditional Christian moral values were attacked as arrogant and intolerant. In America, the thinking slowly shifted from early belief in *the sovereignty of God* affirmed in the religious Reformation to *the sovereignty of the individual* to be free to do what he wants.

6   *Opportunity, or Pandaemonium?*

Secular governments at the federal and state levels, corporate business, the family, and even the churches have been involved in building this selfish man-centered wall of evil. In their present weak conditions, these institutions are not able to help contain these forces. God has let man, in his pride of self wisdom, pervert facts and construct a trap from his own desires into which we will fall. The time of troubles will come as a harvest of man's intellectual bias against the biblical God, and the deceptions that man has built as a result of pride. Man today believes that he can alone build a wonderful world without a transcendent Creator. Indeed, many intellectuals believe, as did Karl Marx, that faith in God is a hindrance to enlightenment and prosperity. These leaders in the western world have sown a harvest that will reap a whirlwind of evil. Man's sins are about to find him out and if God is true, His judgment must be near. The suffering will likely affect every class of individuals and will probably eventually involve the whole world.

Deception of American intellectuals has also resulted in mistakes in informational systems, in economic decisions, and in political social engineering, all of which could trigger a breakdown. These are like a faulty valve or a detonating device. These mistakes have reached a point which are so severe that one simple failure soon could release the walled-up hostility on everyone in America. The moral breakdown will likely introduce confusion, conflict, chaos, and anarchy and destroy most effective institutions of government. Much prosperity and many comforts, pleasures, securities, and health are being threatened. This threat, of course, seems preposterous to Americans who are accustomed to all problems being solved easily.

Most people assume this potential breakdown is a figment of imagination. Such has been the opinion in the times near the collapse of other great civilizations of the world which have died from such deception. There are now growing logical probabilities that detonating forces seem to be converging toward the year 2000 as the time that will cause the long developing forces to break loose and by mid-decade the forces of evil flood in. But because the more visible problems in areas such as the economy, crime, and various other evils seem a little diminished since about 1993, the American people are thinking maybe the rains of evil are about over. The sun seems to be shining again.

Unfortunately, today a great many people are focusing on the problems of a faulty valve, or the detonating charge that might ignite, rather than on the much larger social forces that these things may explode. The urgent need is to understand these and find a way to diminish these. For example, people today are fearful of the year 2000 computer problem that is likely to cause a breakdown of communications and result in the cause of dysfunction of institutions and public services. There are other clear dangers such as the Asian and world economic crisis. But, if there existed unity and respect and love for each other and our institutions, any technological or other problems could be patiently solved regardless of how inconvenient and confusing. The tragic fact is that these fears of chaotic conditions and the efforts to protect ourselves from them appears only to be accentuating an increase in selfish individualism that will cause greater hostilities and suffering. Only after reading and understanding the growth of the evil in America, can we see the real problem is *bias against God and for self* and how faith in God and the good news of Jesus Christ can really be the answer.

The Demonic Deception That Has Led to A Time for Decision and Action

When New York Senator Daniel Patrick Moynihan published his book, *Pandaemonium*,[2] William Safire thought he discovered an error in the title of the book by the learned Moynihan. Upon inquiry he was reminded that the word *Pandaemonium*—meaning "chaos" and "tumult"—was first used in Milton's *Paradise Lost*: "the walls of Pandaemonium, Citie, and proud seat of Lucifer." Moynihan explained that while the accepted spelling of the word has changed to *pandemonium*, Milton's meaning was appropriately chosen, and therefore the original spelling and meaning retained. Moynihan wrote, "Pandaemonium was inhabited by creatures quite convinced that the great Satan had their best interests at heart. Poor little devils." Moynihan describes how both the Marxists and the liberal West have missed what Satan was doing, proceeding in the direction they thought was their best interest. As one of the few men who predicted the fall of Communism, Moynihan is also on target in seeing America and many other nations of the world demonically deluded in believing that the path ahead is successful and pleasurable.

The real issue facing America is: will enough of the people be open to understand the need and reasons for change, *and then have the will to do so?* Malcolm Muggeridge, the outstanding British thinker, once said, "The most extraordinary thing about human beings is that they pursue ends which they know to be disastrous and turn their backs on ways which they know to be joyous."[3] *Man Is Not Enough* presents facts about the path we are taking, and will give difficult and, at times, unwanted solutions that can transform our increasing pain into security and pleasure, both individually and corporately.

I believe this time is not only an hour of peril, but one of great opportunity. The Greeks had a word, *kairos*, which meant "a fixed time, season, opportunity." When Os Guinness, the noted Christian scholar and sociologist, was interviewed by *Christianity Today*, he said, "My notion of the American hour is that it's a *kairos* moment that will be decisive one way or another. I expect the next ten to fifteen years will show which way it will go."[4] I hope this book will help you also see the opportunity and perils.

8   *Opportunity, or Pandaemonium?*

The Growth of Ethnic Hate as an Example of the Growing Forces

In past times, when values of societies had deteriorated into those springing from selfish materialism, the primary hope for the people involved has been to turn back to those people most like themselves in genetic origin, race, class, and religion and to unite together to fight for material objectives. This will be seen in upcoming chapters on Greece and Rome and has been evidenced in other dying societies. These ethnic or class distinctions seem the most prominent remaining foundation for security in a world of economic uncertainty and violence. But these group conflicts from *within* cause great suffering and weaken the nation for attack from *without*. The ethnic sources of the various peoples are now finding strong expression, and are a sign of a final time of trouble and possibly an end of civilization as we have known it.

Daniel Patrick Moynihan in *Pandaemonium* has described what is happening worldwide. He warns of signs of a great turmoil that is coming. Milton M. Gordon, professor emeritus of the University of Massachusetts at Amherst, has on the cover described Moynihan's current book as "a brilliant work of utmost importance. The specter of violent ethnic conflict and the fractious breakup of nations haunts the contemporary world." Moynihan elaborates:

> There are today just eight states on earth which both existed in 1914 and have not had their form of government changed by violence since then ....
> Of the remaining 170 or so contemporary states, some are too recently created to have known much recent turmoil, but for the greater number that have done so, far the most frequent factor involved has been ethnic conflict.[5]

Moynihan had previously stated:

> Obviously, we are at an end of the seventy-five year crisis of the European state system that went on from 1914 to 1989. Just as obviously, there is a halo effect as political economic liberalism makes its way from capital to capital around the world in the manner of *1984*. The age of totalitarians is ended. That claim to the future is over. The obvious question then is what ought we expect now?[6]

He writes, "Nation states no longer seem inclined to go to war with one another, but ethnic groups fight all the time." He points out that Africa and the Soviet Union have come apart and formed states along ethnic lines, with many in conflict.[7]

Moynihan, reflecting on a former book he wrote, warns us against only seeing this trend abroad and not in America:

> Nor for a moment do I think of ethnic conflict as something that happens elsewhere. *Beyond the Melting Pot* was an account of real, if contained, conflict. A third of a century later, the social condition of American cities

is hugely deteriorated. We have just, as I write, suffered our worst urban riot in a half-century [in Los Angeles.] A riot with a difference, new yet old. Asians were among the principal victims of violence against property. The current small-arms fighting in American cities is bound to escalate in terms both of weaponry and of aggression against whites; a role reversal, but the same drama.[8]

Later he refers to the maintaining of peaceful restraint in the current ethnic division of Czechoslovakia, and says:

The United States will need more than a few of these virtues, and will know more than it has known of grief. Grief of a different kind. We have known the grief of caste-imposed subjection; we must now expect caste retaliation. It is already there, on the streets . . . . Race—black—white— has been a primal division in American life, but never the sole division. It will now be dissolved further by the vast numbers of new Hispanic and Asian-Americans (among others) with some surprising role reversals that many of the principals have, as yet, barely noticed.[9]

He is pointing to the festering and exploding immigration problem already at a crisis in some states.

He points out the dilemma the world faces. By the liberal elite emphasizing the equality of all people and the right to individual freedom by all, we are *faced with no criteria to stop fragmentation.* He says, "In essence, it is illegal to aid secessionist or insurgent movements, but equally illegal to use force to prevent 'self-determination'." (italics added)[10]

Adam Roberts, in the foreword of the book *Pandaemonium*, likewise points out:

[Americans are] ill-prepared to come to terms with the central role that ethnicity plays . . . . Being based, however imperfectly, on *individual* rather than group rights and on the idea of the melting pot, the USA is often inclined to underestimate the elemental force of ethnic issues elsewhere. (italics added)[11]

Moynihan himself cites Horowitz on this threatening phenomenon:

The increasing prominence of ethnic loyalties is a development for which neither statesmen nor social scientists were adequately prepared. . . . The study of ethnic conflict has often been a grudging concession to something distasteful, largely because, especially in the West, ethnic affiliations have been in disrepute. . . .[12]

But, I must add to this statement that this step is the inevitable development to obtain individual rights when they are hindered by other groups.

We may soon logically see ethnicity extend its claims in Western countries.

10   *Opportunity, or Pandaemonium?*

Quebec is nearing a democratic decision to leave Canada. Will the renewal of parliaments in Scotland and Ireland lead to secession from Great Britain? Can the liberal elite who have argued so strongly for the individual and democratic rights be able to deny these if they are done by democratic vote? What about states' rights in the United States when the Supreme Court chooses to override the vote of the people of the States and the Congress? Such a right to override is not found in the Constitution.

Political Ethnicity Now a Dominant View in the United States, the World's Leader

When President Bill Clinton nominated Lani Guinier in 1993 to head civil rights in the Justice Department, he stirred criticism. John Leo pointed out that Lani Guinier wanted to toss out America's historic electoral system, replace it with race-based proportional representation, and then perhaps settle down to splinter-group politics in which each ethnic group has its own political party. Guinier sees "America's electoral system of majority rule as illegitimate . . ." and, "favors 'proportionate interest representation for self-identified communities of interest.'" She wants to get rid of whites as a political majority. John Leo concludes, "These are very strange views for a civil rights chief to have."[13]

What was most significant in the failed appointment was the response to the whole matter. Since the years of Martin Luther King's triumphs, there seems to have been progress, but limits to that progress for racial improvement in the United States. Racial leaders and organizations have floundered and argued about which way to go. When President Clinton withdrew Guinier's appointment, almost all of the black civil rights leaders defended her position and drew the focus to the fact that she favored racial quotas as the priority over majority rule, which has long been the cornerstone of American democracy. The feeling for ethnicity, already strong, found new, united vocal support. The vision of Martin Luther King that all men should be considered equal and every man have one vote, faded. It seems that ethnic rights would be the up-front demand in the future. Thus, democracy for the individual is leading to group ethnicity. And affirmative action is a primary tool to gain that objective even if it is unfair to some individuals.

In 1995, the Supreme Court has shown it is not yet ready for affirmative action and overturned in part this principle of group interest for the rights of individuals in regard to affirmative action and the gerrymandered black congressional districts, as in Georgia. For the first time the direction things were going seemed perilous to America's foundation. After the last action of the Court, Jesse Jackson, former lieutenant to Martin Luther King, sought to rally all black support to oppose these changes, focusing protest on Georgia's 11th district. These blacks, in group self-interest, together abandoned justice for the individual, which was prominent in King's movement, for ethnic power. This change in thinking has occurred without much recognition by the people.

While racial confrontations will be discussed extensively in this book, the problem is not only that there is racial and class prejudice, but is also a growing pervasion of the feeling of existent prejudice that resists progress and cuts across the pride of ethnicity. John Hope Franklin, Duke University black historian and Clinton's appointee to lead his committee for racial reconciliation, has said, "The country is so far from being color-blind. This is the most color-conscious society on the face of the Earth. Those who claim [otherwise] merely are ignoring the realities today. We count everything by race."[14] That committee has early shown evidence of black racial bias. The results of the O.J. Simpson trial in October, 1995, shocked Americans into seeing that racial prejudice is a mighty force in America. The Farrakhan march on Washington thrust this into the face of other Americans.

The causes of racial consciousness and anger will be discussed later. But it is important to note that anger is perhaps highest among *middle-class* blacks who are doing well financially. Ellis Cose makes it clear that they are experiencing anger over continued hindrances to reaching the top. In fact, he points out that their anger is higher than that of the poorer or underclass blacks. (He refers to a Los Angeles 1991 poll and other data).[15] The women complaining most about the glass ceiling are those who have already gained the most materially and in position. Thus, the issue is not poverty, but the greed to have more than others.

Race and ethnicity comprise only one of the major problems, but it will be shown that the problems of class, gender, and age all are related and are equally explosive forces that grow from one and the same perversion that promotes self and distorts all values toward conflict.

The Root Problem is Bias against God for Fleshly Self-Interest

Although there is still racial prejudice in America, the underlying problem goes much deeper. It goes back *to unbelief* that turned to materialism, sexual misunderstanding, and actions which affect ethnicity. This misunderstanding is produced by *values based on material progress*. The achievement of material success as a standard emerged after rejecting the value of persons and their purpose in the eyes of God. Ethnic, sexual, and materialistic conflicts produce anger, and anger destroys society and civilization. In subsequent pages, it will be demonstrated that class and ethnic struggles are a symptom of a deeper theological problem. But ethnic class consciousness poses the growing problem which can light the fuse for all self-interest groups and destroy the United States and much of the world's peace. We must not think that these surface problems of group conflict are the main problem that must be solved, or we will be putting on band-aids to solve the serious disease of unbelief.

12   *Opportunity, or Pandaemonium?*

An Anti-Christ Bias Leads the Steps of Decline

The history of mankind reveals men have many times built amazingly brilliant civilizations which have almost all declined and died, or are dying. Arnold Toynbee, the British historian, listed twenty-five such civilizations. Other historians divide them differently, but almost all see a troubled demise. Data will be presented in this book that indicates that the real *beginning of the decline* of a civilization is when man reaches *a point* in his intellectual brilliance in creating a culture, at which he believes *he no longer needs God*, but rather man alone is adequate to solve his problems and build his own utopia on earth, Thus the title, *Man Is Not Enough*. Once the intellectually elite leaders of a society reach that point, they usually lead the people down the same steps in the decline of the society. The reason the same steps are followed is that man is a logical creature with *repetitive desires*, and when he accepts one supposition, this acceptance logically leads to another idea.

The reason for this decline is that *all men have a basic bias against God* which comes from their desire to survive physically and be free to enjoy the pleasures of the flesh. For most men, this bias is not conscious, but it is like a deliberate spiritual gravity pulling toward selfish individualism and self-interest groups, destroying society and *removing faith in a God to whom mankind is accountable*. A small group of intellectual elite become convinced that *the universe is run mechanically by natural laws they can understand* and hope to control. When they gain political control, they motivate the change in education to influence the masses to accept their views, which progressively become more anti-God. Finally, man worships himself, believing he is the climax of mighty forces in nature. This human bias produces the tendency toward man's downfall. While human conspiracies of certain groups may promote this trend, conspiracies are a by-product of man's prevailing anti-God bias. The conspiracies only harness the desires of men that are already leading the trend and are used by the group for their ends.

The True Nature of the Whole Crisis Is Theological

Many critics agree that the United States and the world are facing a crisis. Some see it as an economic crisis, some a political crisis, some an environmental crisis, some a racial or gender crisis, and some a moral crisis. While each of these views may be true to a certain extent, *the root of all* these various aspects of the crisis is *a theological crisis*. Other aspects occur because man has lost a sense of accountability to God. Again, the main point is theological, or removing the idea of God's control. When there is no consciousness of right or wrong before God, and every man follows an individualistic course of what is right in his own eyes, the whole society moves deeper and deeper into division and chaos, and *control of the society is lost.*

Control always assumes some superior authority over all the persons involved. Control also involves a basic teaching unit, such as the family, as the conduit for communicating the will of authority. Man's unwillingness to have anyone control him is the ultimate outcome of this rebellion against God. Through this means, the Devil deceives men into thinking they are moving in the direction of freedom to experience pleasure. He then lures them into the city of Pandaemonium.

Degradation Tends toward an End Time of Great Trouble

Progressively excluding God from society and *rejecting His authority to control* allows crass individualism to emerge. The more this occurs, the more there is *hostility against any form of control.* Paul's description of the end of man's base nature is shocking, "Since they did not think it worthwhile to retain the knowledge of God, he gave them over to a depraved mind, to do what ought not to be done. They became filled with every kind of evil . . ." (Romans 1:28-30). As old institutions of control fail, individuals tend to gravitate toward those people most like themselves in gender and ethnicity. As these groups of natural affinity emerge, there becomes a polarization which seeks power for the self-interest of each group. These efforts of groups of gender and ethnicity to seek power for self-interest further destroy the old institutions and ideals. Inevitably wealth and advantage divide into two poles of growing wealth and poverty. A judgmental attitude dominates toward the end, and war between individuals, groups, or classes weakens the civilization from within, usually before it is attacked from without. Through the confusing conflict comes what I call a "meltdown" without clear leadership, and with great suffering.

A Troubled End Characterized by Group Self-Interest and Conflict

The continued growth of material progress during the progressive rejection of the one true God and His revealed will involves the absorption of diverse people who immigrate either involuntarily or voluntarily to participate in the prosperity and power of the growing nation. The rejection of God and moral absolutes inevitably involves accepting the diverse views of aliens and their gods. Rejection of one true God and His revealed will must inevitably be promoted by the assertion and emergence of selfish individualism. With the dominance of selfish individualism, there results a formation of group conflict for class, race, gender, and ethnicity. Selfish individuals seek support from those most like themselves. These groups form because of the growing confusion and contribute to the confusion that brings the meltdown of control in all institutions. A demonstration of these claims will be made in later data.

14   *Opportunity, or Pandaemonium?*

These conditions that produce the specter of the coming chaos tend to produce a reaction in the conscience of all the people and especially in the community of the believers. When the time of troubles is sensed as growing close, a reaction to the prospect offers one last window of opportunity to bring renewal. If the renewal does not go deep and turn people back to faith in the one true God, the meltdown will occur. The specter of class conflicts seems imminent, but at the same time material prosperity driven by greed deceives the people from seeing that such troubling and chaotic conditions could arise. Thus, the warnings of the secular prophets like Moynihan warn of the Devil who leads into Pandaemonium. How all this occurs will be made more clear later. Here the intent is to present evidence that the time of troubles is near unless America's window of opportunity is effectively used.

America as the World Leader Must Turn People Back to God

United States Leading the Way to Pandaemonium

The United States is today the most prominent influence on the entire world. There are over eight hundred thousand people from all nations of the world studying in our university systems and individual colleges. Our business corporations and banking systems are pivotal in what happens everywhere. The dollar is the standard currency. America houses the United Nations and pays many of its bills. American media are viewed by most of the world, even in the poorest countries. This realization hit me when I sat with many black friends in Kenya around the one TV in the area and all viewed the American reports on Desert Storm. The literate of Europe, Asia, and the United States have embraced the same intellectual presuppositions of the Enlightenment. Many other nations are rapidly being engulfed in the thinking of the degrading materialism and sensualism of the West. The educated elite, primarily of the United States, have set the standards for most of the world, and are leading the moral decline of the poorer and smaller nations by greed, lust, and violence.

The two former major world divisions of Communist nations and the Western social democracies and their decay seem to have roots in the abandonment of spiritual values for material and sensual utopias. My companion book, *Dark Shadows in the New Day of Science: The Story of Perversion by America's Intellectual Elite,* follows the details of intellectual revolt in Western thought. This revolt has over many years moved toward a worldwide humanism without God. The pride of the intellectual elite is that they have dispensed with God as Creator and Controller of the world. Rulers in modern science have little place for God. God and Christians are their chief enemy. This intellectual deception is the root of the problem.

The intellectual secular elite of the world have thought they could bring the world together in a new humanism with scientific socialism. On one hand, the Marxists believed they could use modern science to unite the world and bring peace by the dictatorship of the proletariat. On the other hand, the educated elite of the West thought that through social democracy they could weld the world together in a new oneness of humanism. The hope of both the Communists and the social democrats of the West has been to unite the nations in a "one world" utopia in their own way for their own purposes. They think man alone is smart enough to bring about this change.

Both the educated elite of Communism and of democratic socialism have weakened moral absolutes and sought to eliminate them. The governments of Communism, who early on declared themselves atheistic, are already disintegrating, and there are signs that the Western democracies are also moving toward an anarchistic condition. To achieve firm control, the Communists insisted that what they believed was politically correct and closed education to anything else, especially to religion. Today the American educated elite have also sought to close down freedom in all types of education except for what they believe is "politically correct." Their main intolerance is toward a living God.

The problems of people throughout the world have worsened in recent years. Ideologies that held people together have failed, such as the disintegration of the Soviet Union and Communist states. But the social democracies are also now in trouble and unable to fulfill the promises of cradle-to-grave prosperity and health. While more countries have declared themselves democracies since the decline of Communism, for the part of many, they still remain socialistic dictatorships under the guise of democracy. Significant exceptions are the fragmented Islamic dictatorships that struggle for unity but politically are divided and whose tool is terrorism.

Transitional Opportunity of a Window of Time

The United States is now in a time of reaction and transition which offers either opportunity for renewal of faith in God, or of a triumph of selfishness into a meltdown of all institutional control. This will be discussed more extensively at the end of this book when the reader has more data to see the picture of what is happening. Rationalistic liberalism or modernism which was born out of the Enlightenment has run its course and its failure has become evident. Liberalism began to attain triumph and control in 1960, but after the fall of the Berlin Wall beginning about 1990, the recognition of the failure of human reason alone was manifested. The failure of scientific socialistic engineering of the educated elite of Communism and European socialistic countries finally began to become clear. In America, the extremes of government bureaucracy, economic irresponsibility, criminal violence, sexual deviance, and lack of relational progress in race and class, along with the intellectual failures of liberalism, have awakened the public mind. In the twentieth century, science itself introduced much data that exploded the deterministic or uniformitarian view of the world that was the basis of liberalism's rejection of God. By 1990, that inconsistency was also evident.

The fear of rising crime, drug addiction, premarital pregnancies, and the huge financial deficit cast a shadow over hope, and the public demanded change. Christians began to band together to show disapproval. Public conscience, prayer and fasting, and public demonstrations by God's people have produced a desire of the public for change. This is also clear in the radio medium with those such as Rush Limbaugh and Laura Schlessinger, in the religious marches on Washington by men, in the election of conservatives to Congress, in mass demonstrations against abuses, and in attempts to enact more conservative laws on the budget, failing government social programs, correcting crime, restraining sexually explicit material, divorce, and the disgust with the lusts of a President..

The failure of modern liberalism has produced three major views that are recognized as contesting for control in what I see as a few brief years of a window of opportunity for change. 1. There are the *Hypomodernists* who in desperation blindly push even harder for their agenda while refusing to admit they are wrong. Their inconsistency and unwillingness to admit wrong are further discrediting them. An example is the position of the National Organization for Women. 2. Then there are the *Post Modernists* who are now so committed to selfish individualism and denial of moral absolutes that they want no truth but themselves, whether in old liberalism or in revealed religion. Both of these groups are willing to deconstruct any forms of power and control to achieve their own aims. 3. Finally there are those who hold to absolute principles and for this reason they are considered *conservative*, especially some Christians and Jews. The human conscience has recognized the wrongness of modern liberalism in its extremes, and Judaic-Christian morals seem to have more pragmatic meaning for society. But, true faith in an unchanging God and His absolute will is missing from the polls.

Most of the public mind is even more hostile today than ever to being forced to give up its freedom to any laws for restraint. There are those who fear Christians or Jews who they think want to impose restraints on their actions by political control of government; however, the way of Jesus in persuading the conscience to voluntarily accept what is revealed and reasonable, in a way apart from political coercion, can achieve great change if applied in love. This window of time from reaction to extremes and to growing confusion is *almost certainly the last opportunity for Christians* to present and apply the gospel as the power of God for salvation from the guilt, confusion, and ravages of human sin. The believing churches must see their opportunity and act together or it will be too late, as Judah missed its last opportunity with the revival of Josiah (621 B.C.) and went into meltdown. It lasted until its destruction in 586, which was followed by seventy years of exile by many. As a modern example, Erwin W. Lutzer has shown that the church in Germany missed its opportunity to boldly take a stand and was deceived by Hitler and the prosperity he brought. Hitler gained dominance over the church.[16]

Christian clergy and laymen in America need to understand and rally together to address the problems that have grown out of the nation's long and progressive rejection of God. Understanding that the main reason for moral decay is theological unbelief is strategically presented in this book to help promote Christian renewal.[17] Moreover, the effort is made to show at what points the faith to obey God is needed. May our sovereign God grant us understanding and the commitment and unity to renew faith in Him. It must be soon, because the window of opportunity may be small.

Chapter 2
Biblical Pattern of Moral Decay in the Civilizations

THE PROCESS OF MAN'S SIN AND THE POWER OF DELIVERANCE

A Significant Biblical Passage for Affecting History

This chapter offers the main thesis of this book and shows why America and other civilizations have declined or died. The Apostle Paul, in probably the greatest theological dissertation ever written, his epistle to the Romans, begins the major content of the letter with a perceptive picture of mankind's sin. Paul describes man's sin nature which motivates people to make steps of rebellion against their knowledge of God. This leads men though progressive stages away from God toward selfish individualism and toward anarchy against any institution for exerting divine control. This bias of human nature results in man committing acts against his own best interest and desires, and toward selfish alienation from God and other humans. Man's rebellion results in God abandoning him to his sin and its terrible consequences.

It is important to note that in the first chapter of Romans, Paul has in mind the culture in which he is living as a model reflecting the process of man's sin. As he writes, Paul is thinking expressly about two nations of people, namely the Greeks and the Romans, as two of the Gentiles (the Greek word is "nations"). He states his obligation to both as he contemplates their sinful condition (Romans 1:14). He then describes this progression of sin as he is aware of it in these nations (Romans 1:18-2:4). As we review for you the history of the decline of the Greek democracy and the Roman Republic, these exact steps from Romans 1 that outline the corruption of society by sin can be followed (see chapter 4 on Greece and chapter 5 on Rome in this book). While Paul's intent was to describe the steps of man's rebellion which he observed in these cultures, you will see that these steps turn out to present the historical process of the decline of any nation which is influenced by that sin. I have found that this process applies to most nations throughout history.

It is also important to note that while Paul was conscious of the terrible moral corruption in the Greco-Roman society, he faced it with great optimism. He believed that the gospel (meaning "good news") committed unto him "was the power of God for salvation" for those who believe (Romans 1:16). While that society had many people whom God had delivered over to rebellion, anarchy, and debauchery, Paul believed there were those among them who could be delivered from the power of sin. His optimism of the power of the gospel of Christ was correct because by the early fourth century the Christian church conquered the paganism that dominated when Paul wrote this epistle to the Romans.

Paul quotes the Old Testament prophet Habakkuk and draws his concept of deliverance from that similar condition hundreds of years before in Judah, when evil men were triumphing in violence, greed, and lust. Evil men of that day perceived themselves as gods in their own strength, and seemed to be allowed by God to control things. Habakkuk confronted these terrible acts of men against God's people, and cried out to God for an answer. God's answer to Habakkuk was to await for an appointed time when God would act against the arrogant or "puffed-up" ones. In the meantime he was told, "The righteous shall live by faith [in God]" (Habakkuk 2:3-4). Paul drew upon that answer for his own time period and said, "For in the gospel [good news] a righteousness from God is revealed, a righteousness that is by faith from first to last, just as it is written [by Habakkuk]: 'The righteous will live by faith'" (Romans 1:17).

It is probable that Paul has in view God's imputed righteousness which He will give to the one who believes, as he explains later (Romans 3:21-22). But, it would be wrong to give this passage that meaning alone, or even primarily, without also including the power of God given to enable one to live by faith. That would miss the context of his thoughts, for he is about to describe the terrible power of sin in the lives of men in the Roman world. It would also miss the context of the passage in Habakkuk. The word "save" means not only the gift of justification and deliverance from guilt to be accepted by God, but also and mainly the power of God to deliver one from evil men and enable him to live righteously in the perverse culture around him.

Paul is writing at the *telos*, the ending, of the decline of the Roman Republic. The republic arose near the collapse of the Greek democracy, and the Romans borrowed that nation's pagan thinking after conquering it. Habakkuk wrote at the end of Judah's journey through these steps of sin, and at the time Babylon was invading and rendering punishment to Judah. Examining the steps of sin which Paul observed (and was guided by divine inspiration to record) in those civilizations is pertinent and key for what is occurring today.

The New American Standard Version of the Scriptures in the epistle to the Romans is quoted here, and the steps of decline are indicated with bold type for outlining of the discussion which follows.

THE STEPS OF MORAL CORRUPTION IN ROMANS 1:18-3:2

Human Bias against the Knowledge of God (1:18-20)

For the wrath of God is revealed from heaven against all ungodliness and unrighteousness of men who suppress the truth in unrighteousness, because that which is known about God is evident within them; for God made it evident to them. For since the creation of the world His invisible attributes, His eternal power and divine nature, have been clearly seen, being understood through what has been made, so that they are without excuse.

Revolt against God Intellectually (1:21-23)

For even though they knew God, they did not honor Him as God or give thanks, but they became futile in their speculations, and their foolish heart was darkened. Professing to be wise, they became fools, and exchanged the glory of the incorruptible God for an image in the form of corruptible man and of birds and four-footed animals and crawling creatures.

Revolt against God for Desires of Material Physical Creation (1:24-25)

Therefore God gave them over in the lusts [desires] of their hearts to impurity, that their bodies might be dishonored among them. For they exchanged the truth of God for a lie, and worshipped and served the creature [creation] rather than the Creator, who is blessed forever. Amen.

Revolt against God for Sensual Sexual Desires (1:26-27)

For this reason God gave them over to degrading passions; for their women exchanged the natural function [use or role] for that which is unnatural, and in the same way also the men abandoned the natural function [use or role] of the woman and burned in their desire toward one another, men with men committing indecent acts and receiving in their own persons the due penalty of their error.

Revolt against God and Authority for Anarchy (1:28-32)

And just as they did not see fit to acknowledge God any longer, God gave them over to a depraved mind, to do those things which are not proper, being filled with all unrighteousness, wickedness, greed, evil; full of envy, murder, strife, deceit, malice; they are gossips, slanderers, haters of God, insolent, arrogant, boastful, inventors of evil, disobedient to parents, without understanding, untrustworthy, unloving, unmerciful; and although they know the ordinance of God, that those who practice such things are worthy of death, they not only do the same, but also give hearty approval to those who practice them.

Resulting in Judgmental Attitudes and Judgment from God (2:1-3)

Therefore you are without excuse, every man of you who passes judgment, for in that you judge another, you condemn yourself; for you who judge practice the same things. And we know that the judgment of

God rightly falls upon those who practice such things. And do you suppose this, O man, when you pass judgment upon those who practice such
things and do the same yourself, that you will escape the judgment of
God?

EVALUATION OF THESE STEPS OF MORAL DEGENERATION

Man's Bias against God and His Tendency to Distort Truth

Paul begins these observations about the trend of man's sin by emphasizing
the bias of man against the truth of God, which is the focal point emphasized in
this book. He says, "For the wrath of God is revealed from heaven *against* all
*un*godliness and *un*righteousness of men, who *suppress* the truth in *un*righteousness" (Romans 1:18). The language in the Greek strongly focuses on man's "anti"
or "against" attitude. The words for *ungodliness* and for *unrighteousness* have the
prefix "a," which even in translation to English means "anti" or "against." So the
meaning is "against godliness" and "against righteousness." The word translated
"suppress" is a combination of the Greek words *kata*, meaning "downwards" or
"against" and *echomai* meaning "hold fast." Thus, Paul says these people are
firmly holding down the truth.

In the passage which follows, he then outlines the procedure that unbelieving
men follow in suppressing truth. *The steps resulting from this human bias will be
shown as the key to this book.* This bent toward selfish individual desires and
against God is what causes a civilization's decline. The bias causes man's suppression of truth about God in favor of lies, until he rejects God altogether from
his culture. This whole passage in Romans, chapters 1 and 2, will be examined
carefully, showing the downward progression which it causes. By understanding
these steps Paul gives, one can evaluate history and rationally interpret the path
other declining nations have taken. These steps have been traced in Greece and
Rome (whose histories are recorded in chapters 4 and 5) and a number of other
civilizations and from these the main idea is expanded.

Beginning with a Knowledge of God, a Theistic View

That which is known about God is evident [made visible] within them; for
God made it evident to them. For since the creation of the world His invisible attributes, His eternal power and divine nature, have been clearly
seen, being understood through what has been made, so that they are
without excuse (1:19-20).

Paul is *not* saying here that mankind can look at natural creation and reason
back to evidence for the one true God. This was the argument of Thomas Aquinas

which the Roman Catholic Church used and many philosophers adopt. While the Thomistic arguments show there is a rational force in nature which is greater than man understands, they can never prove this rational power is infinite or that there is a transcendent God above nature. Some modern scientists such as Stephen Hawking and others are willing to argue for a reasonable universe that is favorable for man to a limited degree, but these unbelieving men want to limit God to nature as in pantheism. Actually, Thomas Aquinas' theological argument based on man's logic that the world is reasonably ordered to a purpose is valid only to the limits of nature, and cannot prove by observation that there is an infinite purpose. That is only possible by man using a created innate knowledge.

Paul does not make the mistake of Aquinas, but is saying that man is created with categories of divine light of truth already implanted in his spirit or soul by the Creator so that when he looks at creation he recognizes that the world was made by the God who gave man the power to think. The way the world works and the things in it speak of the One whose image he was created to bear. This truth about God is made visible "*within* [the Greek word is *en*] them." Thus, the reasonable purpose of the world seen by man is only a confirmation of what man knows in his heart by his nature. This knowledge confirmed from nature mentioned by Paul here does not include God's way of forgiveness revealed in Christ by His atonement which he may come to later (Romans 3).

I have shown in chapter 9 of my companion book, *Dark Shadows in a New Age of Science*, that this fact of an innate knowledge of God is precisely what the comparative religionists such as Andrew Lang, and especially the scientific German analyst, W. Schmidt, showed to be true historically. Schmidt demonstrated that all over the world men initially know in their heart there is a supreme invisible God who is the power behind the world. He demonstrated scientifically that the idea of God which evolved from nature worship was in error. This leaves all men with a sense of obligation to worship Him, as Paul asserts. "They are without excuse" for not doing so. But Paul goes on to show that because of their natural disposition toward desires of the flesh, mankind has a bias against this knowledge of God. They thus proceed step by step to reject the revelation within and confirmed in nature about God and His will for them, deceptively thinking they are acting in their own interest.

FIRST STEP—INTELLECTUAL REVOLT:

Reasoning That There Is No Divine Presence, Only the Creation

Man's blessings from creation lead him to feel self-sufficient and without need of God. Paul describes the situation:

For even though they knew God, they did not honor Him as God or give thanks, but they became futile in their speculations, and their foolish heart was darkened. Professing to be wise, they became fools, and exchanged the glory of the incorruptible God for an image in the form of corruptible man and of birds and four-footed animals and crawling creatures. Therefore God gave them over in the lusts of their hearts to impurity, that their bodies might be dishonored among them (1:21-24).

The above description of man's intellectual revolt begins when there are blessings from God so that his needs are cared for and there is no anxiety. Sorokin, the historical sociologist, showed that a civilization arises while the people are "ideational" or inventive, and are related to religious faith. This faith in God enables the people to work creatively by assuming a universe that is united reasonably and with a sense of trust because of feeling an accountability to God. They create culture and prosper. After man has built a productive society, he has what he needs, so he does not feel he must pray for more help. He therefore begins his rejection of God from a sense of self-sufficiency so that he fails to worship God or give thanks to Him. Prosperity, when not accompanied by worship or thanksgiving, is the garden in which the Devil sows his seed of pride and rebellion. Man begins to think that he has provided his own needs without divine help. This is exemplified in Moses' warning the children of Israel that when they entered the promised land not to let such futile thoughts deceive them so that they forget that God provided, blessed, and made them prosperous (Deuteronomy 8:13-14). But history demonstrated the Israelites did not heed his words. Likewise, Paul in this passage of Romans says that man misperceives *nature* as the object of awe instead of God.

The next step in man's intellectual revolt after this assumption of self-sufficiency is to assert the idea that he, man, should be the object of worship: this is humanism. Thus, this assumption that the individual man is of utmost importance is the first evidence of idolatry. When man ceases to worship God, he then places himself at the top in a descending relationship to the other higher creatures: "man, birds, four-footed animals, and crawling creatures." The pride of feeling he knows and can decide what is right and wrong on his own gives him a sense of importance and freedom.

In Hebrew history, this was the motivating idea in the sin of Eve and Adam: the fruit of the tree was "desirable for gaining wisdom," with the promise, "You will be like God, knowing good and evil" (Genesis 3:5-6). Man's direction of thought, ignoring God and now centering on himself, led to the next step of turning his motives to focus on his bodily nature and desires. For the first time, they saw they were naked.

This intellectual revolt away from God initiates and *leads the way in man's thinking* through the next four progressive steps downward until the civilization collapses. Therefore, the intellectual revolt in a civilization will receive major attention in the study of the moral decline. Because this intellectual pride is so crucial in man's path of decline, the companion book, *Dark Shadows in the New Day of Science*, has been written to present the details of the intellectual rebellion in the West that will only briefly be mentioned in this book.

The dynamic of this present book is that the whole historical picture of what is happening in America will make sense as one sees the progressive development of intellectual thought in Western culture and how this has led the conduct of Americans through the centuries. The steps of the intellectual rejection of God began with *deism*—God made the world and left it to run like a great machine; God is the absentee landlord. Secondly, an idealistic pantheism that reduces to a rationalistic *naturalistic* view, or a focus on nature as mechanical. Thirdly, true *pantheism*—the belief there is a mystical power or powers in nature, and man is the highest expression of this god or gods. Thus, the worship of and control by God declines through the succession of these views and ends in the worship of man and the control by one man, antichrist.

This intellectual progression destroys meaningful relationships and increasingly in a zigzag fashion increases lawlessness and destructive violence.

SECOND STEP—MATERIALISTIC REVOLT:
Devotion to Created Things (Idolatry)

When man's thoughts turn from God to self, his bodily desires and needs become the chief object of his attention. Denying God and affirming the priority of possessing the material puts the primary focus on the physical aspect of man. Without God, he has no other power for bodily sustenance and pleasure than created nature. Possession of created material wealth becomes his main pursuit. Paul says:

> For they exchanged the truth of God for a lie [literally, *the* lie], and worshipped and served [worked for] the creature [or creation] rather than the Creator, who is blessed forever. Amen (1:25).

The great lie of the Devil is that God is not trustworthy, and man's freedom will only come from eating the fruit of knowing, and from using the material. His awe or reverence is toward creation and for that he works or serves. Research and knowledge of creation becomes his passion. Man interprets himself as more important than other created beings, and the important thing for him is to acquire and find provision from the materially-created world. One must have food, clothing, and so forth. Money, or "mammon," and the things it can buy, become man's new source of salvation. He follows his desires for the body to meet its needs from the physical world. The belief these will satisfy him is *the lie that damns him.*

Jesus warned, "No one can serve two masters. Either he will hate the one and love the other, or he will be devoted to the one and despise the other. You cannot serve both God and Money [literally, "mammon," the god of wealth]" (Matthew 6:24*). He has just said that this change of focus to worship money makes the whole soul filled with darkness.

Likewise, Paul later warned Timothy:

> But those who want to get rich fall into temptation and a snare and many foolish and harmful desires which plunge men into ruin and destruction. For the love of money is a root of all sorts of evil [The Greek literally says, "is the root of *all evil*"], and some by longing for it have wandered away from the faith and pierced themselves with many griefs (1 Timothy 6:9-10).

The emphasis of Jesus and Paul is that trust in money as the goal in life destroys all relationships. All idolatry grows out of this. In the Old Testament, Baal was the god of agricultural prosperity, and the name of the female goddess, Ashteroth, meant "to be rich."

The male leader of a family traditionally is devoted to material provision. But once the desire to accomplish wealth dominates his life, he will neglect wife and family to procure it. It becomes the source of his self-esteem. Paul has just warned, "If anyone does not provide for his relatives, and especially for his immediate family, he has denied the faith and is worse than an unbeliever" (NIV 1 Timothy 5:8). Paul identified greed as idolatry (Colossians 3:5; Ephesians 5:5).

Changes in All Values and Virtues

When the material becomes the primary value, all values logically change. Men and women are no longer seen as beings in the image of God and distinct from animals. So Paul says man is considered as one with, but above, animals: "*man*, four-footed beasts, and creeping things" (Romans 1:23 italics added). Men are unique from animals because they have the power of reason, can follow God's wisdom in nature, and therefore can worship God. Without faith in God, man sees himself and everything else as being a part of nature, albeit he is the highest creature.

Moreover, the woman is no longer seen as a person being valuable because she is also created in the image of God while physically different to conceive, bear, and nurture children. Under a materialistic view, she is not *equal in value before God*, but is equal in *kind*. And this equality is measured by *the right to have material* wealth and freedom to *choose and act as an individual* in the world for self. The understanding that man and woman are created to be "one flesh" in this life is turned toward an individualism where each, man and woman, acts in his or her own wisdom to gain the most for self.

The *egalitarian concept* of human rights is born out of, and essential to, a materialistic view of life of people who do not believe in God. Men who cease to respect others as equal in value *before God* are brought to the only other alternative, which is to argue for equality *for material wealth* as their ethical basis. This new basis for the value of humans leads to the erroneous view that redistribution of wealth is the need of mankind. Rather than learning to worship and obey God and to care for others because God esteems each individual of equal worth in His eyes, education and government must aim at individual rights to attain material wealth and pleasure. This is the most important motive producing class and feminist movements. *Egalitarianism then becomes the self-righteous motive of the liberal elite that drives the demonic concepts producing conflict and degradation.*

This giant step of changing everything to material values becomes the intellectual foundation from which to take the next steps away from God and toward complete selfish individualism.

THIRD STEP—SEXUAL REVOLT:
Emphasizing Sensual Individual Passion and Sexual Distortion

Once individuals give priority to pursuing their material bodily needs, they tend to use each other for material gain and for sensual satisfaction. This must lead to conflict. Their functions in relationships are changed. Paul describes how this then affects the physical relationship. He says:

> For this reason God gave them over to degrading passions; for their women exchanged the natural function for that which is unnatural, and in the same way also the men abandoned the natural function of the woman and burned in their desire toward one another, men with men committing indecent acts and receiving in their own persons the due penalty of their error (1:26-27).

The pursuit of material gain leads to dishonorable passions or desires. The women then change their natural "use" or function to that which is not natural. The word translated "function" or "use" could likewise be rendered *"role."* The materialistic goal causes women to see their *entire* sexual role or function in a different light, not just in sexual activity. When people apart from God see themselves as important as individuals, and material gain is the main value in life, the woman's role becomes less significant. Having children and helping her husband in caring for the family may become an expense and burden, and motherhood is viewed as a hindrance to her and the family. Her self-worth is radically changed.

To be thought worthy, she must try to avoid having children and get into the competition as a decision-maker, as an achiever, and especially as a money-maker. Moreover, sexual freedom from a husband seems right and liberating. Women demand equal liberty in sex. But, in so desiring, they are exposed to more men with less protection from abuse. In spite of more inventive birth control efforts, many continue to have children, bearing the main responsibility for them, and are thereby hindered from gaining material equality.

Since the man's self-worth has come from respect as provider and protector, his sense of worth drops and his role is depreciated. The husband then abandons the natural relationship with his wife, has adulterous affairs, and exercises the greater physical strength, often in sport, but also in violence. Also, with depreciating relationships to his wife and children, many men find more satisfaction in homosexual relationships. The united family concept—of "being one flesh"—is then broken and encourages more immorality and less fidelity. In this atmosphere of sexual "freedom" which carries less and less relational meaning, there is less and less satisfaction physically, and therefore more and more promiscuity occurs to find a "better" sexual partner. Civil laws then are changed to allow these desires to occur, which further accelerates immorality.

The perverted sexual encounters breed and spread sexual diseases, and the increased conflict in the relationships lowers the immunity level even more. They thus, as Paul said, "receive in their persons the due penalty of their error" (1:27b). In their indiscriminate behavior, these men and women don't want to admit any constraints on their behavior and don't want to admit any guilt. Having dismissed the idea of God, there is little constraint on their conscience to their selfish passionate desires. These frustrating changes in sex, which seem so logical under material values, accentuate the unsatisfied desires and make sex a central focus of thought and public communication. Thus, the tree of materialism generates the fruits of divorce, pornography, adultery, out-of-wedlock pregnancy, homosexuality, and so on.

FOURTH STEP—REVOLT TO ANARCHY, AGAINST CONTROLS:
Individual Human Rights over God and Social Good

When the knowledge of God increasingly has been suppressed, individual pride and worldly knowledge are increased, material progress becomes the main goal, and sexual roles are perverted for individual freedom and sensual pleasure. The family structures disintegrate, children suffer neglect and abuse, and youth are segregated from adults and thereby spend time mainly with their peers. The society then becomes more and more dysfunctional at every level. The opinions of the youth are more and more exalted over the elderly, and the youth rebel. Old ideas are rejected for what is new.

The ethics and morals of the previous generations are considered too narrow-minded. History as a standard of the past is not wanted and is reinterpreted; the older people with standards are not respected; religion is derided publicly and becomes almost entirely therapeutic for the individual, and anything but individual rights becomes secondary. Old government standards or constitutional restraints are attacked, reinterpreted, and changed. The result is every man and woman doing what is right in their own eyes. Tolerance of any view is important, except that which constrains their desires, and all values are relative. No authority is respected. God releases them to their desires. Paul described this fourth step as follows:

> And just as they did not see fit to acknowledge God any longer, God gave them over to a depraved mind, to do those things which are not proper, being filled with all unrighteousness, wickedness, greed, evil; full of envy, murder, strife, deceit, malice; they are gossips, slanderers, haters of God, insolent, arrogant, boastful, inventors of evil, disobedient to parents, without understanding, untrustworthy, unloving, unmerciful; and, although they know the ordinance of God, that those who practice such things are worthy of death, they not only do the same, but also give hearty approval to those who practice them (1:28-32).

FIFTH STEP—JUDGMENT AGAINST OTHERS AND VIOLENCE:
Hypocritical Accusations against Each Other While Being Judged by God

When each individual arrogantly seeks his rights for material gain and sensual pleasure, then the family is soon torn apart and government is used for selfish ends rather than the common good; the result is a society with everyone the judge of everyone else. There is great conflict and confusion in every area of life. Criminals claim equal rights with the victims. Ethnic and class groups turn to infighting; a deep sense of subjective guilt prevails but everything is excused. The end is every man accusing another. Those who trust God and proclaim what is right and what is wrong are the most hated. It is a time when God's blessings are withdrawn and His judgment comes on the society.

Paul describes this last stage of the breakdown of the civilization when the Devil, *the accuser*, causes chaos and violence as God's judgment is falling:

> Therefore you are without excuse, every man of you who passes judgment, for in that you judge another, you condemn yourself; for

you who judge practice the same things. And we know that the judgment of God rightly falls upon those who practice such things. And do you suppose this, O man, when you pass judgment upon those who practice such things and do the same yourself, that you will escape the judgment of God? (2:1-3).

By the beginning of this fifth step, the history of most societies shows that bigots gain control and a dictatorial government is eventually needed to save the economy and bring some form of order out of the division and disarray. Finding real leaders becomes difficult. It is a time when lawsuits abound, government bureaucratic controls abound, there is no end of conflict, and calamities seem to proliferate. Taxes rise out of control and the rich hide their wealth. Man's sins have brought judgment on him for breaking God's laws, but acts of divine intervention also brings tragic suffering. This is the time I have labeled, "the moral meltdown."

LOGICAL PROGRESSION WITH SLOW-GROWING DECEPTION

Each Successive Step Has a Logical Motivation to the Next

The logic of this process is compelling. Each step logically leads to the next. Denial of the spiritual leads to the material. Preoccupation with the material leads to concern for the body and for the sensual for the individual. Preoccupation with the sensual and selfish enjoyment leads to poor family and other relationships, which leads to a breakdown of the home and to more abuse within the family, that then carries over to all society. These things tend to produce anarchy, and anarchy leads to hostile, judgmental violence.

Man's confidence in his self-wisdom makes him feel he can produce progress in material wealth and freedom to give pleasure for all. Moreover, his sense of pride in his developments of civilization increase his sense of self-righteousness. He is compelled to move ahead to the next logical step by his pride and faulty logic. The educated elite feel compelled to control education and legally force compliance on the uneducated "for their good."

Without laboring the details, we have shown above that apart from belief in God, logic compels movement to the next step toward individualistic materialism. Basing security on the material logically forces demands on the government to produce equality, and politicians must vote to please the most people. The evaluation of self-worth of the individual demands greater efforts to equalize by gender and race and leaves the poorer, weaker, and younger to seem to require more government help. To achieve these ends, it seems reasonable to transgress constitutional standards and legal forms of government. Under materialism, the conflict over women's rights and promoting the rights of the lower classes seems logically persuasive. With the neglect and abuse of children, the government's intervening over parents in the rights of children also seems very logical.

Man's pride grows with every achievement, and he becomes more insistent that a belief in God is a primitive idea. Man must have security in this life, since he has no hope of life beyond death. Hence, there is a preoccupation with health and an exaggerated concern about death. But as selfish individualism grows, violence and crime escalate. Rights for material equality and security are demanded by all free men and women, and the only logical way to achieve this seems to be to control the governmental levers to force compliance to what seems so logically right. These conditions must logically lead to hate, rejection, and the persecution of the godly by the lawless, because the only concern for what is right comes from God's people. Desperate demand for social order opens the door to dictatorship. Widespread suffering of the oppressed and poor and the persecution of God's people are the things that motivate God to intervene by judgment on society as a whole.

Each Successive Step Reduces Accountability and Increases Deception

Paul indicates in his sketch of moral decay that these successive emphases build on and overlap each other. For example, the intellectual revolt against God begins, and then continues to lead to greater and greater rejection of Him. While at first man is unthankful to God and ceases to worship Him (in 1:21), Paul later says man moves toward rejection of God for recognition of a hierarchy of beings with man at the top (as in evolution, in 1:23). Then God is given up for worship of creation (1:25), and later man completely rejects the knowledge of God (1:28). This is followed by a complete denial there is knowledge and judgment from God (1:31, 2:1). These intellectual progressions away from God lead the way in the steps toward collapse. The progressive acceptance of these departures from God and His moral commands is so slow that they appear on target for the next generation. But each step of rebellion itself likewise progresses to a growing climax. This will become more clear as we show how this actually occurred in several civilizations.

Zigzag in Progression Is Produced by Offending Public Conscience

We have noted that Paul says God is manifested within man, and he also teaches that God's law is written in the heart. In Romans 2:14-15, Paul says:

> When Gentiles [nations], who do not have the law [of Moses], do by
> nature things required by the law, they are a law for themselves, even

though they do not have the law, since they show that the requirements of the law are written on their hearts, their consciences also bearing witness, and their thoughts now accusing, now even defending them.

Because all men have this innate knowledge of God and His will, when men who are motivated by the Devil to pursue the flesh move too fast in rejecting God and His will, there comes a reaction from the general public and especially from believers who appeal to the conscience and to divine revelation. When this occurs, there is a brief moving back toward God, a backlash, or at least a leveling off in the speed of removal of God's truth. As we shall later discuss, such extremes of rejection of God and His will sometime motivate God's people into prayer and action that moves the society back toward God in genuine renewal. But the natural man's disposition to the flesh soon again moves people to further efforts to reject God.

Thus, the complete corruption of society is *not deterministic*, but on occasion there may be partial and, on rare occasions, almost complete renewal, as shall be demonstrated. However, this seldom happens, and the pattern in history is for civilizations to reach moral meltdown, which promotes a new spiritual minority movement that begins to restore acceptance of God and His will.

Because of the reactions of the offended public conscience, the long-term trend toward rejection of God and His will moves through these steps in successive generations in a zigzag or jerky way. Usually, there are a few major zigs and zags (usually about four) and other minor oscillations. As previously mentioned in this book, the *Devil's deception is slow* and patient, so that *each successive generation perceives that the errors of the previous ones are correct,* because the majority of the people's consciences have been conditioned to accept these views. Moreover, they appeal to the pride of the mind and the pleasurable desires of the flesh.

But the Devil *also* uses the reactions or zigzag motions of thought. His advocates may point back to a time not too long before when there was a backlash, or zag, when morals improved temporarily. The educated elite can then argue that things were not so bad recently and that people should not therefore be disturbed. Thus, the fears of the people are temporarily subdued, but their natural bias to the flesh soon tends to turn toward further sin. In chapter 6 the Devil's use of this will be discussed.

Each Step Develops a Philosophical, Progressive Rejection of God

From study of civilizations it seems the intellectual revolt moves from theism to deism, to spiritual pantheism, to naturalism, and then to natural pantheism. It goes from the spiritual emphasis which produces creative ideas, to a more rationalistic emphasis, then to a sensate one, and finally to a "moral meltdown" in which there is desperation for some spiritual power. Gradually the spiritual becomes submerged under the material. As confusion grows and faith in a transcendent God is denied, desperation for some outside help causes men to seek power from nature, which turns out to be demonic. The philosophical ideas are also zigzagged in the sense that there is usually a movement from a dualism to a monism and back and forth.[1] The emphasis in the main steps outlined by Paul is the dominant idea, but this does not mean that there are no other ideas being advocated at that time. This is still another way the Devil uses deception, because it can be pointed out that those ideas have occurred previously.

Graph of the Steps of Decline in a Society

On page 34 is a simple graph of the steps of moral decline which Paul describes. Notice that soon after the intellectual revolt begins exalting man, the materialistic revolt begins. Likewise, soon after man turns toward materialism, the sexual revolt begins, and as it gets underway the individualistic or anarchistic movement starts. This does not mean there was no emphasis on these before, but that this is the order in which these start and continue as persistently stronger movements. The graph indicates there are about four (from three to five) major zigzag motions in each stage of rebellion.

As all of these movements reach a crescendo of moral meltdown together, they turn into the violent judgmental phase, which must inevitably turn toward a dictator, an invader, or demagogues to try to save it. The anarchistic and judgmental end leads to strong ethnicity or special interest groups competing for power and privilege. When political and philosophical groups break down, those of ethnic background are the main identity left, and become the grounds for affinity. When all the waves of moral decay converge as in step 5, this produces a frightening collapse as under A, which leads the people to take desperate steps to exalt a dictator into power to bring some order, as under B.

Paul was not deliberately drawing a historic pattern. He was a scholar of Greek and Roman history, and he was simply expressing his observation of the pattern that human sin takes, and the final corrupt conditions he observed in the Roman Republic. He wanted to convince his hearers that the good news of Christ contains the power of God to deliver all men from the awesome power of evil.

STEPS OF SIN THAT DESTROY A NATION

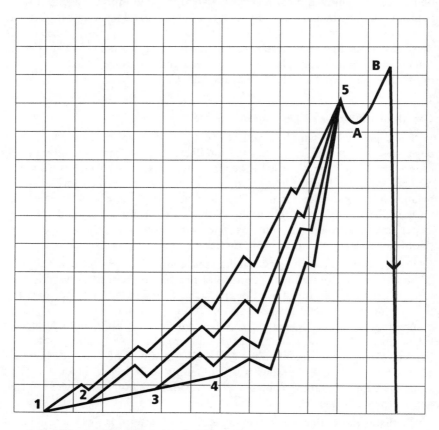

1. **Intellectualism** (Romans 1:21b–22)
2. **Materialism** (Romans 23–25)
3. **Sensualism** (Romans 1:26–28)
4. **Anarchy and Violence** (Romans 1:29–31)
5. **Conflict and Judgement, Human and Divine** (Romans 1: 32–2:2)

As we examine the history of the Greek democracy and the Roman Republic (in chapters 4 and 5) which were the most recent "past civilizations" in Paul's world, it will be seen that these steps given in the passage in Romans describe the path these nations took. I have examined about eight major civilizations and found they all followed the same general path of moral degradation.

The fact that Paul began with a time of faith in God which became characterized by unthankfulness that led man to take the successive steps away from God that led to what Paul presented was a final step of accusations and judgment against each other that brought on God's judgment, is a description of the history of most nations. These steps therefore give us a basis for evaluation of the course of a nation's growth and decline. In describing the path of human nature, they therefore present a tool for use of biblical and also secular history for forming a philosophy of history. Such a philosophy will be found to fit biblical prophecy and the course of civilizations as they play out to a terminus or end of history both for a nation and history as a whole. The applicability of these steps to help describe the course of civilizations and prophecy are in the next chapter and help us evaluate the conditions of America today.

Chapter 3
Biblical Philosophy of History

PAUL'S PATTERN HELPS INTERPRET
THE COURSE OF CIVILIZATION

This chapter is not aimed at debating the various philosophies of history concerning which there are many writers and books. The purpose is to simply emphasize that Paul's description of the path of human sin is logically, psychologically, and historically sound, and that this insight gives a firm foundation for a view of history. In the twentieth century some historians sought to use a more objective scientific view in studying the history. In chapter 4 of my book, Dark Shadows..., I look at what R. G. Collingwood and others generally call "scientific historians." 1

Among them are Oswald Spengler's view that history moves through a succession of self-contained individual units, each with its own character and each civilization going through the same pattern: birth, youthful strength, full maturity and then old age and death. His view is deterministic. Arnold Toynbee in a less deterministic and much more extensive evaluation, sees civilization as developing to brilliance of a materialism and moving to a time of trouble and demise. Pitirim Sorokim with his intense objective sociological studies saw the civilizations moving through ideational, rationalistic, and then sensate phases which end in troubles. These and others describe the civilizations going through a degenerative process that generally are pessimistic of human nature and confirm the steps of Paul as a basis for a philosophy of history.

In chapter 6 more selective aspects of civilizations will be looked at. The science of ethnology developed by the Germans, especially by W. Schmidt, demonstrated that every major civilization began with belief in a monotheistic supreme God and degenerated into a pluralism. This monotheism usually is supplanted by a growing materialism. This has been followed in all civilizations by J. D. Unwins studies in which in 86 civilizations he regulary found a sexual or feminist revolution that produced the decline of the family toward anarchy and conflict. In discussing the end times, Toynbee has said, "When we diagonse each case [in the death of a civilization], in extremes of post-mortem, we invariably find that the cause of death has been either War or Class or some combination of the two."2

Thus, the steps of sin given by Paul are a vital part for establishing the pattern civilizations go though and then decline. By following these steps in

38   *A Biblical Philosphy of History*

civilizations, the rise and then decline of each wave of civilization usually follows the same route.

The Pauline Pattern as a Part of the Growth and Decline of Civilization

As will be demonstrated, the above pattern of moral breakdown applies to the history of civilizations in their decline. Most civilizations have grown to brilliance for more than two hundred years before an educated elite achieves dominance and releases the bias for human nature to express itself against God in this process. These natural expressions of human nature have had subdued manifestations for a short time before in those two hundred years of growth. Because they do not gain dominance, the general faith in God continues. But when the growth of civilization produces what seems to offer unending opportunity for expanding prosperity even for the common man, then an intellectual elite launches what is about two hundred years of the steps of decline that leads to the time of trouble. After this meltdown to confusion, there usually follows a period of many years of confusion, suffering, and recovery. The whole time frame is a slow process of about five hundred years or seventy Sabbaths, according to Jewish chronology. Again, these steps of moral decay take about two hundred years. But this course of decay is not determined—if there is genuine repentance and trust in God, the time of troubles may be delayed. If there is not repentance and little resistance, the time to trouble will be shortened.

By tracing the pattern of human sin given by Paul through the history of civilizations, we are able to discern a pattern of one phase of history. In the next two chapters, the history of the Athenian Democracy and the Roman Republic will be reviewed, and it will be shown that both of these civilizations went for about two hundred years before these nations reached a point when the governing elite accepted a mechanical view of nature and contested the worship of a transcendent God who created the world and held men accountable. It will also be shown that it also took about two hundred years from the early colonization of America to the time an elite gained control of the government which questioned God's sovereign imminent control of the world.

The following graph shows the path a civilization often takes.

GRAPH OF GROWTH & DECLINE OF A CIVILIZATION

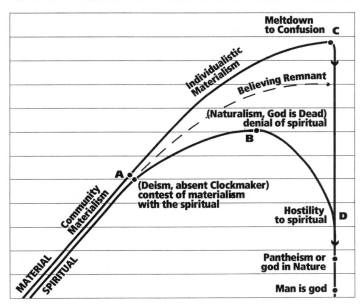

It goes through about two hundred years of growth and then begins the steps of decline as described by Paul. Each civilization has two strains of thinking and interest: *the spiritual*, involving faith in one sovereign God (represented by the lower line), and man's intellectual pursuit of *the material* (represented by the upper line). After about two hundred years of successful growth, it reaches point A, where the steps of the process of sin and the rejection of God described by Paul in Romans begin to occur.

This starts a progressive disjunction of the spiritual faith and material development and begins the definite decline of morals. This continues to widen slowly until point B, when the controlled education of the people has taught a materialistic view of life so as to reach the idea of the "Death of God." At this point, the rejection of moral absolutes rapidly accelerates while attention to material development continues and even accelerates. At point D, the lack of tolerance for anything but materialism and the questioning of all standards of conduct results in a scarcity of clear leadership and produces a meltdown of confusion in all controlling institutions: the state, the schools, business, and especially the family.

At that point, man realizes his inadequacy and, having rejected a transcendent God, he turns more fully toward seeking spiritual help from nature. This involves astrology and celestial objects, the seeing of an intelligent force in all of nature, communication with nature including the dead (as in New Age religions) and, especially, believing that man can be the highest expression of god in nature so that the leader is worshipped as god. Demonic feelings of power motivate great evil. Hedonistic pleasure, greed, and violence prevail. After the meltdown to confusion and the judgment by God by natural disasters or war, a nation often goes through a time of an intermediary government where there is struggle, and little creativity is produced for growth and prosperity. The times of trouble continue and recovery is strangled.

A Nation or People May Repeat this Pattern Several Times

A nation or people may, in folly without heeding history, blindly repeat the same pattern several times to another chaotic time of troubles before it loses its vitality of power and brilliance. It seems incredible that this repetition could happen to the same people, but the fact is that the time period is so long that it is not taught and remembered by succeeding generations. One illustration which is very familiar to historians is that of Egypt. Egypt's history goes through three rises and declines, and then weakens to lesser glory. They are 1. The Old Kingdom followed by the first intermediary kingdom, 2. The Middle Kingdom followed by the second intermediary kingdom, and 3. The New Kingdom followed by the third intermediary kingdom.

The Greeks went through a rise to greatness and decline, with an intermediary kingdom before the Greek democracy. The Romans went through a previous rise and decline under kings before the Roman Republic. Since Paul was describing the tragic conditions after the Roman Republic, that is what will be examined in this book. The Roman civilization was given a new and third beginning through the impact of the gospel so that imperial Rome rose to greatness in power, once again to decline, as described by Gibbon.[3]

RELEVANCE OF PAUL'S PATTERN OF SIN
TO A PHILOSOPHY OF HISTORY

Is a Philosophy of History Possible?

There are many who are skeptical that one can find a pattern of history demonstrating the rise of civilization and the steps of its decline. It is often argued one cannot find a philosophy of history because there are too many facts and one must select a certain principle according to one's own bias.[4] But as one knows a person more intimately, one can arrive at a more appropriate discernment about that person's character and how he acts. Likewise, the more one knows about the history of groups of people, the more certain characteristics can be seen prominently as the keys to a national group action. The wider the examination of the historian, the more accurate. Arnold Toynbee is probably the most exhaustive historian who ever lived, and he certainly may be credited with making many valid observations. The Apostle Paul is acknowledged as having written with a greater insight to human nature than almost any other man. His description of the path of human nature in these steps seem to have furnished a view that has fit the history of civilizations. But there is also another reason Paul's insights are reliable and fit what has happened.

God's knowledge is more extensive than any man's—it is absolute. He knows all men and all events throughout all times and can offer the best insight on history. The *key to this book* is found in God's revelation to Paul in the book of *Romans, chapters 1 and 2*. There, Paul reflects over the history of the conduct of the Greeks and Romans in his world and by divine guidance describes man's degeneration into greater sin. While Paul's objective is to describe the pattern of human sin rather than a philosophy of history, it in effect does so. It is this pattern that the decline of a civilization follows that fits the events of the successive waves of decline to judgment foretold by the prophets. These waves give great insight as to what is happening in America today.

Growth of the World's Nations in Linear View of History

Historians present history as chaotic, circular, or linear. The biblical view of history is the linear one. As Oscar Culmann has brilliantly demonstrated, a line must have a beginning point and an ending point, which is not true of a circular or chaotic interpretation.[5] There is only one way to have history with a beginning and end point, and that is if one believes in the sovereignty of God. God must be sovereign to create all things out of nothing, thereby furnishing the "beginning (Greek, *arche*) point" for time, and He must be able to control all events to bring them to an "ending (Greek, *telos*) point" of judgment. The biblical view is that each of the nations is a group of peoples formed in a specific location by divine determination at a specific time. Paul, speaking in Athens, said, "He [God] made from one every nation of mankind to live on all the face of the earth, having determined their appointed times, and the boundaries of their habitations" (Acts 17:26). Each of these nations in God's plan are given common grace to form a nation until such time as they reject their knowledge of Him and His law in their hearts, at which time they have gone through the process of decay. The time line from the beginning of creation is a succession of nations or aggregate of people who go through the process of growth and then decline as Paul described. The development of a national civilization of a particular people is succeeded to power by another.

Today there seems to be growing a new and final one-world civilization based on the achievements of the industrial movement and information technology of the West which allows the gathering of all nations into its culture. This one-world movement progressively moves toward the antichrist. This worldwide sense of culture has never existed before except in the limited Hellenistic world. There is much talk and some books written about a worldwide conspiracy to promote a one-world government. There is some truth to this. But no such conspiracy as this could be possible without the deception of Satan in using man's disposition to the flesh and the resulting desire to remove the evidence for God. This bias to the flesh and against God produces the great motivation toward world government. Conspiracy only rides on the back of human fleshly bias.

Pride of Accumulated Knowledge Affects Pattern of Moral Decline

The picture of nations is not as simple as one national civilization succeeding the former in one line, but often there are several civilizations, with one being dominant and interacting with others. When a dominant civilization declines, another replaces it. The nation that succeeded the one that has declined gathers up the information and advances of the previous civilization and other concurrent interactive ones, and therefore builds an even greater culture than any before. Thus, after about two hundred years of progress under common grace, the people of the new civilization feel they are superior to any other men who have gone before them, when in fact their intelligence is about average to all previous men.

It is like one boy who is standing on the shoulders of his friend and telling those about him that he is much bigger and better than they. This impression of the nation feeling superior to previous ones is assumed because they stand on the intellectual shoulders of those who have gone before. This accumulative effect is key in causing the educated elite of the growing national civilization to reach a point of feeling they do not need God.

Building on the shoulders of the knowledge of previous generations, the new civilization proudly builds a new and more glorious one: the Amorites and Egyptians build on the Chaldean culture, the Israelis build on the Amorites and Egyptians, and so on. So the Romans assimilated the wisdom of the Greeks, and the Europeans assimilated the knowledge of these two. The Islamic movement from the seventh century A.D. forward gathered up the information and culture of most of the knowledge of the Near East and of the Greeks. Europe received much of the previous civilizations from these Saracens when they entered Europe. Thus, each successive wave of civilization has gathered up not only the culture, but also an increase in the sense of the pride of man. The *great turning point* in each civilization is when the educated elite reach a point where they feel they are superior, and *they accept the lie that there is no God and that man is sufficient with nature. They then proceed to remove the evidence of God and to be free to do whatever they want. But man is not enough.*

This elite then leads the people to finally give up the idea of one God, which eventually causes the moral meltdown. Thus, the line of history from creation shows a succession of civilizations from Adam to more recent peoples of nations known in history and moves toward the final one-world civilization. When a civilization reaches its material peak, there is the meltdown of moral control, and people become judgmental of each other and they are judged by God. Then most often a dictator (sometimes a succession of them) is called in to bring order out of chaos. The dictator is proclaimed god, completing the rejection of God and the replacement of man as leader, fulfilling the role of antichrist in a preliminary way. This man is usually immoral in sexual practices, often homosexual. The Hebrew prophets address many of the surrounding nations about their sins and their accountability to God who will judge them and bring their civilization to an end (cf. Amos 1-2; Isaiah 13-25; Jeremiah 46-51 etc.). This process will be reviewed in the following chapters 4 and 5 on the Greek Democracy and the Roman Republic.

Thus, the bias of men against God for fleshly freedom motivates him through the succession of civilizations. And each wave of civilization with accumulated wisdom moves toward a one-world major civilization that will end in the final antichrist (cf. the vision of Daniel of Antiochus Epiphanes, Daniel 9:27; 11:31 and the future antichrist in Daniel 12:9-11 referred to by Jesus in Matthew 24:15). This succession of rises and fallings of civilizations progresses toward a final end point of antichrist and judgment of all people by God. The last civilization and antichrist will be worldwide. This will end in Armageddon and be followed by the millennium reign of Christ, which consummates with the final point of judgment by God at the Great White Throne of every individual person and all angels, fallen and good. The judgment will be the end point of history and the beginning of a new heaven and new earth with a new civilization in super-history. Paul's steps of progressive rejection of God in most successive civilizations thus have a vital role in carrying out the biblical linear view of history. In chapter 6, the conflict of God and Satan will be discussed as producing the steps of decline traced by Paul and how this fits in the biblical historical process from creation to the time of the final judgment.

In chapter 7 of this book, it will be shown that God called Abraham and his children to form the nation of Israel to specially reveal His character and work for His people, and to produce a Redeemer by whom men from all nations can by faith be accepted by Him, escaping His wrath, and enter His final kingdom. The incarnation or first coming of Christ is in the midst of the line of history and gives meaning and interpretation to all of history from creation to the consummation in judgment. (Humanity as history has recognized this, so that dating by nations is "before Christ" (B.C.) and "*anno Domini*" (A.D.), Latin indicating, "since the year of our Lord.") There were about two thousand years from Abraham to Christ, and about two thousand to our time. The mission of all God's people (the church) since Christ is to use their skills and abilities to build a world that witnesses to the Creator working in them in society for the good of the community and to spread the message of redemption to all men in all nations. A linear diagram of biblical history is as follows:

BIBLICAL LINEAR VIEW OF HISTORY

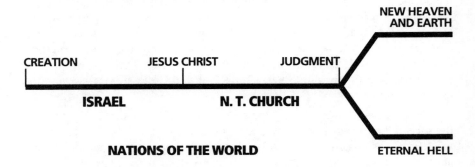

This book, *Man Is Not Enough*, focuses on the impact of the human sin nature (original sin bias) as it is presented by Paul in regard to the Greek democracy and the Roman Republic that preceded Paul. The data will be examined to see if these steps of decline apply to America. It will show our situation and the crisis that will be involved, if Americans continue unrepentant and go through the moral meltdown of our glorious civilization. These steps of moral decline help explain the development of Christian history in the decline of nations. They helps us understand the unraveling of America and its future.

It is therefore probable that there may be a birth of a new worldwide civilization which gathers up all worldwide knowledge. If so, an elect remnant of God's believing people could lead the majority of the world's peoples in establishment of that worldwide civilization to a new point of glory. At some point, the world would eventually follow the path of sin, eventually the final apostasy of much of the church will occur, and the final world antichrist would be revealed. The church in America and the world must prepare to be faithful to Christ, whether it soon leads to witnessing in a final tribulation of suffering and to the final antichrist and judgment or whether we, under God's leading, can contribute to building a new civilization that witnesses to Him.

The idea of successive waves of some civilizations progressing worldwide is illustrated as follows:

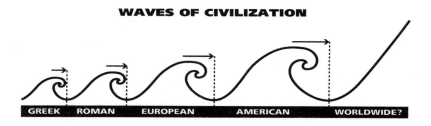

WAVES OF CIVILIZATION

| GREEK | ROMAN | EUROPEAN | AMERICAN | WORLDWIDE? |

Paul's Pattern of Sin Fits the Biblical Linear Philosophy

This wave concept shows the rise of civilization though faith in God as sovereign Creator, and then its decline according to Paul's pattern of sin—all to a point where God is rejected and man is viewed as free and sovereign. At the end, man as sovereign is symbolized in the antichrist's sponsoring lawlessness, thereby bringing the nation into judgment by God. And the repetition of the nations through this pattern of rising and collapsing waves with ever-increasing size and brilliance, until it reaches a world civilization with a world antichrist, fits the repeated biblical emphasis. The beginning point of a sovereign Creator moving to an ending point of sovereign man under demonic world control that ushers in the final judgment as the ending point is the picture of biblical linear history.

Progressively excluding God from society and *rejecting His authority to control* allows crass individualism to emerge. The more this occurs, the more there is *hostility against any form of control*. Paul's description of the end of man's base nature is shocking, "Since they did not think it worthwhile to retain the knowledge of God, he gave them over to a depraved mind, to do what ought not to be done. They became filled with every kind of evil . . ." (Romans 1:28-30). As old institutions of control fail, individuals tend to gravitate toward those people most like themselves in gender and ethnicity. As these groups of natural affinity emerge, there becomes a polarization which seeks power for the self-interest of each group. These efforts of groups of gender and ethnicity to seek power for self-interest further destroy the old institutions and ideals. Inevitably wealth and advantage divide into two poles of growing wealth and poverty. A judgmental attitude dominates toward the end, and war between individuals, between groups or classes weakens the civilization from within, usually before it is attacked from without. Through the confusing conflict comes what I call a "meltdown" without clear leadership, and with great suffering.

A Troubled End Characterized by Group Self-Interest and Conflict

The continued growth of material progress during the progressive rejection of the one true God and His revealed will involves the absorption of diverse people who immigrate either involuntarily or voluntarily to participate in the prosperity and power of the growing nation, as mentioned on pages 13 and 14. This pattern can be demonstrated in a number of nations. The immergrents bring their various gods and their diverse ideas and introduce a demand for tollerance to their views. The process which began with one supreme God who held them accountable to moral absolutes then yielded to relativism and ended in moral chaos that weakened the nation so invaders could conquer. This can be traced in the early Semitic kingdom that worshiped the sky God An and his son Enlid that arose in Mesopotamia and finally ended with the Amoritic take over with the fall of Ur. Or the great Amoritic kingdom that followed which worshipped the great sky God they called El and after the intrusion of the Kassites, Hurrians, and Indo Aryians ended with the collapse and judgment of the great city of Mari. The pattern can also be traced in the growth of the Egyptian culture in the tenth and eleventh dynasties but after the intrusion of many immigrants ended with confusion and division in the fourteenth dynasty when they finally succumbed to the Hyksos. Many of these patterns are analyzed in my book, The Call. In the coming chapters 4 and 5 regarding the Greeks and Romans, a complete cycle of each of these nations will be reviewed with details.

The Pagan Cyclic Views of History as Related to Paul's Pattern

The regularity of a pattern in many nations has often been interpreted as supporting a cyclic pagan view of history. By saying it is pagan, it is not meant these views are primitive and presented by unintelligent men. The pagan view, which is cyclic, is usually presented by leading intellects of the culture to given a naturalistic understanding and hope as the civilization reaches the final phase of unraveling before the meltdown to judgment. The cyclic view is linked to nature's God-given seasonal cycle of renewing in spring, then growth in summer, aging in fall, and death in winter. Spengler's more modern interpretation is an example of this idea.

The cyclic view of history is returning to prominence in recent years and has new proponents who have brilliantly reconstructed this view for Americans who face the impending crisis of social meltdown. Two of the most brilliant are William Strauss and Neil Howe in their recent books.6 They present four historical archetypes of personalities. These successively alternate by reaction of children to parents, going from dominant parents to recessive children, who when adults, have children who are dominant, with the next generation being recessive. The four archetypes of personalities are seen to produce four different kinds of generational reactions, two pairs of opposites. These play out in such a way that their reactions lead to a crisis in the fourth aspect of the cycle, which then usually wonderfully resolves by producing a new solution in a new social contract. Thus history is an unending series of cycles based on human nature and its responses or reaction to parents. The way each generation (approximately twenty-one years) interacts with the previous one and how each archetype generation contributes to the cycle are described.[7]

The eighty-four-year cycle of four generations is called by Strauss and Howe a *salaeculum,* as presented by a Roman historian when the Republic was unraveling in the third century B.C. and is based on cycles of Etruscan history[8]. While Strauss does not mention it, actually the Etruscans ended with an extremely degraded culture that exalted in worship of the phallic and female genital rites. It was this debased culture that the Romans assimilated which brought down their society in the cultural decline of the first civilization under the Roman kings, that preceded the Republic which we will study extensively. These cyclic views seek to explain trends in nature and to encourage people to believe that because of past cycles of human nature, the trend will lead to a successful and happy ending— that man by natural instincts with nature's help will work the coming crisis out for good. While Strauss and Howe do not present this in a deterministic way, this hope is implied and sometimes stated. This cyclic view is really based, therefore, on a pantheistic process, which is essentially New Age thinking, and uses the old Gnostic heretical ideas.

There are three reasons this cyclic view of history, which is gaining popularity in America, is important to this analysis of Paul's presentation of the course of sin. One is that the cyclic view has some truth to it. It is directly related to the zigzags in the growing movements begun by each of the steps of revolt Paul described and that produce the wave of civilization. Why do parents tend to dominate children, and why do children react to parents? Why do parents who were dominated as children tend to be permissive of their children? The answer is that people have the law of God written in their hearts and when the culture is moving too fast in permissiveness, parents want to protect their children and exaggerate authority. When children have been dominated without love, they tend to react and to assert their freedom from authority. The so-called "cycles" explain the zigzags in the trends of the movement of each line of revolt as graphed previously: intellectual, material, sexual, and anarchistic. And these unbelieving historians give recognition that these trends of the cycles lead to a serious crisis in the society which Paul sees as the end of sin. The crisis after the "fourth turning" enforces the idea that there is an inevitable judgment to which sin leads.

Also, Strauss' and Howe's cyclic views are hostile to the linear view which requires a transcendent sovereign God, and they repeatedly debunk linealism.[9] By making historical time a circle, there is excluded the point of a Creator acting to begin history and a future point where men will be brought into judgment. One of the greatest authorities on historic thinking of civilizations, both archaic and others, is Mercea Elliad, who was professor in the department of the History of

Religions at the University of Chicago. His extensive research of peoples led him to the conclusion that the reason human societies gravitate to the cyclic view is because of their desire to escape any sense of accountability for their sins to the transcendent Creator at the end of history.[10] By so doing, the cyclic view encourages people to be indifferent to sin and its consequences and to have false hopes. They are kept from considering the need to repent and receive God's help. After the major crisis at the end of a civilization, it is usually so devastating that the nation only partially recovers.

Paul's presentation of the course of human sin should help people avoid the sin that leads to a crisis. His presentation is important in that it warns people they are under the continual wrath of God (Romans 1:18). The importance of man facing his sin as his morals decline towards God's judgment is that this may cause him to want to repent when he hears of the good news or gospel of God's love in Christ. The cyclic view that human nature will likely enable things to turn out all right without supernatural help only encourages man not to face his sin, or to repent and return to God. It rather makes him want to look back to a mythical time when man was supposedly better, but dooms him to move on to a time of troubles and judgment.

Paul's dark and dismal presentation about sin is given because he believes that the gospel of Jesus Christ is the power of God to save from this terrible power of sin. He is optimistic about the future because he believes Christ is able to overcome all sin. And, as mentioned, historically the Christian movement did make such an impact on the Greco-Roman society that it became the accepted religion of the Roman Empire. The utter chaos at the end of the Roman Republic was given new spiritual foundations that caused Rome to rise to great imperial strength under Christianity. The objective of this book is to enlighten the reader of the way the Devil works and to go on to point out the way the gospel of Jesus Christ can still be the power of God unto salvation. It will help the reader understand what has happened in America and be able to discern what may lie ahead. It can enable us all to know better what can be done to produce genuine renewal of faith and a restoration of our nation. And, even if there is now arising a one-world civilization of the end times, it will help interpret the works of evil and the trend toward antichrist. It will enable Christians to trust in the sovereign God.

Chapter 4

Rise and Pattern of Moral Decline
of the Greek Democracy

Two Preliminary Rises of Civilization before the Athenian Democracy

Only a bare sketch of Greek history with a deliberate focus on the path of the third rise and decline of Greek civilization is possible here. Archeological research in the twentieth century has added amazing dimensions to our previous understanding of Greek history,[1] revealing three rises and falls. The first was the great Greek civilization in Crete (ca. 2000-1500 B.C.), with a middle or intermediate one of lesser importance centered at Lefkadi and ending with the Lilantine war in the eighth century. The third was the rise of the great Athenian democracy, which is the wave before Christianity and our main focus in understanding Paul's description of the steps of decline.[2]

THE RISE AND PATTERN OF DECLINE
OF GREEK DEMOCRACY (ca. 800-300 B.C.)

Faith in a Supreme God behind the Growth of Civilization

Early Theism

The rise of the Greek democracy, centered in Athens, produced one of the greatest civilizations of all times. The evidence indicates that the Greeks began each of their civilizations with the belief in one creator god. The exact events that caused the renewal of faith in Zeus and a reunion under the city-states led by Athens is not clear.

The earliest evidence of Greek belief was in one creator sky-god. Will Durant has said:

> Originally, so far as we can make out, the great god of the invading Greeks, as of the Vedic Hindus, was the noble and various sky itself; it was probably this sky-god who with progressing anthropomorphism became Uranus, or Heaven, and then the 'cloud-compelling, rain-making, thunder-herding Zeus.[3]

Pindar (478 B.C.) said, "Uranus [heaven] is the father of us all." This early faith disintegrated into pluralism and humanism in the first wave of civilization, but was revised and led to the great democracy.

In this wave of Greek civilization, it was Zeus, son of Uranus, who was in the forefront and in control of men, of the world, and of gods and demons. Zeus was no longer the subsidiary of the goddesses and the power of women, or a part of nature (as at the end of earlier cycles) but the ruler of all. In speaking of the origin of Greek gods, H. J. Rose says:

> In point of fact, their origin is extremely varied. The only one whom we can be certain the Achaians brought into Greece with them was Zeus himself, whose name, as has long been recognized, is etymologically the same as the Sanskrit Dyaus and the first syllable of the Latin *Jup-piter* and therefore belonged to the original language . . . . [4]

W. Schmidt adds:

> The figure of the Greeks' Supreme Being, Zeus, has gone furtherest [*sic*] in the direction of anthropomorphism. However, we must distinguish between the later and unrestrained poetical myths and the ritual forms; also, we must allow for the blending with Zeus of gods from non-Indo-Germanic peoples. Even so, he remains the guardian of order, the first and greatest ruler and king, father and begetter of gods and men, superior to all, god of the sky and storms. [5]

Schmidt likewise sees Zeus as supreme over all things and the anthropomorphism of Zeus as later and degenerative. Later, he was reduced to the thunder-god in nature as was Baal, no longer being transcendent. For the reason that this degradation had occurred, Paul never identified him with the one supreme God, as he would have in the early times.

Robert Brow says that Zeus Pater (father) was also called Uranus (heaven). [6] Anaxagorus, and later Plato and Aristotle, argues that God degenerated from a governing intelligence in the beginning to myths. Herod and Hesiod say in the degenerative period that Gaia (earth) was produced from Chaos (void), while elsewhere Uranus is said to have mated with Gaia to produce Zeus and the other gods. This idea is also related to the idea of Cronos castrating Uranus, and Zeus ruling afterwards. While these show how Zeus was degenerated, they point to his early prominence.

Prometheus, a Greek name for God, first created man from clay (as in Genesis 2:7), and only later were men and gods related. He gave men the wisdom and skill to create culture, such as the making of fire and other useful arts. He warned man of the coming judgment of the flood. Prometheus seems to be at times like the Holy Spirit of the Hebrews and the Christians, although this name was also later degraded.

The predominant evidence quoted by the Greeks themselves and stated by leading non-Christian, secular scholars is that the Greek civilizations began with and worshipped a supreme being as the god of heaven, and his son Zeus, who held the father's authority to rule. The degrading of faith in one god led to the decline of the early waves in Greek civilizations. But the renewal of the worship of Zeus was the early mark signifying the renewal that produced the Greek democracy.

The Renewal of the Early Monotheism Began the Democracy

Certainly, the renewed worship that began at Mount Olympus early in the short-lived second surge of civilization had a strong resurgence for the democracy at that same spot of Mount Olympus and in a more prominent way. Perhaps some leaders saw the Greek peoples falling apart again, and by some unknown divine event, were led to renew the worship which had given them oneness before. The evidence points to the fact that the Greeks renewed their relationship with each other by inviting other tribes to participate in the Olympic Games (ca. 776 B.C.) and offering worship and feasts to their original common sky-god, Zeus. The impetus to worship was significant because the commitment to worship one god spread to a dominance in the early generations.

The nature of the Greek experience of living in scattered city-states was part of the reason for their emerging greatness. Being of the same race, they felt kinship, and being in separated communities, they felt competition to outdo each other in the various aspects of the Olympics. The one great point of continuing unity was their original worship of Zeus. Their need for combat against the Persians also brought male prowess to the forefront. The seventh century led to inclusion of many groups in the Olympic Games from about 675 B.C. and then to local games for selecting their representatives in the multiple-city competition in the national games every five years. This competition must have brought worship of the one supreme sky-god to prominence in all the cities.

Practical accountability to Zeus was evident in daily life. The Panhellenic Games were held under the auspices of the Festival of Zeus for one month. Pledges by the athletes to abide by the rules were only one aspect of honesty in society, which involved pledging to Zeus before the open sky. These male endeavors exalted patriarchy and rejected the old feminine power of the goddess worship of past cultures. The Olympic contests were soon spread to include the arts, music, poetry, sculpture, and productive skills. These contests motivated local city-state education, development, and communication.

Renewal of Patriarchal Leadership; Exaltation of Women and the Family

Control through the Reestablished Family

While Homer and Hesiod portrayed the degenerative picture of the gods in the intermediary period, there was a return toward the earlier monotheism, certainly by the time of the beginning of the city-states, that produced the democracy, perhaps by the end of the eighth century.[7] This unity in worship, with the unity in war, produced a patriarchal society with elected leaders that was progressive and intelligent, which revived law and order, the value of family, economic growth, and national spirit.

The need for production of healthy, intelligent offspring gave new value to women as mothers, homemakers, and teachers of children. Charles Seltman of Cambridge was surprised to discover the high regard for women and great freedom for them in ancient Greece.[8] George Murray observes that much later, by the time of Sophocles and Pericles, the status of women in Athens had declined.[9]

Accountability in Government Spread to All Citizens

The monarchical government of the tribes gradually gave way first to elected autocrats whose terms were progressively shortened, then to representative aristocrats, and then to noblemen. This change led to a response to popular demands by the leader of the ruling group, which produced figurehead leaders who did what the people wanted. The figurehead finally gave way in Athens to the landowning population, or demos, to have a vote and then toward the production of a democracy. This democracy did not include free men or slaves at first; women voted through their husbands. Along with this development of government was the development of laws at various places: the laws of Zaleucus at Locri, Lycurgus at Sparta, Draco at Athens, Charondas at Catana, and finally the laws of Solon at Athens (from 660 to 594 B.C.).

A generation after Solon, a more democratic faction emerged. Clisthenes introduced radical reforms, and instead of the four historic tribes, he divided all free citizens into ten tribes and reduced the power of the archons, or chief magistrate. Thus, in Athens, democracy emerged. The religious hierarchy involved with the aristocracy who held political power was a hindrance to its development and lost power in the process. This loss had a negative effect on religion in general. As a result of the Persian Wars that began around 500 B.C., the Greek colonies changed from friendly families in contest to a united people. They had to unite to defend themselves.

While there began to be a departure from faith in God and the supernatural by the middle of the seventh century B.C., it was not until about the middle of the fifth century that a deistic or skeptical view of God gained ascendancy, and there began to be an attack on what had been the prevailing faith in the supernatural. That attack was the moral turning point of the Greek democracy, and it was during that time that the steps of decline began. Also at that time, the intelligence and brilliance of the Greeks continued to ascend to greater glory.

Material Prosperity and Civilization Developed

Divine providence and hard work with an ethical accountability to God began gradually to produce more wealth. From the eighth century, shipping began to increase. Greek trading posts on the Syrian coasts connected with Mesopotamian trade routes, Ischia and Kymen on the bay of Naples, and other posts on the southern shore of the Black Sea. W. G. Forrest writes:

> By 700 B.C. perhaps a dozen states in Greece had been transformed from virtually isolated and self-sufficient agricultural communities into comparatively sophisticated organizations in which, still against a solid agrarian background, both government and individual had become aware that prosperity and even survival depended on overseas connection, on the exchange of goods outside the limits of the state itself.[10]

A generation later, urbanization produced congestion, colonies were exported to relieve population pressures, and imports to the cities grew. Forrest continues:

> With the general increase in prosperity came an increasing demand for luxuries and for quality in everyday goods, and increasing specialization and still more trade . . . . From 800 B.C. onwards, goods were exchanged throughout the Greek world in ever-increasing quantities and profits were made by someone on this exchange.[11]

STEPS OF REVOLT AGAINST GOD AND THE DECLINE OF CIVILIZATION

The Intellectual Revolt

Gradual Pride and Lack of Recognition of God

Education expanded from the aristocrats and nobles down to the people. Peisistratos (ca. 550 B.C.) championed the poor, and promoted popular education, and in the reign of Clisthenes (ca. 515 B.C.), education was finally widely available. The defeat of the powerful autocratic Persians gave a new sense of national pride to the Greeks. The expansion of their commercial markets and the taxes from the colonies and subjugated peoples, along with their intelligent productivity, produced enormous wealth. Self-sufficiency and a lack of thankfulness to Zeus developed.

The Golden Age of Greece lasted 75 years, the lifetime of their great leader Pericles (479-404 B.C.). For more than a generation, it was a time of peace. The brilliance of man overshadowed everything in the areas of art, literature, theater, and the magnificent construction of buildings such as the Parthenon and the Odaem with 20,000 seats. The worshipping of Zeus gradually declined and shifted to the worship of Apollo, the god of manly youth and beauty, as the ideal human. The shift from theism to humanism was occurring.

As the colonies under Athens gradually emerged in strength, unity, and prosperity under an intelligent citizenry, the Greek peoples were deceived again to lose their consciousness of the supreme god, as they experienced foreign cults and secular thinking.

Steps in the Unconscious Humanistic Intellectual Revolt

The intellectual revolt was a slow and deceptive process involving at first a more mathematically precise and mechanical view of the universe. These ideas were made appealing as the Greek people gained self-confidence in their unity through wars against the barbaric Persians, and especially as they grew in prosperity and their citizenry became more educated. The tensions with the conservative religious hierarchy in the face of progress made religion political, and hindered objective religious worship and thought. The steps of thought away from God began like a trickle from a spring and grew to a mighty flooding river that washed away their beginning foundation of belief in the one true God.

The flames of unbelief were ignited by the Ionian School of Miletus, as Greeks from the city-states joined the surge of immense wealth out of Asia Minor. Greeks there subjugated themselves and gave tribute to Croesus, who was considered the richest man in the world.

The first step away from God was a mechanical view of nature. In Miletus, Thales (640-550 B.C.), a scientist who drew on Egyptian, Phoenician, and Babylonian knowledge, was considered the chief of the seven wise men of ancient Greece. He claimed to found mathematics by proving the elementary propositions of geometry. He shocked the world by predicting an eclipse of the sun which occurred in 585 B.C., precisely as he said.[12] The ability to make this prediction was a dramatic example of the power of the human mind and impressed the world with man's ability to understand nature. This knowledge had an effect like the modern post-Copernican views. With his practical and scientific sense, Thales made a fortune.

Thales was followed by Anaximander, Anaximenes, and others who interpreted nature as an infinite and eternal process involved in an eternal being,
inserting deism and/or pantheism, and removing a personal presence of God to
whom man is accountable. This idea was counteracted by Parmenides of Elea
who held that the infinite creator dwelt in the depths of the human mind as "Truth
and Reason," and is changeless.

This idea was followed by the philosophy of universal flux by Heraclitus
(540-480 B.C). He interpreted the essence of Being as *becoming,* which prepared
the way for evolutionary thinking. William Cecil Dampier said:

> The idea of evolution was known to some of the Greek philosophers. The
> Atomists seem to have thought that each species arose independently, but,
> in their belief that only those types survived which were fitted to the
> environment, they touched the concept of natural selection.[13]

Fixity and completeness of the knowledge of nature which is run by universal law was established by Pythagoras and approached a naturalism beyond
deism in nature. Pythagoras developed the Pythagorean theory, or the fourth
proposition of Euclid. He gave all of life a mathematical interpretation.
Anaxagoras advanced the mechanical bent to a belief that the heavenly bodies are
the same nature as the earth; the sun being not the god Helios but a burning stone.
He brought the Ionian school of thinking to Athens, inserting a strong influence.
Hicetas thought the earth revolved on its axis, and Aristarchus held the same
opinion, believing the earth moved around the sun. These ideas were the source
of the modern views of Copernicus.

Atomic theory was forwarded by Empedocles, Anaxagoras, and Democritus,
who declared that indeterminate matter was divided into an indefinite number of
molecules (or *atoma*) differing in size and form, acting out of necessity in
perpetual motion derived from their essence. While Greek scientific philosophical thinking was crude and often inaccurate, it progressively moved from a theistic concept to deism, to evolutionary ideas, to atomistic views, and finally to an
empirical relativism.

The Dominance of Leaders Who Held to a Mechanical World

In the last half of the fifth century, the Sophists introduced the idea that
perceived experience from the senses was the correct epistemological view,
doing away with objective truth and making all things relative, and bringing
empirical thinking to dominance. Man thus became the measure of all things, and
each man's perceptions were as good as those of any other man. The Sophists
developed the dogma of progress and worldly success. Their thinking introduced
religious skepticism into everything. For them, all truth had to appeal to reflection and reason. Protagoras drew a line between time and eternity, and revelation
from God was excluded. Sophistry had widespread impact on all Greeks,

especially in Athens, and made religious skepticism dominant. It became the background for the views and arguments of the classical Greek philosophers who followed–Socrates, Plato, and Aristotle.

The Athenians imprisoned Anaxagoras and exiled Protagoras, who had made these views popular. But the deadly arrow poisoned with the questioning of divine existence and accountability had been driven into the heart of Greek society. By the time of Solon, and a century later with Theognis, their poetry voiced intellectual skepticism by attacking the gods and calling them to account for their misgovernment of the world. They challenged the "god-given right" of the blue bloods to rule. And, as mentioned, they challenged the religious hierarchy for control of the government. By limiting voting to property-owning citizens, they exalted wealth and materialism. In the later educational systems of Athens, these views were incorporated into the knowledge of the common man. This rationalism reached its point of dominance with Pericles.

G. Grotes sums it up:

> When the positive science and criticism and the idea of an invariable sequence of events came to supplant in the more vigorous intellects the old mythical creed of omnipresent personification [belief in God], an invariable schism was produced between the instructed few and the remaining community. The opposition between the scientific and religious point of view was not slow in manifesting itself.[14]

Benjamin Farrington, also studying the Greek development in science for the first three hundred years of the Greek democracy, said, "It offers us for the first time in history, an attempt to supply a purely naturalistic interpretation of the universe as a whole. Cosmology takes the place of myth."[15]

The Materialistic Revolt

In the sixth century, materialism emerged as the "god" of the Greeks. Shipping was intensified, and a new class of nobility grew from trade and production. The decline of worship of Zeus and the turning toward humanistic worship in Apollo developed into prominence. This was accompanied by the providential warning of the tragic Persian Wars.

Then, a new wave of materialism came into prominence. Forrest said, "By the fifth century there were substantial manufacturers, employing as many as fifty slaves, rich men by Greek standards."[16] The Persian Wars took men from their homes, and their wives took over many of the farms and family businesses while the men returned with spoils from conquest. As I have said in another book:

The Greek nation turned strongly towards materialism and the men began to forsake their wives in the pursuit of wealth following the time of the Clisthenes democracy (510 B.C.). This was the time of developing shipping, of discovery and mining silver in Athens, centralizing government and taxing the surrounding areas. The treasury was developed, with banking in the Acropolis, and there was an explosion in education. Materialism reached great heights during the time of Pericles.[17]

These benefits were shared by a new middle class from the end of the sixth throughout the fifth century.

The Sensual and Sexual Revolt

The stage was set gradually for Satan to move the Greeks into an obsession with the sensuous. The Sophists had emphasized that all knowledge came from the senses, and there was no valid metaphysical thought. All truth was now seen as relative. The center of thought and worship, the standard of truth, was man.

While the Greek men had performed naked before Zeus in the Olympic Games (no women were present), the idea of sensual experience now became public. Art included the idea of sexual freedom, and many pottery vases included boys as homosexual objects. Sensuous stories of the gods were widely told by Pindar and others. Aphrodite Paridemas, the goddess of free love, emerged into prominence in Plato's time. Herodotus (484-425 B.C.) presented erotic dancing, and Euripides (480 B.C.) presented it in plays. Attic Comedy exalted divorce as a right. Courtesans became prevalent and acceptable with public officials. Homosexuality became public.

The wars divided many marriages and led to much promiscuity. The Spartans had early been perverted to homosexuality and introduced it into their army, exposing the idea to the military. Education for women increased so that Plato tells us that Diotema had the same education as Socrates, and taught his students. The brilliance of male achievements in the culture made the idea of having babies and raising children seem insignificant, and women's traditional roles now seemed of little value. Margaret Mead, the anthropologist, once observed that when primitive man's achievement involves building only a hut twenty feet tall, having babies appears tremendously important, but when he builds the Empire State Building and a modern culture, a woman's role seems insignificant.[18] The Greek culture, with its glorious architecture and brilliant technology, obscured the role of women, and the materialistic emphasis made children a liability.

Moreover, when the men returned from the wars and assumed control of all production and wealth, removing women from what they were accustomed, women felt devalued and excluded from what they could do equally well, and they resented being denied the power of money. Euripides mentions the poor

58   *Pattern in Greek Democracy*

conditions of women, their restrictions, the double standard in sex, and also the plight of the children and their cries (cf. *Medea*, 213-251). In 451, Pericles tried to restrict women's legal rights.

Having been shown that women and their natures were of equal value in the sight of Zeus, women now demanded the equal material worth and success of men. It also meant viewing sex from a male perspective of enjoying an instant act, rather than from the more common feminine view of a relational closeness and a long-range involvement for children. Emphasis on the woman's role being the same as man's became clear by the last quarter of the fifth century. Pericles' earlier law was bypassed by the popular women's movement.

Plato took a dogmatic position on women being equal to men. He said:

It is sheer folly that men and women should not all with one accord follow the same pursuits with all their might. . . . We shall go on saying that in education and all else our women must participate as far as can be with men . . . in all activities of life.

He argued that women should go to war like men. The only difference, he acknowledged, is they have babies and men don't.[19] But this "only difference" had extreme implications for the future of Greece.

By the end of the century, the women publicly and militantly protested. This protest is displayed vividly in the plays of Aristophanes. In *Lysistrata*, the women are presented seizing the Acropolis and locking the gates. The Acropolis was the center of congressional government and of the treasury in the temple. Women took control and instructed the leaders who wanted money for war that they were now acting as the treasurer and would determine policies of state, leading it to peace. When men sought to interfere, women doused them with pitchers of water and shut the gates in their face. This revolt is displayed also in the play *Ecclesiazusae*. In this play, the women disguised themselves as men, gained access to the assembly, and passed a law giving women financial freedom and power of government.

By this time, the public display of erotica dominated the entertainment of the dance and theater. There were mixed bath houses, and the women participated naked in mixed *gymnasia*. Prostitution proliferated and was permitted and taxed by the state. Divorce abounded, with the law requiring only that any dowry be returned. Leaders kept courtesans publicly.

The sensuous also dominated in religion. Aphrodite Pandemos and Hermaphroditus prevailed. Women became temple prostitutes in service to gods, gaining money for themselves and their gods. The oneness of men and women in the family diminished. While women claimed freedom and equality with men, they were reduced to their lowest level in Greek history.[20] Having healthy, intelligent, beautiful children gave way to child neglect and abuse. Oneness with the husband in worship, work, and family, which had always been a joy of women, was discredited.

The idealism of Plato gave way to Aristotle's emphasis on individual particulars in realism. Individualism found expression in the hedonism of Epicurus, making pleasure the highest good. While Epicurus argued for moderation to achieve it, his followers did not. The reaction was stoicism, which renounced pleasure as an objective and sought to return to the old Greek moral and family values, and to the pride of virtue. But the Stoic source of ethical standards was not to be found in divine absolutes, but rather in changing nature, and the individual man was the only one to set the standards.

Rejection of Control for Anarchy

Egalitarian Teaching Motivated Conflict and Anarchy

The progressive rejection of the authority of Zeus and the religious ideals in favor of a pluralism of various gods placed material success as the highest priority. The exaltation of the material produced the idea of equality, or egalitarianism, based on the right of each individual to succeed. This turned the mind of man to fleshly pursuits and promoted sensualism. The emergence of the individual right to do what one desired for material prosperity and pleasure progressively pushed the way the government functioned from monarchs to oligarchs, to demagogues, and finally to socialism. Plato's city of the poor, in contrast to that of the rich, was a grounds for government distribution of funds.

The intellectual movement that made the mind of individual man the standard, and materialism that led to conflict over achievement of success and wealth, and sensualism that exalted one's freedom to do what feels good, all produced a selfish, individualistic revolt against all authority.

Religious anarchy was evident early. By the time of Solon, the rule of the religious hierarchy was challenged by the deistic view of the world, and new views were discussed while religion was questioned.

By the last of the sixth century, there were large businesses with slaves which eluded governmental controls, and by the time of Clisthenes, there was much speculation and needed controls on banking practices that were irregular. The peak of business anarchy was in the golden age of Pericles, and in time, Athens took material advantage of the other city-states, which ultimately led to rebellion.

The idea of submitting to the social unit of the family and the government that arose from the patriarchal leadership later gradually disintegrated. Carle Zimmerman has traced the family concept of a number of societies, and in his discussion of Greece, he describes this disintegration: The early society saw the family bond as the main tie, and kinsmen composed the armies with family allegiances uniting the army. Even as late as the fifth century B.C., the larger family was bound by public law and definite compositions of the state. The bonds were strong, but family justice was replaced by broader social justice. In the centuries following, there was a great increase in inter-family lawsuits. Zimmerman traces the family changes from "trustee, to domestic, to atomistic." He says that the inner spirit of the nation was lost. Women stopped having babies. There was no allegiance to the nation as a whole by the soldiers. Eventually, the Romans conquered with ease.[21]

After the revolt of the women, the revolt of youth and the underclass followed. Stephen Bertman, as editor of a study of the rebellion of youth, traces the conflict of the generations in Greece. In the introduction to this work, Meyer Reinhold identifies two periods in the classical past that witnessed conflict of youth against the older generation: the fifth century in Greece and the first in Rome.[22] With the conflict within the home and the breakup of the family, the lawlessness of the youth followed.

Rebellion of Youth against All Authority

The rebellion of youth is reflected in the later myths of the gods, in which Pindar says that Uranus was the early father of us all, but that Chronos, his child by Gaia, rebelled and castrated Uranus, and then Zeus replaced him. This was reflected in the myths of Homer and Hesiod. This same act of castration of the supreme sky god is reflected in the myths of other cultures when the civilizations are breaking down. The stories of the gods show that the process went from one transcendent spirit to whom they were accountable, to many gods who reflected their individual desires.

As late as Solon in the fifth century, the youth were still responsible for their parents. In Athens, "laws prescribed obligations of children to their aged parents and grandparents: provision of food, lodging, and burial" was required. They were subject to indictment for failing to do so. This was true at Delphi and elsewhere.[23]

The rebellion of youth and their refusal to obey the laws to respect the elders is identified by Bertman as growing out of the evolutionary development of the logic that everyone is equal and has equal rights. He says this growing idea "increasingly led to the 'de-authorization of the fathers'." He added, "Thus there emerged for the first time the claim of the younger generation to a 'natural right' to disobey and disregard fathers and elders." He said, "This devaluation of the older generation and generational disequilibrium unparalleled in the previous history of mankind was accelerated by the growth of the democracy."[24]

The idea of youth disowning their fathers was in plays of Euripides. The stock figure became the "father beater" in Attic Comedy, and there appeared in the law processes for fathers to disown their sons or to charge them with mental incompetence. Scorn of elders was said to have taken on degenerative practices. As a result, literature and laws cried out for a return to "more authoritarian controls." The moral decay of Athenian youth led to the creation "of a new group of ten officials, one for each tribe, whose duty it was to superintend the training of the ephebes." These were officially called "Sophonistae-Restrainers." Youth associations, *neoi*, formed and began to spread all over the Greek world. These were sports clubs for nineteen- and twenty-year-olds. From the time of Plato, youth rebellion was so bad that the attitude of youth was labeled "anarchy," and the warning was that this would lead to a dictator.[25]

Plato describes the loss of respect and authority that affected the family and then the state:

> The parent falls into the habit of becoming like a child, and the son like the father. The father is afraid of his sons, and they show no reverence or respect for their parents, in order to assert their freedom. Citizens, resident aliens, and strangers from abroad are all on an equal footing . . . . The schoolmaster is afraid of and flatters his pupils, and the pupils make light of their masters as well as their attendants. Generally speaking, the young copy their elders, and compete with them in words and deeds, while the elders, anxious not to be thought disagreeable tyrants, imitate the young, accommodating themselves to the young and filling themselves full of wit and bon mots.

Meyer Reinhold observes:

> Particularly in a democracy excessive freedom, according to Plato, results in loss of respect for the older generation; attendant egalitarian concepts and leveling downward produce a general adaptation on the part of the older generation to the manners and values of the younger generation. In a democracy the fathers therefore do not discipline their sons, who turn to dissipation and abandon modesty and self-control, becoming rebellious, insolent, and profligate, interested only in satisfaction of material desires.[26]

Aristotle says:

> The young, as to character, are ready to desire and to carry out what they desire. Of the bodily desires they chiefly obey those of sensual pleasure and these they are unable to control. . . . Owing to their ambition they cannot endure to be slighted, and become indignant. . . . They are ambitious of honor, but more so of victory; for youth desires superiority, and victory is a kind of superiority. . . . They do everything to excess – love, hate and everything else. And they think they know everything . . . . They think all men are better than they are; for they measure their neighbors by their own inoffensiveness, so that they think that they suffer unreservedly. And

they are fond of laughter, and therefore witty; for wit is cultured insolence.[27]

Judgmental Actions and the Judgment of God

In the closing decades of the democracy before Philip of Macedon took over
as dictator, there was an inward time of disturbances, inability to effect change,
economic disorders, and all kinds of crime and immorality. As previously pointed out, lawsuits exploded in the families and throughout the society. Bertman has
said there were "frequent wars, economic disorders and stagnation, growing
diminution of dignity and worth of the individual."[28]

The Successive Waves against God Reached a Climax

In summary, Will Durant has described most of the conditions at the end
times of the Athenian democracy. The intellectual revolt against God had finally
erased from the leadership the credibility of the supernatural or belief in anything
metaphysical or morally absolute. There was no consciousness of wrong.

> Moral disorder accompanied the growth of luxury and the enlightenment
> of the mind. The masses cherished their superstitions, and clung to their
> myths; the gods of Olympus were dying, but the new ones were being
> born; exotic divinities like Isis and Ammon, Atys and Bendis, Cybele and
> Adonis were imported from Egypt or Asia, and the spread of Orphism
> brought fresh devotees to Dionysus every day. The rising and half-alien
> bourgeoisie of Athens, trained to practical calculation rather than to mys-
> tical feeling, had little use for the traditional faith; the patron gods of the
> city won from them only a formal reverence, and no longer inspired them
> with moral scruples or devotion to the state. Philosophy struggled to find
> in civic loyalty and a natural ethic some substitute for divine command-
> ments and a surveillance deity; but few citizens cared to live with the sim-
> plicity of Socrates, or the magnanimity of Aristotle's 'great-minded
> man'.[29] As the state religion lost its hold upon the educated classes, the
> individual freed himself more and more from the old moral restraints—
> the son from parental authority, the male from marriage, the woman from
> motherhood, and the citizen from political responsibility.

At the end of the intellectual revolt, the materialistic revolt also crested and
promoted the conflict within and without. The new god was wealth. Durant
describes this:

> As the fourth century progressed, a real credit system developed: the
> bankers, instead of advancing cash, issued letters of credit, money orders,
> or checks; wealth could now pass from one client to another merely by

entries in the banker's books. . . . Every transaction was so carefully recorded that these accounts were usually accepted in court as indisputable evidence. Bank failures were not uncommon, and we hear of "panics" in which bank after bank closed its doors. Serious charges of maleficence were brought against even the most prominent banks, and the people looked upon the bankers with that same mixture of envy, admiration, and dislike with which the poor favor the rich in all ages.

The change from landed to movable wealth produced a feverish struggle for money, and the Greek language had to invent a word, *pleonexia*, to denote this appetite for 'more and more,' and another word, *chremastisticke*, for the busy pursuit of riches. Goods, services, and persons were increasingly judged in terms of money and property. Fortunes were made and unmade with a new rapidity, and were spent in lavish displays that would have shocked the Athens of Pericles.

Greed corrupted the government from democracy toward a compulsory socialism that could not satisfy the lower classes and erupted into attacking the right. Durant says:

> In the midst of this wealth, poverty increased, for the same variety and freedom of exchange that enabled the clever to make money allowed the simple to lose it faster than before. Under the new mercantile economy the poor were relatively poorer than in the days of their serfdom on the land. . . . Hundreds of citizens depended for their maintenance upon the fees paid for attendance at the Assembly or the courts; thousands of the population had to be fed by the temples or the state. The number of voters who had no property . . . in 355 B.C. had mounted to 57 percent. The middle classes had provided, by their aggregate number and power, a balance between an unyielding conservatism and a utopian radicalism; Athenian society divided itself into Plato's two cities—one city of the poor, the other of the rich, the one at war with the other. . . . In this conflict more and more of the intellectual classes took the side of the poor. They disdained the merchants and bankers whose wealth seemed to be in inverse proportion to their culture and taste; even rich men among them, like Plato, began to flirt with communistic ideas . . . . Finally the poorer citizens captured the Assembly, and began to vote the property of the rich into the coffers of the state, for redistribution among the needy and the voters through state enterprises and fees.

This led to mounting state debt and increasing yearly tax imposts on the wealthy and the middle classes. Durant says:

> The result of these imposts was a wholesale hiding of wealth and income. Evasion became universal, and as ingenious as taxation. In 355 B.C., Androtion was appointed to head a squad of police empowered to search

for hidden income, collect arrears, and imprison tax evaders. Houses were entered, goods were seized, men were thrown into jail. But the wealth still hid itself, or melted away . . . . The motivation to work was supplanted by the desire to gain and indulge for nothing, and money to maintain the government dwindled . . . [Many] devoted themselves to gambling and profligacy; and the whole people spent more on public banquets and entertainments than on the provision necessary for the well-being of the state.

The sensual and sexual revolution reached its climax in the fourth century. The women of Greece gained access to the wealth they had demanded, and they owned much of the riches. The women also gained recognition and access to serve in all important jobs and places. By the second century, women began to lead in everything. They presided at the Greek games, and they served in the religious leadership in the temples. In at least seven Jewish synagogues in Greece, women presided, though the synagogues were the bastion of conservatism. By the third century, it was called the "Age of Women." As the Greek words could be rendered, "They changed the natural role to that which is contrary to nature" (Romans 1:26).

Sexual freedom exploded in those final days. Homosexuality, which had come out of the closet earlier, now, along with all kinds of sexually explicit ideas, appeared on the pottery and in the art and literature. By the time of Pericles, he publicly maintained a famous courtesan and felt free from political liability to divorce his wife and be married to Aspasia. Even after efforts to enforce law and order and to renew public morality, things only worsened. Durant writes: "But sexual and political morality continued to decline. Bachelors and courtesans increased in fashionable cooperation, and free unions gained ground on legal marriage." Living together out of wedlock freed the men from legal obligations and made the women feel under obligation to treat them well, lest this "live-in" be rejected for another. Theopompus said, "The young men spend all their time among flute-girls and courtesans."

Durant continues, "The voluntary limitation of the family was the order of the day, whether by contraception, by abortion, or by infanticide." Women found various contraceptive means, such as "anointing the part of the womb upon which the seed falls . . . " with spermicidal ointments. Many single women with children ended up dependent upon the state, and many became temple prostitutes. Corinth alone had over one thousand temple prostitutes, and courtesans were so prevalent that the word *corinthiazomai* signified harlotry. But in Athens and all the colonies, men changed and used women freely.[30] In those times of women's great public recognition, the real respect and protection of women and childbearing reached one of the lowest points in all history. Women were used by men for their pleasure and easily discarded, and while women had sexual "freedom," they were the great losers. They had lost the freedom to use their distinctive nature to join in happy union with a husband and to feel loved and securely provided for and protected to bear children.

The growth of selfish freedom could not but reach its climax with this loss of the true concept of women and the breakdown of male obligation to a wife and children. The youth who rebelled had no roots, no security, no feeling of value. Each successive generation was filled with hate from conflict, instability, and none to teach them control. The people, in general, lost confidence in government, from the home to the state. Durant relates:

> The middle classes, as well as the rich, began to distrust democracy as empowered envy, and the poor began to distrust it as a sham equality of votes stultified by a gaping inequality of wealth. The increasing bitterness of the class war left Greece internally as well internationally divided when [at the last] Philip [of Macedon] pounced down upon it; and many rich men in the Greek cities welcomed his coming as the alternative to revolution.

Judgmental Attitudes and the Judgment of God

Already, sources have shown how lawsuits began to proliferate over money, and almost anything else. The public arena became a place of fault-finding and accusations. Durant elaborates:

> At last even Demosthenes . . . [was] one of the noblest of one of the lowest groups in Athens—the rhetors or hired orators who in this century became professional lawyers and politicians. Some of these men . . . were reasonably honest; most of them were no better than they had to be. . . . Many of them specialized in invalidating wills. Several of them laid up great fortunes through political opportunism and their campaigns. Each party organized committees, invented catchwords, appointed agents, and raised funds; those who paid the expenses of all this frankly confessed that they expected to 'reimburse themselves doubly.' As politics grew more intense, patriotism waned; the bitterness of faction absorbed public energy and devotion, and left little for the city. The constitution of Clisthenes and the individualism of commerce and philosophy had weakened the family and liberated the individual; now the free individual, as if to avenge the family, turned around and destroyed the state.[31]

In the end, the once strong, patriotic armies of Greece that defeated the mighty Persians lost their moral and military preparedness. Durant continues:

> Young men received some grounding, as epheboi, in the art of war; but adults found a hundred ways of escaping military service. War itself had become professionalized by technical complications, and required the full time of especially trained men; citizen soldiers had to be replaced with

mercenaries—an omen that the leadership of Greece must soon pass from statesmen to warriors. . . . Greek mercenaries sold themselves impartially to Greek or 'barbarian' generals, and fought as often against Greece as for her . . . . Soldiers shed their blood now, not for a fatherland, but for the best paymaster that they could find.

John H. Vincent says:

Philip was the King of Macedon . . . who by force of arms and skill of diplomacy made the Hellens accept Macedonia as a Grecian State and himself as the Greek commander and chief. . . . No Greek general won fame by opposition to the Macedonians. The quality of the Greek troops had deteriorated, and the soldiers now served for money rather than for love of country.[32]

The Greek freedom and prosperity ended and inevitably came under the judgment of God from selfish individualism and conflict.

The greed of the upper classes led to a gap in living standards, which in turn led to class wars. The Ægean Islands revolted, causing the Social War. The revolt of the Phocians brought on the Sacred War. Then the colonies revolted one after another, because Athens had taken economic advantage of them. With the growth of this anarchy the glory of Greece came to an end. This led to the dictatorship of Philip II of Macedon, the father of Alexander the Great.[33]

The Greek cities were fatigued by the constant conflict, and the mercenaries who were paid to fight had no real allegiance. When Philip invaded, the armies yielded easily and many of the leaders and people welcomed his victory. He ruled briefly (338-336 B.C.), and Alexander the Great, his son, ascended the throne. Alexander solidified his rule, and then set forth to extend his empire, living for the thirst of conquest and spreading the pagan Greek culture.

The End with Antichrist, Man Proclaiming Himself as God

Alexander, in a satanically deceptive way, came to believe he was God, and later declared himself God. Olympias, wife of Philip II, the mother of Alexander, was a beautiful woman with an angry temper who became involved in wild Dionysian rites. One night Philip found a snake lying beside her in bed, and was not reassured by being told that it was a god. Worse, Olympias informed Philip that he was not the real father of Alexander; that on the night of their wedding a thunderbolt had fallen upon her and set her afire; it was the great god Zeus-Ammon who had begotten the dashing prince. In rage against Philip for his love affairs with other women, Olympias told Alexander the secret of his divine paternity.[34] Not long after this revelation, Olympias supported Pausanias, an army officer, in the assassination of Philip and in making Alexander king.

As a youth, Alexander was tutored for greatness by the brilliant Leonidas and Aristotle. He was required by Leonidas to arise and run a two-thousand-pace course up a hill to a shrine. At the turning point of his course, he would reach the white marble shrine just as the sun shone on it. Carved upon it were the words: "I am an immortal god, mortal no more." This set before Alexander his image.[35]

Years later, after his conquest of the Persians and accepting their dress and intermarrying with their women, he saw himself as merging the two great cultures of the Greeks and Orientals, which had so long been in conflict. He was bowed to and flattered by all. In 324 B.C., he sent word to all the Greek states except Macedonia (where the insult to Philip might have aroused resentment) that he wished hereafter to be publicly recognized as the son of Zeus-Ammon. Durant comments:

> It was not so much for a man to be a god in the Greek sense of the term. . . . The Egyptians had always thought of the Pharaohs as gods . . . . The priests at Siwa, Didyma, and Babylon, who were believed to have special sources of information in the field, had all assured him of his divine origin . . . . It is true that after his self-deification he became increasingly irritable and arrogant; that he sat on a golden throne, wore sacred vestments, and sometimes adorned his head with the horns of Ammon.[36]

Many believe his body was interred in Alexandria, the city he founded in Egypt. In late January 1995, a research group of archeologists claimed to have found his resting place in Siwa, the location of the oracle for Ammon.

Thus, the Greek civilization had made its third full-scale move towards degradation and collapsed into complete rejection of the transcendent sky-god, and let man claim his place. The original sin of Adam was repeated. An antichrist who claimed he was as wise as God was manifested. But Alexander still knew of his mortality in his heart, and even continued to offer sacrifices to the day of his early death.

In conclusion, it is quite clear that Paul, in chapter 1 of Romans, was describing the steps of decline of the Greek world that he knew well. He was an inspired apostle, and a great scholar from the city of Tarsus, which had a school that rivaled those of Athens and Alexandria in Greek learning. His knowledge of the Greeks from the time of Crete was obvious (Titus 1:12).

Chapter 5
Rise and Pattern of Decline
of the Roman Republic

INTRODUCTION TO ROMAN CIVILIZATIONS

A Firm Character Forged by Centuries of Conflict

The Romans, after several centuries, developed a reputation that was forged out of the conditions they faced in the midst of the geographic Mediterranean boot. In describing the Roman citizen, one informed historian said:

> To his rude manners, his superstitious mind, and haughty demeanor the Romans added sternness of spirit which at times deserves no better name than cruelty. . . . Callousness to human suffering was a Roman virtue, and the pages of history are red with Roman slaughterings. "As faithful as a Roman sentinel" is the world's highest tribute to fidelity, and, in truth, the Pompeian soldier who was pelted to death at his post by the fiery hail of Vesuvius grandly typified the steadfastness of the Roman character.[1]

Ethnic groups of various languages, from the north by land and others by sea on the Mediterranean, migrated to the boot-like Italian peninsula with Rome near its middle. Michael Crawford, who has diagrammed the map of early Italy, lists the early settlers from the north as Umbrians, Etruscans, and Sabines, and then on the west of Rome, the Marsi, and to the south, the Latins, Samnits, Volscians, Lucanians, and Bruttians.[2] When one adds the Greek colonies and the others who invaded, such as the Carthaginians, it becomes evident that Italy was a place of repeated contests between a number of different people, often with very different languages and customs. To survive as the strongest power and be the conqueror in the Mediterranean world required the building of such a character of sternness. The greatness of the Romans grew out of their fighting, their political ability to assimilate and integrate new peoples into their army, and their legal ability to hold those they conquered accountable as members of the expanding state.

Pattern in Roman Republic

Success Produced Wealth and Pride that Undermined Strength

But if the Romans' strength was in expanding and assimilating, this too became their weakness in bringing down the glorious civilizations which they built up. Their early expansion of civilization was brought down by accepting the Etruscans, and later by inviting in the Greeks, in their final stages of cultural debauchery. Little is known about this earliest phase of civilization. Roman history is plagued by the lack of good historical records in the early times. Andrew Lintott, in writing about the lack of data compared to other civilizations, said, "A small portion of the Roman historians has survived the hiatus in culture and learning that followed the decline of the western half of the Roman Empire."[3]

There are three primary waves of Roman civilization: (1) that of the kings, which was linked to the Etruscans, which has the least historical data (ca. 1000 to 500 B.C.) (2) the Republic (ca. 500 B.C. to Christian era) (3) the Imperial times (to ca. 500 A.D.). The last two are fairly well documented.

Even though there are scant historical records, the story of the earlier rise and fall of the civilization of the kings has historical remnants, even though at times this is linked to their questionable heroic stories. It is the second decline, that of the Roman Republic which is well documented and precedes the Apostle Paul, that seems to furnish the basis of the pattern he gives in Romans and is the focus for this study. As Lintott says, the "real history" stretches back to the records of the consuls at the founding of the Republic.

First Wave of Civilization and the Conditions before the Republic: The Kings

While it is known that the Etruscan civilization had risen to great heights before Rome, which by legend was founded about 735 B.C, "the histories written by Etruscans and other local traditions have disappeared almost without a trace."[4] The record of the years of their agricultural rural history is virtually missing (ca. 200 years), and the cities emerge into history as already growing. Tradition places the line of the Romans from a relationship to an escaped hero of Troy who ruled the Latins.

> Here, from the eighth century onwards, there developed by a combi-
> nation of internal evolution and outside, largely Greek influences,
> (the Etruscan language is neither Greek nor Italic) an advanced urban
> civilization; this civilization was essentially homogenous, although
> the different Etruscan cities remained separated political entities.[5]

During this early period, the city of Rome emerged as a major city involved in the Etruscan culture, and it developed into probably the major center. While there is much doubt about some heroic accounts in the era of the kings, the existing data which reveals the known history of the kings also reveals the same steps of decline that we will follow in the historically better documented Republic that followed.[6]

THE RISE AND FALL OF THE ROMAN REPUBLIC

Interim Between The Demise of Kings and Beginnings of the Republic

The growth of the Roman Republic manifests an awesome trend of human development. The Etruscan-Roman culture collapsed into an individualistic movement of greed and sensuousness. But amazingly, arising from this degraded condition is the phenomenon of a government by the Roman people that became a powerful, extensive republic based on law, justice, and order, that conquered the surrounding world and influenced all of Europe and modern times.

A Great Sky God Was Basis of the Founding of Roman Civilization

Some prominent early scholars, trying to reconstruct the beginnings of the Romans, proposed that their beliefs developed from nature worship. This view was imposed because the evolutionary hypothesis prevailed at the time. But later more scientific German cooperative religion studies have shown that faith in one supreme spirit sky God called Jupiter was original and lasted quite a long time.[7] Statements of a number of scholars say this.

Franz Cumont speaks about "the abode of the supreme God," saying:

Under the Romans he [God] was still simply called Caelus, as well as "Celestial Jupiter" [Jupiter Caelestis, Zeus Ouranios], but it was a heaven studied by a sacred science that venerated its harmonious mechanism. According to this cosmic religion, the Most High resided in the immense orb that contained the spheres of all the stars and embraced the entire universe, which was subject to his domination. The Latins translated the name of this "Hypsistos" by Jupiter *summus exsuperantissimus* to indicate his preeminence over all divine beings. As a matter of fact, his power was infinite.[8]

Barrow says:

One of the earliest powers to be individualized was the power of the sunlight and sky; it was called Jupiter, if indeed Jupiter was not the single Spirit from which other numina [spirits] were individualized. It was an early custom to swear an oath in the open air under the sky, where no secret could be hidden from an all-seeing power.

Earlier he said:

> In the earliest days of the Roman people its leader solemnly took the "auspices" by observation of signs revealed through religious rites, to discover whether the action which the state proposed to take was in line with the God's will, which ruled the world.

He points out that Cicero placed this God first as the principle upon which the state rested.[9]

Early Previous Worship under the Kings Went from God to Man

At the beginnings of the city of Rome, the survivor of the twins, Romulus, is said to have opened a refuge for oppressed and discontented people of the surrounding countryside of the hills; this refuge was identified with the place of the Roman city. A war with Sabine was resolved by the intervention of Sabine women, and the two tribes joined, the Sabine chief reigning jointly with Romulus. Romulus framed the constitution for the state with three tribes of patricians, including also the Latins, each tribe being composed of ten families. From these, one hundred of the wisest patricians were chosen for a Senate to assist the king in ruling. Thus, it began with a ruling oligarchy of aristocratic families. But after these early beginnings, there followed the period of several centuries of the kings in which Rome went though the steps of decline and ended in chaos, ending with the king ruling as god, producing the chaos mentioned above.

Vincent and Joy comment:

> The student of the legends has noticed a strain of violence and despotism running through the stories of the later kings of the Etruscan culture that preceded the Republic. The monarch is no longer the revered judge and priest of the people, but has become a military leader. The throne no longer descended peacefully to the patrician whom the Senate nominates and whom the curies and gods approve.[10]

Finally one king autocratically acted as God and called himself god. All the people suffered terribly under the conflicts, injustices, and judgmental attitudes that pervaded the society. It finally came to the place that everyone realized these conditions could not continue. Rome, in this chaos, was ripe for its internal enemies to assert themselves, and for its foreign enemies to take advantage of their discordant condition. From these conditions, the Roman Republic emerged.

Return to the Great Sky-God, Jupiter, Started the Great Republic

While the details are not recorded, it is clear that there was a unique spiritual renewal in the Romans' view of God and in how He carries out His government in this world. Almost unanimously, the leadership of Rome returned to the worship of the god Jupiter, and also allowed the patriarchs to rule. This was not without struggle and painful conflict, but the return occurred.

The godly, patristic leadership united and asserted their rights in the Senate. According to Michael Crawford:

> The early years of the Republic were marked by an attempt on the part of the patrician families to achieve a monopoly of secular and sacred office. . . . The first century and a half of the Republic saw first the reassertion of Roman leadership of the other Latin communities and then a long sequence of wars against the southern Etruscan cities . . . .[11]

It was the influence of these Etruscan cities that had corrupted and led to the collapse of the first civilization of the Romans.

But at the heart of this patristic reassertion of authority was a deep realization of their accountability to the one sky-god of the universe whom they had forsaken. They called the people of Rome back to the worship of Jupiter. In 509 B.C., the foundation of the Temple of Jupiter was laid on the Capitoline in Rome, indicating the renewal of him as their national god. This was a clear return to monotheistic theism.

This is reviewed in the *Encyclopedia Britannica* as follows:

> In Jupiter we undoubtedly see not only the great protecting deity of the race, but one and perhaps the only one whose worship embodied a distinct moral conception. He is specially concerned with oaths, treaties and leagues, and it was in the presence of his priest that the most ancient and sacred form of marriage (*confarreatio*) took place. The lesser deities, Dius Fidius and Fides, were perhaps originally *identical*, and certainly connected with him. This connection with the conscience, with the sense of obligation and right dealing, was never quite lost throughout Roman history. In Virgil's great poem, though Jupiter is in many ways as much Greek as Roman, he is still the great protecting deity who keeps the hero in the path of duty (pietas) towards gods, state and family.
>
> But this aspect of Jupiter gained a new force and meaning at the close of the monarchy and the building of the famous temple on the Capitol of which the foundations are still to be seen. It was dedicated to Jupiter Optimus Maximus; i.e., the best and greatest of all Jupiters . . . . The fact that the Romans chose the name of Jupiter (in establishing government in other towns they conquered), in almost every case, by which to indicate the chief deity of the subject peoples, proves that they continued to regard him, so long as his worship existed at all, as the God whom they themselves looked upon as greatest.[12]

In September, an annual feast to Jupiter was held, and the counsels made a sacrifice of a white ox, "and after rendering thanks for the preservation of the state, made the same vow as which their predecessors had been bound." The understanding was that Jupiter was the ruler and they were accountable to him.

At a much later time, two female goddesses, Juno and Minerva, were joined in association with this worship. As the same article in *Encyclopedia Britannica* states, "The combination of three deities in one temple is foreign to the ancient Roman religion, while it is found in both Greece and Etruria."[13] In the article on Juno in the same source, it is said, "It does not appear in early cult she (Juno) is associated with Jupiter."[14] As we shall see, the intrusion came in later. The one creator sky-God, in some way at the beginning of the Roman Republic, revealed himself to the Roman leaders and called them to renew the nation's commitment, and a resurgence of civilization began under a theistic patriarchy.

Growth and Establishment of a Strong Government of Laws as a Republic

In addition to the re-establishment of the worship of Jupiter, the Senate negotiated a major treaty with Carthage to the west. This treaty was preserved by Polybius and is the earliest Roman document known in its entirety. The Greeks to the east were engaged in the Persian Wars and were not then the threat. The way was then open for the Roman patriarchal leaders, using the plebeian armies, to seek to consolidate their strength in Italy.

Within about fifteen years of the re-establishment of the Republic, the issue of the struggle of the patriarchal and plebeian orders arose and continued from 494 B.C. until about 287 B.C. The plebeian army launched the struggle, and gradually their rights were opened up to them to enter into government, first in making decisions that affected their own activities and then to be a part of all decisions of the state.

At first, they had magistrates of their own. After 472 B.C., tribunes were elected by the plebeians, and they had the right of veto over the magistrates and assemblies. In 445, when the law allowed plebeians to marry with patricians, the door was opened toward an equality that would move the government by intermarriage as well as by political confrontation of the classes. In 421, the office of *quaestar* opened to plebeians, and so on, until by 367, they had moved from an oligarchy of the patricians to a senate with plebeian participation as magistrates and priestly officials.

By 287 B.C., the plebeian Assembly of Tribes (Comitia Tributa) had become equal with the Assembly of the Centuries (Comitia Centuriata). How the Senate and these two other assemblies fully interacted to decide matters is not known. Through this time, various revisions of the laws were made on the code of Twelve Laws, Licinian Laws, and so forth. As the class controversy continued, it centered on the property taken in military conquest.[15]

As each new city or community was conquered, the Roman form of government was established, with wealth going to patriarchs who were the primary leaders in the Senate, while the military and plebeian assemblies counterbalanced. Certain Roman citizens were transported and given property in connection with the conquered cities, and they taught the language and involved the local leadership in the worship of Jupiter and in government. These Romans who moved retained all rights as Roman citizens. The recognition of the rights of the conquered to be a part of the government lessened the will to resist. From 375 to 275 B.C., the Romans mastered all three races; Etruscan, Samnite, and Greek and were dominant in all of Italy.

The genius of the government that evolved was that it did not for a long time assume egalitarianism, but gave the more educated and wealthy the right to lead, while it gradually recognized the right of each of the groups of the common people to express their opinions. The conquered were included in the expanding government and, to a certain extent, in property rights. Rome did not demand taxes of those on the peninsula at first, but did require soldiers to be furnished from the conquered towns. The main booty of conquest went to Rome.

Family was the center of government. In the early centuries, the concept of the home was sacred and women were the center for warmth and management, while respect for the elders prevailed. The plebeian districts offered the vote to the men. Unlike the Greek democracy, this was truly republican with group representation. The inclusion of so many different groups made this an ingenious and fair way to have a voice. During a period of over two hundred years of progressive growth, the Romans held to a worldview of Jupiter as the one sovereign God and each individual as created valuable and accountable to him.

Christians may hesitate to identify Jupiter with the creator God, because the image identified with this name later became so degraded. But it was this creator God called Jupiter who Paul said they knew at first (Romans 1:19-21). The steps of decline which are traced below follow the path Paul has described.

THE STEPS IN THE DECLINE OF THE ROMAN REPUBLIC

Beginning ca. 250 B.C. and Following

Intellectual Revolt in the Roman Republic

After conquering the mainland of Italy, the Romans developed a navy and gained much ability at sea. They removed much of the piracy that had plagued them and the Greek coastal towns. At the middle of the third century and afterwards, Rome was enjoying great peace, prosperity, and, with less need for a strong dependence on Jupiter, thankfulness and faith in him declined. Because the Greek colonies on the coasts were free from pirates, these "Greek towns, relieved from their fears, admitted their Roman liberators to share their national games and religious rites."[16] The Romans were thus taken into the Greek culture and affected by their degradation.

A renaissance in Greek learning was flourishing toward the beginning of the third century, and slowly but progressively influenced Rome. Alexandria, Egypt, was the leading commercial city on the Mediterranean controlled by the Greeks. The city had a huge library and many prominent teachers during the last years of the third century B.C. Euclid's geometry and astronomy were taught. Aristarchus of Samos revived the heliocentric view of the earth revolving around the sun and astounded the world by measuring the distance to the sun and moon and computing the size of the sun, moon, and earth. The neo-Pythagorean theories of the truth of the universality of natural law, fixed proportion, balance, order, and harmony, on which an intelligent universe is built, developed into a religious mystical order that attracted the Romans and led to a deistic view that excluded the interruption of the world by a miracle. "Pythagorean secret societies, with their mysteries, were maintained and encouraged in the Roman world."[17] Roman intellectual interest grew slowly at first, but grew rapidly after the defeat of Syracuse.

Experiencing their great sense of power, the Romans began to look to Sicily for conquest and engaged in the First Punic War with Carthage (264-241 B.C.). Archimedes of Syracuse had studied in Alexandria, achieving great learning, and returned home to establish a center of learning. By his genius, he expanded motor science by discovering specific gravity, the Archimedian screw, the theory of levers, and the evaluation of *pi*. He invented various machines and was solicited in helping to defend the city of Syracuse from the Roman attack.

> Thus he devised for Hieron engines of war which almost terrified the Romans, and which protracted the siege of Syracuse for three years. There is a story that he constructed a burning mirror which set the Roman ships on fire when they were within bow-shot of the wall.[18]

From this experience, the military leadership which controlled Roman thought gained tremendous respect for Greek science and saw its practicality for war. The interest in scientific education was accelerated after Syracuse and brought in the secular interest which had already begun by interaction with the Greek cities on the continent. Syracuse turned Rome toward the Greeks' intellect and away from trusting Jupiter. By this time, the perversion of Zeus worship in favor of skepticism was dominant in Greece. Thus, the close of the first Punic War was the turning point where the educated elite of Rome accepted human wisdom over faith in Jupiter.

This acceptance of Greek thought was accentuated even more after the defeat of the Greeks in 146 B.C. Vincent and Joy say:

The intellectual eminence of the Greeks remained for a long time unquestioned, and it was customary for Roman youth of the upper classes to seek their education at Athens, or to employ Greeks as tutors. So great was the influence of Greek teachings upon the Romans that it was said, with much truth, "The Greeks captured their Roman captors".[19]

Thus, a skepticism toward supernatural power was progressively gaining dominance in Rome, and the educated elite rejected faith, even though religious form continued to be practiced. Barrow points out how complete this was. He said, "Educated men of the last century B.C., conversant with Greek philosophy and criticism, might regard it as mere form." Nevertheless, these men held religious offices and led in its practice.[20]

As this progressive removal of Jupiter occurred, there was a growth and acceptance of a pluralism of gods. New gods came to the notice of the Romans as their horizons widened, and deities of the Etruscan and Greek cities in Italy found their way into the calendar. "For especially in the fourth and third centuries B.C., new cults were brought into the religious practice of the state, though as regards myth and ritual they were stamped with the Roman mark."[21]

> The people [of Rome] were enlarged by foreigners who were of a temperament different from the Roman and politically were opposed to the Senatorial party. From natural inclinations and for political and social reasons they were indifferent or hostile to the religion and standards of the older Roman tradition, and found greater excitement in newer forms of cult. . . . Pressure was too great, and of necessity the state tolerated all religions as practiced by individuals provided that they were not immoral or politically dangerous.[22]

Argument for returning to the old religion was a source of conflict, and even laws to exclude Greek teaching were passed, but to no avail (ca. 150 B.C.). But the worship of many gods diminished the credibility of faith in any.

With this broadened tolerance, the religions that appealed to the flesh gained dominance, and the gods who exalted wealth and license to indulge the flesh and express violence gained dominance. In the end, the intolerance was toward the worship of Jupiter and the early morals derived from the sky-god. Thus, faith in the one true god gradually lost credibility in several waves.

Revolt to Materialism Following Loss of Faith

If the period before and after the First Punic War began the intellectual revolt against God, the period associated with the Second Punic War was the time when religious skepticism began the revolt toward trust in the material, the burning desire for wealth, and the exaltation of man as an individual.

After the First Punic War (264-241 B.C.), Roman policy went beyond just plunder, colonization, and conscription of soldiers to taxation of their subjects. Sicily was conquered and taxed after the war. The Second Punic War (218-201 B.C.), in which they conquered Gaul (Spain), pushed the accelerator of an already fast-growing materialism into runaway speed. The worship of the great sky-god gave way to mammon.

Otto Kiefer describes the trend:

> About the time of Hannibal's defeat (202 B.C.), the Romans began to come into contact with the kingdoms of the eastern Mediterranean. As these contacts became more frequent, Rome learned to know Greek culture—which, as we shall see, was to influence her in various ways, not always for the better. It was her contact with Hellenism and her overthrow of great kingdoms rich with treasure which first allowed Rome to express her ambition in a new way—in greed and avarice. . . . In addition, wealth brought avarice to Rome, and the multiplication of pleasures brought the desire to ruin oneself and one's country by luxury and lust.[23]

Rome began to taste wealth, and greed replaced thanksgiving and fairness. The small farms had been taken over gradually by the rich patristic landowners and the state. Vincent explains:

> The class of small farmers, who are the strength of any nation by reason of their intelligence, frugality, and conservatism, had disappeared from Roman society. The corn-kings and cattle-kings of the peninsula, with their boundless cattle-ranges and sheep-pastures, had crowded them to the wall. The slave system, importing its human victims by thousands and working them to an early death, destroyed the competition of free labor and left the Italian freeman no recourse.[24]

Otto Kiefer has commented that the greed of materialism brought avarice and demoralized even to the peasant.[25] The men as leaders made mammon their god and this took priority over their wives and families. They neglected them to pursue wealth.

Rome had become a rapidly expanding urban city, with more people pouring into the city from everywhere. Joseph Plescia said:

> Other causes for the urban immigration were the facility by which the migrants could be absorbed into the citizen tribes; the attractions of city life, i.e., the higher style of living ("how can you keep them down on the farm after they've seen Paris"); farm-bankruptcy, caused by competition of provincial imports and local big farms; the hardships and small rewards of small farming; and finally, unemployment in the country, due to the growing use of slaves in the *latifundia*.

In fact, the unusual wealth coming from the wars and provinces in the first half of the 2nd century B.C. (ca. 210-145 B.C.) had promoted the greatest public and private works program in the history of Rome up to that time. This feverish building mood required labor and supplies, which in turn spurred the growth of factories, shops, apartments (*insulae*), etc., to supply the needs of the fast-growing population and of the building projects. [26]

Rome was already overextending its productive means and had to devalue its coin by essentially half of its value after the Second Punic War, showing that greed was a rapidly growing problem. The great concentration of wealth made possible the military potentates and proletarian armies. The aristocrats egotistically envisioned the expansion of Rome as a divine mission for the good of the nations they conquered. The educated elite envisioned spreading Roman government everywhere and this motivated their government spending.

Plescia further describes the conditions:

According to Posidonius, the Roman Empire was actually the realization of the stoic cosmopolis; it had an ideal form of government in which all men could live a just life under the leadership of an aristocracy, enlightened by the divine Logos. Yet, in spite of Panaetius' high tribute to the Roman aristocracy, his disciple, the historian Polybius, after 146 B.C., began to notice that the Roman ruling class was showing signs of a moral crisis. . . . The moral crisis of the ruling class coupled with the economic crisis of the Commons led to the reform movements, i.e., the populares.[27]

The final surge of the wave of materialism was at the end of the second century. The burgeoning materialistic desire drove Rome into an economic crisis in 138 B.C. Unemployment was severe. Some of Plescia's comments or remarks follow. "Rome, or better the Commoners, in the late 130s were in the throes of a serious economic depression." Revolt of slaves in Sicily and wheat reduction caused a food crisis in Rome with inflation of prices. Increase of the clientele of rich families, rise of precinctal bosses, growth of vice and exploitation, and overcrowding of the tenements increased the misery. After the construction of the temple to Mars, no further public building occurred except for the needed Tepular Aqueduct in 125 B.C. Ineligibility of the small farmers because of bankruptcy caused a decline of military manpower. The resulting depression "brought into the forefront the proletarii with all their urban problems, potentially capable of becoming an explosive political force."[28]

The educated, young elite championed the cause of the poor with a sense of self-righteousness, and clashed with the upper-class elders. Behind this was the intellectual cultural revolt, based mainly on Greek ideals. Tiberius Gracchus had been influenced by his Greek mentors. Blossius of Cumae "has been described as the theoretician of stoic socialism, advocating the subordination of individual interests to those of the commonwealth." In their zeal for the poor, Tiberius and his followers threw the state into a constitutional crisis. To take away the money from the rich and from the state, Tiberius demanded a recall of the tribune Octavius.

Joseph Plescia states:

> Previously the people delegated their sovereign power to the tribunes unconditionally; now the recall made the delegation conditional, which entailed the absolute control of the electors over the elected at all times, thus practically nullifying the *Ius intercessionis* (veto-power). Finally, the passage of the resolution to finance the agrarian law with the treasury of Pergamon . . . further undermined the power of the senators who had so far monopolized the finances and foreign affairs more or less unchallenged.[29]

The conflict of the plebeian assembly with the Senate led at first to victory for the liberal young and then to countermeasures by the aristocrats. The warfare, often bloody and in the streets, was over economic issues and involved the question of Italian citizenship.

Plescia describes the final wave of materialism in some detail:

> The economic crisis continued to keep Roman society under strain and stress. The unemployment situation with its extreme and frequent fluctuations was irritating not only because of its hardships, but also because of the fact that the empire was being exploited by a very few families. The monetary chaos and widespread debts further aggravated the crisis.

The following happened: In 91 B.C., Levius Drusus issued silver coins with 1/8 bronze; in 89 B.C., the bronze coin was devalued from 1/2 ounce to 1/3. In 85 B.C., Marius Gratidianue placed markers on some of the new debased coins to distinguish from solid silver ones; in 82 B.C., Sulla decreed the bronze should be accepted at face value, thus refusing to redeem them. Cicero said, "At that time the value of the coins fluctuated so much that no one could tell what he was worth" (Cicero, *De Officiis* 3, 80). Monetary chaos flourished.

People's debts mounted significantly, even among the landed nobility.

> Coupled with the monetary crisis was severe and widespread debt . . . . According to Appian, riots exploded in 89 B.C. between creditors and debtors (Appian, *Civil War 1,* 54). Flagrant usury occurred, in violation of the old law that forbade it. The consul Valerius Flaccus, on account of the magnitude of the debts, passed a law (*lex Valeria*) which enacted that bronze coins could replace silver coins at par value . . . in satisfaction of

the debt. Since one silver sesterce was equivalent to four asses, the law has been interpreted to mean a remittance of 3/4 of all debts, i.e., 75 percent of the debt was canceled. [30]

The government was involved in all kinds of efforts to relieve the debt crisis, not only of the aristocrats, but the commoners. So the final wave of mammon worship led in the end to anarchy.

Wave of Sensualism and Sexuality

The wave of sensualism and sexual revolt came as materialism bred a sense of self-sufficiency after the Second Punic War (201 B.C.). As mentioned, many of the men neglected wives and families to pursue money-making, and the woman's role of childbearing and nurturing became less valued. In the century before, the problem of sensuality and sexual perversion was not pronounced. Otto Kiefer refers to the restraint prior to the First Punic War: "Immodesty was not a vice but a monstrosity."[31] By the time of the surge of Neo-Pythagorianism of the intellectual revolt the sensual perspective had been accepted, and the divine presence was dismissed for the idea of the regularity of nature.

When they returned from the Second Punic War, the Roman soldiers brought back much wealth. Also, they had been away indulging with other women, while their wives carried on at home, so the influence of the Etruscans and Greeks found ready openings for feminist and sexual ideas at this time. Kiefer said, "It can hardly be an accident that all ancient writers mark the end of the Second Punic War as the turning point of morality and social tradition, and so as the beginning of the emancipation of women."[32]

Otto Kiefer describes the women's revolt from the Roman writers of the time:

In 215 B.C. during the terrible pressure of the Hannibal's war, the Romans introduced a law, the lex Oppia, which laid restriction on the use of ornaments and carriages by women. However, after the victory of Rome, these severe measures seemed to be less needful, and the women exerted themselves to have the law removed. Livy tells about it, 'It provided that no woman should possess more than a half an ounce of gold, wear a garment of many colors, or ride in a carriage within Rome or a provincial town or within a mile of either of those places unless for public worship.' When after the war the men returned enjoying their great freedom, there was protest. Valareius, the liberal, countered that the men 'are enjoying these luxuries and have them for their children and even their horses.' He said, 'Shall all other ranks and kinds of men feel the benefit of the country's prosperity, while only our wives are deprived of the fruits of peace and tranquillity?'

The women, already discontent, revolted, and the speech of Livy describes the occasion, and is given by Kiefer:

Neither influence, nor modesty, nor their husband's commands could keep the married women within doors. They beset all the streets in Rome and all the approaches to the forum, imploring the men who were going down to the forum that they should allow their former luxuries to be legalized, now that there was general prosperity in Rome. Every day the crowds of women grew, for they even came into the city from the provincial towns and market-boroughs. And now they dared to go to the consuls, the praetors, and the other magistrates and beseech them.

Livy then describes the response of the legislators. M. Porcius Cato, then head of the Senate (195 B.C.):

Our ancestors laid down that women might carry out no business, even private business, without supervision from her guardian, and they confined them to the authority of their parents, brothers, and husbands. But now we—save the mark!—are allowing them to take part in the government of the country and mingle with the men in the forum, the meetings, and the voting assemblies. What else are they doing at this moment, in the highways and byways, except supporting a bill sponsored by the tribunes and voting for the repeal of a law? Give rein to the head-strong creature woman, the unbroken beast, and then hope that she herself will know where to stop her excesses! If you do not act, this will be one of the least of the moral and legal obligations against whom women rebel. What they wish to have is freedom in all things, or rather, if we are to tell the truth, license in all things . . . . What honorable pretext can be adduced for the revolt of the women? "We wish to be resplendent in gold and purple," we are told, "to ride through the city in carriages on feast-days and working days as if we were celebrating a triumph over the law which we conquered and repealed and over your votes which we captured and carried off; we wish no limits to extravagance and display."[33]

Kiefer then adds, "We may remind our readers that after this memorable meeting of the Senate the women did not rest till the law they thought obsolete was repealed."

The women proceeded to gain their freedom to do anything that men did. By the end of the Republic, women were magistrates, president of the games, presided over temple worship, ruled some synagogues, and occupied offices of civil government. Their feminist movement was successful.

Sexually explicit ideas entered the culture slowly after the acceptance of Etruria as a Roman province (ca. 225 B.C.), and again when the Greek colonies invited the Romans to their national games (ca. 220); the corruption of decadent Corinth prevailed over the colonies with its unbridled sexuality. By the second century, the Romans began to perform naked in the Greek games. The Etruscan farce was performed, and by the end of the third century, the Greek mime was introduced and played at Floralia. The pantomime superseded the mime and was even more sensuous. Dancing instruction, which was considered sexually stimulating, began in 202 B.C. and spread. The first sanctuary of Venus Erycina appeared in Rome soon after, and Bacchanalia and other cults, such as Isis, entered about 186 B.C.

Kiefer observed that the growth of sexual immorality is associated with the women's revolt. He said:

> It is not by chance that one of the first complaints dates almost exactly to the period when the emancipation began. The elder Pliny (N. H., xvii, 25 [38]) tells us that the consul L. Piso Frugi lamented that chastity had disappeared in Rome. That was about the middle of the second century B.C. . . . Similar complaints continued for centuries.[34]

Thus, the tide of sexual immorality continued to bring devastation upon the Roman family.

Edward Gibbon, a historian of the Roman Empire, once said that in the first one hundred years of Roman history there was no record of a single divorce. Just as the father had full control over the children in the law, *patria potestas*, so the husband had autocratic power over the wife in what was known as the law of *manus*. There were three ways this was administered. The patristic families of the upper class held a religious ceremony of *confarreatio* where the wife was under the law of *manus*. Another form called *coemptio*, for mancipation in marriage for the commoner, usually involved the purchase, or dowry, and was secular. In this, the wife also was under the law of *manus*. A third form was the law of *usus*, which was like a common-law marriage, in which the couple lived together for a year, after which time the wife was also considered under the law of *manus*.

The breakdown occurred because when the first wave of Roman civilization under kings was in progress, an exception was added in the law of *usus* in the Twelve Laws, whereby the woman, if absent from the home for three consecutive nights, could avoid the law of *manus*. This exception, *usurpatio trinoctii*, was therefore a legal marriage which allowed escape from the husband's authority.

As the Roman Republic moved into the sensual or sexual revolution, the law of *usus* with this exceptional clause again increasingly became the practice. The growth of materialism and its effect on marriage began to be felt as early as 445 B.C., when the law was changed to allow plebeian marriage to rich patristic families. But after the women's movement in Rome, the shift to *usus* and to the allowance of divorce accelerated. As divorce and living together became prevalent, the law of *usus* also became meaningless.

Kiefer observes:

> In the later Republic, divorce became easier and more general as the status of women improved. An important point was that a marriage without *manus* could be announced simply as an agreement between two parties. This, of course, led to many frivolous results. Valerious Maximus (vi, 3, 12) speaks of a marriage which was dissolved because the wife had visited the games without her husband's knowledge, and Cicero (ca. 62 B.C.) in one of his letters relates that a wife obtained a quick divorce before her husband came home from the provinces, simply because she had made the acquaintance of another man whom she wanted to marry.[35]

In the last century of the Republic, the leaders had repeated divorces: Sulla five times, Pompeius five times, and Ovid three times.

As the importance of the man decreased under the pressure toward equality of the sexes, as his legal power over the family diminished, and as the idea of freedom to do anything one wanted took over, violence also increased, as well as all kinds of immorality.

When a man is not respected in the home, his reaction is to show his superior physical strength and to conquer more women to prove his masculinity; such occurred in Rome. While the first gladiatorial show was in 264 B.C., they became progressively more vicious with the ascendancy of the material and sensual culture. Men fought with each other and wild beasts to the death. In 174 B.C., seventy-four men fought for three days at the funeral games to honor Titus Flaminius. The oldest barracks for gladiators dates to the end of the second century, indicating they were then held with regularity. By the time of Seneca, they were unprotected and hence, bloody and brutal. Near the end of the Republic, the state issued regulations for the games because they were so frequent and gruesome. At the end of the growth of sensualism under early emperors, Christians were placed in the arena with lions.

By the time of the emperors, gladiatorial fights were part of the regular entertainment. Kiefer says:

> Under the emperors, society must have taken the same interest in gladiators that it now takes in boxing matches or films. The underlying reasons for enjoying such things are much the same now as they were then. We hear that children played at being gladiators; the younger generation keenly discussed the most important local fighters . . . The general public and women not least of them, raved about famous gladiators as we do about famous singers and actors. Inscriptions have been found on walls in Pompeii and elsewhere, calling a Thracian gladiator *suspirium et decus puellarum,* 'the maiden's

prayer and delight', or *medicus puparum*, "the doctor to cure girls." Even great ladies of the court seem to have had occasional amours with gladiators.[36]

All classes came under these sensuous and violent influences. Kiefer said:

> Yet we must remember that the mass of the people cared for nothing but *panem et circenses*, food and sport; and that in many of the cultured, rich men of Rome, culture was only a veneer which easily broke and easily disclosed the coarse and brutish instincts of the peasant.[37]

By the early imperial beginnings, sensuousness was rampant.

> Tacitus attributes much of the degradation of women in the Neronian age (54-68 A.D.) to the evil influences of the theater where women even of distinguished birth sometimes undertook most demoralizing parts . . . . The chief danger arose from the character of the pieces presented, as well as from the passion which women often connived for the favorite actors of the day.[38]

Marriage was without *manus* and by simple announcement. Women rivaled men in promiscuity, and chastity virtually disappeared. By 23 B.C., there was public bathing for mixed sexes. Prostitution was rampant.

Tacitus said childlessness prevailed (Annals 3:25), and Pliny the Younger said even one child was thought to be a burden (Letters 4:15). Many fertility drugs and potions for contraceptives existed. Roman soldiers had condoms of animal skins. Infanticide, child abuse, and abandonment were unregulated.[39] Incest increased, along with homosexuality.

Immorality was so prevalent by Augustus' time that he passed a law for the theater compelling "all women to sit together in the upper rows of seats because of [the] immorality bred by men and women together during the theater."[40] The sexual harassment and immorality growing out of the working men and women together caused Lucenius to forbid them to do so.[41] Augustus tried to appeal for change on the basis that marriage is from "the Creator, the first and greatest of the gods."[42] His legislative efforts failed.

Pitirim Sorokin of Harvard has pointed out that by the time of Julius Caesar, in Rome:

> Six hundred thousand of the proletarian population were supplied by the state with rations of oil, pork, wine, clothing and other necessities, and special "cards" (*lasciva nomis mata*) entitling the bearer to the services of the Roman prostitutes.

Sorokin quotes many tombstones emphasizing pleasures of the flesh and says, "Such cynicism, skepticism and sensualism must have been profound and wide-spread to have found expression on the tombstone of ordinary persons." He adds, "This sensate form of Roman culture . . . brought them to their irretrievable decay."[43]

Wave of Anarchy

Following the First Punic War and the victory at Syracuse, religious anarchy was manifested after skepticism gained dominance by the educated. Barrow pointed out that while they still held religious offices and carried out the rituals, they only did it as a form. The degraded, pluralistic religion from Greece poured into Rome and, even though contrary to state religion, it was given official approval and allowed. Disbelief was so dominant by 150 B.C. that there was a legal effort to exclude the Greek teaching and religion but to no avail.

Anarchy in material pursuit began after the Second Punic War. The corn kings and cattle kings of the peninsula illegally took advantage of the small farmers and forced them out of business. The rich also imported multitudes of slaves and destroyed the competition from the labor of the freemen. The financial crisis became so critical that the government devalued its coin by essentially one-half its value. This crisis led to the reform movements, the popularies. The anarchy in materialism caused serious depression in the 130s.

The women's anarchy against the lex Oppia was during the time of Levi (195 B.C.). To break the husband's patriarchal control the women appealed to the law of *usus* to avoid the law of *manus*, and escaped the legal authority of their husbands. Divorce became so prevalent that it could be obtained by the two parties simply announcing it.

For many years in early Rome the total power of the father over the children, even to the point of capital punishment, was unquestioned in the law. But the influx of liberal Greek thought hit the Romans with a cultural impact. Also, the fact that the Roman family was disintegrating as a result of the women's revolution bred more and more youth who were angry.

Meyer Reinhold discusses how the place of youth changed in the first century B.C. He says that in the late second century, rigid family controls changed: "The Roman as an individual emerges out of the rigid Roman family controls and the absolute subordination to the state."[44] Individual freedom and demands for economic benefits ultimately led to government controls and conflict that destroyed peace and freedom.

Consummation of Anarchy

The increasing crisis in the economy and the breakdown of the family led to the final anarchy. The revolt for equality began in the midst of the second century, rising from 144 B.C. until 82 B.C., when all the waves of rebellion against God and authority climaxed into the final meltdown into confusion and judgmental acts. These conditions produced the need for the emperors. Reinhold says:

> But the world crisis during the hundred years from the Gracchi to Augustus eventually had the impact of a generational event that aroused massive disaffection from the Roman government and the ways of the fathers. Cicero . . . was fully aware of the disaffection and alienation of the youth of the ruling class. Indeed, in 44 B.C. he expressed the conservative view that the history of other societies showed that great states were undermined by the younger generation and restored by the elders (Cicero, *De. off.* 2.13.46). [45]

The children of the rich took the lead in believing they could solve the increasing problems of their society. They were called *populares iuvenues audaces,* or "audacious young of the popularis." The rebellion spread to all youth. Reinhold points out that this permeated the whole youth culture.

> Those affected were not only the upper-class youths, but also those among the common peoples in the country, who flocked to the city of Rome preferring dissolute idleness on the dole there to poorly paid manual labor in the fields. Sallust said, "All the youth were utterly thoughtless and reckless, indulging in all sorts of depravity—gluttony, sexual dissipation, selfindulgence, illicit gain, and extravagances." (Catiline 37.7, 3.3-5, 12.1-2, 13.4-5, Epist. I ad caes. 5.5-6). [46]

Sallust continued to describe the youth of the upper classes especially as "greedy for gain, reckless, impressionable, who are attracted to the revolutionary program of Catiline in 64-63 B.C., and who he particularly courted" (Catiline 14.1-4).

Tiberius Gracchus, who was under thirty years of age, was elected tribune in 134 B.C., and caused a war in 133 B.C. when he ran for re-election and the Senate mobilized its opposition to him. Mob rule became prevalent. Gaius Gracchus was elected in 124 B.C. and reelected the next year. There was a bloody confrontation again in 121 B.C. While Sulla conquered the city and tried to restore the oligarchy of patriarchs, it didn't last. Several young men "obtained tribuneship after 70 B.C. and used their political authority to inflame the plebes against the Senate by dole and promises" (Catiline 38.1; cp. 52.26).[47] The rebellious youth continued to gain power.

Among the first emperors, four were teenagers: Nero, Commodus, Elagabades, and Alexander Serverus, and other teenagers came soon after. Many of these young leaders were angry, irresponsible, and carried on wild, illicit sexual relations, as is reflected in Catullus' poetry. The picture of the

Roman youth of the time is amply documented.[48] Young people neglected and at times fought with parents, and even banished them.

Sallust stated the cause of this rebellion against the elderly, "as the result of riches, luxury and greed united with insolence took possession of our youth" (Catiline 12.1). Sallust warned Caesar, "If our youth continue to have the same desires and habits as at present, beyond doubt that eminent domain of yours will come to a speedy end, along with the city of Rome." (Epist. I ad caes.6.1). Horace observed the progressive deterioration, saying, "The age of our parents was worse than that of our grandparents; it made us ever more worthless, and soon we shall produce a more corrupt generation" (Odes III. 6. 21-32, 45-48). Plescia states that the cause is the disposition of human nature:

> General consensus is that there is a universal innate force which drives sons away from their father's power and there is a counterforce which drives fathers to hold their children under their authority. This generational conflict, a private matter between individual parents and sons in normal times, becomes a national generational one in times of economic crisis and cultural revolutions. It resulted in a national generational conflict which in turn brought about the downfall of the Republic.[49]

The anarchy of the period increased and reached its final wave during the last phase of judgment leading to Caius Julius Ceasar and the emperors.

Judgmentalness and Judgment

By the last three quarters of the last century B.C., all moral absolutes had disappeared. The idealistic youth sought to interpret the constitution and the government as one evolving to produce good. The claim of women and the poor for the right to be equal led to the anarchistic times and mob rule. Recalls in government, and court rulings were prevalent. "But in an atmosphere of political freedom and cultural revolution the high-handed judicial procedure of the senatorial commission" provoked a reaction.[50] Enormous debt and accumulation of riches by business and the wealthy resulted in multiple lawsuits. "The praetor, A. Sempronius Asellio permitted both parties to proceed against each other in court, thus to bring before the judges the deadlock between law (*nomos*) and custom (*ethos*). . . ."[51] The cultural revolution . . . brought a new consciousness, a new sensibility that deepened and enlarged the issues, molded the strong personalities, exacerbated the feuds among the family factions . . . ."[52] The conflict of gender, the loss of chastity, and the approval of violence generated conflict in the home, with gender rejection, homosexuality, and violent youth who lacked discipline as results.

"The young men with their instinct of freedom from their elders created a general, pantelic movement, embracing all life and mobilizing everything, government, economy, education, marriage . . . ; in short, it aimed at a new society (*nova aetas*)." The economic and cultural elements tend, "due to their emotional idealism—to turn a significant percentage of them into activism and martyrdom; in the pursuit of justice they will oppose power with power, violence with violence; in these conditions the boundaries of the law are blurred and extremism is justified."[53] Plescia made the further observation, "Such movements tend to be totalitarian, and the result of the Roman Revolution was totalitarian."[54]

The hundred years following the anarchy which had been launched in the time of Gracchus resulted in violent social chaos in the name of freedom and human rights. John Vincent rightly observes:

> A king was inevitable, and the years of proscription and civil murders taught the Romans the folly of resistance. . . . The citizen armies of Rome conquered Italy, Carthage, the Western and Eastern world. But wealth and power brought to the aristocrats decay of morals, greed of power and gain. The slave system destroyed free labor and exterminated the middle class of citizens. With a corrupt nobility and beggared populace the State lost its balance . . . . At last a general and a statesman crushed the whole frail fabric of the republic and made himself monarch of the Roman world.

In 48 B.C. Julius Caesar was given absolute power but this was short lived and ended in division.

> After a dozen years of divided sovereignty Caesarian power was reunited in the person of Caesar Octavianus (Augustus) . . . . Thus the worn-out republic expired, and a greater monarchy took its place, a little less than five centuries after the last Tarquin king was banished . . . .[55]

Augustus "put an end to violence as a tool of change and 'assumed the role of father image for many Romans' and redirected to a new level of submission and duty under emperor and the father in each household." He formed sports clubs with athletics, sports, religious ceremonies, and "generational balance and harmony was restored."[56] While Augustus made noble efforts and the anarchy ended, the civilization was not revived. Augustus was so revered that after he died the senate proclaimed him a god and established altars to him. The third emperor, Caligula, proclaimed *himself* god and demanded worship. The cycle of this civilization ended as the first had with the Etruscans and the kings. The bias against God produced another example of antichrist in Caligula.

This second cycle of the Roman Republic declined like that of the Greek democracy and also followed the pattern of Paul's description in chapter 1 of Romans. In a slow process of rejecting God and enthroning man, the same awful steps had occurred.

Chapter 6
The Devil: His Methods of Deception, Theft, and Destruction

INTRODUCTION: DEMONIC DECEPTION, THE EXPLANATION FOR MORAL DECLINE BY MANY PROMINENT HISTORIANS

F. F. Bruce, professor at the University of Manchester, England, has said:

Modern man may not think in terms of principalities and powers and may consider himself emancipated from outmoded beliefs in angels and demons. But he is all too conscious of powerful and malignant forces operating against him, which he will not hesitate to describe as demonic. He knows that his individual strength is insufficient to resist them, and he is not at all sure that even united action will be more effective. These forces may be Frankenstein monsters of his own creation which no longer obey his commands; they may be subliminal horrors beyond his conscious control. He feels himself to be a helpless victim in a hostile cosmic order carrying him to destruction which he cannot avert. He knows himself to be involved in situations against which his moral sense revolts, if he cannot do anything effective about it.[1]

Best Explanation for the Decline of Civilizations

As mentioned earlier, Senator Patrick Moynihan revealed he deliberately chose the spelling of *Pandaemonium* used by Milton in *Paradise Lost* to emphasize the reign of Satan as the creator of chaos and destruction. He meant that Satan deceptively leads men to think they are acting in their best interest, but is misleading them toward trouble. Moynihan describes how both the Marxists and the liberals in the West missed what Satan was doing, thinking they were attaining their goals of power and wealth, but were proceeding toward their demise. He found that the biblical concept chosen by Milton was the best way to explain the growing chaos in this world, while the followers of socialism feel they are moving to something better. The collapse of Communism exemplifies how this has been true.

When Arnold Toynbee completed his review of the rise and decline of more than twenty civilizations throughout human history, he introduced them with an explanation of his view of history. In it, he told of his struggles to interpret the meaning of history, and how his answer was found in reading Goethe's *Faust*. There, he found Satan's challenge to God to let him test His work. Toynbee says:

God accepts the challenge and thereby wins an opportunity to carry His work of creation forward. An encounter between two personalities in the form of challenge and response: have we not here the flint and steel by whose mutual impact the creative spark is kindled?

Toynbee then refers to Goethe's exposition of the plot of the *Divina Commedia,* and says:

> Yet, if, in response to the Devil's challenge, God genuinely puts His created works in jeopardy, as we must assume that He does, in order to win an opportunity of creating something new, we are also bound to assume that the Devil does not always lose. And thus, if the working of challenge-and-response explains the otherwise inexplicable and unpredictable geneses and growths of civilizations, it also explains their breakdowns and disintegration. A majority of the score of civilizations known to us appear to have broken down already, and a majority of the majority have trodden to the end the downward path that terminates in dissolution.[2]

Toynbee, who was influenced by the Christian West, refused to yield to the Greek cyclic view of history through these rises and declines. He argued that there can be cycles but also be movement in a straight line like riding a bicycle. I must add that this view, which has a beginning point and moves toward an ending point, is possible only to those who believe in the sovereignty of God, His redemption, and His final victory; otherwise one cannot know in which direction things go. As we shall see, it is in the historic process whereby God leads events to a meaningful consummation in which God achieves His purpose for man and gets glory.

Not only do Moynihan and Toynbee (neither of whom accepts an inspired Bible or Christ as the only way to God) resort to the biblical interpretation of history as used by Milton and Goethe, but so do many others who seek to find an explanation of the course of history.

Also significant, the first major heresy of Christendom, Gnosticism, refers to a dualism in explaining history. The Gnostic views are the basis of much New Age teaching today. But in this heresy, they change the biblical scenario, and the God of creation in the Old Testament is made the evil God who promotes destruction, and Lucifer is the promoter of good. Thus, in Gnosticism, the whole biblical teaching is turned around and perverted in favor of the Devil. But even modern man thinks this way—that it is religion which is the cause of deception, wars, and destruction.

Modern thinking is so distorted that a person must be open to understand these profound biblical insights to know how to cope with the problems in America and the world. It is therefore important to understand human nature and the world as given in the Bible, with Satan as the deceiver and destroyer of the world. It is only as this is fully appreciated that the pattern of the decline of civilization can be discerned, and the forces of evil that destroy man and his creative works be counteracted. This view of a conflict of spiritual forces is foreign to the thinking in much of modern education, but that is the major problem with the West.

Deception by the Devil Is Central to the Destruction of Man and Nations throughout the Bible

The view that the Devil is the great deceiver, thief, and destroyer is prominent in biblical revelation in the history of mankind from Genesis to the end of the last book of Revelation. The Devil appeared to Adam and Eve and deceived them to sin and fall from their positions as sons of God and lose their glory and destiny (Genesis 3:1-19). In the concluding chapters of the Bible, in the book of Revelations, Satan, like the serpent, is seen as "the deceiver of the whole world" (12:9), and even after the millennial reign of Christ, again deceives the nations in one last grasp for victory before the Great White Throne of God's judgment of all men, angels, and the Devil himself (20:7-8).

THE DEVIL'S NATURE AND METHODS

Devil's Nature and Objective

Cosmic history in the Bible is presented as a war of spiritual forces (Ephesians 6:10-18). Modern scientific research has demonstrated that man's mind, or soul, is a conscious spirit independent of the brain and transcends the physical realm. This opens the door, as far as science is concerned, to believe that man's thinking can be influenced by other spiritual forces, both good and bad, as the Bible teaches.[3]

The Devil, presented in Scripture as the highest of created angels, led a rebellion of other angels against God. Angels were created to be ministering spirits. The word *angel* means "messenger" and they were designated to communicate messages to the minds of men. Satan's "angelic" followers are called *demons* and are evil spirits.

He is called Satan, the enemy, and is personified as acting in ungodly rulers such as the king of Babylon (Isaiah 14:4, 12-15) and the king of Tyre (Ezekiel 28:1-10). These leaders deceive and control their subjects, leading them in a revolt against God and His people. The Devil is an awesome, influential spirit, but he is finite, not omnipresent, or omniscient. He is therefore dependent on his multitude of demons to help him know what is happening in the world and to influence the minds of men. Satan himself is not present with every person at any time to tempt us, but some of his demons may be. Since he is a non-corporal being, his strategy involves using men, whom he and his demons influence, to carry out destruction. Demons influence men to let their thoughts be dominated by their weaknesses, such as greed, anger, drugs, alcohol, and sex. This explains why men are captured by destructive desires that can overpower them to act against their best interest. The Bible teaches that Satan tempts God's people, but he cannot attack and harm them as he challenges God's kingdom unless God permits attack, and even then, God sets the limits of his damage (cf. Job 1:11-12; 2:6, etc.)

The Devil's attack is supremely against God's incarnate truth, His people, and Jesus Christ, the Son of God. His main point of attack is toward God's Redeemer, God the Son, whom God the Father allowed him to wound and murder. But God's eternal plan has been that in wounding His Son, the Devil's head will be crushed through a man born of woman who he initially seduced (Genesis 3:15; John 8:40-47). Satan and his demons tempted Christ as he tempts other men (Matthew 4:1-11; Hebrews 4:15). Satan's aim was to pervert, accuse, and destroy Christ and those who proclaim Him to the world. But he will be defeated in the end (Romans 16:20; Revelation 12:9-11). It is clear that the whole of the Bible, especially the teachings of Jesus, as well as those of Paul, see the world engulfed in sin and destruction by satanic deception. But the Son of God is superior in wisdom and power and can control him and his demons (Matthew 12:22-29).

Demonic Deception Slowly Leads to Destruction

The Devil's Work through the World's Educated Elite

In both Greece and Rome, it was seen that the educated leaders of each of the nations led them further and further away from belief in God until the whole civilization was in chaos and was finally destroyed. All of their wisest men could do nothing to stop the moral decay. Indeed, the most educated leaders seemed to promote the destruction. Many analysts attribute America's problems to the educated elite. Satan and his demons seek to use the most attractive, wise, and cunning beings to deceive and lead men astray.

This profound truth of what happens in the world is set forth simply and graphically in Genesis, chapter 3. The Devil chose the serpent, who was the wisest, most cunning creature in the Garden of Eden, to speak to Adam and Eve. Later in biblical history, the Devil chose false prophets who were always attractive, able men to influence others. Paul says Satan himself masquerades as an angel of light. Hence, he is called Lucifer, or "shining one." His false teachers present themselves "as apostles of Christ" or as "servants of righteousness" (2 Corinthians 11:13-15). In Jesus' day, it was the highest authorities, many rulers of Israel, and the most religious Pharisees who rejected Him and led people astray.

The Serpent as Representative of Craftiness

Many educated people scoff at the idea of the serpent being the tempter of Adam and Eve. The Genesis account says that the serpent was not in the form presently known, and, other than man, was the most attractive and cunning being created. Since the serpent was the only animal that could speak, the Devil communicated to this crafty animal the ideas he wanted to present to Eve. He was the instrument of Satan to suggest the sin to Eve who then misled Adam, and consequently was cursed by God to be in a different form, as he is today, crawling or slithering on his belly (Genesis 3:14). The biblical story says the serpent lost the position of cunning and exaltation.

People marvel at the results of trainers and researchers with animals such as chimpanzees, thereby accepting the idea that animals might be able to communicate intelligently. But these same people think it preposterous that the Bible says the highest animal God created was used to communicate with Eve (Genesis 3:1-5, 13-15). Actually, the ability of man himself to reason and to think is an amazing ability—an act of creation by God—which science can't explain.

A crucial factor is that Eve was influenced by one she thought was wise or cunning, not by one who was stupid or unattractive. In a similar way, it is the educated elite in whose minds Satan and his demons especially choose to place the anti-God ideas. These are attractive and influential people who know much, and they seem very impressive. It has always been that way throughout the history of man and of nations. It was the wise men of Egypt and of Babylon who were in conflict with Moses, Daniel, and others. Satan's influence to the educated and through them to others comes because he appeals to man's fleshly desires and to his efforts to escape his mortal limitations because of his fear of death.

Consequences of the Devil's Deception for the Original Sin

Those who accept Satan's lies can experience six consequences of demonic deception into sin as with Adam and Eve. (1) Guilt and spiritual death toward God, separating them into selfish individualism (2) Physical death by exclusion from the tree of life (3) Self-knowledge as mortal individuals, offended by nakedness and afraid (4) Loss of the friendly environment or exclusion from Eden (5) Curse of the woman by the multiplication of childbirth and the increase of pain through childbirth (6) A requirement to work hard to provide and to survive.

These changes in man's condition are the points of attack by the Devil to deceive man to give up faith in God and to be destroyed. It will be shown that the moral decline of human civilization is caused by deception by the Devil at the points where God had to make changes because of man's sin, and this results in man's reactions described by the steps of human sin given by Paul in Romans chapters 1-2.

Profound Meaning of the Results of Sin in Genesis 3, Which Are Scoffed at by the World

Modern man looks at the story of Adam and Eve in the Garden of Eden in Genesis 3, and scoffs at it as religious myth. While it is a real story of man's beginnings, in the Bible it is told in a brief, symbolic way so that its truth sticks in our minds and has profound implications for every person. It penetrates to the depth of our being and shows every man the tendencies of his soul and the source of his problems.

The Eating of the Tree of the Knowledge of Good and Evil Reveals an Intellectual Revolt against God.

When Eve and Adam ate of the tree which was forbidden, the result was to make them feel they had become "wise as God." This involved feeling they were the ones to establish the moral standards. They would "know good and evil." The prophet Isaiah describes this effect, saying,

> Woe to those who call evil good, and good evil;
> Who substitute darkness for light and light for darkness;
> Who substitute bitter for sweet and sweet for bitter!
> Woe to those who are wise in their own eyes
> And clever in their own sight! (Isaiah 5:20-21 NAS)

The original sin brought humanity to a condition where an intellectual revolt against God was a tendency of its nature. Man still has an innate knowledge of God and can see God is creator (Romans 1:19-20), and he still has the laws of God written in his heart so he cannot escape some consciousness of God's moral law (Romans 2:14-15). But man became guilty and died spiritually to God (Ephesians 2:1 ff.). Man can no longer communicate with God unless God communicates first with him, though in man's need he may seek after God. After the original sin, man was alive only to his body and to the world. He became bound to see and choose only the world and what it supplies to his fleshly being. Choosing the things of the flesh had become his bent.

The three areas of the forbidden fruit which were attractive—its beauty, its potential pleasure to the body (as in food), and its promise of wisdom in order to become like God—became the dominant motives of man after the original sin. The apostle John describes them as the lust of the flesh, the lust of the eyes, and the pride of life (1 John 2:17), and may be categorized into pleasure, possessions, and pride. Man's righteousness became tied to his right to achieve these.

The Devil as the deceiver knew that God's word was true and that God would bring about the promised results if man sinned. The selfish individualism that resulted from Adam's original sin drives the man and woman toward fulfilling these desires of the world: of possession, pleasure, and pride. The Devil knew these desires would give him points for power to influence men and women to follow his manipulations, to control them, and to destroy them. Every person knows that these are the drives of his life and history shows that wars have been fought to fulfill these.

Paul describes the condition of all men after original sin to the Ephesians thus:

> You were dead in your transgressions and sins, in which you used to live when you followed the ways of this world and of the ruler of the kingdom of the air, the spirit who is now at work in those who are disobedient. All of us also lived among them at one time, gratifying the cravings of our sinful nature and following its desires and thoughts. Like the rest, we were by nature the objects of wrath (Ephesians 2:1-3*).

The Sentence of Physical Death Was Necessary

Man's mortality, and the hostile environment in a cursed world outside the Garden, exaggerates that his disposition is to gain pride, possession, and pleasures for self.

God obviously could not allow man and woman in their sin to continue to be in charge of His world, as He had intended (Genesis 1:25-28). The sentences of God which followed sin were not just punitive against them, but were designed to limit the damage that sinful mankind could do to God's creation and to the persons they would beget, and to force man and woman to henceforth be dependent on each other and on God. We still see the damage which selfishness inflicts on others and the environment. If individuals and groups were allowed to continue to accumulate power by greater information, organization, and use of ingenious instruments, then the exercise of selfish desires would impose devastation to the people and God's created order indefinitely.

So God expelled Adam and Eve from the Garden and from access to the tree of life in the Garden. Moreover, the gate to the Garden was guarded by the cherubim and the flaming sword of God. This meant that God's holiness was to be defended and there would be no return of sinful man to His presence (Genesis 3:22-24, cf. Leviticus 9:24;10:2-3). Mankind's arrogant claim of knowledge and the distortion of God's truth was now limited by impending physical death. From the time of denial of admission to the Garden where God had walked with them and to the tree of life, the genetic powers of the human body were hopelessly degenerated, both individually and collectively. Thereafter, every man's influence has and will end by his physical death.

We dismiss from our conscious minds that our body is mortal. But we humans continually extend much effort to regain perpetuity of life, though that goal is nowhere in sight. Even while progressing to maturity, the body is moving toward physical death and the grave, and we humans cannot forget easily that we are not in complete control. The limit to our days is already set. What each generation of man can achieve is limited to what can be learned and produced individually and together. Even if we pass our knowledge and skills on to our offspring, death imposes limits. Thus after the death sentence, the passions for the world were made more urgent in order to prolong life.

Maintaining good health and avoiding or postponing death is a natural and good motive, providing it is not selfishly exercised so to ignore God and harm others. But as selfish individualism grows in the process of the decline of civilizations, more people become preoccupied with the idea of death and with a concern for good health. This is revealed in the records of all past civilizations, whether in the Amoritic, Egyptian, Greek, Roman, or others. Their writing about death is more frequent, and tombs become larger and more elaborate as the end of the civilization draws near.

In America, we have generally enabled more people to live longer. But modern medicine has not lengthened the span of a person's life. Those who live the longest today do not exceed the length of the longest lives in Colonial America. Health care in America, and the world, is a number one priority, is a growing concern for all, and consumes 15 percent of the United States federal budget and much of the private spending; this expense is increasing yearly. However, the more attention given to better health and longevity of life, the more complex and difficult the problem seems to become.

Other Divine "Curses" Reveal Other Ways to Control Human Sin

The Woman's Curse

After man's original sin, two important things were done by God and recorded in graphic symbols of the reality, one for the woman and another for the man. The Hebrew scholar, C. F. Keil has rendered the Hebrew text of Genesis 3:16a as follows: "To the woman He [God] said, 'I will greatly multiply your pain in childbirth, in pain you shall bring forth children '" [4] The number of pregnancies were to be multiplied and the sorrow or pain in having children was to be multiplied. And Eve was told that the result would be, "Your desire shall be for your husband, and he shall rule over you (Genesis 3:16b)." God has previously told Adam and Eve to "be fruitful and multiply" (Genesis 1:28), so these changes after the sin added something new and different to insure the marriage a success in this.

The Curse Directed to the Man

The second act of God after the sin was addressed to the man. God said:

Cursed is the ground because of you; in *toil* you shall eat of it all the days of your life. Both thorns [Hebrew, *gots,* meaning "to cut or wound"] and thistles [Hebrew, *dardar,* meaning "that which grows luxuriantly, proliferates and is useless"] it shall grow for you; and you shall eat the plants of the field. By the *sweat of your face* you shall eat bread, till you return to the ground, because from it you were taken; for you are dust, and to dust you shall return. (Genesis 3:17b-19 NAS, italics added)

In this statement the earth is placed under a curse that will require painful toil and such great energy in work as to require sweat by the man/Adam. The usual translation from the Hebrew text is that the earth would bear "thorns and thistles" or weeds to make agricultural production more difficult. But it is probable that these words have a much broader meaning of imposed obstacles in nature making man's task more difficult.

In Romans 8:19-22 the apostle Paul, who was a trained Jewish rabbi, shows that the Hebrews understood God's curse as putting *all the forces of creation* into bondage from which it groans and suffers pains like those of a woman in childbirth, and from which it desires to be freed. The idea is that all creation offers things that inflict pain and hurt on mankind and harmful elements that proliferate so that they are out of man's control. Moreover, these are presented as increasing in intensity as the cosmos moves toward the end time, much as a woman in childbirth has greater pain until the baby is born. Thus all kinds of natural catastrophes are included under that which is hurtful, such as earthquakes, storms, fires, floods, famines and the like, the things which proliferate out of man's control including all kinds of germs, insects, viruses, and diseases. All these things make the man's task of providing for his family more difficult.

A Reason for the Curses Is a Counteraction of Individualism

There is evidence of the birth of selfish individualism by the original sin. After eating the tree of the knowledge of good and evil, individualism was born by each seeing himself as wise as God. Now viewing each other as individuals instead of equals to be united together before God, the man and woman for the first time were painfully aware of the threat of sexual differences. Scripture says, "Then the eyes of both of them were opened, and they knew that they were naked; and they sewed fig leaves together and made themselves loin coverings." In response to God's call, Adam said, "I was afraid because I was naked, so I hid myself." (Genesis 3: 7, 10) Recognition of sexual differences had become a source of fear of each other and also before God. This also was the source to cause divorce between Man and Woman and between them and God.

In the beginning God created man and woman of equal value in His sight. He made them both in His image and likeness. He created the woman from the man so that they were of the same essence, but with differences that enabled the woman to complement the man. He then commanded them to be fruitful and multiply, and fill the earth. In so doing they would expand the garden and have dominion over everything on the earth. At the center of His plan was that they should not just be two individuals "doing their own thing," but that they were to marry and be "one flesh." (cf. Genesis 2). They were to unite in body and spirit. Jesus, and later His apostle Paul reconfirmed that it was still His plan for man and woman to be one flesh by leaving father and mother for a new family unit (Matthew 19:6; Ephesians 5:31). This initial purpose of God of unity in marriage creating the family as the source of new children and a school for all of life was threatened by this individualism.

While these two acts of God were so-called "curses", they seem to have meaningful purpose to help maintain dependence on God, oneness in marriage, ands to preserve mankind and its civilization until the redemption comes when "the seed of the woman will crush the head of the serpent" (Genesis 3:15). These conditions require the man and woman to rely on each other, and also on God, for help and dependence for survival. God's "curses" accentuated the importance of each of their separate roles based on their created differences so they would see their need for dependence on each other.

Evaluation of the Woman's Troubles

Evidence in nature reveals some suggestions of the truthfulness of the changes to cause woman's increased pregnancies and pain in childbirth. Virtually no other higher animals have perpetual fertility, but instead have seasons of heat. No animal is like the human race that enjoys regular fertility and constant sexual attraction. Anthropoids normally have fewer offspring. This suggests a change for the human race that led to repeated pregnancies.

Dr. Jan Lever, Professor of Zoology at the University of Amsterdam, has accumulated a number of differences between humans and other higher animals such as anthropoids. While Lever does not reject evolutionary theory, he mentions that these differences have been ignored because evolutionists wish to emphasize man's likeness rather than his difference to anthropoids. These facts Lever gives are suggestive of the biological changes that God may have caused to increase difficulty and bring the pain to the woman in the birth of infant humans, in a way which may not have existed before the sin. These are interesting inferences of the truthfulness of the statements in Genesis. Only a few of Lever's observations are briefly given here without details of the study.[5]

The human infant body weight is much larger at birth than other anthropoids. The following is a graph showing comparisons, in Kilograms.

ANTHROPOID INFANT BODY WEIGHT COMPARISON

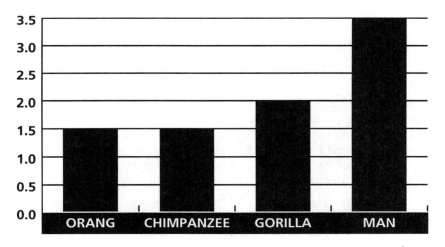

The weight of the human brain is nearly three times more at birth. This difference is proportionally even greater when one considers that the adult weight of a mother gorilla is 2.5 to 3 times larger than the adult human mother.

All young anthropoids are nest-fleeing creatures (nidifugous) and are born with eyes open, well-developed sense organs, and an ability to perform many physical functions within a month to six weeks. They do not lie helpless as human infants. But if the human infant were like most nest remainders (nidicolous) like dogs and cats, he would have to be born at about the fourth month where he exhibits similar characteristics.[6]

These and other characteristics suggest that before the fall into sin, infants may have been born to man after about four months and much smaller, but that God may have caused genetic alterations, making the infant grow much longer and larger in the womb and thereby be more difficult to bear and much more dependent after birth. These factors, combined with more frequent conceptions, would impose greater pain at birth, and a greater burden to care for the infants over a longer period.

Originally, in the Garden of Eden, the birth and care of babies would have been easy without these negative factors, but under normal conditions as it is now, a mother must have help from her husband or other caregiver to take care of her children. Therefore, after the fall, women generally would be forced to have a longer view of a sexual relationship which would require acknowledgment of male paternity and demand for his continued assistance with the babies. To gain this she would grant him respect and recognition as her leader as a compensation for her feminine powers and unique relationship which she has with the children from motherhood.

The Husband's Curse Increased Man's Dependence on God for Provision

Indications of Change after Sin

After an easy beginning existence of leisurely keeping the Garden with his wife and having various healthy fruits to eat, Adam was expelled from the Garden into an unfriendly and threatening world. Here he must help his wife with the children and toil for food, and he was surely shocked in the difference of this new lifestyle over that in Eden. In addition, the changed earth was an insecure environment in which to live.

There is some evidence the world was originally much different. Scientific research reveals there was formerly one continent on earth with stable weather currents and with a possible canopy that shielded life from devastating radiation. If geological disruptions began causing the break-up of the continents and the destruction of such a canopy occurred, it is thought that the world would have become a much different place. These theories cannot be examined here.[7] But this real but symbolic concept of change indicated in Genesis 3 emphasizes that the male has, since the fall, been the main protector and provider for the family with the burden of hard work involved.

Divine Help and Human Ingenuity Could Bring Comfort and Love

Many Scriptures reveal that as man trusts God and cares for his wife, God will bless and prosper him so that his labor for a living is not cursed but profitable (e.g., Malachi 2:9-17; 3:7-11). Conceivably by new inventions, technology, and organization, there could be prolonged prosperity, if faith in God and love for each other were maintained.

Moreover, there is no place in Scripture where planning and limiting children for the wife's and child's health is wrong. Nowhere in Scripture is contraception condemned, except in cases where it was practiced to avoid responsibility to produce children when there was an obligation according to family law (e.g., Genesis 38:9). Why would family planning and the use of contraception be wrong if children were prayerfully and fruitfully produced, cared for, and trained to glorify God as God commanded (Genesis 1:27-28)?

God Himself often hindered conception of men and women for other specific purposes, especially to teach and develop faith in the parents that would be communicated to their offspring who would serve Him (cf. Genesis 16:2; 25:21; 29:31-33; I Samuel 1:5-6; Luke 1:6, 13). In other situations He hindered births to enemies to protect His people (Genesis 20:18). In other words, having more children is not always God's highest priority, and He could lead men and women in planning their families as in every other aspect of their lives. God gave man the understanding to develop contraception; it is the selfish misuse of it that is wrong. Nothing is evil in itself; it is the motive of the heart and how man and woman use it (Romans 14:14; I Corinthians 10:31). Love and trust in God can enable the man and woman to live more comfortably and have a prosperous civilization.

THE DEVIL'S DECEPTION AND DISTORTIONS OF THINKING TO DEGRADE SOCIETY

This chapter aims at understanding how demonic forces motivate fallen man, preventing him from trusting the one true creator God, and destroying a comfortable and prosperous life God is giving him. Paul has said that when man is blessed by God, he becomes unthankful, intellectually revolts, and turns to worship that which is created, rather than the Creator. The first lie man believes is that there is no God, but that creation exists on its own and he must control it to gain his own prosperity. The first demonic deception in man's intellectual perversion is that he must, through his own ingenuity and effort, provide for himself. This then leads down a road where he neglects and oppresses his wife and children so that they start a sexual revolt and reject his leadership. Thus, the purposes of interdependence to overcome the "curses" are perverted. Instead of interdependence, their differences become a tool of the Devil to divide and destroy the family and their civilization. Scriptures which reveal some of the aspects of Satan's deception follow.

The Devil's Deceptive Use of the Fear of Death

Through the fear of death, the Devil keeps men and women in lifelong bondage to sin (Hebrews 2:12). As possessions, pleasure, and pride become "essentials," men and women desire them to the fullest extent. The person who does not trust God is open for the Devil and his demons to encourage him to think he must act for individual gain in these areas to survive. We are tempted by these desires, and then we are carried along by them until we sin, and then sin brings guilt and death (James 1:14-15). Therefore everyone tends to violate the law of love, and hurt others for self.

The Devil can use our peers—often the seemingly wisest individual or even a large group, to influence us to act selfishly in favor of these fleshly desires. When we don't trust God, we feel that we need the help and influence of others to achieve our objectives. We know we ought to care for others and we want to do so, but self is number one in the end.

Deep down we are afraid our peers can destroy us and our worth by rejecting us or hindering the fulfillment of our desires. So our bondage to the Devil by the fear of death is heightened by him using men to intimidate us to join them in their evil, either for profit or harm. Verse after verse in the Bible calls us to trust God and not men (Matthew 10: 26, 28, 31; Isaiah 51:7-8, etc.) Demonic thoughts can cause us to lie awake at night imagining what people might do to malign, control, or harm us. At the root of these fears is the fear of death.

Demonic influences turn people to drugs, lust, or even suicide as ways of escape from worldly pressure and fears. Men become mentally distraught and succumb to controlling drives, being demonically possessed. Why would a person continue these destructive conducts if he were not deceived?

Devil's Motivation to Be Free from God's Law and Will

God tells us through His law in the Ten Commandments how we ought to control our desires to love Him and others so that they will not be destructive. But these commands of God can appear as the chief hindrance to our freedom and the fulfillment of our desires for pride, possessions, and pleasure. They seem to stand in our way to be in control of our lives, or to be like God. The more we think of what God says we should *not* do, the more we want to do it and *exercise our rights and freedom*. The Devil used God's command to Eve not to eat of the fruit of the tree, to call her attention to it and her desire for it. Paul told how Satan uses the prohibition from doing something as a way to enhance the desire to do it in our minds (cf. Romans 7:7-12). The more we live for these desires instead of for God and others, the more we desire to violate God's will. We don't want God or religious people to restrict our freedom.

Paul describes how our fleshly natures are disposed in a war against God: "The sinful mind is hostile to God. It does not submit to God's law, nor can it do so. Those controlled by the sinful nature cannot please God" (Roman 8:7-8*). As John says, "Everyone who does evil hates the light, and will not come into the light, for fear his deeds will be exposed" (John 3:20*). In time, any agency which seeks to govern our lives—whether church leaders, business leaders, human government, parents, or tradition—will be perverted or diminished for selfish individual expression. Thus by promoting the desire for selfish fleshly fulfillment, the Devil causes man to pervert the truth and not trust God's power and love. And he will also avoid human government, or seek to find other men as a group who will help him manipulate to achieve greater individual freedom. When the Devil has convinced man he needs to be free from God and His "religious restraints" to gain the needed possessions, pleasures, and pride of self esteem, he can then attack the differences of men and women, destroy the family, and destroy the civilization.

Demonic Deception to Pervert to Individualism from Sexually Dependence

The first thing men do under demonic deception in their desire to be free is to pursue gain of wealth. This frees them from toil. To get this gain from mammon, men neglect their wives (or push them to work), turn to polygamy to have more wives to work for him, acquire human slaves, invent new machinery, develop ways of storing knowledge, cheat others by deceit in business—all of these to gain economic advantage. Bigger and better organization and management and building of conglomerates in businesses, of farms, unions, and the like show that there is no end to the male ingenuity to free himself from toil against nature. Moreover, wealth has a euphoric, deceptive influence on men, so that they feel they can do anything and get away with it. The husband's relationship to his wife and children becomes oppressive by his arrogance and absence while he deceptively thinks he is doing a better job in providing.

All of this causes low self-esteem in women and children. As Margaret Mead once pointed out, having babies and caring for them is an awesome task when the highest thing a man builds is a fifteen foot bamboo hut. But when he builds the Empire State Building, woman's role and tasks become small.[8] As men build their own little materialistic empires, they exalt the value of money from which women are excluded. Women's anger and envy are generated. Women who have followed their husbands in unbelief, then begin to want worth, not in the eyes of God, but in terms of wealth and freedom as individuals. Contraception, abortion, and child neglect are essential if this path is to be followed. The Devil then motivates the woman to renounce her obligations and calling as a mother and wife in order to have freedom to gain wealth and be free from her husband's control. Thus both men and women depart from dependence on each other, the oneness of marriage is sacrificed for each one to act independently for self, and the family falters and the children suffer.

Demonic Deception Leads Away from the Best Way

As shall be shown, the proper way to freedom for a woman is to seek help from a man whom she acknowledges as her exclusive husband, and on whom she relies. This does not exclude her using her gifts to help him in business, but it puts him and the children first. Her greater good and the good of her children and her husband would require renouncing the male idolatry of pursuing greed and call him back to trust God to provide for her and the family. Instead, under demonic deception she also goes after the idolatry of greed to escape her hurts.

The assertion of feminism to correct male abuses has never been very successful for women. In fact the women's position is worsened and eventually patriarchy asserts itself, and may do so in an even harsher way than before. Stephen Goldberg, in his significant book, The Inevitability of Patriarchy, has shown that patriarchy emerges and cannot be removed.9 Careful historic study shows there are actually no Amazonian societies in real history where women rule, in spite of such claims. These are unattainable wishful visions because of the very nature of women. While patriarchy may become abusive and must be corrected, when women seek to eradicate maleness and man's need to lead, the women and all society suffer. In fact the more feminism asserts itself, the more the family will fall apart, women will be degraded, and in the end a harsher patriarchy will likely emerge. This end time of trouble was seen in Greece and Rome and will be seen as we view the conditions in America.

HISTORY SHOWS REPEATED DECEPTION INTO LIES

Illogical Repetition of Decline to Trouble Is Best Understood As Demonic

The biblical principles that describe the Devil's working in causing the decline of civilization is constantly repeated in society after society, nation after nation. This is why Toynbee, Moynihan and others resort to this idea to explain history as mentioned above. How could human history over hundreds of years follow the same repetitive destructive pattern except that some demonic force leads by playing on the biased desires of human nature? How could this be repeatedly be advocated in culture after culture by the most intelligent educated leaders century after century with such a sense of dogmatic certainty in what they were doing?

There is an obvious bias in human nature that drives men to pervert the evidence they find. In Dark Shadows...., chapter 4 in reviewing the so called "scientific histories", it was pointed out that they all showed a pessimistic view of man and the future, and that while this was unanimous, the trend was for the modern educated elite to reject these conclusions entirely. The views of Oswald Spengler, Arnold Toynbee, Pitirim Sorokin and others were shown to end in a time of troubles for each civilization. It was shown that this rejection of these findings was due to man's desire to remove God's control and especially to remove his since of guilt for sin.

Repeated Rationalization From Nature to Reject God

Man in his pride has repeatedly accepted a mechanical view of the world that made him feel confident he could alone develop material progress. The early mechanical view of the Greek science by the Ionian school of Miletus was imported from the Eastern cultures and brought to Athens by Anaxagoras. This thinking was later taken from the Greek school in Alexandria in Egypt by Archimedies to Syracuse and adopted by the Romans after defeating the city. These views were the basis of Coperican thinking. The development of a mechanical view of nature by perverting these ideas led to the intellectual revolt against the one true great sky God in each civilization. In Dark Shadows the perversion from this thinking in the west is traced out in detail.

. In the nineteenth century when the deistic movement came into being it was based on the presupposition of a deterministic regular view of nature. As European and American intellectuals became caught up in an optimism about man and a hope for material progress, they changed the long held views of sovereign God of the Bible who held men accountable, to accept the idea that man first conceived of gods in nature and eventually developed that of one God.

This speculation of an evolutionary development of God by man for his own needs was the theory used by all nineteenth century comparative religionists (see Dark Shadows, chapter 6). There was no consensus of how this occurred. Andrew Lange early found that this did not fit the facts, because there was evidence of a supreme Being in the civilizations he studied. Lange's evidence and views were by-passed. But in time a scientific method of determining the oldest elements in a culture was devised by E. Grabner and B. Ankermann at the Berlin Ethnological Museum and eventually W. Schmidt applied these cannons to religion. He proved that in every culture worldwide, man began with the idea of one supreme sky God who created and held man accountable.10

In time Archaeologists supported this view. It was found that the Sumerians worshipped .the creator sky God, An, and his Son, Enlil. The Amorites called this God El and the Egyptians early worshipped the same God which they called Horus. The world's greatest archaeologist, W. Foxwell Albright, of Johns Hopkins University strongly attacked the speculative view widely held by higher critics that the God of the Bible was a late development by priests of Israel, and presented the data to contradict this.

But the whole Western intellectual religious community continued to widely teach this speculative view from the theory of evolutionary development. This lie is still believed as a dogma by the intellectual educational and media leaders in America. Michael Weitzman, Near Eastern scholar, University College, London, referring to how Archaeology has upset speculation said, "Even the so-called certainties, on which previous generations ...may have constructed rococo hypotheses, may be demolished overnight by new excavations or some chance discovery."11 Intellectual pride led to rejection of God and materialism.

The remains of Ebla, whose zenith was 2400 to 2250 B.C., and the remains of Ur and other cities show a growing intellectual and material development. The Sumerians developed exquisite art and metallurgy with gold daggers, headdress, and some copper and silver in art and utensils. Cities were well laid out with water culverts, sewerage, and even flush toilets. They built the giant ziggurats and even had early chariots for transportation. All this was before Abraham in the Bible. There were great schools of learning and even inter-city conferences of scholars. These elite intellectuals led the people to a sexual revolution and hedonism, exalting women symbolized by Eshtar or Astarte (who was the same as Tammuz and Ashtoreth), with the sexual implications. Finally, there were development of anarchistic ideas which in the end lead to a society of judgment and to God's judgment.

The intellectual attainments and the material pursuits in Egypt have amazed us to this day, as to how they designed and built the pyramids, temples, ships, and other amazing accomplishments of their culture. Their intellectual pursuits eventually led them to materialism and forsaking the ancient sky God. Egypt's society collapsed after the triumph of feminism under queen Hatshepsut. The same path has been traced among the Amorites and the reign of Ashtoreth. With the male pursuit of materialism, there inevitably was a demonic influence producing a sexual revolution to create an egalitarian society and the breakdown of the family by sexual promiscuity in most societies.

Careful Historical Studies Show Sexual Revolt and Egalitarianism as Destructive

In the review of the decline of civilizations, the breakdown of the family is the most obvious point for moral collapse. J. D. Unwin's work, *Sex and Culture*, is the most massive, detailed, objective and unbiased study and has been mentioned before. He studied eighty primitive cultures and most of the ancient and modern civilizations. His impartial and non-religious work was written at a time when the sexual revolution was popular in Europe and the prejudice against his findings kept it from the recognition it deserves. There are other books that expand Unwin's studies.[12] But he has shown, without a doubt, *that the critical point* for the breakdown in civilizations has been in *abandoning monogamous marriage for sexual promiscuity that follows a sexual revolution.*

Unwin presumed a theory that there is only so much energy in man and that when this is diverted to sexual pursuits, there is a loss of energy for civilization. His theory is called "human entropy." There is much truth to the fact that when sexual immorality gains dominance, much energy is diverted from constructive social projects. But *Unwin himself is not confident that the idea of "human entropy" is* correct, as statements by him will show.

Unwin asserts that the real point of collapse of civilization is the loss of the monogamous family to sexual promiscuity, because this destroys the family, and the family is the principal institution for the transmission of ethical and moral truth and for establishing respect of authority that focuses and controls productive energy for the society as a whole. Pitirim Sorokin has shown that widespread sexual immorality must be preceded by the society moving away from the idealistic (religious) to the ideational (rational) before it goes to the sensate way of thought. This confirms the two previous steps of Paul. Sorokin shows that the ideational society has a coordination of the idealistic and rational that produces a contractual society with a familial basis.[13] But he fails to adequately emphasize that when the point of faith in God (idealistic) is exchanged for a materialistic faith, the next step is to automatically give way to the sensate, which destroys the family and the ability to maintain contracts. Individuals then pursue their desired ends without constraints, and this destroys control for productivity at all levels of society.

Unwin refers to his own important extensive findings and facts which have been obscured or rejected by the modern educated elite:

Owing to the egocentricity in our historical outlook, to which I have already referred (par. 159), it is often supposed that female emancipation is an invention of the modern white man. Sometimes we imagine that we have arrived at a conception of the status of women in society which is far superior to that of any other age; we feel an inordinate pride because we regard ourselves as the only civilized society which has understood that the sexes must have social, legal, and political equality. Nothing could be farther from the truth. A *female emancipation* movement is a cultural *phenomenon of unfailing regularity*; it appears to be the necessary outcome of absolute monogamy. The subsequent loss of social energy after the emancipation of women, which is sometimes emphasized, has been due not to the emancipation but to the extension of sexual opportunity which has always accompanied it. *In human records there is no instance of female emancipation which has not been accompanied by an extension of sexual opportunity.*[14] (italics mine)

Unwin presents evidence that such sexual promiscuity always has produced a decay of civilization. Unwin's argument is that as long as there is prenuptial constraint (premarital virginity) and the practice of monogamous marriage, the creative society can continue to build the civilization. He repeatedly found that when the women revolt, the sexual fidelity goes, and the family will disintegrate.

Destruction of Monogamous Marriage Is Caused by Male Unbelief and Materialism

It is interesting that after all Unwin's exhaustive detailed studies of all the cultures, he ends up with no clear certainty of why monogamy faltered, women revolted, and caused the breakdown and decrease of creative work:

> It is difficult to express any opinion with complete confidence, but as, at the end of my task, I look back along the stream of time, it seems to me that it was the unequal fate of the women, not the compulsory continence, that caused the downfall of absolute monogamy. No society has yet succeeded in regulating the relations between the sexes in such a way as to enable sexual opportunity to remain at a minimum for an extended period.[15]

He then ends his arguments by saying that if desired monogamy is to be maintained so there can be a creative society, women must be treated as equal. But Unwin *never does propose a way to do this.* The answer must not be in denying women's feminine powers and trying instead to masculate them, but in recognizing that they were *created equal but different* by God. Unwin is absolutely right about asserting the breakdown of monogamous sex occurs because women are not recognized as equal.

But Unwin fails to recognize, as did Sorokin also, that the preceding steps that cause the emancipation movements is a loss of faith in God and a movement toward a new concept of equality by women and men—a concept based on materialism. Unwin's failure to find the answer lay in his refusal to look at religion in his studies. He clearly states he would not look at religion.

In summary, the repeated evidence is a slow deception by the devil that causes man to follow the Pauline steps of decline. As Christians we see that the first step of decline is when the Devil deceives man into thinking that he is sufficient without God, and leads him to think that by his own efforts he can be free from toiling to earn his living. His resultant abuse opens the door for the woman to try to avoid dependence on man and to escape her burden of child-bearing. It has been demonstrated that the intellectual revolts and the materialistic revolts preceded the women's emancipation movements in the Greek democracy as described by Plato and the plays of Aristophanes (chapter 4) and in that of the Roman Republic as given by Otto Kiefer from Livy's statements and others (chapter 5). This is true in the decline of most other societies.

Unbelief in God Is the Beginning Point of the Deception which Widens and Destroys Civilization

Thus the evidence is that it is not mainly because of a loss of *energy* (according to Unwin's nebulous use of physical theory and analogy), but *because of the breakdown of all coordinated control of the society that comes from God's loving, patriarchal leadership*. It is this breakdown which causes the loss of creative productivity. Organized efforts at production die when there is no control to lead people in working together. I have shown that at the beginning of each of the creative waves of a new civilization, a worship of the one great sky God was the initiating factor. And that occurred by the formation of patriarchal leadership and vows before God by the men and women of monogamous fidelity to each other and Him. Moreover, in ancient patriarchy women usually had an exalted position of equality in a oneness of marriage, and men taught children to honor them. But when real faith in God is perverted or rejected, then patriarchy becomes oppressive and harsh. The whole society is by then deceived and women are hurting and angry, so that they demand freedom and equal rights to material wealth to be free. They do not evaluate or see the consequences to marriage, the family, and especially to children. They are deceptively led on by the Devil to demand equality which is like that of men. But they do not evaluate that they can never be like men, because they have babies and are physically weaker. Unfortunately the educated elite advocate sexual equality in materialism as the salvation of women. This creates the underclass of poor and a younger generation who hate and are violent, and this produces conflict and a meltdown to confusion that destroys the society.

Unwin's discoveries only confirm the biblical standard and what I have discovered using Paul's guidelines in Romans. It is exceedingly important to see, therefore, that the crucial point for maintaining godly control in society is that the *male avoid unbelief* and not let material pursuit become primary, lest he become arrogant and fail in accepting his wife as an equal before God. Again, *the male's arrogance in unbelief whereby he fails to treat his wife as an equal is the crucial point where the family disintegrates.*

Conclusion: Demonic Deception Produces Blind Destruction of Civilization

The changes which Paul described of man's departure from God that bring down a civilization occur by slow minuscule zigzag trails in a similar way over many generations and a couple of hundred years. While the repeated zigzag or cycles deceptively make the moral decay less evident, the Devil finally leads to the major meltdown in morals from which the civilization never more than partially recovers. This repeated pattern over many centuries cannot be attributed to human conspiracy, since men die out and new generations arise. But there must be a satanic mind that repeatedly is influencing and motivating those generations of men. And this could not occur without a human bias against God from original sin.

As the history of the development of Western thought and the steps of decline in American civilization are followed in the successive chapters, it will be shown that the philosophy and theories of the intellectual elite are perversions by bias and turn out to be lies that they dogmatically will not relinquish in spite of their erroneous and destructive effects (see *Dark Shadows* . . . which exposes the intellectual lies). As Jesus warned, the Devil is a liar and the father of lies (John 8:44). As Moynihan and Toynbee describe: the people are deceptively led because of original sin into the city of Pandaemonium for destruction by the Devil, who is their enemy.

Chapter 7
God's Concern for All Nations
and the Place of Israel

INTRODUCTION

Thus far it has been seen that the moral decline of the Greek democracy and the Roman Republic follows a pattern outlined by Paul in the book of Romans. This decline has been seated in each nation's rejection of faith in God. There are a number of questions to be asked and answered about the premise of a pattern of the rise and fall of nations. Have all nations followed such a pattern? What is God's relationship to and concern for all nations? What is the place of the children of Abraham, or the nation of Israel, and their relationship to this pattern? What is the place of the New Testament Church of Jesus Christ, and how does it relate to Israel, to other nations, and with the climax of history, toward the end times? Is the pattern of rise and fall always the same? Is it proper to identify the God of the Bible with the transcendent God identified at the beginning of a civilization, such as Zeus or Jupiter?

The answers will help us design the church for the trying times ahead. It will help us understand the counter-culture in the West, and in the United States specifically, and what can be done to make changes. The answers will help us see there are many strong indications we are moving toward a time of trouble, and we can better understand the shape those events will take. Some ideas included here may differ from the traditional way of thinking, but will make sense in the light of the overall data presented.

IS GOD'S CONCERN FOR ALL NATIONS?

God's Concern as Creator and Sustainer of All Men

The Bible is clear that God is concerned for all men and all nations. God is the Creator of all men and affects the course of their lives. He directly created Adam and Eve in His image and commanded them to be fruitful and multiply and fill the earth (Genesis 1:26-28). This is not just a deistic concept, whereby God instituted the laws of nature and went off and let the course of genetics and other physical laws develop in whatever way they might. It would be a concession to unbelief to think of natural laws as something separate from God. All natural laws are simply God's normal ways of working, and they would not continue without His personal sustenance. Miracles are God's extraordinary way of working.

When Eve bore her first child, Cain, she made the statement, *"With the help of the Lord* I have brought forth a man" (Genesis 4:1*). She understood God was the force behind the genetic process. David, the son of Jesse, understood God was directly involved in this process of the fetus being formed in the womb (Psalm 139:13-16). God's control of other aspects of nature is seen in the miracles of the parting of the Red Sea for the Israelites, in the timely falling of large hail that helped kill the Canaanites before Joshua's army, and in many more. Moreover, Jesus Christ has been the one who continues this process, "sustaining all things by His powerful word" (Hebrews 1:3*).

After the world was judged by the dynamic flood, and all men and animals except those in the Ark were eliminated, the human race began anew with Noah and his descendants. The Scripture says, "Then God blessed Noah and his sons, saying to them, 'Be fruitful and increase in number and fill the earth'" (Genesis 9:1*). This was the same command given to Adam and Eve and has the same implications of God's superintendence and involvement with the birth of each child.

Further, Paul tells us about God's continued control over and concern for all men. In addressing the Greeks at the gathering at Areopagus in Athens, he said:

> The God who made the world and all things in it, since He is Lord of heaven and earth, does not dwell in temples made with hands; neither is He served by human hands, as though He needed anything, since He himself gives to the all people life and breath and all things; and He made from one man of every nation of mankind to live on the face of the earth, having determined their appointed times and their boundaries of their habitation, they that would seek God, if perhaps they might grope for Him and find Him, though He is not far from each one of us; for in Him we live and move and exist, as even some of your own poets have said, "We are also His children." Being then the children of God, we ought not to think that the Divine Nature is like gold or silver or stone, an image formed by art and thought of man. Therefore having overlooked the times of ignorance, God is now declaring to all men that all people everywhere should repent. Because He has fixed a day in which He will judge the world in righteousness through a Man He has appointed, having furnished proof to all men by raising Him from the dead (Acts 17:24-31 NAS).

These Scriptures show clearly God is not only concerned for all men, but actively involved in their creation and the daily activities of their lives. They are accountable to Him, and He wants them to seek Him, repent, and turn to Him. Jesus Himself taught that God His Father in heaven shows His love even for those who are at enmity with Him because He "causes His sun to rise on the evil and the good, and sends rain on the righteous and the unrighteous" (Matthew 5:43-45 NAS).

God's Concern as the Redeemer of People of All Nations

When God called Abram, His intention was not to discriminate in favor of Abram and his descendants. The Lord had said to Abram:

Go forth from your country, and from your relatives and your father's house to the land that I will show you; and I will make you a great nation, and I will bless you and will make your name great; and so you shall be a blessing; and I will bless those who bless you, and the one who curses you I will curse. And in you all the families on earth shall be blessed (Genesis 12:1-3 NAS).

Abram was ninety-nine years old, and his hope in God's promise was threatened because he had not brought forth the promised seed through whom he would bless the world. But God met with him and instituted the covenant of circumcision, promising to give him His heir. At that time, God changed Abram's name to Abraham. *Abram* means "exalted father," and *Abraham* means "father of a multitude." God's promise was that Abraham would be the father of all nations through faith in the promised redeemer child. Through his child, Isaac, came the descendant Jesus Christ as the Redeemer. By faith in Christ, men of all nations come to the same faith in God that Abraham had. Therefore, God's purpose in the promise to Abraham, after the covenant of circumcision—"You will be the father of many nations"—is fulfilled in Christ (cf. Genesis 17:5; Romans 4; Galatians 3:6-14).

God had a special purpose for Abraham and his descendants, but His intent was to offer a blessing to men of all nations. God revealed His character and purpose to the people of the nation of Israel, and God's Redeemer was to be born from Abraham's descendants, who had that revelation. That Redeemer was Jesus, who bore the punishment for man's sin in order that God might be just and justifier. But God's intent was not to discriminate between one nation or another. God shows no favoritism of persons (Romans 2:11). However, the nation of Israel had a special honor in that through them came the words of God for all men (Romans 3:2). They were the only nation through whom He consistently worked to produce His redemptive revelation in Jesus Christ.

When God commanded Solomon to build the temple in Jerusalem and Solomon dedicated it, his prayer stated it was to be a place for the foreigner to come and pray. When their prayers were answered, Solomon said this would be done that "the peoples of the earth may know Your name and fear You, as do Your people Israel" (I Kings 8:41-43). Jesus reminded the Jews of His day of this dedication and their fault in excluding foreigners, since it was meant to be "a house of prayer for all nations" (Mark 11:17).

God's Special Concern for Nations other Than Israel

God's concern for people in nations other than Israel is clear. The book of Jonah is a striking example. The nation of Assyria was Israel's greatest enemy at that time, and its capital city was Nineveh. Jonah was called to go and preach to that country that they should repent from their terrible sin. He was biased against them and ran away. In a storm at sea, he was thrown overboard. After being swallowed by a great fish, he was spewed out on the beach and commanded again to preach to the city of Nineveh. When he did, the city repented and was spared the judgment of God.

After preaching to the people, Jonah sat outside the city to see what would happen. A gourd vine-tree under which he sat for shade was killed by a cutworm. He grieved over the loss of the vine. God then rebuked Jonah for his concern over a vine when he lacked compassion for the people of Nineveh. "Then the Lord said, 'You had compassion on the plant for which you did not work and which you did not cause to grow, which came up overnight and perished overnight. Should I not have compassion on Nineveh, the great city in which there are more than 120,000 persons who do not know the difference between their right and left hand [many innocent children], as well as many animals?'"(Jonah 4:10-11 NAS)

In many places in the books of the Old Testament prophets, God expressed His concern for other nations. Speaking of Damascus, God said, "Why has the city of renown now been abandoned, the town in which I delight?" (Jeremiah 49:23-27*). To Edom, God said, "Leave your orphans; I will protect their lives. Your widows too can trust in me" (Jeremiah 49:10-11*). Also, for Moab God said, "So my heart laments for Moab like a flute" (Jeremiah 48:33-39; cf. 48:26-27*). There are many Scripture references similar to these.

Jesus angered the Jewish people by reminding them God cared for other people for whom He also performed miracles. He said:

> I say to you in truth, there were many widows in Israel in the days of Elijah, when the sky was shut up for three years and six months, when a great famine came over all the land; and yet Elijah was sent to none of them, but only to Zarephath in the land of Sidon, to a woman who was a widow. And there are many lepers in Israel in the time of Elisha the prophet; and none of them were cleansed, but Naaman the Syrian (Luke 4:25-27 NAS; cf. 1 Kings 17:1-16 NAS; 2 Kings 5:1-14 NAS).

These of other nations showed faith, so God worked in their behalf.

Moreover, God chose the leaders of other nations to bring both judgment and blessing to Israel. Nebuchadnezzar, king of Babylon, was the instrument of judgment on Israel, but he was humbled and then exalted by God when he repented (Daniel 4). Cyrus, the king of Persia, was chosen by God to restore the people of Israel and to be the instrument for rebuilding God's temple (2 Chronicles 36:22-23; Ezra 1:1 ff.; 5:13; 6:14; Isaiah 44:28).

IS ISRAEL SPECIAL AND WHAT DOES GOD REQUIRE OF HER?

Warnings of No Favoritism to Israel over Other Peoples

When God was about to give the nation of Israel victory over the Canaanites to inherit their land, they were warned by Moses that if they committed the same sins, the same diseases and war would come upon them which the Canaanites had suffered (see Deuteronomy 8:1, 9, 20; 28:36-37, 45 ff.). The prophets show that the Jews forgot God's warning. They committed idolatry, immorality, and violence. So God sent Nebuchadnezzar to destroy them, take them captive, and fulfill the warnings of Moses (cf. Ezekiel 6, 22; I Kings 14:21-24, etc.).

Jesus Himself warned the nation of Israel that He had tried to call the nation to Himself over and over, like a hen would gather her chicks unto herself, but they would not come. So God's judgment occurred. Jesus likened Israel to a fig tree that disappointed God, bearing no fruit, which would be cursed and cut down (Matthew 23:37; 21:19-21). Paul likened Israel to an olive tree whose branches didn't bear fruit because of disbelief (Romans 11:20). These examples by Christ and Paul indicate that while Israel held a special relationship to God as a channel of revelation and witness to others, they received no favoritism.

As Jesus confronted the fact Israel would reject Him, and people of the Gentiles/nations were looking to Him in faith, He saw His hour of glory had come. He would sow the seed of His life in death, and it would grow a harvest of fruit worldwide (John 12:20-24). After the Israelite leaders rejected Him and crucified Him, He was raised, and Jesus commanded His Jewish followers to go and proclaim the good news to all nations (Matthew 28:18-21).

Acceptance of People Was Based Only on Faith in Him

When Jesus entered Jerusalem a week before He was crucified, His disciples proclaimed Him the Davidic Messiah of God, quoting Psalms 118:25-26, which gives the words they shouted, "Blessed is He that comes in the name of the Lord" (John 12:12-13; cf. Matthew 21:9). The psalm was to be sung on the Feast of Tabernacles with palm branches in hand, and invites everyone to join in the worship of the King (Psalms 118:27). The Jewish leaders refused to join the worship of Jesus as Christ, and rejected Him. Jesus lamented the fact they did not recognize the day God had visited them, nor the things which would give them peace. He predicted their coming judgment (Luke 19:39-44).

Later that week, Jesus rebuked the hypocrisy of the leadership saying:

Jerusalem, Jerusalem, who kills the prophets and stones those who are sent to her! How often I wanted to gather your children together, the way a hen gathers her chicks under her wings, and you were unwilling. Behold, your house is being left to you desolate! For I say to you, from now on you will not see me until you say, "Blessed is He who comes in the name of the Lord!" (Matthew 23:37-39 NAS)

In this, Jesus predicted God was forsaking the nation of Israel until the nation cried out to Him as the one whom God had sent in His name as Savior. But in so saying, Jesus predicted a time when the whole nation would acknowledge Him in faith as the Son of God.

Paul pointed out that the unbelieving people of Israel were "broken off" like branches of an olive tree because of their unbelief, and the other nations were grafted in as "wild olive branches" joined to the believing remnant of Israel. But he warns the Gentiles that they will remain only because of their faith and only until such a time as they come to a point of disbelief (cf. Romans 11:11-21).

Paul also sees a future time when Gentiles/nations will lapse into disbelief, and the remnants of Israel will bring the whole nation of Israel to faith. He said:

And they [the Israelites] also, if they do not continue their unbelief, will be grafted in, for God is able to graft them again. For if you were cut off from what is by nature a wild olive tree, and were grafted contrary to nature into a cultivated olive tree, how much more will these who are natural branches be grafted into their own olive tree? For I do not want you, brethren, to be uninformed of this mystery—so that you will not be wise in your own estimation—that a partial hardening has happened to Israel until the fullness of the Gentiles has come in; and so all Israel will be saved . . . (Romans 11: 23-26 NAS).

Israel's Role and the Pattern of Degradation and Judgment

Israel has a special place as God's chosen vehicle for revelation. But no Israelites are acceptable to God in disbelief—they must walk in the footsteps of the faith of their father Abraham. Many in the United States want us to give favored privileges to the nation of Israel even in their disbelief, when the Israelites deny the right of Christians to proclaim Christ as Messiah. This is wrong.

In 1973, I was invited to speak to displaced persons in Beirut, Lebanon. One had been a Christian pastor after Israel took over territory in Palestine. This pastor's home and church were taken over by the Israelis, and he and his congregation dispossessed. I heard story after story from these displaced persons about similar injustices done because they were Christians. They were standing true to their witness to their Savior even in the difficult situations in Lebanon where they had fled. In persecuting these Christians, the nation of Israel persecuted Christ. The nation of Israel which does things like this is certainly not in God's favor. But Scriptures such as those quoted show God has a future fulfillment for the nation through faith.

Israel, in such disbelief now, is not under God's blessing, and until they repent, should not be treated with any special privileges by us. Indeed, it is only when the people of Israel see they are about to be destroyed at the end time will the nation turn to Christ in desperation, as He predicted. We as Christians hinder their conversion when we do not hold them accountable for their sin, while at the same time praying they will accept God's grace.

The atrocities of the Holocaust to the Jews under Hitler were terrible, and there have been other persecutions of Jews throughout history. Many Christians have helped them escape and survive, and we should help any humans who are being persecuted. But Israelites are sinners too and have shown injustices to many others. Until we think straight and in agreement with Scripture, we cannot interpret God's dealing with Israel and the other nations correctly. Abraham was chosen because he would teach his descendants to believe and obey God (Genesis 18:19), and like all nations they were to be held accountable. Their special privileges did not give special exemption from accountability to God.

God's Dealing with the Nations and Israel throughout History

This brief survey shows God has been concerned with all people in all nations throughout the history of the world. But it has been seen that all men have sinned against God, and every nation which has rejected God has been judged. All men are dependent on God's grace and mercy for eternal salvation, but God's grace will enable them to persevere in righteousness and do good works (Ephesians 2:10; Titus 3:3-8).

It is impossible to trace the pattern of sin as outlined by Paul in Romans in clear fashion for all nations, but it is visible for most. As mentioned previously, in my companion book, *Dark Shadows in the New Day of Science,* chapter 9, I have presented the evidence from scientific comparative religion that shows that the speculation of the evolution of religion is absolutely wrong, and that every civilization began with a view of one supreme creator spirit as a transcendent God, and that man always perverts religion, as Paul argues in Romans 1. This has been traced here in the Greek democracy and the Roman Republic. The Sumerian god, Enlid; the Amoritic (Ugaritic) god, El; and the Egyptian god, Horus were all one great, sovereign, creator spirit god of heaven over all things in the beginning of those civilizations. But they all, because of the bias of original sin, degraded the image of God and went into greater rejection of Him and into worse sin.

God, as He was known in the beginning of each civilization, fit the description of the Creator Paul describes in Romans. Paul insists that the nations, or Gentiles, had "clearly seen" the character of God by natural revelation and that "they knew God." But, they then followed the pattern of changing and corrupting His image (Romans 1:20-21). Moreover, *Elohim* and *Yahweh* (Jehovah), God's name to the Hebrews, began as the great sovereign Creator-God who chose Israel as a people through whom to give and reveal redemption to and bless all nations of the earth. For about 200 years they prospered under common grace.

I have traced how the Israelites went through the same process of degradation the other nations did, and as a result "the name of God was blasphemed throughout the whole earth" because of them (Romans 2:24). In the last days of Israel, at the time of the judgment of God before the Babylonian destruction and deportation, the degraded pagan gods of other nations were brought into the Jerusalem temple worship and identified as the same god as Jehovah. As Israelites worshipped Baal and other idols, it was as if they were worshipping the Lord. While the early God in the beginnings of these civilizations was the same and only one true God, Paul never identified Uranus and his son Zeus/Jupiter with the God of Israel because the names were so debased in the minds of the people in the Roman world. But the God they first knew was the one Creator.

Successive Cycles of Rise and Fall, Depending on their Faith

Most civilizations go through more than one wave-crest of rise and fall, as was seen with Greece and Rome. I have mentioned the preceding two rises and declines before the Greek democracy (chapter 4) and the preceding one before the Roman Republic (chapter 5) in order to help clarify and eliminate confusion of historical data. In all the civilizations I have studied, the people and their leaders did not learn from the past, and entered again into the same path of demise. A new rise will occur, provided the fall of the first leads to a new spiritual movement that withstands the anti-god persecution of the dictatorship, or authoritarian government, that emerges to save the collapsing one. The blind repetition of human nature can only be understood in the light of demonic deception over the long periods involved.

A new working of God and intense commitment to withstand persecution by the spiritual minority at the end times of each pattern of degradation may gain the following of the majority. The imperial government then must recognize the minority and accept its morals as a basis for government. It was pointed out that the Christian movement influenced the dying Roman Republic so that the people under the imperial government were changed morally and there existed a whole new cycle in the Roman Empire.

Unless the moral renewal of a nation is complete, the successive waves may be of shorter duration. For example, Judah experienced real renewal, but not a complete one, under King Hezekiah, which then relapsed, revived slightly under repentant Manasseh, and again under King Josiah and the preaching of Jeremiah. Judah's renewals extended the kingdom of Judah almost one hundred fifty years longer than the northern kingdom of Israel, which had no renewal.[1] This is evidence of hope that there has been, and can be, God-given renewal and extension of time by His mercy.

It is important to restate the pattern of rise and fall, and trace it as it relates to God's working in major nations which play a prominent role in the Bible. God's working usually involves how the nations relate to Israel as His chosen witness and channel of revelation. It is important to see this and point out certain principles of God's working so we can discern the signs of our times.

Questions about Some Nations Do Not Invalidate the Pattern

No one can dogmatically insist all nations went through the same exact pattern, because there is not enough comprehensive data. But it is clear that the pattern has been followed most of the time, and in the fall of the other nations, the problem has been the sins as listed by Paul, even if the pattern of their unfolding has not always been preserved clearly. But the evidence *is* overwhelming that there was an intellectual revolt against God leading to crass materialism and sensualism that produced anarchy and breakdown. I have presented the evidence from the great Cambridge scholar, J. D. Unwin, who found that in eighty-six cultures which he studied, the materialism was always followed by a feminist revolt and the breakdown of morals that destroyed the family (see chapter 16, where Unwin's and other studies are evaluated). The evidence of materialism leading to the feminist revolts in Greece and Roman has been given in chapters 4 and 5 of this book.

There are many problems in tracing the pattern of rise and decline in some civilizations. In some early civilizations, the culture was reasonably uniform in a number of city-states, but the leadership and direction was not always clear. First, one city-king would lead, and then another, so the focus of the leadership changes for the civilization as a whole is unclear. In others, one nation moves in to dominate another whole nation, or group of nations, and take over their thinking at a certain point, so that the movement is not so clear. But all of these have eventually collapsed because of these major sins, and there is some evidence of the pattern. In the majority of cases, the steps of the pattern are clear. The history of peoples is complicated, and detailed study is required. But the skeptics who reject the warning of the Scriptures about the pattern of sin will in time discover its reality.

122   *God's Concern for All Nations*

Review and Summary of God's Care for All Men, but His Unique Revelation through Israel of Jesus Christ as the Only Redeemer

God has cared for all men everywhere as exhibited by common grace (Matthew 5:45), and His revelation by His Spirit through general revelation (Romans 1:20-21). All civilizations have begun with a belief in the great sky-God to whom all are answerable for the way they live. This God has been revealed as sovereign over the world. He is known by different names in each civilization. The great sky-God for the Greeks and Romans was known as Uranus. This sky-God revealed he has a son through whom he relates and rules. To the Greeks, he was known as Zeus, and to the Romans as Jupiter. This God was present everywhere as a great spirit, who sees all and who holds them accountable through the rule of his son. But their knowledge was only innated from nature.

In time, these great civilizations degraded the idea of God, corrupted his character, and made him one of a pluralistic group of gods. But it is clear that as the preincarnate Word, God was known in early times by the Greeks as Zeus and by the Romans as Jupiter, and that this God was the same God known by Israel.

While the sovereign God has been revealed to all these different peoples through His creation, Jesus Christ is the *"only begotten* Son of God" (John 1:14, 18; 3:16, 18; I John 4:9; Hebrews 11:17). In Jesus, the true character of God's Son is known. He as Jesus (Savior) became incarnate in the world and, according to God's preordained plan, atoned for all the sins of all men throughout the world. The nation of Israel is unique to all nations in that through them came the Savior. Only Jesus was God incarnate and the perfect man whose death would atone for all men's sin. He is the lamb of God chosen before the foundation of the world and all people. Only by repenting of their sins can men chosen and called from any nation come to God through Jesus Christ by faith. He must be proclaimed as the Messiah of Israel who now invites all men of all nations to come to God for forgiveness and let Him reign over their lives. Israel alone was given the oracles of God that led to Christ.

Moreover, God has a future for the nation of Israel, since one day Christ will return to rule the world through His elect people. At the present time, the elect are from all the nations through the church in which both Israel and the nations are one (Ephesians 2). But there will be a time when the Gentiles will be broken off through disbelief, and all Israel will be saved (Romans 11:23-29). God's sovereign purposes for Israel will be fulfilled, for the gifts and calling of God are irrevocable. The nation of Israel has been and is unique in its relationship to God. But Israel is accountable for its sin like all nations. Only when the nation of Israel turns again to faith in Christ will it be saved.

At no time were the men of the nations acceptable for eternal life without faith in the shed blood of the one preordained sacrifice–Jesus Christ. Apart from

Jesus as the Lamb of God, preordained before the foundation of the world to redeem those God calls, there is no forgiveness (1 Peter 1:18-21). Men before Abraham, such as Abel and Noah and the Israelites of the Old Testament, were accepted if they saw their need of the sacrifice of a lamb for their sins. These were a type of the Christ to come. But only God knows whether, before Christ came, people in the beginning of these civilizations could, like Abel, discern and believe in the Lamb eternally preordained to die.

And, it is possible that today God may accept a person who also humbles himself and believes he needs the blood of an appointed sacrifice, as a type of Christ. One man in Africa told me his tribe had a traditional story handed down for many decades that God would send a lamb who would be slain to give them forgiveness. He said, "When we heard the Gospel, we recognized Jesus was that lamb." But God's past use of this type of sacrifice has been superseded in the revealed knowledge of Jesus as the final offering for sin. There never has been, or will be, another way to God. Jesus made clear it is the church's task to witness this to all the world (Luke 24:45-47). All uses of other sacrificial systems are superseded in Christ's work, and there is no other name under heaven given among men whereby they must be saved (Acts 4:12). It seems clear that this is God's message to be blessed by the Holy Spirit and that the church is responsible to proclaim it to all nations.

But God has revealed Himself through common grace to all men through His creation and has wanted to be worshipped by them. His common grace allows them to continue in worldly prosperity if they continue to acknowledge and obey Him. Thus, civilization, whether that of Israel or of any nation or group of nations, may grow and preserve a people who continue in faith and morality. But Israel was chosen through Abraham to reveal God's love and His special plan to redeem men through His Son, Jesus Christ. Only through Israel is the way of redemption and forgiveness made known. But the true son of Abraham must also come by faith in the promised seed (Romans 4; Galatians 3).

CONCLUDING APPLICATION

Does The United States Have a Special Place?

There are many people who believe the United States of America is referred to in some biblical prophecies. While there are prophetic passages that seem to describe this country, it is hard to be dogmatic about these since often the passages specifically refer to other nations of the prophet's time. There is no questioning of the way events occurred in forming and prospering America were providential, and there seems to be a divine hand in making it great and Christian.

Was it an accident Columbus discovered America and the sea lanes had been explored precisely just before Martin Luther ignited the Reformation with his ninety-five theses? Thus, the way was opened at the precise time for the many Protestant groups that emerged to come to the New World. Was it by accident, after the second great spiritual awakening had occurred and means of travel were expanding, that America was able to make the purchase of the western half of the continent from Napoleon for fifteen million dollars in the Louisiana Purchase? It was then that Americans began to move out and settle the continent, as at no other time.

In the rest of this book, the history of America as influenced by the hand of God will be viewed as it began to build a great civilization. But it will also be shown how the same tragic steps of moral decline have come. And America will certainly be judged by God if there is no return to faith in Him.

As you read through the rest of this book on the history of the growth and spiritual and moral decline of America, it is very important to refer back to the summary graph in chapter 2 to see where the material fits into the main theses of the decline of the country, as given by Paul's description on the course of sin in Romans. It is also important to examine ourselves to see if we are men of faith, to understand how we are being influenced by a degraded culture, and what God is calling us in America to do in this hour.

Part II:
An Overview of
the Steps of Decline of America

A. The Steps of Departure
from Faith in God

Chapter 8
America's Foundations of Faith in God

BEGINNINGS OF AMERICAN CIVILIZATION

People of America

American civilization, as it will be considered in this book, began around the sixteenth century. Many years before, immigrants came across the land bridge from Siberia. Asians, islanders, and others are thought to have entered into this country by that route.[1] The descendants of these people were the Native American tribes occupying America in the sixteenth century. Most of these Indian tribes, at the time the Europeans came, with exceptions, basically had degenerated into warring matrilineal groups. In this chapter we will focus on the great European migration into America, and the subsequent events which led to filling the continent and producing the great American civilization.

The immigration of Europeans began slightly after the turn of the sixteenth century. Columbus discovered America in 1492, and in the 1500s subsequent explorers opened up a path across the sea lanes, making it more secure for others to follow. In the seventeenth century, the colonies began to be populated by Europeans. The earliest immigrants were English: the Puritans who came into New England. Within a few decades, there were sixty thousand Puritans in the New England area. They were followed by the Dutch, German Lutherans, Scotch-Irish, and French-Huguenots. An Anabaptist influence came from the Mennonites of Dutch and German backgrounds, the Hutterites, the Amish, and later the English Baptists. Most of these people came to the newly discovered America to escape religious persecution.

Firm Commitment to God in the Churches

Prior to that time, Christianity had spread by the non-conformist denominations as the common people had crowded to hear the preaching of the Word of God. Also, the Puritans had taken a strong stand for truth in contrast to the beliefs of the Church of England. In Scotland and Ireland, the Presbyterians had been very vigorous, and found their way into America.

In establishing the colonies, those who immigrated were true believers. Some brought the desire to evangelize the heathen, which was stated as a purpose in the Jamestown Charter of 1607 (but not fulfilled), and in agreement with Cromwell's vision. But they mainly wanted to find a way to earn a living in a place where they could freely hold their faith and worship God without persecution. God was the center of their lives. The Puritan oligarchy organized their towns around the square with the church at the center. For a man (who represented the family) to vote, he had to belong to the church. Most of the early colonies formed with immigrants who planted their dominant brand of Christianity: Puritans in New England, German Lutherans in Pennsylvania, Dutch Reformed in New York, Roman Catholics in Maryland, and so on. Almost all of the settlers held a Christian worldview, but, according to Cotton Mather, only about 50 percent were allowed into the churches and could vote.

CHRISTIAN FOUNDATIONS IN THE INSTITUTIONS OF SOCIETY

The foundation of all the institutions in the colonies was Christian, so as the nation moved westward these foundations extended. The Louisiana Purchase gained access to much of the West. The pattern of life, with Christianity at the center, continued to expand westward for many years with the camp meetings, circuit-rider preachers, established pastors, and school teachers. Thus, the sixteenth and seventeenth centuries are called "classically Christian" by some. They determined thinking for many years afterwards.

In the early 1700s, there is clear evidence the people in the colonies depended on God and looked to Him to guide the course they were setting. For over three generations, the doctrines and practice of faith in God were established not only in the church but also in the educational system, the government and laws, and therefore in business. God's providence guided the way these foundations were laid.

Christian Roots in Federal and State Constitutional Government

The formation of the nation and of the states reflected faith in God. In general, the people had a firm faith in the God of the Bible, but were from many different Christian denominations. Therefore, some men of less-than-Christian views formulated the documents of government so all could feel free to worship in their own way. A few were followers of the new deistic view.

Declaration of Independence

The Declaration of Independence, written and published in 1776, had been drawn up by Thomas Jefferson and corrected by five men chosen for the committee. It clearly states a sense of dependence on and accountability to God as it speaks of "the laws of nature and of nature's God, entitling them" to be free and separate. It goes on to say, "We hold these truths to be self-evident, that all men are created equal, and that they are endowed by their Creator with certain inalienable rights, that among these are life, liberty and the pursuit of happiness." It states further, after declaring the injustices of the King of England, "We, therefore, the representatives of the independent states of America in general congress, assemble, appealing to the Supreme Judge of the world for the rectitude of our intentions, who in the name and by the authority of the good people of these colonies, solemnly publish and declare" the right to be free and to seek the support of this declaration "with a firm reliance on the protection of Divine Providence." The document continues, "We mutually pledge together our lives, our fortunes and our sacred honor."

While this document reflects a general knowledge or a faith in God as creator, judge, and provider, it does not state a specific religion, such as Christianity. It shows a faith in a supreme God, who is the God who has revealed Himself in Jesus Christ, and it includes all who hold a faith in the one great spirit God who is sovereign, and allows for claiming that the biblical God is that God. This document goes beyond deism.

Foundational Documents of the Constitution

Many of the state charters and other articles of government reflect the truth of Christianity. A former chief justice of the Supreme Court, Earl Warren, spoke at the annual prayer breakfast of the International Council of Christian Leadership in 1954. In his address, he made the following statement:

I believe no one can read the history of our country without realizing that the Good Book and the spirit of the Savior, from the beginning, [has been] our guiding genius . . . . Whether we look to the first charter of Virginia . . . or the charter of New England . . . or the charter of Massachusetts Bay . . . or to the fundamental orders of Connecticut . . . the same objective is present; a Christian land governed by Christian principles . . . .

I believe that the whole Bill of Rights came into being because of the knowledge our forefathers had of the Bible and their belief in it: freedom of belief, of expression, of assembly, of petition, the dignity of the individual, the sanctity of the home, equal justice under law, and the reservation of the powers to the people . . . .

I like to believe we are living today in the spirit of the Christian religion. I like also to believe that as long as we do so, no great harm might come to our country.[2]

These statements from the documents of the various charters of the states, colonies, and the Declaration of Independence make it clear there was a firm faith in God by those people who took part in leadership. Even the deists who participated went beyond a strict deism, speaking of a "Supreme Judge" to whom they were accountable and from whom they needed approval and providential help. [3]

Restored Faith by the Constitutional Convention

When the Declaration of Independence was written (1776), there was a sizable influence of the concept of deism from John Locke and the European Enlightenment. Thomas Paine, Thomas Jefferson, and Benjamin Franklin claimed Lockeian views. But by the time of the Constitutional Convention in 1787, there was a broader involvement of the people's views, which produced a more conservative stance. A great dependence on God grew out of the troubled times of conflict and war. Also, the chaos that came into France and other places, as a result of liberal thinking and the prominence of atheism, caused the American leaders to lean more to faith in God. Already the French king was at war with the Parliaments, and within two years there would be three hundred agrarian riots. Patrick Henry, speaking of the deism behind the French Revolution, referred to it as "but another name for vice and depravity." John Adams, speaking of France, wrote in 1790 he knew not "what to make of a republic of thirty million atheists."[4] So a more sober look at the concept of freedom existed by the time of the Constitutional Convention. Even more so than in the Declaration, God's hand was at work.

C. Gregg Singer said:

> The Convention of 1787 displayed a consciousness of the meaning of the doctrine of sin, and was far less given to illusions about the perfectibility of man and the inevitability of progress. Christian principles and virtues were given a greater hearing than they had been given eleven years earlier.[5]

Some of the more liberal signers of the Declaration of Independence, such as Thomas Jefferson, Richard Henry Lee, and Thomas Paine, were absent.

The Constitutional Convention to form the United States became hopelessly deadlocked in controversy between the individual representatives until Benjamin Franklin addressed the moderator of the assembly, saying:

> I have lived, Sir, a long time, and the longer I live, the more convincing proofs I see of this truth: 'that God governs in the affairs of man.' And if a sparrow cannot fall to the ground without His notice, is it probable that an empire can rise without His aid? We have been assured, Sir, in the Sacred Writings that except the Lord build the house, they labor in vain that build it. I firmly believe . . . that without His concurring aid, we shall succeed in this political building no better than the builders of Babel . . . .

Franklin then made the motion that "prayers imploring the assistance of Heaven and its blessing on our deliberation be held in this assembly every morning before we proceed to business." The selfish interests of the participants began to fall away and the Constitution proceeded to be formed. While Franklin was a Deist and did not profess or practice a Christian life, this call for prayer reflects the impact of Christian faith on the culture and on him.

John Warwick Montgomery has commented:

> Indeed, the eminent constitutional scholar, Edward Corwin, has documented the solid impact of the concept of "higher" or revelational law, as embodied in Christianity from its earliest history, on the making of the American Constitution.[6]

Basic biblical principles are interwoven within it.

In the First Constitutional Amendment, our founding fathers envisioned a government with no sectarian preference or interest in control or in advantage over others. But they did not intend an education of the people excluding prayer and the law of God. The founding fathers only wanted to exclude political control of the view of God and His will that would prohibit freedom of men to answer accountably to God in their consciences. The First Amendment says: "Congress shall make no law respecting an establishment of religion or prohibiting the free exercise thereof." If this meant government not allowing any or excluding all religion for public use in government, it would have excluded the Declaration of Independence, which speaks of a Creator, and the Constitutional Convention itself, which was conducted under prayer, and the Constitutional document which indicated it was signed by all representatives "in the year of *our Lord* one thousand, seven hundred and eighty-seven."

An interesting study was conducted about the virtues or habits of the heart in America in its beginning. A group of scholars examined the statements of the early founders of our nation, and reflected over what they had learned about their commitment to Christian virtues and their realization that these are essential for the government to work. I mention only one statement they made: "Republican government, they (our founders) insisted, could survive only if animated by a spirit of virtue and concern for the public good."[7]

M. Stanton Evans, Director of the National Journalism Center, has documented clearly that the Constitution and the First Amendment did not exclude religion, especially the Christian religion, from expressing its views and initiating prayers in the public forum of education, government, and the like. He presents a tremendous amount of evidence to support the inclusion of Christian views and shows that the present efforts of the Supreme Court and the educated elite in America to exclude any religious views are incorrect. He points out that this view of exclusion is a "fabrication" and is a "prime example of picking and choosing elements from the past to suit the ideological fashions of the present." [8]

Broad National Accountability before the Sovereign God of Heaven

The Bible repeatedly teaches that God Himself gives man freedom to reject or distort His image and to sin against Him. God calls men to search for the truth about who He is and the benefits of accepting His will revealed in their hearts and in His self disclosure of Sacred Writings (Acts 17:26-31). Our founding fathers understood the difference between external political coercion and internal persuasion of the mind based on a reasonable presentation of the truth, with the individual voluntarily choosing what to accept. They wanted to prohibit the former in order to insure the latter. The present conflict for government control either by man or by faith in God reflects a failure by both sides to understand a proper perspective.

God, in His sovereignty, uses the evil of men to accomplish good. Many firm believers in God formed and signed the Constitution, but there were also those who had been influenced by deism and accepted a diversity of religious views. All came from countries involved in religious wars. There were many diverse religious groups, mostly Christian, already in America, and many conflicts already evident. These things, including the views of the deists, influenced the wording and content of the Constitution to allow all religious groups freedom of expression. This established the governing structures of the nation to allow the truth to be proclaimed, so that internal intrinsic motivations could be protected by the federal government without external force.

By the mid-1700s (eighteenth century), the whole of European thought had moved into the phase of carefully categorizing everything. This was a false effort to know the whole mind of God, whether in science, as Isaac Newton's successor at Cambridge, William Whiston, and others, or in theology with the Synod of Dort and others. The denominations found themselves competing and trying to nail down all the details of doctrine. This claim to all-encompassing exactness of theology was but another form of claim to God's absolute religious authority. Authority was declared through absolutely correct doctrine, even as the Roman Catholic claim for control was through the ecclesiastical hierarchy.

Theological conflict had already been experienced, whether that of Roger Williams' efforts at ecclesiastical purity, or of Ann Hutchinson's antinomianism in favor of grace, or Zinzendorf's efforts to bring Lutherans and Reformed Protestants together in a spiritual house. There was also much dispute of methodologies of ministry in evangelizing people and many other differences. While theological error has no virtue, neither does pride of absolute doctrinal or methodological control. All of these issues held some truth, but the conflicts experienced already had manifested the need in the country for a form of government that allowed freedom to worship God according to one's conscience.

At the early stage of the forming of the nation, many of those who were Deists were less rigid in their deism than they were later. Thomas Jefferson coined the phrase, "separation of church and state," which is often quoted today. But, at the time, he never intended that the United States government or its schools should be run without all leaders having a sense of accountability to God. While Jefferson professed to deism, he often reflected belief beyond that. It was Jefferson who proposed the United States official seal picture the pillar of cloud directing the Israelites (Exodus 13:21). This symbolized God guiding His people after their exodus from Egypt and the covenant with Him under His law at Mount Sinai. This is not deism but a sense of God immediately in control.

Biblical Basis for American Law and Legal System

Since most of the people in the colonies were English (at least 75-90 per cent) at the time of the American Revolution, the legal system was loosely based on that of England.[9] However, because of the abuses of the crown of England, only three colonies adopted English law as such by that time. English law in the Colonial period was unorganized, and there were many innovations in America. Scripture played a large part in American law in the Colonial period. Only after the Revolution and independence from England were the colonists open to accept English law more fully.

Roman law, which had ecclesiastical origins, was taught at Oxford in England. English law was not as well organized. Just before the Declaration of Independence (1765), William Blackstone published his *Commentaries* on English law. Frederic Maitland writes:

His (Blackstone's) book set before the unprofessional public an artistic picture of the laws of England such as had never been drawn of any similar system. No nation but the English has so eminently readable lawbook, and it must be doubtful whether any other lawyer ever did more important work than was done by the first professor of English law.[10]

Maitland continues:

In America, where books were few and lawyers had a mighty task to perform, Blackstone's facile presentment of the law of the mother country was of inestimable value. It has been said that among American lawyers the *Commentaries* "stood for the law of England," and this at a time when the American daughter of English law was rapidly growing in stature, and was preparing herself for her destined march from the Atlantic to the Pacific Ocean.[11]

Blackstone organized the concept of law around the idea of the will of God, both in nature and revealed. Frederick Sherwood says:

He advances from the law of nature (being either the revealed or the inferred will of God) to municipal law, when he defines to be a rule of civil conduct prescribed by the supreme power in a state commanding what is right and prohibiting what is wrong. On this definition he founds the division observed in the *Commentaries*. *The objects of law are rights and wrongs*. Rights are either rights of persons or rights of things. Wrongs are either public or private. These four headings are respectively the subjects for the four books of the Commentaries.[12]

Blackstone, therefore, set forth absolutes based on the will of God in his whole legal system. His view of law exerted a powerful influence. He established the precedent followed by many American law books, including the *Commentaries* of James Kent of New York. But the legal system in the United States was firmly based on the idea of the biblical God. This carried over to business and other areas of life. Eminent jurist Roscoe Pound comments on the influence of religion, especially in America:

Social control through law operates on a background of religion, morals, and ethical custom without which it would largely be futile. Religion organized by the church has always been a powerful agency.[13]

But, there was no common law of the United States as a nation. Each of the states had its own common law. The decisions of the lower federal courts that sit in every state and the decisions of the Supreme Court tended to regularize and nationalize the judicial doctrine. But, in time, the American Bar Association prepared various uniform acts for the adoption of all the states. Thus, in time the law tended to change with the conditions or thinking of the country.

Founding of Education in the Colonies in the United States

Few people realize that the whole educational system of our country was based on the church, or the church and state together. The colonies began establishing colleges of higher education, and then sought to establish education at lower levels. Of the first eighteen colleges or universities founded in America, all but one was founded by the church, or the church and state together. These colleges include all of the great Ivy Leagues. The seal of Harvard University was an open Bible with the word *veritas* written across it. "Veritas" is the Latin word for truth. The one university not founded this way was the University of Pennsylvania, and it almost went bankrupt. It was saved from bankruptcy by George Whitfield preaching there and taking an offering that saved it. So, the early form of higher education was basically Christian in its commitment.

There were three basic kinds of schools that fed into the university system. There were New England or Northern schools sponsored by the church and state, there were southern plantation schools, and then the schools as expansion occurred producing Western frontier towns.

The New England and the northeastern colonies sought to implement education among the children, who would then feed into the higher educational institutions. In New England, the Puritans insisted every town of one hundred families was required to have a grammar school under the care of a master capable of instructing in Latin and Greek so the boys could be prepared for college.

These schools were supported by endowment, tuition, and in part by the towns. These were not secular schools, because in most of the towns, in order to be a citizen, you had to be a member of the church to vote. The schoolmasters were chosen carefully, and only orthodox Congregationalists were admitted. Often, theological students helped fill the jobs of schoolmasters as temporarily. "New England colonies made laws requiring education of the children, but left details to local communities, thereby creating the traditions of local autonomy and the district system."[14]

In 1642, the first act by the State of Massachusetts required select men of every town to see that every family would have its children taught to read the English language. In 1645, they required any town with up to fifty families provide a schoolmaster under whom they were taught reading and writing. The motivation given in the laws was they should be able to read the Scriptures and understand the laws of the state. In fact, it was said, "It was being one cheap project of that old deluder Satan, to keep men from the knowledge of the Scriptures."[15]

The Senate of 1679 said in a pamphlet:

After God had carried us safe to New England, . . . and we had builded our houses, provided necessities for our livelihood, reared covenant places for God's worship and settled the civil government; one of the next things we longed for and looked after was to advance learning and propitiate it to posterity, dreading to leave an illiterate ministry to the churches when our present ministers are lying in the dust.[16]

In reflecting over the establishment of the New England school system, Wertenbaker says:

The view that education should be *made to serve the ends of religion* was accepted almost without question by all the groups of immigrants who came to America in the seventeenth century. The Swedish schools in the lower Delaware were strongholds of the Lutheran church; it was the learned clergyman of the Dutch Reformed Church who established schools in New Amsterdam (New York) and on the banks of the Raritan and the Passaic and later founded Rutgers College . . . .[17]

The primers and readers in all the schools used such texts as *McGuffey's Reader*, the *New England Primer*, and others that indoctrinated the students in Christian thought, ethics, and Scripture. Clifton Johnson's study of early

American school books shows how thoroughly biblical they were, not only in Puritan times, but well into the 19th century.[18]

The second type of school was the Southern plantation school where the larger plantations sponsored an educational program for their children and those associated with the plantation, including often sons and daughters. Teachers were often ministers, but sometimes would be an indentured servant. Slaves were not usually included, but some were taught. This schooling was private and so varied in content. These schools were connected to the church and taught many of the same materials which were used in the New England schools. These too, therefore, carried a religious emphasis and were considered important from the point of view of helping the church. There were variations from the Plantation model such as the Old Field, the Dame, and the Charity Schools.

The third type of school in early America developed during the Western expansion. Children were taught at home, or often by a school teacher connected with the church.

> While it is true that there was a certain amount of anti-intellectualism on the American frontier, it is also the case that most pioneer farmers wanted their children to have a greater amount of schooling than they themselves had enjoyed. The frontier tended to support minimum education for every child in theory, although getting the tax money for the support of schools usually met with a good deal of opposition.[19]

The Constitutional Convention passed the Northwest Ordinance of 1787, setting aside property for schools, and repeated it in 1789.

This Congress said:

> The purpose for those schools is religion, morality, and knowledge, being necessary for good government and the happiness of mankind, schools and the meaning of learning shall be ever encouraged.

So it is quite clear the early government and the people in the United States were interested in schools from a religious point of view as well as for building good citizens. Thus, with all three types of schools, there was a strong religious connotation which everyone accepted.

Thomas Jefferson sponsored a law in the State of Virginia establishing schools as non-sectarian, so no particular religion would have use of and control over schools. Moreover, Jefferson built the University of Virginia and invited all church groups to form companion colleges and use the facilities. But Jefferson never excluded the idea of religion being taught in the schools of that day.

The Foundation of the Family Was God and the Bible

In *Our Dance Has Turned to Death*, which is a review of the decline of the family in America, I argued that the family is the germ cell of all institutions and of the social concept.[20] Michael Novak of Syracuse University, in discussing the modern bias in America against the family, says:

> Clearly, the family is the critical center of social force. It is the seedbed of economic skills and attitudes toward work. It is a stronger agency of educational success than the school and a stronger teacher of the religious imagination than the church. Political and social planning in a wise social order begin with the axiom: What strengthens the family strengthens society.[21]

In the beginnings of America in the seventeenth and eighteenth centuries, the family was considered the basis of the society.

The Christian view of marriage was one man and one woman joined in marriage as one flesh (Matthew 19:3-9). Therefore, divorce was not an option and was illegal in the colonies. The family acted together through the father, and the individualism of today was foreign to their thinking. The family worked together. Only the man voted because he voted on behalf of his wife and children. Sex was not a pleasure one sought to enjoy for self, but for the joy of being one together and giving the other pleasure as well as receiving it. While the Puritan view of sex became restrictive when there was growing license to deviate from the acceptable, it seems to have been enjoyable as in most Christian families today, which often express more satisfaction than non-Christian marriages.

Each wife and child was encouraged to develop personalities and abilities to contribute to the unity of the family. Each gained maximum freedom as he contributed to the family under the family government. The conflict and competition which hinder growth and productivity in a strongly individualistic society were not pervasive. While children were punished by the rod, they generally were loved. By the second and third generations, the pastors' messages reflect the relaxation of morals. The sins most often mentioned were drunkenness, breaking the Sabbath, cursing, and the influence of sailors in lowering morals. Adultery was punished severely, and homosexuality was rarely mentioned, as were wife-beating and child abuse. Disrespect for parents was treated severely.

I quote from my book:

> Monogamous marriage was the norm and the law. The earliest government of the Puritans centered in the powerful family leaders who formed the "Puritan Oligarchy." Arthur Calhoun has said, "The fathers adopted the maxim that families are the nurseries of the church and the commonwealth; ruin families and you ruin all. The maintenance of family religion was universally recognized in early New England as a duty and was seriously attended to in most families. Daily the Scriptures were read and worship was offered to God. Fathers sought for their children, as for

themselves, 'first the kingdom of God and His righteousness' . . . . Every town has select men who by law were to enforce family morals and see that family government was upheld. They were also to see that parents educated their children and acquainted them with the civil laws."[22]

One of the books extensively investigating women's positions in the Colonial period is by Rosemary Radford Ruether and Rosemary Skinner Keller. In the introduction, they reveal that their search was to support the women's rights movement that challenged all traditional views of women for about two decades. Their thesis reads: "In what ways did each vision (of women) offer conflicting messages, at once encouraging and repressing new egalitarianism?"[23] In spite of their desire to present the data from the woman's individualistic point of view, they conceded that women in the colonies were content and say women "accepted their subordination without question." While they play up and give inordinate attention to the few exceptions (Ann Hutchinson, Mary Dyer, Jane Hawkins, and the later witch trials), they concede there was a unity and peace in general in the family and society.

They report:

> Carol Karlsen has interpreted the increased worth and dignity of women in the home in relationship to two factors: first, the evaluation of heads of households of Godlike positions in the family, and second, the function of the family in ensuring a well-ordered hierarchical society.

Moreover, they furnish documents of letters revealing a tremendous love and mutual respect between John Winthrop, the first governor of the Massachusetts Bay Colony, and his wife Margaret. Reuther and Keller state that Winthrop and his wife:

> Provide a fitting example of the prescribed relationship of the Puritan couple and the wife's purpose in serving her husband's and family's needs (Document 6). The 'yoke-fellow' relationship consigned them to distinct and separate spheres . . . . They shared a "love of each other as the chief of all earthly comfort" in which their first and ultimate commitment was to God.

Winthrop was chosen as leader because he set forth the example in which the colonists believed. No man or woman could want a more loving, respectful relationship than is revealed in these private letters between the two.[24]

The Dutch Reformed people in New York and New Jersey had the same view of family. The Lutheran families in Pennsylvania and elsewhere also had strong family lives. So it was with all the religious groups in the colonies. All the other institutions found their faith in God because that was the center of the home. The Friends of Society, or Quakers, who resisted Trinitarian Doctrine and put the emphasis on "inter-light" of experience rather than on the authority of Scripture, allowed women to prophesy. But even Quaker families practiced male leadership.

SEEDS OF UNBELIEF BY A NEW TYPE OF IMMIGRANTS

Turnaround of Power in Europe Caused a Change of Immigration into America

In the mid-seventeenth century, there was a slow turnaround in what was happening in Europe. The Catholic and Anglican Churches tried to remove the Protestants from their countries. There had been religious wars in Europe for many decades, killing millions of people, and in some countries destroying a fourth of the population. Finally, peace from armed conflict was declared between the warring religious factions. But in many cases, this peace led to a complete change of power, so the oppression and even persecution then came from Protestants against the Catholic and intellectual hierarchy. The Protestant groups who had been oppressed and persecuted by Catholic or Anglican forces were given favoritism.

The attainment of favoritism can be seen in some of the acts passed. The Treaty of Westphalia was signed in Europe in 1648, which allowed the rulers to choose the religion of their choice for their country or providence. This led to many of them giving priority to Protestantism. In England, Oliver Cromwell was victorious over all armies and established the British Commonwealth in the mid-seventeenth century. He favored Protestantism over the Anglicans. The English Toleration Act was signed in 1689, but toleration was allowed only for Protestants and not for Catholics. This led to a massive emigration to America from Europe of people who were not strongly committed to any Christian church beliefs, and favored the more liberal Church of England.

Those who had opposed the Protestant movement now found themselves on the other side of the persecution, and they fled from Europe to America. Many educated Germans also took their exodus to America. They had embraced the beginnings of the Enlightenment and the deistic concepts. So, a new wave of people from England and Germany immigrated without possessing the same motivation to worship God, as those in the earlier wave. Moreover, some Protestant believers saw conditions favorable to return to their native country where they still had relatives and possessions.

This immigration wave had two profound effects against Christianity in the colonies. Many people came into the colonies competing with the settlers who were already there, in the areas of business, law, and government, and so forth. Many Christians already established in America took their focus off worship and placed it on competing and increasing their control of the world.

In mid-seventeenth century England, Christianity was honored publicly, but by 1730, people talked about politics in the church, and there was indifference toward the truths of God. This was true even of the King and Queen of England. In America, there was also a general decline of the vibrancy of the early Christian commitment. At that time, religion became more doctrinally-oriented and less life-oriented.

In the early 1700s, morality declined because the communities were broken up through the influx of the new people and the changes they brought. For example, the Puritan plan to live in the village and go out to work the farms gave way to their moving permanently out to the farms to take over more land. In 1705, Reverend Joseph Easterbrooks bewailed this condition because people no longer lived together where they could receive spiritual oversight, and they began to absent themselves from church. When this move began, the General Court ruled, without much effect, that no dwelling should be built more than a half mile from the meeting house.[25] The competition for success in business and for new land took men's minds off worshipping God, and focused on the world. Greed and immorality escalated. As early as 1715, Cotton Mather lost control of the direction of Harvard University to those who wanted the curriculum to involve broader studies from Europe, although Christianity was still taught.

Large numbers of unbelieving European immigrants inundated the communities, and worldliness grew in the lives of the church people. These conditions caused a decline in the number of people in the churches to no more than one in twenty, and there was a desire for more to be included. This caused a shift from strict screening for church membership, to one of including as many as possible, and creating new schools of thought. One of the authors of *The Christian Hope* has made the observation that after toleration came, "it was soon evident that something far more valuable had been in large measure lost, namely the presence and power of God."[26]

Following the major immigrations from the end of the seventeenth century up until the time of the Declaration of Independence, most of the people were not in the church. The church had to adjust and try to make an impact to bring these people into the church and convert them to Jesus Christ. At this time, the strong Christian foundations were being attacked by the educated elite. But having the solid foundation of Christian truth in their institutions made revivalistic, evangelistic preaching a tremendous power as evangelists called the people to repent and be born again.

Great Awakening and the Bringing of People into the Churches by Revivalism

The small number of church members in early America is surprising to modern Christians because it is recognized that though they might not be members, many held to a Christian worldview. But the early churches only wanted believers who were living holy lives in the church, while today the philosophy is to get as many people in the churches as possible. Those coming in the later waves in the eighteenth century brought many different ideologies and came for many different reasons. Morality in America was in disarray, and the church realized it needed more members. A new method was needed to try to bring people into the churches and bring about change in conduct. The revivalistic approach began and continued in various forms throughout American history. William Warren Sweet, the American church historian, comments that had it not been for revivalism, the American people would have been "unchurched." Thus, God performed the miracle of the Great Awakening, and brought many back into the churches. That awakening established the presence of God for founding the new national revolution and government.

The following statistics show how God used revivalism to bring the people into the church. There are variations of a few points in different reports, but the following figures are commonly reported.

MEMBERSHIP OF
AMERICAN CHURCHES SINCE 1776

1776	5-6%
1800	7-10%
1850	16-20%
1900	36%
1920	40%
1940	40%
1960	63.3%
1970	63.8%
1975	60.6%
1980	59.2%
1990	59.3%

Preaching of the First Great Awakening

The revival first began with a German-born, Dutch pastor who came to America in 1720 to Raritan Valley, New Jersey. The churches had a dead orthodoxy that did not attract people, especially the youth. Frelinghuysen began fervent evangelical preaching, calling people to repentance and to a new relationship with God. He attracted the masses and was invited many places to preach. He soon drew a reaction from the Dutch Reformed pastors, but the preaching brought many into the churches by 1726. The next year, Jonathan Edwards moved to Northampton where he found similar conditions, especially a breakdown of family government and licentiousness among the youth. In 1734, he preached a series of messages on justification by faith alone to refute Armenian views permeating thinking. He depicted the wrath of God against sin and pointed out man's inability to deliver himself from sin and guilt. Many converted.

There were many other successful revivalists. Gilbert Tennent and his brothers were outstanding in New York and New Jersey. Eleazer Wheelock and Joseph Bellamy became itinerant evangelists with Johnathan Edwards. The most famous of these itinerant evangelists was George Whitfield from Gloucester, England, who had been touched by the Spirit of God in the Holy Club with John and Charles Wesley. Whitfield traveled from New England to Georgia. With a commanding voice, he preached to thousands of people who came into the church this message: "You must be born again!"

The emphasis on Christian love and outreach for others brought a burden for missions and a concern for the oppressed. Jonathan Edwards and David Brainard started to evangelize the Indian tribes. Some Quakers opposed slavery, and Samuel Hopkins also took a stand against it. The influence of John Newton in England and of others no doubt had some influence. During this awakening, there was a new Christian humanism born out of the idea of the love of God and the importance of change in the heart of a Christian.

All of these revivalist preachers emphasized the sinfulness of man and his inability to save himself, and the sovereignty, wrath, and judgment of God, along with God's love in Christ. They held to a Calvinistic view. The results were genuine repentance, moral change in people's lives, and social change in the community. The emphasis on the change of heart resulted in a loss of the overall Puritan view of God in the whole body politic and the church's control over all of life. Also, Christian nurturing was neglected because of the strong influence of the initial change of heart through revivalism. But the Christian belief in God and the Bible strengthened and continued as the main view of life. While the Great Awakening brought forty to fifty thousand people into the churches in New England and elsewhere, initiating the trend to get people into the churches, there was another strong force of conflict that had entered and continued to grow. Tares were also increasingly sown among the wheat.

At the end of the seventeenth century, the Cavalier class from England and the educated immigrants from Germany immigrated and began changing the educational institutions, impregnating them with ideas of enlightenment, and further downgrading the interest in religion. This greatly counteracted the initiative of the first Great Awakening. The deism of John Locke and the influence of Jacob of Arminius on the idea of man's ability and right to choose in the midst of a pluralism of Christian groups led to the emergence of the idea of Unitarianism. Eminent leaders such as Thomas Jefferson, Thomas Paine, and Benjamin Franklin espoused a pluralism of religions.[27]

America's Foundations of Faith

At the end of the seventeenth century and especially at the beginning of the eighteenth, there was a strong influx of unbelievers into the colonies, especially among highly educated people. The worldly influences made people indifferent to Christianity and, even among many of the educated elite, there was hostility to the all-encompassing power of the religious elite. This greatly reduced the favor of religion and the numbers of people in the churches. Had it not been for the Great Awakening introducing revivalist methods into the American scene and restoring favor to Christianity as the prevailing ideology, the continuation of the Christian religion as the major ideology would not have occurred. But, as the number of people who professed to be Christians was restored, so the counter-movement of the educated elite begin to grow to remove the dominant control of the Christian ideology.

Chapter 9
Intellectual Revolt:
Leadership by an Educated Elite

DEISTIC RATIONALISM GAINED GOVERNING INFLUENCE

Governing Elite of Virginia Dynasty Believed in Human Wisdom and Nature

In a companion book to this study, I have presented the growth in the West of an intellectual revolt against God and how, in time, those intellectual beliefs were shown by later secular scholars not to be true.[1] It has been pointed out that the lie of man's superior wisdom is the plan by which the Devil leads man to destroy civilization. These next four chapters will trace how this deception has caused the decline of American civilization since about the nineteenth century.

It has already been mentioned that during the revivals of the Great Awakening, there was a strong element of deistic thinking which diminished religion and morals, and many educated men who were deists had an influence on the Declaration of Independence and the revolution against England. The revivalist preaching in the Great Awakening called the common people away from receiving these deistic views. Gradually, the educated elite influenced changes in the federal government and in the colleges and universities that would eventually filter down to influence the local community schools as well as all the people. Renewed Christian awakening would bring things back somewhat, in a zigzag way. These next chapters will tell the story of the zigzag process whereby the steps of progressive decline occurred on the American scene.

Turning Point from Faith in God to Man: Jefferson and the Virginia Dynasty (1801-1825)

The transition of America from faith in God to faith in man, which began the long steps of decline, was promoted and successfully launched by the men with deistic views of what has often been called "The Virginia Dynasty" (1801-1824). Thomas Jefferson was elected to the presidency for two terms; was followed by James Madison for two, and then was followed for two terms by James Monroe. Madison and Monroe had been closely associated, influenced by, and basically in agreement with Jefferson both in Virginia and in his presidential efforts. While Madison was at first a follower of Hamilton, he later changed and helped Jefferson in forming the Republican Democratic party. They were so successful that the Federalist

Party, which was for strong central government, virtually died out by the end of this dynasty. Of the three, Madison was the least threatening to tradition in the way he communicated.

Thomas Jefferson and the others in the Virginia dynasty were opposed to strong centralized federal government, and for that reason Jefferson is exalted by modern Republican leaders and other conservatives. But these people fail to see the difference in Jefferson's reasons for limited government and theirs today. Jefferson became opposed to strong centralized government primarily because he wanted a government that would allow those who held to a liberal individualism as he did to be more free to pursue what they wanted. Today, those views of individualistic liberalism have triumphed, and advocates of those liberal views have created and used an extremely controlling central government that seeks to force people to conform to their politically correct views. Therefore, most conservative Republicans oppose a strong centralized government for the opposite reasons from Jefferson. The motivations are different. Moreover, as shall be pointed out, it was the rapid promotion of individualism during the time of the Virginia Dynasty and this individualistic opposition to federal control that resulted in the Supreme Court taking steps to restrain individual's and state's rights from going too far in their independence. Thus, Jeffersonian views helped create the beginnings of the expanded powers the court abuses today. This will be considered shortly.

French Connection and Departure of the Presidency from the Biblical God

By the time Jefferson took office as President in 1801, his views were more liberal and anti-Christian than when he had written *A Summary View of the Rights of America* in 1774 and a revision of this in *The Declaration of Independence* in 1776. Jefferson was in France in 1784 to assist Benjamin Franklin and then stayed as the minister to France from 1785-1789. France was predominantly atheistic with liberal morals during that time.

When in France, Jefferson was influenced to adopt a deistic position that bordered on atheism. While he never gave up professing belief in a creator and claimed in 1802 that he was as much a Christian as any other, he also never really believed in life after death. Moreover, he adopted the heretical view that Jesus was the best of men, but not God, as in his writing of Jesus' sayings, often called "the Jefferson Bible." He gives credence to Unitarianism. Through the influence of the teachings of Monsieur Cabanas and Monsieur Flourens while in France, he rejected all metaphysical truth and found confirmation for his life-long materialism. His extensive understanding of nature supported a mechanical view of the universe.

Questions about Jefferson's Morals

Jefferson sought to present himself as a highly principled man, and most of his historians seek to defend him as such. But he violated his own principles in regard to discriminating against the rights of black people by continuing the practice of slavery, even working ten-year-old boys in his nail factory twelve hours a day. Jefferson's conduct elicited persistent rumors about sexual immorality that seem to have valid bases. He is known to have been captured by interest in other women before and after his marriage. When writing about the Ten Commandments, he omitted the command against adultery. This suggests an aversion to that prohibition.

For about ten years as a young man, he had a strong affection for his neighbor's wife and, although there were reports of immorality with her, there is no proof. He married the widowed Martha Wayles Skelton, whom he dearly loved and by whom he had six children; only two daughters surviving infancy. Jefferson is said to have promised his dying wife he would never remarry, which was less than two years before he went to France.

Jefferson went to France with Benjamin Franklin and then became United States Ambassador. At the time, France was filled with an acceptance of sexual immorality and easy divorce. The immoral environment favored relaxed, free sexual relationships. While there, he became involved with Maria Cosway, an English artist from London who was married. They spent time together on trips, and there is little doubt they had an affair. Jefferson kept few of his letters or other records that would document what occurred with any women other than his wife. But he kept detailed records about other things.

Soon after Jefferson went to France, he had with him a young fourteen-year old slave girl, Sally Hemings, begotten by Martha's father from a slave, Betty Hemings. Sally was, therefore, half sister to Martha. Betty and Sally were inherited by Jefferson along with many other slaves and eleven thousand acres from Martha's father, John Wayles. Sally went to Paris with Jefferson's youngest daughter to help care for his children. It is believed that Sally became Jefferson's concubine and that her children were Jefferson's. The records show that Jefferson was present with Sally in Paris and in Monticello when children were conceived and that she was involved in a close relationship to him at these times.

Sally's mother, Betty, had children by four men–black and white–and was the capable slave woman who for many years managed Monticello for Jefferson. Sally's mother, therefore, left an example of promiscuous, sexual relations with various men, and Sally would have had no moral example of sexual monogamy in her mother.

It was rumored that Sally, being a half sister, looked something like Martha, his beloved wife. Sally Hemings was very white, and years later after leaving Monticello and living with two of her sons, all three were listed in the United States Census as "white." She received special treatment from Jefferson that no other slave received. When in France, Jefferson spent considerable money on clothes and jewelry for Sally.[2] There is good evidence that while they were both in France, Sally gained a promise from Jefferson, which was kept, that her children would be liberated when they reached adulthood. Jefferson did not release any other slaves at adulthood. When Jefferson died, in his will he freed five of the house servants and sold the rest, but Sally was left to stay at Monticello, and later freed.

It has been argued that Jefferson was too principled to have a concubine, but the evidence is contrary. His inconsistency in regard to slavery has been mentioned. Also, it is known Jefferson made allowances for concubinage at least once: during Jefferson's second term, James Madison, as Secretary of State, used governmental funds to provide concubines for the ambassador from Tunis, and the record shows Madison wrote to Jefferson and joked about it.[3] Jefferson, therefore, concurred in acceptance and provision of concubines for another person. Why could there not be a loving relationship with Sally, a half sister and much like his wife, for himself?

While this has been contested by some of the most important historians of Jefferson, Annette Gordon-Reed, a black associate professor of law at New York Law School, has done the most comprehensive and recent study of this matter, and she has shown that the preponderance of evidence sustains the view that Sally was Jefferson's concubine and he was the father of her children.[4] Gordon-Reed shows that Jefferson's historians were selective and distortive in dealing with this data.[5] Much of the data presented here is from her book. One group is now studying DNA evidence to settle this question.

Other evidence of Jefferson's paternity is also available. Sally's son, Madison, gave a statement to an Ohio newspaper in 1873 stating that he and his mother's other children were from Thomas Jefferson. His memoirs, which were later revealed, indicated this as a fact. A letter from this third son, Madison, explicitly states this to be the case.[6] William Weaver, a federal marshal, recorded an aside to the census data of 1870 saying Madison was Jefferson's son. This was when Madison was living in Ross County before any public disclosure by him of the matter.[7] Eston Hemings, another son who looked like Thomas Jefferson, confirmed Sally's children were Jefferson's. The evidence of memory of those groups of people closely associated among the Virginia gentry at the time said that Sally's children were Jefferson's. Another slave who worked at Monticello during the time, Israel Jefferson, testified that Jefferson was the father. There is some evidence a son conceived by

Sally in France was named Thomas, and he was sent to live with the Woodson family and was called Thomas Woodson, but this seems inconclusive.[8] Sally begot several children (a total of six or seven).

This matter of Jefferson's sexual immorality is important in that it would furnish adequate reason for him to have a bias against God. He would not want to admit there is the kind of God for which he would be held accountable at the future judgment for immoral actions with married women and a slave girl.

Jefferson's Attitude against Organized Religion

In France, Jefferson was not only influenced by French sexual promiscuity, but he became anti-church in his attitudes. Jefferson's oldest daughter wanted to become a Catholic nun, possibly partly because of reaction to her father's immoral actions and of French unbelief. Jefferson was very opposed to her becoming a nun, and Fawn M. Brodie mentions in her biography that had she joined the religious order, the Pope would have had much satisfaction "upon the daughter of a man whose suspicion of priestcraft and *contempt for organized religion was known all over Europe.*"[9] (italics added)

Anglicanism had educated Jefferson, but this church had become oppressive after it had recovered authority in England following Cromwell in the seventeenth century. Jefferson's great concern about *man* and his rights became more central while in France, and he helped pen *The Declaration of the Rights of Men*. Jefferson was strongly in favor of the First Amendment because he felt religion was the cause of most wars, and he favored only a religion of reason and not revelation; he wanted to keep any religion out of politics. John Adams and others, however, favored the First Amendment to preserve the freedom of all religions to express their views, and saw them as essential for ethics and morality.

This much is certain—Jefferson changed considerably under French influence to a more complete deistic view, one with a strong belief in unchanging laws of nature and a strong humanistic individualism with a more liberal view of morals. Francis S. Philbrick of the University of Pennsylvania has said, "All his ideas were colored by his experience of the five seething years passed in Paris . . . ."[10].

Jefferson's friend Benjamin Franklin also became more unbelieving and less moral from his time in France. Franklin rejected a personal invitation by the great evangelist, George Whitfield, to repent and be born again from the Holy Spirit, and he later wrote a discourse on how to seduce a woman. It is nothing but ironic that the author of the Declaration of Independence which proclaimed all men as *created equal by God* should later influence the nation's departure from God.

When Jefferson ran for president the first time, he was accused extensively of being an atheist. The political implications of this may have caused Jefferson to carefully continue to profess a casual belief there was a God. The first election of Jefferson as president was one of the most hotly debated of all early elections. Moreover, Jefferson did not win a majority of electoral votes, but tied with Aaron Burr. Therefore, it was decided in the House of Representatives by a narrow margin. Because Hamilton distrusted Burr and disliked Jefferson less, he tipped the scales toward Jefferson. There can be little doubt that Jefferson's views as president influenced religion throughout the nation, gave impetus to the feelings of Universalism and Unitarianism, and gave credence to ideas about secularizing education that have progressively gained ascendancy into modern times. The first year in office he did not call for a Thanksgiving Day celebration to God as was common by previous presidents. The second year when challenged about it, he stated that he wouldn't do it because that was the kind of thing a king (as in England) would do.

Late in life, Jefferson founded the University of Virginia, and he chose the teachers and curriculum which were exceedingly liberal and separated from religion. Even when churches of Virginia voiced objections to the board of the university, Jefferson tried persistently to appoint unbelievers, repeatedly trying to appoint a professor from the University of South Carolina who was hostile to religion. While Jefferson opposed state religious support, given the highly religious climate in which he lived as a politician, he did not hold to a strict separation, as some claim today, but allowed state accommodation. As mentioned, Jefferson was willing for religious groups to found colleges in connection with the university and to use its library and other facilities.

The Context of the Times Favored a Shift to Faith in Man over God

People's Loss of Gratitude to God in Exchange for Nationalism

The United States was at a point of development when Jeffersonian ideas were opportune. The economy was growing, new roads and canals were in progress, and more people were moving westward to settle. This prosperity, as well as the victory in the Indian War, gave a new sense of security and freedom. Industrialization was under way in England, but the United States was still dependent mainly on the English to manufacture their goods from their products, although American industrialization was beginning. Jefferson was against the aristocracy and for the individual common man; therefore, he reduced taxes and gained a strong following.

Jefferson ran into major problems on the seas with the French and the English commandeering the ships and pressing American sailors into their service. This led to Jefferson's placing an embargo on goods, which hurt the United States more than the English and resulted in the War of 1812 under Madison's presidency. This ended in a virtual draw. Prosperity had grown strong about 1812. American exports increased greatly and commerce grew. After the war of 1812, American commerce, production, and manufacturing were liberated from English dependence and grew even faster. Madison was capable, but he governed in times of difficulty. Under Monroe, however, there was peace, great expansion, increase in progress in building roads and canals, and communication. Even though Monroe opposed federal help in projects, many expenditures found their way into the federal budget. Pride in the nation came into focus and a new sense of nationalism was born. The Cumberland Road, often called the National Highway, was completed at a cost of seven million dollars to the taxpayer. The Survey Act was passed laying out progressive development.

Thomas Jefferson and his Virginian colleagues believed in the American dream of expanding the nation into a prosperous country of peace and good-will. Jefferson and his two followers believed ***man must and could decide his own destiny in a world run by natural laws.*** They believed man had rights by nature and that there is a progressive goodness in man. The French view of progress was adopted and from it developed hope of a national utopia. This hope increasingly dominated the thinking of Jefferson and his friends and spread to the nation. The dream for America was based on the faith that an elite group of men using science and an enlightened minimum government could produce salvation for all mankind.

Jefferson's acquisition, with the help of Monroe and others, of the Louisiana Purchase (which cost more than the federal budget) from France in 1803 when Napoleon needed money, gave the United States access to the western part of the continent to the Rocky Mountains. Lewis and Clark's successful expedition laid claim all the way to Oregon. These things excited the imagination of the people and substantially boosted the dream of *man* building a great nation from east to west. These providential blessings became stepping stones for human pride.

During the Virginia Dynasty, *faith in a sovereign God who provides by His grace for sinful man disappeared from prominence* and there emerged to center stage a belief in human wisdom and the importance of the individual common man. Most of the people lost a sense of thankfulness and dependence on God and turned in pursuit of mammon. Deism had become dominant among intellectuals, especially in the north and east, and biblical Christianity was criticized. Materialism was the focus of man's labors and worship. But the churches kept the consciousness of God before the nation as they too followed the extension west.

Leading Educated Elite Import the Enlightenment Philosophies of Europe

The new mammon worship was given a further boost by other ideas from Europe. Just as the deism of Europe had made its way and had its influence in America by Jefferson and others, so the European ideas of how man knows things also were being discussed while Jefferson was in France. The philosophers proposed man's ability to know was limited to his sense perception during the Virginia Dynasty. A rejection of objective knowledge of God as revelation in the Bible, and the exaltation of man's knowledge as the one authority, found its way to the educated people. The views of the Enlightenment came into America in full force.

John E. Bentley writes, "Actually the Enlightenment is the voice of Locke carried over the century into action."[11] From England, George Berkeley saw knowledge as *only ideas* from sense and reflection; Hume reduced these mental ideas to skepticism. Kant gave some resolve to how man "knows" by saying man can only know the world through *innate categories* of thought and can know God only by a subjective *sense of ought*.[12] Kant's views led to both the empirical scientific movement and to liberal theology by which man's ability to know the transcendent was reduced to any and various feelings one might have. Any objective knowledge of God was rejected.

George W. Hegel's idealistic evolutionary philosophy helped produce the subjective *liberal theology,* such as Schliermacher's, based on feeling, and Harnack's view based on man's sense of feeling dependent on God as Father of all men, who are all brothers. According to these thinkers, man is free to act and to think about God *as he feels*. Kant's views also led to the transcendentalism of Ralph Waldo Emerson, Theodore Parker, and Walter Channing in the 1840s.

Jonathan Edwards earlier had erred in his metaphysical idealism, "Declaring that bodies have no existence of their own, and that all existence is mental."[13] While being a powerful influence for revival and Reformed theology in his day, he had left the door open to these ideas which have led to modern New Age thinking that says each man can be god. In Europe by 1835, rationalization led to explaining away of miracles by H. E. G. Paulus and then relegation of miracles to myth by Strauss. By 1820 and following, faith in the trinitarian God of the Bible had given way to a Unitarianism and Universalism among the educated elite.

The rise of the common man, the self-consciousness of the laboring class, the westward movement with optimism built on man's strength, and the progressive development of materialism, prepared for the optimism about individual man as the expression of God in the world. Faith in God shifted to humanistic religion, becoming a tool for men to help mankind in social action, slaves' rights, women's oppression by men, and the like. The Virginia Dynasty had lessened the idea of the *importance of authority,* and released it to the authority of how each individual man feels before God. It forwarded the religious idea of optimism in *individual human development* and accomplishment, without any access to or need of objective revelation of God and His will, subjecting the Bible to doubt and ridicule. Unitarianism and Universalism were the result beginning about 1820 and following.

American Education Changed from God- to Man-Centered; from Church Control toward State Control

Foundations by Horace Mann of State-Controlled Education

As the new esteem of man and his pursuit of the material world became increasingly important, the vision for education changed and the educated elite saw it as their mission to educate and control the commoner. Horace Mann gave up his law practice and political ambitions to promote public education (1837). Mann was a Unitarian in belief. He wanted to free education from Calvinistic orthodoxy. He saw himself as "breaking a hole in the wall and letting in the light of religious civilization where it had never shown before." He believed in "the perfectibility of man." He saw a place for religion and for the Bible, but not for piety or worship of God; it was primarily to impart *morals*. He was interested in *liberating man by education* and making a way for America to prosper and become heaven on earth. He saw education as *a natural right* given to every child by creation. He said:

> The will of God, is conspicuously manifested *in the order of Nature*, and in the relations which he has established among men. . . . [It is] the right of every child that is born into the world, to see a degree of education as will enable him, and, as far as possible, will predispose him, to perform all domestic, social, civil, and moral duties, upon the same clear ground of *natural law and equity* as it founds a child's right, upon his first coming into the world, to distend his lungs with a portion of the common air . . . .(italics added)[14]

Mann saw *the state* as having the *parental responsibility* to furnish this. He further said, "Education is not only a moral renovator, and a multiplier of intellectual power, but . . . the most prolific parent of *material riches*."[15] He held to the inherent goodness of man, believing in a spark of divinity in man. He was less and less concerned for character development. He opposed rewards and punishment and especially rejected the motivation of fear. He wanted to secularize education, removing it from the church and having it be a province of the state rather than of the community and parents. He felt that all that was needed was money, and that the failure of education was the people's fault in failing to furnish the appropriate funds. Many of his ideas came from travels and study in Europe where enlightenment ideas were dominant.

Mann was the first secretary of the Massachusetts State Board of Education. He clashed with Boston school teachers, many of whom were true to their Puritan background. Also, because most schools were not in urban cities but in rural towns, his ideas could not be carried out. As Locke was the germ of the Enlightenment, Mann was the germ of the future of education in America. He launched the ideas that have come to dominate American schools. His most controlling innovation was the establishment of teacher training schools and standards. He traveled and spoke, and his writings were read by educators everywhere. The National Education Association, which spearheaded and guided to fulfillment these ideas, was organized in 1848.

Other Educators Held to the State Control of Education

Mann was assisted by James G. Carter, who saw the public schools as an instrument *for influencing and controlling* the future of the people and society. To Carter, the schools were the way of controlling all institutions. Carter passed many laws to influence education. Mann and Carter established the idea of *a new priesthood* for society.[16] Henry Barnard, who saw man as imperfect and who was more religious, also "believed in creating a priesthood of teachers," and to this calling he gave his full allegiance.[17] This cause was central for him and other educators. To the educated elite, the schools were agencies for social rejuvenation. This idea of secular educators as priests to guide the church in a new humanism emerged *in the church* in the 1970s at Harvard and elsewhere, reaching the fruition of these early ideas.

Mann and these others at that time wanted to take over the schools and the religion in them to guide and control them for a better world, an Eden on earth. Their vision was for the state to control the religion for its own purposes and not as separate powers. The emphasis of separating religion from the public schools came only after the intellectual movement embraced scientific naturalism a little later. But this step of controlling all education for the public good was a significant first step. As mankind made the material world his source of life and saw himself as the divine spark of the world, to own and develop it, the elite saw *man*, in his wisdom, using religion for his own ends.

Later Struggles to Implement State Control for Democracy

The struggle in education for the rest of the century emphasized the excitement of the potential of democracy, believing that man, through the state, could guide, indoctrinate, and produce the great utopia. An obstacle was the religious and private schools and the expression of religion in the public schools. Following Mann, Carter, and Barnard there were others such as William Torrey Harris, John Swett, and Francis W. Parker who struggled in various ways to use education to control people toward producing the ideal democracy for a utopia. The imperative of making all education a part of the state emerged, while there was the tacit acceptance of the idea of God as having a place to produce morals.

The National Educational Association was created at mid-nineteenth century, and through it the educated elite gained centralized influence on education through the state by the last part of the century. They thus gained the right to set the standards of education and to guide its formation. Without the church realizing it, the state was taking away the property and control of the schools which it had helped initiate and dominate for about two hundred years. The elite were only a small step away from excluding the church from public education. That significant step could come only after the secular elite had expanded the indoctrination of their vision to most of the people.

Even Evangelical Theology Shifted toward Man's Ability and Perfectibility

The American nation was caught up in a vision of what people as individuals could do to build a great nation. This vision was of prosperous materialism and an advancement of this by democracy. This emphasis on what man could do came from enlightenment on one hand and from a reaction to rigid orthodox religion in the churches on the other, and this changed the emphasis in the churches.

Nathan O. Hatch describes the change in religion from about 1800 ff. in its rapid development in the cities and westward as follows:

> The expansion of evangelical Christianity did not proceed primarily from the nimble response of religious elites meeting the challenge before them. Rather, Christianity was effectively *reshaped by common people who molded it in their own image* and who threw themselves into expanding its influence. Increasingly assertive common people wanted their leaders unpretentious, their doctrines self-evident, and down-to-earth, their music lively and singable, and their churches in local hands. It was the upsurge of democratic hope that characterized so many religious cultures in the early republic . . . .(italics added)[18]

American religion took an upsurge toward an optimism of individual man's ability and perfectibility. This was a reaction against extreme Calvinism and the type of church government control and confessional doctrines expressed by the

Presbyterians, Episcopalians, and Roman Catholics. But before this reaction and the secularizing movement was fully effective, it was impacted by the Second Great Awakening which began under Timothy Dwight as president of Yale with students there, and which spread to other colleges. This tended briefly to revise Calvinism.[19] But the preaching of the time generally took another turn. While powerful preachers brought more people into the church, they emphasized *individual man's power to choose* against *God's sovereignty.*

Nathaniel Taylor emphasized man's choice in his preaching. Charles G. Finney, the great revivalist, preached for decisions by man and stirred many in his great city revivals. He started the method of having individuals come forward in the meetings to the mourner's bench which later evangelists used. While Methodists had previously been seen unfavorably as English missionaries, Francis Asbury and Samuel Cartwright now more effectively launched the Methodist movement with common men who were little trained for ministry, but who rode horseback out across the new territories and built new churches. This spread like wildfire.

Finney, a Presbyterian, was greatly influenced by Wesley's *Plain Account of Christian Perfection* and adopted the view of entire sanctification.[20] Finney and Wesley believed in the *perfectibility of man* and the Armenian view of human choice. Barton W. Stone and Alexander Campbell sought to win the people on the frontier and get them united together in locally-led democratic congregations. There was little emphasis on eternal life and rewards, except in calling the individual to repent before judgment, and the misguided views of the date-setting Adventists.[21] The individual man and his perfectibility were the focus of religion.

Intellectualism Produced a Unitarian Revolt in the Churches (1810 ff.)

As these transitions of thought began, the first of three surges of anarchy in society occurred. The bold religious rejections of the deity of Christ and of God's working as expressed in European ideas produced deliberate anarchy against church confessions and law and came into American churches about mid-eighteenth century. They were readily received by the Unitarians and the educated elite. Under such skepticism about faith in God, unbelieving religious leadership focused on social action for man, especially for the oppressed slave and for women, about which more will be said.

Thus, the mood of the nation and the popular religious emphasis prepared the way for the Jacksonian political appeal to the individual man in a democratic society. While the preaching brought many into the churches, the focus on the individual and his power to choose reduced the emphasis on God's sovereignty in favor of man's ability. While the vision was more on a heaven-on-earth which man could build rather than on a future eternity with God, the one did not necessarily exclude the other. Fortunately, the revivalist outreach of the churches outran the more localized intellectual skeptical revolt caused by the elite in the north and east and in the large urban parts of the country. Man was challenged to trust God as he risked trying to build a new life in expanding westward.

A summary of these secularizing emphases was that American leadership had removed God to irrelevance and promoted *individualistic man to center stage*, focusing efforts on gaining the material world, the second emphasis in Paul's steps away from God mentioned in chapter 1 of Romans.

New Individualism Brought Reaction for Balance in Power from Judges

Reaction of Courts to Restore Balance

In the American experiment in a republican-type government, the forefathers sought to establish a balance of powers. Up until the time of the Virginia Dynasty, the states zealously sought to maintain their independent rights as those who had *voluntarily* entered into a national contract of unity. The government of the nation as a whole was important but was to be balanced with protecting the state's sovereignty. As mentioned, in the era with Jefferson and his successors, a greater sense of national allegiance was born.

The balance in the national government was between the three branches: the President's *executive and administrative* offices, the *legislative branches* with the House representing the people and the Senate giving balance for the smaller to the larger states, and the *federal court system*. During the time of Jefferson and his successors, the test of that system began to come under serious stress. In the earlier days, the tests were between the president and Congress. Jefferson had always argued for the common man and against centralized authority. However, under the Virginia Dynasty, the government grew and the nation did expend money for the National Highway and passed the protective tariff. But when Jefferson's presidential authority was tested, he clearly fought back. The challenge of centralized power soon emerged in the Supreme Court, at least in part because of the dominant emphasis on individual rights.

Supreme Court Claimed Unwritten Powers

Chief Justice of the Supreme Court was John Marshall, a fellow Virginian but a Federalist who believed in strong central authority and who led the court for thirty years. Jefferson had led the Republicans in accusing the court of being too autocratic, and for certain reasons sought to impeach certain judges, but failed. Thus freed from political implications, the courts gained favor with the people. Marshall then took the initiative to establish some important precedents.

He handed down a decree of the court that states must permit the decisions of their courts to be passed on by the Supreme Court in case of an appeal. When Maryland challenged the United States Bank, which was set up by Congress under Madison in 1816, as unconstitutional in their state, Marshall's court ruled that any law within the scope of the United States Constitution was constitutional, establishing the doctrine of implied powers (Art. I, Sec. 8). He also led them to rule that New York acted unconstitutionally by granting a monopoly over steamboat trade and travel while excluding New Jersey and New England, again appealing to the implied powers (Art. I, Sec. 8). He and the court thus struck powerful blows for the court in favor of the national federal government over state's rights, giving the court rights to interpret the Constitution. At the end of the twentieth century, this power of the Supreme Court will be seen as destabilizing to the nation's system of the balance of powers in the government.

THE SECOND SURGE OF THE INTELLECTUAL REVOLT: EVOLUTIONARY NATURALISM AND SECULARIZATION OF MAN

Belief That Nature Is All and Man Is the Highest Being

By the end of nineteenth century, many leaders of the Western world and the educated elite in the United States were convinced there was no God and that man was the highest creature in the world. Deism had given way to the European epistemology, or view of how man knows, and led to the philosophy of an evolution of society and Darwin's biological evolution of man. These views seemed to offer a natural ground for definite progress for the future of America's "brave new world." The Bible was discredited as myth through higher criticism, and religion was useful possibly as a nice tool for morals. But according to the new science of comparative religions, God was created by man for his needs. Everything was in progressive change—nothing was absolute. About 1870-1875, all the pieces of the intellectual puzzle seemingly fit into place for understanding the natural world and man as king instead of God. Important examples follow.

Darwin published the *Descent of Man* in 1871; (his *Origin* . . . was published in 1859*)*, saying man was the highest product of nature and not the creation of God. Marx published *Das Capital*, arguing that through the dialectical process, the world's economy was developing toward the utopia of the classless society through a dialectical process. Julius Wellhausen published his imaginary history of Israel, whereby he claimed power-hungry priests fabricated a fictional view of the development of God and His people to uphold the ceremonial worship of Israel. He claimed this was the true story behind the Bible. The Roman Catholic hierarchy composed and passed the decree of the idea of Papal infallibility, saying when the Pope spoke *ex cathedra* he could inerrantly rule God's church for him. These are only a few of the main ideas that *exalted man* about the year 1875, and reached America within a decade. This was the turning point when the intellectual elite believed that man was the highest creature produced by nature and that God was non-existent or myth.

Education Seen as the Tool to Make Man "King" and to Control the World

Until about 1885, the colleges and universities of America were mostly committed to Christian theism. While there were defections, there was often revival. But after about 1885, the new compelling view of secular humanism began to take over the church colleges to reform the curriculum. Thus, the colleges which Christians had created were now turned over to a philosophy which rejected the supernatural and the biblical view. Evolution of man as a biological basis for progress became dominant in education. The educators in the early twentieth century greatly accelerated the ideas of Horace Mann and others into positions of growing dominance of political influence.

By Darwinian naturalism, man was seen as a product of the forces of nature, and William James envisioned he could be pragmatically controlled by education. Nicholas Murray Butler saw man as an animal who is continuous with community, and that the state should guide his education toward one ideal democracy.

John Dewey effectively extended Mann's desire to exert state control over the education of every child, based on his natural right. Dewey combined the Hegelian idea of developing continuity with that of Darwin in organic revolution. He said every child should be free to develop his natural innate abilities to completion by modern educators who would guide all men into a socialistic state of the Great Community. This would all happen by an inerrancy of the power of nature. By progressive growth, there would be an integration downward to a leveling of the masses and away from aristocracy. With the proper education, this would occur by the democratic process in the ideal state.

This obligation of society to educate every child, first taught by Mann, was again strongly emphasized by Dewey and extended to help forward his new Jerusalem. Thus, the teacher helps the child experience this growth. Dewey believed in the inherent goodness of man. Dewey's influence began to be felt in the colleges and universities in the first and second decades of the 1900s.[22] It was mainly John Dewey and his disciple, J.B. Watson, who presented the schools as the instrument for social engineering. Watson, who *rejected the view of man as evil,* saw him as one who came into the world as mentally neutral, and whom educators (by science) could mold as a force for good.

All of this was seen as a struggle for the rights to gain equality in material things and build a better world. While the vision in Europe became guidance by socialistic Fascism and in Russia by Communism, in America it was by democratic socialism. In Europe, the utopia was to be achieved by extrinsic force and outward compulsion through some form of dictatorship, but in America the elite envisioned it as being produced by the intrinsic power of education and democratic decision-making. But if the dictators of Europe did not succeed and the dogma of the rightness of the educated elite by education and democracy was too slow, this was helped along by the elite through subversion of the forms of government over the people in the institutions.

The National Education Association (and others) began to exert a centralizing control factor by its Committee of Ten and its Committee on College Entrance Requirements. This control progressively increased with teacher training regulations. The educated elite in the Federal Government became increasingly involved and interested in regulating public education. The tradition of the control over education by local boards elected by parents was a chief obstacle to the social engineering of the educated elite.

Under an education centered on God, there were unifying ideals and controlling principles. Under naturalistic philosophy, the idea of many things and the freedom to choose whatever one wished offered a multiplicity of various emerging courses. This produced a departure from the old liberal arts education for a new curriculum of science, psychology, sociology, and many other new courses. The rights of the individual to choose in spite of social consequences gained dominance.

The educated elite discovered a *new tool* for influencing the people and their choices, namely through the growing *mass media.* The secular press used the distorted presentation of what was done at the Scopes' trial over evolution at Dayton, Tennessee, (1925) to effectively discredit Christianity, giving the secular view of man a boost and presenting Christians as narrow and uneducated. This was the planned purpose of the Dayton trial, along with gaining commerce for the town whose main street had been circumvented by a highway. The educated elite became increasingly impatient at their progress, being convinced that belief in God and the Bible was untrue and a hindrance to progress in producing the paradise on earth. The Scopes' trial had demonstrated the powerful ability of the media to persuade people with their new means. The educated elite further expanded its efforts on developing and gaining use and control of the press, motion pictures, and later television, to forward their *messianic vision of providing material equality to everyone* and of discrediting faith in God and religion.

Intellectual Revolt to the Liberal Gospel of Hope of Social Control by the Churches, Substituted for the Gospel of Christ

The second great anarchistic movement within the churches (after that of Unitarianism) came in the sharp controversy from 1890 to the middle of the twentieth century. The impact of Darwinian naturalism and evolutionary higher criticism made its impact in American churches at this time. Many educated clergy were indoctrinated by the liberal vision of the educated elite and were carried away with it, giving up faith in the Bible for proclaiming a "social gospel" of God leading man to form his own heaven on earth by science.

The focus of theological education was changed as was that of secular education. Lefferts A. Loetscher says:

> Before the turn of the century [1900] a few pioneering seminaries [of the church] ceased to require Hebrew and were experimenting with the elective principle, a tendency which was carried much further during the first quarter of the twentieth century. Theological education, like secular education, was now threatened with loss of integrating principles.[23]

Behind this abandoning of *integrating principles* was the emphasis on man and his ability. Worship centered on man. Having abandoned ideals from God, there was only a realism of many things.

Fundamentalist Movement to Avoid "Modernism"

The believers in the churches reacted to this "modernism" and began what became known as "the fundamentalist movement," stating the doctrines they considered as fundamental to the essence of Christianity. These were first formulated at the Niagara Falls conference in 1885 and were later refined. Many believing churches participated in the Bible Institute movement, and after 1880 there were one hundred eighty-six known Bible Institutes organized with over twenty-five thousand students, a very large number when there were less than one million college students. There were other Bible schools that were little known and not included in this number. Publishing companies dedicated to printing only trustworthy books were formed, and the Christian bookstore movement spread across the nation. In time, fundamentalists entered the radio ministry with nationwide evangelistic programs. Prophecy became a vital point emphasizing the return of Christ. Differing views on prophecy emerged, causing an unresolved diversity, but unity against "modernism" was more important. Also, large conferences emphasizing the sending of missionaries to fulfill the Great Commission were developing. Much of the evangelism and missions were motivated by the individual wishing to escape the hardship of the times.

Delineation of "Modernism" as Another Religion

The controversy against liberal, naturalistic teachings in the churches reached its climax when the veiled disbelief became public with the Auburn Affirmation of Harry Emerson Fosdick (1924), pastor of the First Presbyterian Church of New York and leader of the Union Theological Seminary. He had disagreed with the Presbyterian Church denomination, accepting liberal views.

J. Gresham Machen's definitive book, *Christianity and Liberalism*, published about this time, showed clearly that liberalism was a different religion from Christianity. Even the great news columnist, Walter Lippmann, recognized the import of Machen's views. Thus, many churches were torn asunder by those who rejected the essentials of the Christian faith as stated in the standards that governed their churches. The fundamentalist movement gained more unity by 1930 and launched a fight against liberalism and liberals in the church. It was still divided on the coming of Christ and other controversies, but these issues were largely ignored.

Reactions to the Church Conflicts

The sharp attack and clear delineation of the fundamentalists had an effect on the liberal churches. The neo-orthodoxy and existential philosophies such as that of Karl Barth of Europe were started about 1930 and began to find acceptance in America. They inserted a biblical message but had an uncertain foundation.[24] The lack of claim to absolute truth, but with the use of the Bible, divided the liberal camp and attracted many conservative clergy who carried doubts because of scientific claims. Barth appeased both by talking about the resurrection, but he never believed Christ was actually raised from the dead.

The fundamentalist movement basically bypassed the intellectuals and their arguments in the public schools but attacked them head-on in the churches. Denominations were divided, and new training seminaries were formed, as well as new mission boards. The fundamentalists fought the ecumenical movement that tried to unite Christians under one liberally controlled organization, first known as the Federal Council of Churches, and later as the National Council of Churches. As Fundamentalism became organized, it divided into the American Council of Churches, whose leaders were hawks against heresy, and the National Association of Evangelicals that wanted to avoid the errors of unbelief but emphasize a positive message, with a broader organization in promoting the truth.

Gigantic Effort of the Elite to Expand Education for Human Social Control and for Discrediting Faith in God

This optimism about man and the importance of the state furnishing and guiding education as the hope of man's salvation produced an explosion of the state-furnished college and university system. Money on the state and national levels was made available to build universities. Man's drive to gain knowledge to help him control and build his utopia was manifested in the explosion of secular universities and colleges. While there were only one-half million college students in 1900, the numbers have grown rapidly since 1940 with the great emphasis on materialism. This rapid increase in the number of universities and students is an amazing phenomenon never seen before. After the Second World War, this was accelerated by the so-called "GI Bill," which provided education for veterans. This rapid explosion of secular colleges and universities affected the Christian colleges as well. Many Marxists took advantage of this rapid expansion and found their way into the educational institutions and later into the mass media and government

Following are the numbers of college students in America in various years.

1900	0.5 million
1940	1.5 million
1960	4 million
1970	7 million
1976	11.3 million
1985	12.25 million
1990	14 million

This growth in numbers was accompanied by a *gradual change in curriculum*. The loss of the transcendent and the ideal to the naturalism of evolutionary concepts broadened the curriculum and options. With the diminishing of the integrating principles, the idea of having essentials in education diminished and gave way to more electives that further diminished any unifying ideas. The meaning of spiritual control of all life and thought was being lost.

The Secularization of the Church and Its Institutions

Almost all the older universities and colleges started by the church or by church and state have become institutions teaching a secular view of man. Most of them are hostile to the Christian view of the Bible. This applies to many of those institutions to which church people of the old-line denominations gave their money to teach Christianity. A Danford Study done in 1965 showed less than 10 percent of Christian institutions continued to teach biblical Christianity. While they tipped their hat to Christianity in their publicity, their courses demolished the faith in the God of the Bible and dismissed the Bible as a reliable book having the revelation of God.[25]

Nathan M. Pusey, president of Harvard University, in his last efforts to turn that institution and others back to Christian meaning, warned the faculty:

Uncertainty and doubt remain inside and outside the school [of theology], inside and outside the university. Men continue to scorn older formulations of belief, and rightly so, now as in the past; but now belief itself—professedly is consciously eschewed. . . . A new kind of humanism seems to be engulfing even recently updated formulations of the faith. To many no creedal formulation now seems possible because, it is insisted, there can be no supernatural reference to undergird such a creed. And if creeds go, what then becomes of the Church? Would it not be supremely ironic at such a time, when our culture is almost fatally in need of saving grace, if theology, victimized by a new humanism, should choose to run off in pursuit of another man-made illusion?[26]

Many universities have had religion departments that are anti-Christian in their teaching. There have been a few exceptions. At the University of Western Kentucky, for about a decade there was a religion department that tried to present the Christian position and give other religions exposure. That changed, and the department is now anti-Christian. Religion departments of most universities are a clear violation of the proclaimed "separation of church and state." They show the hypocrisy of the educated elite, who demanded the courts keep religion out of the schools, but then used these religion departments, as well as all other departments of the university such as literature and sciences, to demolish students' faith in God without allowing any voice of rebuttal.

The believing churches spawned so-called "parachurch" groups to try to counteract the secularization at the high school and college level. Youth for Christ turned its movement away from just holding Saturday night rallies to focusing on working in the schools. Young Life began social clubs to evangelize high school students, and later I started the high school work of Campus Crusade for Christ with over three hundred staff. On the college level, the Inter-Varsity Christian Fellowship started in America about 1936, and Campus Crusade for Christ began in 1951 with an effort to bear witness in the secular universities. Since then, other groups have begun, such as denominational campus groups, the Fellowships of Christian Learning of Worldwide Discipleship Association which I started, and others. Many of the denominational campus groups defected to teach the secular view of man and to undermine the faith more radically than the universities themselves.[27] More will be said about the student movement since 1960.

THIRD SURGE OF INTELLECTUAL UNBELIEF:
THE "DEATH OF GOD" AND PUBLIC DECLARATION:
MAN IS SUFFICIENT, ca. 1960 ff.

"Death of God" Theology and the Public Rejection of God

In reviewing the intellectual revolt in America and the West, it was demonstrated that rejection of belief in God reached a point of open renunciation of God and His authority in the *"Death of God" theology* and what followed from 1960 ff. The trend from then on was for those *inside the Church* of England (e.g., John Hick), in the old denominational schools such as Harvard (e.g., Harvey Cox), and many others to renounce the uniqueness of Christ and the Christian religion and call the churches to turn to the universities and politics for salvation in building a better world. The standards of the confessions of faith of the churches and the submission to the standards of church government were circumvented or even attacked. Liberal, clerical leadership became militant, and the seeming neo-orthodoxy of existential theology made its way gradually into the churches as "not so unchristian."

Since about 1960, the educated elite gained ascendancy for the secular view of man so that many formerly church institutions (e.g., Harvard) and voices in the old-line churches threw the weight of authority to secular education. The rebellion against the Christian confessional statements of the churches was complete. When I worked with the ministers of one denomination ministering to secular campuses, out of seventy campus workers, there were fewer than three who openly said they believed the Bible was God's revelation or believed in the uniqueness of Christ. The remainder outspokenly planned to take over all our denomination and make it a tool for liberal, social democracy.

In the public schools and universities after 1962, there was a bold rejection of Christianity. In my book, *With Christ in the School of Disciple Building*, I reviewed the secularized trends in the universities and colleges and in the liberal churches.[28] The newspaper, the *Yale Daily News*, in 1974 surveyed four hundred of their graduating seniors and found 54 percent said they no longer believed in God, 33 percent said they were indifferent, 10 percent were anarchists, 24 percent were socialists, and 33 percent called themselves capitalists. A study of fifty-seven colleges by Oklahoma City College about that time revealed 53 percent of the seniors considered themselves "left" or "far left." Considering this, the editor of *Christianity Today* Magazine said:

> The very least that can be inferred is that, one way or another, colleges and universities play a significant role in determining the world and life-views of their students. Quite obviously the drift is leftward, theologically, ethically, and politically. The question this poses for America in general and the Church in particular is whether this state of

affairs can be tolerated. If the leftward movement succeeds, America as we have known it will disappear.[29]

Evangelical Church's Efforts to Restore Faith

Beginning in the 1960s when the student revolts began increasing, evangelical leaders took action to try to restore the teaching of truth and to build new Christian colleges. They also started many Christian day schools that would feed into these colleges. Between 1971 and 1978, evangelical primary and secondary schools increased by 47 percent, with a 95 percent increase in student enrollment. By 1985, there were a total of seventeen thousand to eighteen thousand such schools with an estimated two-and-a-half million students, while there was a drop in enrollment of elementary and high schools in the nation.[30] This also began the Christian home schooling movement which now engages hundreds of thousands of students. These efforts have greatly slowed the secularization in this last wave. During those years, Christian publishers were established and Christian radio and television programs became prominent.

In this last decade of the 1990s, many of these are also compromising their views. Such movements as Inter-Varsity Christian Fellowship are moving toward politically correct ideas like neutering the gender words for God in hymns and other egalitarian ideas. James Davidson Hunter, in his prize-winning book, *Evangelicalism: the Coming Generation,* has demonstrated that the Christian colleges have progressively moved slowly but certainly further away from Christian doctrines and purposes.[31] Almost all Christian schools now have a degree in business and other subjects that relate to material gain, while other subjects relating to Christian vocations and service have been dropped. While this is not wrong in itself, it does reflect the change taking place. Prominent Christian high schools that want to enter their students in leading universities are under increasing pressure by these universities to be "tolerant" to include *non-Christian teachers* on the high school faculty, and some are capitulating under the pressure. An example of this is Westminster Academy in Atlanta. Westminster caved into pressure from Harvard and Ivy League schools and now has non-Christian teachers.

Christian publishing companies that had a mission to present Christian truth against secularization are yielding also. Some have sold out to secular, commercial publishers who have promised not to change the emphasis but have diminished Christian truth. To compete, others have gone through mergers and are pushing the profit margins. One of the largest, Zondervan Publishing Company in Grand Rapids, was planning to neuter the pronouns in the New International Version but retraced under pressure. Many Christian bookstores have yielded to the profit motive and few books of academic quality are now published because of the lack of demand. Many shoppers seem to want light, small, easy-reading books and sundries such as T-shirts and coffee mugs. *World* magazine commented on the compromising nature of Christian publishing and bookstores today.[32] A review of this intellectual assault against God in American life and institutions and its effects on the economy, sexual and other human relationships, and on law and order will be seen in subsequent chapters, along with a summary of the present intellectual conditions in further decline.

Chapter 10

Pursuit of Materialism
following the Intellectual Revolt

INTRODUCTION

It is not possible to give a complete evaluation of the American business and economic cycles in this book because space doesn't allow and informed economists would be required. But it is important to try to see the four major surges that occurred under the growth of materialism and the reactions and troubles that followed. These four surges will be examined for moral implications and for prospects for the future as much as possible. There are some broad trends that give an important message.

There were early debts in the federal government, but they were not significant. There were two hundred years of fiscal restraint, but with slight fluctuations before the Virginia Dynasty. When Jefferson took office in 1801, there was an $83 million debt. He reduced this debt about one-third in his two terms. He also made the significant purchase of the western lands and helped finance interstate commerce. He suffered from personal debt and was aware of the need to be conservative, even with his big dreams.

This chapter will show long-term trends caused by changes in economic philosophy, events, and statistical trends. These four surges resulted from departure from biblical standards of trust in and obedience to God in regard to material priorities. We are now in the fourth surge, which is growing out of control. Under the administration of Franklin D. Roosevelt, there was an increase in federal spending to try to spur recovery from the Depression, but this too was curtailed in time. In the 1960s, there was a radical change in social and financial philosophy by John F. Kennedy which resulted in the present situation that seems critical. This was the end-product of turning away from faith in God and weakening morals that began and reached its peak with the Virginia Dynasty. The change in morals is now beginning to have serious economic effects that could become chaotic in the twenty-first century, as the facts will show and as we will discuss in chapter 14.

FIRST SURGE OF PURSUIT OF THE MATERIAL TO REPLACE GOD

Early Certainty in Ideology and Operation of the Economy Introduced the Nineteenth Century

Europe was deistic by the time the colonies in America made the Declaration of Independence. John Locke and others had made crude beginnings in economic thought, but in the very year of 1776, Adam Smith gathered known ideas about the economy into a meaningful, scientific presentation on the workings of capitalism in his book, *Inquiry into the Nature and Causes of the Wealth of the Nations.* Just as it had been possible at that time to gain an encyclopedic view of the knowledge of the natural sciences, so it was a time when all of the information and views of economics were available and used by Smith. As Robert L. Heilbroner said, "Perhaps no economist will ever again so utterly encompass his age as Adam Smith"[1] Smith skillfully described "the invisible hand" of the working of the market to exert control based on self-interest and competition and presented a picture of material progress based on these forces. Smith expressed great concern for the wealth of the common man and for helping him find equality.

He wrote from a skepticism about God and with a deistic, materialistic perspective of optimistic progress. Those skeptical and derisive of religion were encouraged to find in his writings a scientific approach to wealth with naturalistic controls. Smith's work was praised by the noted Voltaire of France and in England by his skeptical friend David Hume, along with others.[2]

In addition to seeing natural compensation in supply and demand, he foresaw that one of the main drives to possess wealth, other than need that established the demand for goods, was the desire for pride in accumulating wealth and opulence as a mark of superiority. But he did not integrate the problem of hoarding into his theory because it offered an uncertain element that upset the theory of balancing supply and demand. It was like a shadow that did not fit in the sunlight of his optimism. That would not be fully recognized until a century later. Smith presented a view of man in an economy that was ever improving by natural law. Another uncertain and upsetting point was the idea of government intervention.

Conflict and Optimism in Man in the Economy

Smith's picture of a smooth-working and certain, safe economy in nature did not appear in reality. Even in Adam Smith's day, the moral problem of greed as idolatry was beginning, and the wealthy classes of both the landed gentry and the industrialists of England were using their political influence to build their wealth and put down the middle class and poorer people. This greed was behind the crown's governmental taxes without representation that helped foment the American Declaration of Independence and gave grounds for further conflict to gain freedom from England in the War of 1812. As this greed and its abuses grew and began to greatly manifest itself, the rich sought to use Adam Smith's arguments for a free economy to keep government from restricting their efforts, especially in England.

Before the eighteenth century was out, the wealthy were inflicting terrible abuse upon, and misuse of, not only poorer men, but also of women and children in the factories and in slavery, which was rapidly growing in the United States. Moreover, philosophically, the optimism of Smith's capitalism was upset by pessimism in regard to future distribution. Thomas Malthus presented a vision of rising population overwhelming society. David Ricardo incorporated this threat of population into capitalism, emphasized the importance of labor in the value of a commodity, and showed a vision of bitter conflict to survive or to rise up to the top on treacherous moving stairs. In spite of obstacles, he tried to hold an optimism based on worldwide expansion of industrialization. Thus, in spite of unforeseen threats, an adjusting view of optimistic capitalism presided during the Virginia Dynasty that thrust America toward embracing materialism.

Preoccupation with the Priority of Business

The first surge of material pursuit by big businessmen began under the Virginia Dynasty (1800 ff.). The rise of it is called "the turnpike era" when many roads and canals were built. American expansion of commerce was underway overseas. The vision of a paradise in a great nation, having been designed by the Virginia Dynasty, sent the people of America seeking it in hot pursuit. Industrial development by the businessmen of New England and the northern part of the colonies was copied after the textile mills of England and machinery in Europe. The cotton gin was invented and motivated the cotton industry in the South, increasing slavery and hard work in the cotton fields. Other inventions were machines to spin and weave cloth, the steam engine, and the sewing machine. In the early nineteenth century, steam was used in boats and factories.

The Cumberland Road had heavy traffic. Governor Clinton of New York saw the advantage of a canal diverting traffic from New Orleans, Philadelphia, and Baltimore to New York, thus inviting trade. The Erie Canal became one of the largest engineering feats, further opening up water traffic. Many other roads and canals were developed. The newspaper accentuated communication. A protective tariff caused American capitalists to shift their money to manufacturing. A national bank system was established. These great accomplishments were desirable, but the drive of materialistic zeal led to bad consequences. The report of the Lewis and Clark corps motivated westward expansion to acquire land.

Europeans visiting America were at this time amazed at how the men of the country were obsessed with business and industry. Some comments follow: "Men are pressed with the pursuit of fortune, the women are pressed with the pursuit of a husband" (a London newspaper). "The American men are as eager as democrats, genial merchants who spend their time in making money" (book, *As Paris Sees the American Woman*). "The Englishman is continually going home, the American is continually going to business" (*Price Collier*, New York paper).

New states were being formed, and other areas were being outlined for development. They were Louisiana (1812), Indiana (1816), Mississippi (1817), Illinois (1818), Alabama (1819), and Missouri (1821). The new states were more democratic, as is reflected in their constitutions. Many restrictions for voting and holding office were eliminated. The old property requirements for voting were changing in the North. Growth of the nation and material progress were the dominant thoughts among the people.

Value Shift: From God-Given Value to Material Value before Man

Egalitarian Natural Right of All People Based on Materialism

Once the educated elite had marginalized God as the ruling king of the universe and placed their faith in material creation, the value of all things began to progressively change so a person's value was measured by material wealth. This resulted in man's feeling each person should have the right to gain as much wealth as he wished. The emerging new values began to replace the biblical view of the equal value of each individual in the eyes of the Creator and that each man was made for a specific purpose to glorify God and share with others (2 Corinthians 8:14).

As seen in Greece and Rome, when God is rejected and wealth and material creation become the objects of men, the standard of value is changed from the importance of the person to purposes of wealth as a basis of self-esteem. Thus, egalitarian thinking began to grow in America and with it the feeling that these injustices must be corrected by human efforts. The natural rights of the poor, of women, and of children began to be prominent in social thinking of the educated elite.

The anti-slave movement began in earnest at this time. Seeing the injustice and wrongs of that practice, Jefferson and others had considered the slave question before and spoke against it. There was, however, hypocrisy and contradiction in this, since many of them were slave owners and continued to misuse their slaves. Poor labor conditions in business and industry also surfaced at the time of the Virginia Dynasty. All of these obvious injustices were given humanistic solutions.

As in other cultures, the sensual or sexual movement began developing. In the early 1830s, the women's rights movement was born. Thomas Paine, who was an unbeliever, mentioned at the time of the Revolution that women were being defrauded of their rights. New Jersey initially gave women the right to vote, but in 1807 rescinded it. The peace movement based on optimism about human nature was also launched at this time.

Horace Greeley, the emerging New York newspaper tycoon, began advocating socialist policies and government provision for the poor, as state welfare began to be experimented with. He spoke out against slavery. But he inconsistently did not speak for the feminist causes.

Materialism Emphasized Change in Class and Sexual Roles

The slave issue became the primary focus, and after the Civil War, women's and labor rights which had grown, became prominent. The slavery issue went through three stages: 1. a growing matter of conscience. 2. tension and organized protest. 3. the Civil War. In the first stage, George Washington spoke against slavery and emancipated his slaves in his will. Jefferson, Patrick Henry, Madison, and Monroe protested slavery. The liberal churches in New England preached against slavery. Many people in the northern states, instead of emancipating their slaves, hypocritically began to sell them to the South. During this period, the North was becoming more industrialized. They had small farms where slaves were not useful. As mentioned, the invention of the cotton gin; the growth of sugar cane in Louisiana; and the expansion of tobacco in Virginia, Tennessee, and Kentucky spread and increased the desire for slave labor.

The second stage began after the law was passed abolishing slave trade in 1808. This occurred when materialism made the slave's condition appear more intolerable and unjust. The North controlled the House and the southern slave states controlled the Senate. Congressional power depended on whether Missouri would tolerate slavery, as well as what the other new territories would decide. A way of settling the issue of what new states would do found solution by Henry Clay's Missouri Compromise. In the 1820s, widespread tension grew from organized promotion to free slaves. Benjamin Leandy published a journal in Ohio, *The Genius of Universal Emancipation*, and this was circulated widely, spawning other journals. Wilberforce and Zachery Macauley established an anti-slave society in England, and it spread to the United States. The third stage fomented the Civil War, which will be discussed later. These tensions grew out of and were magnified by the new materialism.

Materialism Highlighted Gender Differences

The women's rights movement came into focus in the beginning of the nineteenth century. Materialism influenced the male role, which became more important through growth in business. Male success diminished in significance the women's role with children in the home. Women reacted to male neglect and their own exclusion from access to equal money and ownership. This circumstance has became the source of all feminist movements, as shown in Greece and Rome.[3]

The feminist movement began with social protests against male drunkenness and prostitution. However, the emphasis on individualism in a materialistic world led to the first Women's Rights Congress in 1848. Spokeswoman Elizabeth Cady Stanton declared, "All men and women were created equal." The women made shocking demands which much later became the women's movement.

All the reform movements and the efforts at equality were linked together as a part of the emerging individualism and the material value set on life. Andrew Sinclair said:

> At these times [of surges in promotion of rights], there was an interaction among reforms, and a geography of reform. Those reforms which successfully changed the position of great numbers were the movements for the rights of Negroes, of women, and of labor, the three major groups deprived of the American promise of liberty and equality of opportunity.[4]

These things seem so right in the materialistic world in which we now live. The great problem is when the elite decide something is wrong and they see themselves as the ones who should rectify what is evil, it is hard to see the errors in thinking. To establish equal rights for opportunities for material gain, the crusades almost always are misguided in the long-run and create anger and anarchy that are destructive to everyone's rights. Often the problem is the self-righteous motivation to be a savior of others by coercion, and therefore, the means and the ends become distorted. Sinclair mentions the near-sightedness of these movements and the failure to continue to care.[5] The elite want to use government to force equality, but these efforts only minimally deliver equality in the long-run, and instead turn up the level of anger and violence.

Unethical Practices in Pursuit of Materialism and Depression

The emphasis on the individual and on his pursuit of material wealth continued to grow, eclipsing the idea of submission to God and authority. The nation was shocked by the 1837 financial panic when it went into its first great depression. "Huge quantities of uncertain paper money, scarcity of gold and silver, high prices and bread riots suggest the suffering." At the time, "there was too much speculation."[6] There was opposition to "pet banks" and to forming another National Bank, since the original National Bank was repealed under Andrew Jackson.

A worldwide depression had been going on, and the crisis hit the United States under Martin Van Buren. During this time, there was national disunity over social issues, especially over slavery and the policies for new states in the

Southwest. The strong affirmation of individualism and emphasis on materialism was a prominent factor in the financial confusion and the national crisis. The downturn in business began around 1828 and fell abruptly after the panic of 1837; the beginning of this downturn can be seen nine years earlier and declined significantly three to five years before the panic and collapse.

SECOND SURGE OF MATERIALISM WITH INVENTIVENESS, 1840 ff.

Individual Greed Produced Great Conflict

The second major surge of materialism (or second zig of a zigzag, cf. p. 34) came a short time following the panic during Van Buren's presidency, in or about 1840. The emphasis on individualism continued to grow along with the idea of man as a spark of nature, and in intellectual circles there was skepticism about any revelation of God. These ideas removed restraints on the conscience for the motivation of greed, and the explosion of business continued. Tremendous inventions were made at this time. The telegraph was invented, and the steam engine on boats and trains was expanded and improved, which led to rapid transportation and a boom in trade and business. An example of the growth may be seen in the yearly output of coal used in transportation and industry—15,000 tons in 1820; 7 million tons by 1850; and 33 million tons by 1870, the time of the next major economic panic.

During this second economic wave, the Civil War years (1860-1865) were devastating to the nation, but spurred industrial output. Like the War of 1812, the Civil War was a warning to the nation. There was a self-righteous attitude of the North over their abolishment of slavery; many northern states had ended slavery. While they were not slave holders, the North was using poor immigrants and their children for long hours in factories. The South had based its life on the immoral practice of slavery and had to rationalize it. The North had a larger population, more industry, and more development of railroads and canals.[7] The war depleted the economy for both sides and made the rich richer and the poor poorer.

The Reconstruction Era was a time of great hindrance to the economic recovery of the South. Greed and selfish individualism continued to grow throughout the nation as a part of the thinking of the times. Human development and progress were the religion in many minds. While the uniformitarian scientific views were being taught and biological evolutionary development was known in England and Europe, these were only beginning to grow in America, but would be felt significantly a few years later.

The aftermath of the war led to a second major zag, or decrease, in the economy. The stock market crash of Black Friday in September 1869 was abrupt, although problems had been building through corruption scandals such as the "Credit Mobilizer," a large fraud of a construction firm for the railroad; the "Salary Grab" by Congress to get more money; and other scandals which occurred under President Grant.

By 1873, the nation was in a deep depression. This depression was promoted by men who hoarded a large amount of gold and then persuaded Grant to stop the sale of Treasury gold to the banks except at inflated prices, causing the Panic of 1869. By this, the depression was precipitated two or three years in advance of what might have occurred naturally. There was no immediate rebound, and financial problems continued. Problems with currency (greenbacks, gold, and silver), dishonesty, organization and demands of labor and tariffs hindered the economy until Grover Cleveland's presidential administration. The depression lasted much longer than the one thirty years earlier.

Because of the abuses in the English factories and the turbulence of the times, Karl Marx's communist views were formulated and became popular. It was John Stuart Mill who restored optimism to capitalism in the troubled times in the middle of the nineteenth century by emphasizing production as the important thing and by saying man would see it was in his self-interest to produce and to allow government to tax and distribute wealth so that proper distribution could be obtained. He said government was the key by taxing and distributing goods as the people chose. Such a utilitarian view requires education to enlightened self-interest.

Modern View of Government Welfare

Marvin Olasky demonstrated that the welfare for the poor, up until materialism supplanted faith in God, was personal and "indoor," but from 1840, it became "outdoor relief," or charity, which gave to the poor without personal involvement by the government and other organizations.[8] The shift to the idea of government-sponsored, public charity became an alternative to Christian, private charity. Horace Greeley's views expressed in *The New York Tribune* strongly influenced 10 percent of the voters of the Northeast. He was a Universalist, believing in the inherent goodness of man, and believing in equality by redistribution of funds. He even advocated communal living.

These egalitarian views, motivated by materialistic values, gained a wide hearing and implementation. The Secretary of State of New York said in New York in 1840, there were 11,937 on relief; in 1850, there were 63,764; and by 1860, there were 174,403. Some 70 percent of those receiving help did so because of intemperance and not from inability to find employment; the religious effort to reform people was diminished. Social Darwinism gained prominence, and the personal compassion of the American people decreased. Henry Raymond challenged these egalitarian views to distribute wealth in the new publication, *The New York Times,* and later reversed these liberal views for many.

THIRD SURGE OF MATERIAL PURSUIT
IN CONSOLIDATION OF WEALTH , 1885

Business Consolidation and Emergence of Money Tycoons

The third surge of materialism (or zig) began around 1885. In 1870, there were significant creative ideas in the intellectual revolt. The pieces of the puzzle of humanism that the unbelieving man struggled to find were put together to show a picture of man as king of the world. Man created God to meet his needs, and therefore God was not real; Man could truly understand and control the laws of nature of the world. These ideas were being accepted in the United States a few years later than in Europe.

Before the depressed times, great inventions and progress were made, but as recovery began in this third economic wave, the engines of greed exploded. Men found opportunities and took great risks by speculating to make money. In 1885, only one man was worth six million dollars, and eighteen were worth over one million dollars. There were fifty telegraph companies. New York alone had thirty local transportation companies, and to go from New York to Chicago required seventeen connections. In this new wave of economic effort, great mergers and trusts took over, many tycoons controlled power, and vast sums of money emerged.

This was the era of many modern inventions: the light bulb, the gasoline engine, and the telephone. The national banking system, created earlier, expanded. Trolleys, automobiles, and many other amazing steps of progress developed. John D. Rockefeller gained control over the oil business. Cornelius Vanderbilt united the railroad business. The Bessemer method of making steel gave way to the open-hearth method, and Andrew Carnegie consolidated the great steel-making industry. Great utility companies expanded services across the country. Many multimillionaires emerged.

During this time, federal troops were withdrawn from the South, and the southern whites regained control of local government and set up rules for voting, excluding blacks from the ballot box. Thus, the oppressive segregation system evolved, which in many ways allowed less communication with whites than under slavery, and left blacks in an oppressed state. Moreover, the South was poor because of the high tariff system. By this time, many of the South's farms had depleted their soil, but the West was opened to farmers.

The Evil of Human Greed Became Evident in America

Toward the end of the century, Alfred Marshall, a brilliant economist, focused on seeking equilibrium in the economic cycle to help the poor. In the midst of the establishment of great tycoons and capitalistic empires, he brought a focus on the importance of the consumer. He contributed much to understanding the workings of the cycles of the market economy. J. M. Keynes, his brilliant student, said of him, "(He created) a whole Copernican system, in which all the elements of the economic universe are kept in their places by mutual counterpoise and interaction."[9] While Marshall gave a feeling of certainty in understanding, he found no key for the liberal elite to control the economy except to emphasize abstract time for equilibrium to occur. John Stuart Mill had emphasized the importance to control, and the government soon found this was needed in antitrust legislation.

About the turn of the century, Thorstein Veblen began to develop and more completely expose the weakness of traditional economic ideas. The tragic conflicts of the Civil War and the clear greed of the tycoons made it clear that capitalism was missing some concept. He gave evidence of pride of superiority by ownership as being very important to the economy, and showed it was not competition of products and prices in the market alone, but competition for accumulation of property that drives things in a hidden barbaric way. He showed that in a materialistic society, in striving for superiority, the rich would use monopoly, restriction of new inventions, and oppression of laborers in their efforts to gain. To him, the barbaric spirit of human nature only lay beneath a civilized veneer, and this striving for accumulation (not just savings) to satisfy pride and greed must be seen as a major driving factor in the economy. While the emphasis was not on sin, what he presented showed the human sin nature was a major factor in economics.

As these economic principles emerged, three new systems of government arose to guide mankind to a more certain materialistic utopia in the twentieth century. There was Fascism, which motivated people by pride in racial superiority of their nations as the reason for a dictator and his elite to use modern science to build power for a utopia. On the other hand, the abuses of the rich, especially in England, had motivated Karl Marx to move away from capitalism and devise the system of a dictatorship of the proletariat, which would assume all private property for communistic use by the people. He envisioned an inevitable evolutionary progress by dialectical change that the dictatorship would help along to a utopia for all.

But it was the English, and especially the American, intellectual elite who envisioned they could discern and educate the masses to build a material utopia by a socialized democratic process. The educated elite optimistically believed the masses they enlightened would follow them in a utilitarian doctrine for themselves and others that would give a balance of adequate production and distribution for all. Theirs was a merger of Adam Smith and subsequent economic insights with the belief in the rights of each individual free man in a social democracy. The dreams of Fascism and Communism had built on the failure of the German and Russian governments, but have at the end of the twentieth century failed because a sinful elite of men in those systems took advantage of the masses of people to build their own wealth and power.

Exploding Business and Industry Took Advantage of Exploding Farming

From 1860 to 1890, farm acreage doubled and that under cultivation tripled. Farm equipment was invented mainly in the mid-century, but effective production and distribution of equipment occurred at this time. The land-grant colleges were built during this time, and experimentation on new strains of wheat, corn, and vegetables was done at experimental stations.

Farmers needed money to purchase these advances, and the Northern and Eastern business and industrial men controlled Congress, the banks, and the transportation systems. The farmers mortgaged their farms and paid from 8–20 percent for money. While half the country farmed, the farmers were unorganized with little political influence until the Farmers' Alliance Movement after 1890. The price of farm products moved steadily downward, while the price of manufactured goods moved steadily upward. The greedy businessmen in the cities, and especially in the North, took advantage of the farmer. Many farmers lost their farms, and the small family farm gave way to the large commercial ones.

Alliances of farmers rapidly spread, not only gaining political influence but increasing education, farm journals, scientific research, and cooperative buying and marketing. The two-fold increase of agriculture and industry moved the nation to prosperity. But by 1900, the farm population began to drop and the trend was to move to the cities for employment and prosperity. Not only was making money on a farm hard because of interest rates and the costs involved in farming, there was the allure of the modern conveniences of the cities. There was a consistent decrease in people on the farms, with a leveling off during the depression years, and a rapid decrease to about 7 percent in 1960. While the rate of decline began to slack then, the loss of farmers continued until 1990, when it went below 2 percent. The faith in God and Christian virtues of hard work and cooperation exhibited in the farm communities gave way to the secular spirit and individualism. But the wealthy Americans gained control of agriculture by purchasing and increasing the size of farm industries. The wealthy received money from the government in increasing amounts as farm subsidies.

Influence of Money on Churches Brought in Secular Influence

Materialism had a powerful influence on the churches. Men of wealth were elected to leadership positions, and great amounts of money were given to charities, to build churches, and especially to church educational institutions. It also affected the way the average man participated. William Warren Sweet said, "The most significant single influence in organized religion in the United States from about the year 1880 to the end of the century and beyond, was the tremendous increase in wealth in the nation."[10] The churches became more like a business with more management than relational emphases, and more concerned about facilities than souls.

Tragic Wars and Depression Came to the Nation

World War I and the Great Depression may have been a warning to the people to turn back to God. World War I was a shock to America, and while spurring new developments and requiring great costs, it opened great economic opportunities and new progress. The cost of the war in lives and money was exceedingly high, but there was little American repentance. The war united the people and broke down many barriers between sections. The war time and the sense of achievement from the pride of victory produced an economic boom.

But that boom burst when the Great Depression struck in 1929. The Great Depression continued and worsened with the bank failures in 1932. The results of the depression were devastating. Over one-fourth of the people were out of work, half the factories and most of its banks shut down, and the farmers were being crushed. Roosevelt's New Deal brought hundreds of new regulations and laws, massive public spending, and a host of new institutions, inserting the government into many areas of public life and expanding debt enormously. These difficult times only impressed the American people that the capitalistic system and government limitations were not enough to control the economy. It took five years before Franklin D. Roosevelt could get the people's confidence and for the economy to again began to show improvement.

Because of Japan's aggressions in Asia, the United States spent a large amount on defense, and this spurred the economy. During this time, the radio came into wide use and the motion picture industry was devised, both having a profound influence on culture. New inventions such as aircraft, better automobiles, and paved roads produced faster travel. No sooner were things recovering, than the United States found itself confronted with World War II. It was really the unity of the nation in the Second World War which finally aroused it out of the long depression.

American People Increasingly Yielded to Greed and Pleasure

In the first decade of the twentieth century, America emerged as one of the world's great nations. Foreign involvement became prominent. The Monroe Doctrine was enforced through a war with Spain, and Mexican problems were solved. China and Japan became competitors and open doors were accomplished. In this time, banking became more equitable throughout the nation, antitrust laws developed, labor unions relieved workers, and other checks on greed occurred. It was a time of optimistic belief that paradise could surely be created by man through science. Extensive advertising through newspapers, magazines, and radio announcements presented new material choices. Mass media began to be a major influence on the American mind. Whereas in the second surge there emerged a wealthy class that bought many material things, in this third surge, the desire for things captured the middle class.

FOURTH SURGE OF MATERIALISM AND EMERGENCE OF THE WORLD POWER AND THE GREAT SOCIETY, 1940 ff.

The Emergence of the Scientific Information and Communication Age

In this fourth surge, the educated elite had the vision and sought to extend material ownership to everyone equally. The fourth surge, or zig and zag, of materialism began in the World War II effort in the early 1940s and continues today. More efficient and faster aircraft, first with loran and then with radar, increased accurate navigation. Atomic energy, and later the atomic bomb and color in motion pictures and in television were developed. Jet engines propelled the aircraft industry into worldwide transport, and the development of rocket and rocket fuels ultimately led to space travel to the moon and exploration of the planets. Satellites that gather information about nations, about nature, and about the weather have become strategic. Most importantly, the computer industry has developed to organize and store volumes of information and enable us to examine and evaluate it. This has come from the first computer that consisted of huge buildings of cathode ray tubes to small chips that can be carried and used in the lap. Of great importance has been the development of the Internet.

About mid-century, great scientific breakthroughs with new instruments such as the electron microscope were devised. The use of X-ray technology, radiation techniques and other new medical technology, as well as great progress in biology and pharmacology, genetic engineering, vaccines, and inoculations–all of these have greatly improved health, leading to a world population explosion. New weapon systems have made warfare and destruction awesome. In all, new conveniences were extended to the common man by mass production.

The Information Age has been introduced by improving computers that afford communication for business and for solving the knowledge problems that have emerged. Main frame computers used by business and government have moved to personal computers for every man, and now the Internet is linking individuals with each other and masses of information worldwide, with new Java language-translating type computers taking over. Language translating software is emerging to solve the problem of communicating between major languages. Very complicated computers capable of helping solve the scientific problems of complexity that have emerged by instrumental research have been devised in the last decade. As the new century approaches, individualization and private communication threatens to change and weaken all big business and institutions.[11]

Personal Credit for the People Is Expanded for Business Profit

The idea of the use of credit, which was the undoing of the farmers, soon became attractive for purchase of a variety of things for all the people. In this fourth surge of materialism, credit for everyone and for the government was made to appear right and acceptable. Credit was offered on the purchase of a home for a seven-year term (as in Scriptures) by the 1920s. In the 1920s, people's savings began to decrease from 12 percent to 4 percent. Instead of saving to buy, people began to charge to buy. In 1940 to 1950, there were no loans on consumable goods without equity, or property of value, to back the loan. By the 1950s, there were still short-term mortgages and some short-term automobile loans, but no credit card loans. With the growth of debt under the New Deal, the nation removed all but a portion of gold backing the dollar. In the 1960s, credit was extended for almost anything, first through department store credit, and then on various credit cards to use everywhere–appliances, automobiles, TV sets, college tuition, and so forth.

By 1960, the average income was $6,700; the average home cost was $8,000 with 1,000 square feet, financed on a 21-year loan at 4.5 percent; a new car cost $2,100 purchased with 25 percent down and financing the rest for 18 months. In 1991, the current median income was $36,000, and the average home was worth $72,000, but was valued at $108,000 in relation to disposable income. The percent of budget for a home in 1960 was 22 percent, and in 1990, it was up to 40 percent and continues to rise.

By 1965, credit for purchases by consumers gave retailers huge profits, so there was a rush to make money on interest from financing in various ways. Home mortgages went up in one decade from twelve years to thirty years, adding a tremendous amount to the cost of homes. This demand for credit pushed the interest rates up above 9 percent by 1973. Automobile loans were extended in the 1980s to three and four years. Many different types of mortgages were devised on houses: fixed and variable rates, for up to a maximum of 90 years.

The extension of debt payment expanded the cost of houses, automobiles, and everything else. This also pushed up the original purchase price. In 1937, a new automobile cost less than $1,000, while in 1994, the average cost was over $18,000. Mortgage debt was extended from 45 percent in 1965 to 60 percent in 1987. Installment debt rose from 15 percent to 20 percent during the same time. Household debt on disposable personal income rose from 75 percent in 1965 to 96 percent in 1988. It rose 20 percent between 1983 to 1987. Total consumer debt was $131 billion in 1970, but rose to $794 billion in 1990. Thus, credit has been extended from farm loans and houses to anything a person wants; the time of repayment has been extended over long periods; and the rates have extended.

Because of the increase in the use of credit by the American people, the number of individual personal bankruptcies has risen rapidly, as follows:

Year	Bankruptcies
1970	100,000
1980	259,160
1985	312,000
1990	685,439
1991	900,000
2000 estimate	4,000,000

Because of this, the assets of the people of the United States are greatly overvalued because many assets are not owned but are held on credit. Yet, the people's assets are the primary assets the government has. The government depends on people to pay taxes on the basis of their assets and earning power from their labors. This is the most important thing to remember as federal and other public debt is considered.

John Maynard Keynes' Economic Theory Joined Debt-for-Greed Mentality

As the American debt mentality expanded to fuel the greed of buying more and for continuing growth of business, what seemed the missing piece for managing the economy was offered. Secure control of the economic cycle remained a mystery until Marshall's brilliant student, John Maynard Keynes, seemed to find the key to influencing the business cycle for the educated elite to produce healthy equilibrium. In 1930, Keynes published his book, *The General Theory of Employment, Interest, and Money*, which was an economic bombshell for the Western world.

In Keynes' book, it was recognized that the flow of money is basic to an economy. The people, who always have unlimited desires, have to be employed to buy services and products they desire. And businesses have to have the capital to invest and expand to increase production to meet the consumer demands for the economy to expand. The economy was seen by Keynes as an elevator that would rise to a certain level where the demand met available resources of the people and then would decline because business expansion would decline. There would then come a depression when unemployment grew and the potential for business to increase investment to expand was stagnant. Since many were out of work or making little, there would be little savings. The elevator of the economy would then be stuck at the bottom.

Keynes believed accumulated wealth of the rich would not prime the pump to get things going because in such times they would hold more tightly to their wealth, as was demonstrated in that some of the richest people of the world are in nations such as India which has little or no expansion in the economy. Keynes had served the British government in India and saw this. To motivate the economy to grow, people must get back to work with faith to spend their money and to be able to save so that money was available in the banks to be used for business to further expand. Either this had to happen naturally by some new important invention or product which meets needs that develop in the course of the economy, or the pump of employment could be primed by the government or some other means. For Keynes, this idea of managed capitalism was the main way to get the elevator to begin to rise again.

Hence, a healthy economy depended on employment and expansion of investment by business and every boom would reach its limits, so that a new source to renew must be generated or infused. It was the government which could prime the pump and expand the economy, and therefore government debt and even inflation would not be harmful if controlled correctly. With the new information technology, this seemed possible.

Keynes' influence had been a factor that guided the New Deal of Roosevelt to aid employment and infuse money for recovery from the Great Depression. But the New Deal did not cause the recovery from the depression, because it was upsetting to the people. It did inoculate the people with the thought that debt spending might be helpful. During the depression, it was accepted out of desperation just as many new ideas were accepted. The recovery of the nation came when business and the people rallied to fight the threat of Fascism in Europe and Japan in the Second World War. As computers ushered in the Information Age, they were more and more trusted, and the understanding of the facts and the ability to control and motivate the direction of the economy seemed more certain. Keynes' theories were taught at Harvard and other prominent universities as the significant missing ingredient for future control of the economy.

New Values and Government Deficit and Debt as Acceptable

The turning point in morals about money in the federal budget came in the 1960s. Roosevelt had already used the emergency of the Great Depression to make welfare a major role for the federal government on a temporary and limited basis. The Social Security Act of 1935 was passed to assist needy elderly, and the public assistance programs were implemented for the poor, which we now know as welfare. In subsequent years there have been numerous entitlement programs to help the American people.

While the idea of debt spending had been practiced before and was very much a part of the New Deal for recovery from the Great Depression, the idea was never endorsed openly as a public policy. The minds of the people were not yet ready to accept this. But on June 8, 1962, John F. Kennedy spoke at Yale University and expressed a change of thought. From the view of the 1950s, it was still believed a person should live within his means, and that it was immoral not to. Great debt was still unacceptable. But then Kennedy argued that budget deficits are not wrong or bad, and inflation is not dangerous if managed.

The expanding materialistic desires of the American people and the eagerness of the business community to take advantage of expending credit at a price, also influenced thinking about the federal government and politics. Governmental policies became greatly involved. Under the Nixon administration, silver was removed from coins. Kennedy had grand views of liberal programs which were expanded and implemented by Johnson in his idea of the Great Society. Lyndon B. Johnson removed all gold backing from the dollar, leaving American currency without commodity backing of any value. Social Security and welfare programs began to run deficits in the late 1960s and early 1970s. By the Jimmy Carter administration, inflation had risen to 21 percent, and military defense dropped very low. Eisenhower, who preceded Kennedy, was the last president to consistently balance the budget.

Postmodern Welfare Conceived

The "classical welfare," emphasizing personal involvement of giver and recipient to help with physical needs, also aimed at spiritual and moral change, and was usually given through the churches. This type of welfare had given way, beginning with the Great Depression, to "modern welfare" based on liberal, pure humanism. Under " modern" planning and provision it was believed that people should be helped until they got on their feet. Providing housing, work, and emergency food were right things that government should do.

The New York Times designated the post-Kennedy ideas as "a new philosophy of social welfare," and it was labeled "*post*modern welfare." This new view was seen as furnishing a gate to freedom for the poor. Welfare was payments by society which were to be seized to forward oneself and used to gain dignity and equality. Under this view, the support of the state would last only until man attained his dignity. This was to be chosen rather than menial jobs like shining shoes, working in a laundry, and the like. This was viewed as *the right of the poor.*[12]

The use of public funds as a right to improve was soon applied to every government program both new and old. Social Security insurance, formerly seen as assistance to some elderly, emerged as a retirement privilege. Medicare became not an assistance to elderly but a right for all Americans. Welfare assistance was encouraged to the poor for housing, and food stamps and Medicaid could be had by anyone without money without having to try to pay or seek to get to where one could meet his own needs. So aid to dependent children and children's lunches at school was a government right. By the end of the 1960s and early 1970s, the Social Security program was running a deficit.

The Rapid Increase in the Federal Budget

The spending of the federal government grew gradually over 174 years from a small amount to almost $100 billion by the 1962 change in fiscal philosophy. The debt was not then burdensome.[13] The expansion of government spending relates to this idea of credit and inflation, as influenced in part by English economist John Maynard Keynes and others. Also, this was linked to the Kennedy-planned programs for the poor and to the so-called "entitlement programs" which gave away money to the American people. The idea of everybody being equal had moved from the rich to the middle class, and now this idea was being extended to the poor. While envisioned under John F. Kennedy, these programs for the needy became government policy under Johnson.

The graph shows it took 174 years to incur the first $100 billion to 1962, then 9 years for the second, 4 years for the third, 2 years for the fourth, and 1 year for the fifth. By 1995, it reached $1514 billion, or more than 1.5 trillion dollars, and is still expanding rapidly. During this time, the population expanded from about

180 million people in 1962 to about 270 million, or added about 90 million people. Also, fiscal policies caused the purchasing power of the dollar to erode to about 22.7 percent of what it was in 1962 (estimated by using the Producer and Consumer Price Indexes). But even when taking these things into consideration (which are factors in the change), the federal budget has in the 35 years since 1962 increased more than 2.5 times per person what it was. More importantly, it is rapidly moving toward another point in which almost all authorities agree it will exceed any measures to correct or control it.

GROWTH IN U.S. BUDGET SPENDING

(in billions of dollars)

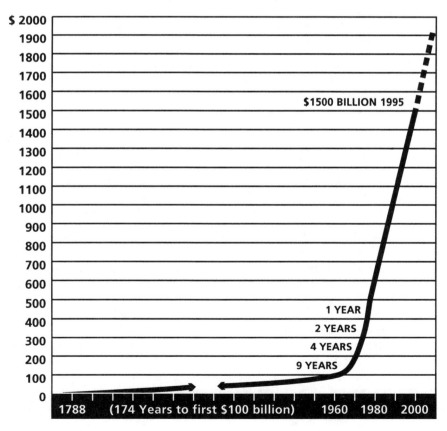

This change in financial policy was a part of the climax of intellectual thinking that denied God and freed man to do as he wanted. The rapid acceleration *began immediately following the "Death of God" theologies* which were talked about by the educated elite and spread in the media. It was therefore directly but unconsciously related to the theological thinking of the American people, developed and taught in the public universities and the liberal theological institutions.

Increasing Awareness of the Need to Rectify Federal Budget Excesses

In 1978, during the Carter Administration, William E. Simon, former Secretary of the Treasury, Chairman of the Economic Policy Board and of the Federal Energy Office, said:

> There is . . . a substantial awareness in our political leadership that our fiscal and economic policies have gone awry and that the multiple promises of cradle-to-grave security for our citizens can no longer be responsibly expanded, if indeed they can be fulfilled. This is true not only in America but also in all the Western social democratic nations that are guided by the same egalitarian-redistributionist philosophy . . . .

Simon stated that from many talks with Western leaders, none of them knew how to stop this expanding desire of the people. He warned, "Unless the lethal pattern is changed, which means, unless the philosophy that shapes this pattern is changed, this nation will be destroyed." He pointed out that, unrecognized by the public, there has been laid:

> The groundwork for an economic dictatorship which is expanding geometrically year after year . . . . We are careening with frightening speed toward collectivism away from individual sovereignty, toward coercive centralized planning and away from free individual choices, toward a statist-dictatorial system and away from a nation in which individual liberty is sacred.[14]

His comments indicate the basic problem is one of human ideology that must be corrected, although he did not articulate or understand it fully.

All efforts to curtail deficit spending have failed. When Ronald Reagan returned the presidency to conservative Republicans, the programs causing the budget build-up were moving into full swing. But the Cold War against Communism demanded that Reagan rebuild American defense capabilities, which had declined under Carter, to restore American world influence and restore American confidence. His idea of new confidence, reduced taxes, and expansion of jobs offered no immediate help in reducing the budget. His budget director, William Stockman, resigned in desperate exasperation as he looked at what lay ahead. The Grace Commission, appointed to study the matter, reported hard but significant choices, but little was accepted.

In 1982, Social Security was near a point of crisis, and a joint commission of Congress revised the program and increased taxes in order to save it from bankruptcy.

Repeated changes in the entitlements have been initiated. The steady rise of the number of people receiving benefits, the continued increase in the maximum wage taxed, and the maximum taxes on Social Security are shown in the following graphs. What once was seen as a help to needy people became the rights of everyone in the future.

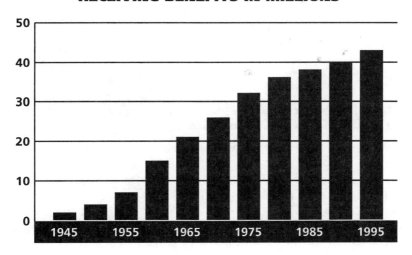

NUMBER OF PEOPLE
RECEIVING BENEFITS IN MILLIONS

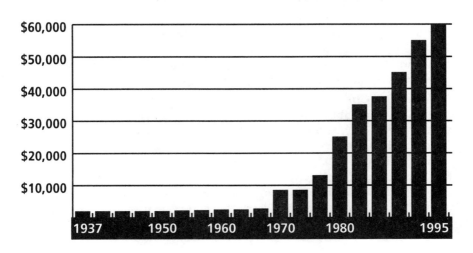

MAXIMUM WAGE TAXED

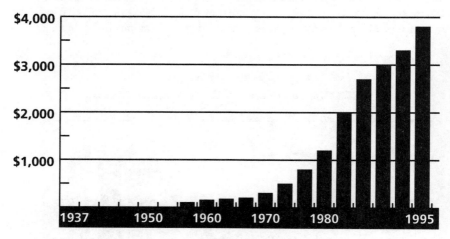

MAXIMUM YEARLY TAX FOR SOCIAL SECURITY

Worker's employer puts in the same amount. Self-employed pay double.

Also, Congress had to seriously consider the matter. By 1985, the Balanced Budget and Emergency Deficit Control Act, popularly known as the Gramm-Rudman-Hollins Bill, was passed. It sought to fix deficit targets for decline each year, but exempt major items like Social Security. By the next year, it was evident the accepted guidelines would not be kept. By 1990, they were overspent by $121.2 billion. In its place, President Bush offered the Omnibus Budget Reconciliation Act of 1990, with new budget procedures and the intent of greater enforcement to reduce the budget by $482 billion. Then followed a bill crafted as the Second Omnibus Reconciliation Act of 1993 to reduce cumulative deficits over 1994-98 by $433 billion.[15] In the meantime, Rudman resigned, feeling the effort was futile and that he did not want to participate in the demise of the government. The balancing of the budget became the focus of much talk.

When Bill Clinton ran for president, the federal budget and the growing debt had become the major American problem. In the election, the whole seriousness of the matter was laid out before the American public by Ross Perot on charts showing in no uncertain terms that the American government was in deep trouble. The great issue of the election was on curtailing the budget. For the American people, the moral decline found its most important focus on the continuing fiscal irresponsibility of the government as symbolized in the budget. There is now great fear that the government is headed for another serious crisis.

SUMMARY REVIEW OF THE PATTERNS OF AMERICAN ECONOMY

While it is not possible to fully analyze American business cycles here, two perspectives are given in graph form to show what has been occurring. Shorter recessions appear every three to five years. Ravi Batra of Southern Methodist University sees major depressions occurring every thirty to sixty years. From an interview with Jay Forester resulting from his use of a multitude of factors in a computer at Massachusetts Institute of Technology, Bill Hendrick with staff artist Randall Grant of the Atlanta Journal present a theory of long waves of forty-five to sixty years.[16]

Also, a chart accentuating the major depressions from 1812 to 1990 is given on page 192 and taken from Larry Burkett's book.[17] They are meant to show general trends. Both of these help show the zigzag pursuit of materialism as it developed in America, and can help in evaluating what may lie ahead.

Certain things are clear. The zigs have an increasing economic wave promoting greater change, and the zag depressions come with greater severity and last much longer. The depression during Monroe's presidency was shorter and less severe than the one during Grant's, while the later 1929 depression was more severe. This characteristic of the successive waves being deeper and longer will be considered in looking at the last surge of this civilization toward which society is now moving. Each successive major depression had an increased length of time between them. The MIT model did not allow for enough lengthening of time between each depression or it would have pushed the last over to about 2000 A.D. They rather assumed an average in estimating the time of occurrence.

The tremendous increase in budgets and the continued growth in public and private debt indicates that the next recession will be far greater than anything that has yet occurred.

MIT VIEW OF RIDING THE LONG WAVE OF ECONOMICS

Riding The Economic Long Wave

Researchers at the Massachusetts Institute of Technology claim the economy moves up and down in 45 to 60 year cycles. The stylized chart represents major fluctuations in such measures as consumer prices, factory production and unemployment

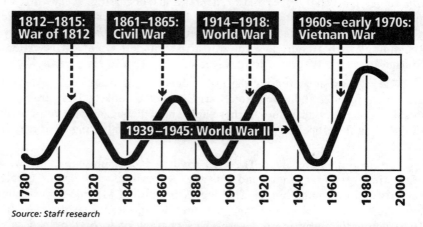

Source: Staff research

CYCLES OF BUSINESS ACCENTUATING DEPRESSIONS

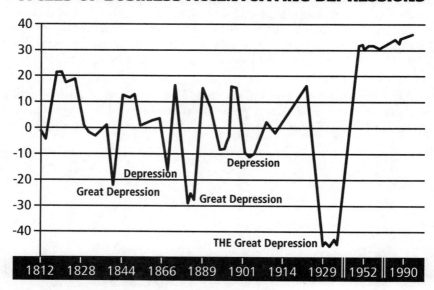

Note: Chart is designed to highlight periodic depressions

Most alarming is the continued increase of American voters who are profiting from the government programs that cause politicians hesitancy about reducing these entitlement programs. The decline of moral commitment to do what is right, by not only the politicians but by the voters, makes the crisis of will to change much greater. Moreover, the expansion of economic involvement introduces wide areas of unpredictability that are outside American control even though there is much more information known and available in this computer age to help adjust.

Before the last surge of the decline of the culture is evaluated, it is important to look at the sensual and sexual revolt of America, which began about 1830 and is now in full swing leading to the final decline. As mentioned before, materialism inevitably leads to sensual and sexual concerns that change the way each sex looks at the other. And the sexual revolution so changes values that the way people react materially is greatly affected. The presumably last surge of materialism in which we will be involved will also be evaluated under the final surge or step of anarchy and the approaching time of judgment in succeeding chapters.

The patterns presented in this chapter offer a warning to pursue a significant spiritual renewal for change. These matters will be discussed further as the results to the economy are discussed in chapter 14.

Chapter 11

Sensual or Sexual Revolt in America

INTRODUCTION

As explained earlier, a materialistic revolt soon initiates the turn to a sensualist revolt, and each surge of materialism motivates the sensual and sexual even further. A materialistic view of life focuses man on the physical aspects of his nature. Adam and Eve became aware of their sexual differences and were ashamed in the Garden after eating the fruit in disobedience to God. So in America, sexual differences were accentuated by a sexual awareness that produced a revolt. It led to the breakdown of the family, and therefore to the breakdown of control over upcoming generations.

An overview of the sexual revolution follows. Mrs. William D. Sporborg, in a lecture on "Women as a Social Force," traces the movement as "stirring" (1833-1866), "moving" (1866-1900), and "marching" (1900-1933). I have adjusted this slightly and added that it was "permeating society" (1930-1960), and "politically fighting" (1960-present). A brief review of these developments and the results on the family and American life follows.

PROVOKING CONDITIONS STARTING THE SEXUAL REVOLT

Male Pursuit of Mammon and the Building of Civilization

In the early nineteenth century, women were neglected by their husbands and denied wealth as the male pursuit of mammon grew. Men were absent from their homes for business, leaving women with all of the home responsibilities in exchange for small material gifts but no real access to wealth. Andrew Sinclare observed:

> Most of the feminist leaders came from homes where the father was a professional man, interested in Eastern reforms. They lived continually in the ferment of speculation, which characterized the speedy development of the West. And yet they [the women] could not occupy themselves in the business of money-making, which kept their menfolk busy from morning to night.[1]

When men distort their roles and gain a sense of power, when they develop a civilization and gain wealth, they have a sense of importance and pride that leads to abuse, neglect, and unfaithfulness to their wives. Men with wealth and power tend to be promiscuous. This is the repeated pattern causing the decline of civilizations. This produced frustration and anger of wives in America and led to a feminist revolt. There are few things more humiliating to a woman than infidelity and neglect. This was what happened in America in the early 1830s.

Comparative Population of Men and Women

During the nineteenth century, the population rapidly rose, both by natural births and also by immigration. In 1820, the total population probably did not exceed 10 million, with about 103 males to every 100 females. In 1860, the population had risen to over 30 million, of which just over 4 million were foreign born and the males being about 105 to every 100 females.

At the close of the century, the population was estimated at nearly 76 million, with only a slight drop in the male surplus. With many people taking advantage of increasing mobility by roads, and later by trains and by canals, there were many people moving westward into new communities, and this produced growing differences between urban and rural populations. More people were moving to big cities.

Many Women Employed in Factories

Community influence was broken up and relationships destroyed by the changes in society. In addition to the larger amount of people working, there was a change in jobs, so young women were separated from their families by their work. In New England by 1860, one-third of all factory workers were women; in the country as a whole they were one-eighth the total of factory workers. In 1834, Michel Chevalier stated that 6,000 women were employed in the Lowell mill factories, and 5,000 were between 17 and 24 years of age, most being daughters of farmers and rural workers from Massachusetts, New Hampshire, and Vermont. Chevalier commented that their habits and ideas were very different from those in France, and he attributed this to their Protestant Christian education. These women lived in supervised boarding establishments which were locked at ten o'clock each night.[2]

Henry C. Carey, an overseer, stated he knew of only three cases of "improper connexion [*sic*] of intimacy". However, *The Boston Times* and *The Boston Quarterly Review* published critical articles upon the character and condition of the female workers. As immigration and natural population increased, more young women went into the work force. "And by 1860 there seemed to be few occupations where they had not found some kind of employment." As a result, there were public outcries about the lack of suitableness of the hard work and conditions under which they lived.

Double Standard of Greedy Men Who Neglect and Abuse

It is amazing that the purity of the factory girls remained high for as long as it did. There seems to have been a growing laxity of morals among the factory workers over time. Also, in the South, there was a growing abuse of black female slaves by the white men. The earliest problems of immorality in all the colonies, including Maryland, Virginia, and the Carolinas, were with servants or slaves. This was a peculiar condition dealt with harshly in the early Western days. But the nineteenth century began to introduce views of women as equal with and competing with men, and this began to open the doors to sexual immorality as a right to pleasure.

The upper-class women, in the absence of their husbands, were the first voices for the feminists. The large numbers of hard-working women in the factories were an interested audience. The fact that men were dedicated strictly to work and business, and women were committed to the home and social activities, caused a separation between ladies and gentlemen. "This social dichotomy led many Americans to seek escape into a world of phantasy [*sic*] and romance."[3] It also produced hostility of women toward men.

Fantasies of Fiction for Women

The middle of the nineteenth century was a time of romantic novels and magazines. Best-sellers were melodramatic romances, and there were many of them.

> Apart from books, magazines for women began to be increasingly popular and in New England twenty such journals had appeared before 1830, and another thirty were published between that date and 1860. In the 1850's the three most important magazines were the *Ladies Magazine* of Boston, *Godey's Lady's Book* of Philadelphia and the *Ladies Companion* of New York.[4]

Also, French books were being imported. These opened the way for a greater feminine interest in the outside world and for the rise of feminism. Certain sexual evils accompanied the breakdown of morals, and tight-lacing and masturbation were the subjects of diatribes against what was going on. Outspokenness about female physiology and anatomy grew.

Pornography and Prostitution for Men

Prostitution was prevalent in some eastern cities, such as New York and Boston, in the early part of the nineteenth century, but there is a difference of agreement as to what extent. The Gold Rush led to prostitution in California, and the river boat traffic also produced much in New Orleans. There were prominent fashionable houses in New York, and some travelers said that one in thirty women in Boston were involved. As men traveled away from home more, prostitution increased.

John Dingwall reports:

By the middle of the century prostitution and vice were a general feature of the social scene, and books began to be issued, on the one hand of an avowedly fictional character, and the other more or less founded on facts.[5]

By 1880, there were 600 brothels and 90 assignation houses in New York, together with 487 panel houses. Abortion houses also began to appear and proliferate. One of the main efforts of the upper-class feminists was social reform of prostitution. This is clear evidence that an increase in abortion is an outgrowth of the breakdown of the relationships of men and women in the family, which is motivated by egalitarian materialism.

Social Reform, Including Women's Rights

Outspoken feminist writing occurred earlier in England, with Mary Wollstonecraft's *A Vindication of the Rights of Woman* (1792), which drew much of its impetus from the freedom expressed in the French Revolution. Abigail Adams, the wife of President John Adams, wrote letters that were published and gained attention for women's rights. Anne Royall published a newspaper in Washington that addressed the issues of anti-slavery and the woman's right to vote. The issue of "women's rights" legally was in debate and summarized in a book by Mrs. A. J. Graves, although this issue was not greatly challenged until later.

Many women gained prominence through writing, speaking, and leading movements, and some were involved in sexual affairs as an aspect of women's rights. Francis Wright, and in a more sophisticated way, Margaret Fuller, became known. They later joined Mary Wollstonecraft and George Sand in France. So, by mid-century, the sexual revolution was underway.

Inventions that Assisted Women's Liberation

As I have pointed out, inventions in the first half of the century gave added freedom to women and to sexual promiscuity. Efforts have aimed at reducing the rate of conception and making child care easier to give women more freedom.

The movement was aided by the invention of the vulcanization of rubber in the early 1800's and the application of this to mechanisms for birth control. It was also aided by the invention of the baby bottle in 1841 and also the invention of refrigeration and better stoves. These released women from the necessity of having and nursing babies.[6]

Birth control and abortion gave freedom for sexual involvement, reducing the responsibility of bearing children.

THE FIRST SURGE OF SEXUAL REVOLT, WOMEN STIRRING (1833-1866)

Women Shifted Focus from Social Reform to Their Rights

Upper-class women involved themselves in organizing social reform, and especially against slavery. Finally, they focused on women's rights. The first women's rights conference was held at Seneca Falls, New York, in 1848. By this time, the neglect and abuse of women by men was felt deeply. Women of the upper-class had little self-esteem. Men spent their time earning money, which set the value of life. Women were excluded from money-making, except in low-paying jobs and from places of importance. Their significance was gained in women's clubs and in social movements, and they were lonely. Many of the aristocratic women came to feel important and tasted the power of public influence in the anti-slave movement. Their ability to have children was little appreciated, and they were a financial liability to the husband. As Margaret Mead once pointed out, having a baby is very important when the largest thing a man builds is a twenty foot hut. But when he builds a railroad and great buildings, the woman's role is diminished. Women began to consider their status, which seemed unfair and demeaning.

Under these circumstances, the prominent speaker Lucretia Mott met with Elizabeth Cady Stanton. They had met at the World's Anti-Slavery Convention in London eight years previously. Since that time, Elizabeth Stanton had married a successful businessman. She began to bear children, eventually having seven, and moved to Seneca Falls, New York. With her husband's money, she had been able to hire a Quaker woman who was in her employ for many years. The woman looked after all the children who were a lower priority for Elizabeth, and this allowed her to be involved outside the home.

Mrs. Stanton reports as follows:

My experiences at the World's Anti-Slavery Convention, all I had read of the legal status of women, and the oppression I saw everywhere, together swept across my soul, intensified now by many personal experiences. . . . In this tempest-tossed condition of mind I received an invitation to spend the day with Lucretia Mott. . . . I poured out the torrent of my long-accumulating discontent with such vehemence and indignation that I stirred myself, as well as the rest of the party. Then and there the decision was made to call a woman's rights meeting.[7]

A few days before the conference, Mott, Stanton, and a few other women met and drew up the *Seneca Falls Declaration of Sentiments and Resolutions* using the *Declaration of Independence* as a model.

It was a particularly appropriate time for revolutionary thought.

In 1848, in England, France, Germany, Austria and elsewhere, people were taking to the streets, seeking the fulfillment of liberal democratic rights proclaimed in the great documents of the French and American Revolutions and, in many instances, demanding new economic rights for workers. Presaging the political and social storms of the future, that very same year Marx and Engels penned and issued the *Communist Manifesto*.[8]

About three hundred people attended the convention, which was chaired by James Mott, Lucretia's husband. Frederick Douglass, whom they had supported in the anti-slavery cause, attended at their invitation. The *Declaration of Sentiments and Resolutions* was presented by Elizabeth Stanton. Eleven resolutions were adopted unanimously, and a twelfth for granting women elective franchise passed by a narrow margin only after Frederick Douglas stoutly defended it from the floor. The declaration that day formed the foundation of the women's movement. Part of its power was in copying the *Declaration of Independence*. In part, it said the following:

When, in the course of human events, it becomes necessary for one portion of the family of man to assume among the people of the earth a position different from that which they have hitherto occupied, but one to which the laws of nature and of natures' God entitled them, a decent respect to the opinions of mankind requires that they should declare the causes that impel them to such a course. We hold these truths to be self-evident: that all men and women are created equal; that they are endowed by their Creator with certain inalienable rights; that among these are life, liberty, and the pursuit of happiness; that to secure these rights governments are instituted, deriving their just powers from the consent of the governed. Whenever any form of government becomes destructive of these ends, it is the right of those who suffer from it to refuse allegiance to it. . . .

The document ends declaring the wrongs of men to women as the Declaration ended presenting the grievances against the king of England. Its lead statement follows, "The history of mankind is a history of repeated injuries and usurpation's on the part of man toward woman, having in direct object the establishment of an absolute tyranny over her."[9] There is a list of fifteen abuses, accusing men of every kind of evil against women, claiming these have occurred throughout human history. It ends with this statement:

> Now, in view of this entire disfranchisement of the one-half the people of this country, their social and religious degradation–in view of the unjust laws above mentioned, and because women do feel themselves aggrieved, oppressed, and fraudulently deprived of their most sacred rights, we insist that they have immediate admission to all the rights and privileges which belong to them as citizens of the United States.

To this end, they pledged total effort using every available means to achieve this.

Douglass reported this meeting in his newspaper, *The North Star*, editorially saying:

> Standing as we do upon the watch-tower of human freedom, we can not be deterred from an expression of our approbation of any movement, however humble, to improve and elevate the character of any members of the human family. . . . We are free to say that in respect to political rights, we hold woman to be justly entitled to all we claim for man.[10]

Evaluation of the Declaration and Resolutions and the Feminist Movement

Hatred and Eradication of Men

Dr. Marynia Farnham, one of the foremost psychiatrists, reflecting over this movement in the mid-twentieth century, said:

> The real goal* of the feminist movement was to eradicate men. A document more against men you cannot imagine than that formed by the American feminists when they first met in 1848. They demanded the instant abolition of marriage as a form of slavery for women. They demanded the institution of uterine descent, namely, no child to be named for its father, but always for its mother. The mother was to dictate the nature of the union and disposition of the child. I have seen recent documents (by feminists) demanding that men be ousted from all public office except engineering, and that women take over the control of all party politics.

Farnham continued:

> Now, this is sheer annoyance. It is not common sense. It is hostility, it is rage at being dispossessed, at being made into a nobody, having no

known function, and there is one thing you cannot do to any human being with impunity—you cannot take away his self-esteem. If you do, he is going to get mad and do all sorts of irresponsible things and not know why he does it. Nor did the women who had lost theirs know what they were doing. . . . They looked around for a solution, a good solution—a bad solution—and like most dispossessed people, they looked around to see what the "haves" had. They found that men are "haves," men are the enslavers, men are the conspirators. The poor miserable men who had also been enslaved by the machine. . . . Such thoughts lead to the idea that the best thing women can do is to look over what the male "haves" have, and try to get it for themselves. . . . The feminists said, right out loud, "We want what men have. We want masculine rights for ourselves." The feminists had no idea of sharing. No ideas about just quietly getting together.[11]

Thus, this third step of sexual revolt toward the decline of society was taken. The obvious right solution was to recognize that equality of the sexes means something different for each and to call men away from the materialism and their idolatry. The right thing was for men to return to God and to caring for their wife and children, as Farnham suggests. But the cause was not just the bad conditions into which the material passion of men had thrust them, but the individualist thinking of the time period which demanded individual freedom.

The early feminist stage focused on a woman's right not to marry yet still have sexual affairs. "By the early twentieth century there were a number of 'advanced' women who not only denounced marriage, but openly advocated sexual freedom." This extended, as Isadora Duncan said, "to fight against marriage and for the emancipation of women and for the right of every woman to have a child or children as it pleased her."

Another theme of central importance to the old as well as the new feminism is the economic dependence of women. . . . Serious feminists of every generation have advocated financial self-sufficiency as a prerequisite for independence, personal fulfillment and socialization of women.[12]

This involved attacking low wages, and calling for remuneration for house-keeping work. But importantly, it also involved attacking property laws and rights.

Focus on Material Privileges

The first moves of American feminism, as in Greece and Rome, were to gain material privileges in the worship of mammon. Stanton was integrally involved in the Married Women's Property Act of 1848 and was dissatisfied with its limitations. She addressed the New York State Legislature in 1854 about other rights, such as trial by jury, but especially about property rights, and claimed women had no more rights than slaves.[13] Susan B. Anthony was also heavily involved in state-wide canvassing to pressure the legislature. And in 1860, Stanton was able to get another Married Women's Property Act passed guaranteeing a woman the right to keep her own earnings, the right to equal powers with her husband as joint guardian of the children, and with property rights as a widow equal to those her husband would have in the event of her death.[14] Thus, the first phase of the sexual revolt was directed at declaring sexual freedom from marriage and gaining material rights.

THE SECOND SURGE OF THE SEXUAL REVOLT, WOMEN MOVING (1866-1920)

Dissolution of Marriage by Divorce: Individual Freedom

The second surge of the sexual revolt turned against marriage itself. "In 1860 Elizabeth Cady Stanton introduced the subject of liberalizing divorce laws at a woman's rights meeting." Some delegates immediately saw this as an attack on marriage itself, and some even asked the suggestion be stricken from the minutes. In 1853, Stanton wrote to Anthony saying:

I do not know whether the world is quite willing or ready to discuss the question of marriage. . . . I feel, as never before, that this whole question of woman's right turns on the pivot of the marriage relation, and mark my word, sooner or later it will be the topic for discussion.

In 1860, she wrote again, "How this marriage question grows on me. It lies at the foundation of all progress."[15] In 1870, she demanded the unlimited freedom of divorce.[16] Tennessee Claflin, in 1871, reminded women that demand for suffrage was not the fundamental issue if women were still enslaved in marriage. She said:

At the ballot-box is not where the shoe pinches. . . . It is at home where the husband, as in prehistoric times. . . is the supreme ruler, that the little difficulty arises; he will not surrender this absolute power unless he is compelled.[17]

This intense focus on the ability to break the marriage by divorce began to achieve its end.

In 1867 divorces numbered some 10,000; in 1929 they numbered more than 200,000. In other words, the rate of divorce increase advanced. . .

about five times as fast as the proportion of the married people over a period of sixty three years.[18]

Reduction of Children for Greater Freedom

The feeling that having many children kept women in bondage made the reduction of children a major objective. Contraceptives greatly increased in use, as well as an increasing number of abortions. Observer after observer, and study after study report the gradual decline in the birth rate of this period in spite of the increase of immigrants during the time who bore more children than nationals. There were 5.25 million immigrants from 1880-1890, and they bore 5 percent more children than American women. The rate was lower than any Western country, except perhaps France. Calhoun refers to numerous writers on this with varying statistics, but all agree on a gradual decline because of the deliberate desire of women to have fewer children.[19]

Education of Women

Another major emphasis during the second stage of the women's movement was the beginning of higher education for women. Correlated with the opening of industrial careers for women were the opening opportunities for higher education. Advanced education for women is practically a development of the post-bellum period. Vassar was founded in 1865. In 1870, the University of Michigan was opened to women. Even at Oberlin, however, as late as 1870, it was considered improper for a woman to address a mixed audience. There were still many alarmist articles against women's higher education, but much progress was made during this second surge of feminism. The main emphasis at this stage for women was on separate institutions, but not exclusively. Increasing education of women usually leads to reducing the size of family and therefore is related to the previous subject of lower births.

Black Women and Their Rights After the Civil War

While black males were active in the emancipation movement, the white women with their social movements became their champions. After the Civil War, though, the black woman's condition changed only minimally. Those who went to the North sometimes inter-married with white men. They joined the whites to work in industry. Those in the South found themselves with large families and in the old slave houses or alley houses in the towns. It was commonly accepted for black girls to have children before marriage. This early pattern has direct relevance to present modern problems of black women. Infidelity of a married, black woman was looked down upon, but adultery was not uncommon. The prostitution or red light districts in the South were most often black.

Unfortunately, because of federal pressure on southern civil governments after Southerners regained control, it was common to leave blacks alone and not enforce laws or try to punish outside of the courts. Civil laws of marriage were seldom enforced by the white Southern governments on the black family. Black clergy held a position not only of religious leadership, but often they were also a political boss. They were reputed to have widespread sexual involvement with the women of the congregation, so the religious emphasis of sexual morals had a negative impetus from the center.[20]

Some studies show many blacks, especially those who gained education, moved toward greater sexual purity. The high birth rate and mixed families in small quarters were conducive to lowered morals. Black women often had absent husbands, so demand for freedom from men was not at first as strong among black women as it was among the white feminists.[21] The far greater laxity in sexual morals was not because of race, but because of previous practices as slaves and resultant conditions economically and legally after the Civil War. This led to the tragic conditions for the black family at the end of the twentieth century.

Organizing Women's Suffrage Efforts: Gaining the Voting Right

The issue of women's suffrage became a major focus in this second stage of the sexual revolt. From the outset at the Seneca Falls Conference in 1848, the gaining of the right to vote was primary. The women recognized this as important, but also felt great opposition to the vote at that meeting. That particular resolution was passed only by a persuasive speech of Douglass, and then barely. While the women continued to talk about this, no great push came until this second phase of the movement.

It has been mentioned that Maryland had the vote for women at first, and then it was canceled later (1807). The Mormons in Utah had been a source of conflict because of their polygamous practices and threats of the United States Government. When the railroad reached Utah, the Mormons feared being overrun by non-Mormons, or "Gentiles." To increase their voting power, they passed the women's right to vote. But just before that time, the territory of Wyoming, in its first legislature, adopted woman's suffrage in 1868.

In 1867, the main leaders of the women's movement made an effort to pass the right to vote in Kansas, which had been a main turning point for women involved in anti-slave efforts. Much effort to register people and put pressure on the legislature was made.

About this time, Emily Collins resided in Rochester, New York, and a women's society was organized there which saw the voting franchise as the only solution to women's problems and began to petition the legislature. A decade later, when she was living in Louisiana, there was a convention to form a new state constitution, and Elizabeth Stanton addressed the convention about the franchise for women. It did not pass, but they did receive other privileges and were promised the right to vote soon.[22] In New York City, the National Women's Suffrage Association formed in 1869 and held a meeting every year for the next fifty years.

Early Militancy for Women's Right to Vote

Susan B. Anthony, who lived in Rochester and whose ability was in organizing and petitioning, made much effort at a state-wide canvas for six years in New York to put pressure on the state legislature. In 1872, she led fifty women to a polling place in Rochester, New York, where they registered to vote. She urged women everywhere to do the same. Within two weeks, Anthony and the others were arrested and charged with voting illegally under a statute designed to be used against freed slaves, which carried a three-year jail term. She made a plea for women's rights, but was found guilty in court by the United States in June 1873, and given a fine, which she never paid. This brought the matter before the women of America.[23] Susan Anthony brought Carrie Chapman Catt into the movement. She succeeded Anthony as the leader, and she focused on the suffrage issue.

THIRD SURGE OF SEXUAL REVOLUTION: WOMEN MARCHING (1900-1930)

Women's Aggressive Threat to Men

In the last of the nineteenth century, the feminist movement took a militant approach to producing change which frightened and intimidated men, and gained much newspaper support. There were five million women employed in American industry, and they gained access to the labor unions by the tens of thousands from 1909-1912. They organized a strike against the garment and textile industry, and stayed out for months protesting their low pay and miserable working conditions. This hit the businessmen of America where it hurt—their profits.

Emmeline Pankhurst, an English feminist, led many women in a dozen hunger strikes, and was convicted and sentenced to three years of penal servitude. She was allowed to leave England for the United States in 1913, and by 1917, had added to the militancy of the American women's move-ment. Under her leadership, there were ninety-seven American women in prison on charges which were later thrown out of court.

The whole movement to promote the vote was accompanied by the emphasis of equal economic opportunity, which was seen as the key to women's freedom and the same self-realization as men. Charlotte Perkins Gilman's works at the end of the nineteenth century and beginning of the twentieth century emphasized this (e.g., Gilman's book, *Women and Economics*). Emma Goldman, an anarchistic, Russian Jew emigrated to the United States, received a divorce and declared her sexual freedom. She became a forceful public speaker, inciting male hatred and rebellion. She emphasized marriage as a male arrangement for economic advantage, and urged legal and political involvement. She publicly gave out information on contraceptives and was sentenced to a fifteen-day prison term.

All of this public turmoil helped produce an in-depth, four-year study by the United States Senate published in 1911 as *Women and Child Wage-Earners in the United States*. Helen L. Sumner contributed to this (vol. IX), and argued for the goal of occupational equality for women. This led to the establishment of the Women's Bureau of the United States Department of Labor, aimed in that direction.

By this time, there were many organizations formed to promote the vote, such as the Federal Association, the College Equal Suffrage League, the Friends' Association, the Mississippi Valley Conferences, the Southern Women's Conferences, a Congressional Union in Washington, and a National Men's League for Woman Suffrage. The National Republican Convention in Chicago in 1917 adopted the name "National Woman's Party."

Finally, after many states had already adopted the right for women to vote, both houses of Congress passed the Nineteenth Amendment to the Constitution in time for women to vote in the 1920 presidential election. It said, "The right of citizens of the United States to vote shall not be denied or abridged by the United States or by any State on account of sex."

Religious Support of Women's Liberation and Equality

During the third surge of the women's movement, the theory of evolution gained dominance, the higher critical views of the Bible gained dominance, and the liberal theology of knowing God subjectively as taught by Schliermacher, Harnack, and others gained dominance. While Darwin taught that women evolved as inferior, the women's movement saw their dominant emergence as the next stage of evolution. The argument that women had always been tyrannically treated and neglected by men seemed persuasive, since this was apparently true during this phase of the material revolt and the industrial revolution.

The readerships of the old-line denominations embraced liberal theology and were leaders among the educated elite who were seeking to forge a new society through the social gospel and social democracy. There was great pressure to give women theological education. Lucretia Mott was a Quaker minister, and so were others. Some of the other women leaders had theological education and were ordained, including the distinguished educator, Anna Garlin Spencer, who will be referred to again in the next stage of the movement.

But most importantly, women became important as missionaries. The churches embraced the idea of "evangelizing the world in this generation" in the Student Volunteers Movement (S.V.M.) and the modern missionary movement which consummated in the International Missionary Conference in Edinburgh in 1910. Liberal and conservative elements were involved in this strategic effort. The initial motivating force of the student movement had been the Young Men's Christian Association, and the focus continued to be on male leadership, but the Young Women's Christian Association was also formed and grew. Moreover, there was no sexual distinction in the S.V.M. At the end of the nineteenth century, or twenty years before the Edinburgh Conference, over six thousand young men and women from Western countries, two-thirds of these from the United States, went to the mission field as laymen and teaching leaders.[24]

The numbers were a growing tide of youth with an increasing number of women that eventually became a majority. Men were still highly involved in pursuing business, although the leadership in missions focused on the male. However, the heroic and good work of many women did much to promote the Christian idea of equality of women, or at least was so used by the women's movement. A. J. Gordon, a leader in the missionary movement and founder of Gordon College and Gordon Seminary, strongly argued for ordination of women on the basis of their participation in the missionary movement. Those groups that emphasized the common man and the Holy Spirit more than Scripture moved toward ordination of women.

FOURTH SURGE OF THE SEXUAL REVOLUTION, WOMEN'S IDEAS PERMEATING (1930-1960)

Reevaluation and Regrouping for New Goals

The sexual revolution went through a generation of struggle for a number of reasons. The main reason was that the feminist movement became organized and focused on the main objective of gaining the vote for women as the answer to all other problems. When the vote was won, the reason for existing melted and so did the impetus, so that much of the organization died. The feeling of women was that now, by the right legislation, many of their problems would be solved. Moreover, during World War I, millions of men had gone to war, and the women ran the homes and took over much work in industry. The men came back as heroes, and anti-male sentiment among women was not as strong.

Also of great significance is the fact the United States went through the Great Depression beginning in 1929. Jobs were scarce, and everyone found he had to work together to make ends meet. With fewer jobs, the preferential choice was for the male provider of the home to work. These conditions created more intimacy and interdependence between men and women in general. Women therefore were not as free to be involved in social programs. Since real recovery from the depression was not until the early 1940s, materialism and the motivation behind the sexual revolution were not as prominent.

Woman's Freedom through Birth Control

Freudian psychology became popular by advocating sexual freedom and the evil of suppressing sexual desires. It became scientifically right to be immoral. This was a great opportunity for those who were still militant feminists and saw the enemies of women's freedom as men and giving birth. The great champion of women's freedom during this period was Margaret Sanger. Her mother had eleven living children and died at forty-eight years of age. Sanger was a nurse who saw the terrible economic conditions of poor women who repeatedly had unwanted children that were inadequately cared for.

Sanger left her husband and children to study the birth control efforts in Europe, and especially in Holland. She returned to America with a righteous zeal to free women. She divorced her husband, neglected her children, and her own life became immoral. Her self-righteous zeal for the cause of freeing women sexually grew tremendously. She saw herself as women's savior in this next step of evolution to free women from the tyranny of motherhood by "family planning," or especially by birth control. She organized what is now known as Planned Parenthood. But for her, the purpose was for women to enjoy the freedom of sex without the responsibility of bearing the child. In her book, *Woman and the New Race* (1920), she proclaimed birth control as the "key to the temple of liberty." In this book, she said:

> The most far-reaching social development of modern times is the revolt of women against sex servitude. The most important force in the remaking of the world is a free motherhood. . . .[25]

Her life's mission was to give each woman the right "to control her own body" and escape from the dominance of men. This included widespread abortion, as well as increased knowledge of birth control. Margaret Sanger was willing to be imprisoned and maligned to save women. She and her followers sold the idea of pro-choice for women to the American public.

By 1955, a study revealed that seventy out of every one hundred couples practiced some form of birth control, and by 1960, a study showed this had increased to eighty-one out of one hundred. Excluding those who have infertility problems, it is thought today this would be eighty-nine out of one hundred. Thus, the idea of birth control has thoroughly permeated America. While birth control is as old as mankind and some birth control is acceptable to Christians, the point is that birth control became widespread before the great change that began to take place in the 1960s.[26] The radical changes for women would not have occurred in the 1960s had not Sanger formulated her ideas and developed the organization to promote them. It was in the last surge of the women's movement that all previous objectives came together to promote women acting like men in every way, including sexual freedom. But the implications of sexual freedom for women have not worked because sexual freedom also introduced premarital pregnancies. Since the 1960s, premarital pregnancies have increased rapidly, and sexually transmitted diseases have spread extensively.

Continued Promotion of Equality among Educators and Clergy

During this struggling period of the women's movement, American education, both in building universities and especially in building high schools, exploded in the United States. The National Education Association was led by the educated elite's endorsement of women's equality, co-education, and promotion of women's education. Moreover, the Senate study mentioned promoted women's equality in all vocations, and there was considerable advancement of women in the work force.

World War II moved women into traditionally masculine jobs. They built ships and airplanes, worked in steel mills, and did everything the men had done. Songs like "Rosie the Riveter" popularized women's participation, as did the sex appeal to the men in the appearances of movie stars to entertain the troops. Women were needed in every vocation, and by the thousands they went into the armed forces. Women's Corps for women in the Army, Navy, and Marines were organized to fill non-combatant jobs. Again, women became in charge of home and business. The war brought the United States out of its depression and launched business into another round of rapidly expanding materialism.

Religious Liberalism and Promotion of Women's Equality

The old-line denominations promoted the idea of ordaining women to the ministry toward the end of this period. Also, the World Council of Churches and the National Council of Churches (formerly the Federal Council of Churches) were born and professed liberal theology. There was a combined effort to promote equality of women and men. The World Council of Churches commissioned a study on women's roles with the intent that this study would exalt a woman's role in the work place and in churches around the world. Much to their surprise, this report did not say exactly what they wished. Sarah Chakko and Kathleen Bliss, who wrote the study, concluded:

> There is real danger in this equalizing process. Equal conditions of work and living do not guarantee women's freedom, for women need different conditions from men to give them equal freedom with men.[27]

Males still dominated business outside the home, and pursuit of money was still the goal for them. They left the care of the children to the wife and mother. Women gained a place of dominance over men in the home by running the homes and increasingly controlling their sons. Moreover, the public schools were now booming, and the teachers in the lower schools were almost all women. So boys were trained and raised by women for the most part. The dichotomy between the sexes was still there socially, but through public schools and other factors, the scales of influence had tipped to the woman as the dominant influence. Much of the literature and studies of this time deal with the problem of "Momism," and of fathers fearing their sons would be "sissies."[28] The result was that the men of society were less the traditional alpha male, and more passive and reserved towards women, or even angry at them. Homosexuality became an evident option and was increasing toward the end of this period.[29] Dr. Toby B. Bieber and his team of researchers determined that poor parental relationships, especially dominance by the mother, was the major cause, and that this began by a boy's tenth year of age.[30]

Radio, motion pictures, and extensive advertising appealing to women began to have a powerful impact on women and their self-image. The reduction of the price of printing and the proliferation of romantic novels and other stories in the motion pictures had a profound impact. There became a standardized image of young women and their romantic involvement. Since the motion pictures and literature were censored, there was passionate lovemaking with the hero but no explicit sex. Thus, the standard morals of "spooning" or petting were accepted without sexual intercourse. There was accommodation to this since the automobile became more common, plus the frequented movie house, and certain housing arrangements made a place for this. Thus, the moral ideal was not set by the Bible, but by modern motion pictures and other media. As this practice became more prolific and the standards more explicit, the morals generally changed for the masses of young men and women to premarital intercourse.[31]

Re-evaluation of Women's Role and Dangers of Feminism

During this time, intelligent, educated women emerged. Some of these increasingly gave warning for women and for society as a whole against the revolt of the women's movement and the role of equality and competition against men. Anna Garlin Spencer, who held evolutionary and liberal views and who taught social science in leading American universities, was a dissident voice. She traced the contributions of women from primitive to modern times in the evolution of civilization and their important role in industry, education, the arts, and other aspects of national life. She strongly disagreed with efforts to remove the domestic responsibilities of women. "She defended the home and family and emphasized their central importance to the personality development and socialization of the child."[32] Her emphasis on the importance of the mother in caring for the child would be seen as crucial by the end of the century. Modern social studies have shown conclusively the chaos for children because of the neglect of both parents in the home, validating Spencer's views.

The psychological movement began to discover women in particular were not finding satisfaction in marriage and sex. Also, the psychological movement came into full bloom, emphasizing the importance of sex for pleasure for women as well as men but revealing a tremendous frustration and frigidity in women. Famous women psychiatrists, such as Dr. Marynia Farnham and more recently her successor Dr. Marie Robinson, argued strongly that for women to try to be like men was sexual suicide. Farnham's book, *Modern Woman, the Lost Sex*, was discussed previously. Robinson's book, *The Power of Sexual Surrender*, helped women accept their womanhood and their husband's role, and was also important in emphasizing the way for women to find genuine satisfaction in the sexual experience was in marriage when women accept and appreciate the male's role. She found trust in the husband was a key element for sexual climax.

Popular magazines began to report consensus in these matters of gender roles; in *Life*, a study by psychologist Cleo Dawson for the National Management Association revealed most women preferred male managers and different conditions, while *Look* magazine's "New In-Depth Study for the American Woman," and studies by McGill University and others backed these findings. These popular reports quoted the psychologists in agreement on these findings. As a result,

Margaret Mead, the anthropologist who had argued that men's and women's differences were socially learned, began to fall in line.[33] Thus, the psychological movement urged women toward a more feminine role and men toward a more distinct maleness.

By 1940, the United States Census shocked people by announcing there had been a significant drop in the number of men, and for the first time in American history, the women outnumbered men. This made women reevaluate their attitude to men. As the United States moved into World War II in 1942, the country moved toward greater sexual permissiveness.

A Warning to Radical Feminists

At the end of this period, the women's movement faced a decision. Women had gained the right to vote and registered many women across the nation. Moreover, the population had tipped in their favor, since women now held the dominant number. But many of the most brilliant leading women, as well as men, were warning society through studies that to try to make women equal in terms of sameness was wrong and dangerous. Anna Garland Spencer and others in social studies, leading women psychologists and spokesmen about women, and the world study by the World Council of Churches, all said women were strategically important as mothers in the home, and women were not happy when competing with men. Most women really wanted caring husbands as their leader.

Since 1960, the American family was clearly in trouble. Men were absent from home, women wanted to have the same rights as men, and each year there was no moral constraint of the conscience about not wanting children and even less about caring for children.

FIFTH SURGE OF SEXUAL REVOLUTION, POLITICAL ATTACKS (1960-Present)

Women's Demands to Be Like Men in Every Way

In the late 1950s, the women's movement was reborn and the Equal Rights Amendment for women was conceived, and became a major issue in Congress in the 1960s. Women demonstrated publicly, burned their bras, and even threw them at authorities. The ethos in government thinking was opportune for all seemingly righteous causes, and the woman's cause was one of these.

As Betty Friedan said:

By the end of the nineteen-fifties, the average marriage age of women in America dropped to 20, and was still dropping into the teens. Fourteen million girls were engaged by 17. The proportion of women attending college in comparison with men dropped from 47 percent in 1920 to 35 percent in 1958. A century earlier, women had fought for higher education: now girls went to college to get a husband. By the mid-fifties, 60 percent dropped out of college to marry, or because they were afraid too much education would be a marriage bar. Colleges built dormitories for 'married students,' but the students were almost always the husbands. A new degree was instituted for the wives—'Ph.T.' (Putting Husband Through).[34]

The wives worked and provided for the husband.

As the 1960s progressed, many angry women increasingly sought to break into equality with men in terms of earning power and positions of prestige. Every area exclusive to men was challenged, and the demand for men to care for children and the house became prominent. So many educated elite had never before been so angry and determined to gain equal rights.

The renewed feminist movement presented itself with racial issues as a human rights effort, and promoted their aims along with the racial agenda. The feminists wanted to eliminate all barriers against gender in hiring, in advancement in jobs, in freedom in sexual conduct, and against male initiative in sex. The feminists considered all courtesies and protection for women as sexist. They considered themselves objects of prejudice and sought minority support and homosexual support to help gain their ends. Eliminating the double sexual standard took the direction of demanding open sexual promiscuity for all, rather than arguing for both men and women to live in abstinence until marriage.

Reference has been made to what psychiatrist Marynia Farnham diagnosed as a result of the statements of the first women's rights movement and her observations over the years. She said, "The real goal of the feminist movement was to eradicate men." The leaders of the feminist movement have been women who have been abused by men and are rebelling against men having any control over them and what they do.[35] Their goals have been unlimited freedom in sex, a choice to have children without a husband, unlimited opportunity for divorce, destruction of any patriarchal rule of the home, and elimination of male political leadership.

In the 1960s surge of feminism, they sought every effort to achieve their goals.

The hard-core, extreme feminists of today are clearly continuing to aim at the dissolution of the family, although they have no clear alternative. They see more clearly than the moderates that removal of the male role in the family is the only way to achieve their objectives. Some are aiming at the goal of dissolution of the family by 2000 A.D.

Such leaders as Ti-Grace Atkinson, former leader of the National Organization for Women, Kate Millett, and others are insistent on destroying the family. Kate Millet, whose book *Sexual Politics* became the handbook for the feminist revolution, says that "the family is patriarchy's chief institution and cell for sexist brainwashing, which not only encourages its own members to adjust and conform, but acts as a unit in the patriarchal state which rules its citizens through the family heads." She admits that an end to patriarchy will probably destroy the family.[36]

The feminists who initiated and gave leadership to the movement of the 1960-70s were not mainstream women. Midge Costanza, one-time aide to President Jimmy Carter, said in regard to homosexuality, "I get very emotional about this issue because I feel very strongly that you should have the right to love whomever you want. I do." Gloria Steinem, editor of *Ms.* magazine, (hostile because of an abusive father) said, "The overthrow of capitalism should accompany the overthrow of the institution of marriage." She also wrote, "By the year 2000 we will, I hope, raise our children to believe in human potential, not God." Bella Abzug, New York Congresswoman and chairperson of the Commission of the Celebration of the International Women's Year held in Houston, Texas, and former chairperson of the president's advisory committee on women, introduced a "civil rights" bill for homosexuals. Jean O'Leary, a former nun, now co-executive director of the National Gay Task Force and an appointee to the President's Commission on Observance of I.W.Y., advocates studies in our schools to help children accept the idea of homosexuality as an alternate lifestyle. Eleanor Smeal, former head of the National Organization for Women, advocates government-run nurseries into which a child must be put at two years of age. Kate Millett's autobiography tells of a lengthy and turbulent affair with a dominating lesbian. Betty Friedan announced her objective to be restructuring all society for women with an inclusion of lesbianism as normal.[37] Angry with men, these women have been an able group who hold a sense of messianic mission to control from their limited perspective.

Sexual Freedom Is Hostile to Women's Nature and to the Social Benefits of Children and Men

The nature of women is unquestionably designed biologically for bearing and nurturing children. A woman's body shows this as the obvious. I have reviewed the extensive biological differences of men and women, and there have been other studies showing additional factors.[38] This is obvious to even a child, and any person willing to make an objective analysis of women's and men's differences must conclude that to be true.

Without women's acceptance of this, the human race will end. All of the trends reveal a complete rejection of femininity. The feminist's motivation has been to act like men to gain material power and influence and to act independently in sex like men do. To achieve these abnormal objectives has made women deny their very natures. The provision, protection, regulation, and honor that civilized societies usually have given to women as women have been sacrificed to individuals selfish to achieve "equality" as one group of feminists understands equality. Women thereby give up the husband and father's protection of them from other unprincipled men.

Women by Nature Have Reason to Be the Gatekeepers

While women do not bear the whole blame for permissive and indiscriminate sex, biologically, women's different sexual nature enables them to be the chief gatekeeper in sexual relations. This has usually been seen as desirable and even necessary for women because of the potentially greater, direct responsibility if there is conception and birth of a child. Maryina Farnham, Marie Robinson, George Gilder, and others point out the double standard results, because in the past, most women held a more long-term view of sex and chose not to follow the promiscuous sex route of many men.[39]

Men are motivated more by the sight of the sexual and then initiate interest and affection. Women are motivated more by caring communication and touch. A woman's desire for and ability to bear children motivates her to want the man to maintain an abiding relationship to help care for any child born. If the woman gives the man recognition as father, she gives him a sense of self-esteem. Most women find a sense of fulfillment in having a baby, and they need the man's help. Women therefore must be the chief barrier in preventing indiscriminate sex and promoting stable families. Hence, because of long-term concerns, women bear the most responsibility and reap the most harm from casual sex.

Many men are willing to use a woman, and they will default their responsibility to help, if the woman permits. Men are also willing for a woman to initiate sex, since she saves them from the risk of rejection. But in accepting the woman's initiative and promiscuity, the man loses his feeling of importance as husband and father in the long run.

The Women's Rights Movement towards Sexual Freedom Reached Its Climax in the 1960s

The educated elite in America have gone through several attitude changes making a rebellion against sexual morals more viable. This has been affected directly by the emphasis of individualism in men and women.

A definite, progressive promotion of sexual freedom occurred since the dismissing of God and the turning toward mammon by Jefferson. The steps toward immorality and sexual freedom are as follows.

1800 ff.	Secret immorality
1900 ff.	Open-mindedness (influence of Freud, Havelock Ellis, etc.)
1955 ff.	Anything is normal and should be legal (Kinsey ff., H. Hefner)
1990 ff.	Hostility to those who believe anything is wrong

How Sexual Freedom Was Unleashed in the 1960s

The educated elite rebelled against any moral restraint as harmful, as taught by Freudian and humanistic psychology. The women's movement used these teachings as a rationalization for freeing themselves from the responsibilities of motherhood. The feminist movement chose to rebel against their nature and to remove sexual restraints in trying to make women become like men. They rejected the natural, long-term view of sex in favor of a short-term view of sex. They were thereby saying maleness is better. To achieve such freedom, the feminists also had to reject any obligation of a man to protect women from other men. Thus, women cast themselves into promiscuous sex, rejecting any social protection except from the civil government. Since sex involves interpersonal, private relationships, it is very difficult for government to offer safeguards. Only close family supervision and the individual conscience offer protection.

Not surprisingly, the women's movement joined with the homosexual movement politically, since both are a rejection of nature for freedom to yield to fleshly desire. Because these are both acts of anarchy against nature, it is not surprising that the most radical sexual abusers of women end up being their allies and representatives in Congress. Senator Ted Kennedy has sponsored legislation and spoken at feminists' conferences of NOW and other organizations. His abuse of his first wife, Joan, and his involvement with many women in sexual affairs are public knowledge. Senator Brock Adams has been a chief activist in sponsoring feminist legislation, but has been accused of drugging, seducing, and even raping his women associates. Senator Bob Packwood, who resigned from the Senate for his many abuses of the women working for him, has been a chief proponent of feminist legislation. It seems paradoxical that these men are chosen as feminist representatives, but these men find common ground in removing boundaries of protection for women, so they can express their individualistic indulgence.

The proclamation of the death of God, the rejection of Christian morals in favor of pure secular humanism by most universities, and the rejection of God from the schools, along with acceptance of the liberal agenda by the Supreme

Court, enabled youth to feel free to give themselves over to immorality during the youth revolts in the 1960s. This was encouraged by the FDA approval of oral pills for contraception in 1960, which enabled women to avoid the mechanical means and feel they had a high degree of protection against pregnancy. But this method of birth control was expensive and required a doctor's advice, and therefore was useful only to middle class women. "The Pill" was useless to the lower classes. Because it required faithfulness in regularity and timing, there were many failures. It also allowed women the resumption of fertility at will, in theory. Hence, the risk for women was rationalized by the feminists.

The legalizing of abortion in Roe v. Wade in 1974 by the Supreme Court also encouraged women's freedom. The organization of Planned Parenthood was in place and ready to persuade women to leap into promiscuous sex as never before.

Thus, in the 1960s and 1970s, the feminist movement fulfilled this aspect of their plan from the 1848 women's rights declaration. Women removed and burned their bras in the student revolts on campuses, and they demanded coed relations as never before in dorms, and often even in bathrooms, to demonstrate sameness with men. The result has been an explosion in living together out of wedlock and premarital pregnancies. The government and educational institutions talk about birth control and how to use it, so the message is that immorality is okay if you don't contract diseases. Immorality and its consequences continue to increase. Bill Clinton's Surgeon General endorsed the ideas spread by Planned Parenthood and the radical feminists. Most sex education has been more harmful than helpful in that out of wedlock pregnancies and STD diseases increased.

Sexual Pleasure without Men

In this frame of mind promoted by feminists, women are motivated to seduce as many men as possible to prove their superiority. The modern emphasis on beauty, often involving anorexia or bulimia and excesses of makeup, are a result. On the other extreme, women reject sex with men, or seek sex in a solitary way, or in lesbian relationships. Studies of and counseling of women by Dr. Marie Robinson and Dr. Seymore Fisher have demonstrated that respect for male authority and trust in surrender to a husband have produced much deeper and more satisfying sexual experiences.[40]

But women's desire to be free of men has gone about as far as possible. Shere Hite did a study by and for the National Organization for Women in 1976 based on interviews of women biased to feminist persuasions. This ended up strongly inferring that masturbation is equally as satisfying for women as regular sex.[41] The importance of masturbation for sexual satisfaction is being taught by feminists throughout American society today. Joycelyn Elders, as Surgeon General, made statements advocating teaching masturbation and other feminist ideas, which angered the public and led to her removal from office in 1994. She has even written a book on masturbation since leaving office. At present, courses on female masturbation are taught by women in public schools and in colleges and universities. Professor Joanne Marrow of California State University is currently facing a lawsuit for her lecture and slides about nuances of women's genitalia and the use of dildos and masturbation.[42] American society is inundated with such blatantly uninhibited, perverse teaching. These represent the end of the line in anti-maleness and anti-marriage by feminists.

Conception without Men

The idea of the feminists about no need for relationships with men reach also to the idea of having children from sperm banks as single women. In this way, all relationship with a man is removed. But sadly enough to them, the male sperm is still necessary. However, the feminists have pushed the issue of rejection of men as far as they can. John Leo, in his recent article, "Promoting No-Dad Families," points out the number of women having children alone by artificial insemination has reached three thousand per year, and this act is clearly aimed at eliminating the father figure. He said:

> Feminists, some strongly hostile to men, have been prone to portray all procreative issues as principally a female concern. Fathers and fatherhood have virtually dropped out of the literature and the discussion of reproductive matters.[43]

This kind of procreation is presented as a woman's right. There is no question that the demand by feminists for sexual freedom has been achieved. But is this real sexual freedom?

CONCLUSIONS ABOUT FEMINIST PURSUIT OF FREEDOM

This survey of the feminist movement indicates that they have achieved most of their objectives to a limited degree. The idea that women ought to be "like" men in terms of equality has been so well established in most of the American people's minds that it is hard to muster resistance against their extremes. Today, most women work outside the home (approx. 77 percent) according to which study is used, and every job is virtually open to them, including the interviewing of male athletes in the locker room by female reporters. Also, being "alike" tends to make the line between homosexual conduct blurred also. The elimination of the need for males in relationships to promote complete individualism for women, even removing sexual involvement for conception, has brought human thinking near confusion. As George Guilder warned, "We are very close to a small step for man–a giant leap for mankind–over a genetic precipice."[44]

It is not only a genetic leap, it is a leap removing traditional meaningful *social relationships*. But there is no such thing as absolute freedom, except for God and redeemed followers in eternity. Freedom must be limited to the nature of the creatures and the interest of all. The law of "love your neighbor as yourself" still must set the boundaries for freedom. An individual may act with such freedom, that he or she not only harms others, but one's own freedom so that those acts may harm and destroy the person. Have we been led by the lies of the Devil into the city of Pandaemonium for destruction?

Americans are committed to freedom, but many have never thought through its limits. It is important to see that the feminist movement since the 1960s has taken freedom into the realm of licensee. In chapters 16 through 18 the resulting implications of this will be presented and discussed. In the conclusion of this chapter, the direction of free conduct is illustrated in the graphs which are mostly self-explanatory and show the direction freedom has taken us. These graphs show that the thinking of the 1960s was the turning point where the rejection of God and public removal of Him in various ways (e.g., prohibiting prayer in public schools) primarily removed restraint from immoral acts and their consequences.

The graphs omit minor fluctuations giving the long-term trends. There are some significant fluctuations, such as a significant rise in divorces in the two World Wars, but these reduced to the level one would expect from the former trends in a few years, and then the rise in divorce rate continued on the same trend upward.

The following graphs used to illustrate these trends only go through early 1990. One of the reasons is that these graphs had not been corrected for these early years. Many of these show a decline or a leveling off. I believe these are the zig of a zigzag and that the trend will continue in a more radical way than before. But in future chapters, the events after 1993 will be discussed, along with other trends so that they can be understood.

Graphs showing trends of sexual conduct since the 1960s follow:

INCREASE OF DIVORCE FROM 1850 TO 1995

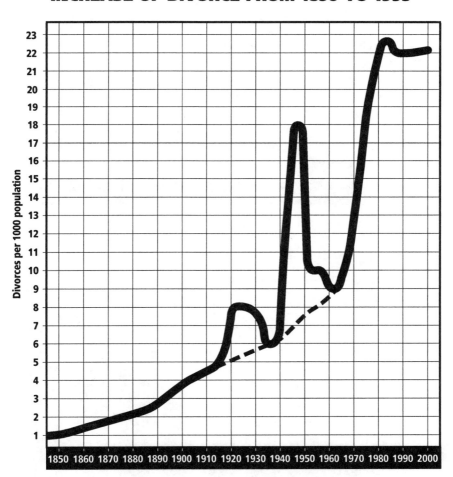

By Carl W. Wilson derived from reports of 95% of the counties before 1960 (as given by Arthur Calhoun, op.cit., p. 261) and from National Center for Health Statistics.

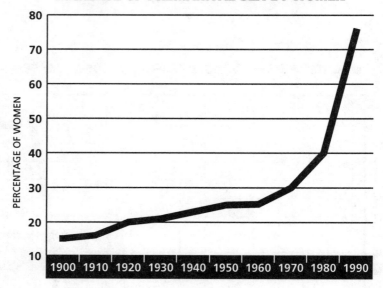

INCREASE OF PREMARITAL SEX BY WOMEN

(figures for males are usually 18% to 20% higher)

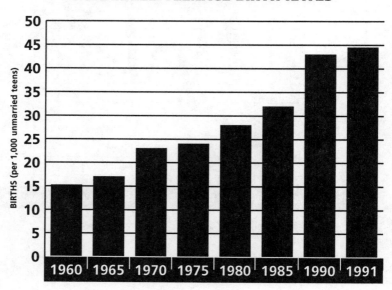

UNMARRIED TEENAGE BIRTH RATES

Source: National Center for Health Statistics

UNMARRIED TEENAGE PREGNANCY

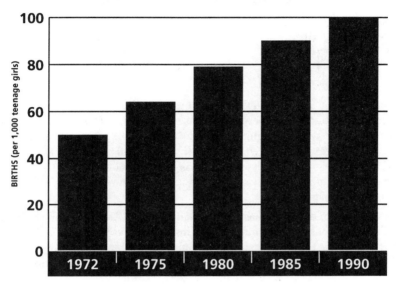

Source: National Center for Health Statistics; Centers for Disease Control; Alan Guttmacher Institute.

ABORTIONS
(per 1,000 teenage girls)

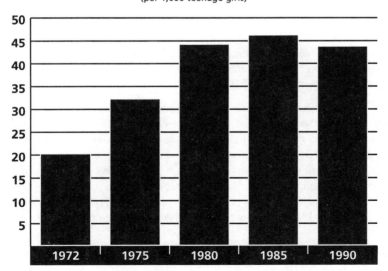

Source: National Center for Health Statistics; Centers for Disease Control; Alan Guttmacher Institute

224   *Sensual or Sexual Revolt in America*

Summary of Information

Premarital sex by women—1960 = 27 percent; 1990 = 77 percent

Percentage of illegitimate births:

	All	White	Black
1960	5.3	2.3	23
1991	29.5	21.8	69.9

Charles Murray argued that the point where there is a loss of control is 25 percent illegitimate births. That percentage was surpassed by blacks about 1963, and is now close for whites. Children born to unmarried women: 1960–1 of 20; 1970–1 of 10; 1995–1 of 4. Illegitimate births are up 400 percent. In numbers per 1,000, this means unmarried teenage girls were: 1960–15.3; 1991–44.8. For teenage mothers, about 90 of black babies are born out of wedlock and 55 percent of white babies.

The number of abortions has risen steadily since 1972. There have been over 35 million abortions since. Summary showing rise of abortions: 1972–.6 million; 1991–1.7 million. The number has been consistently about 1.7 million until the early 1990s. About 40 percent of all teenage pregnancies end in abortion.

Aim of Abolition of Husband and Father for Democratic Individualism

Hard core feminists have now fully embraced the idea that women, children, and men should all be equal in whatever family this may be. Shere Hite who has done books sponsored by the National Organization for Women wrote a recent book claiming to be a *Report on the Family*. She says the old model with a father was detrimental and to be blamed for the growing violence in society. According to her, children do not need training and discipline and should be given freedom to decide for themselves in a democratic family. She has never raised children and gives no documentation, but said,

> What is happening is that finally democracy is catching up with the old hierarchical, father dominated family; the family is being democratized. No one wants to go back to the days before women had (at least in theory) equal rights in the home, before there were laws against the battering of women, before the freedom of men and women to divorce if they could not longer sustain a loving unity. . . . All these things are advances. Signs of the development of a more ethical and 'true' sense of family and human community. And there are many more advances we are on the threshold of achieving. . . .[45]

Women have gained their objective of sexual freedom, and the younger generation is increasingly practicing that freedom. But it is also clear that men are practicing greater freedom, leaving the women with health risks, abortion decisions, and care of illegitimate children. While the majority of women have entered the work force, they are making a little more money, but not much. The children are in many cases receiving inadequate child care and certainly much less love and attention. In chapter 16, these results of this will be evaluated.

Chapter 12

The Steps to Anarchy
and Breakdown of Control

Anarchy Is the Increasing Threat from Other Steps

In Paul's description of decline in the book of Romans, and as observed in Greek and Roman civilizations, the growth of anarchy began shortly after the sexual revolt and became prominent in the last stages of a declining culture.[1] All of the stages of decline contribute to producing anarchy. The surge of anarchy finally leads all other aspects of revolt to the final breakdown of a culture and to judgment of man-against-man and God-against-man.

Rebellion against authority is seldom one instantaneous act. Our rebellious nature knows that rebellion is most effective when there are several successive acts subverting authority before the rebellion can be effective. But man's ingratitude–leading to believing himself wise, to the worshipping of creation, and to perverting the sexual roles–ends in anarchy described by Paul.

> And just as they did not see fit to acknowledge God any longer, God gave them over to a depraved mind, to do those things which are not proper, being filled with all unrighteousness, wickedness, greed, evil; full of envy, murder, strife, deceit, malice; they are gossips, slanderers, haters of God, insolent, arrogant, boastful, inventors of evil, disobedient to parents, without understanding, untrustworthy, unloving, unmerciful . . . (Romans 1:28-31).

Paul then lists the kinds of evil that follow this step of anarchy.

In this chapter of this book, the effort is to review the development of the preliminary anarchistic surges of decline, and then to describe the rejection of God from knowledge in America and the acts of anarchy that have followed. Only enough details are given to highlight the flow of anarchistic development. Anarchy in human relations involves actions against government in the churches, the civil governments, and the family. The preliminary acts of anarchy will be reviewed first, and then the final public rejection of God.

The Definition of *Anarchy* in this Discussion

Anarchy, strictly speaking, means "without a leader" or "social confusion." The dictionary also lists "lawlessness" as a meaning. Here, anarchy is used to describe the point in a society or civilization where people break from lawful government and take it on themselves to do what they think is right. This break results in confusion and a lack of control. Anarchy in one area of human society tends to influence the promotion of anarchy in another.

There are no situations where there is not a leader. In a mob, someone initiates and others follow. As a civilization declines, there are groups that feel they have been treated unjustly, and after many efforts to seek redress, in desperation they act anarchistically. Having tried the intrinsic force of logical persuasion, they turn to the use of extrinsic pressure to make people comply to their wishes. This force may be intimidation, non-violent intrusion, or, finally, violence. When the law seems unjust and the lawful means of change are too slow, it seems right to act anarchistically. Power groups form to do this and in time a point is reached to cause a melt-down of lawful control.

In tracing the rise of anarchy, each person or group holds some aspects of truth which gives them a sense of self-righteous zeal to achieve their cause, and at some point, they feel this truth justifies breaking the law to achieve their ends. These are usually half-truths as bait from the Devil. Examples of truths that motivate this way: all persons should have equal material blessings regardless of race; women should be considered of equal value with men; children should be loved and considered equal in worth to adults.

When a group feels they are superior to others, the process of righteous zeal reaches a point of hate, causing a breakdown into anarchy. This elect group of people eventually see themselves in the place of God as having the right to rectify abuses and enforce equality. When they encounter a situation that stops their advances, they become frustrated, and by self-righteous hate and determination to succeed, they go over the line of obedience to lawful authorities in the state, the church, and the family. The result is increasing confusion, harm to others, and loss of security.

The first acts of anarchy are violations of theological confessional agreements because of lies presented in the intellectual revolt. Having rebelled from God to exalt man, leaders turn to social causes. These causes lead to material concerns for freeing oppressed groups and violations of the law. In America, this involved the racial and women's movement. It also led to concerns giving people sexual freedom, and the lawlessness to achieve these freedoms. When those seeking to achieve these aims find they are failing and have a high level of self-righteous frustration, there is a massive anarchistic outbreak. America is nearing that point. This chapter gathers together the anarchistic tendencies previously mentioned so that growth of anarchy is seen.

THE PRELIMINARY PROGRESSIVE ZIGZAGS, OR SURGES, OF ANARCHY

Intellectual Perversion and Anarchy in the Churches

The intellectual revolt in America in the time of "The Virginia Dynasty" relegated God to insignificance and exalted man and what he could do. This progressively and deceptively led to steps of greater departure from God until today. During this process, there were the three surges, or zigs, of religious anarchy against the established church government. These led to three successive surges of materialism and anarchy against government in regard to the oppressed, women, labor, and youth.

In the intellectual revolt, the major apostasies from the church followed the steps of intellectual revolt. A summary of those apostasies follows:

1) **1810 ff.** Anarchy existed primarily in the Northern and New England states in rejecting the Trinitarian view of God and forming Unitarianism. This rejection of the most important doctrines of Christianity and biblical revelation found its source of ideas in the European enlightenment teaching of deism, based on a uniform working of nature, and on individualism. But God poured out His Spirit in the Second Great Awakening and revivalism, renewing many of the colleges and cities of the North. This movement followed the westward expansion with hundreds of camp meetings sometimes attracting as many as twenty-five thousand people and resulting in the founding of churches by trained laymen wherever the people went. The churches outgrew the spreading of the Unitarian apostasy.

2) **1890 ff.** The anarchy of Darwinian naturalism and biblical higher criticism produced a liberalism or "Modernism" in the old-line denominations which rejected the God of the Bible and viewed the Bible like other literature, rejecting the Deity of Christ. But God raised up the Bible School movement and the fundamentalist movement which circumvented and separated from the disbelief. At this time, the educated elite captured most of the Christian colleges and rejected their commitment to the creeds on which they were founded, expanding the secular view of man into the universities. The educated elite thereby gained increasing control of American thinking after the two World Wars, and the whole culture was impregnated with a scientific naturalism. The new preaching of neoorthodoxy, which rejected the Bible as inspired, deceptively penetrated many of the conservative churches.

3) **1955 ff.** The third most dominant and pervasive apostasy in all of American history was the view of the "Death of God." While few people studied and understood these writers, there was a powerful impact from the media in emphasizing that the American culture no longer took God seriously. By the 60s, the educated elite gained dominance over key departments in most universities, colleges, and theological seminaries and indoctrinated the students to subvert their religious views. From this theological view, the educated elite caused many leaders to consider religion evil. There has since been a hostility to Christianity in the public arena. This has led the American people to the final surge of anarchy leading to judgment.

Preliminary Anarchy in Regard to Race

The First Surge to Anarchy over Slavery

The surge toward anarchy in government began in the middle of the nineteenth century over issues that seem clearly wrong. At root, it had an economic or materialistic cause for the South, but was linked to a sense of self-righteousness by the North. The *Dread Scott v. Sandor* case raised the long simmering issue of black rights. Scott argued when he was carried by his owner from the slave state of Missouri to a free territory, that he should be freed. The Supreme Court disagreed.

William Lloyd Garrison began to publish critical articles in *The Liberator* promoting the liberation of slaves, after reading *Uncle Tom's Cabin* by Harriet Beecher Stowe. He publicly buried a copy of United States Constitution at a Fourth of July service and ignited a spirit of rebellion. This is one of many such incidents at the time. The spirit of lawlessness which had been fermenting came to the surface, generating anarchy under the guise of promoting righteousness. In a few years, it fermented into the terrible Civil War of the South against the North, killing six hundred thousand men and taking a great economic toll on both North and South.

Slavery came to America from Europe. At first, the slaves were of all races and nationalities; also, there were indentured slaves. The black slave trade soon eclipsed the others and found its home mainly in the South on the large plantations. The black slaves became the source of prosperity for the Southern farmer, especially the cotton farmer. The anti-slavery movement had Christian humanistic (Quaker, Mennonite, etc.), as well as secular humanistic roots in Europe, and then in America. There were inconsistencies. While the northern states became free from slavery, they did it by selling their slaves to the South, thereby regaining or increasing their investment. Anti-slavery was tied to materialism, as has already been mentioned in regard to Jefferson, who kept slaves because of his debt. Many Christian slave owners rationalized the New Testament instructions to treat slaves equally as brothers (e.g., Philemon) .

Anti-slavery sentiment grew, and the movement became more organized and political in the middle of the nineteenth century. The slavery issue had been increasingly a matter of concern as materialism grew in the eighteenth century, and by the middle of the nineteenth century, there was impatience in the New England and northern states where Unitarianism and humanism were strong, and slavery had been removed. Not only was there no faith in God in regard to the slave issue, but finally it resulted in a lack of faith that the matter could be resolved through the government.

The issue finally burst into anarchy as a means of bringing resolution. Many in the North wanted to force the South into compliance, and the strong remembrance of states' rights by the southern states pushed the anarchy into a national conflagration and the Civil War. This explosion led to the legal emancipation of slaves. But in the bungled Reconstruction efforts, it produced a segregated society that was another form of humiliation and bondage.

Transition to a Second Time of Anarchy over Race and Class, and Supreme Court Activities

The years from 1865 to 1877, called "The Reconstruction of the South," have been called by Nevins and Commager "an almost unmixed tragedy" and "probably the worst (of governments) that have ever been known in any English speaking land." Lincoln, who would have led a moderate transition, was assassinated. Angry, self-righteous, northern zealots wanted immediate compliance of equality in all ways for the former slaves. They did not understand the time required to produce an orderly and effective transition for all. Whites and blacks suffered, and finally, federal troops were withdrawn from the South with whites regaining governmental control under close federal observation.

In the transition, the Knights of the Ku Klux Klan became a terrible way for whites to redress abuses from bad government by northern carpetbaggers and often uneducated blacks. The segregated society which resulted could have been avoided or minimized with a quicker recovery for all if more sane, moderate policies had been followed.

During the time following the Emancipation and the end of the Civil War, many blacks worked hard and prospered. Many in the South, sometimes with the help of white friends, gained their own farmland. But the segregation system, established firmly in the schools, extended to the restaurants, places of entertainment, public transportation, public meeting places, and even public rest rooms and drinking fountains. This was a constant humiliation for the blacks as a class. The autonomy of the southern governments and the continued advocacy of the constitutionality of "states' rights" left the southern black at a severe disadvantage.

White anarchy contributed and led to new black anarchy. The Knights of the Ku Klux Klan of the Reconstruction Era regained new strength during the 1920s. While the organization professed constitutional and Christian allegiance, it was based on white supremacy and submission primarily to a human hierarchy and militia, and acted anarchistically. Also, it was not uncommon for white men who were not in the Klan to carry out reparations for justice by pistol and whip against blacks who stole or committed a crime against them. The black population endured many tribulations in compliance with the southern governments.

During the Depression years, the black population suffered severely, especially in the South. The black population was fast losing what land it had gained. They lost over four million acres of farm land. The Klan exercised tyranny with occasional lynchings and other intimidation tactics, and there was little justice for blacks in the courts. They were excluded from jury duty, and were not allowed to vote. Education for black youth was inadequate, and unemployment was high.

After the Civil War, the Supreme Court took little aggressive action, favored big business, and gradually intruded on states' rights. The Thirteenth through Fifteenth Amendments (1865-1870) were passed and cleared the way for civil rights legislation. The "due process" and "equal protection" clauses of the Fourteenth Amendment became points of leverage for egalitarian civil rights, welfare distribution, and control. The Supreme Court struck down voting requirements, which aimed at restricting blacks from voting (*Guinn v. United States*, 1915), and ruled the state could not restrict the right of blacks to live in particular neighborhoods (*Buchanan v. Warley; Harmon v. Typer*, 1927). Other cases recognized equal rights such as removing political party restrictions, unlawfulness of segregation of interstate buses (*Morgan v. Virginia*), and removal of restrictions on graduates schools (*Missouri ex. rel. Gaines v. Canada*, 1938; *Sweatt v. Painter; McLauren v. Oklahoma*, 1950).

Emergence of Black Identity and Organization

The black community gradually acted in legal and effective ways. In 1935, black leadership offered a call to a national Negro Congress which called for commitment from the black people, and sought to unify the black organizations, such as the National Association for the Advancement of Colored People, the National Urban Leagues, the International Brotherhood of Sleeping Car Porters, and others. They set goals for the Negro Congress–the right to jobs; relief and security for every family; aid to the farm population; fight against lynching; right of youth to equal opportunity in education; equality for women in pay and work; and opposition to war and fascism, as was being demonstrated in Ethiopia.[2]

In September 1942, at a policy conference of the "March on Washington Movement," conference members expressed their deep concern for the world effort of totalitarian power to oppress blacks. They further committed themselves to definite goals. They said, "Thus our feet are set in the path toward equality–economic, political and social and racial." Records show they clearly delineated their objectives, and they said:

> But our nearer goals include the abolition of discrimination, segregation, and Jim-Crow in the Government, the Army, Navy, Air Corps, U. S. Marine, Coast Guard, Women's Auxiliary Army Corps and the Waves, and defense industries; also they desired the elimination of discrimination in the hotels, restaurants, on public transportation conveyances, in educational, recreational, cultural, and amusement and entertainment places such as theaters, beaches and so forth.[3]

Their methodology of attaining their ends was spelled out. They said:

> Our first job then is actually to organize millions of Negroes, and build them into block systems with captains so that they may be summoned to action overnight and thrown into physical motion.[4]

They pointed to the success of the people of India as a model. Thus, the blacks moved toward promoting success for their cause after the Civil War and into the beginning of the twentieth century.

The first half of the twentieth century was a time when, by organization and planning, the blacks of America rose to the point where they had an identity together, made their condition known, realized their power, and were encouraged by favorable rulings of the Supreme Court. Having attained some strength, they were poised so they could rapidly forward legal changes. But unfortunately, because of long-suffering, these actions prepared them for the next racial surge of anarchy and pressure on the government. In the meantime, the women's movement surged toward anarchy.

The Anarchy against Human Government over Women's Equality

Review of the Growth of Women's Hostility

In the 1830s, slavery and other social issues, such as temperance and prostitution, became a focal point of the women's movement. As mentioned, Frederick Douglass became a major supporter of the women's movement, and the two movements offered support to each other. But by the Women's Rights Congress, a number of women felt their insignificance so deeply they were ready to move beyond the peripheral matters resulting from the materialism to try to rectify the problem of their own self-worth.

As materialism grew, women's roles as housewives and mothers were less meaningful, while the role of men was enlarged. Modern inventions and manufacturing left less to do in the home, especially in the urban cities. In early America, women helped with the farm or in the family business, washed clothes by hand, cooked from scratch, and made soap, clothes, and many other things. With washing machines, clothes bought from the store, pre-packaged foods, gas and electric stoves, and so on, women seemed less important. Moreover, with birth control and the baby bottle, there were less responsibilities for children.

In contrast, man's world became more fantastic, with skyscrapers, trains, automobiles and many other things he produced for larger amounts of money. Therefore, man's worth was magnified and woman's worth was demeaned. This contrast in the value of women and men became accentuated by the progressive growth of male education and materialism. The dissatisfaction of women with their role grew. Moreover, the double standard in sexual pleasure became more unacceptable and painful for women.

Women's Adoption of Lawless Tactics

This weakening of women's roles deepened for over a generation until anarchistic actions were taken. After Elizabeth Cady Stanton focused the women's movement on breaking the bonds of marriage by divorce as the main obstacle to women's equality in the late nineteenth century, the divorce rate soared. It rose five times as fast as the proportion of the married people in the late nineteenth century and the early twentieth century. The matter of divorce for unhappy women was at first solved by going from a state with strict divorce laws to one with slack laws. These avoidings of the law, along with women's conflicts in marriage, gradually lowered the requirements for divorce. Thus, the source of law and order for which the family was the school, began to be subverted by lawless tactics.

Repeated legal efforts of women to gain the right to vote and to get various property rights seemed to progress very slowly. Moreover, the women's movement became more organized and widely influential, but saw little significant progress. In frustration, the women's movement began to break the law. Susan B. Anthony led women to violate the voting laws by registering. Women labor leaders began to demonstrate. Emmeline Pankhurst led women on hunger strikes. Emma Goldman, and later Margaret Sanger, promoted contraceptives and abortion. All these women challenged the law, were imprisoned, and punished for illegal actions. Disrespect for the law grew among the feminists.

Efforts for Matriarchy Asserted in the Home

Finally, after the suffrage amendment passed, the idea of women as equal with men was disseminated everywhere, and women were given more educational opportunities. A woman's main enemy, according to the feminists, was still the husband in the home. After suffrage, many women asserted a sense of dominance over men in the home and increasingly had fewer children. While access to most jobs opened up legally, women were still mainly homebound in marriage. Psychologists found conflict and efforts at female dominance in the home, and that with this women were sexually "frigid." Moreover, this seemed to be causing gender rejection or homosexuality among sons. Women's unhappiness led to a social reaction through psychology in calling women back to submission.

Even after two world wars when opportunities opened in every kind of job in manufacturing production because of the absence of men, many women still felt imprisoned in the home. One of the major problems of the women's movement was many women did not look on marriage as the feminists did. Most women did not desire independence from their husbands, but enjoyed marriage and so did not join in the feelings of male hostility. Earlier, Henry Blackwell, who willingly signed a paper giving up male leadership privileges to marry Lucy Stone (who kept her own name and separate domicile), said, "I believe nineteen women out of twenty would be unhappy with a husband who, like myself, would repudiate supremacy."[5]

So the gaining of the right to vote did not yield the feminist's objectives. There seemed to be the need for some other bold initiatives. This led to their last surge for freedom in more anarchistic terms from about 1955 ff. and is producing women's power groups today.

Surge of Anarchy for Blacks, Women, and Youth after Second World War

After the Second World War, the United States recovered from the Great Depression, and some of the most amazing material progress ever seen occurred. This explosion in prosperity and materialism again created a great contrast between those who had and those who had not. Many blacks served in the military services and gained new government privileges for education under the GI Bill. The issues of equality and freedom again came to the fore in American life.

The prosperity and opportunities of whites in America made the lack of opportunity for the black people even more evident to the educated leaders. When the contrast worsened, with the poverty of the poor seeming darker and the wealth of the rich seeming brighter, the demand for change screamed out. Segregation laws seemed clearly wrong. In the 1950s, the movement for the rights of black people exploded. The social agenda of the educated elite for government help to the poor was promoted by the media and stirred up the anger of the black community to violate the segregation laws.

Anarchy by the Homosexual Lobby

Homosexuality is a practice that had been little known. But toward the end of the nineteenth century it surfaced in the medical journals and laws against it were beginning to occur. In the twentieth century after the women were given the right to vote and momism became more evident, so did the problem. After the middle of the century more books and studies about it seemed to appear. After the time of the death of God theologies, talk about homosexuality became more public as deviant and a sickness.

With the sexual rebellion in the sixties, there came an open belligerency by homosexuals to their social rejection. Following the "coming out" of homosexuals after the Stonewall incident in 1968, they were brazenly breaking the laws of many states and began to try by every means to change their status in society. Eric Pollard, who organized the Washington DC chapter of ACT-UP, a prominent homosexual group, admitted in the homosexual newspaper, *The Washington Blade*, that the group had studied Hitler's *Mein Kamph* and other sources to learn subversive tactics.

They infiltrated and organized a small group of homosexuals in the American Psychiatric Association, deflected a scientific presentation on the topic by forcibly taking over the microphone in a scientific presentation on the subject by Irving Bieber, accused the APA of waging war of extermination against gays, and then persuaded the committee on Nomenclature to say homosexual behavior was not a sign of disorder. The gay lobby, financed by and outside group, took a poll by a mass mailing to the APA members. They claimed a majority of the respondents voted for this, and used this to pressure a change in the definition. In fact only one third of the members returned the vote and later a survey showed that sixty nine percent disagreed. But this change was released to the media and used later to pressure the American Psychological Association to accept this, and still later these two were used to promote a change of the much larger National Association of Social Workers. In none of these organizations was the decision made to reclassify by an objective study of the knowledgeable scientific authorities, and most existing scientific evidence at the time opposed the change. Thus by unlawful means the public media was turned to their acceptance[6]. More details of their deceptive activities are given in chapter 18.

THE WARREN COURT SETS AN EXAMPLE OF ANARCHY TO FORWARD THE EDUCATED ELITE'S EQUAL RIGHTS AGENDA

The Context of the Warren Court's Reasoning

Following the "Death of God" theology, circa 1960, man's reliance on his own wisdom led to a surge of anarchy. Until the time Earl Warren became the Chief Justice of the Supreme Court, the rulings by the Supreme Court made most decisions for racial justice in agreement with laws of the Constitution and of Congress. The Warren court was dominated by liberal activists of the educated elite who seized the broad powers of interpretation begun in limited form by Chief Justice John Marshall much earlier. But, in a unique way, those on the Warren court felt a calling to expand the court's authority to what they thought was right rather than what agreed with the intent of the framers of the law.

Warren held the principal leadership as Chief Justice from 1953 to 1969, but others on the court contributed in his effort. Later, the main engineer of the social revolution became William J. Brennan, Jr. In fact, Brennan renounced as arrogant the idea of trying to understand the meaning of the original framers of the Constitution; actually, as Robert Bork argued, for men to give their own new meaning to law rather than what was intended by the lawmakers, is really the arrogant and lawless position.[7] This change by the court angered many and caused a loss of faith in the court and the government as arbitrary and lawless.

There was some logic to the court's actions. Clearly, the early national and state laws accepted slavery, and after emancipation, the nation adjusted by producing segregation with its humiliating subjugation of blacks as a lower class. Moreover, the women's movement led to recognizing the lesser privileges accorded them. The first efforts at civil rights seemed slow, if not stymied, until the Supreme Court took a stance.

In the light of the dominance of Darwinian thought at the time, the educated elite believed in an evolving society which man must help along. Those on the Warren court saw it not only as their right, but their obligation to progressively promote equality for all. Warren was a graduate of the liberal law school at Berkeley. He was a doer, rather than a law researcher, having twice been governor of California, and he would have been the Republican nominee for president had not Eisenhower been chosen. Eisenhower gave Warren the job as Chief Justice in deference to superseding him in the Republican party.

The Feeling of Correctness Was Encouraged by Scientific Naturalism

The new, naturalistic humanism dominated modern thought after the 1960s with the leaders believing that enlightened men must take charge and socially engineer things. Having been unable to outlaw biblical and traditionally historic morals, which they deemed unscientific, through the legislative branches of government, the educated elite managed to place people with their perspective into power in the Supreme Court and on other lower federal courts. In this position, they became a new legislative arm in American government. Instead of interpreting the Constitution and the laws, the Supreme Court and the lower courts soon became makers of the law by their personal private opinions. Thus, in a subtle way, the justice system shifted from a basis of common law to case law and to an abandonment of set standards except their own thinking.

The judges of the Warren Court became an authoritative oligarchy acting above the President and the legislative bodies of Congress. Moreover, from their modern educated perspective, it was not important what the framers of the Constitution thought. They essentially saw themselves as the lawmakers over and for the people with the right and obligation to override the elected officials. Robert Bork commented:

> What is worrisome is that so many of the Court's increased number of declarations of unconstitutionality are not even plausibly related to the actual constitution. This means that we are increasingly governed not by law or elected representatives but by an un-elected, unrepresentative, unaccountable committee of lawyers applying no

will but their own. Moreover, in departing from the meaning of the constitution's principles, it has invariably legislated an item on the modern liberal agenda, never an item on the conservative agenda.[8]

Bork concurred with Bickel in saying of the Warren Court:

> They engaged in civil disobedience, a disobedience arguably more dangerous, because more insidious and hence more damaging to democratic institutions, than the civil disobedience of the streets.... There are heavy costs for the legal system, heavy costs for our liberty to govern ourselves, when the Court decides it is the instrument of the general will and the keeper of the national conscience. Then there is no law; there are only the moral imperatives and self-righteousness of the hour.[9]

The Court's Anarchy Influenced Others to Anarchy

By the justices having placed their own opinions above the meaning of the laws of America's forefathers, they had encouraged a sense of anarchy in others. The disadvantaged felt a right to rebel, and the majority of voting people felt a loss of respect for their rights through the law-making bodies. This feeling of the court's new power was reflected in the fact that demonstrations by the public groups shifted from the capital to the front of the judicial building. It had become the new center of government.

These actions of the court encouraged anarchy from 1954 and following, especially in the 1960s. A spirit of anarchy was released first in regard to rights of the black people in the civil rights movement, then in regard to women and sex, and in regard to the economy in the name of capitalism. In these last years of this century, judges have even overturned the decision of juries, and FBI illegal actions such as in Waco and Ruby Ridge have helped foment militia groups.

This affect on the law was recognized in a case in 1968 when Justice Hugo L. Black, a strong liberal, voiced a dissent and said:

> I deeply fear for our constitutional system of government when life-appointed judges can strike down a law passed by Congress or a State legislature with no more justification than that the judges believe the law is "unreasonable."

The Court's New Legislation Changed Black Separation

No one denied there were social injustices needing change. But the way the change was to be made was a step of anarchy. The social revolution by the initiative of the few men on the court began with the initial decision to break down the door of segregation in the public schools in 1954. The old standards of 'separate but equal' education for blacks and whites (*Plessy v. Ferguson*, 1896) was abolished in *Brown v. Board of Education* and the *Bolling v. Sharpe* cases, which mandated that segregation was inconsistent with the equal protection clause of the Fourteenth Amendment, and that segregation imposed a stigma on blacks.

The court clearly invalidated all state-imposed racial segregation. While in some states this brought quick conformity, in the areas of greatest practice of segregation where it would require large economic costs, there was no evidence of compliance. Because it was an arbitrary decision by the court, even some blacks disregarded it. At Fort Valley State College, Georgia, which was all black, the students protested and refused to integrate.

Blacks Follow Court in Non-Violent Anarchy

A significant change occurred in 1955 when Rosa Parks refused to comply with the segregation law involving seating in the back of the bus in Montgomery, Alabama. The result was a city-wide boycott of the Montgomery transit system. Ninety pastors were jailed for anti-boycott law violations, and for nearly a year, 42,000 blacks walked or shuttled each other to work. It ended with the passage of a Supreme Court ruling that segregated buses were illegal, although in a previous ruling the court had ruled only for interstate bus transportation. Martin Luther King, Jr. soon implemented the use of the nonviolent resistance which had been used successfully by the Congress for Racial Equality. It had been the tool of Mahatma Gandhi in India against British power.

As Joanne Grant said:

The style of the Negro protest movement changed drastically in the 1960s with the large scale use of the technique of non-violent resistance. Other methods of protest were by no means abandoned but a qualitative change took place when the youth shifted the emphasis from the slow process of court suits to direct confrontations.[10]

Violation of laws and ordinances through public protests with marches and sit-ins was a use of anarchistic, extrinsic force, even though it was against long-standing injustice. It led to beatings, deaths, and in the calling out of the National Guard in one case. Mob action and violation of many unjust laws occurred under the black leadership's endorsement of anarchy as encouraged by the educated elite, because the laws had long imposed injustice.

Other Governmental Shifts toward Care for the Oppressed Were Motivated by the Court's Actions

Every major frontier of racial segregation was attacked and new court cases invalidated segregation in restaurants, parking facilities, hotels, and other public buildings. Blacks marched into large churches with the intent to break the existing segregation. Under the impact of the Supreme Court rulings and compliance by the states, the Democratic Congress began to move toward a program of social improvement. The United States Congress passed the Civil Rights Act of 1964 and the Voting Rights Act of 1965. These included not only racial but sexual laws based on gender.

The championing of the underclass and the forcing open of doors by the courts made liberal politicians boldly think they could gain the vote of the new voters. At this time, President Lyndon B. Johnson launched his war on poverty, begun by Kennedy, to help the poor and the oppressed. Many of the social programs were enacted to take public tax dollars from the rich and middle classes and distribute this money to help certain groups. Thus, social programs were expanded and new programs to disperse taxpayer's money were born.

The self-righteous commitment to helping the underprivileged was the popular rage. The precedent set by Franklin Roosevelt under the New Deal to help all the poor and get the whole economy started after the depression had begun again in another less-challenging way which was more acceptable to people of all races in this desperate time.

The door to open-ended spending launched by John F. Kennedy's policy–that deficit spending was permissible and inflation not necessarily evil–became the excuse for allowing deficit expenditures in the budget. Johnson and successive presidents accepted this spending on social programs because of the protests for rights by various groups and the Vietnam War. The results of this elitist governmental ideology of the liberals which gives license to spend according to individual and group need were the public welfare system, food stamps, Medicaid, Social Security, and Medicare for the elderly. The social program based on race was the catalyst leading to changes in gender, parent/child relationships, and generation gaps which grew to unmanageable debt.

Supreme Court's Rejection of God and Denial of Christian Free Expression in Public Education

The boldest and obviously most arbitrary ruling by the Warren court was in the exclusion of religion in the public schools. The secular, anti-religious views which had become generally accepted by the educated elite were also expressed by the Supreme Court (in the cases *Engel v. Vitale,*

Murrary v. Curlett, and *Abington v. Schempp* on June 25, 1962 and June 17, 1963), namely the exclusion of teacher-lead prayer and the teaching of religion in the public schools.

The justices referred to the Jeffersonian phrase "the wall of separation" as an interpretation of the First Amendment. That amendment does not refer to a "wall of separation" and only says, "Congress shall make no law respecting an establishment of religion, or prohibiting the free exercise thereof; or abridging the freedom of speech, or of the press . . . ." The court ruling did in fact violate the amendment itself by deliberately "prohibit[ing] the free exercise" of religion and of "freedom of speech" in the precise area which is most vital for religion, namely the teaching of children to help them integrate truth with life and vocation. Thus, Christians who had built the foundation of America's schools, both elementary and higher educational, were prohibited expression within them.

This moved Christianity into a position where it was no longer recognized as a legitimate voice in the public arena, which was a blow to its prestige. Everyone except Christians now had freedom of speech, and they were expected to pay taxes to subsidize this system. Christians' rights gradually were limited to their churches, and even there the rights to educate children were narrowed. Crosses and religious symbols, such as advent scenes, were prohibited on public civil property. Public prayers, which still continued in Congress, were eliminated from any publicly supported gathering. The court dared not cross over and limit Congress.

Liberal efforts in this direction had been tested before. In 1892, the Supreme Court reviewed hundreds of historical documents and concluded "that this is a religious people . . . a Christian nation." In 1931, Justice George Sutherland reviewed the 1892 decision and reached the same conclusion. There were eighty-seven precedents for allowing Christianity in the public schools and any religious expression by way of accommodation. The First Amendment was, according to the founders, only to exclude a state-controlled religion of any kind. In 1952, Justice William O. Douglas affirmed "we are a religious people and our institutions presuppose a Supreme Being." Previously, a review of many Colonial documents and the same conclusion were quoted by Chief Justice Earl Warren early in his time on the bench. Moreover, he even stated that the nation had Christian origins.

While the court had struggled with religion in the public schools since 1948, in the 1962-1963 decisions, the men on the court ruled in contradiction of what were the facts of the Constitution, of rulings of previous courts, and in contradiction to what Chief Justice Earl Warren had said. He stated from his research that the United States was founded as a Christian nation.[11] They shut out the Christian voice and view which is the only contrary view to secular humanism. This decision was therefore the height of intolerance and bigotry for the men on the court. Moreover, they gave no pretense to any precedents to their ruling, which indicates its arbitrariness. In these decisions, and from that point on, the men on the court took the law into their own hands and imposed it on the people, contrary to the consent of the governed. Nothing could have been more contrary to the spirit and purpose of the people of the thirteen colonies who voluntarily came together to form the government of the United States.

Thus, the shift in the tide of intellectual views in the late 1950s to a position against the inclusion of God in American public life was voiced in these 1960s rulings against prayer and religion. It was a radical, arbitrary, and arrogant shift, and forwarded the liberal agenda. Most of the American people knew little specifically about the history of the past and the implications were not fully realized immediately. But the public was shocked, and the biased liberal news media applauded these rulings as in keeping with the Constitution.

FINAL SURGE OF ANARCHY IN THE INTELLECTUAL REVOLT WHICH LED UP TO THE TURN IN 1960s

Shift of Curriculum from Learning to Promoting Humanism

When the secular humanistic view gained dominance in the universities and acknowledgment of God was excluded by the Supreme Court, an immediate change in the churches and their institutions occurred. James Davidson Hunter pointed out that the conservative Protestant churches remained committed to the doctrines of the Bible until the 1960s. He said:

> By the 1960s, conservative Protestants had not altered their views appreciably. . . . This is seen, for example, in a survey conducted in 1963 where church members overwhelmingly affirmed the complete authenticity of the biblical miracles—that "Miracles actually happened just as the Bible says they did." They also maintained absolute certainty in the deity of Christ, His virgin birth, His actual return to earth, and a life after death.[12]

This view was held by the people in the churches in spite of the avalanche of naturalistic teaching infiltrating the public educational system and the old-line denominational liberal literature.

While the infiltration of naturalism into public education progressed in the early 1900s, it exploded after the end of World War II. In the rapid expansion of the universities, the curriculum gave way to Messianic concepts of the educated elite to establish an ideal individualistic humanism. The idea of building a wonderful materialistic world, where all would be provided for and happy, dominated the ideas of the professors who taught. Darwin's evolutionary concepts prevailed. Marxism and social democracy gained ascendancy. Existentialist philosophy became popular. Asian religions, African studies, women's studies, environmental studies, and a number of easy courses took over, and even old-line liberalism became conservative. The lies that damn spread everywhere. Professors dared not differ with the approved naturalistic views of the universities or they would be intimidated and possibly lose their jobs. Thus, true freedom of expression stopped. To even hold the idea there was intelligent design for the world without mentioning God, which even Darwin at times taught, was considered a violation of law.

Domination of Schools by Secular Humanism

Previously in chapter nine (cf p 165) on the Intellectual Revolt it was shown that with the turn of the nation to building of a multitude of universities and the taking over of the religious schools by the secular humanists, unbelieving teachers dominated higher education and within a generation changed the views of college students so that a majority no longer believed in God and were committed to the agenda of the liberal elite.[13] This was interpreted as a clear warning to Christian leaders that the position of Christians was one where there was little tolerance of Christian views and a radical change in the nation from what it previously had been. Thus the whole view of allowing freedom of speech for all ideas including those of Christianity, which since the founding of the nation had prevailed, was about to change.[14] Thus the legal position of openness to Christianity was secretly subverted and a new position was taken toward God, which had hither too been illegal, had triumphed and was made new law by the Supreme Court.

These secular views filtered down from the universities into the primary and secondary public schools and to the producers of textbooks. In 1983, Paul C. Vitz, professor of psychology at New York University, did a government-funded study of many of the standard textbooks for elementary and high schools and concluded, "Religion, traditional family values, and conservative political and economic positions have been reliably excluded from children's textbooks." History, sociology, science, and other studies are presented purely from a humanistic point of view. This had systematically been going on for many years. Misconceptions and fear of the laws as rendered by the court led many principals, teachers, and school boards to prohibit ideas which were later seen as clearly legal.

OUTBREAK OF YOUTH ANARCHY COACHED BY INTELLECTUALS

By the 1960s, except for those in the so-called para-church groups on the campuses, the prevailing view among students was God was not important. A change was imperative in the government and the schools to remove the past. The Students for a Democratic Society–a small, organized, neo-Marxist group, many of them wealthy, disillusioned, upper or middle class youth–stirred up the multitude of students who were uneasy about race, sex, Vietnam, and the like. They had been taught by the educated elite, and some of the most radical students turned from democratic Socialism to Communism. Anarchy broke out against the educational system itself, but also against all tradition, and the student movement with its flower children defied not only any sexual or language restraints (four-letter words were in), but also all laws. Illegal drug use was advocated.

Students not only rebelled, they took over in some institutions and the administrations cowardly gave in to their requests and, to the far left, had faculty who motivated them. At Harvard, the faculty voted 248 to 149 not to criticize the violent seizure of the administration building. At Stanford, militants pelted Vice President Hubert Humphrey with urine and excrement, and the students were forgiven. At Dartmouth, radical students drove Alabama's Governor George Wallace off the campus by rocking and pounding on his car, and no punishment was offered. President John Sloan Dickey was so intimidated, he conceded to phasing out the ROTC, and when a courageous dean resisted, he was pushed down a flight of stairs. Yet, twenty-two Dartmouth professors defended the students as "sincere, dedicated, and thoughtful young people." At Cornell, the Afro-American Society enforced its demands literally at rifle point, seizing Barton Hall. College President James Perkins melted in fear and called the revolt a "constructive force." These are only a few of the many student revolts across America. Even in some Christian colleges, like Wheaton in Illinois, there were student demonstrations and demands that went unpunished. Student revolt raged until the shootings at Kent State University.

Anarchy in Business for Selfish Materialism
While there have always been thefts and underhanded dealings in business, a study of the way business has been handled reveals growth in the

loss of trust. The first real material anarchy and loss of confidence in the business community and the government in financial dealings occurred at the first Great Depression. Trust diminished on a national scale and became widespread, causing the depression under Van Buren in 1837. The explosion of business greed produced dishonesty in businesses and in the government in finances. The conflict over "pet banks," the controversy over forming another national bank, excessive issues of notes by poorly regulated banks, the scarcity of gold and silver, and the uncertainty over paper money, as well as widespread speculation in business dealings, led to loss of confidence. The source of depression was speculative dealing and questions about the value of currency and checks.

The second major period of anarchy in business came as greed exploded again with ruthless efforts to form large trusts and monopolies in business after the Civil War. Under President Grant, corruption multiplied in business and in government. Disastrous fires in Chicago and Boston (1871-1872) put strains on big businesses in these key centers. There were high interest rates and significant banking house failures (e.g., Jay Cooke & Company). With all this there were the corruption scandals such as the "Credit Mobilizer" and the "Salary Grab" by Congress to get more money. The depression was triggered by the hoarding of gold by a group of prominent businessmen who persuaded Grant to stop the Federal flow of gold to the banks. Many problems over currency, labor demands, accusations against business, and problems over tariffs continued much after the crisis of the panic and depression in 1873. Unfairness to labor, and unlawful corruption motivated by greed that created fears, were the principle causes of crisis triggered.

The third surge of anarchy in materialism came after the victory of the First World War. As business prospered in the North during the Civil War and laid ground for prosperity following it, so did the World War launch much industrial development. But the productive capacity of the nation was greater than it could consume, and the small number of rich were making much more money from the farms and the factories than the ordinary worker. Moreover, they were hoarding and not spending it. The high tariffs and the war debts to the United States affected the foreign markets. This was so serious, President Hoover had to suspend payments to business at times. Private and government debt grew during the war to well over $100 billion. Mortgage loans and installment buying were instituted by businesses. Before the Great Depression, there was a massive transfer of assets to American lenders.

Also, trust companies, which were rare before 1850, began to proliferate after the Civil War. These companies practiced without adequate regulations and allowed monopolistic tendencies by the influential rich. While laws were passed, the courts liberalized these anti-trust limitations, and clearer laws came in after the Great Depression and partly because of it. The greed of the small wealthy class restricted the re-distribution of wealth and goods which caused the Great Depression. This anarchy of business occurred in the usurious rates of farm loans, the monopolistic violations of laws, and the misuse of the banks.

America is now in the final critical period of materialistic anarchy. As previous wars launched industry in growth and production, so too was there a great leap forward in American industry during and following the Second World War. In reviewing the growth of materialism since the Second World War, the general population, businesses, and government have moved progressively into greater debt to allow more consumer spending to avoid the limitations of the Great Depression. Greed pushed capitalism into the insistence of progress in expanding the economy. This mistaken abuse of capitalism reduced American savings to a minimum, and credit increased to the point where the American economy became a superficial prosperity. Since the depression, the orderly lay-away plan of credit has given way to buying on credit with little or no assets to pay for the goods if there were to be a major financial collapse. The government has itself promised the people much for less in a great Ponzi game of entitlement benefits.

Business interests have gone through great buy-out sprees using "junk bonds." Those investors doing the buy-outs then sell off the assets piece-by-piece and make huge amounts of money. Fraud and conviction of the most prominent businessmen—such as Solomon of the famed Solomon Brothers; Boskey in stock fraud; and Michael Milikan, who was the main creator of "junk bonds"—are but a few. The scams of the savings and loan businesses and many others are preparing the way for a future depression. Agribusiness giant Archer-Daniels-Midland has been fined $100 million for rigging markets, and Microsoft has been under a million-dollar-a-day fine from the Justice Department for monopolistic dealings. The company World Com Incorporated, having assets of only $169 million, bought out MCI Communications with assets of $37 billion by realigning stock assets in a tricky mega-merger that is contrary to the goal of the Telecommunications Act of 1996. There are many other questionable acts.

EFFORTS OF CHRISTIANS TO COUNTERACT
THESE TRENDS TOWARD ANARCHY

Early Efforts to Influence the Colleges

The takeover by the educated elite with their disbelief in the public arena and the exclusion of the Christian voice by mostly illegal measures led to significant reaction by Christians to institute change. The churches' reaction was slow at first but accelerated after the secular triumph of the 1960s.

The churches realized secularized education in colleges was destroying the faith of the students. The lies that damn were in contradiction to the Christian faith. Interdenominational groups were organized to evangelize and give mutual encouragement, and to some degree, counteract teaching of humanism. Youth for Christ, a cooperative, fundamentalist, city-wide rally of youth on Saturday nights, began in the 1940s and, later in the 1960s, shifted toward a high school campus student group, Student Life. Young Life, a ministry forming social clubs for high school youth to win them to Christ, began in Texas and spread nation-wide. InterVarsity Christian Fellowship began in 1936 and spread nationwide. Each campus group functioned like a Plymouth Brethren local church that was serviced by visiting staff who were college graduates.

A high school version of Campus Crusade for Christ, later called Student Venture, was started in the 1960s. Campus Crusade for Christ was founded to evangelize and train college students in 1951, and using these students to lead the local groups, spread to many colleges. The evangelical ministries were joined by many denominational ministries that combined the likeness of these and added emphases of their own. Others, such as the military ministry called the Navigators, started on campuses, as did Worldwide Discipleship. The groups on campus were a place where Christian views could be discussed and people of Christian values could gather and have fun. But liberal church groups also organized on campuses and helped the educated elite with a contrary view. The old-line denominational groups became centers of liberal theological teachings and undermined the churches' views.

By the 1960s, there were representatives of these various groups on most colleges and university campuses. The problem was that conservative groups lacked intellectual ability to confront the educated elite, nor was there time available in a demanding academic setting. Jim Williams started Probe Ministries, out of Dallas, who took groups of Christian professors on campuses to speak in various classes and to debate the secular view from a Christian perspective. I started Worldwide Discipleship with limited Fellowship of Christian Learning groups to present the Christian perspective and help students grow in faith. Our efforts were worthy, but were so limited that they were overwhelmed by the view of scientific determinism and the naturalist perspective. These college ministries reached their peak in 1970 after the eruption of student anarchy.

Neo-Evangelical Ministry Focused to Influence Intellectuals

About 1950, some Christian leaders decided there were obvious weaknesses in the fundamentalist movement. Not only was fundamentalism disengaged from human concerns about social problems, but some leaders felt it focused mostly on the Bible, theology, and eternal life, and failed to speak to the intellectual community of American universities. Fuller Theological Seminary, founded in 1947 in Pasadena, California, was the central focus. Other schools across the nation took the same direction: Trinity Evangelical Divinity School in Chicago; Gordon Conwell in Boston; Dallas Theological Seminary, and others. Billy Graham, who had become a national figure, joined this group led by Dr. Harold Ockenga, Charles E. Fuller, and others.

James D. Hunter made this incisive analysis:

> The irony in the Evangelical case is that the emphasis placed upon gaining intellectual credibility for the Evangelical position (from the late 1940s to the present) may ultimately have the unintended consequence of undermining the Evangelical position. What began as an enterprise to defend orthodoxy openly and with intellectual integrity may result in the weakening or even the demise of orthodoxy as it has been defined for the better part of this century.[15]

What George M. Marsden missed as the main flaw of the Neo-Evangelic effort in his book, *Reforming Fundamentalism,* was many Neo-Evangelicals blurred the line between revealed truth and human learning and insight to gain respect.[16] One of the great driving desires of some leaders at Fuller Theological Seminary where I was in attendance, and elsewhere, was to make evangelical Christianity acceptable to the secular educated elite. They wanted to be published by distinguished, liberal publishing houses, and to be read and listened to by the prominent colleges and universities. Since the secular worldview is opposed to the Christian view, that point gradually weakened some Evangelical schools, especially Fuller.

Ironically, Fuller Seminary offered a doctoral degree in psychology before it offered one in theology. It prided itself in seeing God's revelation in secular disciplines along with the Bible, and eventually gave up the uniqueness of the Bible's revelation, while claiming it had not changed. Admittedly inspiration of Scripture is hard to define, and John 3:16 is not equal to an Old Testament genealogy, but does that undermine accepting the Bible for what it says? In time, Fuller's faculty and board, in anarchy against its original signed standards, gave up and changed these standards. While intellectual respect is admirable, to court the world's favor rather than win the world and bring it to commitment to Christ was a demonic trick.

Not only has commitment to biblical beliefs changed, but the curriculum has been altered to fit the world's thinking. For example, almost all Christian colleges now have a degree in business, management, and other subjects relating to material gain, while subjects relating to Christian vocations and service have been disappearing. While this change is not wrong in itself, it does reflect the influence of a world no longer focusing on Heaven and God, but on mammon and the present.

Evangelical Responses to Change the Anarchistic Trend

The anarchistic movement of students in the universities met with a "Jesus Movement" of Christian students, with thousands of students joining in a rebellion against the materialistic culture by accepting Christ. These were promoted by the para-church and Christian groups, and found expression in new movements and new churches rejecting traditional ways that appealed to youth.

Also, beginning in the 1970s when the student revolts were manifested, evangelical leaders acted to restore the teaching of truth and bypass the perverse educational system. They built new Christian colleges, and Christian primary and secondary schools that would feed into these institutions. Between 1971 and 1978, Evangelical primary and secondary schools increased by 47 percent, with a 95 percent increase in student enrollment. By 1985, there were almost eighteen thousand such schools with an estimated 2.5 million students, while there was a drop in enrollment at secular elementary and high schools in the nation. This change started the Christian home-schooling movement which now engages more than a million students. This latter effort is an object of attack by the liberal elite in the courts on grounds of lack of parental qualifications to teach. But, in most of the cases, home-schooled children do well when tested in standardized methods.

During those years, Christian publishers grew, and Christian radio and television programs became prominent. The Christian bookstores and publishers organized into the Christian Book Association, which is committed to the Bible. Along with these came distribution companies, such as Spring Arbor Christian Book Distributors, and there developed a formidable network to produce and distribute Christian material. The many Christian radio stations, along with the development of the Christian television networks, such as Christian Broadcasting Association and Trinity Broadcasting Association, have disseminated truth and ideas to many American homes. New evangelical mission boards were established and the National Association of Evangelicals began to bring Christians together.

Political Efforts to Stop the Elite's Agenda Politically

The Christian churches understood that the government agenda had shifted to the liberal agenda, and soon the government would become anti-Christian. Jerry Falwell, a formidable fundamentalist leader with a national television program, launched the Moral Majority. His effort to bring together people across America sought to restore Christian morals by passing laws to enforce them. After expending millions of dollars and much effort, the Moral Majority failed to accomplish its mission.

Pat Robertson, also a formidable leader of Christians with his impressive, widespread television forum, The Christian Broadcasting Network, made a continuing effort to change the political scene. He launched the Christian Coalition with a more knowledgeable understanding of politics. Robertson, the son of a United States congressman and well-acquainted with politics, ran for president and lost. But he has continued to build a grassroots voter constituency under the leadership of Ralph Reed, director of the Christian Coalition. Reed was a major factor in leading the Coalition to help Republicans regain the House and Senate in 1994. The Coalition is often derogatorily labeled "the conservative right," but has well-respected, long-range goals. The success of the Republican Congress forced Clinton to reduce the national debt and act to reduce welfare and crime. These efforts by evangelicals put the process of moral decay into a temporary zag. But there is evidence that a new zig to collapse the morals is coming.

Continued Loss of the Christian View to Social Secular Humanism

Continued Decline of Seminaries and Colleges

James Davidson Hunter demonstrated that the Christian colleges (nine liberal arts colleges) and graduate schools (nine of the most prominent seminaries) have moved slowly, but certainly, further away from Christian doctrines and purposes.[17] He evaluated the significant fundamental doctrines and found gradual departure in each. His observation was that Christians know what they ought to believe, but have difficulty committing to these beliefs in modern culture. Included in this is the doctrine of the uniqueness of Christ and the fact there is no forgiveness and acceptance from God except through Him. As Hunter observed, this is the stumbling block of Christian belief. By the departure from conviction of the main concept of Christ's deity and His death to take away sin, the controls of the Spirit fell to anarchy in many churches.

Para-Church Student Groups Yield to the Agenda of the Secular

Many of the evangelical student organizations gradually have given in to the secular agenda. Young Life began to use Paul Jewett to train their staff in the summer. Jewett, more than any person, influenced Fuller Seminary away from its original confession of faith and weakened the view of Scripture, claiming Paul's teaching about women was non-binding since it fit a dead culture. Such movements as Inter-Varsity Christian Fellowship are still prominent on secular campuses, but are giving way to secular, politically correct ideas, like gender words for God in hymns. This was demonstrated at the Urbana 1993 World Missions Conference, and has been expressed by the president.

The departure of InterVarsity from biblical Christianity manifested in two other instances in which spokesmen denied the reliability of the Bible as revelation from God. In a four-page promotion of academic books, InterVarsity Press editor Rodney Clapp interviewed Richard Middleton and Brian Walsh about their book, *Truth is Stranger Than it Used to Be*. In the book, they deplore propositionalist theology where God gave words to men, and they dispute that Christian culture has truth, making Christianity unique. InterVarsity also sponsored a theology conference of post-liberal speakers with Wheaton College in which criticism focused on traditional, evangelical orthodoxy and its view of the Bible as the propositional Word of God. These examples could extend to other evangelical organizations which stand against secular humanism on the campuses, but are now conceding to them. Campus Crusade for Christ and the Navigators have been accused of yielding in some places on the gender issue, but the leaders still seem evangelical in their beliefs and committed to male leadership. But both are so large and diverse, there is less centralized control. More importantly, they are evangelistic in orientation and have not been able to counteract the agenda of the intellectual elite.

Yielding of the Churches to Humanism

Many of the people in the churches who profess belief in Christ have a strong individualistic orientation. Many in the Neo-Evangelical movement turned back to human concerns psychologically and socially, and gradually made doctrine that is centered in God secondary. The ministry of many churches has been diverted toward therapy and meeting mankind's needs. For that reason, people gravitate to the "mega-churches" which offer a better variety of services for meeting their family's needs. But in such large churches, accountability is greatly reduced and little is known in most mega-churches about people's personal lives. Hence, those needs don't find their fulfillment primarily in commitment to God and His glory, but more in how to solve human relationships and find human fulfillment.

Some churches are filled with "how-to" and "counseling" solutions. Seminars on many areas of life tell how to correct problems of a family, parent, children, and so forth. Much evangelism is aimed more at getting the sinner into the church and in finding Christ for his individualistic needs. Because Jesus' ministry was primarily through house churches, there was more relational accountability.

The result is the church suffers humiliation by prominent preachers and leaders of charities who have been immoral, such as Jim Baker and Jimmy Swaggart. In 1995, The New Era Foundation, led by Jack Bennett, was exposed as a giant Ponzi scheme, and over two hundred of the most reputable Christian organizations were taken. The leaders of the United Way and other community charities have also failed morally. The evangelical book publishers and their Christian Booksellers Convention have been criticized as promoting the superficial and moneymakers, more than promoting the truth of God. The National Association for Evangelicals, the largest cooperative organization for evangelical churches has capitulated so that it receives 60 percent of its overseas budget from the federal government. In so doing, it is engaged in programs of government relief and family planning, distributing condoms, the use of IUDs, and the promotion of sterilization by tubal ligation, even though these are not devised by NAE leaders.[18] Such actions blur the lines of truth.

More importantly, Gallup and Barna surveys show a large number of the American people are professed believers, but they also find that only a small percentage of these live any differently from society. Large numbers of people who are doctrinally discerning have a loose attachment to a particular church—they attend but are not members, and cannot be counted on to aid God, His glory, and His church. Thus, the failure of church members to live for Christ grows daily, and churches often seem to have a shallow following because its members seldom attend church; the numbers of church attendees who practice divorce and sexual immorality are only slightly less than that of the general public.

Moreover, the clergy in many places are trying to accommodate the people by using more of the music of the world, reducing the time and way of worship, and even often dressing very casually. The mega-churches have as their aim reaching the people who are not Christians, but the result is that very often the people in these churches have less accountability; this is reflected in their lifestyles.

The following graph shows the membership and attendance in church.

NUMBER OF PEOPLE IN THE AMERICAN CHURCHES

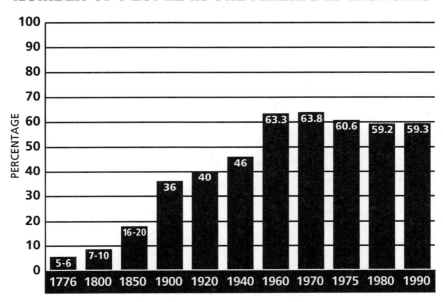

William J. Bennett, commenting on the trend, said that it is not religion or profession of faith, but commitment to God that is significant. More people are going to church and membership is proportionate with population growth. But only 20–28 percent attend in any given week. Sunday school attendance has declined significantly in recent years. While there may be as many as forty-eight million Christians participating in small groups during the week, Robert Wuthnow has pointed out that these may be an accommodation to our secular culture. Therefore, even in small groups, conformity to the world is seeming to win. He said:

> Indeed, it does not overstate the case to suggest that the small group movement is currently playing a major role in adapting American religion to the main currents of secular culture that have surfaced at the end of the twentieth century. . . . When spirituality has been tamed, it can accommodate the demands of a secular society.[19]

As the above graph shows, since 1990 there is a decline in church membership. but more importantly, an analysis shows that the people do not respect authority or the importance of membership. Church activities are seen as being for their benefit, rather than to glorify God. Accepting vows of commitment to the church are ignored by many as unnecessary, and violation of the laws of God are sometimes not seen as significant. In the Roman Catholic Church the people often express views and practice activiities directly contrary to what the clegy pronounce. Sometimes prominent clergymen who sin continue to be used without repentance or loss of face.

Part II:
An Overview of
the Steps of Decline of America

B. Results of Unbelief in God

Chapter 13
Education and Art

INTRODUCTION

The second section of this book (part 1, chapters 8-12) traced the way the people of the United States succumbed to man's sinful nature, and for over two centuries, have been drawn to follow the path of moral degradation outlined by the Apostle Paul in Romans, chapters 1 and 2. This section defines the present conditions in which Americans find themselves as a result of this moral degradation. It discloses how the educated elite led American thinking to positions that are not working, are outright failing, or have reached conditions beyond which human beings cannot continue to go without accepting views contrary to reasonable physical science, or which will bring devastation to the institutions of family, education, business, and government.

The next five chapters show the results of the liberal efforts to free people from unenlightened ideas about God and His will. These ideas were believed to restrict human beings from a life of prosperity and freedom from religious restrictions inhibiting the pleasures of life. Their proponents felt they were teaching people to recognize their individual rights and equal worth. They saw themselves as releasing people from antiquated "Victorian" or "Puritanical" principles to enjoy life. However, the results of their interpretation of the facts reveal that the vision of the educated elite perverted truth, and by deception, led us to the door of pandemonium rather than freedom. The efforts of the elite to educate people and lead them by democratic socialism to their vision are deluded.

But worse, these elite are unwilling to admit their errors and are now in such positions of power they seemingly can't be dislodged before they blindly produce a melt-down to confusion. Their position of dogmatic intolerance and inflexibility against faith in God or against allowing a fair presentation of the truth of God is important for Christians to understand. Otherwise, Christians will not have the commitment to change the trends. Bold measures must be made to take advantage of this brief window of opportunity.

These chapters indicate what needs to be done to change things. At present, it seems reasonable that steps can be taken to right the world that is turning upside down. But evidence will be given that the real problem is the sinful bias of human nature that has caused the gradual moral degeneration which is now so strong and unrelenting that only by God's grace can it change. The real problem is the lack of will to change before the melt-down to confusion occurs. The present trend is being driven by pride, greed, and hedonistic pleasures.

There is an even more important factor than this trend to consider: The fact that when man withdraws from God and refuses to repent and return to Him, God's supernatural acts of judgment occur. After a certain point, God gives mankind up to his sin. God is not unkind, but His words are irrevocable, and therefore His judgment is inevitable when grace is spurned. The liberal elite will, of course, laugh at this idea. I argue that American leadership is near that point today.

TIME OF TROUBLE BECAUSE OF CONDITIONS IN EDUCATION

Intellectual Perversions Have Led to a Crisis in Knowledge

The bias of the intellectual elite against God has slowly perverted how the American people interpret the facts, so that the meaning does not fit the theories taught by the elite. And there is now such a vast amount of data that cannot be integrated that life seems an unrelated hodgepodge. The more data accumulated, the more mysterious and complex things are and the more the facts go contrary to the foundational theories. This chapter summarizes the development of these views of a world run by natural laws without God, and the dilemma faced by the people who accept these views. [1]

The growth of the secular worldview first developed in Europe, and since most early Americans were from there, the views traveled to the young United States. Thus, American thinking was affected by those views, and in time made significant contributions to them. By the end of the eighteenth century, there was a new humanism giving great confidence in man's mental ability. This led into scientific exploration to bring forth knowledge of what appeared to be a regular working of all of nature. This thinking developed a linear sense of certainty with the work of Isaac Newton. This impressive new knowledge about the world was organized and disseminated in an encyclopedic way by 1800, influencing many men to feel the human mind could soon encompass and control how the world worked. The educated elite believed man could understand and explain all of nature.

Man's natural bias of pride, which excludes God, was motivated at this time in history because religious clergy sought to dominate Europe selfishly and caused bitter wars that left suffering and abuse. Human reason could easily blame religion and discredit the conflicting ideas of God.

Under these biases, the formation of the earth was interpreted to have evolved to its present condition by a regular, slow process of nature, including wind and water erosion, fire, and gravity. This view of the world was known as determinism, or uniformitarianism. Also, the accepted view of the way man knows truth, or epistemology, was defined to fit such a view and limited to certain categories of thought natural to man. Thus, the biblical idea of a worldwide flood and of the earth being divided into continents to confuse the tongues of the earth's people were rejected; judgments by earthquakes, the collapse of the walls of Jericho, the parting of the Red Sea and the Jordan River, and other miracles, were ignored or explained away. Intellectuals who accepted this deterministic view of the earth had to reinterpret theology.

Also, to explain the biological forms and fit them into such a uniformity, Darwin presented his theory of the development of biological life by chance and by competition for the survival of the fittest. He wanted to exclude all mystery, miracle, design, and any control by a higher power. The educated elite developed social theories based on these scientific theories, such as Fascism, Communism, and Western social democracies. The elite thought by expanding naturalistic understanding, they could lead the common people in building a glorious new world. By the time of the Virginia Dynasty in America, enlightenment science accepted this view of nature excluding cataclysms, chaos, mystery, or miracles.

This view developed into a reductionist-materialistic view of nature. As Heinz R. Pagels described:

> The entire vast universe from its beginning in time to its ultimate end, from its smallest quantum particles to the largest galaxies, is subject to rules—the natural laws—comprehensible by the human mind."[2]

This idea excluded God and any need for Him.

Twentieth Century Science Disclosed Perversion in Scientific Determinism

But unexpected things occurred that now expose this reductionist-materialistic view as untrue. Science in the twentieth century developed new instruments and made new findings which showed the deterministic and uniformitarian views of the late eighteenth and nineteenth centuries to be incorrect. The fact is now clear that there are many things about nature man cannot fit into a logical and uniform closed understanding. Geology cannot be explained simply by uniform daily changes of wind, rain, and fire. Biological life does not fit the evolutionary hypothesis of gradual development, and the history of religion is not one of how man created myths about God to meet his own needs. That view of the world is now turning out to be a myth perpetrated by fundamental and dogmatic uniformitarian scientists and by journalists, most of whom were indoctrinated in these views in colleges and universities.

This does not invalidate much of the knowledge that has been accumulated and used to build our civilization. But it does call into question the theories devised to say man is equal or superior to God, and that he knows all about the universe so that he can exclude God. Such views are at least suspect, and at most arrogant and untrue.

The Crisis in Science

In the early twentieth century, the quantum theory and the recognition of indeterminacy in the atomic world were the first evidence that the physical world is a mystery. The discovery of quantum activity and the "standard theory" of quarks has been attended by finding other mysterious particles of the atom and exploding the deterministic view of matter. The general and special theories of relativity gave a different view of gravity and the operation of the universe from a purely linear view. The "Big Bang," or origin of the present galaxies and stars, the discovery of black holes and that more than 90 percent is made up of dark matter that is unknown, confront the astronomer with singularities and a multitude of mysteries about formation of matter and the forces that work in it.

The understanding of the history of the earth is now not that of nineteenth century, uniformitarian geology, but of movements of the continents with great tectonic plates that in the past by great force have divided, collided, and are now forming the continents and mountains. The repeated changing of the magnetic poles of the earth are mysterious, and the changing of the temperatures and climate of the earth are now known to be much shorter than the old uniform Ice Ages. There is the discovery of the multitudes of large asteroids, and the existence of millions of comets that have and may collide with the earth. Also, there is the discovery of aberrant weather-disturbing forces, such as El Nino, which are mysteries little recognized until this century. All these things have affected life. Also, man and the human mind have been shown to be far more complex and mysterious than thought. Following are a few quotations revealing the place of modern physical knowledge:

Timothy Ferris, an award-winning emeritus professor of physics at the University of California-Berkley, has recently commented on the present view of the universe. He said:

> The standard [or "big bang"] cosmological model is broad and pliant. It comprises an arena within which many narrower theories and experimental programs thrive and compete. It is incomplete: Scientists don't yet know exactly how old the universe is, how big it is, how rapidly it expands, or how much matter is in it. [As the English astronomer royal, Martin Rees, remarks, "It's embarrassing that 90 percent of the universe is unaccounted for."] Nor is it clear how the matter we do see organized itself into stars and galaxies. There are a great many things we do not know. But it is quite possible that all these issues will be resolved, one way or another, without leaving the basic precepts of the standard model behind.[3]

In this statement, the idea of an established theory about the universe is clearly in limbo. Even the "standard theory" he says is "incomplete, broad and pliant" and has views within that "compete." He mentions many things that "we don't know." Even this view that he called the "standard model," which was mathematically demonstrated by Stephen Hawking, was questioned and rejected by Hawking himself because it was based on a mystery that the theory of relativity could not explain.[4] All of this led to the development of the theory of probabilities about nature which is often called "the theory of Chaos," which of course is the opposite of determinism and uniformitarianism.

Dr. Barry Parker in his book, *Chaos in the Cosmos: The Stunning Complexity of the Universe*, traces how in the last thirty years the deterministic view of the cosmos, which was used to rule out biblical truths, has gradually become evident and is gaining ascendancy. Dr. Parker is a professor of physics and astronomy at Idaho State University. In his epilogue, he writes:

> This brings us to the end of our journey into the world of chaos. We have seen that chaos theory is one of the most exciting developments in science in the last 30 years, a development that has completely changed the way we look at nature. At one time the universe was considered to be deterministic. With enough machinery, we could follow every particle in the universe throughout its entire history. We could, in effect, calculate everything that is to be known about the universe. But this assumed that nature was linear, satisfying linear equations that were easy to solve, and scientists gradually began to realize this wasn't the case. Much, if not most, of nature is nonlinear, and with this nonlinearity comes unpredictability and chaos. Yet strangely, the chaos is not completely random; it has structure. Chaotic trajectories don't wander randomly through space; they are confined.[5]

Also, Darwin's view of the origin of the species, and the views of Huckley about the origins of life by accident, have yielded to changes of view that bear no resemblance to the original ideas. The original evolutionary ideas of Darwin were exciting because they gave a natural basis to fit the ideas of man's view of progress which dominated the age. But these ideas were soon found faulty and without a workable mechanism for forming new characteristics that could be transmitted. So in the twentieth century, a neo-Darwinistic view was formed which taught that genetic mutations could furnish such characteristics over long periods of time. But it is now clear, after many years of intensive research, there is not a known instance where mutations have produced a new species. No mechanism for evolution has been observed and tested.

Moreover, the science of molecular biology, which emerged since the middle of the twentieth century, has now shown that the workings of molecular systems are so irreducibly complex that the possibility of gradual emergence by chance through survival of the fittest or of any other known mechanism is so improbable that it requires more than a miracle. Michael J. Behe, Associate Professor of Biochemistry at Lehigh University, in his best-selling book, *Darwin's Black Box*, demonstrates the impossibility of the Darwinian evolutionary theory in regard to the development of several important bodily functions such as blood clotting. Behe said:

> Science has made enormous progress in understanding how the chemistry of life works, but the elegance and complexity of biological systems at the molecular level has paralyzed science's attempt to explain their origins. There has been virtually no attempt to account for the origin of specific, complex bimolecular systems, much less any progress. Many scientists have gamely asserted that explanations are already in hand, or will be sooner or later, but no support for such assertions can be found in the professional science literature. More importantly, there are compelling reasons–based on the structure of the systems themselves–to think that a Darwinian explanation of the mechanisms of life will forever prove elusive.[6]

In addition, many of the more competent scholars admit the science of paleontology has not produced the multitudes of fossil intermediaries to support the descent of the various species as Darwin promised they would. This result in paleontology would be precisely what one would expect from the observations Behe and others have made. The present theories argue for evolution of one form to another without evidence. While there are admittedly many unique and strange forms of fossil life, there is no evidence they evolved.[7]

In spite of these facts, evolution is the prevailing view of life forms dogmatically taught by the educated elite.

The same is true about the origin of life. There is no scientific evidence produced anywhere showing how life originated. New theories and ideas have been produced throughout this century, and none have been conclusive. In fact, the New Information theory and the New Revised Second Law of Thermodynamics, which say that information as well as energy is always lost, not gained, are contrary to the idea of evolution to greater size and complexity. Scientists have used powerful computers to figure the probabilities of life originating from nothing, and also of the evolution from simple to complex organisms, and these reveal improbabilities so large that these could occur only by the miracles which they reject.

Hence, many leading scientists (e.g., Fred Hoyle, Francis Crick) have abandoned the arguments for the view that life must have began by chance on earth, and have accepted the view that it began elsewhere in the universe and migrated to the earth. That is why there is the desperate, and yet futile, attempt to find other planets with life on them. At present, the evidence of life elsewhere, contrary to the impression given to the public, is zero. The view life began elsewhere avoids the lack of evidence on earth, and is simply another argument.[8]

Repeatedly, application of the theory of evolution to anthropological studies has hindered or clouded the picture. Some of the greatest secular scientists have found this to be the case. W. Schmidt, the greatest of the German comparative religionists, found it to be so in the field of comparative religion.[9] William Foxwell Albright, perhaps the greatest archeologist of Palestine, rejected the evolutionary interpretation of the history of religion by Julius Wellhausen's *Introduction to the History of Israel* as fraud and contrary to what was discovered in Palestine.[10] J. D. Unwin found that those who sought to interpret sex in culture by the evolutionary view completely missed the sexual roles in social development in eighty-six societies.[11] Many times, modern medicine found that to apply things true to other animals to man was deviant.

Society believed the computer revolution would help resolve the complexity problem.[12] Thus far, it seems to have given more validation to the Chaos Theory and produced more data for more complexity and more mystery about the universe. Evidence seems to point away from uniformitarianism or determinism in all areas, and therefore against the reductionist-materialistic view. There is no reason modern man cannot accept the biblical view of God and His working in the world.

Perverse Social Theories Have Led to the Door of Pandemonium

With distorted theories centered around scientific determinism that excluded God, scientific progress focused on man and his individual, material well-being. This distorted view of the world was a shaky foundation on which to build society. The educated elite's ideas about man's social and political evolution led many intellectuals today far astray into errors and failures. Modern Fascism and Communism were built on the same enlightenment ideas that prevailed in the West, and all claimed to lead to a new utopia. The enlightened elite in America portend the same dangers if there is no moral regeneration.

No person has reviewed the modern history and modern thinking of the Western World in more depth or with more respect than Paul Johnson in his book, *Modern Times.*[13] In a more recent book, *Intellectuals*, he begins his study by saying:

Over the past two hundred years the influence of intellectuals has grown steadily. Indeed, the rise of the secular intellectual has been a key factor in shaping the modern world. . . . With the decline of clerical power in the eighteenth century, a new kind of mentor emerged to fill the vacuum and capture the ear of society. The secular intellectual might be deist, skeptic or atheist, but he was just as ready as any pontiff or presbyter to tell mankind how to conduct its affairs. He proclaimed from the start, a special devotion to the interests of humanity and an evangelical duty to advance them by his teaching. He brought to this self-appointed task a far more radical approach than his clerical predecessors. He felt himself bound by no corpus of revealed religion . . . . For the first time in human history, and with growing confidence and audacity, men arose to assert that they could diagnose the ills of society and cure them with their own unaided intellects; more, that they could devise formulae whereby not merely the structure of society but the fundamental habits of human beings could be transformed for the better. Unlike their sacerdotal predecessors, they were not servants and interpreters of the gods but substitutes.[14]

He points out that at the end of World War II, "there was a shift of emphasis from utopianism to hedonism" among these intellectuals. This shift began slowly and gained speed and momentum.[15]

Johnson questions what conclusions should be drawn from his review of the thinking of a dozen of the most prominent and influential intellectuals, and in his final chapter on "The Flight of Reason" writes:

I think I detect today a certain public skepticism when intellectuals stand up to preach to us, a growing tendency among ordinary people to dispute the right of academics, writers and philosophers, eminent though they may be, to tell us how to behave and conduct our affairs. The belief seems to be spreading that intellectuals are no wiser as mentors, or worthier as exemplars, than the witch doctors or priests of old. *I share that skepticism* . . . . But I would go further. One of the principal lessons of our tragic century, which has seen so many millions of innocent lives sacrificed in schemes to improve the lot of humanity, is—*beware intellectuals* . . . . That is what makes them, en masse, so dangerous, for it enables them to create climates of opinion and prevailing orthodoxies, which themselves often generate irrational and destructive courses of action. Above all, we must at all times remember what intellectuals habitually forget: that people matter more than concepts and must come first. The worst of all despotisms is the heartless tyranny of ideas.[16] (italics added)

Johnson points out the efforts of the educated elite, to control the masses for social good, squandered more money and killed more people than in any previous era of history:

> The state had proved itself an insatiable spender, and unrivaled waster. Indeed, in the twentieth century it had also proved itself the great killer of all time. By the 1980s, state action had been responsible for the violent or unnatural deaths of over 100 million people, more perhaps than it had hitherto succeeded in destroying during the whole of human history up to 1900.[17]

Thomas Sowell, who has taught at Cornell, UCLA, Amherst, and now is a senior fellow at the Hoover Institution of Stanford University, devoted his book, *The Vision of the Anointed*, to exposing the failures of the social ventures of the educated elite (i.e., The Anointed). Moreover, he shows their complete unwillingness to accept their failures. He reviews their many methods of denial, avoidance, and rationalization. He says, "Today, despite free speech and the mass media, the prevailing social vision is dangerously close to sealing itself off from any discordant feedback from reality." He gives several significant examples of the opposite effects of the programs of these "anointed" elite. He shows the declared purpose of the war on poverty, begun by President Kennedy and legislated by President Johnson, was to reduce dependency and break the cycle of poverty.

Sowell points out that before the legislation was introduced in 1962, the number of people below the official poverty line had already declined by about half from what it had been in 1950. As a result of the legislation, the number of dependent people grew, and there were more people below the official poverty level by 1992. "All government-provided in-kind benefits (welfare, public housing assistance, food stamps) increased about eight-fold from 1965 to 1969 and more than twenty-fold by 1974." This meant not only a rise in dollar terms, in real terms, but also in the percentage of the nation's gross national product going from 8 percent in 1960 to 16 percent by 1974.

Sowell shows when the elite launched the sex education program, teenage pregnancies had been declining for more than a decade since 1957. Venereal disease was also declining. Afterwards, premarital sex among teenage girls at every age from 15-19 rose by 1976. The pregnancy rate among 15 to 19 year olds rose from 68 per 1,000 in 1970 to 96 per 1,000 by 1980. The venereal disease rate skyrocketed 350 percent in 15 years. The crusade to spread sex education into the public schools and through other channels spent less than $500,000 in 1965 and expanded its sex education more than five-fold by 1966. By 1968, nearly half of all schools in the country–public and private–taught sex education. The object of sex education to reduce pregnancy and venereal disease was disputed by the statistics.

The program for reducing violent crime is the same. The number of murders in 1960 was less than any of the three previous decades, even though the population was growing. In 1960, the murder rate was half that of 1934. But the elite proposed protecting the rights and rehabilitating the criminal. By 1974, the murder rate had doubled since 1961, and the arrest rate of juveniles for murder more than tripled from 1965 to 1990, even allowing for population increase. Sowell shows all the increasing problems in American society arose out of the years after the educated elite gained control, after the years America reached the "God is Dead" mentality.[18]

The perverted views of the educated elite in physical science that encouraged these abuses in social and political actions have produced such strong individualism and grouping together for ethnic-, gender-, and now age-conflict that each group is deconstructing present knowledge. This anger and uncertainty is moving us toward the post-modern mind with culture wars brewing on the horizon. Reaction by the public to these views since 1992 led to improvement.

Review of Resultant Conditions in American Education

The visions and motives of Horace Mann and his followers stated each child was born with an individual right to an education which the state must ensure so each person could earn a good living. The Freudian psychology was added saying sex and human desires should be freely expressed. Moreover, the rights of women included having roles like those traditionally held by men in sexual relations; in addition, homosexual conduct was now considered normal, and equality for homosexuals taught in the public forum. Any individual was to be guaranteed such rights by the state.

This view of education, which now dominates is in strong contrast to the early beliefs that education was to teach children to read the Bible and develop into good citizens. Then, every individual was responsible for loving God and his neighbor as himself. But the right and autonomy of selfish individualism has now reached the point of political correctness, and everyone is threatened under law to conform.

In the process, the individual's rights are based on building material prosperity. The school curriculums have diversified with an emphasis on meeting individual and unique group needs with man at the center. All creatures are seen as individual creatures of random chance. Man's psychological and social needs, and his specific individual or group identity have become most important. By the 1950s, there were diversified courses for man to build and control a better world with everybody equal in the same way. Better instruments for research and storage of information dominated the scene, accumulating a great mass of facts. Knowledge of the world became the passion, and knowledge of God or the metaphysical was spurned.

Pursuit of Massive Accumulation of Facts

American schools have amassed such a huge amount of facts about the world with new technology that the various people of the world come here for education. But it is education centered on the individual and materialism with few standards, ideals, or morals. The individual is beset by a multiplicity of specialized facts with no meaningful coordination, and with new information and choices coming into view every day. Moreover, according to the intellectual elite, there is no one to whom the individual conscience is accountable—no God, parents, church, or community—only the state. There are no morals or absolutes; everything is said to be in evolutionary change. But everyone is assured the change will lead to better people and a better world. However, the teaching is only the fittest will survive, and they, as an individual, are the most important

Alvin Toffler, the great analyst of change, described the situation:

Never before have so many people in so many countries, even educated and supposedly sophisticated people, been so intellectually helpless, drowning, as it were in a maelstrom of conflicting, confusing and cacophonous ideas. Colliding visions rock our mental universe . . . . Every day brings some new fad, scientific finding, religion, movement or manifesto. Nature worship, ESP, holistic medicine, sociobiology, anarchism, structuralism, neo-Marxism, the new physics. Eastern mysticism, technophilia, technophobia, and a thousand other currents and crosscurrents sweep across the screen of consciousness, each with its scientific priesthood or ten minute guru.[19]

Commitment to Blind Evolutionary Destiny

Toffler and others so believe in evolution and the goodness of man that they see a new civilization emerging that must be encouraged, although they do not know a transcendent designer and have no idea of the ultimate outcome. Many are New Age naturalists who believe in an intelligent power of nature, but such a view does not fit in with the strict empirical knowledge from nature. But they are excited about—and encourage—giving in to nature and following natural urges. All we know that has worked and given stability to our lives is being swept away by this flood of change. As Toffler said, "This new civilization brings with it new family styles, changed ways of working, loving and living; new economy; new political conflicts; and beyond all this an altered consciousness as well."[20]

Edmund Fuller, the chief book critic for *The Wall Street Journal*, gave a college commencement address in 1982 in which he warned the graduating students against "junkyard minds." He said:

It is possible that you may become the best informed generation in history–quantitatively. It is also possible that you could turn out to be one of the worst-educated generations qualitatively. . . . You could be cursed with knowledge without wisdom, with data without direction.

Education to a Time of Troubles?

The educated elite assure us through social democracy we will arrive at the best and most harmonious world. But they feel they must guide and compel us to follow them, like the communists did the proletariat. But their lives are not models of happiness and harmony. They are sure that blind chance evolution will guide us, but there is no evidence it is a meaningful evolution. What evidence is there they will have success, when the communists who trusted in the same evolutionary process failed? The result of Communism was arrogant, brutal leaders who built plush Dacas, private recreational facilities and a health system, and the people suffered. Yet, the Soviet Union had more oil, minerals, forests and the like, than any country in the world. In their greed, they bled the soil of the farmers and used the funds to build worldwide political and military power and personal possessions, rather than build the infrastructures of the Soviet Union. By the time Nikita Khrushchev became the Soviet leader in the 1960s, the problems were so evident that change was demanded and removal of restraint begun. By 1985, when Gorbachev came to power, the society was too far gone to recover.

When the American educated elite finally gained control of the educational system in the 1960s, society began to disintegrate. The nihilistic and existential philosophies, which led to the rejection of God from the school system, led a time of change for the schools. Man's intellectual aims were denuded of most meaning except to promote man.

The Scholastic Aptitude Test (SAT) scores progressively declined from an overall average of 975 in 1960 to 890 in 1980. The National Assessment of Education Progress, or NAEF, showed science achievement scores dropped from an overall average of 305 in 1970 to 183 in 1982. In 1983, the National Commission on Excellence in Education alarmingly reported in "A Nation at Risk" that American students showed poor performance on international tests, and declining scores on the standard tests and in knowledge of critical subjects. The Commission warned of a rising tide of mediocrity threatening the future of the country.

Efforts to Solve the Education Crisis

In the years that followed, there was an effort to improve test scores. Schools began to train students on how to take the tests, giving them exposure to the type of tests so they were more familiar with them. There was a trend back to basics. But, by the 1991 National Assessment of Educational Progress, there was no continued improvement. In 1992, the International Education Survey revealed the United States ranked ninth in science and tenth in math to other countries.

The tests devised by the educated elite led to bewildering obstacles. For example, in helping the underclass, Murray's report in *The Bell Curve* confronted them with a problem. The tests they developed to find and educate the most qualified proved an obstacle to their preference by affirmative action in education. So the response of some of the educated elite was to add a handicap of a certain number of points to all blacks so they would qualify. This purpose contradicts the reasons why the educated elite created the tests.

It is acknowledged by all that the public school systems are in deep trouble. While there cannot be a review of all aspects of the crisis in education in America today in this book, it is suggested that the reader review William Bennett's discussions and the references he gave[21] in *The Devaluing of America* and chapter 4 in the *Index of Leading Cultural Indicators*. He has served as chairman of the National Endowment for the Humanities, Secretary of Education, and Director of the Office of National Drug Control Policy.

The solution to the troubles of education has been to allocate more and more money. However, Bennett relates:

> The fundamental problem with American education today is not lack of money; we do not underspend, we underproduce. A review of some 150 studies shows no correlation between spending and educational achievement. The American people have been remarkably generous in their contributions to our schools. In 1990 we spent $414 billion on education, roughly $140 billion more than national defense . . . . In absolute terms we spend more on education than any other nation in the world. And expenditures keep climbing. In 1950, we spent (in 1989 dollars) $1,333 per student. In 1989, we spent $4,931. As John Silber, the president of Boston University, has written, "It is troubling that this nearly fourfold increase in real spending has brought no improvement. It is scandalous that it has not prevented substantial decline."[22]

Better, more enlightened management seems to be the answer. Public school systems have been turned over to prominent universities to run or to commercial businesses to manage, but with little positive results. In talking with educators who are leaders in universities in various parts of the country, there is tremendous reorganization going on in many departments, partly to improve but also because of a money crunch.

In the inner-city schools, there is little discipline, rising crime, and assaults against teachers. Lack of interest continues to grow. There is a loss of teachers from these schools, and the forecast of a shortage of 220,000 teachers per year for the next decade. Many studies with new answers from prominent educators were published in *U.S. News & World Report*, "The Perfect School: Reforms to Revolutionize American Education."[23] Their answers have all been tried with only moderate improvement. A prominent option today is to give vouchers to parents and let them choose the school for their child. The competition, as in private enterprise, is believed to force the bad schools out and improve the ones left. But again, this assumes the main problems are money and management. If private, religious schools were also an option, there might be more improvement. Strangely, one of the largest groups sending their children to private schools are public educators.

Intolerant Claim for Tolerance by the Elite

When Allan Bloom, educator and philosopher of social thought at the University of Chicago, published *The Closing of the American Mind*, it shook the educational establishment and became a bestseller. He charged that higher education had failed democracy and impoverished the souls of today's students because it "unwittingly played host to vulgarized Continental ideas of nihilism and despair, or relativism disguised as tolerance."[24] The educated elite have, in the name of tolerance, shut out all views suggesting moral absolutes to protect their own bigoted view of relativism.

One book which seems to explain the dilemma brought up by Bloom is Ron Nash's *The Closing of the American Heart*. Nash taught for twenty-five years in public universities, and for twenty years was chairman of the Philosophy of Religion Department at Western Kentucky University. He argues that no teacher or author is neutral and all present their own point of view. The educated elite have shut out the religion of the transcendent God from which moral absolutes or virtues must be derived. Every person operates from his heart of beliefs, and his objectives, purposes, and conduct come from here. Nash reveals the problem is one important step deeper than Bloom.[25]

William J. Bennett concludes:

> After nine years of public service and heading up three government offices, I have come to the conclusion that the issues surrounding the culture and our values are the most important factors in the improvement of life . . . . The ideas of the mind and the "habits of the heart" [in de Tocquevilles's phrase] determine almost all important issues.[26]

This is the heart of the matter in the culture-wars confronting America. The issue is the intolerance by the secular, educated elite and their determination that biblical religion be excluded from public schools and the public arena. The agenda of the elite is founded on the absolute wisdom of man to control and be free from moral restraints of God. They, like all elites of the past who have destroyed civilization, are seeking to free man from God and His control of their lives in His world. Yet, that is the most basic cause of the failure of the public education system. Education in America has arrived near the end of the line, and society is poised for tremendous conflict in their determination to continue against the people who now want a change back to faith in God and moral absolutes.

William J. Bennett has said, "Unfortunately many of today's intellectuals have overstepped the bound of common sense and seem to have given up on the disinterested pursuit of truth."[27] Elsewhere he said:

> The American people's sense of things is in most instances right; the liberal elites sense of things is in most instances wrong. Still and all, the elite exercise enormous influence in shaping public policy and the terms of public debate.[28]

He pointed out that the NEA embodies the philosophy of liberalism, is controlled by the elite, and is the largest union in America with 2 million members and a budget of $135 million used for lobbying. He concluded what was needed to improve education was "not exhortation or lectures," but was "more on the order of a demolition squad" and replacing it.[29] He made little headway.

AN INTELLECTUAL CRISIS REVEALED IN THE ARTS

Trend of the Arts Reveals Degrading Mind

The expression of all ideas of the mind is most vivid in its art. H.R. Rookmaaker, professor of the History of Art at the Free University of Amsterdam, in referring to art as the expression of our modern culture said, "Modern art did not just happen. It came as a result of a deep reversal of spiritual values in the age of reason, a movement that in the course of a little more than two centuries changed the world."[30] Art reflects the thoughts of the mind taught by perverted science.

Aleksander Solzenitsyn was awarded, in absencia, the Medal of Honor for Literature of the National Arts Club in New York in February 1993, and his son read his remarks entitled, "The Relentless Cult of Novelty and How it Wrecked the Century." He observed each artist has successively sought to outdo the other in the meaninglessness, the vulgar, the obscene, the ugly, the blasphemous, and the violent, in order to shock and gain attention. He said:

> For several decades now, world literature, music, painting and sculpture have exhibited a stubborn tendency to grow not higher but to the side, not toward the highest achievements of craftsmanship and of the human spirit but toward their disintegration into a frantic and insidious "novelty." ... If we, the creators of art, will obediently submit to this downward slide, if we cease to hold dear the cultural tradition of the foregoing centuries together with the spiritual foundations from which it grew—we will be contributing to a highly dangerous fall of the human spirit on earth, to a degeneration of mankind into some kind of lower state, closer to the animal world.[31]

In modern times, the arts have joined together to communicate in a powerful way. Narrative tells the story in papers and books, poetry expresses the flow of the spirit, song makes aloud the feeling of the heart, design and color in pictures impress the image from one mind to the other, and sculpture encases the story of a person or thing in life-like image. The radio carried the message and song. The motion pictures of modern times gather all the sound, story, and image to communicate it with dynamic impact upon the heart. The Internet and modern compact discs send it all where the individual can choose which communication he wishes. America and the modern world will soon access all that human art can craft in order to communicate in the most dynamic ways imaginable.

I have attempted to show that through the centuries, as the rebellion against God progressed, there has been a slow degrading of the arts. They departed from the spiritual to the rational and meaningful (reflecting the divine mind in man) toward the modern splashes, blobs, and discord. This reflects rebellion against meaningful expression left from the thoughts of the Creator. But the blobs and discord also report the story and feelings of the modern soul.

When the outbreak of secular humanism was expressed in the 1960s, there was a rapid degeneration which inspired strong reactions and which resurged again in the 1980s to continuous acceptance. *Lady Chatterley's Lover* (1959), which was allowed import by the Supreme Court, all but demolished the censorship law in New York and opened the door for other foreign movies. The foreign movie, *I Am Curious (Yellow)* (1968), which would have been previously rejected by the judges, found ready acceptance with its tumbling bodies and explicit sex acts. The reason for its acceptance was it had "some redeeming social value," and this phrase was rapidly applied by liberal judges to other movies. The voluntary censorship of American movies by Hollywood immediately caved in to overt sexual acts and greater violence. Acts performed on a stage as art, even sexual intercourse, were approved "for artistic value" (in a California Federal Court).

In the 1960s, rock music's rebellious, sensual themes dominated the sales of music and the radio. Hard rock with suggestive performances by the stars became the craze around the nation.

By 1969, Senator Everett McKinley Dirksen stated, "The United States is overwhelmed with smut. Like some medieval plague, the mounting flow of obscene books, films, and magazines surrounds us, threatening our national health." Topless bars, night clubs, and eventually full nudity gained acceptance. Slowly, the bounds of propriety and decency crumbled, leaving nothing for suggestion or shame.

New Crisis in American Education in Technological Revolution

Since the 1960s, American education has gone through a new and significant transition in how it views truth in television and the emerging technologies. While the American educational system created this transition, and the people it has educated control it, the new electronic and photographic systems threatened to go completely out of anyone's control. The main reasons it is so dangerous is it aims at the baser desires of human nature, and the owners are greedy to make money.

Neil Postman, in *Amusing Ourselves to Death*, persuasively argues America has entered a new era. Until now, the country has been geared to a literary society born in the sixteenth century. But, television offers new and different ways of communicating, and results in a different way of thinking. Moreover, he argues and I show, the country has passed the point of critical mass, so everyone in America is now dominated by the media. This medium does not control so much by logic as by impressions implanted in the consciousness subtly. It has now gripped the nation, and controls politics and social issues with emotional impact more than facts.[32]

Today, television has a greater power over American thinking than any other media. The growth of the influence in America, especially since the educated elite gained control of the schools and mass media, is as follows:

> 1950 - 4.2 million homes with 2 channels
> 1960 - 45.2 million homes with 4 channels
> 1970 - 59 million homes with 9 channels
> 1980 - 76 million homes with 15 channels
> 1990 - 92 million homes with 30 channels

The total continues to increase in numbers of homes and numbers of channels. The turning point of influence on the masses occurred after the 1960s when the daily TV viewing hours increased dramatically.

AVERAGE DAILY TV VIEWING PER HOUSEHOLD

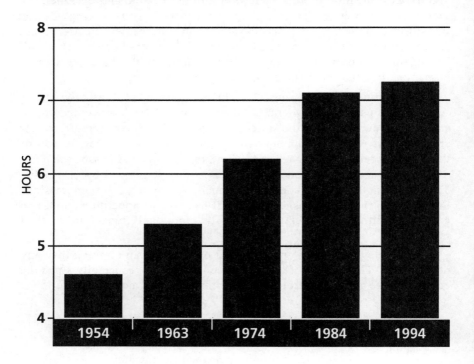

The Extreme Degradation of Visual Arts

Television broadcasts many programs about unusual sex, violence, dysfunctional homes, and conflicts. Sitcoms and comedies make fun of everything from God, religion, marriage, sex, politicians, government, and the home. A British comedy, *Absolutely Fabulous*, portrays two women firing off jokes about masturbation, bulimia, killing in Grozney, and male prostitution, and is being remade in an American version. Even the news focuses almost entirely on violence and sex stories to the point that they are commonplace.

It is for this reason that television can be so lethal. It is the newest, most dynamic form of idolatry where a multiplicity of images are pressed into the mind in fractions of seconds. Michael Medved, a motion picture critic, wrote *Hollywood vs. America: Popular Culture and the War on Traditional Values.*[33] He shows the motion pictures chosen for production by Hollywood are not those that attract people and make money. Hollywood produces the kinds of pictures it does because that media is committed to the liberal agenda of selfish, individual freedom to express sex, language, and power in any way desired. The men who control the industry are at war with the values still held by many Americans. But, they are gradually persuading the children to follow their destructive path. Many American leaders, such as Bob Dole, feel the need to attack these productions because of protest by a majority of Americans. Hollywood stays alive by producing a few good movies the average American likes.

The motion picture industry and music industry are closely linked to television, and T.V. producers are now agreeing to ratings. All entertainment is controlled by a few big companies and produced by a few hundred skilled people. Many of the leaders came out of the 1960s rebellion against tradition and morals. In 1993, Gayle White reviewed the tallies on the Academy Award Best-Picture nominees such as *The Crying Game*, *Scent of a Woman*, *Unforgiven*, and others in an article entitled "Hollywood or Babylon." The ratings were high on the use of the "F-word", other profanity, and various kinds of sex. When there is criticism and public outcry, there is a slight improvement in content, but studies indicate over recent decades the overall trend is increasingly worse in spite of the efforts at ratings guides.

Great controversy has swirled around use of public taxpayers' funds through the National Endowment for the Arts, which sponsored artists who contradict the feelings of the American public. There was so much controversy that John Frohmayer, former chief administrator of the NEA, was forced to resign during the Bush administration, and there have been efforts to terminate funds for this federal extension of grants. The once reputable arts are now on a level with "the crude and lewd."

Federal grants from the endowment have been made for a cross in a glass of urine (Andres Serrano), the image of Christ with a hypodermic needle (Wojnarowicsz), and explicit images of homosexual acts (Robert Mapplethorpe). Of course, there have been legitimate projects of value sponsored, but Americans have been inundated with these perverts as heroes who get rich off their abusive communication.

Drawing, painting, and designing have become almost an expression against the rational: irrational forms of art produced by untrained, uneducated artists are becoming popular. Tinkling, or forms of folk and primitive art, is becoming popular. Charlie Lukas, "The Tin Man" from Pink Lilly, Alabama, uses scrap metal with blow torch welding to create meaningless figures which sell to art collectors. His work is controlled by Judge Mark Kennedy who makes the most profit from his work. There is also art made from twisted roots of trees by Bessie Harvey. And Thornton Dial paints figures reminiscent of pagan face masks and grotesque figures similar to those connected with African witchcraft. Many of these artists are controlled by Bill Arnett, an Atlanta art merchant.

Even the art involved in clothing design has yielded to the new, innovative, and shocking. The change from the traditional has gone so far clothing designers don't know what will appeal. One clothing designer in an interview said his company had given up on the upcoming generation. Jerry Adler in *Newsweek*, "Have We Become a Nation of Slobs?" , said, "Lets just say that the concept of 'proper attire' is hanging by a thread." IBM and many of the biggest corporations are no longer strict and regimented, but "dress down." Even in churches, the pastor may not wear a tie. Young women and men wear almost anything they want. Individual self-expression rules.

The revolution in communications where the computer is linked with TV. and the telephone is now moving into the image communications field. The Internet makes available, upon demand, information in visual, audible, and written form at the choice of the individual. This vast system is only in its infancy. In 1995, the Internet comprised 14,000 networks connecting more than 4 million computers and 30 million people around the world. It is doubling in numbers each year. The information is sponsored by a vast aggregate of organizations and groups: government offices, businesses, non-profit organizations, major universities, and colleges. This is the ultimate concept of communication by art and sound.

The Internet and the computer are the product of modern education for the individual and make up its main tool for the future. It allows easy communication for personal messages and for consumer purchases. Because it may be anonymous and lend itself to fraud and evil as well as good, it is the ultimate expression of individualism. James Dale Davidson and Lord William Rees-Mogg see it as making the individual sovereign in the years ahead, and may therefore threaten all institutions of family, school, business, and state as we know them.[34]

End of the Line for What Is Called "Art"

Already, all kinds of pornography and other forms of art are available on the Internet. The United States Congress is seeking to curb the availability of unsavory information which is free to anyone who wishes to access it. The system can then involve those who access "information" in various ways to encourage further devious conduct. About ten new pornographic entries are discovered each week. Software and screening laws are being studied. This vast access to knowledge will soon extend into every home and become as common as the telephone. This is at present a massive threat to change what Americans believe. But in the last part of this book, I will argue that this may be one way God uses to draw His people to Himself and together. This new revolution has one thing that television did not have: it involves a two-way communication, and a way of choice that is important. But, presently it offers another threat in the hands of the educated elite.

Degrading of Music to a Point of Extreme

Music is an art in deep trouble. Popular music that influences the youth has almost dropped out of art and become militant and sensual. John Leo recently informed us that there are nineteen recording bands with human genitals in their names. *Time* magazine listed a dozen rock bands with at least four hate labels each.[35] Rock has given way to rap singers and MTV. Sister Souljah, who came to the Washington convention for Jessie Jackson's Rainbow Coalition, has a solo album, *360 Degrees of Power*, in which she repeatedly demonized white men, calling them "the weasel." There are two references to cop-killing and an emphasis on black militarism and race war. Ice-T features a rape with a flashlight and a cop-killing, and threatens Korean merchants that their stores will be burned down. Time Warner association sponsored him, 2 Live Crew, Metallica, Snoop Doggy Dog, Nine Inch Nails, and the late Tupac Shakur. Some rap albums advocate rape, murder, and violent abuse of women. Some "artists" have themselves been charged with violent crimes.

Are Arts Expressing an End of Intellectual Rebellion?

Today the arts express hate, lust, rejection, and blasphemy. The modern soul has lost its way from spiritual and aesthetic beauty, and slid to the area of pornography conveying heterosexual, homosexual, and incestuous acts, with masochism, gynechism, and in some cases, bestiality. Extreme violence is a daily fare.

Beverly Sills, the opera star, told a New York audience:

We have laws today that tell us we can't smoke on airplanes, but you can freely sing—if you'll pardon the expression—about the joys of violating a woman's body in monstrous detail on commercial recordings because its a constitutional right. . . . Now, I'm all for artistic freedom—I used to be a performing artist myself—but we as a society are growing dangerously out of touch with our conscience.

Education by the elite has not promoted freedom of speech and learning; it has promoted bondage to lust and evil which our forefathers in America would never have allowed.

CONCLUSION OF THE ROLE OF EDUCATION
IN DECONSTRUCTION OF THOUGHT

The loss of faith in the old liberal views and values, along with the lack of faith in God created by the reductionist materialism and the merging of individuals together in power groups to achieve their ends, have led to what has been called deconstruction of our culture. Walter Truett Anderson has seen three processes in this tremendous conceptual transition. They are: 1. The breakdown of belief systems of all kinds; 2. The birth of a global culture where there is an awareness of the multiplicity of belief systems; 3. A new polarization by conflicts of ideas over critical issues and morals in education.[36] It would appear the unbelieving educated elite are entering the city of Pandaemonium.

Chapter 14
The Economy

INTRODUCTION

The resultant conditions of the visions of the unbelieving, educated elite on the economy and on the egalitarian efforts for the various classes of individuals are intricately linked. Without trusting a benevolent God to provide, the alternative for the unbeliever is to depend on material wealth to furnish freedom for self-esteem, security, health, and pleasure. Thus, the result is for individuals to group together to gain their materialistic and prideful objectives. This chapter will segment economy from the problem of class for examination; the issue of class will be discussed in the next chapter. However, the pursuit of mammon is linked together ideologically with class objectives because of the selfish extremes to which human nature is drawn. The economy and class conditions have approached points of difficulty for which there are no clear solutions apart from either violence or spiritual renewal of faith in God. In chapter 10 the process of economic thought in Western ideas was followed, and it was observed how the trend of thoughts led Americans to act. The trends were not only demonstrated by the statistical changes but through thought trends. In this chapter, the focus is on where this economic thinking has led to, the validity of those ideas, and the options which are in the American future.

CRISIS POINT IN ECONOMIC THINKING

Review of the Trends of Modern Economic Thought

The pursuit of modern economic trends of thought was based on the view that man could understand nature and that there were natural economic principles which, once understood, could be controlled by well-intended men to make mankind sufficient without supernatural help. The invisible hand of nature presented by Adam Smith to control supply and demand to produce necessities, did not work out as he presented them. Too many factors were omitted. Thomas Malthus showed that under a coming population explosion, the survival of the fittest would upset the law of supply and demand. David Ricardo focused on the value of labor as well as products, and he emphasized the struggle of men to survive and to rise to the top of the escalating stairs under population growth.

John Stuart Mill expressed optimism that good men in a democratic government should and would control the supply and distribution of goods according to everyone's need. Alfred Marshall evaluated all the aspects of the economy to seek equilibrium in the economic cycle to help the poor and to emphasize the worth of the consumer as foremost. But in the light of the events of the past and of the ruthless accumulation by tycoons at the end of the nineteenth century, Thorstein Veblen argued that the drive to accumulate wealth for superiority was one of the major factors in the economy, and that past economic theories left out this pride-of-gain that disrupts all other factors.

The devastation of the Great Depression was a major attack on the belief in the ability of man to control the economy. But about that time, John Manard Keynes brilliantly argued that the government must prime the pump to get men back to work so they would have funds to buy goods and to give businesses the ability to produce goods. The flow of money by government pump priming was key. In this situation, he agreed deficit spending and inflation of money was the right thing to do for a brief time. It was this view of economics that allowed the thinking of government leaders since the great depression to expand the budget, which ended up with huge deficit spending as the United States entered the end of the twentieth century. It has been argued that this rationalization was in a major part due to the whole society feeling free from accountability to God because liberal theologians and the media had proclaimed the "Death of God" theologies. After the recovery from the depression, with the Keynesian view of economics, and with the government use of expanding information and ability to analyze the economic factors by computers, there has been *a growing feeling of certainty* that man can keep the economy reasonably under control.

Feeling of Certainty about Knowledge and Control for the Future

Beginning about 1930, the mainstream economic elite believed that they could have an overview of the facts and regulate society. Israel Kirzner said:

> To the standard mainstream view in economics, since about 1930, the view of the world has been one in which the future is essentially known, in which the participants in markets are in effect completely informed about the relative decisions made throughout the market by fellow participants. This is a world of equilibrium, a world in balance, a world in which quantitative economics predictions are entirely feasible.[1]

Ronald Nash, in quoting Kirzner, made the comment, "Such mainstream views led economists to believe that sufficient knowledge about the future made it possible for them to predict successfully the future effects of governmental intervention on the economy."[2]

Adam Smith's vision was very limited and blind to the coming of the full Industrial Revolution, to modern transportation, development of trusts and conglomerates, protective trade unions, government power through bureaucracy and mass communication, modern weapons that promoted gain by war, modern population migrations, and modern technical innovations like the computer. But the economists gradually found that certain indicators could help predict trends, and the Federal Reserve Board helped insert new control elements along with budget controls by Congress and the administration. While there was much more known by the economists, by the 1960s, the impression was of greater certainty than was in fact true.

Discovery of Uncertainty and the Dilemma of the Future of the American Economy

In the 1980s, other new factors began to enter the picture that had been hidden or unaccounted for. In the 1980s, the Austrian School of Economics showed that values may be subjective and changeable, and that this upsets certainty in linear quantitative economic understanding. For example, the absence of one good product may affect the value of others. Also, the value which one person or group may put on something may be much more than what another places on that good. So the cost of goods is to a certain extent in the eye of the decision-maker. They also showed that values are often based on anticipation from cultural and other factors and therefore may greatly vary. To this has been added the many widespread service jobs that add no concrete products. But more importantly, the Austrians showed that the market is a continually changing process, and there never really is such a thing as equilibrium. The Austrian School in effect gave a revolutionary change in viewing the market, much as the wave and particle views of matter did with physics. Ludwig Von Mises, Friedrich Hayek, and Israel Kirzner were some of the Austrian proponents of these ideas which radically changed the way Marxists and many others view the science of economics.

Another major force to change the feeling of security in economics was the collapse of Communism. The Central Committee of the Soviet Union allowed—indeed had fostered—a wealthy, privileged class. The need of the privileged classes to retain power caused depletion of the soil, the closing of trade and important technical information, and the weakening of the infrastructure, so by 1985, there was hardship for the people, a large black market, and declining hope. To bolster the control of the Central Committee, multitudes of people were misused, imprisoned, and widely disappointed. The highly controlled system destroyed productivity and improvement. Moreover, the closed system excluded learning new technology and inventions, causing the Soviet Union to fall behind the West. Recognized in the Khrushchev era, the system was so far gone when Gorbachev tried to open up the society, he could not revive it. For a nation progressive enough to explode atomic bombs, be first to put a man in space, and repeatedly gain control of so many nations of the world, it was a surprise to most people that its economy could collapse so quickly. This completely managed society failed. Along with the collapse, the unexpected drop of the American stock market in October 1987 showed the American people the economists did not have complete control.

But more important still, in the late 1980s, American businesses began to look overseas and expand worldwide. Many companies have had their greatest gains overseas since. The collapse of Communism caused many anti-American countries to court the free enterprise system and welcome new business, making this possible at that time. Communism had been tried and had failed in developing countries. Coca Cola, Caterpillar, and many large American businesses began to see tremendous gains in the overseas markets, and their profits skyrocketed in the 1990s. The recovery of Latin American countries and the surge of capitalistic production in South Korea, Taiwan, and other countries created a tremendous opportunity for American business expansion.

This opportunity expanded business so that trade, banking, and credit opened on a worldwide scale. Also, the use of the Worldwide Web on the Internet has taken business into a sea of exchange that is almost unlimited.

Many leading American and other economists believed that with computer information and the use of the Keynesian idea of pump priming, international markets could be reasonably conrolled. Governments could take measures under the elite's direction and with other international instruments such as the World Bank and the International Money Fund, adequate pump priming could occur.

HIDDEN LIMITS OF AMERICA
FOR ECONOMIC GROWTH AND CONTROL

Keynes-Managed Economy Used in the World

The United States has been the jump-starter for business, not only in America, but in much of the world. We helped rebuild Europe with the Marshal Plan. We have subsidized many nations through the IFM and World Bank, especially in Latin America. Mexico was rescued by American funds.

But conditions in America have reached a point where resources cannot be extended much farther. It is not only that the limits are stretched way too far, but moral responsibility has not been taught to Americans and to people in other nations, so that the lack of honesty and the use of the money of others for satisfaction of greed has become endemic. This has become common in talk by the media, and most Americans know that this is so, but few know how really far American funds have been depleted because the government and businesses have hidden this. The following are some of the facts.

Growth of Non-Federal Public Debt

While the debt of individuals and of the federal government has risen rapidly, so had non-federal debt. Debts of cities, counties, and states have also risen. The 1995 bankruptcy of Orange County, California, which was considered one of the richest counties, gained national attention. Washington, DC is now under the supervision and control of Congress because of near bankruptcy. The great political issue in many governor's race became balancing the budget. By 1995, the non-federal public debt had risen as shown on page 284

The Growth of Debt and Formation of Corporate Conglomerates

American businesses have never before shown such an addiction to greed in high places. The landslide of mega-mergers of savings and loans, banks, insurance companies, production corporations, farm companies, giant stores, and service organizations have resulted in high corporate debt and reduced jobs and benefits for the workers.

There were 4,000 Savings and Loan companies in 1979; by 1991, there were less than 2,500, and more failing or merging daily. The S & L problem cost the taxpayers $175–$200 billion. In 1991, there were about 12,000 commercial banks and by the end of the decade, this could be down to 6,000 or less.

We have gone through a period of bank failures similar to the last half of the 1930s. By early 1993 probably 100 more banks of the 40 percent which are weak among those left will close, bringing the number of bank failures close to that of the Savings and Loans. Less than five major banks control about 40 percent of United States banking with more big mergers occurring. The struggle to survive proves a tooth-and-nail melee–a disorderly scuffle in which top executives wrestle on the edge of a cliff while regulators act as referees.[4]

Since this statement, some of the largest banks in America have merged, such as Nations Bank with Bank America, in October 1998

The same thing is happening in the insurance industry, another capital source. There are now only 4,600 companies, and Joanne Morriseey, an authority says, "We're going to see more and more companies needing outside help and more and more mergers." [5] In 1990, 41 of the largest "multi-state" insurers bit the dust.

GROWTH OF NON-FEDERAL PUBLIC DEBT
(in billions of dollars)

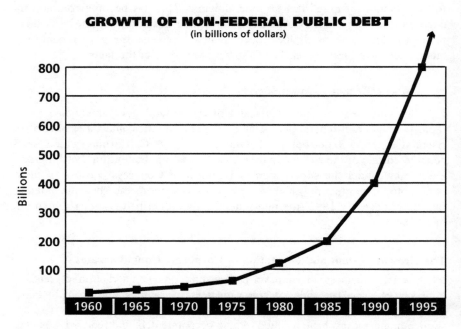

Standard and Poor downgraded 20 insurers and related entities and are at a snail's pace in upgrading any.

Buy-outs and mergers have produced larger businesses. While bigness is not necessarily bad, the present immoral environment allowed less efficiency, with rare exceptions (Wal-Mart). The largest American corporations that have been idolized for success went through deep trouble in the early 1990s and scrambled to reorganize, and there was a question as to whether they could succeed. General Motors and IBM are two of the better known. It now appears there will be only three or four major airlines left when the dust settles. Some of the oldest and largest being victims, such as Eastern, Pan-Am. TWA, and Continental are now seeking to make a comeback after bankruptcy and reorganization. A few are competing in limited sectors with reduced service and pay. Mergers and "downsizing" are feared by employees. Because of government opposition and other reasons, airlines have recently moved toward linking together in cooperative agreements rather than outright mergers. This new effort to eleminate small competitors is having difficulties.

Even the farm industry is now succumbing to mega-mergers in chicken and beef production, and beginning in pork as well. All other areas of farming are following with increasing speed. Large farm mergers make it very difficult for individual small farmers to compete.

Many of the highly successful and much-esteemed business leaders have been convicted of fraud and secret dealings that wrong the American people. Leaders in the stock and bond markets have been exposed as fraudulent, such as the confession and conviction of Milikan in the bond market, Soloman in stocks and securities, and others. This has shocked the public at the lawlessness of top executives. The Securities and Exchange Commission reported a growing list each year of offenders. While most brokers and businesses are honest, credibility has suffered on the top levels. This gives many others a feeling of freedom to take a bigger piece of the pie. Even Hillary Clinton, the president's wife, has made questionable gains in commodities.

In 1970, business debt was $62 billion with an interest rate of 3.8 percent. By 1990, the debt increased to $700 billion with an interest rate of 7.7 percent. In spite of the scandal of junk bonds, while the buy-outs have been more restrained, corporations still continue. Debt for acquisition and expansion has become risky, since it is difficult to produce the yield for profit. Joel Klein, Chief of the Justice Department, Anti-Trust Division, successfully fined Archer-Daniels-Midland $100 million for rigging markets; twenty states and Joel Klein of the Justice Department have filed suits against Microsoft for anti-trust practices.

The problem with such huge businesses is that if there comes a time when the government lacks leaders of principle, it could be controlled by lobby groups of these corporations. They will run the government for their own interests and contrary to the good of the people. There are now few leaders in government who stand for principle.

Result of the Debt of the Federal Government

Accumulated Failures in Federal Subsidies and Generous Loans

Chapter 10 discussed the growth of the United States budget and debt and its rapid acceleration after the university-thinking reached the "Death of God" idea near the 1960s. But a brief summary of what resulted is enlightening about the future. There are many irresponsible uses of federal funds. In fact, when the administration asked for an accounting of federal funds in 1998, it was discovered that sixteen of twenty-four major government agencies could not account for their spending. The Pentagon could not account for 25 percent, and Medicare could not account for 23 percent. There has been much waste going on for years.

Farm subsidies are an area of misuse. Abraham Lincoln founded the Department of Agriculture in the 1880s when one-fourth of the people lived on farms and there was one employee in the department for 227,000 farms. In 1992, there was only one person in fifty living on a farm, and there was one federal employee in the department for every 16 farms. There were then 36 farm agencies, 135,000 employees, and a total annual budget of $54 billion. Subsidies to farmers were originally given to help the small family farmer, but farming has now become big business in most areas of production.

The subsidies for farms are now going into the pockets of the large business conglomerates that make millions of dollars in profits each year in the large industries pertaining to sugar, corn, milk, peanuts, forestry, cattle, chickens, and pigs. Most of these big companies still claim to be "family farms" to claim these government subsidies. The government is artificially keeping prices up by paying farmers not to grow crops, and buying up millions of gallons of milk products (about 5 percent annually), which costs the American consumers $9 billion a year. We have millions of gallons of milk, mountains of cheese that are spoiling, and the like. James Bovard tells how this is robbing from the poor and giving money to the rich.[6] The United States has reached a budget of $54 billion in about that many years. Large corporate farms, employing thousands of people, are listing themselves as "family farms" and receiving government subsidies of millions of dollars. For example, 21 of 25 of the largest poultry-producing companies are listed as family farms. Tyson Foods, the largest, employs more than 25,000 people, and has more than $1.5 billion in annual sales. Yet, Bill Clinton, while governor of Arkansas, got them a $900,000 tax break, and they were exempted $37.6 million in federal taxes in one year. In 1997 Congress did take minimal steps to alter this situation.

The youth of America are also misusing government money and adding to the debt. The college loan funds were originally established to help the poor be able to go to college and then repay the money. There are now hundreds of thousands of students who do not qualify, and who could go to college without these loans and grants. There are about $2 billion student loans that are unpaid. Colleges, and especially private trade schools, are cheating the government. Federal grants for housing for the poor, funds for highway construction, other transportation construction, and contracts for defense are being fraudulently handled with millions being pocketed.

Aid to Families with Dependent Children (AFDC) and Supplemental Security Income (SSI) now exceeds $130 billion a year. Mortimer B. Zucherman has said this welfare system has "deterred parents from marrying, and consigned untold children to lives of bitterness and failure; dismaying numbers of them have sought revenge on the society that intended to help."[7] For children born in the year 1980, 22.2 percent of white children and 82.9 percent of black children will be dependent on welfare before reaching age 18 (in 1998). Senator Patrick Moynihan points out that America is going through a profound social crisis, and we pretend it isn't happening. In some places, 60 percent of the people who applied for welfare were not eligible.[8] Food stamps have become a second currency for many to use at half of their value for luxury items or crack cocaine, and the abuse is by the certified dealers and the people who receive the stamps. Yet virtually no one is prosecuted. The welfare bill passed in August 1996 has returned welfare jurisdiction to the states and moved toward requiring "workfare." After a two-year safety net, welfare is supposed to be withdrawn.

Entitlements in Retirement and Health Benefits a Bottomless Pit

The biggest abuses and the greatest threat to the future is in the area of retirement funds and health subsidies. In 1993, 98 percent of elderly people received Social Security and Medicare, or 33 million of the 37 million eligible. The American Association of Retired Persons is the largest, richest, and most unbending lobby in America, and it is growing. It has a tremendous political influence, and no politician is comfortable reducing its benefits. We have all heard about this, but most do not understand the seriousness of it. To this must be added the federal pension system, insurance, and other liabilities, and also the other publicly held treasury debts like bonds. On the next few pages, there are graphs showing how serious this is and how it will accelerate shortly because of the aging of the population

There are other hidden factors involved that most people are not aware of. The surplus in Social Security funds is not really an amount available, although this is not counted as government indebtedness. The government has bought treasury bonds with them, or has given IOU's to the Social Security trust fund of the Social Security payees amounting to $58 billion in 1994 (or $62 billion, if the second trust for the disabled is counted). The government reduced the report of the announced deficit to the American people for budget spending by this amount, or from $251 billion to $191 billion. This is a deception because neither that $58 billion or any of the hundreds of billions paid into the trust fund of Social Security are there. It will be an estimated $1.3 trillion by 2013. Graphs on this are on the following pages.

Moreover, there are over 120 government trust funds for projects such as highways and pensions. These all had funds confiscated and given IOU's as treasury bonds, which are not included in the budget deficit. These bonds are owned by Americans, Japanese, Arab nations, Europeans, and so forth. But they are also debts owed. The United States Treasury does not want Japan or anyone to cash these.[9] The federal government's only source of income would then be new taxes on the American people or to print useless money. At present, the federal government has a much larger debt than the American people have been told. The following are graphs of the actual conditions within the last few years.

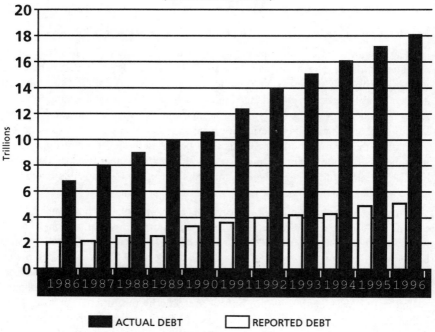

THE PUBLIC DEBT
(In trillions of dollars)

By normal accounting standards the federal government is drowning in a sea of red ink. The following graphs are taken from Peter G. Peterson's *Will America Grow Up before It Grows Old? How the Coming Social Security Crisis Threatens You, Your Family, and Your Country*,[10] The first shows Uncle Sam at the bottom of the sea liabilities and his ship at the surface floating with only a few trillion assets. These are the total assets and liabilities in trillions of dollars of federal government at the end of year 1995. Graphs on this follow.

The other three of Peterson's graphs which follow show how the accounts on Social Security will go into serious deficit, and Medicare, already in deficit, will drop even faster. This serious portent is due to the aging of the population, and less younger people to support them. In 1994, there was a surplus payment in Social Security of $58 billion, which by 1995 dropped to $29 billion. These indicate that in a few years the already huge sea of debt will rapidly become deeper with little prospect of getting out alive because there will be fewer workers to support social security and Medicare.

In addition to the debt of the unmentioned treasury bill. There is a second hidden factor, which is that Social Security and Medicare are paid for, mostly by monthly payroll taxes. In 1994, there was $308 billion with 90 percent or $276 billion paid out. But when America has another deep depression, there will be millions of people out of work and the payroll taxes reduced greatly.[11] In a short time, money previously available would be unavailable to the government and millions of elderly would be without funds. Such events would cause massive bank failures and claims on the FDIC for the guaranteed insurance of up to $100,000 per account.

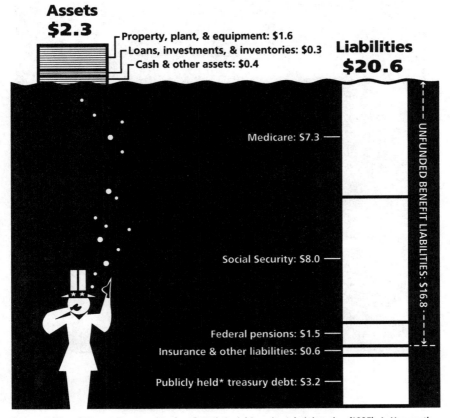

DROWNING IN A SEA OF RED INK

**Total assets and liabilities of the federal government,
at the end of FY 1995, in trillions of dollars**

**Assets
$2.3**

┌Property, plant, & equipment: $1.6
├Loans, investments, & inventories: $0.3
└Cash & other assets: $0.4

**Liabilities
$20.6**

Medicare: $7.3 ——

Social Security: $8.0 ——

Federal pensions: $1.5 ——

Insurance & other liabilities: $0.6 ——

Publicly held* treasury debt: $3.2 ——

UNFUNDED BENEFIT LIABILITIES: $16.8

Source: Office of Management and Budget (1996); Social Security Administration (1995); A. Haeworth Robertson, Social Security: What Every Taxpayer Should Know *(1992); and author's calculations.*
* Excludes debt held by the Federal Reserve System

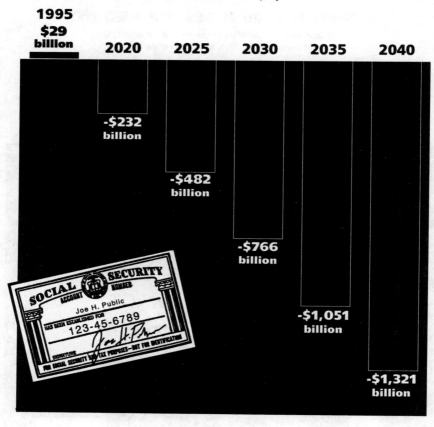

ANNUAL OPERATING BALANCE
of the Social Security* trust funds.

*Old Age, Survivors, and Disability Insurance
Official "intermediate" projection

MEDICARE ALREADY RUNS ANNUAL CASH DEFICITS
that are projected to grow explosively in the next century.

Annual operating balance of the Medicare (hospital insurance) trust fund:
official "intermediate" projection

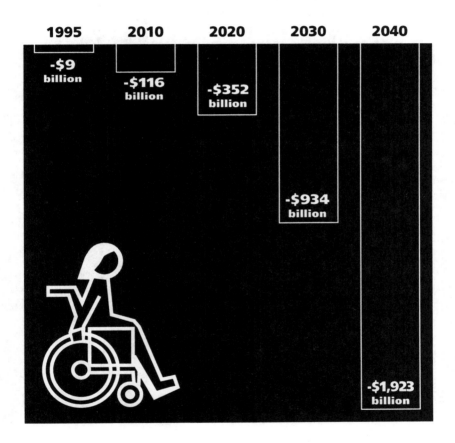

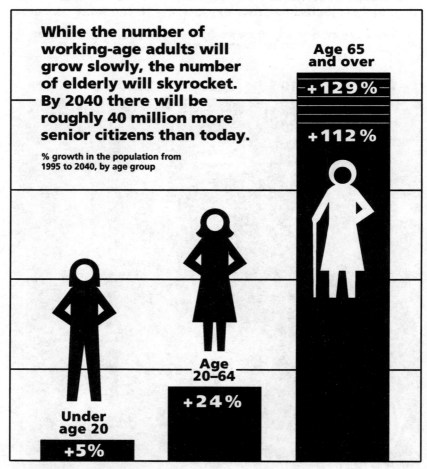

While the number of working-age adults will grow slowly, the number of elderly will skyrocket. By 2040 there will be roughly 40 million more senior citizens than today.

% growth in the population from 1995 to 2040, by age group

Age 65 and over
+129%
+112%

Age 20–64
+24%

Under age 20
+5%

Source: Social Security Administration (1995)

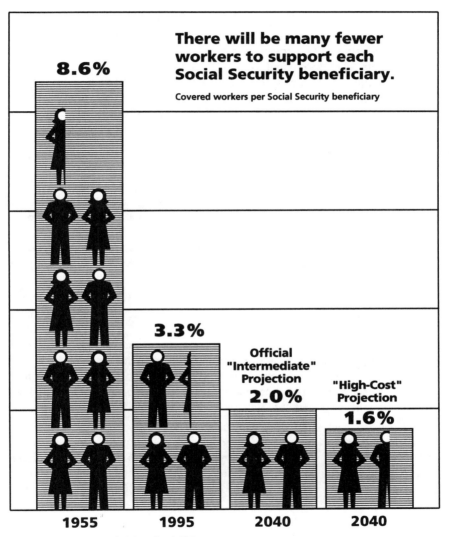

There will be many fewer workers to support each Social Security beneficiary.

Covered workers per Social Security beneficiary

8.6% — 1955

3.3% — 1995

Official "Intermediate" Projection 2.0% — 2040

"High-Cost" Projection 1.6% — 2040

Source: Social Security Administration (1995)

Delusion of Our Certainty of Materialistic Improvement

The advancement of the American civilization has been exceptional in the twentieth century, and especially in the last half. Part of this advancement is the result of the tremendous inventiveness of the American people, smart management, and the God-given natural resources the country has. In recent years, extensive retooling of American industry after being challenged by Japan has downsized its labor force, multiplied the number of jobs worked by women, transported jobs to cheaper labor overseas, and started many new businesses. These measures upped the production by the average worker and produced more taxes. Since World War II, there has been an average growth in the economy of .4 percent per year.[12] But can growth be maintained?

Near Limit of Financial Debt

Since the 1960s, we have expanded the idea of personal and business debt to its limits. Individuals gained more and better houses, cars, and wealth, but progressed further into debt. We are living an illusion that these things are ours, when they really belong to the money lenders. Most Americans are at a point where they could easily lose everything should there be a serious economic decline or breakdown. The increase of personal bankruptcy was shown on page 183 and projected to reach 4,000,000 by the year 2000.

The personal debt system progressively developed: first Americans paid a certain amount down on products, and then made mortgages on houses, liens on cars, and then from secured loans moved to lay-away purchases for commodities. Then there were term loans with longer payments and amounts based on presumed income. Then the door opened to credit cards for anything to be paid for in the future by the consumer. Real financial responsibility is no longer taught. For example, there are estimates that 65 percent of high school students at graduation have a credit card with over $1,600 debt on it.

Business moved from private ownership, to trusts, to conglomerates, to leveraged buy-outs with junk bonds, to overseas sales for credit. We have moved from credit on farms and equipment, equity loans, to short-term loans, to long-term loans and credit on everything, to poorly-backed bonds for buyouts, to heavy charging to foreign nations. This is about the end of the line for the credit train.

The federal government started with currency secured by gold and silver, and now it has paper notes with no value except the promise of a government in deep debt, with only the resources which the American people have or can generate. Very few of the American people are aware of how much paper money is being printed, and that the more printed and circulated, the less it is worth. The bonds of the United States Treasury now operate and support a partial Ponzi scheme for promised entitlements, taking money from some programs and its citizens and giving to others to try to establish equality.

The American government loaned trillions of dollars to business, to farmers, to students, and to national governments overseas. It has pledged itself to cover billions of dollars in mortgages: FAA, FANNYMAE, SALLYMAE and others. These debts are owed to banks with the government guarantees. The government guarantees up to $100,000 for each personal bank account. These guarantees are beyond the large debt the federal government already owes. A treasurer of one of the largest financial corporations in America once said to me, "There is no way the federal government could in a crisis cover all that it guarantees."

Individual savings were formerly placed in savings accounts, then in c.d.'s, and money market funds. When the last two dropped in interest earnings, the common man in the late 1980s and 1990s played the stock market through mutual funds for the best returns. More people shifted their funds into mutual funds and stocks. This increase of investors in stocks continually supplied business with the ability to expand, especially in overseas markets. But this continued increase of mutual funds from the people is a semi-Ponzi scheme limiting their use in expansion of business and profits. Even Keynes agreed. When the investment in mutual funds slows or expansion of business reaches its limits, a collapse occurs. The troubles in overseas markets may be one of the places where brakes are already being applied.

The Illusion of Recent Debt Improvement

In the early 1990s, the financial trend to reduce the federal budget began, and in 1997, there seemed to be improvement. More money was coming into the government treasury, and it appeared the budget would be balanced soon. Some in Congress, and the president himself, talked about what would be done about the surplus we would have in a year or two. There was little talk of repaying the debt. The budget for 1998 could have balanced, but Congress and the president added billions for children's health insurance and other areas. The following graphs show recent financial history involving the national debt and the national deficit under Regean, Bush and Clinton.[13]

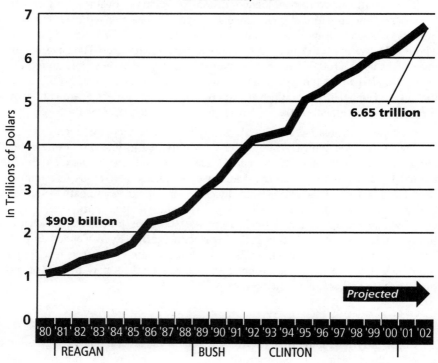

NATIONAL DEBT
as of Oct. 29, 1997

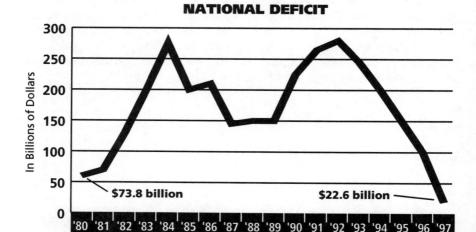

NATIONAL DEFICIT

From the graph on the growth of the federal debt, it is obvious it has contin-ued to climb through the Reagan, Bush, and Clinton years, adding an increasing tax burden to the American people. The graph on the national budget deficit indi-cates significant growth under Reagan's early years, then decline and leveling off in 1987 and 1989, a resurgence during the Bush years, and a decline in 1992 that continued toward balancing in 1997, with only a $22.6 billion owed. The budget office announced in October 1998 that there would be a $70 billion surplus with both Bill Clinton and the Congress claiming credit.

Improvement in Economy Due to People's Moral Reaction

The changes in budget must be viewed in the context of what has occurred. The morals in America took a nose-dive after the 1960s because of the liberal moral practices of many liberal leaders in Clinton's boomer generation, and a majority of people in the decade of the 1980s saw these as manifestly wrong. This reached a point of alarm by the 1990s, especially for the economy. The num-ber of people below the poverty level and on welfare, in criminal abuse, in sexu-al promiscuity, in out-of-wedlock births, with abortions, in breakdown of the family by divorce and living together, in growth in AIDS and other diseases, in the decline of the educational institutions, in the loss of confidence in govern-ment, and in regard to morals in general- all these things seemed to be going out of control.

By the 1980s there began a strong reaction by the America people, especial-ly by Christians. This led to the election of Republican administrative presiden-tial leadership in Ronald Reagan and George Bush and to improvements. National defense and national confidence needed restoration by Ronald Reagan. Under the Carter administration, American defenses had greatly declined; the United States had been humiliated by the Iran hostage situation and the terrorist acts against Americans. The shortage of oil, the rise of oil prices, the tremendous inflation of the dollar, and the growth of the national debt caused a loss of con-fidence in the American economy. There was diminished world influence of the American government in the light of the victories of Communism in much of the world. Especially worrisome was the spread of Communism's influence into Nicaragua and other Latin American nations. Under these conditions, most of the nations of the world voted against America in the United Nations; and Communist leaders openly threatened the United States with military and inter-continental nuclear warfare.

Ronald Reagan and George Bush reduced inflation, built up national defense, gained world confidence, and stood up to, and helped cause the collapse of Communism. Then Bush dramatically showed America as the central world power militarily and politically by the Desert Storm war in which the United Nations, including the other Arab states, gave backing against Iraq in Kuwait.

The continued military expenditures of the Bush years, along with the social programs started by the Democrats, alarmingly expanded the budget. The failure to restrain the budget deficit and national debt was made central to the entire nation by Ross Perot, so that the election in 1992 produced the saying emphasizing the central issue, "It's the budget, stupid."

But most important is the fact that the respect and confidence of the people for the American government had been renewed by Reagan and Bush, along with an optimism about the future. The also accomplished a second important aspect for growth, namely it began to rapidly expand the Ameircan economy on a worldwide scale. Moreover, the poorer nations turned their faith from Communism toward the American democratic and capitalistic system, which opened the door to a global economy in a new way. The growing budget deficit continued to disturb most people and paved the way for the promises and election of Bill Clinton and his seemingly centrist position.

The continued decline of sexual morals and widespread abortions disturbed religious people and most people who are strong family advocates. These things spurred Christian involvement in politics Following the failed political efforts of the Moral Majority movement, Pat Robertson ran for president as a Christian against George Bush and began to build a Christian political base, but lost. Then, Pat Robertson, working with Ralph Reed, formed the Christian Coalition and focused on establishing a grassroots political effort to change politics. The reaction of the American people expressed through the CC leadership, led to the election of the conservative Republican Congress in 1994, with the demand that the budget be balanced and family values be reinstated.

Reasons for Budget Improvements

The budget improvements occurred because both Clinton and Congress knew they politically had to. Several important things occurred that improved the budget deficit, but these did not solve the real problem of curtailing spending, and they make the future even more fragile. First, there have been large tax increases. Because the budget was exploding under Bush, he violated his pledge of "no new taxes" and approved a tax hike by the Democratic Congress. Bush lost to Clinton because of this. But Clinton, in his first term, also included a hefty tax hike because he wanted more spending and the deficit was still high. By 1997, taxes reached 19.8 percent of the GDP from 18.4 percent in the 1980s.1 Secondly, to reduce the costs of the debt, with the help of Lloyd Bentson as Secretary of Treasury, Clinton began to try to refinance long-term debt into lower-rate, short-term obligations. Today, at least a third of federal debt is financed at one year or less. While this significantly reduced the amount of interest, it has also made the debt more vulnerable if there is economic trouble and all interest rates go up.

Third, Clinton began to take advantage of national peace that Reagan and Bush produced and he greatly reduced defense spending. Under Reagan, defense spending was 6 percent of the GDP, but in 1998 it is only 3 percent, amounting to a decline from 20 percent to 15 percent of the budget. Since 1990, army divisions dropped from 18 to 10, ships in the fleet from 546 to 357, and tactical air fighter wings from 24 to 13. This alone was a major factor and decreased the budget by $150 billion. Lack of defense funds is now approaching the low point of the Carter years, and today the military is in a transition to even more costly weapons for the future.2

Fourth, many new businesses have been started, employing more people and creating more income taxes. The revival of national confidence under the Reagan-Bush administrations allowed Clinton to promote the formation of new businesses. In addition, to the public's renewed optimism, the downsizing by companies had removed capable middle-age people from big corporations who, along with young expectant entrepreneurs, stepped out to form many new businesses. This was made possible because Congress and the Clinton administration relaxed lending laws to form new businesses to help boost employment and income tax revenue. Many of these loans are risky. From 1983 to 1996, small business loans went from $8.5 billion to $24.6 billion. Since the government has guaranteed these loans, Susan Tanka of the Committee for a Responsible Federal Budget has said she is fearful that if there is a depression, many businesses will go into default and greatly expand the federal debt.

Three other factors have produced an increase in income taxes that reduced the government deficit. Because of the long bull market and the stable economy, many middle-class people are investing in mutual funds and other stocks for their place of saving. Because of the bull market, some have borrowed money to do this because the stock market increase gave a better return. These yearly profits have brought in much new income taxes. But everyone knows the bull will not continue to run indefinitely, and the available funds to keep it rising are reaching a limit. Also, the high tech industry has exploded, and many young computer people have made millions. Along with this, incomes of CEOs of many corporations have continued to much higher levels. These too have added to government income taxes. Everyone admits that these increases of income must reach a peak level beyond which they can no longer go. In 1997, there was $72 billion more in federal taxes than was expected and this increase is much greater for 1998 and was expected to be even greater in 1999 allowing the predicted zero level of deficit..

Fifth, Clinton has showed no courageous leadership in reducing the entitlement programs, and the so-called coming surplus is a deception. Between 1988 to 1998, entitlement spending went up from 10.2 percent of GDP to 11.3 percent. Domestic discretionary spending rose from 3.2 to 3.4 percent of GDP and represents a real increase in spending of 25 percent.3 The coming surplus is based on plans for Social Security reforms to give reserves for Social Security. But these are not real savings, for they have been and will be loaned out in federal bonds, or T bills as discussed previously. This money is " 'called Reserve Pending Social Security Reform.' It starts at $9.5 billion in fiscal 1999 and rises to $258.5 billion in 2008 and consists of the difference between federal receipts and federal outlays. In other words, what would normally be called a surplus is now called Social Security reserve."4 But these changes in Social Security and other programs have not yet been adopted or occurred, and unless there is a change in the will of the people and Congress, they will not be.

In summary, increase in taxes; restructuring to short-term, lower interest rates; great reduction of defense costs; increase in new businesses giving more employment; increase in tax payments by the rise of the stock market and the surge of mutual funds for savings; and the rise of CEO's salaries and new high incomes by new technological fortunes all account for budget balancing. Congressional cuts and administrative reduction of costs are minimal, budget costs have continued to grow, and tax rates have reached a level so that further raises will be resisted or avoided.

The Delusion of Financial Optimism

In spite of improvment in the budget, in 1979 Charles L. Schultze evaluated the possibility of continued growth in the economy of around .2 percent a year, considered all other ways of boosting this growth, and concludes this will not significantly remove the approaching problems. He said, "Here, as elsewhere, we will have to make progress the old-fashioned way-by working for it. To eliminate the budget deficit, there is no substitute for spending cuts or tax increases."5 But soon even those will seem impossibilities. Robert D. Reischauer, former director of the Congressional Budget Office and now Senior Fellow in Economic Studies at the Brookings Institution said:

The decade from 1997 to 2007 offers an opportunity-perhaps a final chance-for the nation to deal in a measured but preemptive way with the major adjustments in policy required to accommodate the baby boom generation's retirement in the second and third decades of the twenty-first century.6

Not only was it foreseen that the growth in the economy would certainly slow down, but certain unforeseen factors were occurring. Greed to make fast gains in riches has created new instruments such as hedge funds that use leverage to bet on complex derivatives and futures contracts. They use expert investors with highly complex computers to predict. Major investors and American and international bands have money in these to make exorbitant gains if the investments are right. There are no regulations and laws governing these hedge funds and no one knows how many and how much money is involved. It is estimated that there are probably over 3,000, some involving many billions of dollars. Also, the investments of corporations and loans by banks in the rapidly expanding world markets involve tremendous amounts of money which is not rally known or under any control. As David Shulman, Chief Equity Strategist at Soloman Brothers said in June 1995, "The economy is too big and too complicated to be piloted by a few central bankers sitting in Washington, DC and other world capitals."7

Approaching Time of Troubles in the Economy

Moreover, can defense cuts continue with a failing Clinton foreign policy? The Serbian war has spread to Albania and American troops have not been brought home as Clinton promised. There are about one third of a million refugess and nothing short of military tactics will stop the Serbs. Moreover, a 1998 congressional committee's warning about soon possible missal attacks with lethal weapons was met with dismay by the White House. But, within two months the North Koreans fired a missile over Japan that is capable of reaching parts of America, and intelligence has revealed the North Koreans now have nuclear capabilities and a massive new underground production center. China, with nuclear and rocket capabilities is helping Pakistan, and Iran. Iran has unveiled a new missile they claim can reach Europe. India has jointed the nuclear club. China has gained our technical secrets, and gained marine facilities at each end of the Panama Canal. Clinton has proclaimed there is one China, and in essence said Taiwan belongs to mainland China. Haiti is without an effective controlling democratic government and is in shambles from the hurricane George. It is said Iraq will have renewed military capabilities in biological and chemical warfare within six months because Clinton failed to push inspections. Our military in Saudi Arabia have been pushed off into confinement in isolated desert conditions so our military personnel are miserable. Arab nations who are male dominated have been offended by a pushy woman as Secretary of State. The Israeli and Arab peace accords have little progress and Arafat has just announced a plan for a Palestinian nation with its capital in Jerusalem. America is in a declared war with fundamentalist Islamic terrorist factions when nuclear materials and chemical and biological weapons are available. Moreover, America's mercenary military is in trouble. Many much needed American pilots are rapidly resigning for higher paying, more comfortable Airline jobs; and military enlistment in all our forces are down. Thus the Clinton foreign policy has drastically reduced our military strength and left us spread thin and without resolution throughout the world. Military expenses will have to increase in the future to meet the needs.

Domestic social issues are not resolved and new problems are unaddressed. The 1996 welfare bill that moved control to the states may be reaching a point of difficulty. The moving from welfare to workfare contained the promise of removal of the safety net in 2 years. This will run out next year and could become an explosive issue with the underclass. Moving people from welfare to jobfare has been minimal. For example, in 1997 in the Atlanta area, only 154 people of the 1,278 referrals were hired. If the 2-year limit is enforced, there will be a rebellion in the lower class. Bill Archer of the House Budget Committee has said that Clinton's recent additions in coverage for children who have no medical insurance, coverage for child care for working mothers, inclusion of early-retired persons into Medicare and Social Security, and educational programs amount to another $150 billion addition to the budget. So Clinton domestic efforts are reaching a limit.

The Asian countries experienced a depression in October 1997. The collapse of the stock markets occurred in Hong Kong and in nations all around the Pacific Rim. It soon was revealed the poor conditions of the banks in Japan, South Korea, Indonesia, and other less modern nations. Even China, which is thought to be the most promising, has since been found to be hundreds of billions of dollars in debt. These events were a shocking surprise. Banks in these nations are at a point of bankruptcy, and there has been much corruption. The conditions in these nations were a product of the Keynes theory, whereby the governments picked certain industries and motivated business leaders to invest in them using the banks. But bad loans were made, and the companies overreached their GDP. Their foreign debts soared in the 1990s.

While Asia was a growing area of trade for the United States and the immediate impact on American business was small, there are long-range implications for the future. Moreover, how could the world economists miss this uncontrolled condition and allow it to happen? In hopes of stopping the hemorrhaging of some of the major nations, the International Monetary Fund and the World Bank, following Keynesian economics, has invested, some say, $160 billion of American money to jump-start the recovery of these nations. The Pacific Rim and Latin American countries have already significantly devalued their money, which means they seek to flood America and other nations with their products and undercut American business.

Moreover, the confidence of the nations in an American world economy are said by Robert Samuelson, George Soros, and others to be in crisis. Russia's economy is in such bad shape that state control instead of capitalism is now certain. It is believed there is over 200 billion in one hundred dollar bills held in Russia. The failure of the Russian economy is a demonstration of the failure by the American liberal elite under Clinton to influence one of the largest nations and build a managed social democracy based on capitalism. Since the end of the cold war, American intellectuals have sought to guide Russia's economic course. With the collapse of the Russian economy, few other nations will continue to follow the present American model of managed democratic capitalism, and this will certainly hinder or even end the openness to capitalism and democracy and to a global economy. The global economic expansion has been a key to American continued prosperity. Moreover, the International Monetary Fund is nothing more than a credit union of $195 billion, which about $40 billion are contributed by the U.S.A.

Russia's economy has been run primarily by a small group of former Communist leaders who appropriated the assets when Russia went through efforts of privatization and by the Russian moffia. In Russia, Indonesia, Japan, and other Asian countries the money given by the IFM to prime the pump of their failing economies has gone into the pockets of corrupted leaders. Latin American companies are showing significant decline. By the beginning of 1999 the low cost goods from other nations will significantly compete with American goods and affect American profits.

In September 1998 the American stock market took a significant nose dive and has vacillated with loses that wipe out gains for the year. This has certainly significantly slowed or stopped investment in the market for the immediate future by private citizens. Near the end of September it was discovered that the Long Term Capital Management hedge fund who had loans of over $100 billion from banks and securities was discovered to be in deep trouble. Under leadership of the Federal Reserve Control Board, who feared the failure of this fund would spook a collapse of the American market, rallied major banks and investment funds to inject $3.5 billion more in one day into the fund. It is not yet certain that this fund that was considered one of the best, will survive, and no one knows if there are a number of others that are in deep trouble. This alone indicates that the Federal Reserve Board and most American economies recognized the American economy is on the edge.

CONCLUSIONS

The arrogant view that man now understands the laws of nature and how to control the economy has reached a crisis point. But the facts reveal Americans have built up such a huge debt they will have to act soon to make improvements or they will be swamped by a tidal wave of commitments at home and abroad among the nations. It is clear the problem is the lack of human will driven by demonic desires. No one is willing to change. Repeatedly, there have been efforts to change this apathy: the Grace Commission by Reagan, the Graham-Rudman-Hollings Bill (GRH), the first and second Omnibus Budget Reconciliation Acts (OMB 90 and OMB 93), the Balanced Budget Act given to Clinton in 1995, and the resultant Budget Enforcement Act in 1995. These legislative acts forced some reduction in the budget, but all failed to alter the course and change the flood of debt ahead. The problem has been the bias of the will of the American people. Recent improvements are described in chapter 19.

There has been an unyielding continuation of the appetites of pride and greed of American government, business, and people. The classes of people formed are at a point where they are poised to force the other classes, if necessary by violence, to achieve what they feel are their just ends. In the first chapter, I pointed out the classes in America and in the world are poised at the door of the city of Pandaemonium to light the fuse of meltdown which will lead to confusion and violence.

Chapter 15

Class Conflict

INTRODUCTION

Class conflict is a result of giving up faith in God for a materialistic view of life. People living for the material logically think justice means each individual should be equal in the same way with an equal amount of wealth and an equal opportunity to gain an equal amount. To gain equality, individuals of like kind unite to gain the most power, and to gain the opportunity to gain the most for themselves. In America, as in the Greek Democracy and the Roman Republic, this has produced groups based on race, gender, and finally age. These produce class struggles and conflict that in the end accuse and excuse each other. It produces a time of each person *judging others.*

In Greece and Rome, this ended in mob conflicts and internal wars that led to internal weakness, exposing the nations to attacks by outside enemies. This internal conflict led to the end of democracy–of any representation, deliberation, and joint decision-making. The establishment of a dictator seemed the answer to bring order and direction. As Paul said in Romans 1:28–29, "God gave them over to a depraved mind, to do those things which are not proper, being filled with all unrighteousness, wickedness, greed, evil . . . ." Because the violence and abuses cause so much pain, destruction, and persecution to His people, God brings supernatural judgment on the society. thereby ending its power.

This meltdown occurs when each group seems to reach an impasse to accomplishing their vision, and is so certain their own cause is right they are unwilling to hear and negotiate with other groups. All other objectives and standards are rejected, and all things deconstructed for their own selfish ends. This delusion and self-righteousness of the groups cannot but end in conflict and loss of any unified control in the society. Each group sees truth as relative only to them and there is no prevailing–and certainly no absolute–truth for all. This chapter shows the racial issues in America are close to that point of moral meltdown. The chapter which follow these will look at the sexual conflict and the point of impasse that results for women, men, and children.

Development of Racial Issues

In previous chapters, the primary ethnic struggle through most of America's history involved those who are from African decent. The most common name of these people changed from "nigger," to "Negro," to "black Americans," and now the proper definition is African-American. The changes of status, motivated primarily by materialism, began with slavery; the Civil War led next to an oppressive segregation, and following this, black identity became recognized through slow legal changes. This was followed by the civil rights movement in the late 1950s and early 1960s at the time of the "Death of God" theology.

The civil rights movement was initiated by the liberal Supreme Court which made arbitrary decisions for social engineering. Also, the liberal elite convinced blacks that government-induced socialism was the way to justice and promoted illegal black protests against unjust laws. The liberal determinists took this opportunity to offer their vision of government help for the poor: a financial safety net, integrated education, health assistance, affirmative action for education and jobs, and sex education. That led to changing these unjust laws, but launched the black leadership into dependence on the liberal government's social agenda. Liberals thereby expressed their superiority by encouraging blacks to feel victimized and dependent on the liberals for salvation.

Tony Brown accused white liberals of racism, saying:

They have demonstrated their belief in the inferiority of Blacks by enacting policies that place Blacks at the mercy of welfare and other socialistic entitlement programs for the middle class as well as the poor. This perpetuates dependence by Blacks on them, rather than encouraging Black self-reliance and economic independence. Many of the problems that Blacks face today—material poverty, dysfunctional families, illiteracy, and so on—can be traced back directly to the organization of the Black protest movement by Whites, many of whom were socialists.[1]

The goal of the civil rights movement at first aimed at legal representation and equal opportunity for each individual as "whites" had had. The record of the failure of the liberal agenda given by Thomas Sowell and others showed that the conditions of blacks worsened when they were improving, and their views of sex and victimization actually hindered the improvements they were making, and helped produce the lower class (see chapter 13).

Three main groups of African-Americans today are defined by scholars according to material wealth. The dividing line between these classes is not clear in most presentations, but generally is as follows:

The top (20–30 percent) are wealthy blacks. Their status has barely changed, having 67 percent as much wealth as whites in 1967 and having 68 percent in 1995. But their wealth has grown significantly, as has the white upper class, creating a greater disparity between the rich and the poor.

The middle class of more than 50 percent of the black population had 58 percent of the wealth of whites in 1967, but 63 percent in 1995, this being significant progress for most.. These people live integrated mostly into white suburban neighborhoods with some primarily black suburban neighborhoods.

The bottom sector (20–30 percent) have declined, having had 58 percent of that of whites in 1967, and only 52 percent in 1995. There were almost 30 percent of African-American families below the poverty level in the early 1990s. These mostly live in the inner-city neighborhoods with poor schools and a degenerating moral environment. There is an increase of single parent families. The number under the poverty line improved slightly in the early 1990s.

In summary, the rich African-Americans remained virtually unchanged in their status in relationship to European-Americans, but are much richer. The status of middle class blacks increased significantly, while the lower class continues to decline and degenerate into near chaotic conditions.

COMPARISON OF AFRICAN-AMERICANS
TO EUROPEAN-AMERICANS

Considerations of African-Americans

Orlando Patterson has given a useful factual overall evaluation of the place of the African-Americans today with numerous graphs and a discerning evaluation of the perspective of the various views. Much of my discussion draws from his work, except where corrections must be made from the perspective of biblical faith.[2] He shows that, on the whole, African-Americans have made tremendous improvements in their conditions in the last 40 years.

Comparison in Education of African-Americans with European-Americans

In 1940, there was a 4-year gap in median years of schooling; in 1995 it was reduced to a few months. In 1940, completion of high school by ages 25 to 29 years went from 12.3 percent to 86.5 percent, compared to 41.2 percent to 87.4 percent for whites. Three-quarters of all African-Americans over age 25 have at least a high school diploma. Between 1971 and 1990, the reading achievement gap for 13-year-olds was cut in half, and the ethnic gap in math scores from 1973 to 1990 was reduced from 46 to 27 points in relation to the European-American average of 276. For African-Americans over 25 years old, completing college has grown from under 1.5 percent in 1940 to almost 13 percent in 1995, but is still barely more than half of the European-American rate of 24 percent. But for blacks this represents a *tenfold* increase in college completion.[3] Far more blacks are attending college, especially women, but the percentage of all who finish is diminishing.

Comparison in Income and Wealth

Top income class: While not closing the gap between them and European-Americans, the top 5 percent went from $82,387 per year (in 1995 dollars) in 1967, to $122,558 in household income.

Middle class: Using $35,000 as the median income, at least 35 percent of black males are solidly middle class. In 1995, the median income per year of African-American families was $25,970, which was 60.8 percent of European-American median family income of $42,646. Married couples earned 87 percent of similar European-American couples, while in 1967, they only earned 68 percent. Black men's median earnings jumped from 64 percent in 1967, to 75 percent of white male income in 1995. Black women's income increased from 74.6 to 90 percent of white women's earnings in that time. Black women's income increased faster than white women's income. Patterson said, "This marked a stunning improvement when we compare individuals working full-time."[4]

Bottom Class: Over 25 percent of all black families and nearly 30 percent of all black people were poor as of March 1996. They are 2.6 times more likely to be poor than whites, and their families are slightly more than three times more vulnerable to poverty. In 1995, 4 out of 6 children, or 4,552,000 black children under age 18 living in families were poor. Very important is the fact the poverty rate for blacks 18–64 years of age is almost twice that of whites and one-and-a-half times of those over 64 years of age. Nearly 60 percent of all black children are in homes where the head of the household is female, and 45 percent are in poverty. All but 6 percent of the poor black children are in homes where the head of the household is female.

Unemployment of black youths in urban areas is high. The technicalization of industry and the beginning of new jobs involving communication technology in the suburbs has put jobs out of reach geographically and educationally because of the demand for skills they don't have. Moreover, the creation of the feeling that black youths deserve better paying jobs than seem available in black neighborhoods, and the fact that illegal jobs such as selling drugs are available, reduces incentives for legitimate, beginning jobs. The breakdown of morals in the black underclass has been accentuated by crack cocaine sale and use, and by the spread of AIDS, which is heaviest in the black race. Drug arrests in blacks have risen from 24 percent in 1980 to 39 percent in 1993.

Patterson asserts: "The *most serious of these problems* is, of course, the rise in *families headed by single women* . . . . Unemployment is about the same in 1997 as it was in 1970, while the overall female-headed family rate has escalated from under 30 percent to over 46 percent" (italics added).[5] The birthrate of blacks diminished about 34 percent from 1960 to 1990, due to the availability of contraceptives, abortions, and public and government pressure to restrain payment of welfare for more children. But, the *black single birth rate* among teens and young adult women has grown to 70 percent, and if the trend continues, will soon be 90 percent. Patterson concludes, "This is an internally generated disaster . . . ."[6]

This is generating a self-perpetuating poverty and is having "a devastating effect on the Afro-American lower class." [7]This affects education and depraves the home environment causing cognitive impairment, greater child abuse, and greater risks of children being put into foster homes. Most important is the absence of a caring father-image for teaching discipline, which the black single mother does not furnish for her sons.

Unfortunately pregnancies of young black women usually involve men 5 or more years older who leave, are never known by the children, and offer no care. Patterson says, in addition to the emotional and moral costs, the financial cost of black teen mothering by the state is about $30 billion a year to the taxpayers. But the greater cost is the sense of entrapment and lack of male discipline which yields to gang affiliation and warfare, arrests, imprisonment, and often death.

Status of African-Americans Generally

The general state of the majority of black Americans is amazingly improved and improving. Not only is there great improvement for the majority of blacks in education and financial attainment, but in regard to full legal rights in most areas of the country that count. Full integration first occurred in the military between 1948 and 1965, and following the civil rights act, affected all areas of life. Patterson discusses:

> On the one hand, there is no denying the fact that, in absolute terms, Afro-Americans, on the average, are better off now than at any other time in their history. The civil rights movement effectively abolished the culture of postjuridical slavery, which, reinforced by racism and legalized segregation had denied Afro-American people the basic rights of citizenship in the land of their birth. Afro-Americans are now very much a part of the nation's political life, occupying positions in numbers and importance that will go beyond mere ethnic representation or tokenism . . . . Being Afro-American is no longer a significant obstacle to participation in the public life of the nation . . . . The enormity of the achievement of the last forty years in American ethnic relations cannot be overstated. For better or worse, the Afro-American presence in American life and thought is today pervasive. A mere 13 percent of the population, Afro-Americans

dominate the nation's popular culture: its music, its dance, its talk, its sports, its youth fashion; and they are a powerful force in its popular and elite literature . . . . So powerful and unavoidable is the Afro-American popular influence that it is now common to find people who, while remaining racists in personal relations and attitudes, none-the-less have surrendered their tastes, and much of their viewing and listening time, to Afro-American entertainers, talk-show hosts, and sitcom stars. . . . This is a truly amazing situation, which finds no parallel in any other society or culture in the world today . . . .[8]

Patterson follows these statements by pointing out that, whether genuine or not, polls show "the United States came out far ahead of all other nations in its level of ethnic tolerance . . . . In comparison (to other nation's prejudices which showed 49 to 21 percent), only 13 percent of Americans responded that they disliked the Afro-American minority."[9]

Distorted Interpretations of the Racial Picture

Andrew Hacker's book, which is basic for today's liberals, presents a number of facts blaming all on racial bias. [10] He claims that in spite of all the laws, blacks are losing out in many ways. Much like in the Depression, black farmers are losing their farms. From 1982 to 1987, land cultivated by black farmers dropped from just under 3.5 million acres to just over 2.5 million acres–a loss of 25 percent. The loss of total farms was only 2.3 percent during the same time. But Hacker's is a superficial observation, since far greater losses of farms in America by white and black farmers occurred in the third quarter of the century under democratic liberal rule, when all farmers were encouraged, almost induced, to use government loans and caused huge debts that became unbearable because of inflation. Those were the civil rights years, and there was reluctance to foreclose on blacks, which favoritism ended with the Republican victory in 1980 under Ronald Reagan.

It is argued that blacks in the inner city have been discriminated against in bank mortgages and other loans, yet they actually have a better repayment rate. The reports of the Home Mortgage Disclosure Act and studies by the Federal Reserve Board showed lenders rejected 34 percent of black borrowers and 21 percent of Hispanics, while the rejection rate for whites of comparable income was 14.4 percent. Thus, blacks were 2 1/2 times more likely to be denied a mortgage in 1991. Records show people with more expensive home mortgages, mostly whites, are more likely to default than those with inexpensive homes. Most of this given by Hacker is true. But this was in the time of the tremendous rise in crime rates, even riots, and blacks acquired a poor image for loan risks as a result of the liberal media. Since that time, loans to blacks have increased.

Almost all authors of black studies admit there are serious, growing dangers in the American racial situation in spite of the improved conditions for blacks and the improved tolerance of whites for blacks. There are three major problems between the races that threaten to ignite conflict. These are discussed next.

Problems of the Inner City

Some problems of the inner city have been discussed before, but a better look at these current conditions and attitudes are important. Black people had tremendous expectations from the liberal elite that all their problems would be solved when the human rights laws were passed. But since 1964, the emergence of the high proportion of single homes led by women, the flight from the cities and the technical revisions of industrial jobs, left a sense of being trapped in poverty. The absence of male leadership in the home helped produce the male-led gangs. Also, crack cocaine has proliferated and added to the pain, as has the spread of AIDS and venereal diseases.

While the anti-police attitudes emerged in the sixties and seventies, they have increasingly become a dominant attitude among black males today. A study of 32 states showed that of 4,558 hate-crime incidents, six of ten involved racial motives. The Rodney King beating and the 1992 riots in Los Angeles resulted in more than a thousand injured and at least 46 killed. This sparked similar riots in at least ten other cities. Quotations from black rap lyrics are filled with hate for cops, whites, and women. Following the 1992 riots, the Los Angeles County District Attorney Ira Reiner estimated there were about 1,000 gangs there with a total membership of 150,000. There had been a county increase of gangs of more than 200 percent between 1984 and 1991.

Inner-city crime proliferated in all major urban areas and spilled over even into rural communities. It is believed that half of all black males, 21-24 years old, are involved in some kind of gang activity. Gang members commit 6 times as many crimes as people from similar backgrounds who are not in gangs. Moreover, some gangs have used drug money and thefts from National Guard armories to procure rapid-fire weapons, bullet-proof vests, and all kinds of explosive and military devices. Many police in the cities are now overpowered and outgunned by the gangs and other criminals. As a result, at the end of 1997, there are special police SWAT teams, or special forces units, created in 33 American cities with the latest weapons and many with armored helicopters operating around the clock to be called in to deal with these conditions. There is already a large potential for armed war by hundreds of thousands of gang members in major cities.

Patterson describes these conditions of violence and hopelessness:

What this cry of anguish fails to emphasize is the fratricidal nature of underclass criminality and the fact that the victimizers are almost all

Afro-American. Afro-Americans constitute 25 percent of all of those arrested in the United States, and 47 percent of all those arrested for violent crimes, nearly all against fellow Afro-Americans. Murder is the leading cause of death among Afro-American men ages 15 to 24, and Afro-Americans in general are 6 times more likely to be murdered than Euro-Americans. . . . A 1995 report of the Sentencing Project shows that on any given day almost one in three (32.2 percent) of Afro-American men between the ages of 20 and 29 is under some form of criminal justice supervision, in either prison or jail, or on probation or parole . . . . When the flow of persons coming under the control of the criminal justice system in the course of a year is considered, the rates escalate even further. A 1987 study of California, which calculated such rates, revealed that two thirds of all Afro-American males between the ages of 18 and 29 had been placed under arrest at some time. . . . What has skyrocketed is the arrest rate for drug offenses, which increased from 24 percent of all drug arrests in 1980 to 39 percent in 1993.[11]

These trends indicate an increase in criminal justice control rates involving an increasing number of blacks and a distrust of the system. False ideas have been spread and believed. In 1996, it was reported that federal law enforcement offices were actually promoting the sale of drugs to blacks in the Los Angeles area. There was widespread belief among blacks that the drug business is government-sponsored against black people, which was not proven. But the anti-government fears in the inner city is held broadly.

In addition, there is widespread belief that AIDS involves a plot of whites against blacks. Hanna Rosen points out:

Blacks, 12 percent of the population, account for one third of all AIDS cases. Three out of five new AIDS victims are black, up (in 1995) from one in five in 1986. Black women are 15 times more likely to have AIDS than white women, and their children 18 times more likely.

In Atlanta and some other cities, AIDS is the main cause of death among blacks. Dr. Stephen Thomas, associate professor of Behavioral Science at Emory University, conducted a study for the Southern Christian Leadership Conference with surveys among 1000 black church-goers in each of 5 cities: Atlanta, Charlotte, Detroit, Kansas City, and Tuscaloosa. Rosen, in reporting results of the study, said in the same article:

More than one-third thought AIDS was a form of genocide against blacks; another third were unsure. And more than a third thought HIV was produced in a germ-warfare lab, a theory shared by 40 percent of black college students polled in Washington.[12]

The average white American does not realize the extent of the anti-white, anti-government feelings among blacks in the United States.

Rage of the Middle Class Black American

These prevailing misconceptions about drugs and AIDS were not just among the bottom portion of blacks. There is much evidence of a strong rage among the middle class blacks of America. When Lewis Farrakhan held his "Million Man March" in Washington in 1995, the media interviewers were shocked to find the marchers were primarily middle class black men, many of whom were not there because of involvement as Black Muslims. They were the middle class black men who were doing well financially, but were deeply angry over the condition of the black people.

Earlier, African-American media reporter and author, Ellis Cose pointed this out in his book, *The Rage of the Privileged Class: Why Are Middle-Class Blacks Angry? Why Should America Care?*. Cose does not believe most white people are racist. He is aware many black people have become good friends with white people. What lingers in America is an abiding lack of general acceptance of blacks by whites. Every day black people who have moved into white business-es, government offices, and schools are encountering a sense that white people do not yet treat them as equals. It is not only that blacks rarely make it to controlling levels in white-owned corporations, but that white people are generally better treated. Cose said:

> This is not to say that white Americans are intent on persecuting black people, or that blacks are utterly helpless and fault-free victims of society. Nothing could be further from the truth. Nonetheless, America is filled with attitudes, assumptions, stereotypes and behaviors that make it virtually impossible for blacks to believe that the nation is serious about its promise of equality—even (perhaps especially) for those who have been blessed with material success.[13]

Cose gives the response of many blacks to his interviews as follows:

> I have done everything I was supposed to do. I have stayed out of trouble with the law, gone to the right schools and worked myself nearly to death. What more do they want? Why in God's name won't they accept me as a full human being?[14]

Cose makes it clear they are experiencing anger over continued hindrances to acceptance to continue progress. In fact, he points out their anger is higher than that of the poorer or underclass blacks. (He refers to a Los Angeles 1991 poll and other data).[15] Thus, the issue is not poverty, but the greed to have more than others.

Sinful Bias for Self-Interest Is the Basic Problem

What Cose does not acknowledge is that all men and women–black, white or whatever–are sinful human beings with a bias towards self. Everyone acts in his own self-interest, and it is precisely because of that self-interest that he wants to be treated equally. That general bias of humans will come out, especially when the white population is 75 percent and the blacks are only 12 or 13 percent. And blacks must acknowledge that because the daily media are inundated with the repeated violence and crimes of the black underclass, whites carry a fear of any blacks they don't really know well, and so do some blacks.

Moreover, the black middle class themselves, even if they have come out of the underclass, while greatly troubled with the problems of black people there, really do not care or seek to help them, when they could probably do more for them than anyone else. Cose tells when he was working on his book, he consulted with Daniel Patrick Moynihan, the New York senior senator, who replied, "The big problem, is, 'What are we going to do about the underclass? And a particular problem is that [the] black group your talking about [the middle class] doesn't want to have anything to do with them.'"[16] Middle class blacks are angry about the underclass conditions, but they want to place the blame on whites instead of accepting some responsibility themselves.

The growing number of other minority groups that compete with blacks also brings out the black selfish bias. Since the civil rights laws, there has been massive immigration from Asian and Latin American countries. The Asians and Latin Americans generally have more stable marriages, so they have fewer single parent homes and succeed in school and business better than the blacks.[17] As a result, there are feelings of hostility toward these other poor people. In the 1992 Los Angeles riot, blacks burned stores and homes of other races, especially of the Koreans in the district.

Mixed Races: Growing Loss for Blacks in Political Numbers

The United States has long classified any person with any part or "drop" of black racial background as black. But the existence of multiracial backgrounds is now accepted as more accurate. The Miss USA who also won the title Miss Universe in 1995 chose her identity as "biracial" when introduced. When Tiger Woods won the Augusta Open Golf Tournament, he chose to be identified with Asian and African heritage.

Newsweek did an extensive study and found a large number (figures are uncertain) of people, who normally were called black, are really bi-racial.

Class Conflict 315

Studies show interracial marriages grew by at least 6.5 percent in the 1980s. Interracial married couples numbered 310,000 in 1970; 651,000 in 1980; 964,000 in 1990; and 1,195,000 in 1993. Moreover, cross-racial adoptions are increasing. Many biracial people are nearly white and have passed for white, and throughout American history there are many people who have some biracial blood in their background.

The trend is toward doing away with racial categories, but this is resisted by liberals because it could end the social engineering for race. Several states have passed this new designation of "biracial," and in 1997, the Census Bureau added a category of mixed race. The point is that a large number of people who are considered part-black, or Hispanic, or Asian, no longer view one heritage as their preference. Hence, politicians who still hold a liberal racial agenda are disturbed that the number is rapidly diminishing. When the public makes the shift away from racial distinctions, it will upset their whole vision as social saviors. There are millions of people in America with more than one kind of racial blood. Color of skin is no longer a sufficient definition of people. Many things are involved in determining what group a person is in, and many more people each year don't want to choose between their ancestors.[18] Many whites prefer the place of ethnic origin (Poland, Italy, etc.) as a listing, over just white.

At present, those counted as black are about 13 percent, but if the "biracial" people are subtracted, it will be much lower. Hispanics are now 10 percent of the population, but at the present rate of growth by immigration and a higher than normal birth rate, they will be the nation's largest minority by 2010, and one-fourth of the nation by 2050. Whites are 74 percent. But how many listed in any of these specific groups are completely identifiable there? The Asian population has also grown, and is much more prominent and influential than in 1960.

Race and Affirmative Action

Until the 1960s, little progress had been made in doing away with inequality of the races. Only after the 1960s when there was government compulsion through affirmative action programs did there seem to be much progress for blacks. As we shall see, there had also been little progress for women. At that time, court rulings sought to extend laws to require businesses to equalize opportunities and wages to make up for the past discrimination. The laws for equal rights allowed for preferential treatment for enrollment in educational institutions, opportunity for jobs, promotions in jobs, pay in jobs, government permission for ownership of mass media such as radio and TV stations, grants for education and research, and other areas given to minorities.

There is no question some blacks in America have apparently been helped, and they have helped themselves. But they still earn less than whites on average. Also, only 28 percent have executive, managerial, or administrative jobs. This increase happened under affirmative action requirements and by virtue of the fact that many young executives of corporations and institutions of the educated elite have controlling positions, and as educated elite, they are committed to the agenda of affirmative action. The top executives, most who do not favor affirmative action as such, chose to exercise some affirmative action to avoid government pressures for not doing so. Such preference is offered for race and sex, which explains why black women have made greater advances than even white women.

It is an evident fact that most blacks would not have made their gains without civil rights pressures to help the public overcome its selfish bias. This does not deny the equal ability of most. Liberal colleges and universities have given preferential treatment to minorities, claiming students need to experience diversity in relationships with minorities. Because there has been so much gained by government pressure, there is fear that advancement of blacks will diminish, and even regress, if this stops. A study by Sharon M. Collins on black executives argues that their positions were gained by "politically mediated opportunity structure" and that this will erode in the absence of a sympathetic political environment.[19]

But other black leaders argue there would have been and would be greater advancement if blacks weren't given this concept that they were victims and were motivated to be responsible without preferential treatment. Moreover, there is evidence that the black community might as a whole be much further advanced if it had governmental backing only for equal justice and not affirmative action. Supreme Court Judge Clarence Thomas argued in the concurring decision on a ruling against affirmative action by the Court on June 12, 1995, that the Court cannot make people equal and said, "These programs stamp minorities with a badge of inferiority." This gives them the victim mentality and a bad attitude that demotivates them from trying. Moreover, their reverse injustice only angers many and increases resistance to help. Arguments by Joe Klein, one of many writers on affirmative action, and the writing of others, show blacks have often gained less when given affirmative action help.

For example, Joe Klein, in his review of current problems, relates:

> Affirmative action—the accepted, if imprecise, shorthand for ethnic and gender preference programs—has insinuated itself into every aspect of American public life and most of the private sector as well. The policy has evolved with a minimum of democracy—almost entirely by executive order and court fiat, almost never legislatively, almost never as the result of public debate.[20]

Every company, place of employment, school, and place of government work has been fearful the government agencies and courts will apprehend them and they will get involved in litigation at significant costs. Therefore, to avoid costs, they advance blacks that are less qualified to avoid litigation expense. This question will surely be one of the most important in politics in the days ahead. Klein said, "In fact, we may be hurtling toward the most sensitive moment in American race relations since the 1960's . . . . The most basic American idea—that people from all races and religions can co-exist as equals—may be on the line."[21]

The problem is these efforts to equalize the society have not pleased even all of those that seem to win. It has also made running institutions and companies at times nearly impossible and confusing. The "inescapable conclusion: discrimination can't be cured by counter-discrimination. It is not only divisive but fundamentally unfair, and, in some ways, the results are more costly for blacks than for whites."[22] Proposition 209 in California, and lawsuits in many states, seek to end affirmative action.[23] But indications are there are other ways to create diversity for those who wish to continue to promote preference.[24]

Dangerous Direction of Black Leaders in America

Black leadership is divided, and most of the organizations are still run by older people who represent the old, traditional, liberal civil rights views, and resentfully are not yielding to younger leaders. They still march for affirmative action causes with lessening effect. Jessie Jackson's march, in May 1995, against the Republican Contract, drew small crowds. Manning Marable, author on race related issues, sees the black professionals, educators, and entrepreneurs as having different interests than welfare mothers, the unemployed and the homeless, while these make up one of the largest group of blacks.

Marable sees three distinct political ideologies:

1. *Separatists*, such as Louis Farrakhan of the Nation of Islam, and Dr. Khalid Abdullah Tariq Al-Mansour, who oppose integration or coalition

2. *Inclusionists*, favoring racial integration, and access to opportunity within America's democratic institutions. Many are of the old deterministic liberal elite who dominate the social sciences will not allow themselves to accept the racial progress in America, and they interpret the data to preserve the idea of a remaining "two nations" controlled entirely by prejudice.[25] They must blame "racism" in order to continue the need of the liberal control of the social programs of government. Hacker's "two nations" is their textbook argument. John Hope Franklin's remarks about everything for blacks is viewed by a racial perspective have been referred to.[26] While the old line liberal black leaders still held this view, most of them have not seen progress from the government to achieve their ends and have gravitated to the next view of transformationists.

3. *Transformationists*, such as Marable and Lani Guinier, with the key issue being equality of power relationships between social groups. They also interpret the nation as two races. These are abandoning the one person/one vote

idea of American democracy for ethnic power positions. Their views are growing in acceptance,[27] and these call for the empowering of black voting areas by unnatural geographical configurations, which is now seen as unlawful. Some in the last category would like for Washington, DC to become a state. But Washington, DC is already near bankruptcy and is now under financial control of the federal government. Others that seem to fit these ideas are James Foreman, and V. P. Franklin, who argue for self-determination of blacks in a separate area or state. Lewis Farrakhan's idea of an Islamic black nation is not far removed.

All three of these black groups still are committed to the old liberal, racial purposes of helping blacks, but they are merging toward the postmodern transformations view to achieve their ends. The transformationists have abandoned the American ideal of all men being equal as the foundation of American democracy, which was also the vision of Martin Luther King, Jr. of equal opportunity for all, and which was the idea of the old liberals who envisioned accomplishing their utopia by persuading the votes of the masses to accept equality in a social democracy. At the head of this new postmodern effort for ethnic power positions are Bill and Hillary Clinton.

It was mentioned in chapter one that the appointment of Lani Guinier to head the Justice Department by Bill Clinton failed because this was a departure from the basic concept of the United States government of one man one vote, and replacing it by representative power groups, as John Leo and others pointed out.[28] As mentioned, this was also a departure from Martin Luther King, Jr.'s declarations in his vision, which unsettled many old line blacks. But since they had made little progress, they supported her and protested. Soon afterwards the Supreme Court had to face political gerrymandering of political districts to gain power centers for blacks (the same things southern whites had done to limit black influence). The Court rejected that concept of manipulating power centers and forced realignment. Giving up the justice of the democratic system of one man one vote was just not acceptable for the alternative of group power.

During the Court's considerations in 1995, Jesse Jackson sought to rally black support to the maintaining of these power positions, focusing protest on Georgia's 11th district. While the Court rejected the districting, it is interesting that the black representatives who gained power in the eleventh district of Georgia and elsewhere were all elected by whites anyway, showing capable blacks could win without empowerment centers. Thus, democracy for the individual is facing the pressure to give ground to the power of special groups in the thinking of group leaders, and the way is being led by black ethnicity.

In 1997, President Clinton acknowledged the critical racial situation in America and formed a President's Advisory Commission on Race to help develop better relationships as a top priority of his second term. Clinton appointed

John Hope Franklin, the Duke University professor who believes race figures into everything, to head this, and six other members, all who favor affirmative action. A sympathetic board member, Angela Oh, an attorney, asked that the board's discussions be broadened to talk about all races, but she was told by Franklin the main issue is black and white. When Ward Connerly, a leading opponent of affirmative action asked to be heard, he was denied. When this group sought to hold a dialogue on race in Dallas in December 1997, with the moderator being Transportation Secretary Rodney Slater, only blacks were invited to participate. It is now evident that this advisory group has the narrow perspective of modern, deterministic liberals and the transformationists, who seem bent on gaining racial advantage at the expense of democratic processes. While the president surely knew the views of the advisory group, it has been so blatantly biased that he is losing political approval and, at least publicly, is seeking to influence decisions. White reaction is sure to occur, and we now face great tension in which there could be an explosion ignited. Black liberals are at an impasse, and are willing to force the acceptance of selfish positions that even the Supreme Court recognizes are against the basic premise of the Constitution of the United States and against the original liberal dreams. These are countered by conservatives who oppose the liberal dream and all continued racial change.

There is a another group of black leaders who realize most whites are not racists, and blacks and whites must work together to save America. These differ concerning continuing some form of affirmative action but want to drop race as an issue and work together while helping disadvantaged people. In this group, there is Tony Brown, Orlando Patterson, Thomas Sowell, Supreme Court Justice Clarence Thomas, and other intelligent blacks. While they may lean toward some old liberal ideas of help, they and others see the urgency of friendship of all ethnic groups and of promoting self-reliance. Christians must take the lead in bringing together a new approach soon. The situation is urgent, and an economic crisis or misunderstanding with blacks could ignite a bomb such as America cannot imagine. Tony Brown, the PBS television commentator and syndicated radio talk-show host, warns both white and black people:

> But I fear we are on the path of self-destruction as a nation; that the United States of America is committing national suicide. I do not want to see this country destroyed because we fail to see the truth about where we are headed . . . . Unless America confronts its racism, its greed, and its moral rot, we face at the very least a drastically reduced standard of living. At the worst, I fear a racial conflagration and national bankruptcy. To avoid these catastrophes and to ensure economic growth, Blacks and Whites must join together to work for the common good on a national scale . . . . If we fail to unite, there will be no Black or White winners, just American losers.[29]

Coss concluded his search for the anger of blacks with a solemn warning before exploring new alternatives. "It there was one sentiment that consistently came through in interview after interview with very successful black people in all walks of life, it can be summed up in one phrase: *We are tired of waiting.*"[30] America had better hear the warnings of these discerning black men.

Chapter 16

Women

INTRODUCTION

In earlier chapters, data was presented showing that when a people begins to reject God and turn to materialism, the civilization begins to view women and children in terms of material worth. Men and women are no longer seen as equals before God, though with created differences. This was reflected in Plato's statements and those of others. As shown, this change of perspective resulted in the feminist movements in Greece, Rome, and America. The materialistic human perspective adopts an egalitarian view in regard to women and men, which means women should be equal to men in every way, except men can't have babies. This chapter evaluates what changes have occurred for women as a result of the sexual revolution in the United States; chapter 17 will look at the results for men and children, and chapter 18 for homosexuality. While male-driven materialism is the founding cause, the feminist movement has been a strong promoter of the changes for men and children in each society, and therefore is the focal point in viewing these changes. Most feminists were driven by the convictions of the injustice from the materialistic prospective, and really thought they were doing right.

THE SEXUAL CHANGES FOR WOMEN BY FEMINISM

A Review of the Steps of Sexual Change by the Feminists

The story of the changes made by the women's movement was given in chapter 11, but it is helpful to review some of these to have a clearer picture of the results. The feminist movement began because men were forsaking their wives and children to make money, and were also feeling their independence from God (cf. chapter 10, "Value Shift"). Being indifferent to God, wealth seems to give men a euphoric feeling of individualistic power, the men neglected or dominated their wives and often engaged sexually with other women. Thus, as psychiatrist Marynia Farnham pointed out, the women's movement began in

America as a reaction of hate for and competition with men (chapter 10). Feminism promoted women's rights for status and materialistic gains and was a companion with the cause of slavery and civil rights for the underclass. The alternative for women might have been to call the men away from the idolatry of mammon back to love God and their wives and children in order to regain equality. The architect and early chief motivator of the feminist movement was Elizabeth Cady Stanton. She gave the primary emphasis of each of the early steps and envisioned the demise of the family as the ultimate end for women in order to gain their freedom (see chapter 11).

The first surge of the women's movement in the nineteenth century aimed at gaining recognition of women as separate individuals with a right to own property and be treated equally in earning money. The second surge was to liberalize divorce laws so women could be free from men, and the rate of divorce increased five times as fast as the proportion of married people over a period of sixty-three years. The graph on divorce showed a consistent rise in the divorce rate from 1866 till 1960. To promote this independence from men, there was a growing emphasis on educating women the same as men, and an emphasis on their bearing fewer children. The birth rate began declining. At the time of the Civil War and Reconstruction, it was noted that it was acceptable in the black community for young women to have children out of wedlock. Unfortunately, there were few male sexual role models for black men, even among the preachers. The breakdown of monogamous marriage among blacks was allowed by Southern white governments after they regained control in the Reconstruction era. The governments by Southerners did not enforce the marriage laws among blacks, ignoring violations of laws that did not affect them, lest the federal government again interfere. During this time of the second surge of feminism, beginning efforts to organize to promote women's voting rights were led primarily by Susan B. Anthony, the friend and assistant to Elizabeth Cady Stanton, and others.

The third surge of the women's movement (1900 ff.) was a time of militancy, and of finally gaining the vote for women. After obtaining the vote in 1919, women had grown so numerically that they outnumbered men, and there was a sense by most women that they now would be treated more equally. This concept of individualism rather than oneness in marriage resulted in tremendous conflict in the home. Counselors and psychologists discovered many women were "frigid" sexually, and they were told to be more feminine. The effort of many women to dominate the home resulted in "momism" or women controlling the sons. There was more gender rejection by boys and evident growth of homosexuality.

The World Wars resulted in a skyrocketing rate of divorce, and women entered into all kinds of jobs which before were exclusive to men. The motion picture industry and the media encouraged romance and immorality.

Contraception began to be practiced and birth control ideas discussed. Margaret Sanger launched the idea of planned parenthood and of widespread use of contraception. The fourth stage brought Freudian psychology to the forefront, and the idea that sexual restraint was harmful and freedom of sexual expression was the ideal. Sanger made the idea of a woman controlling her own body by birth control methods popular, and was the forerunner of the concept of "pro-choice" by women.

The fifth surge of the feminist movement called for militancy. The women's movement had turned back toward accepting the role of women, women were marrying earlier, and efforts at women's education were diminished. While contraception was accepted by 70 percent of Americans, it was not practiced effectively. The renewed feminist movement, which was launched during the "Death of God" theology, was given a shove by Betty Friedan and the formation of the National Organization of Women. This promoted women as victims of men and demanded change of many kinds, especially seeking political emancipation and enforcement of women's freedom to gain economic advantage and equality in achievement for earning. Sexuality was taken into politics by Kate Millet and other extreme feminists, and a women's agenda gained approval along with civil rights legislation. The invention of the birth control pill promised greater sexual freedom for women. Premarital and extra-marital sex by women, cohabitation, extramarital pregnancies, and single-female-parented families rapidly escalated (as shown in the graphs). These were all promoted as that which was "natural" for the woman in order to control her own body.

Feminists Sought Force of Government Where Aims Were Unacceptable

By 1975, there were 500 women's studies programs, with 20,000 courses on women and 40 research centers. Women's studies turned to emphasizing "womancenteredness" on a worldwide basis, envisioning women would come to control the world. Some male clergy joined in promoting these things, feeling they were rescuing women from past oppression. Researchers presented evidence of female goddesses in many ancient cultures, and feminists argued that women in the holy of holies produces peace, while male leaders, they insisted, had promoted war. Women turned to witchcraft as a way of rebellion against men and as an expression of women's leadership. The worship of female goddesses became a logical part of the objective to remove male leadership and establish female leadership.

About 1980 women realized their positions of control in business and earnings had not increased appreciably to that of men, and black leaders also realized this. Women and blacks joined together, and through the educated elite, promoted the Affirmative Action movement to try to compel change in industry and government to make greater gains in pay, in positions of authority, and in government administration and Congress. The liberal news media led the way, and Hollywood presented women as not only equal, but superior to men in their roles in films and in commercials.

The liberal elite argued social democracy was the way to freedom. The feminists argued families should be run as a democracy with men, women, and children equally having a voice. There was to be no patriarchy, but rather equality, or a historical compensation by matriarchy. Children were to be raised with the help of the whole community (a village), especially the democratic government and not just in the family. Satisfaction of sex by masturbation, extra-marital relations, and homosexuality were to be applauded because they did not involve male control. Children could be conceived and born without a relationship to a man by artificial insemination, and could be aborted up to the final term by the woman's choice, without the father having any say. Women could get off work without penalty (leave of absence without pay) to have or care for children according to the Family Medical Leave Act of 1993. Women asserted that there should be business or government support to put children in child care facilities, and men should give equal help at home with the children and house-work. Also, it was seen that teenage girls should be able to have sex and abor-tions without parental involvement or consent. These ideals were perpetrated by the feminists and sought politically with Affirmative Action for job positions and pay.

Apparent Victory for Women to Be Like Men

Today it appears all the feminist's objectives have been accepted by many in American society, and most have been endorsed legally. Women are given a position not only of equality with men, but a preference over men in many instances. Almost all colleges have co-education, and many have mixed living in dorms with mixed bathrooms. Today, 54 percent of college students are women, and more are getting graduate degrees. Records indicate the following changes in degrees offered: in life sciences in 1968, 15 percent, while in 1983, 33 percent; physical sciences in 1968, 5 percent, while in 1983, 15 percent; computer information in 1968, 0 percent, while in 1986, 14 percent; engineering in 1968, 0 percent, while in 1986, 14 percent; with even greater increases in law, business, and so forth. These numbers continued to rise and therefore opened doors for better jobs in business and industry.

It is true that some women in the workplace in America (as in other Western countries) have received improved status and pay. The average pay compared to the male dollar earned by women changed *by virtue of affirmative action* in the U. S., and rose from 59.9 cents in 1979 to 71.6 cents by 1990. The picture feminists give is of women's conditions constantly getting better, and they will soon take over corporate America's leadership. The Department of Labor reports that of the Fortune 1,000 companies, the percentage of women senior managers of Vice President or higher rose from 1.5 percent in 1980 to 5 percent in 1994. (Some feminists claim up to 10 percent). Two researchers, Leslie Kaufman-Rosen and Claudia Kalb, claim, "If current trends continue, women could reasonably expect to have as much as 15 percent of Senior corporate posts within 10 years." They base this on the much higher percentage of women getting graduate degrees.[1] Moreover, in the economy as a whole–in business offices, retail stores, and so forth–about 43 percent have managerial positions. Among these are the 6.5 million women who own their own businesses, and many others where the work force is almost all women. In 1900, only 15 percent of married women worked; in 1960 about 30 percent, and in 1990, there were 59 percent. But many worked part-time.

The marriage laws, which in the colonies prohibited divorce except in extreme circumstances, have become progressively weaker, so divorce may now occur at a whim under the "no fault" divorce laws. There has been rapid increase in divorce, and the widespread cohabitation without marriage is accepted.[2] Women are now legally free from men, and law prohibits any distinction in hiring or promoting women. Today, women have many options in contraceptives with no legal prohibition, with only medical direction and guidance required. The so-called "pro choice" ruling of the Supreme Court (*Roe v. Wade*, 1973) has consistently increased abortions from about 700,000 in 1972 to about 1.7 million in 1990, so that few children are born in America that women do not "choose." The Supreme Court excluded the father from having any choice in women's abortions of their children. Men have increasingly been excluded from having a voice in the family. Recent changes in these laws will be discussed later.

In universities, women hold positions on the faculty from heads of departments to research and teaching positions, and all government supported colleges admit women. Women in the military have increased from 4.6 percent in 1975, to 8.4 percent in 1980; from 9.8 percent in 1985, to 13.2 percent in 1996. In many cases, until recently, they have trained with the men and even lived with them. They hold leadership and combat positions in the military. More women have been elected to Congress, and President Clinton has appointed a large number of women to Cabinet and other positions in his administration. Two women now hold positions on the Supreme Court, and women hold many other judicial positions. In most modern videos and movies, women are the judges. They became police chiefs in many large cities, mayors, governors, and heads of universities.

Women in sports have increased rapidly, in scholarships, media coverage, and Olympic participation (19 in 1900 to 3,779 in 1996). Women are given equal if not more priority as media reporters of all kinds, even in men's sports and in economic reporting. There is now a professional women's basketball league, and women in other professional sports such as golf are becoming prominent. Some even perform in professional boxing matches. They are given preferential treatment for government loans and contracts, preferences in education, and places of visibility in the media in all roles, including sports announcing and interviewing, even in male locker rooms after games.

The feminist's ideal of a women is accepted. The selection committee of the Mother's Day Committee for outstanding Mother Award in 1995 chose four women who fit the feminist ideal. Women hold leadership positions in many churches, preside in national church offices of organizations, and now even para-church Christian groups, such as Young Life and InterVarsity Christian Fellowship, are promoting parity of women in leadership. *Christianity Today* indicated Campus Crusade for Christ and Navigators are also moving in this direction.[3] In many churches, the masculine pronouns for God are made feminine and many pray, "our Mother who is in heaven." Some Bible publishers have changed the text to a neuter gender where the pronouns are masculine. The so-called feminist's agenda is certainly well on its way to completion, if it has not arrived. Many boundaries between men and women have been erased.

FEMINISTS PERVERT DATA TO PROMOTE THEIR CAUSES

In order to achieve advancement against men, the feminists have not only used government pressure on business and civil sectors, they have perverted much data which they publish to put men in a bad light. Christina Hoff Sommers, associate professor of philosophy at Clark University and a W. H. Brady Fellow at the American Enterprise Institute in Washington, DC has been a feminist writer for a number of leading magazines. She has written a popular book, *Who Stole Feminism*, in which she exposed many of the distortions of facts by feminists leaders. [4] The reader should consult the book for these, since it would be tedious to repeatedly give the page references. Other sources in the following discussion are referred to when applicable.

Men Cause Thousands of Women to Die of Anorexia?

On a number of occasions, it has been said that men are the chief cause for many women's deaths from eating disorders. Joan Brumberg, former director of women's studies at Cornell University, wrote *Fasting Girls: The Emergence of Anorexia Nervosa as a Modern Disease,* and used the figure of 150,000 women who are plagued by the disease, as women scholars believe, because of a "misogynist society that demeans women . . . by objectifying their bodies." Naomi Wolf, in her book *The Beauty Myth: How Images of Beauty Are Used Against Women,* says 150,000 females *die of* anorexia each year. She says the reason is men pressure them to be beautiful, and she likens the disaster to that of the Holocaust.[5] This projection was then repeated by Gloria Steinem,[6] and in turn by Ann Landers in April 1992, and more recently, this figure of 150,000 deaths was quoted in the preface of a women's study text, *The Knowledge Explosion*.

Disputing with these "facts," Sommers traced the story of such a "holocaust" against women back to a figure Brumberg used from a 1985 newsletter by The American Anorexia and Bulimia Association which said there were 150,000 to 200,000 *sufferers* (not fatalities) of anorexia nervosa. Ms. Sommers found studies reveal *less than 100 deaths of women* among one hundred million women, which is a very small percentage, and no proof was offered anywhere that men were responsible.

Abuse of Pregnant Women by Men Is the Main Cause of Birth Defects?

Sommer's tracking of the "fact" that male abuse was the main cause of birth defects, revealed another distortion. Caroline Whitehead, a maternal nurse and child care specialist in Raleigh, North Carolina, had introduced Sara Buel at a nurses' and social workers' conference in 1989. Sara Buel is a founder of the Domestic Violence Advocacy Project at Harvard Law School. In her remarks, Whitehead mentioned, according to the March of Dimes research which she had seen, there were more women *screened for birth defects* than are ever screened for domestic battery. She *did not attribute birth defects to battery*, but was saying less attention was paid to battery than to birth defects. Buel distributed this statement about battery as the cause of the majority of defects (which she later admitted was a misunderstanding) in an unpublished manuscript she circulated among family-violence professionals. On November 4, 1992, Deborah Louis, president of the national Women's Studies Association, quoted this misinformation on the Women's Studies electronic bulletin board. Then, journalists around the country quoted it in articles in *Time, Boston Globe, Dallas Morning News, Arizona Republic, Chicago Tribune*, and so forth, and educators, governors' offices, and Washington politicians began to stir into action over this lie. Thus, men have been incorrectly blamed for a multitude of birth defects.

Wife Beating Is at Epidemic Proportions in America?

Wife abuse by men is a serious problem and *has increased significantly since the conflicts introduced by the women's movement*. But it is now *greatly exaggerated* by feminists. For example, Barbara Mobley and June Hegstrom, members of the Women Legislators Lobby and of the House of Representatives in Georgia said:

Violent attacks by men have become the leading health risk for American women which costs taxpayers billions each year in health-care expenditures, lost wages, litigation, welfare and homelessness. Feminists argue that such violence against women must be viewed as a national epidemic, and one that demands a national solution.

They give the figure of 4 million abusers, while other feminists have said there are 60 million (although there are not that many women living with a man).

This is a malicious exaggeration. A leading authority, Murray Straus of the University of New Hampshire, said, "There are about 1.8 million women who suffer real violence from husbands or boyfriends, meaning one or more incidents of hitting or kicking each year, with about 10 percent requiring help from a doctor." This means about 3 percent of the 56.8 million women who are living with men suffer at least one violent act a year, with about .33 percent requiring medical help. Actual statistics for 1996 of women abused were only 837,899, with about 1,326 killed by their spouses.

There is another aspect that feminists omit. Straus and his co-author Gelles say, "Women *initiate assaults* (not self-defense) against their partners at the same rate as men."[7] Another study in 1990 concluded 24 percent of domestic violence is initiated by women, 27 percent by men. There is a rising number of serious sexual abuses in America which must be addressed, but it is much smaller than feminists say, and it is certain some of it is a result of the conflict caused by the distortions of hate promoted by feminists.

Male Belittling of Women Is Hindering Their Education?

Christina Hoff Sommers also tells of a study by the American Association of University Women (AAUW) which had been founded in 1881 to promote excellence in women's education and which now has over 140,000 members. The organization commissioned a study as a part of its "Initiative for Educational Equity," which was done by the firm of Greenberg-Kake Associates, to measure the self-esteem of girls and boys between the ages of 9 and 15. In it, they claimed a drop in self-esteem for girls of these ages in education, and published under the title *Shortchanging Girls, Shortchanging America*. This was highly promoted through the media. As a result of this report, conferences were held on boosting girl's self-esteem. The AAUW commissioned another study with the Wellesley Center for Study of Women and promoted the passing of a bill in Congress for $360 million. The AAUW claimed that because young women were demotivated, America was losing great achievements through those women in the future. The study was never submitted to other scientists working in the field, and the AAUW was extremely reluctant to sell or make available the study to others. The AAUW study gave no definition of "self-esteem" or even what they meant by it. Sommers "found that the AAUW's finding that girls' self-esteem plummets did not square with what most of the experts in adolescent psychology were saying." Barron J. Hirsch, a professor of psychology at Northwestern

University said, "Its findings are inconsistent with the recent literature." Moreover he pointed out that no one has been able to establish a clear correlation between self-esteem and behavior. But the AAUW continued to assert its unfounded claims.[8] In fact, it seems girls of this adolescent age have their self-esteem more affected by whether they have friends and have acceptance and a close relationship to their fathers, than perhaps anything else.[9]

Related to this falsification, the Gender Equity in Education Act was passed in April 1993. It instituted numerous other activities in education by using this study. As a follow-up, in October 1997, Donna Shellala, Secretary of Health and Human Services, at a conference in Washington, DC, entitled "Creating Safe Passage for Youth," announced the allotment of 1 million dollars to exalt self-esteem for girls 9-14 years old, and to help prevent teen pregnancies and other problems.

In the subsequent Wellesley Report, the AAUW continued to promote the idea women were the gender at risk and received over 1400 articles in the media and promoted their education venture to bolster equality for women not only in the bill, but before all the foundations of America that furnish funds. Sommers points out the Wellesley Report never made any comparisons between participation and achievement and progress for women, nor did it evaluate the indications that boys are really the ones in trouble. Sommers points out that today 55 percent of college students are female, and in 1989 they received 52 percent of the B.A.'s, 52 percent of M.A.'s. While they received only 36 percent of the doctorates, there is rapid increase in this, having increased 185 percent since 1971. She said:

> In a study of self reports by high school seniors, the United States department of Education found that more boys than girls cut classes, fail to do homework assignments, had disciplinary problems, and had been suspended and had been in trouble with the police. Studying transcripts for 1982 high school graduates, the Department of Education found girls outperforming boys in *all* subjects, from math to English to science.[10]

When one examines the evidence, the facts seem to support that the gender at risk is not that of the female, but that of the male.

Rape Is a Frequent Experience, Especially on the College Campus?

There are many other feminists claims that are distortions out of hate for men. Ellis Cose, in *A Man's World,* casually mentions some of these, such as the distortion of the number of rapes by men. In regards to this Cose says:

> Statistics have been widely disseminated indicating that more than one in four women in college have been sexually assaulted. A number of critics recently have pointed out that the statistic is misleading at best. The high number of assaults is derived by lumping together rapes; attempted rapes; assaults before entering college; and 'rapes' of women who, in many cases, don't believe they have been raped.[11]

Sommers gives even more extensive research to the misleading data used by feminists on rape.[12] Much of the misleading data came from a study by Mary Koss who believes rape is an extreme behavior "on a continuum with *normal male behavior within the culture*," and much of her teaching is given by Gloria Steinem of *Ms.* magazine in 1985, and also a 1992 National Women's Study by Dr. Dean Kilpatrick of the Crime Victims Research and Treatment Center at the Medical School of South Carolina. Sommers showed that in these studies, the questions were designed to count rapes when the majority of the so- called victims did not consider themselves to have been raped. Sommers lists a number of polls and studies by social scientists that regarded these figures as greatly exaggerated for political reasons, including Louis Harris and Associates; Eugene Kanin, professor at Perdue University; Margaret Gordon at the University of Washington; Dr. Linda George of Duke University; Dr. Naomi Breslau at the Henry Ford Health Science Health Center in Detroit, and others. While feminists claimed as high as 1 out of 4 women have been raped, the figures are much lower, or about 2–5 percent according to other studies. The feminists have especially exaggerated "date rape" on campuses, yet Peter Hellman of *New York* magazine found fewer than 1000 recorded in the police logs of all the campuses in the country in 1990. Campus rape seems to be much lower than rape in general across the country. Many young women who had been on drugs and alcohol and participated in kissing and fondling and later regretted their conduct were falsely considered raped. As a result of these feminist claims, there has been $20 million allotted by the Senate in the *Title IV, Safe Campuses for Women in the Violence against Women Act of 1993.*

Exaggeration of Women as the Main Providers for Families?

The feminist movement sought to depreciate homemaking and caring for children as a main vocation for women. They exalted women as the main providers of the family and say women are happy leaving the children and doing the job of provider. Many women writers in the media have accepted these ideas and have helped promote this as politically correct.

In an article on a study done by the Families and Work Institute, Sue Shellenbarger, staff writer for the *Wall Street Journal*, begins by saying:

> Women in the workplace not only are *major breadwinners* for their families but also have little desire to give up that role. A broad new study . . . shows that *55 percent* of employed women bring in *half or more* of their household income and 53 percent say they don't want to give up any of their responsibilities either at work or at home. (italics added)

The impression is that most of the homes in America are dependent on women, and women like these conditions. But this is not true. The following is a graph of the report of the percentage of women working and their earnings:

MAJOR CONTRIBUTORS

Proportion of family income contributed by employed women.

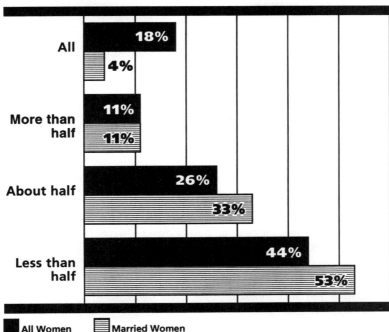

All
18%
4%

More than half
11%
11%

About half
26%
33%

Less than half
44%
53%

■ All Women ▤ Married Women

Sources: Louis Harris & Associates; Families and Work Institute; Whirlpool Foundation

The contributions of employed women (18-55 years old) to their families' income.

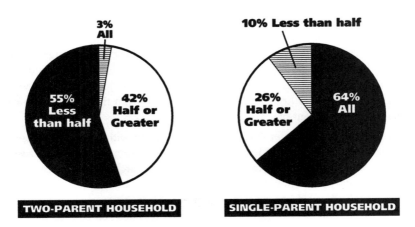

3%
All

55% Less than half

42% Half or Greater

TWO-PARENT HOUSEHOLD

10% Less than half

26% Half or Greater

64% All

SINGLE-PARENT HOUSEHOLD

Sources: Julie Brines, Univ. of Washington; Louis Harris and Associates

This shows that 15 percent contribute all or more than half of the income, while 33 percent contribute about half, or a total (15 percent + 33 percent) of 48 percent. But it also reports that 53 percent of *married* women, and 44 percent of *all* women contribute less than half. Important is the fact that these are *percentages on only 45 percent of the full-time work force who are women.* Thus, *less than half of less than half* (48 percent of 45 = 21.6 percent) of the work force who are women are providing the needs of the American family. While more women are helping, the predominant amount is by far still provided by men.

Married Women Have a More Successful Home if Working?

Moreover, Sylvia Ann Hewlett, a woman economist, recalls male wages were increasing until 1973, at which time women began entering the job market. But she points out, changes have not made two wage earners as profitable as it looked. She said:

> By 1987 the male wage, adjusted for inflation was back down to $19,859, a 19 percent decline. To shore up family income, wives have flocked into the labor market, but their earning power is low. In 1988 the average family income was only 6 percent higher than in 1973, though almost twice as many wives were at work. In many households, one well-paid smokestack job with heath insurance has often been replaced by two service jobs without benefits.[13]

There are many obstacles women have found that the feminists did not count on when they planted the seeds of the idea of entering the market place, and they do not warn other women about these. With the wife and husband working, the family *needs on average 30 percent more income than the one-earner family,* including financial cost of child care, more clothes, more transportation. Another important factor is working women usually end up with very *little retirement* for their work. This is true not only for those who work part-time and receive few benefits. Women often leave their jobs and then go back; they change jobs more frequently, so they seldom get vested in a retirement plan. A 25-year-old woman is estimated to spend only 44 percent of her remaining life on a payroll, whereas a man would spend 70 percent. Seven years away from the job during a career usually cuts retirement benefits in half.[14]

Also there is far greater stress, a continuous fight with time, since there is no full-time person at home to tend to household chores and other necessities. Leaving children, especially teenagers, at home as "latch-key" kids leads to their indiscriminately watching television and having guests, even girls have boy friends in. The incidents of sex and pregnancies have increased from this. Moreover, *Newsweek* says over one million couples have been forced to live apart in separate locations with two homes to keep both jobs because companies want one to move. These things put exceedingly high stress on marriages.

The picture is distorted about men doing housework. The following graph shows men help more in the home when the wife works up to where she provides 50–60 percent; but after that, if she provides more–up to 100 percent, the husband's participation falls. It seems that when she provides the most, his self-image drops and so does his motivation. Usually, the wife comes home to doing housework, and studies show it is usually not because the husband and children are unwilling, but the wife wants to help her husband and children; the woman's desire is to be in a helping role. Thus, married women who work are faced with

SHARING WORK AT HOME

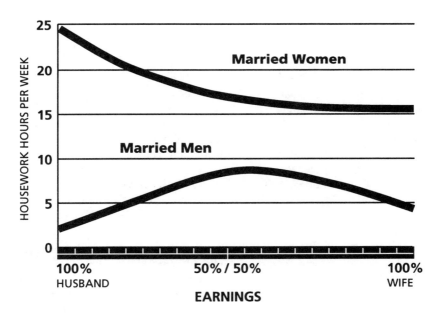

back-breaking work away and at home, and with increased tensions, as the following graph shows.

Betty Friedan has decried these unexpected conditions and said, "We told our daughters, 'You can have it all! Well can they have it all? Only by being super-woman. Well I say no to superwoman!"[15] Sara Davidson interviewed 300 women in writing her book, and found they were "disillusioned, with many women realizing that they can't have it all–marriage, career, and motherhood." This view of wives and mothers who work is substantiated by many others.[16] Many women feel torn and concerned because they leave the children, and also many would like to have more energy for their husbands.

The real desire of most women is to be at home. The optimistic report by Families and Work Institute (given above) also claimed, "Rather 48 percent of women surveyed say they would choose to work even it they already had enough money to live as comfortably as they would like . . . ." But a Labor Department Women's Bureau study done only months before said, "Although 79 percent of women say they 'love' or 'like' their jobs, *many* would be just as *happy not to* have to work so hard."

> Just 15 percent of those in a 'New Providers' survey said they would work full time if they had enough to live comfortably. Instead 33 percent would work part time, 31 percent would care for their families, and 20 percent would do volunteer work.[17]

The claim that women really prefer to not be at home, but rather working, is just not the true story when all the women are included. This is a feminist misrepresentation of the heart of most women.

Women Are Better Off as Singles?

Look also at the real situation of single women. The picture of single women is surely not rosy. In the single-parent household, 64 percent must supply all the income, 26 percent supply half or greater, and 10 percent less than half. But even Gloria Steinem has admitted that by the year 2000, the majority of people below the poverty line will be single women with children. The tragic story is of women becoming pregnant as teenagers, having children out of wedlock and ending up with the heavy burden of caring for them alone. The number of fatherless homes is growing at alarming rates. Many women have divorced their husbands thinking, as a single mother who was reasonably educated, they would be free to do as they pleased and could do well financially.

But as Dr. Lenore Weitzman, associate professor at Stanford University, points out, divorced women and minor children experience a 73 percent drop in standard of living in the first year after divorce, while the men experienced a 42 percent increase. The census data shows 85 percent of divorced women are awarded no alimony. When it *is* granted, a divorced wife typically received only $350 a month for 2 years. Child support (as of 1985) averaged $200 per month, which is less than half the actual cost. Ninety percent of non-custodial fathers pay no child support, and 55 percent who are supposed to pay do not comply with court orders. Since Weitzman's study, Congress has passed a law allowing garnishing a man's salary, but this remains a major problem. While the number of non-paying fathers is not as large as the feminists would portray, since a large part of non-paying fathers are in jail and can't pay and often back-debt is allowed by courts when a man is out of work, the number is still formidable. Part of the problem for non-support is the anger, vindictiveness, and harassment of the former wife, who harasses the man at his work until the employer perhaps even terminates him.

There are additional problems for young, unmarried women. Young single women have found that they have to postpone marriage to get into a career, and they find themselves increasingly in a "marriage crunch." *Newsweek* said a woman at 20 years old has a 75 percent chance of marriage while one at 35 has only a 5 percent chance.[18] For some time, it has become known that women who sacrifice marriage and children for a career later regret it. Dr. Matina Horner, president of Radcliffe College, said:

> Today, some women who pursued careers are saying that the price of success is too high. They are beginning to want to have children and deeper relationships. They viewed the career route as the primary source of their hopes and now are questioning that decision.[19]

Some are taking the difficult route of opting to be single parents. Many are choosing to be "the other woman" to a married man, with many tensions and disappointments.[20]

ADVERSE EFFECTS FOR WOMEN RESULT FROM COMPETITION, PERVERSION, AND GOVERNMENT PRESSURE ON MEN

At superficial observation, the feminist's movement seems to accomplish good for women. But the effects in the long run turn out to be not in the interests of women. A few of these can be observed from overall study of what occurs.

Threat of Male Uniqueness Results in Abandoning Work to Women

In America and all the Western countries which have been influenced by an enlightened educated elite, there have been similar feminist movements that preceded America's. And as women have increasingly entered the work force, the men have exited. In Britain, where the women's movement preceded America's, there is a precedent. "Male participation in the British work force actually fell from 93 percent to 84 percent between 1973 and 1992, while female participation rose from 53 percent to 65 percent. By 1991, one third of unskilled British males were jobless." Women's jobs are predicted to grow by 700,000 in the next 5 years, while those carried out by men will fall by 200,000. "In Britain, France and Germany, the unemployment rates (of men) have tripled. Seventy percent of the jobs created in Europe in the second half of the 1980's went to women and new entrants to the labor market"

> In the United States the total number of registered unemployed workers plus those too discouraged to look for jobs–has doubled for men between the ages of 25 and 55 since 1970.[21]

There are several reasons for this. One is many new jobs are service sector jobs more fitting for women; another is many jobs are part-time and women look for these; and another is businesses can pay women less than men. But there are two far more important factors. One is many men are not comfortable competing with women, and they abdicate the kinds of work where women enter. Men intuitively want to love, not fight, women. Also, men cannot have babies, and they desire work known as important male work in order to find meaningful identity.[22]

It is very important to recognize that the male desertion of many jobs and their letting women take over in increasing numbers is caused mainly by a basic need of men. By flooding the work places of men to be like men, women are in fact causing the men to leave. And, as in many third world countries, women in the West could some day find they are doing two-thirds of all the work because they challenged men in the jobs that were known as typically male. This is increasingly occurring.

Also, as male identity is lost (especially when men have been dominated by women in the home when growing up), men then devote themselves increasingly to pornography, to sexual promiscuity to conquer more women, and to violence to prove their male identity. Most rapists are not motivated by lust as much as by vengeance. The same is true of violent abuse; men act violently to prove their manhood when challenged by women. In America this is the great problem of black men in the black matriarchal society where there is only the single mother.[23] Men need a distinction as men, and if women do not grant this, they will seek it by greater physical strength.

Margaret Mead long ago said:

As far as I have been able to distinguish in the whole of human history, the importance of male work is the most universal social difference between the sexes, aside from the basic physical one expressed in reproductive activity [by women].[24]

All over the world men's work has been considered more important than women's to give men an identity to equal the power of motherhood. This is true within a particular culture. The same jobs may be switched in another culture so that what was woman's work one place will be more important as man's work in another. If the men fish in one culture, it is most important. But if women fish in another, it will be less important than what the men do. But if men and women do the same things, the male identity is confused and men withdraw to war and sexual conquest.

J. D. Unwin's study of 86 different societies found when a sexual revolution captures a culture, the culture declines. Unwin said, "I offer no opinion about rightness or wrongness." But his conclusion was, "In human records there is no instance of a society retaining its energy after a complete new generation has inherited a tradition which does not insist on pre-nuptial and post-nuptial continence." Pitirim Sorokin of Harvard confirmed the same phenomenon in his studies. Unwin led Sorokin to the conclusion that this was because all their energy in a sexual revolution was focused and expended in sex, which is no doubt partially true.[25]

But George Gilder has shown in his book, *Sexual Suicide,* the main reason for societal decline is that men withdraw from jobs invaded by women, jobs which are key to building and maintaining the culture. I have encountered other illustrations. For example, when women entered the medical profession in the Soviet Union, men began to withdraw from the field of general practice to specialties. And the numbers of male doctors dropped altogether leaving general practice, pediatrics, and medical service areas to the women. These changes, along with the rebellion of the youth from lack of training in discipline by the father in the home, are the two major reasons a civilization dies.

Gilder described the phenomenon of men leaving when women enter male domains:

> Because of the amorphous sexuality of the males, they must be given specific and exclusive tasks, not to accomplish the business of the society but to accomplish and *affirm their own identities as males.* If such roles are not given them, they disrupt the community or leave it. Or else they subside into a torpor, punctuated with rituals of sexual self-exaltation. Such patriarchies overburden the women with all the community's real work, both procreative and productive. (italics added)[26]

Thus, this general process in time diminishes the work energy on the whole and causes the women to become more subservient to the men, when they think they are gaining ascendancy over them. This seems to be occurring in America to American women.

Equal Sexual Freedom Has Widened, Not Reduced, the Double Standard

The process of removing patriarchy completely (not just oppressive patriarchy), and claiming to be free to interact with any men in any job or situation for sex or any other reason, has removed all sexual protective cover of husbands for their wives and especially their daughters. The demand of women for equal freedom in sex has not only given then freedom of choice, but greatly accelerated vulnerability and sexual promiscuity at a rate almost unbelievable. In the past, patriarchy could protect precisely because it controlled.

When the liberal theologians arrived at the "Death of God" theology in the 1960s and 1970s, the liberal elite were influenced by Freud and his followers and by the perverted report of Kinsey (with the practical application by Playboy and others). With this influence, they brought fulfillment to the feminist aspiration for sexual freedom.[27] As Paul Johnson mentioned, it was in the 1960s that the trend of the intellectual elite turned toward hedonism. That is still the one of the main themes of the educated elite as manifested in the emphasis of the Clinton Administration.

Gertrude Himmelfarbe, distinguished professor of the Graduate School of the City University of New York, in her recent book, *The De-Moralization of Society*, traced this change. She said:

> The combined effect of defining deviancy up and defining it down has been to normalize and legitimize what was once regarded as abnormal and illegitimate, and, conversely, to stigmatize and discredit what was once normal and respectable. This process, too, has occurred with startling rapidity. . . . What is striking about the 1960's 'sexual revolution', as it has properly been called, is how revolutionary it was, in sensibility as well as reality. In 1965, 69 percent of American women and 65 percent of men under the age of thirty said that premarital sex was always or almost always wrong; by 1972, those figures had plummeted to 24 percent and 21 percent. For women over the age of thirty, the figures dropped from 91 percent to 62 percent, and for men from 62 percent to 47 percent - this in seven short years.[28]

Feminist's Promotion of Sexual Freedom Resulted in Greater Promiscuity for Men than for Women, with Adverse Effects

Sex education is now advocated for elementary school children and even, in some cases, for preschool children, and the incidence of sexual immorality has increased. Courses on masturbation in college, courses in the public schools that imply nothing is wrong with sexual intercourse outside of marriage, the Surgeon General of the United States advocating masturbation and sex with condom use, and all the media presenting all kinds of sex as good–these together have produced a wide-open society. Sex, both oral and otherwise, has been reported as occurring in some public school classrooms while teachers were present. Sexual education has produced far less birth control and had engendered many choices for women which are apparently bad ones. Thomas Sowell's work given above traced how liberal-sponsored sex education actually made premarital sex and teenage pregnancies worse, when they were in fact diminishing before that.

In 1992, about 80 percent of women and 90 percent of men actually engaged in premarital intercourse. This reflects that their views of what they felt is wrong has declined much further. What is most disturbing is how widespread and repetitive sexual immorality is. It is said that, on average, men have 11.4 sexual partners while women have only 3.5. Obviously many men are involved with a more limited number of the same, more promiscuous women. Also, the evidence is that promiscuity increases with the amount of education one has.[29] While women were protesting to the promiscuity and the double standard in sex for men in the early days of feminism, the evidence is the promiscuity of men has expanded rather than women gaining an equal standard. Women's greater freedom has really meant men's greater use of women for their pleasure.

It is also now manifested that removal loving patriarchal protection of wives and daughters has exposed women to great indignities and offenses by unwanted males who make sexual advances and no government anti-harassment laws can ever stop these. Six women who were sexual accusers against the Army's top-ranked non commissioned officer, Sgt. Maj. Gene McKinney, ended up being publicly sullied in reputation while he was only convicted of a minor count of obstruction of justice. The women accusers of President Clinton found the law exonerated him in the Paula Jones case, while the women's reputations were sullied. Apparently today any man may fondle, expose himself, ask for favors, or embarrass any woman on a whim of desire if there are no other witnesses. Women who respect their sexuality and who want a long term relationship with men, now find themselves open to misuse, and to heartache over broken relationships. And they often found they have served as a prostitute without pay.

The Sociological Claims of the Educated Elite for the Family Are Disillusioning

The sociological views of the 1970s based on feminist's assumptions have been reviewed and the evidence is that they had no scientific basis. There were three basic assumptions. Their claims were:

1. Women could now afford to be a mother without also being a wife.
2. Family disruption would not cause lasting harm to children and could actually enrich their lives.
3. The diversity in family structure would make America a better place.

It has been shown before that studies by women scholars in some of the liberal universities were already showing these were not true. Barbara Dafoe Whitehead, in a famous article where she discussed these three, has given a summary of studies since showing they were in grievous error.[30] The fact is that it is women and their children who have been hurt the most. Other studies substantiate this.

In the previous chapter, the tragedy for the black community in producing single-female-parent families was reviewed as the primary cause of the black underclass. Charles Murray warned that black births out of wedlock were at 23 percent, and that when they reached more than 25 percent they would get out of hand. Orlando Patterson was quoted as saying the figure of births out of wedlock is now 70 percent but if the trends continue they will reach 90 percent. In the early 1990s, white pregnancies out of wedlock were at 23 percent and are also moving in the same dangerous direction. Some polls show that more than 30 percent of Americans now believe there should be no shame or stigma to a woman having a baby out of wedlock. Acceptance of such a view would open the door for many more women to end up in single parent families with all its burdens. Many Americans have accepted the Hollywood sexually-promoted morality and are moving toward the same condition as the black community, although up to now it has been better hidden. The tragedy is that it is the single women with children who are getting the worst part of the changes.

Crisis Today in Child Care

The long-known bad child care conditions which are used by many working women have recently been made more public. President Clinton has proposed to subsidize child care facilities with $21.7 billion to expand and improve it 10 percent per year over five years, seeking to offer more training for workers, more inspection, and to raise the pay of child care workers. American businesses are also getting more involved through the American Business Collaboration for Quality Dependent Care. United States companies estimate they lose $2 billion per year to hardships on parents because of child care. All of this means that all people, including the families whose wives and mothers stay home will end up paying for the women who leave their children to work. They will pay by the higher costs for goods and services from the companies who spend more on child care and more taxes to the government. Clinton has proposed that these costs come from the settlement with the tobacco companies.

The issue is this. Feminists have told women that staying at home to care for a husband and children is below their dignity—they need to be out making money and using their brains and abilities. The result is that more and more women have forsaken child care. Yet child care is probably the most important task in America, and the early years of a child's life have proven to be the most crucial. But because the quest of women in working is to make more money, that means they will pay as little as possible for child care. Hence we are moving toward managed day care or socialized child care.

Yet child care personnel are poorly trained, often are not kind, and from one third (ca. National Center for Childhood Workforce in 1997 report) to two thirds[31] leave child care centers every year, mostly because the pay is so small (average $6.17 per hour) and they can make more working at Wal-Mart, or Pest Control Companies (approx. $10.25 per hour). Barbara Willer, of the National Association for Education of Young Children says, "When children experience disruption in early relationships, its problematic. You don't trust anyone and you don't look up to anyone."[32] There is government inspection for only about 10 percent per year, and increasing inspections raises the cost of child care. To find more women to expand and improve child care, there is no place to get them except in competition for women in other work. Yet we are told that over 1 million public school teachers are retiring before the next century. Where will they come from? Can the system expand and improve in quality?

Census reports show that women from poor homes tend to leave children with relatives (usually older women), while middle class women use child care centers. As discussed in chapter 15, the poor are mostly single women families who live where there is more drug use, more crime, and more dependency. This is the place from which the government is demanding more women go from welfare to workfare, thus putting pressure from both ends. These unstable conditions for children are breeding increased crime. When children are shown they can't trust those over them, the matter of authority everywhere diminishes.

Moreover, the system is breeding resentment, especially from boys toward older women. Yet as shown in the results to the economy, the largest group who are expecting to receive social security and medicare from the government in the next generations will be older women. Mary Mallard of the Brookhaven Christian Child Development Center in Atlanta has said, "If we don't value taking care of them, how can we expect them to value taking care of us when the time comes."[33]

Marcy Whitebook has a ditty that expresses the problem in a nutshell, "Parents can't afford to pay. Teachers can't afford to stay. There's gotta be a better way." [34] But is government-supported and inspected child care a better way? Is not the real issue that God made the family so that there are two parents and one must take care of the children. No one else but parents really has a higher interest in or for the child, and the cost in money, emotions, and guilt to parents, children, and society is too high to forsake the child's care by the mother. No amount of argument from the feminists can really change the facts.

The feminist's never envisioned this scenario. They believed that with new birth control and with provided child care, they would be liberated and society would be improved. That has not turned out to be the case.

Manifestation of the Deception of Artificial Birth Control and Abortion

The two-pronged efforts of the feminists have been to be free women from man's control for importance and wealth, and to be free to have sex whenever and wherever they wish, like many men do. Birth control has been an essential element. When the women's movement first began, it was aided by the invention of rubber that produced condoms, the diaphragm, and the baby bottle. The greatest invention for women came in the launching of this last surge toward anarchy in the 1960s when the birth control pill allowed hormonal control.[35] Since condoms were not discussed publicly and involved interrupting passion, and the birth control pill depended on it's being taken on schedule, it did not work well with some women. Therefore, the women's movement has hoped for another better and more foolproof method. Insertion of capsules for regular release over a period of time to control hormones was invented but the process was unpleasant and unreliable.

The final answer at first seemed to be RU-486, which was invented by the French firm Roussel Uclaf. It has been almost completely effective as a pill that could be used for an early and easy abortion. But this drug, while effective, is not popular because it is expensive (about one-third the cost of a surgical abortion) and must be administered by a physician because there is heavy bleeding involved, so much so that one of a thousand women must have a blood transfusion. Its limitation for countries where doctors and blood transfusions are not available is obvious. It was expected that this abortion pill would have cleared the FDA and be on the market in the United States by 1994 and would be available by the Cairo conference of 182 countries where a feminist document of 113 pages was presented for world population control in large part by "legal abortion." The FDA approval did not occur. In September 1998 the FDA did approve a new drug, PREVEN, which is designed to prevent an egg, unfertilized or fertilized (therefore and abortion) from attaching to the uterus within three days after intercourse. The effectiveness is yet to be seen for wide practice.

The problems with all birth control methods relate to safety and effectiveness, part of the latter resting on a willingness of participants to use it. The injection of progesterone took 25 years to win FDA approval and wasn't popular. The sponge wasn't used correctly, and so was taken off the market as too costly to upgrade. United States firms have refused RU-486 because of risks and because of the fear of boycott and bad publicity of anti-abortion groups. Michele Ingrassia and others. say, "Its not just RU-486. Companies have fled the entire contraceptive market because the risk of lawsuits outweighed any possible jackpot."[36] If the companies have fled production of contraceptives, women themselves have given up and 42 percent of them have gone to surgical sterilization, mostly by tubal ligation but also by pushing husbands for vasectomies. Is this the end of the line for sexual sameness? Michele Ingrassia asks the question:

> Is this where the Sexual Revolution was supposed to lead us? Symbolism aside, the pill was designed to let women control when and if they got pregnant. Of course, it also freed them to go to work and allowed them–and their partners–to view sex as recreation. But that was before sexual freedom gave way to increasing numbers of out-of-wedlock births. In the years since, policy makers have grown frustrated trying to stem the tide–to the point where a new unabashedly conservative Congress threatens to take welfare benefits from single mothers who bear more children. Abortion isn't a solution. With anti-abortion protests becoming more violent, the number of

counties with doctors willing to perform abortions has shrunk to 16 percent.[37]

Planned Parenthood, which spearheaded birth control for the feminist's movement, has launched other early abortion efforts because RU-486 has such difficulties. Using new, more accurate, ultra-sensitive early pregnancy tests and better ultrasound imaging to locate the gestation sac within 8–10 days after conception, abortions can be produced using a hand-held syringe, thereby avoiding the vacuum pump and other devices that are so destructive of the fetus. Training of people in abortion clinics in this is spreading. But the use of abortion as a means of birth control has been increasingly recognized as the killing of an infant.

The Jane Roe in the Supreme Court Ruling of *Roe vs. Wade,* which legitimized all abortions as a freedom of choice for women, was Norma McCorvey. In 1995, McCorvey confessed Jesus Christ and was baptized as a Christian, admitting her heart was changed about abortion, and that it was a wrong moral choice. She also admitted signing the affidavit to activate the lawsuit, even though she had not had an abortion but was a strong advocate of abortion. But as a result of her testimony and of other prominent feminists who have confessed deep guilt about abortions, no less a feminist than Naomi Wolf wrote an article published in the *New Republic* and in many national newspapers calling for a change in feminist statements about abortion. She concluded women should not say an abortion is just "pro-choice," but women should be honest about the moral wrong it is as one of the responsibilities for women's freedom. Wolf said:

> But to its own ethical and political detriment, the pro-choice movement has relinquished the moral frame around the issue of abortion. It has ceded the language of right and wrong to abortion foes . . . . We lose the millions of Americans who want to support abortion as a legal right but still need to condemn it as a moral iniquity. . . . But we are also in danger of losing something more important than votes; we stand in jeopardy of losing what can only be called our souls. Clinging to a rhetoric about abortion in which there is no life and no death, we entangle our beliefs in a series of self-delusions, fibs and evasions. And we risk becoming precisely what our critics charge us with being: callous, selfish and casually destructive men and women who share a cheapened view of human life.
>
> I argue for a radical shift in the pro-choice movement's rhetoric and consciousness about abortion. We need to contextualize the fight to defend abortion rights with a moral framework that admits that the death of a fetus is a real death; that there are degrees of culpability, judgment and responsibility involved in the decision to abort a pregnancy; that the

best understanding of feminism involves holding women as well as men to the responsibilities that are inseparable from their rights; and that we need to be strong enough to acknowledge that this country's high rate of abortion–which ends more than a quarter of all pregnancies–can only be rightly understood as what Dr. Henry Foster was brave enough to call it: 'a failure.'[38]

Here, prominent "pro choice" leaders admit abortion is a choice to kill one-fourth of America's babies and that this is a failure, but, they insist that for a woman to be free, she must accept the responsibility for her act of murder. Wolf and others may feel this becomes more moral to admit the wrong of killing babies, but for them a necessary wrong to have freedom. But is she willing to say anyone has the right to kill another person, such as a husband his wife, in other circumstances if it grants them more freedom? This is absurd!

Since that time, Congress on two occasions presented a bill against "partial birth abortions" whereby a late term baby is brought out breach and when the feet and body are out, the baby's head is pierced while in the canal by a surgical knife. After the first bill was vetoed by Bill Clinton, the abortion authority who testified to Congress the procedure was seldom used, and always to save the mother, later admitted that he lied. He said it is used frequently and by teenagers who concealed their pregnancy until the fifth or sixth month. It is used for medical reasons less than 10 percent of the time and never to save a mother's life. A large number of pediatricians spoke out against the procedure. Jean A. Wright, associate professor of pediatrics at Emory University, testified the baby at that time "is more sensitive to pain than a full-term infant would be" and said if it was done on an animal in work at Emory "it would not make it through the institutional review process."

The liberal elite have fought for this process to stand because they feel to give in on any abortion will open the door against all abortions. They fought to keep this abortion even against the clear will of the American people. Polls showed 79 percent of the American people opposed the partial birth abortion. The bill was modified and passed a second time, being endorsed by not only conservative Republicans, but by 72 Democratic votes including Richard Gephardt, the Democratic leader and the whip, David Bonior. Yet Clinton vetoed the bill a second time. In the state of New Jersey, a law banning partial birth abortions was passed, and the legislature overrode Governor Christine Todd Whitman's veto. But the liberal U. S. District Judge, Anne Thompson, issued an order blocking the law. These rulings have made it clear to most American people that abortion as such is not based on logic, medical facts, or the will of the people. This symbolizes the attitudes of conflict around the country, and enrages the people because their voice by the democratic process is subverted. It seems that the liberal agenda is ready to hold to the sacrifice of children in order to maintain their ideas of the freedom of women. This is a serious moral failure.

Insecurity in Attempting Maleness and Exaggeration of Women's Power

As women intuitively realize they are handicapped by their differences and cannot completely win by playing at the level of maleness, they have tended to react by an exaggeration of women's power. God has given women a unique power different from that of men to influence men. They have the ability to physically attract, to give pleasure to men, and to complement them mentally and emotionally; all this power over men is linked to the immense power to have and nurture children. To be like men, much of her power must be denied and set aside. The early triumph of the women's movement in the 1920s resulted in the "boyish bob," or short male-like haircut, and dresses flattened the breasts and de-emphasized the wider hips. Then there was a return in the 1930s and following to a sexy female emphasis. But in the 1960s and following with the new surge of feminism, many women stopped wearing bras, and in protests, even took them off and flung them at the authorities, wore dungarees and other male attire, and again went to short hair.

But in the late 1980s and 1990s, in the face of frustrated feminist's goals, women have sought to deceive men and exaggerate their female powers to draw and control them. This is the real story behind "the beauty myth." Women are being taught and driven by women and men in the fashion and beauty fields to gain acceptance and self-esteem by exaggerating femaleness. This is done by the exaggeration of thinness of models pointing out their breasts and hips, the emphasis on diet and exercise, the practices and ultimately sicknesses of anorexia, bulimia, breast implants, and cosmetic surgery–all are driven by desire to exaggerate femaleness.

For example, in spite of the media prominence of health risks and lawsuits, breast implants have continued to occur. Eighty percent of the 2 million American women with breast implants chose the surgery for non-medical reasons, to enhance the kind of self-esteem of themselves as women that relies on breast size.[39] In the 1998 Miss United States beauty contest, forty of the fifty one state winners competing admitted they had breast implants to enhance their feminine look. This is illustrated also by the widespread sale of the "miracle bra" or "wonder bra" which gives an appearance of bigger breasts. Many mix the exaggeration of feminine appeal with seeking to be like men in other ways to gain maximum power. This clearly shows that women do not feel secure trying to make their way in the world on the same grounds as men. Their efforts to enhance female power indicates that they have a power over men and children which gives them control. Many want not only the natural power of womanhood, but the power that men have exercised as well.

CONCLUSIONS

There is much evidence that the replacement of faith in God for materialism has resulted in conflict of women with men and adverse conditions for children whom they bear and have the greatest power to nurture. Moreover, it can be argued that this has reduced their quality of life, the quality of life of men and children, and poses a threat to society. Many women experience guilt over abortions, the feeling over not having children they wish they had born but prevented, tragic effects of broken homes and loneliness to spouses and children, the diminished love and often rejection of men they want, the loss of a man to protect from the world and from unwanted men, the embarrassment and burden of single parenthood, and the lack of future care and support of lost children and men.

While men and children are hurting greatly and share the causes for pain (as shall be been in the next chapter), women are insecure and seeking to make a statement and find help together for the separation they have seen. Women have responded to the Million Man March and the Stand in the Gap Promise Keepers rally in Washington, with the black women's gathering in Philadelphia, and in the response mostly of white women to conferences around America. In 1998 there will be about 600,000 women gathered together in conferences at different locations (about as many as attended Promise Keepers rallies in 1997). Many of these are organized by Focus on the Family, Aspiring Women, and Women of Faith who focus on the theme, "Bring Back the Joy." The leaders of these sponsoring groups say the main problem of women is "loneliness."[40]

The Feeling of Betrayal by Many Women over Feminism

After about thirty years of feminist promises or near the dawn of the 1990s, there began to be a realization for many that what feminism promised it was not delivering. The feminist movement had certainly proved women are equally as intelligent as men and can do many things that men can do, and just as well, if not at times better. But it has also ably demonstrated for any who want to know, women are not like men; they are strikingly different in many ways. And to try to equalize women as being the same has tragic consequences for women.

Under the guise of justice and truth, the feminists have made distorted claims to coerce other women to leave the women's role in the family and compete all-out against men. Dr. Toni Grant, distinguished psychologist and star of the award-winning national radio talk show on the Mutual Broadcasting System, "The Dr. Toni Grant Program," wrote a *New York*

Times best-selling book entitled, *Being a Woman,* in which she claims to have exposed "The Ten Big Lies of Liberation." She said:

> At its inception, the feminist movement, accompanied by the sexual revolution, made a series of enticing, exciting promises to women. These promises sounded good, so good that many women deserted their men and their children or rejected the entire notion of marriage and family, in pursuit of 'themselves' and a career. These pursuits, which emphasized self-sufficiency and individualism, were supposed to enhance a woman's quality of life and improve her options, as well as her relations with men. Now, a decade or so later, women have had to face the fact that, in many ways, feminism and liberation made promises that could not be developed.[41]

This Jungian psychologist was reporting what she found to be true in the lives of millions of women as she interviewed them. Grant's conclusion was that the feminist's movement was a mass deception about liberation. It led in a majority of cases to great difficulties and painful loneliness.

Many women are now seeing that the feminist promises are empty. They are angry at feminists because they were led by them to leave a marriage they could have worked out. Kay Ebeling, writing in *Newsweek,* said:

> To me feminism has backfired against women. In 1973 I left what could have been a perfectly good marriage, taking with me a child in diapers, a 10-year-old Plymouth and Volume 1, Number One of Ms. magazine. I was convinced I could make it on my own . . . . Today I see feminism as the Great Experiment That Failed, and women in my generation, its perpetrators, are the casualties. Many of us, myself included, are saddled with raising children alone. The resulting poverty makes us experts at cornmeal recipes and ways to find free recreation on weekends. . . . Feminism freed *men,* not women.

She describes her ex-husband's life of "living around" and financial prosperity.[42] Hers is only one of thousands of women who have been disillusioned by walking the feminist's path. But the tragedy is that an increasing number ȯf young women are still believing this lie of freedom and are following the so-called "feminist dream." The real betrayal is forsaking the idea of oneness in marriage by faith in the transcendent God or trust in man's ability to understand nature and natural laws.

But the feminist movement is in growing trouble. There is a dwindling support for women's organizations such as NOW and magazines such as *Ms.,* which indicates women have awakened to the fact something is wrong with feminism. There is now a strong division about feminism by the women in America. It is not only that the far right is more vocal and more women are listening to Focus on the Family, reading their books, and books such as Dr. Brenda Hunter's, *Home by Choice*, or Mary Farrar's, *Choices*. But there is defection from hard feminism of people like Christiana Hoff Sommers, Elizabeth Fox-Genovese of Emory University ,[43] and others that come from liberal sources. Even Betty Friedan, in her book *The Second Stage*, called for feminists to tend more closely to families. When she did so, Friedan was attacked by feminists like Ellen Willis, Catherine Stimpson, and Susan Faludi for being a traitor and for backing away from the freedom that feminists had fought for. Anyone reviewing the original and consistent purposes of the feminists from their origins with Elizabeth Cady Stanton know this accusation is right. But Friedan and many other women are now seeing much that feminism has done has been disastrous.

Present Difficulties from Feminism, Much Worse Than Early History

There is no question that from the materialistic worldview, feminists showed increasingly that from the time of the Virginia Dynasty, women were treated as inferior and were mistreated. As was shown in Colonial America, women had a unique role but also were highly honored. Before the Virginia Dynasty, a woman's position in the United States was in general a very high and happy one. Alexis de Tocqueville said of American women, "I have nowhere seen women occupying a loftier position." Historian Midge Yearley, writing on "Early American Women," said:

> Women taking important roles in business, politics, the army, the ministry and the arts is not a recent phenomenon. During the Colonial period, the Revolution, and the early years of our nation, women were also active in these fields. Businesses were centered in the home or in nearby offices, and women and children as well as the men worked to make a success of the family business. It was not until the 19th century when most occupations became unsuitable for women.[44]

In early America, the wife in particular as well as the older children were considered as partners in the family economic efforts and all felt important. The children grew up learning to do adult things with the adults and felt a part of the family, church, and community. Unbelief, materialism, and the feminist movement changed this. The increasing turn to materialism left women feeling more and more inferior, being excluded from jobs that were away from home and from their participation; their husbands were away, and children became a greater cost and restriction to their lives. The feminist movement certainly proved that women could do many things men could do and as well, but what did this do for their unique nature as women? Has this materialistic interpretation of sex been good for women?

While their earning power was pushed up more than 11 cents compared to the male dollar, from 1990 till 1994, the average declined from $.716 back down one cent to $.706 for the man's dollar. While women seemed to be gaining some progress in management of big business, the Federal Glass Ceiling Commission reported in 1994: "Even after two decades in the work force, women have made little progress in winning the power posts of corporate America. At the highest levels of business, there is indeed a barrier only rarely penetrated by women." The expected continued increase because of graduate degrees did not occur. At the same time, the male CEOs increased their earnings 200 percent more than that of the average worker and significantly above the women.

Moreover, mysteriously, women's added income did not boost the income of the family very much, especially considering the added cost of their working and the frustration of two parents working, creating difficulties at home. Sylvia Ann Hewlett recalls that male wages were increasing until 1973, at which time women began entering the job market. But as pointed out earlier in this chapter in her quote, changes have not made two wage earners as profitable as it looked. She has not even mention how much it added to costs for the second person to work. So with two working, the family is not appreciably better than when only the man worked. An the loss to the family and to the witness for Christ is large. The lack of real progress materially for married women working away from home has been confirmed with practical applications by Linda Kelley and others.[45]

Feminists Feel Backlash or Impasse to Progress

Feminist leaders in America now feel they are facing rejection in much they have stood for. Their dream of being free to be equal in business, governmental power, and to do what they want to gain "womancenteredness" worldwide is now threatened. They are deceived in thinking that modern Westerners, especially those in the United States, are the first to conceive of equality like men for women. They believe the evolutionary process in history must now move to produce female superiority, and they are its agents. They are adamant to move ahead, no matter what their agenda does to the unity of the family.

Susan Faludi, the Pulitzer prize-winning journalist, in her book, *Backlash: The Undeclared War against American Women,* searched but could not find any conspiracy against women, but won't admit that much of feminism has been contrary to the very nature of women and extreme. She is convinced feminism has seen things correctly, and at any cost must promote their just cause. She said:

Because there really is no good reason why the '90s can't be their [women's] decade. Because the demographics and the opinion polls are on women's side. Because women's hour on the stage is long, long overdue. Because, whatever new obstacles are mounted against the future march toward equality, whatever new myths invented, penalties levied, opportunities rescinded, or degradations imposed, no one can ever take from the American woman the justness of her cause.[46]

The National Organization for Women meeting July 1998 celebrating 150 years since the first meeting of the feminist, drew up a new Declaration of Semtiments expressing a two year plan and determination to achieve its radical demands. They are aiming at passing the Equal Rights Amendment, which was three states short in 1982, achieve equal pay and job opportunity by affirmative action, complete abortion rights, and birth control. Hillary Rodham Clinton was the keynote speaker for the meeting.

The feminists are now a group deconstructing every standard to fit their own, and they are not hearing what is being said by other women who want union with a man in marriage and the freedom to care for their family. A meltdown to final confusion and anarchy in judgmental attitudes is not far away.

Chapter 17

Men and Children

Men Led the Way to the Changing of Roles

Men led in unbelief in the 1800s and following, and they have promoted the intellectual views of a mechanical view of nature that diminished their faith in God and turned them toward materialism. Almost no significant women participated in this process until recently. Man exalted himself as the one who had a vision for a glorious new world he could build, and it was the man who began to neglect his wife and children for business. Many American men began to exalt themselves, to act more selfishly, to indulge in alcohol, to enter into sexual relations other than with their wives. At each step, when men enhanced their power, wealth, and pleasure, they progressively alienated their wives. This idolatry of the male, and his euphoria about his power, promoted the sexual revolt and the feminist movement, exactly like what occurred in ancient Greece and Rome.

Historic Review of Male Leadership Changing Roles

For almost two hundred years from the Colonial beginnings until the Virginia Dynasty, the American male was husband, father, provider, role model, and leader of his home. While he held his wife in high esteem as his partner, helper, and mother of his children, and of equal in value in the sight of God, they recognized their differences and the importance of their roles before God. As was shown, during the Virginia Dynasty that began to change, this change occurred not solely because of the national leaders and their views, but because of the changing opportunities in the nation.

The first efforts of most men focused on doing a better job in providing for the family and nation. During the Virginia Dynasty and for twenty-five years more, the expanded trust in man's ability to understand a mechanical nature and to use it for himself opened before him. The new faith in human reason and the Uniformitarian view of the way the world worked, along with the opening of new opportunities to create industry and to expand westward for more land and adventure, offered temptations many men gave into so that their wives and family become secondary. While it was easy to reason that this was best for the family, it took many away from home to spend much time in business.

Secondly, men felt it was all up to them, and they wanted to achieve for themselves. After mid-century, the conflict over slavery and the mistreatment of the lower class immigrants in factories brought disruption, and Darwinism introduced the idea that all evolved and man was alone dependent on an impersonal material nature. But a false optimism about man emerged because of his great engineering and scientific developments, and the idea of the perfectibility of man was one of the aims. Men plunged even harder into creating industry, and from this arose the financial tycoons who manipulated and gathered control and great wealth. The optimism of liberal clergy brought businessmen into control in the churches, and science and philosophy into the teaching positions of the private and mostly Christian colleges along with state universities. The liberal elite took over most of the Christian colleges. Women were excluded from most higher education and business ventures, and the jobs of homemaker, mother, and keeper of the children seemed insignificant compared to men's exploits. The efforts towards divorce, custody of the children, and separate provision from the husband increased.

Thirdly, men wanted to help women be equal, but this implied that men would still be in charge. As the twentieth century opened with belief in a great utopia, women's efforts for the vote and equality in sexual freedom were encouraged by many men who saw themselves as champions of women. But their neglect increased, and women's efforts to assert their rights and abilities as individuals grew. They gained the vote, and found they were more than a majority. They asserted their equality at home and found great conflict and pain, lost the affection of their men, and backed away again. Two world wars thrust women into industry and business while husbands were away. The peace movement began and they were busy in it. The idea of a world government had small beginnings producing the League of Nations, and ultimately, the United Nations. Science produced new marvels, which were mostly men's work.

Fourth, men saw it was their obligation to build an equal world. Following World War II, the liberal elite began to build state universities and federal research programs, and this elite had a social plan to construct a paradise; equality for the lower class and for women began to find an expression. God was removed further from the American scene as at least irrelevant, and for many intellectuals, a hindrance. Credit began to open up the way for expansion and gain. The hope was that social democracy, and in many cases even communism, would be the way for achievement. Equality for all in one world was the goal. When human thought reached extreme individualism with the recognition of sin in Hitler's Germany and Japan's dictatorship, liberal optimism turned towards existentialism and skepticism. Intellectual rejection of God in the "God is dead" theologies released restraints in the late 1950s. The races and students rebelled, women recognized they had regressed, and the great surge of women for position, wealth, and sexual freedom broke down sexual images and opened the door to claim freedom.

Man's social engineering took over in government, and it was men who graduated from the colleges and universities into government and business that led these changes in the name of progress. The Supreme Court, following the educated elite, asserted their view of justice and righteousness, and as the new high priests of a secular religion, it excluded God from the public schools and from the public arena. The liberal religious leaders were the voices leading government. Man had now changed faith to materialism for health and pleasure; God was given a place off to one side in the churches, there only to help seekers find community and build self-esteem. But He was not to control. Finally, the true nature of what is considered a family was now nebulous.

Men Have Progressively Less Meaningful Lives

Lost Leadership and Custody

Man progressively has lost his position in the family and has defaulted in all his responsibilities except providing funds. He progressively lost his relationships and control of his family. While he verbally and legally has assented to giving equality to women, he has taken advantage of women for his own selfish ends. While women have been given more opportunity in the business world, man has increased his own income more. When women protested the double standard in sex and was socially given sexual freedom, man used this freedom to increase his own promiscuity. What is happening in America is the same as happened in the ancient civilizations. Men offer women more freedom, and then they claim more of the same vices for themselves.

At the time of the Declaration of Independence, divorce was at a minimum. Man was esteemed as the head of his home, and he alone voted for his wife and children. In any divorce, the custody of the children went to the man. Most women were dependent on men, and men controlled the funds to provide for the children. An orphan was defined as a child that did not have a father.

As a result of the Civil War, as in all wars, there was an increase in the number of divorces. After the Civil War, many people forsook farms and moved to the city, with a rapid increase in urbanization, especially in the East. At the same time, new farms and rural housing developed in the westward movement. During the last of the 1800s, business exploded and the good jobs were in the city. Due to a lack of houses, many families lived in hotels and rooming houses, which reduced the significance of women's work in the home and the ability to have children. The feminist demand for divorce and child custody grew at this time. During this period, out of wedlock births began to occur. These trends were a major zig in moral degeneration. Robert Lerman estimated these out-of-wedlock births to be about 30 percent, although this is doubtful for anywhere but in the North and East. In the early 1900s, the women's movement strongly emphasized equality for women and the right to be equal with men in voting. In World War I, women went to work to provide for the war effort. During the last of the nineteenth and early part of the twentieth centuries, when there was an explosion of divorces, the courts began to favor giving custody of the children to the mother and to require men to provide alimony and child support.

Since 1960, easy divorces developed for women, education of women became more prevalent, and most kinds of jobs began to open up for women. Since the 1960's women have almost always received the custody of the children in a divorce. In two out of three cases, women have sole physical custody. Men say they desire joint custody in one out of three cases, and sole custody in 1 out of 3. But men do not file for sole custody in 40 percent of these cases where they say they want sole custody. In the 1970s and following, many women and men lived together out of wedlock, and when children were born, the men had no claim to the children. In 1960, a single parent was 5 times more likely to be a divorced mother, but in 1993, about 50 percent of single mothers had never been married. Three-fourths of divorced women have been awarded support payments, and 1 out of 4 women never married received some payment.

In the last generation, the removal of dads from the home has accelerated. Government census studies show children living with one parent, usually only the mother, are as follows:

> 1960   5.1 million with single parent
> 1993   15.6 million with single parent
> Today, of 66.8 million children, 47.1 million
> are with both parents, 17.8 with one.

Money for Child Care vs. the Family

Government policy has been to deny welfare payments when the husband lives at home, so the policy has driven men away. When a child is born into a family where there is no marriage and the couple has lived together, the government policy has been to try to identify the husband and collect support payment, part of which goes to the government. The men deny their paternity and stay away to receive money. All experience has been that when men have contact with their children, they are more likely to give support. Thus, government policy tends to keep men out of the family and away from giving support. Federal collection policies have raised $204 million less per year than is paid in support and for government services. As pointed out, an increasing number of women who opt for the single life are choosing to have children by artificial insemination, or as John Leo called it, promoting "no-dads families."

These facts show the man progressively has lost recognition, power, and love in the home. From a position of recognized leader of the home in the eighteenth century, he has lost almost all public recognition. And his image has changed by feminist's propaganda, as Ron Henry said, "'from father knows best', to 'all men are rapists.'"

Contest for Power and Money Has Increased Hostility

More and more homes are without a man, and even when there is no divorce, men spend less time with the children than in previous generations. There are various reasons, from the declining income of middle class men and the need to work more to earn more, and from voluntary absence because of the competitive attitude of wives. Conflict between men and women in and out of the home has grown. There is an increase in wife beating, but there is an equal amount of increase in husband beating, and regardless of who began the assault, the man is usually arrested. Hate and fear of the opposite sex has increased gender rejection in the children, especially among the boys who are more often allowed to see and hear arguments. Rape, which is more a crime of hate and violence than passion, has been increasing. Official reports show in 1960, there were 17,190 rapes, or 9.6 per 100,000 women, and in 1992, there were 109,060 rapes or 42.8 per 100,000 women. There is an increase in the number of men who do not claim to be the fathers in extramarital situations. While there is an increasing number of deadbeat dads, when women who are non-custodial are asked to pay allotments, they are equally deadbeat moms and refuse to pay. The problem is not the male or the female, but sinful nature.

Men Continue to Be the Leader but Lose Much

The man still has the levers of power in the economy. For example, 95 percent of the CEO's of the Fortune 500 companies are still men, and more complete figures have been quoted. Men still earn much more than women. About 99 percent of the men say they favor equal pay for women in equal work, and 88 percent favor women working outside the home.[1] But men are not giving this equal earning power to women, not just because they are unwilling, but because of the reasons attached to being women. Women are earning less alone, and families with 2 parents working are not earning much more than they did with one working before the trend began. Men are dropping out of higher education while women are entering. Men are dropping out of the work place while women are entering. While women make about 3 times as many attempts at suicide, men have twice the rate of suicide and are 4 times more likely to succeed when they try. There are many efforts to explain this, but no conclusive reasons for it.[2]

Life expectancy has been affected mostly by man's scientific developments in living and health services. In early America, women died earlier because of childbirth. About 1900, both men and women died about age 50. By 1920, women lived slightly longer than men (men - 53.6 years, women 54.6 years). By 1992, men averaged 72.2 years while women 79.1 years, or almost 7 years longer than men. But there are signs that women in the work place are now showing some of the same problems of heart trouble and other health problems which have killed the men. Men are now the first to die, while formerly women died first. The New York City's Fertility Research Foundation reported 8 percent male infertility in 1960 and 40 percent in 1996. Sperm count for men is declining 2.1 percent annually and, according to the *British Medical Journal,* men born after 1970 have a 25 percent lower sperm count than those born before 1959. One out of 8 men has a problem with impotency, although there is some hope of chemical help for erections.

By way of summary, the husband and father's losses are many. His great achievements in business and political government are rapidly proceeding to a great time of trouble. His earning power as a single-parent provider dropped, and often he worked two jobs; his wife works, with added expense, and also expense for day care. As previously cited, he has lost his position in the family over his children. He commits suicide twice as often as women; he dies much earlier than his wife. His fertility is declining. He is turning from the labor force and is filling the prisons of America. And women and children are suffering from the male idolatry of money and the loss of protection for them. The male's declining sense of value is compensated for by increased sexual conquests and exercise of his greater physical power in violence.

Male are Confused with the Feminist's Redefinition of Their Role

Confusion over "the Sensitive Man"

Women have asserted men are too demanding and not sensitive enough. There have been books and seminars on "the Sensitive Man." Men were told they should be more open, more revealing, more emotional, more in touch with women and children. By the early 1980s, men had become turned off. Bruce Feinstein's bestseller, *Real Men Don't Eat Quiche,* lamented the rise of the "wimp." Aaron Kipnis, in his *Knights Without Armor*, conceded men had become more sensitive and socially responsible males, but less effective in the world. *Time* in 1990 said it was time to say good-bye to this "wimp and object of derision." After trying hard, Harry Stein, in *Esquire*, denounced the idea of the "sensitive man" as a "screwy bit of social engineering." Even women bemoaned the loss of male leaders. Many other writers kissed this emphasis off as more of a confusion than a help.[3] No doubt it was a message men needed that was taken too far.

The other call by radical feminists was for men to leave the market place and become mom at home so women could have their shot at earning the bucks and providing. Many men have tried to help. Fathers caring for preschool children did rise from 17 percent to 23 percent, or one-third from 1977 to 1991. But few men really wanted to become the ones who cared for the children and the home. The Family and Medical Leave Act of 1993 was designed to make room for men to help at home more, but it has shown virtually no effect. Also, as the *Wall Street Journal* observed, men have found corporate America does not particularly want caring fathers. There is "daddy stress," where men are trapped between work and the family. The feminists had a fantasy in thinking most men would opt for being "Mr. Mom." The great problem is that women are naturally the nurturers, and the job is not distinguished as masculine.

The efforts to redesign the male image to accommodate the feminists have failed. They certainly offered lessons for men to learn in trying to understand their wives and in making men more willing to help at home with the house and children. But they have a reaction from men because they sought more than that—they pushed men out of their role.

These changes, along with affirmative action, have caused men to be passed over for jobs and promotions in favor of women less qualified, and have produced anger and resentment. At the same time, men are tremendously frustrated and confused. A male movement was discussed, but only recently has begun to manifest, as shall be discussed later. The Islamic teachings, (e.g., Farrakhan), that endorse extreme domination of women by men has appealed to black men.

Confusion of Aggression in Sex and Harassment

With the exception of the hard-core feminists (many who often act as lesbians), most single women still are interested in being loved by men and getting married. Many women, even today, still recognize there are reasons men should initiate offering affection—having the male aggressive hormones that motivate, and the way man are affected visually by women. While the women's movement has tried to redefine the role of women as equally the aggressor, many women still feel it is up to the man to initiate interest in knowing her and beginning a relationship. Indeed most women still seem to desire the man be the leader, though various women do not agree on these matters.

Men are confused about harassment and the laws for this offense. Just as there are some men who are rapists, there are also some men who do not respect women except for sexual encounters. But the majority of men do respect women and want to treat them kindly. Today, when there are women whom men are interested in spending time with, the men are confused about how to proceed, especially at their place of employment. There is no good legal definition of harassment, and no clear delineation as to what is evidence of this act. There are clear cases of harassment, but often the decision is in the minds of the woman and her friends as to when it occurs. It is even more confusing that the very congressmen who have been the champions of feminism and speakers for their conferences are those who have been accused of harassment

It was thought that the Supreme Court case, *Teresa Harris v. Forklift Systems*, would clarify matters including a definition. The Court did determine that guilt did not have to involve psychological harm, but it gave no clearer definition of what harassment is. In this case, Cose said, "The argument, in essence, was that women see sexually obnoxious behavior in a different light than do men, and that the judicial system is tainted by a male perspective and controlled by a 'gender hierarchy'."[4] The Court essentially said male and female perspectives are part of the problem. But that means the difficulties will remain. This matter will certainly produce increasing problems for men, and it is questionable whether it can be defined any better. This problem will exist as long as men are men and women are women and they work together, and as long as there are extremes of differing perspectives by various men and various women. If sexual conflict continues to increase, as in the past, and produces anger and hate, the matter will be an increasing burden for both sexes.

Sexual harassment as a result of integration and coed living and training in the military has led to prosecution and exposure in harassment cases. The problems for women in bootcamp have been large, and the Marines have abandoned this effort. The widespread problem of harassment of people working together in business is not resolved.

The Black Man Is Hurting the Most

Black men in America are brought up primarily by black single women, and yet many black women are not attracted to black men and often feel mistreated by them. Black men are the most wounded part of American society. Cose, an award-winning black writer, gives some of the evidence.

If there is one thing black men are sure of, it is that this is not *their* world. Whether they punish women for the 'ills of society' is debatable, but certainly those ills seem to find black men in grossly disproportionate numbers.

The statistics are compelling. Black men are less likely than either black women or white women to go to college and are twice as likely as white men to be unemployed (for those 20-24 years, they are less than two thirds as likely to have jobs as white males). They are roughly 9 times more likely than white men to kill, and 7 times more likely to be killed. Though they are less inclined to commit suicide than are white men, the gap is narrowing—particularly for young black males ages 15–24, whose suicide rate has quadrupled since 1960. In 1991, young black men are 10 times as likely to kill themselves as are young black women.

Their problems with law enforcement have been presented earlier, and Cose summarizes:

In a widely disseminated 1990 monograph, *The Sentencing Project* reported that nearly 1 in 4 black males in their twenties was in prison or jail or on probation or parole. The comparable figure for whites was 1 in 16. "We risk the possibility of writing off an entire generation of black men from having the opportunity to lead productive lives in our society", wrote Marc Mauer, the study's author and assistant director of the nonprofit research and anti-prison advocacy organization'.[5]

If men in general are hurting and have a growing anger about how society treats them, the black male is experiencing more than any. It is not surprising that especially black men have flocked to urban gangs, weapons and fighting in recent years. If black people constitute about 12 or 13 percent, and half are black males, then we must have about 2 or 3 percent of the population as black male Americans who are in serious trouble and pain. This constitutes a serious problem for America. People who hurt in this way and associate in armed groups with modern weapons will not long be silent. The black, single-parent family has been the major cause of this problem. Alarmingly, the growth in white single-parent families is moving white men rapidly in the same direction.

RESULTS OF SEXUAL REVOLUTION
FOR WIVES AND CHILDREN

Consequences for Women and Their Children

The consequences of the loss of husbands and fathers for women is important. Wives and daughters no longer have protection or guidance from men with regards to extramarital sex. Older and stronger men take advantage of them. Thus, women have become exposed to harm by many men for sexual pleasure, rape, abuse, and disease. Women have been great losers economically. Men no longer seek to show deference or honor to women because women claim to be equal to them. In 1994, teenage mothers were more likely to have a total family income below 50 percent of the poverty line. Almost half of unwed teen mothers went on welfare within one year of the baby's birth. By the time the first baby is 5 years old, 72 percent of white teens and 84 percent of black teens have received financial; according to support from the 1994 Aid to Families with Dependent Children Act.

In 1970, 10.4 million children lived in poverty, but by 1992 it grew to 14.6 million. The percent of children in poverty 7 years or more was about 22 percent in 1-parent families and only 2 percent in two-parent families. Black children, whose rate of fatherlessness is much higher, are nearly 3 times as likely to be poor as whites. The National Center for Health Statistics reports black babies suffer twice the mortality rate of white infants even when both parents have completed college. In 1993, 46 percent of black children were living in poverty compared with 17 percent of white. This difference is clearly related to higher percent of fatherlessness among the blacks.

As mentioned before, Charles Murray warned the results to black families would be disastrous if the number of children with unmarried mothers went over 25 percent, the number is now 69 percent. The warning is that the same disaster will occur when the number of white women having children exceeds 25 percent, and it is now near 23 percent.

Direct Effects to Children of Not Having Their Father in the Home

The effect of fatherlessness to children is clear. Adolescent girls reared without fathers are much more likely to be sexually active than girls raised in two-parent families. Teenage girl runaways disproportionally come from *stepfamilies*. After completing a study, Synthia Tucker commented, "The odds that a girl will grow up into an emotionally healthy young woman are better when she has a loving and attentive father in her life." A number of studies have revealed this fact.[6] Significant emotional or behavioral problems occur in children 3 to 17 years old: 19.1 percent experience such problems if they live only with their biological mother and 23.6 percent of those living with their biological mother and *stepfather*. The figure is that *only 8.3 percent of children have serious emotional or behavioral problems if they are living with both biological parents, their father being present.*

In 1993, 80 percent of adolescents in psychiatric hospitals come from broken homes. About 50 percent of suicidal youths came from single-parent homes in 1991. Suicide for teenagers has tripled since 1960. Schooling of children is greatly affected by the single-parent family. Fatherless children were twice as likely to drop out of school in 1993. Children from low-income *two-parent families outperform in school* the students from high-income *single-parent* homes. So the primary issue is not economic but *two-parent presence.* School children from divorced families are absent more, are more anxious, are hostile and withdrawn, and are less popular with their peers than their classmates from intact families. The higher percentage of absence of fathers in black families certainly has a relationship to the lower SAT scores for blacks. Since America has the highest divorce rate in the world, this surely has some relationship to the fact that among literate countries, American students score lower than most.

Child neglect and abuse is motivated and promoted by a number of things that are growing out of the change in the roles of men and women. The financial burden of children, the increased conflict between husbands and wives due to changes in responsibility, and the great burden of children to single mothers are some of these. But *the primary reason for child abuse*, sexual or otherwise, surprisingly contrary to feminists, *is the absence of the real father to guide and protect* the children. The presence of unconcerned other males in the house–boyfriends of the mother, stepfathers, others in the home when parents are not present, all contribute much more to incest and abuse than real fathers.[7] Moreover no one knows how much father abuse stems from alcoholic or drugged fathers who seek to escape conflict with their wives, or are denied love from their wives. Since men want to be the leader, when there is conflict with the mother, they lose with the children. No feminist wants to discuss this situation.

Incest is a growing problem and is very difficult to measure. Kinsey in his early studies, claimed one out of sixteen women had experienced an incestuous relationship, but as indicated above, his studies were flawed. Robert L. Geiser, Chief Psychologist of the Nazareth Child Care Center in Boston, claimed in 1978 that 10 percent of our population may have known such an experience. But as indicated, stepfathers, brothers and stepbrothers are a larger part of the problem. The percentage of incest has certainly grown since 1978, but reliable figures are hard to come by. Benjamin DeMott in his article, "The Pro-Incest Lobby" (people who actively advocate incest) said, "The movement to weaken the incest taboo demonstrates the force in our time of a particular sense of *self*."[8]

Harm from Divorce and Fatherlessness Overlooked by Feminists
Preferring "Freedom"

Documentation of Harm Long Known and Willfully Rejected

The adverse effects of the absence of a father to women and children has
long been known, but feminists have not acknowledged it. Prominent *women*
in family research in *liberal universities* were the first to discover the harm of
divorce and the absence of the father or of either parent. Judith Wallerstein in
1970 began study at the School of Social Welfare at the University of
California Berkeley of 131 children whose parents were divorcing. She
continued to follow these and other children of divorce for 25 years. She found
over half of them had serious psychological problems and argued that divorce
is silently altering the social fabric of the entire society. At Princeton
University, Sara McLanahan long ago also found the same thing and says that
children of divorce drop of out of high school, become teen mothers, and are
jobless far more frequently than their peers. Barbara Dafoe Whitehead's work
and her synopsis of the studies show the same things that have been referred
to previously, especially her article summarizing research on children in
Atlantic, "Dan Quayle Was Right."

Whitehead is a colleague of David Blankenhorn. He, in his book as a
researcher at the Institute for American Values spoke of *Fatherless America:
Confronting Our Most Urgent Social Problem*. He said:

> A generation ago, an American child could reasonably expect to grow
> up with his or her father. . . .Tonight, about 40 percent of American
> children will go to sleep in homes in which their fathers do not live.
> Before they reach the age of eighteen, more than half of our nation's
> children are likely to spend at least a significant portion of their
> childhood living apart from their fathers. . . . If this trend continues,
> fatherlessness is likely to change the shape of our society. Consider this
> prediction. After the year 2000, as people born after 1970 emerge as a
> large proportion of our working-age adult population, the United States
> will be a nation divided into two groups, separate and unequal. . . .
> They will live fundamentally divergent lives. One group will receive
> basic benefits—psychological, social, economic, educational, and
> moral—that are denied to the other group.[9]

There are many feminists (e.g., Shere Hite[10]) who deny there is any
evidence that divorce and loss of the father is having adverse affects. They
claim there is a transformation of culture to a family *democracy* that will
produce new and happier situations. These feminists are putting their head in
the sand as to the real problems of our society, and what history shows. They
are not even familiar with the family studies *by prominent liberal women* and

also know little about history, even recent historical studies about the Western nations, such as one by Gertrude Himmelfarb of the Graduate School of the City of New York.[11]

The present data about the importance of father in the home for children is so overwhelming that the effects of divorce and the loss of either parent has disastrous effects for the society. In 1978, I wrote *Our Dance Has Turned to Death*, and the main thrust of the book was to warn that the demise of the family and the loss of the father as the leader of the home would become a disaster. Many subsequent studies have confirmed what I said. [12]

Of significance is David Popenoe's statement in his comprehensive new book on the decline of fatherlessness in the last three decades. He said:

> No one predicted this trend, few researchers or government agencies have mentioned it, and it is not widely discussed, even today. But its importance to society is second to none. Father absence is a major force lying behind many of the attention-grabbing issues that dominate the news: crime and delinquency; premature sexuality and out-of-wedlock teen births; deteriorating educational achievements; depression, substance abuse, and alienation among teenagers; and the growing number of women and children in poverty. These issues all point to the profound deterioration in the well-being of children.[13]

Fatherlessness Has Significant Effect on Children in Crime and Social Disorder

Exclusion of Father and Correlation to Crime Increase

There is perhaps no more significant effect of the presence of the father than in preventing crime. The father figure represents *controlling authority* with love, and respect for authority is very important in crime prevention. There is a direct correlation in the rise of crime and the disappearance of the father from the home. From 1982 to 1991, the arrest rates for juveniles increased 93 percent for murder, 72 percent for aggravated assault, 24 percent for forcible rape and in 1993 car theft increased 97 percent . Seventy percent of juveniles in state reform institutions grew up in single or no-parent homes. Young black men raised in single-parent families on welfare and living in public housing are twice as likely to engage in criminal activities than black men raised in two-parent families also on welfare and in public housing, according to the 1993 study. Sixty percent of rapists grew up in homes without fathers, according to a 1990 study. Of adolescent murderers, 72 percent grew up without fathers. In many of the current flagrant shootings in 1998, the youth are from divorced home without their biological father. Such was the 13 year old boy in Jonesboro, Arkansas who led a 11 year old friend in an execution-style shooting of their school mates, killing four students and a teacher, and wounding others.

In 1957, when it was obvious the United States' crime rate was beginning to grow, Samuel S. Leibowitz, senior judge of Brooklyn's highest juvenile criminal court, concluded his intensive search among various peoples of the world for the cause and prevention of juvenile delinquency. He concluded there is one main solution to the problem that can be summed up in nine words, "Put *father* back at the head of the home."[14] This was before the full storm broke of the 1960's and 1970's to remove the father by the educated elite.

The rise of crime has followed the time of the "Death of God" theology, the rise of divorce, and the cohabitating of the sexes outside of marriage, which have produced the single parent, primarily not the father. All of these cause a child to have no sense of accountability. A discussion of proper control through theistic marriage will be discussed in the last section, but it is important to see this important parallel at this point. [15]

Fatherlessness Homes Escalate the Number of Prisoners, Prisons, and Their Costs

The rapid rise in crime, especially violent crime, and crime related to drugs, has produced and increasing nightmare for government. Mary Cronin, after reviewing the trends, has said,

> In the past decade, the war on drugs and tough mandatory-sentencing laws have helped double the number of inmates, which reached a record 1.1 million this year [1992]. To house and feed this army of incarcerated souls, states have poured $30 billion in construction in the past 10 years. This year they will spend $7 billion more, while the Federal Government will plow $2 billion into a system that is demanding 1,100 new beds every week. After Medicare, the cost of corrections is the fastest-growing item in most state budgets, eating into scarce funds earmarked for health, education transportation and social services.[16]

This much is clear: until the early 1990s *more and worse prisoners were serving less time* because of the explosion in numbers and the demand that prisoners be released to make way for more. It is now known that criminals breed other criminals. The United States Bureau of Justice Statistics in a study of serious juvenile offenders reported they "found that 52 percent had one or more close relatives who had been incarcerated." Moreover, the upcoming criminals are increasingly more violent. According to the Justice Department, based on 1991 figures, about 80 percent of state prisoners are recidivist; the majority are violent recidivist which means the crime that landed them in prison was a violent crime (murder, rape, robbery, or assault), or they were convicted in the past of a violent crime. Of the remainder of these recidivists, about 40 percent are nonviolent criminals, meaning they had no current or prior violent crime convictions, but a significant portion have two or more of some prior convictions.

It was this type of information that helped law enforcement officials to put violent criminals in jail to stay that helped significantly reduce the crime rate in the middle of the decade. Along with longer imprisonment of recidivists, large cities have adopted computer software designed to help the police locate the areas of a city where the most crimes were occurring so they could concentrate most police action there. So in the last of the decade actions have been taken that have reduced crime, but not its causes. On the next page are charts showing the growth in violet crime into the early 1990's and the fact that new policies to reduce crime are increasing the size of our prisons even more.

The United States already has more people incarcerated per 100,000 people than any other nation, except Russia. There are 519 compared to Canada's 116, Germany's 80, and Japan's 36. Almost 1 out of 4 American households have one member victimized each year. In America there are far more black men in prison and for more serious crimes than any others. All people are demanding something be done to improve their security. The following are graphs showing the imprisonment of Americans.

GRAPH OF GROWTH OF VIOLENT CRIME

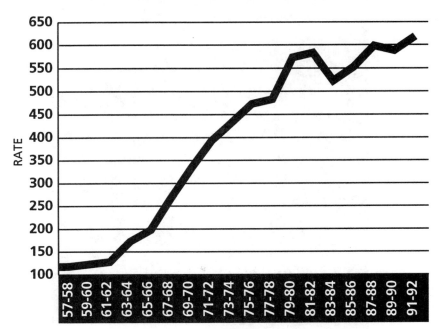

STATE AND FEDERAL PRISON POPULATIONS

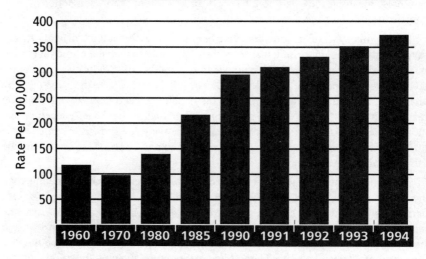

ESTIMATED INMATE POPULATION BY AGE (1992)

Age	Male	Female
18-19	24,000	1140
20-24	141,500	7300
25-29	189,300	12,000
30-34	170,825	11,160
35-39	115,200	7500
40-44	73,600	3900
45+	80,000	3500

(source: Correctional Populations, Bureau of Justice Statistics, 1992)

RECIDIVISTS AND CURRENT OFFENSES (1991)

CURRENT OFFENSES	FIRST-TIMERS	RECIDIVISTS Prior Violent	RECIDIVISTS Non Violent
Violent Offenses	65%	55%	35%
Property Offenses	10%	22%	32%
Drug Offenses	22%	16%	24%
Public Order Offenses	3%	7%	9%

(source: Survey of State Prison Inmates, 1991)

AVERAGE TIME SERVED FOR VIOLENT CRIMES

Murder — 8 Years
Rape — 5 Years
Robbery — 3 Years and 3 Months

(source: National Corrections Reporting Program)

The Tragic Effects of Children's Freedom from Parents by State Control

The tragic abuses to children by the optimistic programs of the educated elite in regards to the family, has created another wrong for the educated elite to make right. Instead of correcting the wrong by aiming for stable families, they have moved in the opposite direction to *free children from parents*. In the late 1970s, concern for children's rights emerged because child abuse was growing. Richard Farson wrote a "Child's Bill of Rights" which was published in *Ms.* magazine and legislation was proposed in the senate in 1979. The International Year of the Child proposed by the United Nations was the beginning of the liberal use of that organization to promote the agenda worldwide.

Previously it has been observed that welfare laws and collection procedures for child support drive many fathers away from their children. H. W. Brueister, President of Children's Rights Council of Georgia, and Stuart Miller, legislative director of the American Father's Coalition, both feel that the court system in America follows current gender tradition and is not aware enough of children suffering from lack of parental guidance. Many of the cases are those that come to the public attention because of abuse.

The idea of children's rights has swung too far and threatens to further diminish parental control in our society. In the Danforth case from Missouri (1976) ruling mentioned previously, the Supreme Court also ruled it unconstitutional to require written consent of a parent or guardian for an unmarried woman under the age of eighteen to obtain an abortion. In those rulings, John W. Whitehead observes, "In the area of abortion, then, the Court has created the autonomous wife and the autonomous child to the detriment of the traditional family statute."[17] In 1977 the Court also held it unconstitutional for a state statute to restrict the sale of contraceptives to those over sixteen years of age without parental consent. The Court was vigorously implementing the agenda of the educated elite on sexual freedom to the detriment of parental authority.

An underage teenage daughter was allowed to divorce her parents in 1994. Later she returned home asking to be reaccepted. Laws have been passed by state or federal government, and rulings have been made that prevent parents from exercising control in their children's education. Parents are unable to find runaway minor children in Oregon and bring them home without being charged with kidnapping. The trend goes on.

These, and other similar court rulings are only preliminary to *placing the state between children and their parents* and asserting the *rights of teenagers over parents or state*. Such were the implications of *Tinker v. Des Moines Independent School district* and other later rulings which are clearly presented by Whitehead. These and cases of parental rights in deciding on the education of their own children, show that the educated elite feel they should free children from parents and let the state social workers determine their future. Whitehead shows the Court did not relate this to age but to *the inherent right of the child* even as a minor. Such claims have been a basis for state control of children as far back as educator Horrace Mann in 1800s, but are now becoming law.

Whitehead's conclusion from the reviewing of these cases led him to say:

> Recent decisions of the Supreme Court seem to indicate that the family is no longer the basic institution for determining values for children. Instead, that is the state's province in and through its various agencies–in particular, the state supported public schools. . . . The family, like all other institutions, has been seen through the lens of social evolution. It, with the individual, is evolving.[18]

Thus, mother and father are being excluded from control over youth in favor of freedom and state control. This assertion of child independence will be shown in the next chapter to be tremendously important in the future.

Lawsuits concerning the way school authorities and social workers are assuming the right to control minor children over their parent's wishes are growing. For example in the little conservative town of Toccoa, Georgia, Wayne Earls placed a 3 million dollar lawsuit against the county school district. He and his wife discovered his 2 daughters, 14 and 15 years old, had a bag of condoms. On further inquiry, they found the wife of the school superintendent as a school counselor, had also taken the girls to a local health clinic to be tested for AIDS and cervical cancer, and given a prescription for birth control pills. The parents were not notified and were denied access to the tests. Thus, children are being put in conflict with their parents over vital issues.

Thomas Sowell, in attacking the educated elite for their programs that intrude into the family, has pointed out that "protections afforded criminals are not afforded parents." Quoting Elena Newman, he has said:

> Somewhere between 2 million and 3 million allegations of child abuse and neglect tie up the nation's hot lines every year. Of that number, 60 percent are deemed false and dropped. Of the remaining 40 percent that lead to investigations, about half (involving nearly 700,000 families) eventually are dismissed, but not before children have been strip-searched, interrogated by a stream of social workers, police officers, and prosecutors, psychologically tested and sometimes placed in foster care. Such actions usually occur without search warrants, parental consent, court hearings or official charges—and often solely on the basis of the anonymous telephone call.[19]

These children are often taught by social workers to suspect or even reject their parents. If ever there was a violation of the personal rights of parents, these are the incidents.

As Blankenhorn pointed out, the next generation will be marked by a significant number of people who have not known paternity and who have little stability or control in conduct. The liberals who took over the institutions in the 1960s and 1970s are now the ones raising the children of tomorrow. The movement to let children do as they wish without parental guidance, but require them to be under the inefficient public schools of the state, is to say the least, frightening. It would not be so threatening if we were referring to a few cases of children, but it poses social chaos because it is so pervasive.

In the review of the demise of the Greek democracy and of the Roman Republic, it was the final chaos brought on *by the youth who had rejected parental and all authority* that brought such tragic internal judgment on the societies. The daily news is filled with numerous crimes of great violence and harm done by children, and the number and horror of these seem to increase.

Individualistic Democracy Aims at Children without Fathers

Shere Hite's latest report on the family sees the home led by the father as an outmoded model that was detrimental and is now giving way to a much better *democratic* system. She blames the growing violence on the old patriarchal authoritarian system.[20] The American Association for Marriage and Family Therapy in 1994 gave a major press award to a magazine article that argued that fathers are unnecessary, and while conducting hundreds of workshops it seldom mentions marriage as a topic. The concept of the traditional family is now shifted to think "it takes a village" to raise a child. This radical concept of democracy in the home is the extreme individualistic view of the liberal elite where there is no one in charge.

This view of individualistic freedom is causing the loss of family and the loss of control in the United States, England, and much of the world. Maggie Gallagher in her book, *The Abolition of Marriage*, has said that marriage has been ruthlessly dismantled, piece by piece, under the influence of those who. . . believed that the abolition of marriage was necessary to advance human freedom.[21] This is an uncritical optimism that contradicts the lessons of history.

The problem is that for the individual to be able to participate in society, he or she must be trained and learn to care for others and keep his desires in control. Throughout all history the father has always been the leader in the family to do that. The major difference between humans and animals is that humans can train their young and pass on an ethical code that controls society so that they can live together and build a civilization.

It is now clear to any who want to know that the problem of crime, drugs, suicide, and so forth in America are directly tied to the breakdown of the home. The absence of the father with an authoritative voice and masculine presence is of greatest significance. All the money, all the additional police and social workers, and any efforts to solve educational problems are not likely to be successful until the educated elite's *politically incorrect democratic views* on which the family is based are corrected.

Danger of Segregation of Youth from Parents to Be Alone or With Peers

In America, the youth have been increasingly segregated from their parents to other caregivers who do so because they are paid and not because they have a relationship to care. In the last chapter this was discussed in regard to inadequate care for small children in child care centers. But this trend has been extended to free up parents from their children as much as possible in almost every way so they can earn more money and enjoy their freedom more. When the youth are not under paid supervision, they are left to be with their peers. One of the great attractions of the megachurches for parents is that they provide paid youth workers for extensive youth ministries where the youth are away from the adults with their peers. Schools offer after-school programs for peers to play together. While I once led one of the largest youth programs in the nation with 300 full-time staff, I now believe a new approach to youth is desperately needed. I began this in the 1960s to help reach youth in the midst of the youth revolt. Now all this needs rethinking.

Armand M. Nicholi II of Harvard has said:

> If any one factor influences the character development and emotional stability of an individual, it is the quality of the relationship he or she experiences as a child and both parents. Conversely, if people suffering from severe non-organic emotional illness have one experience in common, it is the absence of a parent through death, divorce, a time-demanding job, or for other reasons.[22]

One of the most noted child and youth specialists is Urie Bronfenbrenner. After some thirty studies over a twenty-five year period since World War II, the following has been said regarding his findings:

> He shows that the American way of adults forsaking their children to the youth peer groups is a major cause for growth in antisocial behavior. Moreover, he points out that studies by Condry and Simon indicate that the age at which the peer group gains dominance over adult desired behavior has gotten lower in recent years. Youth in America now spend two or three times as much time with their peers as with their parents.[23]

Bronfenbrenner has offered us a profound warning:

> We cannot escape the conclusion that, if the current trend persists, if the institutions of our society continue to remove parents and other adults and older youth from active participation in the lives of children, and if the resulting vacuum is filled by the age-segregated peer group, we can anticipate increased alienation, indifference, antagonism, and violence on the part of the part of the younger generation in all segments of our society—middle class children as well as the disadvantaged. . . . If adults do not once again become involved in the lives of children, there is trouble ahead for American society.[24]

Already it has been more than a generation where the trend has continued, with some rare and interesting exceptions which will be discussed later, but the masses of youth continue to experience this alienation. We are already paying the price with a growing number of problems, not only in the lower class, but with the middle class youth rebelling against adults by drug use, criminal acts, and sexual immorality which often leads to premarital pregnancy. But Americans are now building toward a great tumult of rebellion of the whole class of youth against adults. In the student revolts in the 1960s and 1970s it became common to say that anyone over thirty was suspect. But this expression of alienation is nothing compared to the hate and rejection that may soon occur.

Coming Financial Burden to Youth Is Breeding Hostility Toward Elders

As in previous civilizations there is a giant storm building between the youth and the elderly. Not only have youth been left alone or segregated to caregivers or their peers, but in the whole of the commercial markets, senior citizens are offered discounts, senior citizen fares, and privileges which used to be for the kids. As described in previous chapters, older generations have added more personal, corporate, and governmental debt. This expansion of credit has been described in previous chapters, and in their future old age through "the entitlement programs" the younger generations will have to care for them.

The elderly have voted themselves privileges of medical care and social security for retirement that will be a heavy burden on the shoulders of the young. This occurred not only by appealing to the politicians for more benefits, but by husbands and wives deciding they wanted fewer children. While there are less children to be cared for, there will also be less young adults to care for the elderly. But, also very important is the fact that through women's aborting babies who would have been inconvenient, there will be 35–37 million fewer children growing up to work and help pay the price of these entitlements. Twenty seven times as many unborn babies have been killed since 1973 than all the American soldiers killed in all the wars since America began. Moreover, the elderly are through modern medicine living much longer. This means the young will have to pay more and longer to care for the elderly. These selfish acts of American adults are placing exceeding great burdens on America's youth of the future, acts that are already beginning to light the fires of rage among young men and women. A summary of the facts graphically presented in chapter 14 follows.

The demographics are startling and few people want to face the facts of the future. Like the alcoholic who denies he has a problem even though he is wrecking his life, he won't admit he can't stop, and that drinking is causing great future problems. Peter G Peterson, who is one of the top American economists, has ably described the problem in his current book, *Will America Grow Up Before It Grows Old?*[25] American adults are rapidly undermining the future of the youth of this country. And the present elderly or parents of the baby boomers are the ones who started this financial catastrophe into which the ship of state is sailing. Most people do not think things would ever get to the apparent crisis. But the fact is that politicians vote the wishes of the greatest lobby, and the American Association of Retired People have the biggest and richest lobby in America to sustain their benefits. As summary of the data given in Chapter 14 is needed here.

Peterson has pointed out that in 1900 there was 1 in 25 who were 65 years or older, and they were all virtually self-supported by themselves and their families. At the present rate of births and average longevity there will be one 1 of 4 or 5 over 65, and virtually all will be supported to some degree by the government by taxpayers money. The number of senior citizens 65 and over will double between 1995 and 2040. Moreover, those that are 85 years and older and who require the most expense, are increasing rapidly compared to the young. In 1970 the kids 5 years old outnumbered those 85 years plus by 12 to 1 . By the years 2040 the number of 85 years plus will be equal to kids 5 years old (In 1970 there were 1.4 million 85 and older, and by 2040 there will be 14.4 million or 10 times more.) The high-cost elderly will increase 129 percent, those of intermediate cost will increase 112 percent, but those 20 to 64 years old will increase only 24 percent and those under 20 will increase 5 percent. So hospital and nursing bills will skyrocket. Also, because men now die sooner than women, two thirds of those 85 years plus will be women, and 4 of 5 of them will be single, divorced, or widowed.

There are more older people asking fewer young people to bear the responsibility of providing for them. We have all heard of the changing ratio of working people who will have to care for the elderly. In 1955 there were 8.6 people caring for 1 retiree; in 1960 there were 5.1 workers to one retiree; in 1995 there were 3.3 to 1, and in the year 2040, there will be 1.6 to 1. This means that 1 working couple will have to support 1 unknown retired person, before they begin to pay the other taxes for the other costs of federal, state, and city governments.

As a result, Social Security will grow from a $29 billion surplus in 1995 to a $1,321 billion deficit in 2040. Medicare will go from $9 billion deficit to a $1,923 billion deficit. Moreover, of those younger workers who bear the burden of these older, mostly white women, 25 percent of them will be non-white. Peterson warned, "This creates a potentially explosive situation in which the largely white senior Boomers will increasingly depend on overtaxed minority workers."[26] A further irony in the situation is that those dependent on this age of workers will be mostly the women, many of who chose to prevent or to abort the children that would have greatly swelled the ranks of this diminished group that must support them.

Time May Be Much Shorter Than Demographics Indicate before Youth Explode

The demographics were thrown off, not only because of the drop of the fertility rate and the abortions, but by great advances in medicine enabling longer life, and the high increase of the cost of medicine by new machines for doctors, and new pharmaceuticals and medicines that have been invented. But there are now new breakthroughs to lengthen life even more, and these will increase the number of people living longer and with even greater costs than are given in the demographics quoted by Peterson. At the National Institute for the Aging, demographer James Vaupel said that a whole new paradigm of aging is coming, and the average life expectancy could reach 100 or more.[27] Many of the factors of this new paradigm could begin late in the next decade or about 2008, or the very time when the Baby Boomers begin to start retiring.

Peterson warns, given the present trend, 2008 is the likely time that concerns for what is happening will begin to cause trouble. In a current book with contributions about areas of the expertise of the authors, the editor and former United States Budget Director, Robert D. Reischauer gives warning and also sets that time as a terminus by which some significant changes will happen.

> The decade from 1997 to 2007 offers an opportunity–perhaps *a final chance* for the nation to deal in a measured but preemptive ways with the major adjustments. . . . (italics added)[28]

All this dismal outlook is really very optimistic about the government being stable until that time, assuming that there will be no major crisis such as an outburst of war or terrorism or a stock market crash. Peterson warns:

> Since financial markets try to anticipate future events, the reaction will surely come years before the first boomers start retiring on social Security in 2008, when and if the markets determine that America has irretrievably lost any chance to deal with this challenge in advance.[29]

A collapse of the markets, the growth of unemployment even on the scale of the 1929 ff. debacle will leave many in the lower class without help and jobs, and could be the match to light the fuse of racial conflict. Most certainly there would be widespread tax evasion, as was described in Greece and Rome. The wealthy who would be taxed even more and mean's tested to get what they think they deserve, will hide their wealth and evade taxes. But more importantly, the average worker will have taxes that Peterson says could reach "35 to 55 percent" of every worker's paycheck just for the entitlements for the elderly. He warns:

> The experience of runaway pension systems in Latin America and Eastern Europe suggest that if payroll taxes begin even to approach these levels, tax evasion will become widespread, and much of the economy will go into the tax-exempt gray market. In other words, it may be impossible to

fund the future cost of our current benefit promises no matter how willing we are to legislate higher tax rates.[30]

It is not likely that things will continue even until the window of opportunity seems to close. Many other factors are involved in creating anger and unrest that will likely cause the meltdown of morals before that point. If trends go like those in other civilizations, as the great disorder and unrest breaks out, men will - abdicate the leadership of government to certain women, and soon after youth will take over with mobs and arrogance. Everyone will be at each other's throats in the name of justice for the cause of themselves as the underdogs. Also, the rejection of the traditional family concept to accept homosexuality is close at hand. This will be a denial of the created purposes of the male and female roles and the ultimate perversion and abuse of children. And at that point our society may encounter the hand of God's judgment.

Chapter 18

Homosexuality

Orientation to the Sexual Revolution and Homosexuality

The feminist movement has aligned with the homosexual movement because there is a mutual desire for freedom from sexual restraints and because male homosexuals break with the father image. Homosexuality is highly related to the male dilemma in society, since there are twice as many male homosexuals as there are lesbians. Moreover, homosexuality is related to children in the sense that it is highly related to trauma and conflict that affects children, especially male children.

A look at homosexuality is important for understanding the place of crisis to which the decline of our civilization has come. Homosexuality is not only a crucial element in the limit for the sexual revolution, but for the whole process of moral decline. As the intellectual revolution was a progressive revolution against the idea of God and the control for His will through the institutions, homosexuality is the greatest expression of individualism. The revolt of the sovereign individual against the sovereign God produced the progressive material revolution, and homosexuality is the ultimate point of effort to equalize everyone for individualistic selfish achievement. It is the supreme expression for individualism in the sexual revolt.

The homosexual has fulfillment of sexual self-pleasure as his goal without any abiding responsibility, and for all the talk about homosexual families, that is not the major concern for the homosexual movement. Homosexuality does not aim at producing offspring and continuing society, so it is really a-social and very pro-individual. If it were applied universally, society would end in one generation. Homosexuality is the ultimate end of man's intellectual journey of selfishness and inevitably leads to the point of individualism where each one judges others. The political battle to make homosexuality normal as a human right hides the definition of man as human and tells whether he can maintain society as we have known it. If and when homosexuality is accepted as normal in a society, it will in a final way usher in a complete meltdown to confusion and demand the exaltation of man as God. This has happened in a number of societies.

Jeffery Satinover, one of the best informed psychiatrists about the homosexual issue in America, writes:

> Because it is not really a battle over mere sexuality, but rather over which spirit shall claim our allegiance, the cultural and political battle over homosexuality has become in many respects the defining moment

for our society. It has implications that go far beyond the surface matter of "gay rights." And so the more important dimension of this battle is not the political one, it is the one for the individual human soul.[1]

Therefore homosexuality is not only the end of the objectives of the sexual revolution, but the end of the journey toward almost complete anarchy, to the final breakdown of society, and to judgment. The biblical story of the destruction of Sodom and Gomorra presents "the whole city" controlled by homosexuals who want to use the messengers of God. God's destruction of the city is used in later scriptures as an example against such rebellion (Genesis 19:4, Amos 4:11, Luke 10:12; 17:29 et. al.). Homosexuality is also prominent in the leaders at the end of many great civilizations. The next chapter will seek to more clearly show evidence for why we seem nearer to that point today, and why at the same time everything seems to be going so well.

If any matter, especially homosexuality, is to be interpreted correctly, a consciousness must be maintained that homosexuality involves an act of human beings who must be cared for, and that all of us as human beings commit wrong acts and are sinners who dishonor God, harm ourselves, and damage others for our own selfish ends. Unless we see ourselves as all in the mess of sin of which homosexuality is only one kind—albeit a very important kind of sin—we cannot perceive what is true and cannot help ourselves, much less others, including homosexuals. We must withhold judgment lest we add to the process toward meltdown in judgment. Let us leave all judgment to God. A man who practices homosexuality is human like all other sinners, and our aim must be to understand him and help him while avoiding hurting ourselves. Homosexuality involves a multitude of psychological emotions as well as acts of bodily desire and because of its complexity, it is difficult to understand.

Overview of Historic Development of Homosexuality in America

This is a brief overview of the development of homosexuality and makes no claim to comprehensiveness, but seeks to focus on what might be helpful.[2] In the last quarter of the nineteenth century, the increasing manifestation and study of homosexual acts began to appear in Europe and especially in Germany. Havelock Ellis has reviewed many of these studies in his book, *Sexual Inversion*.[3] Some interest and writings about the matter of sexual inversion appeared about this time in America, but became more prominent in the early part of the twentieth century. In the 1920s and 1930s, there was concern about the domination of women over their sons in the phenomena of "momism," and the manifestation of concern about homosexuality becoming more widespread.

While monogamous marriage was still the preference for women, having won the right to vote and thereby feeling they had established their equality legally, the expression of that equality was manifested in the home, and the conflict for control of the children led to more gender rejection and to a distance between some men and their sons.

The victory of the liberal agenda in the schools about mid-twentieth century established the perverted idea that freedom to fulfill all sexual desires is best and right. This was taught widely. In the last quarter of the nineteenth century, Freudian psychology and the writings of Richard von Krafft-Ebing, and especially Havelock Ellis, seemed to give a scientific credibility to this right for sexual freedom. While most of the early writings on the subject saw homosexuality as an undesirable illness, these acts, along with sadism and masochism, were *no longer viewed as sinful* and morally wrong. That was a big step toward the idea of today that homosexuality is normal.

Freud's claims that guilt over sexual acts were unenlightened became accepted by mid-twentieth century. Also, the anthropologist Margaret Mead argued that sexual freedoms were practiced by other people all over the world and were culturally established; she also argued there were grades of sexual identity.[4] After Alfred Kinsey published *Sexual Behavior and the Human Male* (1948) and *Sexual Behavior in the Human Female* (1953), his studies seemed to say sexual freedom was natural and that about 10 percent of the American public acted homosexually. He claimed it was a much more *acceptable practice* than was thought.

When the rejection of God reached the "Death of God" theologies of the late 1950s and early 1960s, the human conscience felt more free to act the way it pleased. As the sexual revolt was unleashed by a renewed surge of feminism in the 1960s, homosexuals were encouraged to go public. In 1969 at the Stonewall Tavern, a revolt occurred and its leaders called homosexuals to come *"out of the closet"* and be proud of their identity. From that point on, they sought to change the traditional views of homosexuality in America as a perversion and illness.

Promoting Homosexuality politically has proceeded rapidly. When Edmund G. (Jerry) Brown, Jr. ran for governor of California, he endorsed and sought the help of the homosexual community. In 1982, senator Ted Kennedy from Massachusetts was given a $1,000 plate dinner as a fund-raiser by homosexuals. In 1985 there was the Gay Pride march in Los Angeles. In 1988 George Bush entertained homosexuals in the Rose Garden of the White House. In 1992 Bill Clinton actively courted the homosexual vote, and soon after his inauguration he issued an executive order to make homosexuality acceptable in the military. This was rejected by the military for a compromise saying they would not be prosecuted if they did not speak out. In 1997, a school board of Massachusetts endorsed teaching the normalcy of homosexuality in the public schools. Also in 1997, President Bill Clinton was the speaker at a national meeting of the homosexuals. He also met alone personally with Ellen DeGeneres, an actress who had recently come out of the closet as a lesbian on her media promoted TV. show. He thereby gave open support to the homosexual community, and only a short time later spoke in Massachusetts in favor of supporting the curriculum endorsing the normalcy of homosexuality. Also, late in 1997 Al Gore spoke in Hollywood and commended the TV producers for helping to educate the public on that human rights issue by airing the show about DeGeneres making known her homosexuality. Thus the administration clearly gave this practice their endorsement.

Evaluation of Homosexuality

In American society, there are several concepts about homosexuality that have been predominantly accepted as tradition throughout the history of the nation. These have been the views for the foundational years of most civilizations as they have grown to prominence and were basic to the views and practices in the Greek democracy and the Roman republic, as they also were in colonial America until after the Virginia Dynasty. These accepted views were as follows:[5]

1. Homosexuality is *a moral choice* and not a necessity. While other pleasurable choices such as eating, drinking, and protection of body temperature are essential for life, they are necessary for maintaining life. While sex provides a pleasure, it is not essential for the individual to live—one can refrain from it; and since homosexuality is one route to sexual pleasure, it is a choice.

2. Homosexual acts are chosen on the basis of psychological and mental desires stimulated by visual image and physical contract, and therefore *homosexual behavior may be controlled, changed, and reversed.*

3. Homosexuality is not the predominant practice for men and women, and for this reason is *not considered normal* but a perversion from God's created plan and does not conform to the best health for individuals or society. More importantly, *it is considered wrong and a sin against God and others*. This practice favors promiscuity and is unhealthy for the individual and for the public.

4. Homosexuality, if widely practiced, is antisocial, *tends to racial suicide, and therefore is a social disease.*

Because homosexuality is a practice for selfish fulfillment of sexual pleasure, it promotes individualism and makes an individualistic lifestyle progressively more acceptable. For it to become accepted, it must change traditional institutions that influence society, such as family, school, church, and government. Those who practice homosexuality therefore progressively will seek to persuade everyone else to accept their lifestyle as normal to remove social stigma and guilt. That means they must change the above traditional views. Therefore, homosexuals seek to establish the following ideas that contradict the traditional ones.

1. Homosexuality is *based on innate genetic biology* which is different from that of most people and is the necessary direction for the homosexual to practice sexual desires. It is therefore normal for them, and heterosexual practice is not always normal. They are unique from most people.

2. *To try to reverse the practice of homosexuality is to deny the self* and harm the typical psychology of the person. It is like asking a black to deny his color or a Jew to deny his race and religion.

3. Homosexuals are *a distinct minority group whose human rights must be politically defended* and their practices treated as normal and healthy for them. To argue against homosexuality is bigotry, like racial hatred, denying their rights and is "homophobic."

4. Homosexuals *can promote a united society, even forming families* and adopting children, and they should be accepted into society with their practice.

The facts need to be examined to determine which are correct, traditional views, or the modern homosexual claims.

Is Homosexuality Caused By an Innate Bent Required by Nature?

Individuals committed to homosexual practice are seeking to convince the public that this practice is a result of some innate, biological factor, genetic or otherwise, and that this is natural for them. Therefore, to treat this practice as wrong and harmful to society is unjust. Homosexuals want to link their preference for same sex interaction to a cause of physical differences, and argue this from certain scientific claims. If these claims are accepted, then their argument is that they are a group under necessity, their practices are not morally wrong choices, and they should be accepted. They then claim that to be treated as perverted or ill is wrong. They then appeal to the public as victims of injustice.

Claims are that this innate desire can be seen from differences in certain brain stem parts, from the discovery of a certain gene causing homosexuality, and from tests suggesting influences of prenatal hormones. They argue that because this is so, the psychological and sociological professionals have accepted homosexual practice as normal and the public should do the same. They therefore claim they are treated unjustly, and their handbook for political activism seeks to promote them as victims. Like the feminist movement, some homosexual leaders have led homosexual groups to influence the media to believe these claims.

Perversion of the Facts by Homosexuals

Is Freedom for All Kinds of Sexual Practice Based on "Science"?

The claim that it is healthy for mankind to be free to experience all kinds of sexual pleasure is basic for homosexuality, and therefore those who practice it are hostile to restraints. Freud's driving motive was not primarily to heal sick people, but to establish human sexual freedom. Freud claimed this freedom was based on scientific research. But it has been discovered that while Freud had certain insights of truth, he did not follow scientific procedure, and his theories were based on guesses and a desire to justify his own rejection of God's law and religion and the guilt it caused. Thus, his followers have distorted images of Victorian and Puritanical ethics and opposed these as damaging. Freud was an immoral man, involved not only in perversions of adultery, but also homosexuality, he also indulged in what we know as crack cocaine use for his migraines.[6]

Freud's perversions have become increasingly clear. Paul Johnson, the noted modern historian said, "After eighty years' experience, his (Freud's) methods of therapy have proved on the whole, costly failures, more suited to closet the unhappy than cure the sick." Johnson quotes the famous philosopher Karl Popper, "Far from formulating his theories with a high degree of specific content which invited empirical testing and regulation, Freud made them all-embracing and difficult to test at all."[7]

Most of Freud's theories were questioned or rejected by other secular psychologists or psychiatrists in technical writings.[8] In the 1980s, the psychological and psychiatric associations in America generally renounced Freud's theories. Also, because they were not definitive, there were so many methods that were used, the associations selected certain approaches that seemed best. On February 18, 1991, a presentation made to the American Association for the Advancement of Science showed that Freud was more a slick salesman than a scientist and used connived data, often derived from others, which he sometimes censored to fit his ideas. Frank J. Sulloway of the Massachusetts Institute of Technology was involved in the report and said that Freud's theories were based on "outmoded assumptions from the 19th century."[9] This agreed with what Freud's prized student and later famous writer, Havlock Ellis, said, which raised Freud's indignation. He told Freud he was not a scientist but an artist. Yet Freud's perversions were the basis of the liberal elite's teachings for promoting sexual immorality, including homosexuality.

The view that Jewish and Christian morals are damaging and sexual freedom should be promoted for good health has been at the heart of the message in liberal education and entertainment. For example, Madonna's motive was to enlighten the world through her music, acting, and her book, *Sex*, and this motive is behind most of Hollywood's emphasis. President Clinton accepted the educated elite's secular view of sexuality, and these led him to appoint Joycelyn Elders as Surgeon General and for him to promote free sex and homosexuality through his administration and legal efforts. The homosexual groups sincerely believe in these false teachings and are committed to promoting them. Individuals promoting homosexual conduct are the most promiscuous of any group.

The Kinsey reports were prominent in communicating that practice of sexual immorality was widespread in America and that about 10 percent of its citizens were homosexuals. The prominent psychologist Abraham Maslow warned Kinsey that forming statistics from volunteers as he had done would not give valid results. In 1990, Judith Reismam, Edward Eichel, John Court, and J. Gordon Muir did a study published in *Kinsey, Sex, and Fraud*, showing that Kinsey repeatedly falsified his statistics to produce the results he wanted–that everything sexual is "natural" and therefore "normal."[10]

The first truly scientifically conducted survey to discover sexual practices in America was by the Alan Guttmacher Institute and was published in the March/April 1993 issue of the institute's journal, *Family Planning Perspectives*. After about forty-five years more of the sexual revolution, one would expect a much higher rate of homosexual practices in their study, but they found only 2.3 percent of men reported any homosexual contacts in the last ten years and only 1 percent said they were exclusively gay. The figure for women was much lower. Thus, the expansion of sexual freedom that followed Kinseyís report was based on fraud and produced the surge of change in sexual morals discussed previously.

Deception of the Public by Promoting a Change of Status in Psychological and Sociological Professional Groups

In chapter 12 on anarchy the high handed and anarchistic ways were used by homosexuals to gain acceptance and approval by the mental health organizations and by the liberal media. These events have been reported in several places, but Satinover gives many of the details.[11] More details are given here to help see what homosexual conduct did to gain acceptance by the scientific community, but rather goes contrary to the interest of health.

In 1970, a small faction of homosexual psychiatrists planned the takeover of the American Psychiatric Association. Using funds from the outside National Gay Task force and working through the APA's Committee on Nomenclature, in 1973 they achieved a vote of the Trustees stating the committee no longer lists homosexuality as a psychiatric disorder in the *Diagnostic and Statistical Manual*. This faction then mailed a letter to the over thirty thousand members in the American Psychiatric Association. Because a majority of the small sector of those who responded voted to support the change in the classification, the decision of the Board of Trustees was accepted. But less than one third of the members responded, and four years later a survey published in the *Medical Aspects of Human Sexuality Journal* found that 69 percent of the psychiatrists disagreed. Thus, the position of this scientific professional organization was changed by political maneuvering and not by scientific study.

Two years later, a faction of well-placed homosexuals in the American Psychological Association, which is three times larger than the American Psychiatric Association, was able to get them to also remove homosexuality as a disorder. This minority influence was next extended to the largest body of mental health practitioners in America, the National Association of Social Workers. The homosexual factions having gained approval of normalcy, sought to force another step. In 1992, through the Committee on Lesbian and Gay Issues, there was a lobby of the NASW to change its Code of Ethics and in 1994 sought the same change through the Trustees of the American Psychological Association to make it a violation of the codes of conduct (which would disqualify them as members) to try to help a homosexual change his practices, even if he requested help to change.

While they were unable to pass this change, it is evident the homosexual lobby is increasingly bold. These seeming endorsements by these professional organizations have been used by the liberal press to persuade the American people that homosexuality is a normal, healthy lifestyle. The next effort by homosexuals has been to find an innate scientific necessity for their practices.

Perversions of the Biological Data

Among others, Robert Gorski at UCLA has a team studying brain differences, and found the brain's "anterior commissure," a small bridge connecting the two hemispheres, is larger in females than in males, and also is larger in gay men. Laura Allen, a member of the team, discovered a portion of the hypothalamus (a bundle of neurons smaller than a grain of sand) is more than twice as large in men as in women. Simon Levay, a neurobiologist at the Salk Institute in San Diego, then explored a sample of ninteen supposedly gay men, sixteen heterosexual men, and six women. He found the gays' hypothalamus was also about half the size of the heterosexual men, as were the females.

But what might this prove? Levay admitted this was such a small sample that there was no scientific certainty of results, and others pointed out there was no certainty about the sexual preference of homosexuality of the brains because the specimens were dead and no investigation about them was possible.[12] Moreover, research has shown that the brain areas adjust in size as result of experience. For example, a blind person who learns to read Braille eventually has brain enlargement related to the reading finger. K. Klivingston, assistant to the president at the Salk Institute for which Levay worked, and others believe these differences may have been caused by the homosexual practice, rather than the practice caused by the brain difference.[13] Moreover, Levay's real motivation was revealed in that, soon after given prominent recognition by the press, he resigned and went to work in a homosexual organization.

A study by Dean Hamer announced that he and his research team had done a "linkage study" and found a gay gene in the chromosomes in the region know as q28 (xq28).[14] Having found that in a small number of families, the maternal uncles of homosexual men—but no other relatives—were disproportionately homosexual, they sought and located a variant in the genes of the male x chromosome. Geneticists from Yale, Columbia, and Louisiana State Universities looked at the work and made the following conclusion:

[The study's] results are not consistent with any genetic model . . . . Neither of these differences [between homosexuality in maternal versus paternal uncles or cousins] is statistically significant. . . . Small sample sizes make these data compatible with a range of possible genetic and environmental hypotheses . . . .[15]

Satinover pointed out that in the Hamer study there were only six sons of homosexual males, a very inadequate number for a meaningful test. Hammer presented four families as consistent with x linkage and only one homosexual male in these four has a child, a daughter, thus a lack of male reproduction.[16]

Yet the media communicated the implication to the public that these findings in the Hamer study were an innate biological cause for homosexuality. *The Wall Street Journal* article on July 16, 1993 read, "Research Points Toward a Gay Gene", and *The New York Times* on the same day read, "Report Suggests Homosexuality Is Linked to Genes." There were no articles to inform the public that these findings were inconclusive and with no definite meaning to the community of genetic scientists. The Levay study on brain parts and this on genes are two of the most significant of many studies which the homosexual community used in the media to bring people to believe there is an innate cause of homosexuality.

William Byne and Bruce Parsons, two geneticists of Columbia University, reviewed one hundred thirty five research studies in *The Archives of General Psychiatry*. This covered the entire literature up to that time and concluded as follows:

There is no evidence at present to substantiate a biologic theory, just as there is no evidence to support any singular psychological explanation [for the cause of homosexuality] . . . . Critical review shows the evidence favoring a biologic theory to be lacking. . . . Because such [personality] traits may be heritable or developmentally influenced by hormones, the model predicts an apparent non-zero heritability for homosexuality without requiring that either genes or hormones directly influence orientation per se.[17]

The homosexuals sought to use the studies of twins to prove heredity, but with no success.[18] Thus, the desire for the homosexual community to find some conclusive biological basis for their behavior is missing, but the liberal media has persuaded many that homosexuals have a legitimate basis for claiming they are a biological minority with the right to have public and government support. They claim they are victimized when their conduct is considered wrong.

Claim That Homosexuality Is Irreversible Is Refuted

Causes of Homosexual Conduct in America

There are many different factors that make biological and environmental contributions that offer persuasion to those seeking to choose homosexuality as a lifestyle. Genetics and environment only increase the option for homosexuality. Factors which increase desire in that direction are no doubt stronger in one person than in another, but the individual chooses that kind of conduct, seems comfortable in it, and becomes addicted to it. These factors follow:

1. There is a sexual culture claiming to be backed by science. Because of the sexual revolution and the deceptive idea that science supports that giving in to sexual urges is good and resistance is harmful, we now live in a sexually saturated culture that encourages all kinds of sexual perversion. Sex is used to entertain, to promote sale of intimate items, and in many ways to bring sexual pleasure to mind.

2. Normal sexual experimentation begins in early adolescence. It is possible anyone, male or female, can sexually excite another under the right circumstances. Older men who have become homosexual tend to seek out younger boys and introduce them to homosexuality. Experiments show that these men are on the average eleven years older than the partners they seek. A younger boy finding himself being led by such an older person yields to the authority of age and, because of his ignorance, may give in to a homosexual experience.

3. The family may have a strong influence on increasing the choice towards homosexuality. High stress situations during a mother's pregnancy may cause a reduction of testosterone in the fetus and result in greater homosexual preference in the male.[19] A wife may feel, perhaps from

feminist influence, she should compete with her husband for equality causing conflict and stress. This may also result in the mother and father vying for the affection and control of the children. This choice of favoritism for one parent against the other may lead to gender rejection. Studies show that when there is intimacy between father and son, there is almost never a son who becomes homosexual, and conflict in the home is usually present in a home where children become homosexual. Thus, the failure of the man to be the loving leader, or the feminist attitudes toward the husband and father, offers problems.[20]

4. Certain physical features or gestures may be the results of testosterone differences or other factors involving the fetus and may have a part in gender rejection. There are certain mannerisms, ways of movement, and emotional desires that are different which increase criticism from peers and enlarge the option for practicing homosexuality. But these same deviations may exist in heterosexuals and may not exist in the same way in others practicing homosexuality. Therefore these deviations are not determinative.

5. Sex offers an increasingly constraining desire leading to orgasm, which under the right conditions gives the greatest unexplainable bodily pleasure. Sex in humans, unlike in animals, can be a continuous desire, and to gain the right conditions for pleasure, to maintain health, and to direct society, one needs to be trained and disciplined for control. All bodily desires need to be controlled, but sexual urges take particular discipline to curb.

Satinover has explained this:

> The chemical released [in orgasm] is a special type called an "opioid," meaning "opium-like." None have such an intense but of internal opioids as sex. This is similar to a heroin "rush" which is called "orgasmic." Heroin and cocaine addicts quickly lose interest in sex, it being a substitute. [Without bringing this under controlled by will] the pressure to seek their immediate fulfillment becomes deeply embedded in the neural network of the brain. Furthermore, the particular, individualized patterns by which we seek this fulfillment will also become deeply implanted.

> Once embedded, sexual fantasy life in particular cannot be erased. New fantasies may be learned "on top of," so to speak, the earlier ones . . . . We may learn new behaviors that prove as gratifying or even more gratifying than the old ones; the old ones will weaken and wither, yet they will always be there- the "old self" and the "natural man" does not die entirely in this life. Few are so strong that given sufficient duress, the old patterns of fantasy and behavior could not be provoked again into near-overwhelmingly seductive strength.[21]

The homosexual fantasy and drive seems to be one of the most insistent and consuming. Homosexuals have twelve times as many different partners as do heterosexuals. While there is talk about homosexual marriage, this is only another claim for normalcy and acceptance that is not true. Of one hundred fifty six couples studied, only seven had maintained sexual fidelity; of the hundred couples that had been together for more than five years, none had been able to maintain sexual fidelity. Satinover goes on to say, "A 1981 study revealed that only 2 percent of homosexuals were monogamous or semi-monogamous- generously defined as ten or fewer lifetime partners.[22] And a 1978 study found that 43 percent of homosexuals estimated having sex with five hundred or more different partners and 28 percent with a thousand or more different partners. 79 percent said that more than half of these partners were strangers and 70 per cent said that more than half were men with whom they had sex only once.[23] In contrast, he points out that according to the study *Sex in America,* 90 percent of heterosexual women and more than 75 percent of heterosexual men have never engaged in extramarital sex.[24] While the strong warnings against AIDS in the last decade have caused greater caution, the promiscuity of homosexuals is unquestioned.

Major Evidence Homosexuality Is a Choice Is the Conversion of Many

The leaders of the homosexual groups are unwilling to admit that anyone addicted or involved in the homosexual lifestyle can be sexually reversed in practice and be reoriented to heterosexual living. This goes against their whole political effort to claim normalcy and refutes all scientific claims. Yet many homosexuals are miserable people and desperately desire to change and do change. As Satinover has said:

> If homosexuality was once a taboo, what is taboo now is the notion that homosexuals can be healed, if they want to. Few articles in the popular press ever mention programs that aim to reverse homosexuality; those that do are derisive and uncritically repeat activist's claims that the programs are rarely successful. And almost no articles in the professional literature discuss the treatment of homosexuality as homosexuality.[25]

This fact is the exact opposite of the claims printed before many came out of the closet and the successful political activities since successful lobbying of the professional groups. While there are differences in homosexuals, these were considered perversions and, except for physical sexual deformities, they were all considered correctable illnesses. Since 1975 and the changes in the APA by the homosexual lobby, articles about the matter have become almost nonexistent.[26] Earlier, there were articles that reported following up treatment of homosexuals, with a significant 61 percent in sexual reorientation. Satimover quotes those who decry this rejection of this data as a turn of events that is a "disastrous disregard of knowledge gained through painstaking psychodynamic and psychoanalytic investigations over the past seventy five years."[27]

I believe Satinover is correct in arguing that, while calling sexual addiction an illness removes the judgmental attitude, the problem is really spiritual and deals with the "progressive erosion of the ability to choose differently." It therefore needs to be approached like alcohol and drug addiction.[28]

He reviews the studies of secular, Christian, and Jewish treatments and their results. An extensive survey reveals that secular psychological efforts showed 23 percent changed to heterosexuality and 84 percent benefited "significantly" from treatments. Of some two hundred Christian groups that work in this area, he found, for an example that about 33 percent make little progress, about 50 percent make substantial progress, and about 25 percent went on to marry and their marriages lasted as long as those of heterosexuals.[29] Thus, a significant amount of reversal of sexual orientation is now being achieved in spite of the opposition of the homosexual leadership, of the professional organizational changes toward treating them, and in spite of opposition from the public media. Because homosexuality has many unhealthy effects, this is tragic for them and for the public health that is involved.

The High Risk and Lethal Indifference of Homosexuals

Homosexual conduct is far more risky to health since it involves oral and rectal organs with their secretions. Anal intercourse is the preferred choice of homosexuals, which is only about one thirteenth as common even in perverse heterosexual acts, and at least 40 percent never use a condom. This causes them to be exposed not only to AIDS and other diseases, but to a suppression of their immune system which is thought to be related to sperm antibodies and other factors. According to 1996 CDC figure the government spends $39,172 on AIDS/HIV per patient compared to $5,449, Diabetes; $3,776, Cancer; $1,056, Heart Disease; $765, Stroke. These affect much more of the general population.

Their extreme promiscuity exposes homosexuals to more disease and causes them to spread sexually transmitted diseases (STDs) widely. About 78 percent of homosexual males have had at least one sexually transmitted disease, and they have an abnormally larger proportion of the group who contact urethritis, and 20 to 50 percent more hepatitis A and B than do heterosexual males. They account for over half the cases of syphilis, much more gonorrhea and other diseases such as venereal warts, and 30 percent of all AIDS cases, even though it is estimated that only 1.4 percent of the adult population consists of homosexual males. Since many of them are also heterosexual, they pass these on to women. Satinover refers to W. Odets who said:

But shockingly and frighteningly, yet consistent with concentration of AIDS cases among high risk populations, epidemiologists estimate that 30 percent of all twenty-year-old homosexual males will be HIV-positive or dead of AIDS by the time they are thirty.[30] This means the incidence of AIDS among twenty- to thirty-year old homosexual men is roughly 430 times greater than among the heterosexual population at large.[31]

He then lists the problems that a homosexual male faces.

- an unsuccessful marriage
- a twenty-five to thirty- year decrease in life expectancy
- a chronic, potentially fatal, liver disease–infectious hepatitis, which increases the risk of liver cancer
- inevitably fatal immune disease including associated cancers
- frequently fatal rectal cancer
- multiple bowel and related infectious diseases
- a much higher than usual incidence of suicide
- a very low likelihood that the adverse effects listed here can be eliminated unless the condition of homosexuality itself is
- at least a 50 percent likelihood of dying through lengthy, often costly, and very time consuming treatment in an otherwise unselected group of sufferers (although a very high success rate, in some instances nearing 100 percent, for groups of highly motivated, carefully selected individuals)

It is sad that American leadership is allowing homosexual leaders to promote this kind of conduct which is responsible for such tragic conditions of so many people in order to justify their practices.

Point Is Near Where Homosexuals Will Insist Americans Accept Their Lifestyle

What is even more alarming is that homosexual leaders are trying to outlaw telling people the truth about homosexuality and how they can be returned to heterosexual health. As mentioned, in 1992 and 1994 they sought to make it a breach of ethical conduct for anyone in the National Association of Social Workers and the American Psychological Association to try to treat people, even if the person wanted restoration to heterosexuality. Only by bold opposition of some members were these efforts thwarted. But it is only a matter of time before they succeed in some way by their political, not scientific, efforts.

When homosexuals make laws in the various states on the basis of human rights homosexuals can legally marry, they already plan to seek to disallow licensees to clergymen to marry anyone at all, if they deny homosexuals the right to marry. The chaplain at Emory University in Atlanta recently received permission to hold marriage ceremonies in the Emory Chapel. Recently a New Jersey judge allowed an adoption by a homosexual male couple, and it is now considered legal for homosexuals to marry in New Jersey.

Homosexual Conduct Uses and Pursues Sex with Children

Homosexuals are seeking to promote sex with younger children. Satinover quotes L. S. Doll:

> 1,001 adult homosexual and bisexual men [who were] attending sexually transmitted disease clinics were interviewed regarding potentially abusive sexual contacts during childhood and adolescence. Thirty-seven percent of participants reported they had been encouraged or forced to have sexual contact before age 19 with an older or more powerful partner: 94 percent occurred with men. Median age of the participant at first contact was 10; median age difference between partners was 11 years . Fifty-one percent involved use of force; 33 percent involved anal sex.[32]

Pedophilia is statistically closely associated with homosexuality, and to cause a shift in values that makes homosexuality normal along with other sexual freedoms, the leaders must promote laws of consent for pedophilia. The homosexual leadership is working hard to communicate the idea to the public that involving children in sex is not wrong. Satinover refers to articles that have been circulated to communicate these ideas to the press in *The Journal of Homosexuality* by an editor who sits on the board of Paedika: *The Journal of Paedophilia*; the *San Francisco Sentinel*, which is a Bay area gay-activist newspaper, and others.[33] They are pushing hard to get sex education in the public schools that include these ideas..

Shocking, according to *World*, the President of the United States was spokesman at the "Human Rights Campaign" dinner for gay, lesbian, bisexual, and transgendered people. Speaking at the dinner, he suggested that as people grow older they become "somewhat limited in their imaginations." The implication is that people must be taught while young if their views are to change. He expressed the idea that morals change to meet the ideal and used the illustration that Thomas Jefferson believed all men were created equal, he kept slaves, but that in time Americans evolved to the ideal. He was saying that homosexuality must be taught to children as normal if Americans are to ever evolve to accept the human rights of homosexuals. In another speech only days later at a "Conference on Hate Crimes" at George Washington University, Clinton and several members of his Cabinet endorsed a K-12 plan to teach children tolerance of racial minorities, homosexuals, and the disabled.[34] This form of education is now being promoted in a number of school districts, with the objective of spreading it all around America. People who oppose these teachings are being labeled "ignorant" and "bigots."

Homosexual leaders are insistent on brainwashing the public to accept them and to allow children to become involved with their conduct. They have often tried to infiltrate the Boy Scouts of America, and they have fought lawsuits against them to make them change the organization's commitment to the traditional family, but lost. At present there is a nationwide effort by the gay leadership in the Unitarian Universalist Church charging the Boy Scouts with being homophobic. Gays are introducing books in the public schools to gain acceptance of their lifestyles. One company has published books even for children of two to six, one being *Heather Has Two Mommies*, and another showing men kissing with a child looking on, entitled, *Daddy's Wedding*. Gays are seeking to create "gay-straight" youth alliances, which are homosexual groups in schools, and are pushing for the rights of gay teachers to proudly affirm their homosexual identity. They are also advocating a Gay History Month for public schools.

Homosexuals are pushing hard to gain governmental backing for claiming the gay lifestyle as a human right. In May 1998, President Clinton issued an executive order banning "discrimination" against homosexual federal employees as an amendment to an order mandating affirmative action, so now homosexuals will be given preferred status. In 1996, the United States Senate came within one vote of passing the Employment Discrimination Act which would have made sexual orientation a protected class equivalent to racial minorities under federal civil rights laws. The Republican leadership is moving away from the position of the conservative right, claiming they are wanting to take the centrist position of the American people. Recently Jim Nicholson, Republican National Chairman, called to offer best wishes to David Catania, a homosexual, as a member of the District of Columbia GOP Council saying, "We were and are fully supportive of him without equivocation." One of the largest political action committees of its kind in Washington, The Human Rights Campaign, which spent one million dollars last election, has described itself as taking "the lead role in bringing lesbian and gay issues into the mainstream of American politics." This group has just produced a thirty-two page gay manual to advance the homosexual political agenda for both parties and the foreword was written by former Clinton advisor, George Stephanophoulos and Bob Dole's former chief of staff, Sheila Burke. Thus leaders of both parties are promoting this. The Human Rights Campaign is one of a number of gay activist groups. Gays have won political races in almost half of the states, and a number are running for United States Congress in this next election. While Senator Trent Lott recently spoke out, identifying homosexuals as "sick," there are few voices other than Gary Bauer and the Family

Research Council who are opposing gay efforts, and it seems homosexual conduct will soon be considered a right by federal law, and taught in our schools.

If homosexual relationships are treated as legal families there is no way to limit the family from that point on: polygamy, incest, and every imaginable perverted sexual practice will become acceptable. If one state accepts deviant marriages, many other states will be forced to do so. Moreover, clergy who refuse to perform such marriages could be denied the license to marry anyone.

Tragically, some homosexual leaders are poised to try to force the American people to comply with accepting their lifestyle and with allowing them legal access to children to lead them into their unhappy and unhealthy practice. America is only a short step towards judgment, because God's word against this practice cannot be broken. God would have to apologize to Sodom at the final judgment if He allows these things to continue.

Chapter 19

Terminus in Judgment:
Man Judging Man and God Judging Man

INTRODUCTION

In the United States in 1998, the President announced the state of the union to be in excellent health: it has had a long time of economic growth, unemployment is very low, interest rates are low, the budget deficit is almost gone and promises a surplus, the welfare roles are decreasing, and crime is down. Also, AIDS is leveling off, abortions and premarital pregnancies are decreasing, and so are divorces. There have been significant problems, but they seem to have been solved. But is "good health" a correct diagnosis of the state of the people and the nation?

In this chapter, I will show the nation is at a point of serious deception. The Devil is a deceiver. He is Satan, the enemy, and his purpose is to destroy. In recent years, an all-American football player who had a small growth removed from his face seemed in the peak of form and the leading contender for the Heisman trophy. So he continued to strive with great effort to win. But before the season ended, he died from melanoma cancer. A young girl won the title of Miss Texas and was a leading contender for the Miss America title. She never made it to the contest because a crippling nerve disease, for which she earlier showed symptoms, eliminated her from participating. These two young people, while seeming to be the best, exhibited evidence of disease without knowing its seriousness and pursued their courses until it was too late.

Close analysis indicates America, which is considered the strongest nation on earth, is likewise stricken with a disease of moral decay that can bring her destruction. Previously presented data suggests this decay, but this chapter evaluates events seeming to negate this course and the continuing seriousness of our condition. America, like the two young people mentioned, would do well to heed warnings of trouble, get a better diagnosis, and find an early cure. The nation is more at point C in the graph on page 39, which described the growth and meltdown of a nation, and is the climax of all waves at point 5 on the graph on page 31 in Steps of Decline. This condition of the nation is also confirmed by looking at the deception of the Devil as we discussed in the trends of thoughts (cf. chapter 6). This will be shown by comparison with the steps of decline of other national cultures, by the conditions at the time of their meltdown to confusion, and with the final deceptions near the end.

COMPARISON WITH DECLINING CULTURES
SHOWS AMERICA NEAR ITS END

America is nearing the end of moral decline as seen by comparison to already dead civilizations. The following is a brief review of the steps of moral decline in the Greek democracy and the Roman Republic, which parallel the decline of morals in the United States.

GREEK DEMOCRACY
Intellectual revolt:

Rejection of God for a mechanical, naturalistic world (late 6th century B.C.)

Materialistic revolt:

Devotion to wealth and prosperity (early 5th century B.C.)

Sexual revolt:

Revolt of women for money and freedom (mid 5th century B.C.)

Anarchy begins:

Conflicts for power between internal groups (late 5th century B.C.)

Judgment, Human and Divine:

Meeting of all trends ending in meltdown (mid 4th century B.C.); resulting in Macedonian conquest and dictatorship.

ROMAN REPUBLIC
Intellectual revolt:

Rejection of God for a mechanical, naturalistic world (late 3rd century B.C.)

Materialist revolt:

Devotion to wealth and prosperity (last of 3rd century B.C.)

Sexual Revolt:

Revolt of women for money and freedom (early 2nd century B.C.)

Anarchy begins:

Conflicts for power between internal groups (mid 2nd century B.C.)

Judgment, Human and Divine:

Meeting of all trends ending in anarchy (late 2nd century B.C. and early 1st century B.C.); Caesar dictator.

UNITED STATES OF AMERICA

Intellectual revolt:

Rejection of God for a mechanical, naturalistic world (late 18th and early 19th century A.D.)

Materialistic revolt:

Devotion to wealth and prosperity (early and prominent in mid 19th century A.D.)

Sexual Revolt:

Revolt of women for money and freedom (begin mid and prominent late 19th century A.D.)

Anarchy begins:

Conflicts for power between internal groups (last third of 19th century A.D. but prominent in mid 20th century A.D.)

Judgment, Human and Divine:

Meeting of all trends ending in anarchy (Next decade?)

This brief comparison of the facts presented indicates the United States is near some end point. The Greek democracy and the Roman Republic both went through steps of moral decline until they reached the point of moral meltdown, bringing them into utter confusion with internal conflict leading to dictatorships that ended their prosperity and greatness. At the end, they both gained prosperity and seeming strength until there was a surprising collapse. There now seems to be the same kind of deceptive conditions present in America at or near the same time this occurred in other cultures.

Apparent Prosperity and Surprising Meltdown

In the middle of the fourth century B.C., Greek democracy seemed at its height and as if nothing could shake it. Greek influence had affected the whole Mediterranean world, and wealth flowed into Athens along with the cultures and religions of many nations. The Golden Age of Pericles had yielded to the politics of the flamboyant and popular Archibiadies, who knew the art of promise and compromise. While the old beliefs in one God had long gone, prosperity made it seem safe to allow anyone to pursue his choice of the declining morals. The strong contest for more power and wealth of the different classes was troubling, but most people seemed better off. The middle class had declined in property ownership, while the upper class grew more wealthy. The large number of declining middle class individuals provided an "unyielding conservatism and a utopian radicalism" of intellectuals who sided with the poor and the disadvantaged. There was a growing state bureaucracy with increasing requests for taxes from the government that were resented. Then, it all melted into confusion of conflicts between the groups.

As the third quarter of the second century B.C. approached in Rome's stately streets, the power of its empire was indisputably reaching its heights. What nation wanted to combat powerful Rome? The magnitude of business conglomerates and large farms produced tremendous wealth for a small number of families. The capital city of Rome became very cosmopolitan with many cultures and religions spreading licentious pleasures, many absorbed from the decadent Greeks. Violence marked everyday activities, as well as contests in the Coliseum. Then, revolts tore the city-nation apart. Men of principal were scarce, and youth and women became leaders.

The feelings of power and wealth of Greece and Rome in the last days deceived the leaders and most of the population. There were few who really anticipated the eruption of underlying financial problems and of the seemingly senseless outbreaks of conflicts between the groups. When outbreaks came, the meltdown to confusion was unmistakably painful, paralyzing, and destructive to rich and poor alike. America, like the Greek and Roman civilizations, seems to be in a similar condition.

Because America is prominent in the modern world and exercises wealth and military genius, does not mean the nation is well and secure. The same internal divisions and competition for power and pleasure that were in Greece and Rome are manifesting their presence. The same diseases are lurking in our system and must be dealt with soon or they will be lethal. Judgmental attitudes will break out into accusations and attacks directed mostly toward those who stand for integrity and righteousness. These attitudes will bring divine judgment to terminate the diseases of pride, greed, and lust.

Point for Close-Minded, Self-Righteous Insistence is Near

Structures of Intolerance for Tolerance

The intellectual elite have achieved the position of control in the universities; now, in American government, the intellectual elite use this control to intimidate, and often disallow any presentation of data evidencing a transcendent Creator, or that He as a designer gives ultimate meaning and control to all things. That would contradict their premise of the sovereignty of the individual person and his freedom to act as he pleases, and especially, of the elite's certainty they are right in their agenda and they must, by virtue of their feelings of intellectual superiority, have the right to tell the masses what is best for accomplishing equality for all.

Most importantly, these intellectuals resent believers in God calling them into account for the fact that this elite almost always give themselves a preferential place and special benefits derived from their control. Their agenda keeps others in submission by causing them to believe they are victims and cannot do better without their government help. The intellectual elite sell the masses on believing their hope must be in an elite-run government which takes from others and gives to them, the victims.

But it was shown in chapters 13-18 on results, that each group of victims now has reached a point where it sees it has not attained its objectives of equality through the government by the intellectuals, much less will those of each group have a time of superiority, as the members feel they deserve. Thus, each group is now reasserting itself and rejecting not only the absolute standards of God, but rejecting the control and standards of the educated elite themselves. Such rejection of the help of the educated elite was not anticipated as a part of their liberal agenda.

Near Terminus Point of Exclusivism by Each Group

As the end of each culture approached, intolerance–or an exclusivism which elite leaders developed to maintain their control–was rejected. The views of the educated elite were now in question, because all of their theories of determinism had been questioned by other intellectuals. Some groups that rejected scientific determinism have discovered the lack of facts to support this. Also, some deterministic scientists discover contradictions to the elite's views in the data and disclose these to gain personal recognition, even when it is not politically correct. These findings have shown the "vision of the anointed" was not based on a correct understanding of the facts and didn't promote the good of the so-called "victim" groups, but actually, for some, have caused more and worse oppression from the elite-run government. In chapter 13, the collapse of intellectual views both in basic science and in sociological theory was presented as increasingly evident and was rejected by some considering the authors. Moreover, it was shown at the end of each chapter 15-18 that each group is disillusioned and angry at the lack of fulfillment and are at the end of waiting.

The deterministic and uniformitarian view of nature is being increasingly exposed as untrue. Indeed, in *Dark Shadows . . . ,* I show that a view of probabilities, questionably rendered as *chaos theory*, is gaining dominance in leading universities, and the idea of possible catastrophes as causes of past events and as threats for the future is now real. As an alternative to a return to belief in God, "New Age" thinking, which includes the idea of design and power in nature, or paganism, is reasserting itself. And the social theories of control by the educated elite, whether fascism, communism, the socialistic democracies in Europe, or in the emerging countries of Asia, are now in economic trouble. The troubles in America now call into question the correctness of the educated elite. As Paul Johnson and others have shown, societies in the twentieth century, controlled by a secular elite, have been responsible for more brutal deaths and unjust imprisonment than by any other controlling elite in the centuries past.

Most elite are unwilling to allow views which oppose what they consider politically correct. Numerous books pointing out and challenging these closed views of the universities and of Hollywood have been mentioned (see chapter 13). The most significant factor behind this is the organized groups educators have established to protect their views. Some of these views are as follows:

National Education Association and Sympathetic Groups

Examples of this political control to force acceptance of their ideas by American society can be given. William Bennett pointed this out in regard to Education. He said:

> The National Education Association is the largest union in America (with 2 million members and an operating budget of $135 million) and the most influential and powerful force in the education establishment. . . . The modern-day NEA is primarily a political action organization. It routinely takes liberal and even left-wing stands on political conditions and on many national and international affairs . . . . The record then is clear and beyond dispute: the NEA is an organization embodying the philosophy of modern-day liberalism.[1]

Most of the teachers who are members of the NEA disagree with the leadership of their union. Bennett points out that two-thirds of teachers polled by the NEA in 1985-86 classified their political philosophy as conservative or leaning towards conservative. And more than half of them voted for Ronald Reagan, both in 1980 and 1984. To improve education in America, Bennett came to a radical conclusion. He said:

> But what was needed was not exhortation or lectures. What was needed was more on the order of a demolition squad. My target was the entire mediocre education enterprise in America, and my goal was to replace it with a better one. That meant going head-to-head with the guardians of the education system—its powerful interest groups, its political protectors on Capital Hill, its assumption of full entitlement to the public purse, and its pathetic performance and record.[2]

In almost every area of study, there were watch dog groups which were controlled by people committed to the dominant view of the educated elite working with the NEA and other associated educational and political groups. For example, the National Center of Science Education (NCSE) located in Berkeley,

California, opposes appointments of teachers or selection of textbooks not agreeing with a deterministic, scientific view of the universe or not accepting the Darwinian theory of evolution. They dogmatically insist any other views are unenlightened, harmful, and ignorant, much like going back to holding the idea that the world is flat. But they never consider that facts to support their views have never been demonstrated, as in the case for the views of Copernicus and Newton, both authors who held to belief in a transcendent God.

Since the takeover of the universities, the rejection of God and the idea of creation has been almost total in spite of the lack of evidence. The Federal Court of Arkansas in 1982 and the Supreme Court in 1987 ruled evidence for creation could not be taught as being in agreement with science in the public schools. One participant who heard and reviewed the evidence of these court hearings referred to them as exercises in bigotry. He compared them to the Scopes trial in 1924 and pointed out the only change is the bigots were on the opposite side. In fact, Daniel Dennett, in his book, *Darwin's Dangerous Idea,* advocates the teaching of anything but Darwinian evolution be outlawed in America.[3] That is narrow dogmatism indeed!

As pointed out in chapter 11, increasingly in recent years, the scientific truth is emerging that evolution has no foundation. It is debated publicly in major universities. These scientific, fundamentalist leaders, who more and more hold to a deterministic view of science, proclaim their dogma as the only correct one, and their aim is, even in private schools and home teaching, that the views of creation be eliminated.

These watchdog groups of educated elite are prompting that President Clinton and other leaders adopt national examinations for students. These tests will then gradually change to insist there will be an exam which all teachers must pass to be allowed to teach. Since their view of correctness will require acceptance of their secularized views on everything from their views of science and human rights for women, all races, and homosexuals, they will try to disqualify any teachers from teaching children anywhere in America who won't accept their ideas. Since their publicly controlled schools cannot compete with most of this private education, they will therefore try to reduce them to the level of those schools they already control. This dictatorship would never be accepted by masses of Americans, and a cultural war would erupt with massive arrests and blood in the streets if that should be legally attempted.

Hard-Core Feminist Control

What is true of prejudice, in regard to science in education, is also true in regard to sexual issues in education. Christina Hoff Sommers revealed a planned takeover and control of the universities by radical feminists. Her review of the bias of the AAUW's studies on self-esteem and the Wellesly Report have already been referred to. But she has a chapter tracing the plans by these feminists, including a "handbook for transformations" and a five-phase theory to grade teachers and their classes. Sommers writes:

> Feminists' [gender feminists, by her definition] academics have worked hard and successfully to get people "who carry a new consciousness" into administrative positions at every academic level. These now do their best to ensure that new appointments are not out of line. To criticize feminist ideology is now hazardous in the extreme, and even to have a "clean" record is no longer sufficient. Aspirants to university presidencies, deanships, program directorships, and other key posts are aware that they will probably have to show a record of demonstrated sympathy with gender feminist doctrines and policies. The same is rapidly becoming true for faculty appointments . . . . The Association of American Colleges (AAC) itself one of the "power structures" that have been colonized by women of the right consciousness, disseminates a widely used questionnaire entitled "It's All in What You Ask: Questions for Search Committees to Use." Prospective candidates for faculty or administrative positions are asked such questions . . . .[4]

The questions center on support for the position of the hard-core feminists. The public is well aware of the strong feelings and open conflict concerning sex education for children, especially abortion.

Other Exclusionary Control Groups

This same kind of bureaucracy and companion political groups are in existence for black studies, economic studies, political studies, and religious studies. These groups are backed up by organizations like the People for the American Way and the Americans United for Separation of Church and State; further legal action is furnished by the ACLU. The education establishment is no longer a place for the free exchange of ideas in which truth will be given a chance to win the minds of the students. This restriction has led to a position that is degenerating through a lack of moral control and fragmented meaning. This exclusivistic condition is similar to that of established Communism which, in the long run, diminished the power of the Soviet Union and led to the demand for Glasnost and Peristroika. By then it was too late; Russia missed out on information for scientific and other developments, putting its country behind.

These exclusivistic conditions have been countered by an extreme right position which is headed for conflict with these groups in the political arena. Many of these right-wing groups are militantly Christian who see the bigotry of other groups, but often do not see that they themselves appear to offer compulsory, exclusionary views that they would seek to impose by gaining political force. Thus, they are ceasing to fight their battles against the spiritual forces causing acceptance of these views. The matter of the spiritual attack and the place of politics will be discussed in the last chapter, but the dangers for Christians are simply mentioned here. Fighting on a spiritual plain rather than a political one is most important.

All of the different groups for self-interest are rejecting all standards claiming truth–biblical and liberal–except what is good for their own self-interest. Groups in the post-modern age are skeptical of any certainties and see all things relatively. Thus, all views and values are now going through deconstruction, which involves reinterpretation and rejection of other peoples' meanings. This deconstruction, because of strangling intolerance, is indicative of a dying civilization. This was true of communism until efforts were made for change at the end of the 1980s.

What Is Involved in Deconstruction by the Various Groups

Views Being Rejected and Why

God's creative act enabled man to think His thoughts and understand His revelation, and the Word of God conveyed to man His wisdom, which gave meaning. As such, Jesus Christ was the Word of God incarnate, the "logos." This theological basis for logic was the grounds for insisting on non-contradiction in meaning. The integrated meanings of words were then rejected by the educated elite, removing God from the American culture.

In its place, the liberal elite established their own absolute system of deterministic science and logical positivism which accepted only empirical truth that came through the senses. It began with the presupposition or *a priori* belief, that there is no God: nature operates only by natural laws as a mechanism, true knowledge can come only by the senses, and man's knowledge of the universe will increase and he will progress towards building a better world. The educated elite created this new metaphysical system. From their altered science, they created a vision of social theories whereby they, the elite, would control and help the masses of individuals to become wise, free, rich, pleasurable, and important.

But theories of the enlightenment that constructed the new absolutes around the view of deterministic science increasingly have been proven false. Moreover, the physical world is not a limited pool of knowledge where man can know everything within its shores. The universe really has an infinite number of pools of information hidden off the shore of every island and every peninsula of investigative knowledge. Man really can't know and control everything in the universe.

Moreover, the individualism supporting the system has produced a fight for selfish advantage that is infecting our world. The social visions of the educated elite have led to disunity and conflict with little direction. Now, in order to find fulfillment, every group has its own agenda and desires. Each group which failed to get its promises fulfilled by the liberal elite is now increasingly promoting only to its own advantage. Past governmental/social control is suspected as oppressive. The educated elite taught that the male white man is the chief oppressor. But these victim groups have come to believe any other group with a different agenda can also become the enemy.

What Is Deconstruction?

There is much said today about deconstruction of thought. What is meant by deconstruction?[5] The metaphysically constructed system of scientific determinism failed and must be rejected or reconstructed around power centers of control for each group. It was shown around the world that the trend has been towards group interest and conflict, and often ethnic interests. With Lonnie Guinnier, the issue emerging for blacks has been to establish power centers, rather than believe in "one man, one vote." This is true for each ethnic and religious group, for feminists, for homosexuals, and the elderly, and finally, will be true of the young.

The center of meaning for these various political groups is increasingly only that which fits their culture and purpose. In this century, the trend has been away from the logos of God to the words of deterministic science and social control. Now, the move is away from any other standard and towards the words meaningful only to each group. A common language of meaning is diminishing. Society moves towards an anarchistic, nihilistic philosophy like Friedrich Nietzsche's "the will to power." This philosophy produced Nazi Germany and Hitler. Because each group has its own meanings of the words it uses, communication is difficult, which is ironic since we boast this is the information age. While we have more stored information of words, the words have less common meaning. Other groups are rejected, especially Christians. Most groups of gender, class, and ethnicity consider Christians the one source of absolutes restraining them from the freedom to reach their goals.

Selfish individualism thus has run its course in producing judgment of one group against the other and individuals in the group against each other. The period of judgment inevitably must be one in which there is less understanding, because there is less common meaning to words or life. This process of deconstruction is accelerating, and the cultic groups find less in common with the majority of people and feel conflict towards anyone not representing their self-interest.

Review of Intolerance Indicates Point of Outright Conflict

There has been an increasing sense of opposition to public education, and the educated elite see the increasing effectiveness of private and, especially, religious schools. They are angered at the large number of children in the homeschool program. This homeschooling gives direct control to religion and to parents, which undercuts the main views of the liberal elite and empowers teachers who they feel are unqualified. It especially angers educators who are insulted by the idea that private, and especially parental, teaching can do as good or better a job than the teachers they trained. The resurgence of conservative thinking in the nation alarms them, and because they believe they are right in their views, these educated elite feel it is urgent to indoctrinate the public to accept their radical agenda. Since President Clinton and his wife Hillary espouse the intellectual agenda, the elite feel this administration is the opportune time to make people accept their agenda.

The old guard of black leaders feel blacks have not achieved equality and affirmative action is completely necessary for blacks to have their day. Since the Supreme Court has acted against affirmative action and laws in California have rejected affirmative action, black leaders feel it is urgent to replace the "one man, one vote" system with power centers that influence giving equality to every black person. John Franklin and other leaders of the President's committee for resolving racial issues refuse to allow opposing views to theirs and want no reconciliation, except complete surrender, to their position.

The extreme feminists, or "generic feminists," as some call them, sense there has been a backlash slowing down their sense of advantage attained through affirmative action, but is even reversing their progress. Now they feel is the hour they must act to break through to complete equality with men, even if it means the sacrifice of children and the traditional family, even if it means that the families in which women wish to stay home with their children must be taxed to help pay for their child care so they can be free to work. Shere Hite and other spokeswomen for feminists insist freedom demands the abolition of male leaders of the family, as existed in colonial patriarchy.

The homosexual leaders feel they are right, and their sexual desires and promiscuity ought to be accepted as normal. They demand that this normality must be taught to the children of America if their homosexual rights are ever to be attained, and if they are to open minds, so most of America will allow children to be involved in their view of freedom of sex. They want the privilege for older men to seduce young boys who have been taught that this sexual conduct is right. They want their lustful passions to be considered normal, and to achieve this view, they want it taught in all public school systems, as is the case in some counties of Massachusetts. They are pushing for pedophiles to be accepted.

The youth of America are increasingly angry with the elderly. When they begin to reach adulthood, they will be saddled with taxes on their income to pay for Medicare and Social Security for many unhealthy, older people who already seem to have the most accumulated wealth.

These older people have built up one of the largest political lobbies, the American Association of Retired People (AARP), which exercises such political power that elected officials dare not take away the entitlement programs the elderly feel they have earned. It seems that promises of Social Security and Medicare are really a growing Ponzi scheme that will fall on the backs of the youth. Because of older peoples' power with money and politics, the stores, airlines, and services of all kinds give them special discounts and privileges. The youth are told by the liberal elite that their parents and grandparents have exercised authority without considering their wishes.

Christians are angry because they have been excluded from a voice in the public schools which were established in colonial days by Christian efforts with money for teaching religion. Now, the public schools are used to teach against Christianity. Also, Christians are paying taxes to support public schools, yet must carry a double load by paying for private education of their own children as well. But, if Christians want to speak up for their rights, they are accused of sponsoring conspiracies and treated as if they are doing something wrong. The Christians who helped build this country are now labeled derogatorily as "the religious right" and considered intolerant and unworthy.

Laws and Public Thinking Have Been Turned Towards a Victim/Adversary Mentality

Accusations of Law for "Our Rights," Dominate

The judgmental and fragmenting conditions in America have become a major theme in American journalism. George F. Will talked about "Our Expanding Menu of Rights" and the trivial lawsuits deluging us.[6] So the victim mentality grows. Robert J. Samuelson said:

> The increase in crime, divorce, regulations, and government, accounts for much of the rise in lawyering. But things have gone beyond that. Lawyers pander to the American illusion that all problems have legal solutions and the result is a society that requires lawyers to do almost anything.[7]

Mortimer B. Zuckerman said, "Beware of the Adversary Culture," and warns that "divisiveness and anger" are replacing "*E pluribus unum*" as America's theme. He warned the media, "The adversary culture provides a certain spurious drama that the media have been overly tempted to exploit. Too often, the only way to break into the realm of public attention is through controversy . . . ."[8]

In an article entitled, "The Greatest Danger to America," Pulitzer Prize-winning historian Daniel J. Boorstin cited the fact "of the emphasis on power rather than on a sense of community." He said, "The separate groups in our country are concerned about their power—whether it be black power or white power, the power of any particular group." This greed, he said, robs us of the unity in community.[9]

Change in Ways of Litigation for a Judgmental People

Our lawmakers have changed our laws to make judgments against each other more possible. David Gergen, writing about "America's Legal Mess," said, "Over the past quarter century, . . . courts and state legislatures have rewritten the rules so that a lawsuit is no longer an option of last resort but a weapon of choice, a reach for the jackpot."[10] John Leo called us "The world's most litigious nation." After naming many trivial lawsuits and the costs in insurance premiums and court and attorney's fees, he cited changes that have occurred. He said:

> Before the 1970's, formal barriers and an informal understanding made it hard to haul someone into court without first laying out a plausible basis for a suit. Judicial decisions made it easier to sue, the legal profession grew more profit hungry and the rise of so-called Rambo litigators brought us into the era of the silly lawsuit and the jackpot settlement.[11]

Matthew Cooper and others wrote of 159 laws and programs being contested in courts by NASCP, handicapped groups, and other special interest groups, calling it "marching to a new war." Under another article, "Our Hypersensitive Society," he pointed out "Bias is real, but the air is thick with all these accusations, mostly because of our elaborate victim culture. Many charges are breathtakingly trivial . . . ."[12] He quoted William Raspberry as accusing feminists of distorting the facts about men because they keep portraying women as victims.

Lawyers and Experts Motivate Increased Judgments

The multiplicity of lawyers is cited repeatedly as one of the problems. In 1970, there were 355,000; by 1990, there were 805,000 with a prediction there will be one million lawyers by 2001. We are said to have 5 percent of the world's population and 70 percent of the world's lawyers. Everyone concedes the courts are clogged with litigation costing America billions of dollars, much being wasted, with tremendous frustration of justice. Samuelson said

there were 100 million cases filed in the state courts every year. [13] Not much
is known about how many of what kinds of cases, but usually it is said from
18–30 million cases a year with awards from $40,000 to $625,000. The confusion
is that 50 states have 50 different ways of recording the cases. Most are still on
paper and not on computer, so they are difficult to study. It is known that the
criminal filings increased 69 percent since 1980. Many cases have to do with
crime, tax violations, violation of government regulations, and private litigation
in a multitude of areas. Samuelson lists contract, personal injury, product liability, medical malpractice, and employment discrimination over racial, sexual and
age issues. [14] Lawyers are the most criticized group and one of the most frustrated, yet they are promoting this litigation. But greed for money motivates many of
the lawyers and their clients.

Along with the lawyers is the existence of a multiplicity of kinds of experts
to advise and help in lawsuits. Samuelson says the 1995 *Yearbook of Experts,
Authorities & Spokespersons* lists 900 pages of experts on everything. He says:

> And the Yearbook, of course, just scratches the surface. James A. Smith,
> author of *The Idea Brokers: Think-Tanks and the Rise of the New Policy
> Elite*, estimates that there are now about 1,200 public-policy institutes.
> Many of them, plus a lot of universities and trade associations, publish
> their own guidebooks. Johns Hopkins University has a 301-page catalog
> of its experts, the Heritage Foundation's encyclopedia runs to 412 pages
> and the American Council on Education has a pamphlet of 36 pages. As
> in most things, America leads the world in experts. [15]

Of course, all experts are not involved in litigation, but they dogmatically argue
conflicting views. The existence of so many experts reveals our individualistic
specialization and many exist to furnish information to those in conflict and present an exclusive view.

Crisis in the Justice by the Court System and the Threat to Law

The implications of the division into ethnic and other groups for our
judicial system and for justice across America is now becoming clear. Paul
Butler, a professor in George Washington University, in an article in the
March 1996 issue of the *Yale Law Journal,* advocated that black juries should
render a verdict that all black people arrested and charged with crack cocaine
violations be rendered innocent as a move for black power. He saw this as a
tool of black power in possibly other cases also. He argues that white juries
have long made racial decisions in favor of whites in certain cases. His former
law professor, Randal Kennedy of the Harvard Law school and also a former
prosecution attorney under whom he served, among others, have labeled
Butler's instructions as anarchy. It is obvious that if an increasing number of
juries followed suit for their race or group, the injustice in American courts

would be rampant. It would be especially bad for blacks, since they are a serious minority—more white juries would convict innocents, or render guilty persons innocent on the basis of race by virtue of their greater frequency in the courts. The frightening possibilities of this include the tremendous anger between races that would emerge from such court cases. This ethnic policy could breed indifference and a near abdication of serious police action, since their arrests would be meaningless. This trend needs stopping now.

The crisis of our court system is amplified in a book by Harold J. Rothwax. His prominent position and reputation as a liberal prosecuting attorney and judge makes what he said very weighty. He is a judge on the New York State Supreme Court, has been a senior trial attorney for the Criminal Defense Division of the Legal Aid Society, been vice chairperson of the New York Civil Liberties Union and lecturer at Columbia Law School, along with receiving many awards and much recognition. In this book, *Guilty: The Collapse of Criminal Justice*, he clearly describes with many examples how our criminal justice system is in great crisis. In addition to showing other very serious problems with the jury system (on p. 197 ff.), he deals with many other areas such as the problem of fairness that repeatedly lets criminals go free, the ineffectiveness of the Miranda clause with a quagmire of coercion and confession, the misuse of plea bargaining, the failure to give speedy trials and justice, the use of the fourth amendment and suppression of evidence, the use of the fifth amendment to withhold evidence, and the overwhelming number of cases in the system.[16] The use of jury decision as racial power as in the O.J. Simpson case is criticized. Americans cannot ignore our growing problems in finding justice and the consequences for our society.

Moreover, the end of the line for liberal intellectuals has been reached theologically, and leaders are now giving up the pretense of supporting Christianity. They are beginning to admit they are atheists. Commenting on this, reporter R. Albert Mohler refers to statements by Gerd Luderman, professor of New Testament and director of the Institute of Early Christian Studies at Göttingen University, Germany, as saying, "The game is *now reaching its end stage* having denied virtually every essential doctrine; the liberals are holders of an empty bag." Eugene Genovese, Marxist historian, said about liberal Protestant theologians, "When I read much Protestant theology . . . I have the warm feeling that I am in the company of fellow non-believers."[17]

The Bureaucracy of Government Aggravates Judgment

In addition to blaming lawyers and experts, much blame is placed on the growth of bureaucratic government and excessive regulations and laws. Philip K. Howard's best-selling book, *The Death of Common Sense: How Law Is*

Suffocating America, is frequently referred to. Howard shows many ways the government is frustrating the American people and causing much anger and disillusionment about government.[18] Americans should not forget that the bureaucracy really runs the government and changing one's political party does little to change it.

No doubt lawyers, existence of experts in a technical society, government regulations, loss of a sense of knowing people and being friends in community, specialization in business and health care, racial and sexual bias, technology on things that are little understood, and many other factors help cause anger and these many law suits. But behind all these things and driving them are two main conditions in our society.

Two Main Causes for the Growth of Judgmentalness

There are two main reasons why a judgmental attitude increases in the last phase of a declining society. One is that any *fear* of God (not talk about God) is almost completely removed, so that the freedom to act in the interest of selfish individualism expands because there is a decline in the conscious value of other individuals. In almost every article just quoted above on the growth of judgmentalness, the authors comment on the growth of individualism since the 1960s and 1970s (the time of the "Death of God"). The loss of faith in God is also related to the other major reason for judgmental attitudes towards others which is considered next.

Many authors also refer to the philosophy that each person has the right to be equal in freedom to enjoy material prosperity and pleasures. The egalitarian view has prevailed since secular humanism came to ascendancy and dominance in the middle of this century. Many writers refer to the idea of equality as basic to the judgmental attitudes. John Leo has said, "Other changes can be chalked up to an amazing *new conception* of equality" (italics mine).[19] Mortimer B. Zuckerman, in discussing the problem has said, "We are the only nation founded on the notion that all men are equal in their claim to justice and that the government exists to enable all who can to realize their fullest promise."[20]

In his article, John Leo is perceptive in labeling this *new*. The view of equality mentioned in the *Declaration of Independence* was very different in that it was based on being "created equal." The equality was the worth of each person *in the eyes of God* until modern times. The equality existed by the endowment of the Creator and did not have to be established but only needed to be recognized. Thus, equality was not a widespread purpose or objective of a group or of the federal government until recent years after the dismissal of God as dead. Since the 1960's, it has emerged as a main function of government derived from the domination of the view of the educated elite. The claim that we should make people equal is a denial of the equality they already have been given from God and is sure to promote that inequality even more.

The situation in America has gotten increasingly worse. Zuckerman describes how difficult it is to lead in the present judgmental conditions. He said:

> In such a vindictive culture it is virtually impossible to rally the nation or to bind its wounds. We are living in a time of accelerating social and economic turmoil that strains the connective tissues of many individuals to marriage, family, school, church, nation, job–indeed to any sense of responsibility. . . . Even more worrisome than the crazies is the depth of anger and alienation felt by ordinary people for government, our politicians and our bureaucrats. Government is feared as too intrusive, too big, too powerful and to imperious. One *U.S.A. Today*-C.N.N. poll found that 39 percent think that the federal government has become so large that it poses an immediate' threat to the rights and freedoms of ordinary citizens.[21]

So instead of promoting individual rights, the "vision" of the educated elite has reduced the recognition of those rights. Moreover, the intolerance of the educated elite for any opposing views has become manifested.

APPARENT IMPROVEMENT GIVES IMPRESSION PROBLEMS ARE SOLVED

Public Reaction Demanded Changes

Near the end of every dying civilization, there has occurred a reaction to moral decay that gave the appearance of improvement and good health that was deceptive. This was the last zag in the zigzag trend or worsening morals. It has been shown that by early in the decade of the 1980s, the conditions in America were headed in the wrong direction, and this reached a point of alarm by the 1990s for the economy, in the number of people below the poverty level and on welfare, in criminal abuse, in sexual promiscuity, in out-of-wedlock births, in abortions, in breakdown of the family by divorce and living together, in growth in AIDS and other diseases, in the decline of the educational institutions, in confidence in government, and in regard to morals in general.

This led to a strong reaction by the Christian community and to the election of Republican administrative leadership in Ronald Reagan and George Bush and to improvements that will be mentioned. But the failure of the Republican presidency to restrain the budget deficit and national debt was made central to the entire nation by Ross Perot so that the election in 1992 produced the saying emphasizing the economy. On pages 295 through 303 arguments were made that while Clinton had changed many things that reduced costs- the long term to short term debt, made government loans easier to start and expand small business, and he had cut defense spending- he had actually increased the budget more than Reagan and Bush and the adjustments he has made, make the economy more tenuous for the future.

But what was pointed out was the main problem was the lack of will for the American people to accept sacrifices to do what is necessary for the future. This is further confirmed by the most alarming thing, and that is when the evidence of the special prosecutor, Kenneth Starr was released and the House voted to proceed to review the evidence to impeach and the American public also were given the data, everyone admitted that Bill Clinton was obviously guilty of gross sexual perversion and of lying to a grand jury while under oath. But the public opinion polls all showed the people did not want Bill Clinton impeached because of the so-called "good state of the union."

The affirmation by the media and the consensus of the public approval made it so America was unwilling to remove Bill Clinton from the presidency. This means that the country has made a decision that prosperity is more important than honesty, fidelity in marriage, and sexual purity. We must face this head on: the country has made a decision that prosperity is the most important thing and that lying and hedonistic conduct is acceptable. In William J. Bennett's book, The Death of Outrage, he gives numerous testimonies about the results of this on the American conscience. The impression in the media, to school children, to politicians and to everyone is that gross sexual immorality, infidelity and lying is OK if you can get away with it. Unless this is corrected soon in the public mind by bold punishment of such conduct, there will be no way to prevent violations in the future and those punished for these things in the past will bring outrage to the criminals instead of change. The fact that the public has indicated it is tired of talking about the president's failures and wants to move on confirms Bennett's claims that outrage about morals is now dead.

Another tremendously important turning point has been reached in the body polity because of these attitudes by the public. The failure of the Republicans to make further gains in the Senate and their loss of some in the House, while still having a slim margin, has greatly influence the future of the Republican party. The resignation of the Newt Gingrich as speaker and a representative in the House indicates a significant shift in the thinking of leaders of the party. Gingrich left to give unity and to avoid being reduced from a powerful man to being one vote among many. While Gingrich has always been first of all a politician with a conservative view especially in economics, he was not a leader for political morals. Gingrich had lost the backing of the moral conservative right who were against abortion, for the family et. al, but he had lost the confidence of the moderates who had not won greater gains. A centrist position did not leave a striking vision which Gingrich could promote. The election of Bob Livingston of Louisiana as speaker changes the vision of the Republican Party from a party who will lead significant change, to one that will likely be managed in the old political way by lining up votes for a more centrist and popular position. Renewal of American morals by Republican leadership in every area is now likely dead. This death has occurred, not because Gingrich left, but because Americans have voted against supporting moral change and shaking the boat in any way. His leaving was an indication of this.

This indicates important things. One is that the real failure is the church's fault. The church no longer significantly influences the moral thinking of the nation to cause a desire for change. The church's failure is that it does not furnish a strong moral nucleus that the people are willing to follow. The church must return to its purpose of spiritual power and influence in order to have a political impact for moral living. Second, the church must now form its own minority political group for influencing both parties. But that cannot be effective until the church regains spiritual commitment to Christ that the public sees is worth following. While the church needs a political voice, the way to make that effective is to give attention to being salt and light for Christ to the world. Those who hold to conservative moral principles, Christian and Jews and others, now need a party with a clear moral objective. The leadership must be bold and loving in enunciating its objectives. But the church must not make passing Christian laws its primary objective. The new political entity must by the channel for Christians to cast their votes because the political entity espouses what the church stands for. The power of the good news of the church must be the primary thing. The new party should be open to all religious groups who can endorse what the party stands for. It therefore should not be called Christians but something like Foundationalists, for early morals.

The apparent improvement in many area of American life such as crime, divorce, premarital pregnancies, drug use, and the economy are deceptive. Spiritual renewal is the only thing that will really change the American will.

Deception about Economic Correction of Trends

There are two things that have driven the economic tends of growing indebtedness by individuals, by corporate business, and by the government. The first is personal motivations of greed for more wealth to make the individual important (e.g. Verblin's theory) desire to be free from restraints to what can be done by having more money, and the desire for money to buy pleasure. The kind of self esteem that money gives is superficial and is accompanied by growing fear of loosing it; freedom to get things often imposes more restrictions and problems in maintaining them and in protecting them, and pleasures that are bought that do no conform to truth bring guilt and imprisonment to continue to indulge. These personal desires are never satisfied but become increasingly driven. There are far higher rates of suicide among the wealthy than among people who are moderately poor or even in the middle class who trust God. In other words the benefits of wealth are superficial and not long lasting. But the motivation of the consumer is the obsession of the world, and getting the most wealth and quickly is one of the greatest driving forces of men in finances. Almost all self esteem, security, health, and pleasure is thought to be satisfied by money and is the driving force of every self interest group.

Secondly, the trend of increasing of debt continued to accelerate, not diminsh, the pursuit of these motives. These demands by the people is the great controlling factor of the political governments in a democracy. When there is no moral restraint because there is no feeling of accountability to God toward the nation or other people, the people continue to demand that the politicians give them more of what the government has. The care for others and commitment to the community of the nation is the oil that makes democratic government and the capitalistic system work. Selfishness has only pragmatic reasons for honesty and integrity. So the politicians manage the government to take as much as it can and gives more than it has, to please the unrestrained will of the people. The unrestrained will of the people is the problem.

It was demonstrated in chapter 14 that, even though everyone knew that when one spends more than he earns and uses up more than he can produce, there is a point when the process cannot continue. The masses demanded the budget be balanced. But as shown, President Bill Clinton has continued to spend more to satisfy more people, and congressmen corporately have not had enough courage to deny what most people want. People will continue to demand that their representatives give them more for less to get their vote if they want to stay in office. People will continue to gamble if it seems they will get more out than they put in, and for many it gets more and more addictive. What is true in government is applied to business. The rise in the mass mutual funds that have driven the stock markets was based on more and more people thinking that was the best way to get the most, so more and more money was put into these markets and the price of stocks were driven higher and higher, and more and more jointed. But the decline of the stock markets in the Fall of 1998, and the obvious turning point for profitably investing these moneys with the Asian, Latin American, especially

Russian and other nations who are in trouble, now portends this joy ride is slowing and will stop. The illusion that Keynesian pump priming can continue on the international scale and that the financial elite can solve the problem by this kind of management, is now becoming a reality.

The reservoir of moral principles in American business and government are almost drained dry, and the lack of virtually any morals by business men and government leaders in the atheistic an secular societies in most nations of the world has now been demonstrated. The principals on which the government has operated on which have caused these debt trends have not been solved, and apart from a spiritual renewal by the power of God and the humble work of the churches, the national economy must continue to lead to a collapse, and probably very soon.

Any Real Changes in Public Education?

The outcry of the American people and the strong criticism of William Bennett has generated pressure on the associations leading the public teachers to do something for real change in the public schools. An even greater pressure has come from the political effort for issuing public vouchers to parents to choose schools, private or public. School conditions are bad–nearly a quarter of newly-hired teachers failed to meet state licensing requirements, and nearly one-fifth of those hired leave in five years. Only 1 out of 5 high school teachers have ever majored or minored in the subjects they are teaching. There is the need of filling 2 million teaching jobs in the next decade.

Yielding to these public and political pressures, the teachers' unions have elected new presidents in favor of change. Robert F. Chase in 1996 was elected president of the National Educational Association, which has 73 percent of the teachers, and Sandra Feldman was recently elected president of the American Federation of Teachers, which is the second largest. Both ran on a plan to reform schools by endorsing standardized tests, charter schools, and peer review of teachers. It is expected they will reduce the use of money of these organizations for political purposes to the Democratic party. [27]

But this does not change the control of the liberal educated elite in these organizations and the public schools, and this certainly does not get rid of the controlling cliques of intolerance in favor of the old scientific determinism, liberal social ideas, feminism, and black racism. Even if new leaders achieve the changes they have promised, the intolerance against moral absolutes and faith in God will remain strongly in place. These organizations will still have intense efforts against private schools and home schooling. Thus the efforts to restore faith in God, discipline by fathers in the homes, and controlling discipline that makes possible good education will not be addressed by changes the new leaders now advocate.

No Real Change in Causes of Crime

The reduction of crime has been a relief, but the fact is that there has been *no significant change in the causes of crime.* Isolation, neglect, and abuse of children is certainly no better, and the learning of discipline in the home continues to deteriorate. Reduction of crimes by apprehension and incarceration are not likely to continue much further. The prisons are already reaching capacity with residents so that many jails are having to release offenders on parole early. The further improvement of computer software for locating areas of crime for police concentration are not likely to be more than incremental. The entertainment of youth by a diet of violence, whether by Nintendo-like computer games, television, or motion pictures, all continue and magnify violent acts by youth. Fatherhood in the homes is not being significantly revised. Most importantly, within the decade ahead, the chairman of the house committee on crime, Bill McCollum of Florida, warns that there is a large wave of youth coming that seem more violent than in the past. Moreover, the percentage in gangs has doubled in this decade. Respect for authority is eroded by the continued increasing demand for youth to support the elderly, of which many youth have a growing resentment. If we continue to allow the increase of sexual and homosexual abuse of the young, we will heap up an accumulation of lust and anger that will be difficult to abate.

Continued loss of unity in marriage and community and unwillingness of the Republican Congress to speak out and take a stand for moral and family issues shows that no political correction seems possible. James Dobson of Focus on the Family has announced there will be no continued support for the Republican party by him among his five million listeners unless this changes. Other Christian leaders have expressed similar feelings. The reputation of Bill Clinton for immorality, lack of honesty, and efforts to distort facts for personal gain reflect a new low in moral standards for the people.

Since 1993 there has been a significant decrease in divorces, in premarital pregnancies, and other sex-related statistics. But sexual immorality is increasingly accepted as a lifestyle and promoted through the media and schools. In 1960 the number of couples living together out of wedlock was one-half a million, but at the end of July 1998, the Census Bureau announced there are now four million. While there is temporary statistical improvement, the underlying structures to destroy life-long monogamous marriage are not changed.

Along with this, the idea of each individual operating for his own selfish advantage is reaching a peak in American life. There is a new wave of the unfettered individualism and the morality of selfishness promoted by Ayn Rand whose inner circle included prominent people such as Alan Greenspan, Federal Reserve Chairman. New motion pictures, TV promotions, theatrical productions, and books about her and these ideas are just now reaching the public. More importantly, the quest for information and communication of knowledge is moving toward expansion by the computer and the Internet which will allow anyone to move his money and location from place to place and do it with anonymity and radical selfishness. Davidson and Ress-Mog describe how we are only now in the beginning of the second phase of the information age and that the third will bring radical operation of the individual. This will produce the ultimate of selfish individualism that began with the Enlightenment. Women have reacted to the efforts to reform the male image as loving leader. Black women counteracted the men's gatherings with a large rally in Philadelphia of their own, and feminists are rejecting this.

Most importantly, the efforts of Christians seem to be losing power and influence just when they were thought to be succeeding in turning things back to God's standards. The Promise Keepers movement has seriously declined in attendance and funds, and the Christian Coalition has had leadership problems, lawsuits, and theft, and is in deep trouble. Pat Robertson's television influence is waning. Under pressure from the IRS, the Christian Broadcasting Network spun off the Family Channel in 1990 to the cable giant, TCL, which in 1997 was bought by Rupert Murdock's secular Fox Kids Worldwide. On August 15, 1998, the Family Channel with its sixty-nine million viewers will be replaced by the Fox Family Channel, and there will be little left at Virginia Beach in Robertson's center. While there are some signs of Christian cooperation rather than church competition, real local unity is not occurring.

THE COMING CRISIS COULD BE WORLDWIDE IN SCOPE

America Has Spread Its Idolatries to the Whole World

The United States is today the most prominent influence on the entire world. There are close to a million people from all nations of the world studying in our universities and colleges. American media are used and viewed by most of the world, even in the poorest countries. The whole literate world of Europe, Asia, and the United States has embraced the same intellectual presuppositions born out of the Renaissance and the Enlightenment. This includes the communist areas as well as those influenced by the vision of social democracy.

As the Greek civilization spread worldwide under Alexander the Great and the Roman civilization dominated their world by the first century, the exchange of faith in the true God for gods, and the spread of the secular view of life, fragmented and generated ethnic divisions. So today, the unbelief and trust in a mechanical view of nature, or naturalism, is succumbing to a pantheism because man is desperate for some spiritual help, since it is increasingly evident that "man is not enough." This trend toward accepting past occult views, or spirit worship, is spreading from the West, especially from the United States and producing an increasing ethnic and fragmented consciousness. Most of the world is caught up in the pursuit of Western materialism and sensualism. In most of the world there is respect for American power and wealth, but there is also a resentment against American greed and arrogant dominance.

The Demand Is for World Egalitarian Government

The whole world is moving into the view that world institutions should be the tool to forward their own selfish individualism through their group. Government is viewed as an institution to primarily make everyone and every nation equal. What "every person, group, and nation" really means, is that government should give *me* a bigger share. The world's educated elite see themselves as the "anointed ones," called to force all ignorant common people to accept their vision. The United Nations has become their instrument through which to exert their ideas and control. For the educated world elite, the major problem as they see it is income distribution.

This was seen by Communism as the solution, and is a major objective of social democracy in the United States and the Western nations. The United Nations is increasingly seen as the focal point to solve the world's problems. Today it is at a crucial turning point mainly over the very great problem that most of the members of the world organization are poor developing countries, and the increasing conflicts of the nations within and between nations is over wealth. Until the collapse of the Soviet Union, developing countries saw their hope of wealth redistribution in Communism. Hope then shifted to the United States, the West, and democratic capitalism. Now the growing economic problems in the United States and the West shows little hope from this source. Now the leadership of the poorer countries is advocating a much bolder suggestion—that of setting up a world government and from the money saved by nations in defense and military spending, these funds would be distributed to the developing countries.

In the 1994 Human Development Report of the United Nations, on the back of the front cover and placed to be a strategic guide, is a graph to illustrate what could be saved by a defense dividend (primarily of the United States) for redistribution to undeveloped nations. Jan Tinbergen, winner of the 1969 Nobel Prize for Economics, has written for the United Nations Human Development Report of 1994 a proposal for "Global Governance for the 21st Century". Tinbergen, speaking for the undeveloped countries in the United Nations about their low level of development and income within their countries and in the world, said:

There is a strong case for much more redistribution with developing countries. But there should also be redistribution at the international level through development cooperation. How much should the industrial nations make available to the developing countries? In 1970, the UN General Assembly decided that 0.7 percent was needed. By 1991, the average for the OECD countries was only 0.33 percent. But the UN target figure is itself too low. In the 1970's and 1980's, the gap between the developing and industrial countries widened. To have prevented this would have required aid equivalent to 1.3 percent of GDP. As the world economy becomes increasingly integrated, so the redistribution of world income should become similar to that within well-governed nations.[29]

The economic conditions which cause conflict and ethnic and class struggle are growing ever more desperate. The world looks to the United States as the world leader and the champion of human rights, and as the wealthiest nation in the world. But the United States is on the verge of the same kind of crisis that Greece was in as a world leader under Alexander the Great when it collapsed, and as the Roman Republic was when it collapsed. Another time of worldwide judgment and troubles seems near.

The idea that the United Nations might become a world government led by the United States and might seek to redistribute wealth from the industrialized civilized countries seems improbable. This could only happen if the United States ends up under a dictatorship that claims worldwide power, as happened in Greece and Rome. As J. Tinbergen said in the close of his plan for the United Nations, "Some of these proposals are, no doubt, far-fetched and beyond the horizon of today's political possibilities. But the idealists of today often turn out to be the realists of tomorrow."[30]

World Economy May Pose Worldwide Trouble

Many men who research and think on a worldwide scale see us racing toward a time of troubles. This is described as one of "hysteresis economy" by Harold Trudler of the Institute for the Future, and by several as "eco-spasm." They believe that there may be a time of run-away inflation in the advanced rich societies and of hyperdepression in the poor. Alvin Toffler has said, "Imagine not merely the soft collision suggested by such euphemisms as stagflation, but a combination of erratic super-inflationary forces and super-depressive forces striking at once." Certainly the promises in Communism have failed and in the Western democracies, including the United States, that promise cradle-to-the-grave prosperity and security, are nearing an end. The results of this could be worldwide pandaemonium. These warnings come not only from the doomsayers, but from many who want to be optimistic. Surely America is headed for such a trauma before too many decades unless there is change. But must this be the last time of troubles? An opportunity for the last great Antichrist?

Worldwide Loss of Control from Loss of Divine Absolutes

Spread of unbelief by Western thinking has reduced the sense of moral control worldwide. Zbigniew Brzezinski, who served as foreign policy adviser to Jimmy Carter, has also written a book, *Out of Control*. While he mentions ethnicity, he rightly focuses on it more from a point of loss of cohesion in our world. He said:

> Discontinuity is the central reality of our contemporary history, and that demands an intensified debate regarding the meaning of our era. Moreover, our ability to understand the wider ramifications of the present–not to speak of the future–is impeded by the massive collapse, especially in the advanced parts of the world, of almost all established values.

> The role of religion in defining moral standards has also declined while an ethos of consumerism masquerades as a substitute for ethical standards. . . . At the same time, our societal criteria of moral discernment and of self-control have become increasingly vague. Ethical perplexity does not enhance historic comprehension.[31]

He speaks of "a global crisis of the spirit" and warns that in our "world of contingency", morality becomes the "central" and the "only source of reassurance." The loss of social control is his great concern.

When Aleksander Solzhenitsyn, the famous Russian dissident, received the 1993 United States National Arts Club medal of honor, he remarked:

> Behind the ubiquitous and seemingly innocent experiments of rejecting "antiquated" tradition [Christian and human] there lies a deep-seeded hostility toward spirituality.[32]

He said the post-modern norm has a "relentless cult of novelty" in which "there is no God, there is no truth, the universe is chaotic, all is relative." Solzhenitsyn has put his finger on the real problem as "a deep-seeded *hostility toward spirituality*."

It has been shown that man's hostility to God is what repeatedly has been the undoing of all civilization, the thing that changes man's wisdom into his folly, and produces the chaos that divides into ethnic wars. All of these leaders are decrying *the loss of control* and many point to the *loss of spiritual and moral authority* as the root cause for the loss of control.

The stage of our world is that of Western civilization in decline; yet all peoples seem to *want* these decadent values which plow the ground for planting ethnic conflict and the loss of civilization. Because of the length of this book, the decline of the United States has been the main focus, and details of events in other areas of the world are omitted. But the problem of American decline affects the world, and the solution for the world will likely be linked to that of the United States as the present world power.

All Secular Solutions Are Inadequate to Give Moral Control

There are secular answers to the loss of control and moral decay which are inadequate. Moynihan believes the only answer is one-world governmental law under the United Nations, but admits there are difficulties in present thinking to curbing ethnicity. Adam Roberts rightly observes that the recognition of the rights of every group to freedom can lead to pandemonium. He says:

> Yet if every ethnic, religious or linguistic group claimed statehood, there would be no limit to fragmentation, and peace, security and economic well-being, for all would become ever more difficult to achieve.[33]

The same would be true if every group in the United States had its own districts of power.

Joel Kotkin also insightfully bemoans the failure of the liberal individualistic democratic dream:

> Born amidst optimism for the triumph of a rational and universal world order, the twentieth century is ending with an increased interest in the power of race, ethnicity, and religion rather than the long-predicted universal age or the end of history. The quest for the memory and spirit of the specific ethnic past has once again been renewed; the results will shape the coming century. In the words of sociologist Harold Isaacs: "Science advanced, knowledge grew, nature was mastered, but reason did not conquer and tribalism did not go away." . . . As ideologies such as "scientific socialism" have collapsed, the world has experienced a renaissance of interest in the symbols of the tribal past.[34]

But Kotkin sees a new world economic unity emerging through five global tribes, "The Jews, British, Japanese, Chinese and Indians." He recognizes the strong influence of religion, but hopefully sees that the present driving force for one world order that has emerged is an economic one. However, his vision has a fatal flaw: he believes economic motive will be the unifying force. However, this cannot furnish the ethical bases for such a world economy any more than the materialistic ideologies of Communism or social democracy. In fact, they were the undoing of Communism and are the present poison in the West. Individualistic materialistic and sensual desires can only divide–they cannot unite. Greed is the leaven that produces the decay of the morals of the whole lump. Already since he wrote these words of economic hope, his vision has failed significantly in Asia.

THE PROBLEM IS SIN AND THE ANSWER GOD

Greed Accelerates and Breeds Hate to Promote Anarchy

Each group, whether by class, or gender, or race is seeing its own selfish advantage that has moved us toward a termination of judgmentalness and divine judgment. The real problem is human sin that has progressively gotten worse as God has been removed from society. But when is selfish advantage enough? If people are treated as of lesser importance, they want more recognition in power and more opportunity to gain wealth and advantage. If they gain more, they want more still. Ellis Cose emphasized that it was the successful, privileged-class blacks who are the angriest. It is the women who have gained power in the women's movement and the women who have moved up in wealth and power in the business world who are angriest and want more power to get through the so called "glass ceiling." The selfishness of men and women of every race and class is the real problem. Race, sex, and class are used to promote self interests. The lusts of the flesh and of the eyes, and the pride of life, increasingly dominate.

Selfish Groups Pervert and Destroy Government

Under such a selfish perspective, all institutions of government then become tools torn apart by groups seeking advantage, and cease to be an instrument for orderly control and exercising laws for justice to the individual. Politics can be turned from its God-given purposes to administer justice and protect (Romans 13:1-3), to promotion of selfish advantage. The governments of Greece and Rome were used by differing leaders of conflicting groups to gain their advantage. The same is happening in America. Education can be a tool for godliness and promotion of the common good, but it increasingly has become a tool to indoctrinate for more power and for discrimination against others. It has been shown this has been the case in America since the 1960s. Again, *the great problem* socially is mankind's *selfishness or sin*. The problem is *in the human heart* and no institution run by man can solve the problem; self-interest groups usually makes matters worse. Again, **the problem is human sin** that has been expanded and motivated by demonic deception.

Historians Have Acknowledged Human Sin the Source of Demise

While Arnold Toynbee was far from infallible, he was probably the most comprehensive of modern historians. Referring to the cause of death of all previous civilizations, we again quote him as saying:

We invariably find that the cause of death has been either War or Class or some combination of the two. . . . The institutions of War and Class are social reflections of the seamy side of human nature–or what the theologians call *original sin*–in the kind of society that we call civilization.[28]

The root idea of original sin is the human bias or disposition against having God or anyone else interfere with our individual freedom to get the pleasure, security, and recognition for control that we desire. It is precisely this selfish individualism that results in the anarchy and final judgmentalness of society. In chapter 7 it was shown that behind this persistent bias of man that carries civilizations down the same steps of decay over hundreds of year, is the conflict of the Devil with God over man's soul. Toynbee was right in this analysis, and so may Moynihan be right in seeing this as the direction America and the world now moves: it is toward Pandaemonium, or the city of all demonic control.

It is precisely the fact that our world is set against recognizing God and sin that it seeks solutions that cannot change human selfishness in the heart. But more detrimental is the fact that society increasingly is focused on selfish individualism which promotes transgressing the will and control of God, and inevitably is increasingly hostile to God and His people who witness to Him. God's elect people in the church represent the standard of righteousness that sinful men are rebelling against. For that reason His people are the answer. The Biblical prophecy that the world will climax in exalting man as antichrist in a world government that is hostile to God's witness, is a logical climax for the whole world. It could occur in our time.

The Better Way Is through Spiritual Power

The present trend is to try to fight this battle as a political conflict. That was the case in Greece and Rome, and in most other dying civilizations. The results were pain, death, and heartbreak. At present churches are fighting on the political level of mobilizing money and people to try to pass laws to force humans to conduct themselves in the churches' ways in regard to religion, sexual roles in the family, abortion, and all the others.

There is another more effective way. As Charles Colson and others point out, there is a difference between political and spiritual power.[35] Spiritual power is what Paul used in confronting the declining culture he described in Rome. It is the spiritual power of the good news of Jesus Christ (Romans 1:16, 17; cf. Ephesians 6:10-18). The New Testament approach of changing minds and hearts by voluntary persuasion by truth is the most challenging. Even in this post-modern world that asks, as did Pilate, "What is truth?"–even one witness committed to truth will reveal that faith is the only way to salvation, not fighting with the sword (John 19:36-38).

It will be shown that this is the only effective way to change men's hearts, apart from bitter conflict and bloodshed. Men's hearts must be changed first, in order to change a culture and society. By spiritual power the primitive church was victorious and Christian virtue conquered the Roman world. Because many of the churches are focusing on political power, they are therefore not only losing the fight, but angering the general public who feel Christians want to force their morality upon them. The Moral Majority had this as its main reason for failure.

While Ralph Reed, then the organization's leader, saw the main objective of the Christian Coalition as being political, he wisely discerned that the greatest need in America is for the church to be the church and bring change in lives first. He said:

No lobbying or arm-twisting can take the place of a change in public attitudes through moral persuasion. If religious conservatives are wise, they will resist the temptation to replace the social engineering of the left with the social engineering of the right by forcing compliance with the moral principles that motivate us so deeply. . . . It is a path defined by its spiritual arrogance and by its faulty assumption that the most efficacious way to change hearts is through the coercive power of the state. [36]

It is true that the law is a teacher, but it can only teach for the whole community what God has implanted as a consensus in the hearts of an exemplary religious minority. It is the demonstration of truth that establishes it for law.

The urgent need is for the churches of America and the world to recognize that their great power is witnessing, through suffering love, to God's forgiveness and change through the cross and resurrection. The hour is late and the churches must awaken to the dynamic of their mission. It is not only the answer for America, but for a world under the growing demonic deception to which the Lord sent us to witness.

Toynbee has commented on his observations of our possible near destiny as seen by parallels of past history of the end of civilizations. He warned:

If the analogy between our Western civilization's modern history and other civilization's "time of troubles" does extend to points of chronology, then a Western "time of troubles" which appears to have begun sometime in the sixteenth century may be expected to find its end sometime in the twentieth century; this prospect may well make us tremble; for in other cases the grand finale that has wound up a "time of troubles" and ushered in a universal state has been a self-inflicted knock-out blow from which the self-stricken society never has been able to recover. Must we, too, purchase our Pax Oecumenica at this deadly price? [37]

It is entirely possible that if the church fails in this hour to adequately present the "gospel as the power of God unto salvation," the final terminus of judgment and judgmentalness may be the final time of troubles for the whole world (cf. Matthew 24: 21). The Bible is clear that God's judgment of the flood on the whole earth at the time of Noah was because of sexual promiscuity and violence (Genesis 6:1-13), and the same was true of the cities of Sodom and Gomorra (Genesis 18:20; 19:4 ff.). In my book, *The Call*, I show the same conditions were true of the Chaldean culture, of Egypt, of the Canaanites, of the Israelites at the end of the Judges period, and upon the Nation of Judah before the fall of Jerusalem. America, like them, has gravitated away from God to tremendous greed, violence, and sexual lust.

America stands at a crucial point of decision. The president of the United States has committed some of the most perverse and heinous sexual acts of infidelity in the very offices of the White House where he administers the government. As the highest official of government, he has under oath perjured himself in a court of law. The Attorney General who is the highest office for justice has appointed a special prosecutor and he has presented conclusive evidence of these acts to the house of Representatives. The worst act of degradation of women is for a man to pervert loving affection for his wife to sex for his own pleasure with another woman in violation of the trust he has promised that wife. Honor in marriage is lynch pen for all social relationships. All law and order rests on truthfulness by legal authorities and by witnesses in the courts. Truth in our legal system is the diamond pivot point of law and order. When credibility in the legal system is forfeited, law and order will disintegrate.

The majority of the people of the United States have reviewed the evidence and formed the opinion that Bill Clinton committed gross acts in the White House and that he lied under oath. The House of Representatives of the people forms the decision to impeach and sends the case against the President to the Senate of the United States for trial. Failure of the Senate to impeach Clinton will remove the glue of law and order from America and condone perjury for every citizen. Such an act would begin the meltdown of moral order in the nation. The time is NOW for the church to take a stand and to speak and act against all evil in a courageous way.

God, His character, and His will has not changed. His word cannot be violated without the consequences being the same again. The American people have chosen and given their approval to leaders who are against the expressed word of God. Without genuine spiritual renewal, God's judgment will surely come soon. The options for renewal are narrowing, and the time is getting shorter to promote change.

PART III: CONCLUSIONS

Chapter 20

Steps of Faith to Counteract
the Devil's Points of Attack

INTRODUCTION: BIBLICAL AND RATIONAL PLAN FOR RENEWAL

The Urgency for Leadership against Demonic Deception

If the terminus of judgment is near as asserted in the last chapter, it is urgent that the churches in America realize what they must do. The final major zigzag where all standards are being deserted for selfish group values seems to be upon the nation. Scientists now are giving up the deterministic view of nature for a view of probabilities, which they call chaos, and this opens the door to either believe nature has an occult mystical power as pagans do, or return to design by a transcendent creator who has left room for His sovereign acts that are beyond human reason. Psychology is returning toward the concept of the gnostic, dualistic heresy that explains the conflict with evil. In an effort to justify man in his sin, these teachings tend to distort and identify the biblical view of God as the source of evil and make the god of human self-enlightenment the way to freedom and personal power. Sociology and economics are in a quandary. Marxism has collapsed, and social democracy is increasingly not working.

The self-interest groups representing ethnic groups, gender, and age, which were created by the old liberal determinism, are ready to demand justice for their rights and an advantage which they feel they are due. They have rejected biblical standards and are now deconstructing the liberal standards, with their own group standards as supreme. Each group is at a point where they ready to demand that the government act primarily in its self-interest instead of in the interest of the majority, bringing selfish, elected politicians to a point of confusion by trying to please all. Social economic promises have reached an impossible point where there is little room for more debt and taxation, and hard decisions must be made to limit the greed of those who have the most power politically. As presented, in this post-modernistic position, groups can only tear the social fabric of the nation by accusations of judgment and utter confusion. In order to end the pain, God will bring judgment to end the conditions.

In traditional history, at the end, final confusion is ushered in. Government does not work, there is a confusion of many gods in religion. Homosexuals assert the claim that their conduct as normal, confusing sexual distinctions, which is lethal to marriage unity and human propagation. Many historians, who long ago gave up meaning to life through the deterministic view of nature, are now returning to reinforce the appeal for pagan cyclic views to find some source of hope. Intellectually, historians with a cyclic view of history predict that America is nearing a fourth turning and that social confusion or chaos is near. They are insisting that for people to have hope they must adopt the pagan cyclic view of history. By this they say we must blindly believe nature will by occult processes produce a better day ahead. But opening one-self up to the occult gives direct control to the demonic. These so-called cycles are changes in human thinking caused by periodic zigzags. As shown, the zigzags move by the bias of fleshly desire and deceptions, and by the "wrong" progress of human public conscience. But as shown, the zigzags are part of the long-term trends toward moral decay. The world is awaiting some final event that will release the confusion and set off pent-up anger. It seems Judge Robert Bork is right in asserting we are "slouching toward Gomorrah."[1]

There may be a trigger cocked and ready for release to cause the final death to morals and bring on the meltdown. In man's long passion for knowledge, he has trusted in computers and the Internet which will give him freedom to escape almost all human governmental control.[2] But those who rely on computers are now faced with a possible introduction of mass confusion because all computers up to a few years ago indicated the date of year by two digits instead of four. This is called the Y2K problem for the year 2000. It is crucial for this problem to be fixed by that time. If not there could be mass confusion in business and government after the calendar turns. This poses a much bigger problem than is recognized by the ordinary citizen in America.

The White House Office of Management estimates that thus far, with only months to go there are only 35 percent of the government's 7,850 "mission critical" systems that have been fixed; some that are not fixed involve the Defense Department and the Treasury Department, which include IRS and Social Security bookkeeping. Moynihan said, "This is terminal if you don't get it right." Many big businesses are still working on it and some just don't have the money or can't find the technicians to fix computers. General Motors is investing a half billion dollars, Citibank over $600 million and others equally as much to fix things. The Wall Street Journal specialist Edward Yardeni predicts there is a 40 to 60 percent chance of a global recession from this. Fed Chairman Alan Greenspan said to the House Budget Committee, "All you need is a few . . . major glitches in the system and the ramifications [could] be really awesome."

It is thought that because there is now interaction of all major computer systems worldwide, the ones not corrected will infect and confuse other systems. No one knows the extent of damage that will be caused by the year

2000 computer problem. Many people naively believe that nothing adverse will happen because it would be too catastrophic and some last minute simple solution will be found. Reason would call us to recognize that this irrationality in rational software systems will cause significant difficulty if it has not been corrected. Besides the Y2K problem, the growing possibilities of terrorist acts against major American cities and utilities could paralyze things. A major racial incident could set off a chain reaction. The impeachment of the president or a number of other unknowns could occur to trigger the meltdown at any time.

The Best Alternative Is Renewal of Faith in God and His Will

Today there are those who cling to the old liberal agenda, and there are many post-modern advocates who are really following their illogic toward the old occultism or paganism. Neither of these views can solve the dilemma but only exacerbate it. Return to faith in the transcendent sovereign God is the viable solution. Also, there are really no other people who can exhibit and proclaim that faith in God except His elect remnant in the churches to whom God has given His revelation of Himself.

And the objective must not be for men to try to save their own souls from their chaos and trouble, but to return to love for God and a desire above all else to give glory to Him at whatever cost. We must lose our lives to find them again. This will surely lead to fulfillment of God's plan to glorify His Son Jesus Christ by obedience that leads to the fulfillment of the great commission to the church to extend God's reign through the kingdom of Christ worldwide (Matthew 28:18-20).

The Believing Remnant Must Look to God to Initiate Renewal

In the most profound sense, a renewal and salvation cannot be created by man—even by Christian men. When men devise their own religious agendas, this only leads to an expression of the selfishness by the clergy in control. The initiative must come from a true admission of God's people that "man is not enough" and that God alone can save. Utter humility before the Sovereign God in prayer is needed for Him to act in their behalf to lead them to see His worth and His values which can truly recreate their own hearts and their values and objectives, according to His revealed will.

Some years ago, A. W. Tozer warned us that we were moving toward the place where every individual pastor of a church and various other leaders would have more authority over the churches than Jesus Christ. He warned that we are governed more by customs and traditions of our groups and our intellectual ideas of how to meet peoples' needs, rather than biblical truth of how to glorify God.[3] The time has come when most of us must admit that we have led our own way and helped forward Tozer's warning at least in part to a perilously confused church. That is why we must look to God to supernaturally initiate His will for renewal.

This does not mean that there are no guidelines for renewal that come from what God has revealed in the Bible, or that we should give up our convictions, but it means that apart from His leading and motivation of power by His Spirit, no renewal can ever truly take place. Recognizing the need for God's initiating and revealing Himself has always been the central factor to change His people.

In Egypt, it was only when the people of God cried out for Him to act in their behalf that God called Moses and produced the exodus and the forming of the independent nation at Sinai (Exodus 2:23-25). It was only after the people of Israel had fallen under the domination of the Philistines and Samuel led them to admit their sin and cry out for the need of God's leadership that God raised up His kingdom under the kings of Israel (1 Samuel 12:14-25). When the people of Israel had been oppressed by the Assyrian world power, King Hezekiah sent a proclamation to all the tribes to turn to the Lord in repentance and prayer, invoking the Lord to return to them and initiate their deliverance and restoration of the power of the kingdom (2 Chronicles 30:1-9). These instances involve the formula that God led Solomon to enunciate when he dedicated the temple (2 Chronicles 7:14) that is more frequently quoted today. While men's hearts must be receptive, the living God can and will initiate change in His own way.

The renewals in other civilizations also show that the divine initiative was central for renewing faith. The renewal of the Greek civilization began by a supernatural work of God that brought the people together at Olympus to reinstitute the worship of Zeus, the Son of the Sky God Uranus. There was also a mysterious working that led the Romans to turn back to worship Jupiter (linguistically related to Zeus), the Son of Uranus, and to build the temple on the Capitoline in Rome for his worship. Other instances of earlier national renewals might be given. The original pilgrims to America all came with a desire to not only find a new opportunity in life but to freely worship the God of the Bible. Not to be ignored is Christopher Columbus' conviction that he was being led by God to find the new world. As in the past, for renewal to occur today, it must be a result of prayerful expectation of God's sovereign working. Renewal of faith must start by the living God showing a fresh act of His presence that directs us to trust Him, yield our own biases, and search His word.

Conclusions 431

God's Guidelines for Renewal Based on Scriptures in This Book

The steps of faith for renewal suggested here are based on the evidence given in this book and its companion, *Dark Shadows* . . . . Because this book is long, the full details of God's call to His people for renewal will be given more completely and with more explanation in an unfinished sequel book, *The Call*. There the biblical data showing the degeneration in previous biblical societies (Chaldean, Amoritic, Egyptian, and others) are reviewed and what God called His people to do in those times of dying civilizations is used as a light to help instruct us. But in this book, it is important to at least see the basic principles of Paul in Romans as seen in the data on Greece, Rome and America, so that churches can humbly ask the Lord to empower and lead by the Holy Spirit for the guidelines for bringing renewal.

The steps toward moral renewal can be derived by looking at the steps of decline and how faith may be renewed to change these. The points of deception by the Devil, causing these steps which progressively destroy man's faith and removed divine control, are logically the very points that must be progressively counteracted by faith in God's truth. The apparent loss of divine control through the loss of faith ultimately leads down the road to the loss of all governing control, and that is what destroys the civilization. These points where man departs from obedience to God's word and will are where the confusion, trouble, and judgment follow. That fact in itself is evidence that God's word is true and His will is for man's good. A review of the steps of decline in civilization (chapter 2) and a summary of the main biblical answer are given first and then a brief explanation is given to suggest what God would have us do according to His word.

Summary of Answers to Steps of Revolt against God

Step one: **the intellectual revolt.** *Answer:* Offer men reconciliation and faith in God through the gospel of Jesus Christ, showing the implications for now and eternity. This opens the way to renewed trust in God as creator and Savior. A bold faith in the God of the Bible revealed in Jesus is essential before restoring a renewal of how to correct the Devil's deceptions in the other steps.

Step two: **the materialistic revolt.** *Answer:* Call men to trust the Creator and Recreator to provide all things and not to look to or fear men.

Step three: **the sexual or sensual revolt.** *Answer:* Lead men and women to return to accepting the *equality* of the sexes *before God* (not based on material success), and emphasize the divine plan of oneness in marriage with different roles for complementation. Emphasize the importance of the individual before God, but also the call to be one in marriage before God who will provide for the family. The woman exercises the power of attraction and control by nurture, and the father the power of loving sacrificial leadership, protection, and provision under God.

Step four: **anarchy and violence,** growing out of each man's thinking he is right in his own eyes and each living for his individual selfish desires. *Answer:* Institute God's control through death to self and resurrection with Christ, and extend Divine control through the patriarchal leadership of the family, the church, and the local community.

Step five: **judgmentalness and judgment,** where many self-righteously accuse and enter into conflict against each other, so that God must execute judgment. *Answer:* Call Christians to live by faith and exhibit God's sacrificial love when wronged, trusting in God to avenge evil in the world and at the last judgment. Witness to God's suffering love by loving the unjust.

A brief discussion and reflection on some of the data will make these answers more clear.

GUIDELINES TO COUNTERACT DEMONIC STEPS OF DECEPTION

Step One: Refuting the Intellectual Revolt against Faith That Leads

The Initiating Point for Renewing Faith

The Intellectual Revolt Is Based on a Bias against God

It has been man's confidence in his knowledge about nature that made him feel he could be king of the world without God, save himself, and build his own paradise. Those intellectual steps have been given for the Greeks, Romans, and America (cf. chapters 4, 5, 9). In the light of this, only a change away from man's intellectual pride in the leadership's beliefs that the world is run by mechanical, natural laws to a recognition that nature is controlled and run by the Creator, can begin true renewal. While only God can initiate this, the church needs to understand the biblical instructions in this regard.

The main theme of this book, *Man Is Not Enough*, points out that man's problem is he sees himself as intellectually sufficient without God. It is important to realize that it is a trick of the Devil to make the church think that the proper way to attack man's intellectual perversion is by focusing directly on the intellectual lies and discrediting these. But man's intellectual arguments are the wrong point *to begin* in order to dismantle man's intellectual revolt.

It was argued that the process of moral decay began by man's self-sufficiency, unthankfulness, and accepting of a mechanical interpretation of the world. But it was indicated repeatedly that this was *motivated by man's natural bias against God* in order to maintain that he is sufficient and free. Because of man's fleshly mortal nature, he has a bias to rationalize away any evidence for God in the world. The foundation of man's moral decline is not men's rationalistic interpretations that have been exposed as false in my companion book, *Dark Shadows . . .* , but *the sinful bias of the human heart*, or man's original sin.

In *Dark Shadows . . .* , and to a certain extent in this book, it has repeatedly been shown from the quotes of intellectuals themselves that the perverting of various theories was motivated not by facts of nature, but by *the desire to free mankind from God and accountability to Him* as shown in the Bible. The perversion of science has been and is philosophically motivated against God because man does not want to face his own sin and guilt. Man wanted to be free from God and His will. That is why it has been argued that the root and foundational problem is theological.

As the first goal, trying to answer the infinite and continuous rationalizations of the intellectual elite of men is futile. The intellectuals hold their views and persuade others of them because men want to deny their finiteness, their mortality, and sinfulness. Their error is that they believe the demonic deception that they can be free from divine control and be "as wise as God" in building their own kingdom in their own way in this world. Man's sinful bias will always lead him to other perversions in argument.

This has been true since Adam and Eve. Man's sin nature, established since Adam's fall, is the foundation on which the Devil has repeatedly built his kingdom of deception for man's destruction. *To try to first refute the intellectual rationalizations of unbelievers is to move to their ground and not to use the power of God and spiritual weapons.* The Christian can only use the sword of the Spirit the way God has instructed us. By attacking the foundational motivation behind unbelievers' arguments, then the rationalizations can be exposed and accepted by them. They must be disarmed by the gospel of God's grace and kindness. The *presupposition of men's hearts must first be changed* by the objective evidence of God's grace in Christ through the Holy Spirit. The hearts of unbelievers must be prepared by the Spirit through the troubles created by their sins, and as the end of a civilization is approaching, trouble increases and many hearts are softened.

Paul Began with the Hope in the Gospel, not in Wisdom

In the early section of this book, when Paul presented the pattern of degeneration of human sin, he began by saying the gospel of Jesus Christ is the way of salvation through faith and can free a man from the sin, guilt, and the wrath of God under which he stands (Romans 1:16 ff.). It was argued that to limit this to the idea of justification and acceptance alone, only so man could go to heaven, is to miss the context of those verses. In Romans, chapters

1 and 2, the gospel tells us that man can be saved from sin and the degrading pattern of his sin. Also, to focus only on justification and forgiveness omits the fact that Paul goes on in Romans chapter 5 and following to show how this leads to identification with Christ in His resurrection and to presenting our bodies as instruments of God for living in this world. The gospel of the cross and resurrection has *relevance in this world now* where the church is to witness to the redemption in Christ's death and His resurrection. Christ "gave himself for our sins that he might rescue/deliver us from this present evil age/world" (Galatians 1:4; cf. Peter's words, Acts 2:40).

Beginning with the cross and resurrection of Jesus Christ, God's Son, is the only way of salvation. It is a fact that nowhere in the New Testament did Jesus or His apostles begin by arguing against the rationalizations of the intellectuals, whether it be the wisdom of the Greeks in their natural philosophy or the legalisms of the Jews. Paul makes it quite clear that his approach to Greeks who "seek after wisdom and the Jews who want miraculous signs" was always to present *the cross and the resurrection of Christ* which deals with man's sin.

Paul said:

> For Christ did not send me to baptize, but to preach the gospel, not in cleverness of speech, so that the cross of Christ would not be made void. For the word of the cross is foolishness to those who are perishing, but to us who are being saved it is the power of God. For indeed the Jews asked for signs and the Greeks search for wisdom; but we preach Christ crucified, but to the Jews a stumbling block and to the Gentiles foolishness, *but those who are called* both Jews and Greeks, Christ the power of God and the wisdom of God. And when I came to you, brethren, I did not come with superiority of speech or of wisdom, proclaiming to you the testimony of God. For I determined to *know nothing* among you *except Jesus Christ, and Him you crucified.* And I was with you in weakness and in fear in much trembling, and my message and my preaching were not in perceived words of wisdom, but in demonstration of the Spirit and of power, and so that your faith would not rest on the wisdom of men, but on the power of God. Yet we *do speak wisdom among those who are mature*; a wisdom, however, not of this age nor the rulers of this age, who are passing away . . . (1 Corinthians 1:17-18, 22-24; 2:1-6; cf. this whole passage of 1:17-2:16; italics added).

The same principles apply to modern intellectual leaders today. In the companion book to this one, *Dark Shadows in the New Day of Science*, it is demonstrated that the efforts of intellectuals to interpret facts were perverted by their bias. This was seen to be true in forming a deterministic view of science and of comparative religion. Also, the key ideas for the meaning of Jesus in "the quest for the Historical Jesus," all critics subconsciously or consciously avoided the question of man's sin and the interpretation of Jesus' ministry in the cross and the resurrection (cf. *Dark Shadows* . . . , pp. 183-205). Quotes are given there by prominent scholarly critics, men who favored this pursuit for another purely human Jesus, in which they themselves make the observation that the critical interpreters all were driven by their *bias of hate* against the supernatural aspect of Jesus' life. And also in the section on history, the findings of the research of Mercea Eliade are reviewed which show that it is man's desire to escape his guilt from sin that leads him repeatedly to pervert the evidence of history to a cyclic view and a pantheistic theme, which avoids a future point of judgment for sin (cf. *Dark Shadows* ..., pp. 79-82).

The Apostle Paul says that he always focused entirely on the gospel of the cross and resurrection of Christ with the unbeliever. By revelation, he knew that all men have an intuitive knowledge of God and that the law of God is written in their hearts, and they have an inward consciousness that the secrets of their hearts will be judged by God's Christ (Romans 1:20-21; 2:14-16). It was this knowledge of God that they were always suppressing or being willfully blind to. But Paul also believed there was a group of people (the elect) that the Holy Spirit was speaking to and who were open to God. He therefore always confronted men about the coming judgment by the Risen Christ (cf. Acts 17:26-31). Having proclaimed Christ as coming judge, Paul told them of the good news that on the cross Christ paid the penalty for their sins and that by accepting Him as their Messiah they would receive forgiveness and the gift of the Holy Spirit. Peter also referred unbelievers to Christ as the coming judge (Acts 10:42).

Unbelievers are without hope in the world, suffering from the captivity to their desires and selfish deceit (Ephesians 2:1-3; 4:17-24). It is with those in this condition that God the Spirit uses the "good news" of the cross and resurrection of Jesus Christ to awaken the elect to the goodness and love of God, to the hope of forgiveness, and to the deliverance from the power of sin. But more, for those who trust God, the Spirit confirms in their hearts that they are now in God's family, that God is guiding them, and they *can have power to live* for Christ (Romans 8:14). Paul believed that God had certain persons that He had appointed to life whom God would call to believe as this message of the cross and resurrection if it was preached in the power of the Holy Spirit. It is important to notice that for Paul the acceptance of evidence for truth was based on the presuppositions of a man's heart being changed by the Holy Spirit. Acceptance of the cross and resurrection produces the ability to trust the wisdom of God about the world.[4]

One purpose of this book which shows the course of moral decline is to confront men with the fact that their growing troubles reveal man's sin against God and that they need God. Today, the church needs to believe that God is at work preparing hearts, and they must boldly proclaim to the unbelieving world the message of the cross.

Incompleteness of the Modern Gospel

One of the problems is that the complete good news is not preached. The gospel not only proclaims that sinners may be forgiven and accepted by God's grace alone, but that when a man really trusts God and dies to self with Christ, God's grace makes available the power of the Holy Spirit for him to live in this sinful world. The faith of Habakkuk that Paul quotes (Romans 1:17) and that the author of Hebrews quotes (10: 38) is emphasizing that the man of God is enabled to live for God in this present evil culture.

In the midst of a dying civilization such as America's, people want to know that God's grace also involves the power to be victorious over sin around them. This is a *deliverance from the controlling power of sin* and a freedom to live for Christ under God's kindness. This does not mean reaching perfection, but an acceptance by God and power from God to break with the demonic control in the world when we trust Him. That involves having the power to suffer for Christ with the hope of reigning with Him when He comes again.

Faith in God's Love and Power Frees One to Understand and Trust the Creator's Wisdom

The whole process of reversing the steps of demonic deception as outlined by Paul depends on faith in the foundation of redemption in the cross and resurrection of Christ. That is why this book, and also especially *Dark Shadows . . . ,* is addressed *to men who are converted* and have their hearts already opened by the Holy Spirit and God's love. This new perspective to accept their sinfulness and faith in God makes them open to want to see the truth about God in the world, whereas formerly they were biased against it.

I read of the testimony of a scientist that demonstrates this. An intelligent, beautiful, young woman married a college professor who was skeptical about God and the Bible. Soon after the marriage and the birth of her first child, the wife accepted Jesus Christ as her Savior. Her husband accommodated her by going to church with her and the baby girl, but often made fun of the message and the church. Gradually the marriage became troubled, and the husband became worried about his relationship.

One day one of his intellectual colleagues asked him, "Are you always right?" For the first time he began to question his judgments, and realize his mistreatment of his wife. At church the next Sunday, he heard the message of man's sinfulness and God's love in the cross. He was touched and accepted Christ. His published testimony told how his view of everything began to change after this. He said that facts about science, about the world, and about human relationships began to be seen from a new perspective, and his doubts began to be answered.

This testimony has been repeated many times. C. S. Lewis once told of how, as a young man, he felt he had gained freedom by rejecting God and interpreted facts by doubt, but then later in life he saw his folly and God's love. This changed the way he interpreted the facts.

The believer's trust in Christ will restore faith in biblical and other history. He will like history because it helps him see how man has sinned before and how he can avoid the same errors. The love of God in the cross will enable him to daily accept his sin, review his and all mankind's failures in history, and live looking forward to the coming of Christ and His eternal rewards. He will have intellectual integrity with all the data of scripture and science that examines the works of God's regular working in the world. He will not want to seek to use scripture to build a righteousness and kingdom for himself. He will recognize that it is a lack of respect for God's regular working in nature when someone always wants some miracle. Yet he will respect the past miraculous, special revelations in the Bible that led to revealing Christ as His Son and God's miracles of providence in guiding him daily. And he knows that God still judges the nations in this world and that Christ will miraculously come again one day in a momentous time of judgment and final freedom from evil. This first step in removing a person's bias must occur before solving the other steps of deception. Then the truth of the Word of God can be applied to the other steps with acceptance and discernment.

Step Two: Counteracting the Materialistic Revolt

When a person has given up his intellectual bias against God by accepting the gospel of God's grace, he is then ready to be shown that he now can return to trusting in Christ for his daily material provisions. In his new-found faith, he will be open to see that trusting in material wealth is wrong. It is tremendously important that to bring about renewal, the churches need to challenge those who truly believe in Christ to trust Him to provide all their needs. The believer needs to see how uncertain trusting in money is. In Proverbs 28:22 it says, "A man with an evil eye hastens after wealth, and does not know that want will come upon him." Jesus refers to this and warns:

> For where your treasure is, there your heart will be also. The eye is the lamp of the body; so then if your eye is clear, your whole body will be full of light. But if your eye is bad, your whole body will be full of

darkness. If then the light that is in you is darkness, how great is the darkness! No one can serve two masters; for either you will hate one and love the other, or you will be devoted to one and despise the other. You cannot serve God and wealth . . . . Do not worry then, saying "What will we eat?" or "What will we drink?" or "What will we wear for clothing?" For the Gentiles eagerly seek all things; for your heavenly Father knows that you need all these things. But seek first His kingdom and His righteousness, and all things will be added to you. So do not worry about tomorrow; for tomorrow will care for itself and each day has enough trouble of its own (Matthew 6:21-24, 31-34).

Paul said:

But those who want to get rich fall into temptation and a snare and many foolish and harmful desires which plunge men into ruin and destruction. For the love of money is the root of all sorts of evil, and some by longing for it have wondered away from faith and pierced themselves with many griefs (I Timothy 6:9-10).

A man's personal success involves self-esteem and achieving financial gain. Even in Christian ministry, the motivation may be to have a bigger church, make more money, and have nicer things. These are of the world, and only by knowing you are God's son, highly valued by Him, and called to do something for Him through your home, family, and church, can you be free from this earthly and demonic drive. All of the Christian's needs should come from his faithful trust and prayer to God. Only by a man seeing God's call for him is to provide for his family and the kingdom of God can a man be free from idolatry and treat his family properly. James said:

Who among you is wise and understanding? Let him show by his good behavior his deeds of gentleness and wisdom. But if you have bitter jealousy and selfish ambition in your heart, do not be arrogant and so lie against the truth. This wisdom is not that which comes from above, but earthly, natural, demonic. For where jealousy and selfish ambition exist, there is disorder in every evil thing. What is the source of quarrels and conflicts among you? Is not the source your pleasures that wage war in your members? You lust and do not have; so you commit murder. And you are envious and cannot obtain; so you fight and quarrel. And do not have because you do not ask. You ask and you do not receive, because you ask with wrong motives so that you may spend it on your pleasures (James 3:13-16; 4:1-3).

The first two commandments that define man's love for God are: 1. "You shall have no other gods before me." This sets God Himself as priority. 2. "You shall not make for yourself an idol in the form of anything in heaven above or on the earth beneath on in the waters below." No images that focus on prosperity in earthly things and on pleasure should be devised. (Exodus 20:3-4). Greed is idolatry (Ephesians 5:3, Colossians 3:5) and is at the root of the male revolt that starts the moral breakdown of society.

Church leaders and the agenda of the churches themselves need to focus on the adequacy of Christ and show their love for and trust in God by their giving to others. "Seek first the kingdom of God and His righteousness, and all these will be added to you" (Matthew 6:33). The giving of a tithe to the Lord, and resting in God to provide by worship and not working on the Christian Sabbath, are good test points. While these may help indicate "God first," they ought not to become legalistic for self righteousness or judging each other. Leaders should be chosen for their trust in, and love for God, and not for how wealthy they are.

Step Three: Correcting Sexual Distortions by Equality in Monogamy

In previous chapters, it was shown that when selfish individualism causes one to turn from faith in God to trust in materialism, the value of people changes to how much they have and to believing everyone should be financially equal. These motives in regard to sex soon seek to erase all sexual difference and lead in ways described to homosexuality. The promotion of sameness of people is at the root of the egalitarian social efforts. After returning to faith in God and making it clear that God is able to supply all the material needs of His people, the groundwork will have then been laid to return to a proper view of sex and gender. Egalitarian efforts always create classes and do not eliminate inequality in terms of being the same.

The way to change sexual or gender perversion is to again seek to restore the idea that while men and women are equal individuals, God has created and called them to be *one in marriage*. Their commitment to that oneness should be made the supreme priority of the man and woman to each other. But acceptance of differences to complement each other is what makes oneness useful and enjoyable. Churches should reemphasize physical differences of sex and promote the pursuit of voluntary sexual distinctions in dress and behavior. Legalism in these regards should be avoided. No work for business should be more important than one's wife or husband, and no child should have priority over one's spouse. To try to establish each individual as separate, equal persons who are alike destroys dependence and oneness and should be recognized as wrong.

While unity as one in marriage is generally acknowledged by many church leaders as right and has been taught by Focus on the Family, in books, in seminars, and in other ways, local church leaders have been timid to take a stand on this and on the biblical roles that are necessary for this to occur. All the how-too instructions and helpful ideas of how to relate which are now being taught will begin to be effective only if the churches have boldness to publicly take a stand on the idea of oneness according to the biblical roles.

This means church leaders should publicly declare to their congregations that it is the churches' policy for men to be sacrificial leaders of their wives, and also that women should respect and obey their husbands. This does not mean a return to abusive patriarchy as in the mid 1800s. Women are now suffering from a lack of monogamous marriage in which faithful, loving men exercise the responsibility for provision, protection, and integrity of their families. Women are open to unsavory sexual advances because there is no male protection. Women, for their own good, need to insist that the church do this. Wives, who are equal in value by submission to their husbands, are the *key to exemplifying* the importance of God's governing authority. If children observe their mother's respect by submission in the home, they, too, will submit to the control of parents and to other governing authorities everywhere else. But the husband's leadership must be just and loving.

Step Four: Divine Control Must Be Communicated through Patriarchs of Faith

All civilized societies have arisen out of God's control through the family to build society. The Father of heaven (Uranus) ruled through his Son Zeus in Greece, who was known as Jupiter in Rome. This rule through His Son in those societies points toward the *only begotten Son*, Jesus Christ who became incarnate, and is worshipped in the Christian churches. The Son of God began the civilization by communicating and controlling through the human fathers of the families in these and all past civilizations. Every major civilization has begun with patriarchal control. The wife and mother was co-leader of the family under the father and highly honored by him in early Greece, Rome, and early America.

This is unquestionably the way divine control was exerted and the way moral law was transmitted to every known society. It is certainly central to the Hebrew-Christian religion. In the Old Testament, God called Abraham (Genesis 18:19), and the religion was transmitted through the father of each successive family unit (Deuteronomy 6:4-7; Psalm 78:5-8). Then, through these family leaders, control was extended to the religious, business, and civil governments. In the New Testament, the same was true (Genesis 12:1-3; Romans 4; Galatians 3.; Colossians 3;18 ff.; I Timothy 3:2-5; Titus 1:6-9; and others). These are tasks to which God has called and appointed the man and the woman.

No man can be worthy of such leadership, but neither is any wife worthy to ask the man to deny himself and love her as Christ loves the church. They both must die to self in their roles. This does not mean the father is an autocratic leader, but that both man and wife are subject to God and to each other. But being a servant leader does not mean that he has no authority to lead (John 13:13-15), but that he leads by sacrificial love of his wife as Christ leads the church (Ephesians 5:21-33). He must seek to understand her and give preference to her needs (1 Peter 3:7-9). Our different roles are our obligations in order to glorify God. This unity in the family helps exemplify the unity in which the Son is subject to the Father and the Holy Spirit is subject to the Father and the Son in the Trinity. It is the only way oneness in marriage can be attained.

Since each feminist movement has aimed at establishing selfish individualism and destroying patriarchal leadership because it has often been abusive, the aim of the churches must regard it as highly important to restore oneness in marriage and loving patriarchal and parental government. Through this, divine control can then be established and passed down generation after generation. This will do more than a thousand sermons to restore morality and control to the church and America. The church must be bold in this and unafraid of the so-called "politically correct" views advocated by the feminists through the educational and public media.

As men and women die to self to establish oneness in marriage, the husband will seek to uphold God's will, but he will administer it under the expression of divine grace, kindness, and forgiveness. Under proper male leadership, women will grow and be effective wives, mothers, and workers in church ministry. Effective women are as necessary as men for the church, and this is manifested in Jesus' (Luke 8:3) and Paul's ministries. Elders of the churches should monitor and oversee that the husband's leadership is loving, as did the minutemen in the early Puritan societies. Older spiritual women should be appointed who can teach the younger women how to love their husbands and help care for the children. Today the greatest problem is failure of men to lead.

There is a place for single women and single men to reveal and maintain the value of the individual before God, which enhances the mystery that God unites individuals so they become one in marriage. Single women should have their rights to work and own property without greed. But they also should maintain sexual purity, with an openness to later be called to serve God in a monogamous marriage and bear children for His glory. But singles should submit to the broader patriarchal leadership to uphold divine control of society as singles. Premarital immorality and independence is widespread among church singles and must be spoken against as wrong.

Premarital chastity and sexual fidelity in monogamous marriage are essential for all character. The greatest act of fidelity is to sacrificially keep the marriage covenant. If a man will not keep his promise to his wife, he cannot be trusted to abide by his word in anything. The same is true of a woman. There is nothing that treats a woman with greater degradation than for a man to give himself to another woman when the wife has given herself to him in a life-long trust. Men greatly demean any woman that they simply use for selfish sexual pleasure. Immoral practices soon reduce sex to frustration for those who selfishly seek pleasure for themselves without a willingness for long-term care for the other person in the marriage bond. Studies show there is no greater sexual pleasure than that between a man and a woman who both trust each other and go to the marriage bed because they care and want to be a blessing to their partner.[5]

Step Five: Remove Anarchy by Renouncing Selfish Individualism

Selfish individualism is at the root of anarchy. Anarchy is the opposite of control and is the exercise of self to do what the individual or group chooses over governing authorities. This book has presented evidence that it is the product of all the previous steps of departure from God. When there is a strong individualism as in modern America, every person begins to see himself as right in his own eyes. And under the dominance of materialism, self-interest groups form, and in self-righteousness feel it is just to transgress what "seem to be" unjust laws to attain their ends. This especially occurs when no further progress of a special interest group seems possible by legal means. But when one segment gains by anarchistic means, this encourages others to do so in a progressive escalation until the final breakdown.

Standing Firm for What Is Right Stops Anarchy But Requires Accountability and Growth

The antidote to anarchy is faith to live righteously in submission to God's authority. But, in such a time there needs to be training in accountability to respond in obedience to authority. Children have to learn control to do right to operate as a family unit. And most adult Christians still need to be held lovingly accountable so they progress in growth of character to where they can stand for what is right in spite of criticism. Social order is the result of individuals who have learned to submit to authority so that they can work together in an organized way.

Any organization is like an organism which is composed of individuals who harmoniously work together under a control center. At times, submission and obedience cause sacrifice and sometimes suffering. But the end result is that each person contributes to the working of the whole effort and produces much good for all individuals in the society. The plan of redemption by God required the Father to give His Son, and the Son learned obedience by the things He suffered. The cross and the resurrection that brought forth the power of the Risen Christ and the birth and growth of the church testify to the power released by suffering. The church is the body of Christ working together in Him (Ephesians 4:11-16). Christians must break with the present day individualism which disregards what leaders say. We must especially learn respect for parents and church leaders. After we have expressed any dissenting view, we should then obey, even if it causes suffering to us. The only exception is that we should not disobey any clear command of God if asked by a leader because their authority is from Him.

Present Church Structures Don't Provide Means For Good Accountability

Today, where the emphasis is on large congregations, no one presiding pastor or even a staff of pastors can offer personal influence for most of the congregation to live under accountability. In America, there are millions of people in small groups and about 40 percent are Christian groups. But most of these are not groups with effective relationships and accountability. There is a lack of lay leaders who care about the people in a small group or who are trained to teach and set an example for the people as in the New Testament. Small house groups today are mostly fellowship groups for study or help in overcoming addictions.

The presiding pastor of a large congregation can only have its people in an accountable relationship by forming small house churches and training leaders to care for them. Some of the most effective big congregations in America have discovered the forming of house churches with a sub-pastor to care for the people is the only way to effectively and lovingly care for the people. Early primitive house churches existed in Palestine and today thrive even without congregational ties in China and elsewhere. The seminaries need to train pastors to train lay leaders who can care for the people in small groups.

The church needs to reinstitute small house groups with trained leadership to pastor small segments of the congregation. Jesus began His church and discipleship teaching in His own house (John 1:37 ff.; Matthew 13:36, Luke 5:17-26; and others). The early disciples first planted churches in houses in the community to which they went (Matthew 10:11 ff.). In Jerusalem, in addition to meetings in the temple, the house churches were the vital centers (Acts 1:13-26; 2:42-47; 4:23-31; 5:42; 12:12). Paul and the apostolic band established house churches wherever they went (Acts 20:20; Romans 16:15; I Corinthians 16:19; Colossians 4:15; Philemon 2). Teaching elders were appointed for these (Acts 14:32; 20:28; 1 Thessalonians 5:12,13). The small group is the most effective way to help people grow into Christ-like maturity because there is the power of personal influence of Christ from one life to another.

Upholding What Is Right in a Local Community Requires Extending Patriarchal Accountability

To establish social accountability, the patriarchal control which is based on loving accountability in the family needs to be extended to the church. Then the church needs to exercise this influence through the united elders of all the churches with voluntary control over the local community. In the New Testament, obedience to parents in the family (Ephesians 6:1 ff.) was to be extended to the caring elders in the small house churches (Hebrews 13:17). It was the working together of all the elders in the local community or city that influenced the city to stop the use of idols and occult books and to instead trust God (e.g., see elders in Acts 19:17-20, 23-27; 20:13-37). It is obedience that grows out of loving trust in the home, in the church, in businesses, and is extended by the united influence of the church leaders in the whole community that changes anarchy and brings people under divine control.

The primitive churches extended the controlling influence of the house churches to the whole local community by bringing all the leaders of all the churches together for fellowship and witness in a local presbytery. All the congregations united at times for worship and teaching and influenced the whole community. The example of Ephesus has been given. The local community where people live and shop and send their children to school is the only place where social influence can be made for change by the churches. The local churches have long seen themselves as competitors against each other. But the Christian church is in a war for survival against pagan, demonic forces and churches need to see that they must join together in this vital spiritual warfare against evil. There is a desperate need for a united spiritual impact against evil in every local community by all the church leaders together.

Elders of the community should begin to meet together across denominational lines in prayer for leading in cooperation. The scriptures show this is God's requirement for renewal that will distinguish the righteous from the unrighteous (Malachi 3:16-18). These efforts to unite should not be antidenominational but transdenominational in loving trust. But united work together should be limited only to the churches who accept the apostolic teachings of the New Testament that centers in the Christian trinitarian God. This was the basis of unity in the early churches. But this unity of witness is desperately needed if the culture is to be influenced toward Christian obedience. This unity should aim at spiritual objectives and not allow their spiritual warfare to be diverted to political ends.

A local community is defined as the place where people usually shop and participate as a family. Elders in a local community should begin to meet together and plan for emergencies, jointly establish places for reserve food, and other essentials such as water and soap. Should a national meltdown occur, some advanced planning could save much confusion and save many lives. Individuals could invest savings in a joint project that could be drawn upon for their own use and for others in need.

While there is a place for political efforts, the church must first fight with spiritual weapons for spiritual objectives. Unbelievers react toward the idea of being forced by law to comply with Christian ideals. Only after the majority in a community endorse Christian truth can Christian laws be enforced. The church influences the minds, then the state can police the enforcement of community laws of conduct. Too much energy has been expended on political action when the church has not yet entered the spiritual warfare and exhibited the moral integrity and love that will influence the world around us. As more local communities become strong in their Christian witness, then people will increasingly turn to the God we trust. As the church unites in local efforts, there will be a natural linking of these communities for a national witness that will produce political action.

Step Six: Counteracting the Coming Judgmental Acts in a Time of God's Judgment

Urwin Lutzer has warned Americans that the churches in Germany waited too long to relate to each other, and then too many people were not mature enough to stand against Hitler and his forces. Lutzer is right in insisting that now is the time for American churches to prepare.[6] If America does not turn back to faith in God soon, the church may find itself under great persecution and opposition. This, of course, is a great time for witnessing to the cross and faith in the resurrection. The death of Christ and His resurrection occurred in a time of trouble for the nation of Israel. The church needs to prepare now for the coming time of confusion, accusations, judgments, and depravation. The scriptures repeatedly remind the righteous to trust God, and He will be adequate to meet their needs.

In the modern world, people are breaking up into self-interest groups that fight for their own rights. Under these conditions, Christians need to manifest *acceptance of all others* who are true believers no matter what class, race, gender, or nationality. The church needs to rise above the ethnic and other divisions. God's plan in calling Abraham was to produce one people for Himself from all peoples and sexes (Genesis 12:1-3). The blessing God planned was to offer forgiveness and reconciliation through Christ's death and then to impart new life through the gift of the Holy Spirit so that they would be born into the spiritual family of Abraham (Galatians 3:14; Acts 3:25-26). All groups of people now can be one under the Lordship of Jesus over the church (Ephesians 2).

Christian acceptance is not a matter of social integration. It is based on our spiritual rebirth into God's family and our common purpose and life in God's

446 *Conclusions*

kingdom. As we have all come from the first Adam, so we should all be one in the second Adam, Jesus Christ. Favoritism and discrimination is a denial of the royal law of love by God's people (James 2:1-12). While men are called to different roles than women and each individual has different gifts to exercise in the kingdom of God, we who are indwelt by the Spirit should accept each other as equal in God's family (Galatians 3:28). Differences are a tool which the Devil uses to divide but which the Holy Spirit harmonizes in the body of Christ to do God's work through His church. Our acceptance of our differences should be a witness against the ethnic and other divisions of the world at this time.

In the Midst of Evil There Must Be Faith in God's Sovereign Power to Judge and Deliver

Such a confusing time of accusation and hypocritical living are the times that God will act in judgment for His people (Romans 1:31; 2:1-3). These are the times when God's people are told *to hold undeviatingly to their faith* and not give in to these tests. This is true of Habakkuk in Judah before the Babylonian invasion. The author of Hebrews gives the same exhortation to those he writes about the trials they are enduring (Hebrews 10:32-39). Paul quoted Habakkuk as he faced the evil of the Roman world which "suppressed the truth in unrighteousness" (Romans 1:17).

In such times, the people of God are asked to watch in prayer and wait for God to act. All events are under the sovereign control of God, and God has His schedule to intervene and deliver (Habakkuk 2:1). And surely there will be a day when "the knowledge of God will fill the earth as the water covers the sea" (Habakkuk 2:14). Paul was committed to preaching the gospel to everyone everywhere because he believed it was the power of God unto salvation to every one who believed.

God's people need to fix their eyes on the future glorious return of Jesus Christ when He judges the world and gives final deliverance to His people (Habakkuk 3). The prophet prayed for the soon coming of God in glory for his people and focused their attention on that event. The author of Hebrews also encouraged his people to persevere so that they will receive the promise because Christ's coming to earth is soon. Jesus urged His disciples to lose their life for Him now in this world, knowing that when He comes in glory He will reward them (Matthew 16:24-27). Jesus said His servants should be expectant, like a person assigned to feed his household and ready when his master returns (Matthew 24:45-50).

Lastly, believing Christians should accept evil against them and respond in love, thereby heaping coals of wrath upon the evil person's head (Romans 12:14-21). The Christian must believe that God is just and will give recompense, and therefore trust vengeance into the hands of God. Likewise, the author of Hebrews counsels that Christians should accept wrong treatment, knowing they have a better reward (Hebrews 10:32-36). Instead of joining the judgmental groups, Christians are to be a witness to trusting in God. In so doing, they will overcome evil with good. When the evil is life-threatening, the Christian can appeal to civil government, as God's temporary judge, whose proper function is to protect the righteous (Romans 13:1-5). Civil government has been instituted by God, and we should pray that God will control those in authority for good (I Timothy 2:1-4).

CONCLUSIONS

For many who have done intensive studies at what is happening in the post-modern culture with all its complexities, what is advocated for guidelines will seem extremely simplistic and unworkable. The reason is that they are seeing too many multi-cultural trees close up and do not see the long perspective of the rise and decline of the civilization, which is the forest.

We need to remember that every major civilization has risen and declined in time because of man's sinful nature. It seems the time of troubles for the United States and the whole Western World may be near. If men turn in judgment against each other and against Christians who believe, God may intervene in judgment with natural catastrophes or a terrible world war to end the conflict. But we must also remember that God in His grace has renewed some civilizations, often for a long period of time. Scriptures teach that God offers renewal, and we are not determined to troubles. By His sovereign grace, God may begin a new and powerful movement that could be worldwide.

It may be that the ending of this great American civilization will usher in the final Antichrist and the Lord's return. But we do not know that hour or day, as Jesus did not. Therefore, it may well be that we are the Christians who God will use to spark a new beginning for a worldwide civilization, just as Paul's preaching of the gospel brought a new beginning to the Roman world.

This much is certain: The gospel of Jesus Christ is still the power of God unto salvation to anyone who believes, to the Jew, or Greek, or Roman, or anyone. Perhaps as each of us is willing to be accountable and die to self to live unto the Savior, a new civilization will emerge through the faithfulness of the church. Our purpose on earth is not to build a great civilization. But as we obey, through the grace of God and the power of the Holy Spirit, and together use our gifts and each walk in the good works for which God called us (Ephesians 2:10), God might create another great civilization with a witness to Him.

In doing this, we can build a better world for ourselves and our children, and we can show the world the power of Christ's future glorious kingdom working in the church in the world in these evil days. Perhaps then many people will join us and begin to obey and witness with us. We are now citizens of heaven, and we look for the eternal city whose building and maker is God. But our obedience now can show that every great civilization must be built on God's eternal truth and that when we forsake God, every civilization will fall. There is always hope, and "the just shall live by faith." But our study of the word of God and of history shows clearly that "man is not enough!"

Mature, Christian men have been called *Andragathia*, the Greek word for "brave, good men." Christian *Andragathia* are "brave" because they trust in God alone, "good" because they are committed to obey God through the grace and power of the Holy Spirit, and "men" because they are committed to grow and be like the only perfect man, Jesus Christ.[7] When they unite together, they present a mighty spiritual force for proclaiming the gospel which is the power of God to save. This is the great need of the hour in America.

Endnotes

Chapter 1: Opportunity, or Pandaemonium?

1. In a freak storm in 1976, fourteen inches of rain was dumped on the eastern face of the Continental Divide flooding the Big Thompson River, surprisingly endangering hundreds, destroying many with their property, and killing some of our friends. This is recorded in Mary Farrar's book, *Choices* (Sisters Oregon: Multnomah Press, 1994), 23-26. The idea of the danger of this tragedy has been adapted to serve as a parable to show America's serious conditions today.
2. Daniel Patrick Moynihan, *Pandaemonium: Ethnicity in International Politics* (Oxford University Press, 1993).
3. Quoted by Carl F. H. Henry, *Twilight of a Great Civilization: The Drift Toward Neo-Paganism* (Westchester, Illinois: Crossway Books, 1988), 20-21.
4. Guinness interview, *Christianity Today,* May 17, 1993, vol. 37, no. 6, 49.
5. Moynihan, op. cit., 10-11.
6. Ibid., 9.
7. Ibid., 4-5.
8. Ibid., 23.
9. Ibid., 70.
10. Ibid., 151.
11. Ibid., xi.
12. Ibid., 157.
13. John Leo, "A Controversial Choice at Justice," *U. S. News & World Report* (May 17, 1993), 19.
14. John Hope Franklin, *The Atlanta Journal*, July 16, 1995, R3.
15. Cose, *The Rage of a Privileged Class* (New York: Harper Ellis Collins Publishers, 1993), 38.
16. Erwin W. Lutzer, *Hitler's Cross* (Chicago, Moody Press, 1995), see especially chapters 5-7.
17. The crisis condition of the churches is frequently reviewed with authoritative facts. The crisis in the churches in America is presented by George Barna, *The Second Coming of the Church* (Nashville: Word Publishing, 1998); the crisis in the churches' world mission is presented by Jim Engle, *The Cloudy Future* (Milwaukee: Christian Stewardship Association, 1996); the crisis in reaching American youth, by Thom S. Rainer, *The Bridger Generation* (Nashville: Broadman & Holman Publishing, 1997), and others.

Chapter 2: Biblical Pattern of Moral Decay

I have written an unpublished paper tracing the general trend philosophically, but have not included it in an addendum here because of the great length of this book. Available at Christian Growth Books, P.O. Box 642, Fayetteville, GA 30214-0642.

Chapter 3: Biblical Philosophy of History

1. See my extensive discussion of this controversy in Dark Shadows, chapters 5 and 9 and W. Schmidt, *The Origin of Religion*, 184 and all of chapter XIV.
2. Arnold Toynbee, *Civilization on Trial* (New York: Meridian Books, Inc., 1959), 32-33.
3. Edward Gibbon, *The Rise and Fall of the Roman Empire* (1776).
4. Oscar Cullmann, translated by Floyd V. Filson, *Christ and Time: The Primitive Christian Conception of Time and History* (London: SCM PRESS LTD, 1951), 51 ff.; cf. D. W. Bebbington, *Patterns in History: A Christian View* (Downers Grove, IL: InterVarsity Press, 1979), 43 ff.
5. William Strauss and Neil Howe, *Generations: The History of America's Future*, 1584 to 2069 (New York: Quill of William Morrow, 1991) and *The Fourth Turning, An American Prophecy: What the Cycles of History Tell Us about America's Next Rendezvous with Destiny* (New York: Broadway Books, 1997).
6. Strauss, *Generations*, e.g., 56 ff. *The Fourth Turning*, 25.
7. Ibid., 11.
8. Mercea Eliade, *Cosmos and History: The Myth of the Eternal Return* (New York: Harper Torchbooks, 1952) xi, 52, 75, 81.

Chapter 4: Pattern in Greek Democracy

1. Emily Vermule, *Greece in the Bronze Age* (Chicago: The University of Chicago Press, 1972). See v-vii for reviews many of the mid-century excavations.
2. Not much historical details exist about the first two. But in order to exclude data that is not relevant for the Athenian democracy, I have studied the data and written and unpublished review of these.
3. Will Durant, *The Life of Greece* (New York: Simon & Schusterr, renewed 1996), 177.
4. H. J. Rose, *Gods & Heroes of the Greeks* (New York: Meridian Books, 1958), 17, 202.
5. W. Schmidt, *The Origin and Growth of Religion*, H. J. Rose, trans., (New York: Dial Press, 1931), 45.
6. Robert Brow, *Religion: Origins and Ideas* (London: Tyndal Press, 1972), 14, 128.
7. George Gilbert Aimes Murray of Oxford has said of Homeric times, "It corresponds to the type of society that we find in many parts of the world under particular historical conditions. It occurs where and old and rich civilization is in process of being broken up by barbarian conquerors." *Encyclopedia Britannica*, "Homer", v. 11, 692.
8. Charles Seltman, *Women in Antiquity* (London: Pan Books, 1956), 52 and following.

9. George Murray, 761.
10. W. G. Forrest, *The Emergence of Greek Democracy: 800-400 B.C.* (New York: World University Library, McGraw-Hill Book Company, 1966), 69, 74-75; see also chapter on "Economic Expansion."
11. Ibid.
12. Benjamin Farrington, *Greek Science: Its Meaning to Us* (London: Penguin Books, 1953), 36-37 and following.
13. William Cecil Dampier, *A Shorter History of Science* (New York: Meridian Books, 1958), 119-120.
14. G. Grotes, *The History of Greece* (New York: E. Dutton, Everyman Library), v. XII, 89.
15. Benjamin Farrington, 33.
16. Ibid.
17. Carl W. Wilson, *Our Dance Has Turned to Death* (Fayetteville, GA: Christian Growth Books, 1979), 80.
18. J. E. Fairchild, ed., Margaret Mead, "One Aspect of Male and Female," *The Way of Women* (New York: Fawcett, 1956), 21.
19. See Plato, *The Laws, Book vii,* and *The Republic*, 451-457.
20. See Carl W. Wilson, 80-82.
21. Carle Zimmerman, *Family and Civilization* (New York: Harper and Row, 1947), 211-322. He also discussed the Roman family, 323-383.
22. Stephen Bertman, ed., *The Conflict of Generations in Ancient Greece and Rome*, (Amsterdam: B. R. Gruner, 1976), 11.
23. Ibid., 25-26.
24. Ibid., 28-32.
25. Ibid., 38-45.
26. Plato, *Republic* 562D-563A.; Meyer Reinhold in Bertman, ed., op. cit., 43.
27. Translation by John Henry Freese in the Loeb Classical Library edition of Aristotle, *The Art of Rhetoric* (London: 1926), Found in Bertman, 172-173.
28. Ibid., 47.
29. Will Durant, 464-469 contain all the following quotes in this section, except when others are noted. Durant gives the Greek references.
30. Durant, 459, 91, 299-301.
31. Ibid., 459.
32. John H. Vincent and James R. Joy, *An Outline History of Greece* (New York: Chautauqua Press, 1883), 181.
33. Carl W. Wilson, 82.
34. Will Durant, 481.
35. Harold Lamb, *Alexander of Macedon* (New York: Bantam Books, 1953), 5-6; Carl W. Wilson, *From Uncertainty to Fulfillment*, (Fayetteville, GA: WDA Books, 1992), 381.

36. Durant, 548-549.

Chapter 5: Pattern in Roman Republic

1. John H. Vincent and James R. Joy, *An Outline History of Rome* (New York: Chautauqua Press, 1889), 32-33, 249.
2. Michael Crawford, "Early Roman and Italy" (in *The Oxford History of the Classical World*), 388.
3. Ibid., quote of Andrew Lintott, "Roman Historians," 636.
4. Ibid., Michael Crawford, 387-391.
5. Ibid., 391.
6. I have studied and written a short history of the kings so that I would not confuse that data with the later history. It is omitted here.
7. Carl W. Wilson, *Dark Shadows in a New Day of Science,* chapter 9.
8. Franz Cumont, *The Oriental Religions in Roman Paganism* (New York: Dover Publications, 1956), 127-128.
9. R. H. Barrow, *The Romans* (Baltimore ll, MD.: Penguin Books, Inc., 1960 reprint), 18, 13-14, 45.
10. Vincent and Joy, 57.
11. Michael Crawford, 397.
12. *Encyclopedia Britannica*, Vol. 13, 188.
13. Ibid.
14. Ibid., 187.
15. Michael Crawford, 406.
16. Vincent and Joy, 89.
17. John E. Bentley, *Philosophy: An Outline-History* (Ames, Iowa: Littlefield, Adams & Company, 1956), 28.
18. Sir Thomas Little Heath, *Encyclopedia Britannica, vol. 2*, 271. Heath is author of "Archimedes."
19. Vincent and Joy, *An Outline History of Greece*, 119-120.
20. Barrow, 17.
21. Ibid., 16-17.
22. Ibid., 145.
23. Otto Kieffer, *Sexual Life in Ancient Rome* (New York: A.M.S. Press, 1934), 4.
24. Vincent, 116.
25. Otto Kiefer, 5.
26. Joseph Plescia, chapter 9 on the Roman Revolution, *The Conflict of Generations in Ancient Greece and Rome*, Stephen Bertman, ed., (Amsterdam: Br. Gruner, 1976), 154. The source *was An Economic Survey of Ancient Rome, Vol. 1*, T. Frank, ed. 109 ff.
27. Ibid., 158.
28. Ibid., 154-155.
29. Ibid., 160-161.

30. Ibid., 164-166. The quotes are from here, but the discussion is from 157-166.
31. Otto Kiefer, 22.
32. Ibid., 41.
33. Ibid., 52-54.
34. Ibid., 45.
35. Ibid., 33.
36. Ibid., 103-104.
37. Ibid., 5.
38. Ibid., *Compl. of L. S.,* 187, 237.
39. John T. Noonan, Jr., *Contraception: A History of Its Treatment by the Catholic Theologians and Canonists* (Cambridge: Harvard University Press, 1986), 12 ff.
40. Ibid., 187-188, #231.
41. Cathline Bliss, *World Council of Churches Report on Women,* 15.
42. Kiefer, 37, cf. *Casmus Dio 56,* 1 ff.
43. Pitirim Sorokin, *The American Sex Revolution* (Boston, MA: Porter Sargent, 1956), 96-97.
44. Meyer Reinhold identifies two periods in the classical past that witnessed such conflict of generation, the fifth in Greece and the first in Rome. See Stephen Bertman, ed., 48 ff.
45. Ibid., 51.
46. Ibid., 52.
47. Ibid., 52.
48. *The Conflict of Generations in Ancient Greece and Rome,* Stephen Bertman, ed., cf. chapter 10, "The Generation Gap in Caliullus and the Lyric Poetry of Horace."
49. Ibid., Joseph Plescia, 143-144.
50. Ibid., Plescia, 161. His source for this was Andrew W. Lintott's *Violence in Roman Republic* (Oxford, 1968), later published as *Violence, Civil Strife, and Revolution in the Classical* City (New York: Chapman and Hall, 1987).
51. Ibid., 165.
52. Ibid., 157.
53. Ibid., 69.
54. Ibid., 159.
55. Vincent, 176-177.
56. Meyer Reinhold, 53-54.

Chapter 6: The Devil

1. F. F. Bruce, *The Epistle to the Ephesians* (London: Pickering and Inglis, Ltd., 1961), 129.

2. Arnold Toynbee, *Civilization on Trial* and *The World and the West* (New York: Meridian Books, Inc. 1958), 22.

3. Carl W. Wilson, *Dark Shadows,* chapter 18 has a lengthy discussion of scientific research and the findings about the mysteries of the human mind. For examples, see Maya Pines, "The Human Difference," *Psychology Today,* September 1983, 62-68; John C. Eccles and Karl Popper, *The Self and the Brain* (Springer Verlag International, 1977).

4. C. F. Keil, *Biblical Commentary on the Old Testament,* Vol. I (Grand Rapids: Wm. B. Eerdmans Publishing Company, 1951), 102-103. (Both the word *heron* for conception and *etseb* for grief or sorrow, are each attended by the word *rabah* for multiply.)

5. Dr. Jan Lever, translated by Peter G . Berkhout, *Creation and Evolution,* (Grand Rapids: Kregel Press, 1958), 182-191.

6. Lever, 184-187.

7. See my book, *Dark Shadows*, chapter 9 for a review of scientific data on some of this.

8. Margaret Mead, J. S. Fairchild, editor, *The Way of Women* (New York: Fawcett Publications, 1956), 21.

9. Stephen Goldberg, *The Inevitability of Patriarchy* (New York: William Morrow & Company, Inc., 1973). This is a comprehensive study which demonstrates that historical and scientific studies do not show matriarchy but only matrilinialism, and that patriarchy always emerges.

10. See my book, *Dark Shadows,* chapter 9 and W. Schmidt, *The Origin and Growth of Religion,* H. J. Rose, trans. (New York: The Dial Press, 1931), see chapter XIV, "The Historical Method and It's Result for Ethnology," 219-250.

11. Chaim Bermant and Michael Weitzman, *Ebla: A Revelation in Archaeology* (New York: Times Books, 1979), 14.

12. J. D. Unwin, *Sex and Culture* (London: Oxford University Press, 1934). See also Appendix II, III; Pitirim A. Sorokin, *The American Sex Revolution* (Boston: Porter Sargent Publisher, 1956),when viewed with his other great work that helps put this sexual revolution and the breakdown of the family in context, especially in chapters iv and v , and *The Crisis of Our Age: The Social and Cultural Outlook* (New York: E. Dutton & Co., Inc., 1941); Gertrude Himmelfarb, *The De-Moralization of Society: From Victorian Virtues to Modern Values* (New York: Alfred A. Knopf, 1995).

13. Pitirim Sorokin, *The Crisis of Our Age* (New York: E. P. Dutton & Co., Inc., 1951), see chapter V, with previous chapters in view.

14. Unwin, 344-345, 161.

15. Ibid., 431-432, 172.

Chapter 7: God's Concern for All Nations

I have covered, in much detail, the rise and steps of decline in Israel and Judah in my yet unpublished book, *The Call.*

Chapter 8: America's Foundations of Faith

1. Martin E. Marty, *Pilgrims in Their Own Land: Five Hundred Years of Religion in America* (Boston: Little, Brown and Company, 1984), 3-9.
2. Jim Nelson Black, *When Nations Die* (Wheaton, IL: Tyndale House Publishers, Inc., 1994), 253.
3. Gary T. Amos, *Defending the Declaration; How the Bible in Christianity Influenced the Writing of the Declaration of Independence* (Brentwood, TN: Wolgemuth & Hyatt Pub., 1989).
4. John Warwick Montgomery, *The Shaping of America* (Minneapolis, Bethany Fellowship, Inc., 1976), 66.
5. C. Gregg Singer, *A Theological Interpretation of American History* (Philadelphia: Presbyterian and Reformed Publishing Company, 1964), 45.
6. Montgomery, 65.
7. Robert N. Bellah, et al; *Habits of the Heart: Individualism and Commitment in American Life* (New York: Harper and Row Publishers, 1985), 253.
8. M. Stanton Evans, *The Theme Is Freedom: Religion, Politics, and the American Tradition* (New York: Regnery Publishing Company, 1994); this chapter was reprinted in *The National Review*, January 23, 1995.
9. Alan Nevins & Henry Steel Conniger, *Pocket History of the United States* (New York: Pocket Books, Inc., 1943).
10. Frederic William Maitland, "English Law," *Encyclopedia Brittanica*, 1953, vol. 8, 568.
11. Ibid., 568.
12. Frederick William Sherwood, "Blackstone, Sir William," *Encyclopedia Britannica*, 1953, vol. 3, 687.
13. Roscoe Pound, in the "Introduction," Morris Ploscowe, *Sex and the Law* (New York: Ace Books, 1962), 8.
14. John D. Pulliam, *History of Education in America* (Columbus, OH: Charles E. Merril Publishing Company, 1968), 22.
15. *The Laws and Liberties of Massachusetts*, 1929, 47.
16. Thomas Jefferson Wertenbaker, *The Puritan Oligarchy: The Founding of American Civilization,* (New York: Grosset & Dunlap, 1947); 143-146; Charles Scribner's Sons; *Necessity of Reformation*, 14-15, quoted from Wertenbaker's book, 137.
17. Ibid., 136.
18. Montgomery, 66.
19. John D. Pulliam, 37, 46.
20. Carl Wilson, *Our Dance Has Turned to Death* (Fayetteville, GA: Renewal Publishing, 1978), 10 ff.
21. Michael Novak, "The Family Is the Future," from *Harper's*, April 1976, cf. condensation in *Readers Digest*, March, 1978, 111.

22. Carl Wilson, 15; I refer here to Thomas Jefferson Wertenbaker, 41-77, and to Arthur Calhoun, *The Social History of the American Family*, Vol. I: Colonial Period (New York: Barnes and Noble, 1960), 72, 74-76.
23. Rosemary Radford Ruether and Rosemary Skinner Keller, *Women and Religion in America: Volume 2: The Colonial and Revolutionary Periods* (San Francisco: Harper & Row, 1983), xiii.
24. Ibid., 138. For the letters see 163-165.
25. Wertenbaker, 188-189.
26. Ian Murray, *The Puritan Hope* (Edinburgh, Scotland: Banner of Truth Trust, 1971), 107.
27. Montgomery, 47-68.

Chapter 9: Intellectual Revolt

1. Carl W. Wilson, *Dark Shadows in a New Day of Science* (published with *Man Is Not Enough*). Sections I and II cover the ideas presented, and III and IV show how these were shown as untrue.
2. Fawn M. Brodie, *Thomas Jefferson: An Intimate History* (New York: W. W. Norton & Company Inc., 1974), 239.
3. Annette Gordon-Reed, *Thomas Jefferson and Sally Hemings: An American Controversy* (Charlottesville, University Press of Virginia, 1997), 231-232.
4. Ibid., read her whole book, but especially the summary of evidence, 221-223.
5. Ibid., 224-235.
6. Brodie, 28, for a copy of the letter.
7. Gordon-Reed, 9.
8. Ibid., 20-24, 67-75; Brodie, 359, 531-532.
9. Brodie, 239.
10. Francis S. Philbrick, "Thomas Jefferson," *Encyclopedia Britannica*, Chicago, 1953, 988.
11. Bentley, 71.
12. Cf. Wilson, *Dark Shadows*, the last half of chapter 2.
13. C. Greeg Singer, 28-29.
14. Mann, *Life and Works*, Vol. IV, Tenth Annual Report, 115 ff. for the above quotes.
15. Mann, *Life and Works*, Vol. VII, Fifth Annual Report, 1841, 109.
16. For a good review of these developments, see Rousas J Rushdoony, *The Messianic Character of American Education*, (Nutley, NJ: The Craig Press, 1976). Cf. also Merle Curti, *The Social Ideas of American Educators* (Patterson, Littlefield, Adams & Co., 1965).
17. Rushdoony, 53; Curti, 142 ff.
18. Nathan O. Hatch, *The Democratization of American Christianity* (New Haven: Yale University Press, 1989), 9.
19. J. Edwin Orr, *Campus Aflame* (Glendale, CA: Regal Books, 1971), 25-30.

Endnotes 457

20. John Woodbridge, Mark A Noll, Nathan O Hatch, *The Gospel in America: Themes in the Story of America's Evangelicals* (Grand Rapids, Zondervan Publishing Company, 1979), 37.
21. Ibid., 38.
22. I suggest Rushdoony for a comprehensive review of these and about John Dewey, 144 ff.
23. Lefferts A. Loetscher, *The Broadening Church* (Philadelphia, University of Pennsylvania Press, 1954), 74-75.
24. See Wilson, *Dark Shadows*, chapter 6.
25. See Carl Wilson, *With Christ in the School of Disciple Building* (Grand Rapids, Zondervan Publishing Company, 1976), where I discuss the loss of the public schools in discipling Christians. 17-44; this report is by Manning M. Pattillo, Jr. and Donald M. Mackenzie on 27-28 and in footnote 17 on 44.
26. *Christianity Today*, Vol. XII., No. 2, October 27, 1967, 24-25.
27. I personally served in the Campus Christian Life Ministry of the Presbyterian Church U. S. in the early 1960s and all but two or three leaders were completely secularized. Most of the leadership in the other old line denominational groups were that way.
28. Wilson, 25-31. See this for most of the following quotes.
29. "One More Time: The Crisis in Higher Education," *Christianity Today*, Vol. 19, no. 21 (July 18, 1975), 20.
30. James Davidson Hunter, *Evangelicalism: The Coming Generation* (Chicago, IL: University of Chicago Press, 1987), 6-7.
31. Ibid.
32. Gene Edward Veith, "What Ever Happened to Christian Publishing?" *World,* July 12/19, 1997, 12-15.

Chapter 10: Revolt to Materialism

1. Robert L. Hilbroner, *The Worldly Philosophers* (New York: A Touchstone Book of Simon & Schuster, fourth edition, 1972), p. 71.
2. Ibid., p. 40.
3. See Carl Wilson, *Our Dance*, chapter 4, *History of Role Changes and Their Effects in the U. S.*, 50-77.
4. Andrew Sinclair, *The Emancipation of the American Woman* (New York: Harper & Row, Publishers, 1965), xii.
5. Ibid., xviii.
6. Edith Latane and John Holaday Latane, *American History* (Boston, MA: Allyn and Bacon, 1949), 306-307.
7. Nevins, 238-239 and following.
8. Marvin Olasky, *The Tragedy of American Compassion* (Wheaton, IL: Crossway Books, 1992), see 42-79. His whole book is an excellent discussion about the changes discussed here.

9. Ibid., 200-201.

10. William Warren Sweet, *The Story of Religion in America* (New York: Harper & Brothers Publishers, 1950), 345.

11. Cf. Heinz R. Pagels, *The Dreams of Reason: The Computer and the Rise of the Sciences of Complexity* (New York, Simon & Schuster, 1988 and Bantam Books, 1989); James Dale Davidson and Lord William Rees-Mogg, *The Sovereign Individual: How to Survive and Thrive During the Collapse of the Welfare State* (New York: Simon & Schuster, 1997).

12. Cf. Michael Harrington, *The Other America: Poverty in the United States* (New York: Penguin, 1981), 37. See also Marvin Olasky, "Culture of Irresponsibility? Important to Define Terms", *World* magazine, May 23, 1992, 7.

13. I have reviewed this in *Our Dance,* 92-96, where I rely on William E. Simon, former Secretary of the Treasury, from his book, *A Time for Truth*, (New York: McGraw Hill, 1978), 63, 181, 212-214, 222; cf. Robert J. Samuelson, "The Year of Sobering Up", *Newsweek*, December 23, 1991.

14. William E. Simon, *A Time for the Truth* (New York: McGraw-Hill Publishers, 1978), 212-214, cf. also 63, 181, 222.

15. See Robert D. Reischauer, ed., *Setting National Priorities: Budget Choices for the Next Century* (Washington, DC: Brookings Institution Press, 1997), 14-15. This is a current discussion by the leading authorities on much of this.

16. Bill Hendrick, "Americans Swept in Long Wave," *Atlanta Journal*, February 23, 1992, G 1, 5.

17. Larry Burkett, *The Coming Economic Earthquake* (Chicago: Moody Press, 1991), 85.

Chapter 11: Sexual Revolt

1. Andrew Sinclair, *The Emancipation of the American Woman* (New York: Harper & Row, Publishers, 1965), xix.

2. Eric John Dingwall, *The American Woman* (New York: Signet Books, 1958), 67.

3. Arthur Calhoun, vol. 1, chapter XIX, "Servitude and Sexuality in the Southern Colonies," 313-329.

4. Dingwall, 73-74.

5. Ibid., 87-88.

6. Carl Wilson, *Our Dance,* 38.

7. Miriam Schneir, ed., *Feminism: The Essential Historical Writings* (New York: Vintage Books, 1972), 76-77.

8. Ibid., 76.

9. Ibid., 78.

10. Stephen Douglass, *The North Star*, July 28, 1848.

11. Dr. Marynia Farnham, "The Lost Sex," in *The Way of Women*, J. E. Fairchild, ed. (New York: Fawcett Publications, Inc., 1956), 31-32. Farnham with Ferdinand Lundburg is the author of *Modern Woman, the Lost Sex* (New York: Harper and Brothers, 1947) in which she extensively evaluates women and the effects of the feminist movement.
12. Schneir, xv.
13. Ibid., 110-116.
14. Ibid., 122-124.
15. Ibid., xvii.
16. Calhoun, vol. iii, 107.
17. Schnier, xviii.
18. Dingwall, 111.
19. Ibid., 225-254 gives studies by Monett, Burn, Dixon, Dike, Potts, et al.
20. Calhoon, vol. iii, 44.
21. Calhoon, vol. iii, 27-64.
22. Alice S. Rossi, 413-470.
23. Schneir, 133.
24. John R. Mott, *The Decisive Hour of Christian Missions* (Missionary Education Movement of the United States, 1911), 135.
25. Schneir, 325.
26. Alan F. Guttmacher, *The Complete Book of Birth Control* (New York: Ballantine Books, 1961), 8.
27. Sarah Chakko and Kathleen Bliss, *A Study of Man-Woman Relationships* (London: S.C.M. Press, 1952), vii.
28. Dingwall, 128-131; cf. Ralph Wentworth-Rohr, "Momism," Fairchild, ed., *The Way of Women*, 101-110.
29. Edmund Bergler, M.D., *Homosexuality: Disease or Way of Life?* (New York: Collier Books, 1956), 7.
30. Toby B. Bieber, *Homosexuality: A Psychoanalytic Study of Male Homosexuals* (New York: Basic Books, 1962), 106; cf. Peter and Barbara Wyden, *Growing Up Straight* (New York: Stein and Day Publisher, 1968), 49.
31. Dingwall, 133 ff.
32. Schneir, 268-285. See Spencer's significant book, *Woman's Share in Social Culture*, chapter III on "The Drama of Woman of Genius."
33. Wilson, 58-61. References on this data are given in footnotes.
34. Betty Friedan, *The Feminine Mystique* (New York: Dell, 1963) 12.
35. Cf. Wilson, *Our Dance,* 64 ff.
36. Ibid., 66-67; cf Kate Millett, *Sexual Politics* (Westminster, MD: Doubleday, 1978).
37. Ibid., 67 ff.
38. Ibid., chapter. 3, 19-20; Anne Moir and David Jessel, *Brain Sex*, 1991. A study by Sally Shaywitz of Yale University's School of Medicine.

39. See my discussion of this with reference to authorities, Wilson, *Our Dance*, 23-28.
40. Dr. Marie Robinson, *The Power of Sexual Surrender* (New York: Signet Books, 1959), 40-58; Seymour Fisher, *Understanding the Female Orgasm* (New York: Basic Books, 1973), 187; See my discussion on this in *Our Dance*, chapter 3, "Equality, Differences, and Freedom in Sexual Roles," 19 ff., and 71-76 of other studies.
41. Shere Hite, *The Hite Report* (New York: Dell Books, 1976), 199-200.
42. cf. George F. Will, "Sex in Sacramento," *Newsweek*, April 3, 1995, 76.
43. John Leo, "Promoting No-Dad Families," *U. S. News & World Report*, May 15, 1995, 26.
44. George Guilder, *Sexual Suicide* (New York: Bantam Books, 1975), 268.
45. Shere Hite, *Report on the Family* (West Emoryville, CA: Publishers Group West, 1995), 345, cf. 54 ff.

Chapter 12: Steps to Anarchy

1. Review chart 2a in chapter 2 showing the beginning of the wave of anarchy as the sexual revolution gets underway.
2. Joanne Grant, ed., *Black Protest: History, Documents, and Analyses, 1619 to the Present* (Greenwich, CT: Fawcett Publications, 1968), 240-243.
3. Ibid., 244-245.
4. Ibid., 249.
5. Andrew Sinclair, *The Emancipation of the American Woman* (New York: Harper and Row, 1965), 47; cf. Wilson, *Our Dance*, 66.
6. Cf. Carl W. Wilson, *Dark Shadows*, chapter 20; see chapter 18 references.
7. Robert H. Bork, *The Tempting of America: The Political Seduction of the Law* (New York, NY: The Free Press of Macmillan, Inc., 1990), 162.
8. Ibid., 130.
9. Ibid., 132.
10. Ibid., 251.
11. See chapter 7, 105.
12. James Davidson Hunter, *Evangelicalism: The Coming Generation* (Chicago, IL: University of Chicago, 1987), 23.
13. Carl W. Wilson, 29; cf. 25-35.
14. "One More Time: The Crisis in Higher Education," *Christianity Today*, vol. 19, no. 21, July 18, 1975.
15. Hunter, *Evangelicalism*, 33.
16. George Marsden, *Reforming Fundamentalism: Fuller Seminary and the New Evangelicalism* (Grand Rapids, MI: William B. Eerdmans Publishing Company, 1987).
17. Hunter, *Evangelicalism*.
18. Mindy Belz, "Whose Calling the Time," *World*, March 28, 1998.

19. Robert Wuthnow, *Sharing the Journey: Support Groups and America's New Quest for Community* (New York: The Free Press of Macmillan, Inc., 1994), 7.

Chapter 13: Education and Art

1. Carl W. Wilson, *Dark Shadows in a New Age of Science: The Story of Perversion by American and Western Intellectual Elite* (to be published in late 1998; write Christian Growth Books, P.O. Box 642, Fayetteville, GA 30214-0642).
2. Heinz R. Pagels, *The Dreams of Reason: The Computer and Rise of the Sciences of Complexity* (New York: Simon & Schuster, 1989), 11.
3. Timothy Ferris, *The Whole Shebang* (New York: Simon & Schuster, 1997), 14.
4. Stephen Hawking, *A Brief History of Time* (New York: Bantam Books, 1990), 50-51.
5. Barry Parker, *Chaos in the Cosmos: The Stunning Complexity of the Universe* (New York: Plenum Press, 1996), 287.
6. Michael J. Behe, *Darwin's Black Box: The Biochemical Challenge to Evolution* (New York: The Free Press, 1996), x.
7. Carl Wilson, *Dark Shadows*, chapter 17.
8. Ibid., chapter 19.
9. W. Schmidt, *The Origin and Growth of Religion* (New York: The Dial Press, 1931, H. J. Rose, trans.), 14-15, 171.
10. William Foxwell Albright, *Archaeology of Palestine and the Bible* (New York: Fleming H. Revel, 1935), 129.
11. J. D. Unwin, *Sex and Culture*, 327-329.
12. Pagels, 13; cf. the whole book arguing this may produce a new synthesis of science.
13. Paul Johnson, *Modern Times: The World from the Twenties to the Eighties* (New York: Harper & Row Publishers, 1983).
14. Paul Johnson, *Intellectuals* (New York: Harper Perennial, 1988), 1-2.
15. Ibid., 306.
16. Ibid., 342.
17. Johnson, *Modern Times*, 729.
18. Sowell, *The Vision*, see chapter 2, "The Pattern" 7-30.
19. Alvin Toffler, *The Third Wave* (New York: Bantam Books, 1980), 289.
20. Ibid., 9.
21. William J. Bennett, chapter 1, *The Devaluing of America: The Fight for Our Culture and Our Children* (New York: Summit Books, 1992); and chapter 4, *The Index of Leading Indicators* (New York: Simon and Schuster, 1992).
22. Bennett, *The Devaluing*, 55.
23. *U.S. News & World Report*, cover story of January 11, 1993.
24. Allan Bloom, *The Closing of the American Mind* (New York: Simon & Schuster, 1987).

25. Ronald H. Nash, *The Closing of the American Heart* (Waco, TX: Word Publishing Company, 1990).
26. Bennett, *The Devaluing*, 36.
27. Ibid., 29.
28. Ibid., 37.
29. Ibid., 45-47.
30. H. R. Rookmaaker, *Modern Art and the Death of Culture* (London: InterVarsity Press, 1975), 11.
31. Aleksander Solzenitsyn, *The New York Times Book Review*, February 7, 1993.
32. Neil Postman, *Amusing Ourselves to Death* (New York: Penguin Books, 1987).
33. Michael Medved, *Hollywood vs. America* (Grand Rapids: Zondervan, 1992).
34. James Dale Davidson & Lord William Rees-Mogg, *The Sovereign Individual: How to Survive and Thrive During the Collapse of the Welfare State* (New York: Simon & Schuster, 1997).
35. Christopher John Farley, "Rock's Anxious Rebels," *Time*, October 25, 1993, 60-66.
36. Walter Truett Anderson, *Reality Isn't What It Used to Be: Theatrical Politics, Ready-to War Religion, Global Myths, Primitive Chic, and Other Wonders of the Postmodern World* (San Francisco: Harper & Row, 1990), 6.

Chapter 14: The Economy

1. Israel Kirzner, "The Open-Endedness of Knowledge," *The Freeman*, 36 (1986), p. 87.
2. Ronald H. Nash, *Poverty and Wealth: The Christian Debate over Capitalism* (Westchester, IL: Crossway Books, 1986), p. 39.
3. *The Wall Street Journal*, June 12, 1995, p. C 1.
4. See *Business Atlanta*, August 1991, p. 30 and p. 27.
5. Ibid.
6. James Bovard, *The Farm Fiasco* (San Francisco: I. C. S. Press, 1991).
7. Mortimer B. Zuckerman, "Fixing the Welfare Mess," *U.S. News & World Report*, January 16, 1995, p. 72.
8. Mortimer B Zuckerman, "Showing the Way on Welfare," *U. S. News & World Report*, May 22, 1995, p. 72.
9. "Stumbling Giants," *Time*, November 24, 1997, p. 75.
10. Peter G. Peterson, *Will America Grow Up before It Grows Old? How The Coming Social Security Crisis Threatens You, Your Family, and Your Country* (New York: Random House, 1960). He is the Director of the Federal Reserve Bank of New York, Chairman of the Council on Foreign Relations, Chairman of the Institute for International Economics, Director of the National Bureau of Economic Research, Chairman of the Blackstone Group (a private investment group), and others. He is not an insignificant alarmist without knowledge.

11. For more study see C. Eugene Steuerle, *Retooling Social Security for the 21st Century* (Washington, DC: Institute Press, 1994); or Larry Burkett, *The Coming Economic Earthquake* (Chicago, IL: Moody Press, 1991), pp. 55 ff. and articles: Robert J. Samuelson, "Social Security; the Facts," *Newsweek,* April 24, 1995, p. 37; George J. Church and Richard Lacayo, "Social Security," *Time,* March 20, 1995, pp. 22-29; Susan Dentzer, "The Case of the 'Stolen' Trust Funds," *U.S. News & World Report,* April 3, 1995, p. 49.

12. Charles L. Schultze, chapter 2, *Setting National Priorities: Budget Choices for the Next Century* (Washington DC: Brookings Institution Press, 1997), p. 69.

13. Michelle Mack, staff of the *Atlanta Journal-Constitution,* November 2, 1997.

14. Robert Samuelson, "The Surplus: An Accident," *Newsweek,* February 16, 1998, p. 44.

15. Carl W. Wilson, *Our Dance Has Turned to Death,* (Fayetteville, GA: Renewal Publishing Company, 1978), pp. 192-195.

16. Robert J. Samuelson, "Judgment Calls, The Peace Dividend," *Newsweek,* February 16, 1998, p. 49.

17. Allan Sloan, "The Budget: Books, Cooked D. C. Style," *Newsweek,* February 16, 1998, p. 42.

18. Ibid., p. 55, see the whole chapter pp. 35-74.

19. Robert D. Reischauer, *Setting National Priorities,* op. cit., p. 33.

20. *The Wall Street Journal,* June 12, 1995, p. C 1.

Chapter 15: Class Conflict

1. Tony Brown, *Black Lies, White Lies: The Truth According to Tony Brown* (New York: William Morrow and Company, Inc., 1995), 50.

2. Orlando Patterson, *The Ordeal of Integration: Progress and Resentment in America's "Racial" Crisis* (Washington, DC: Civitas Counterpoint, 1997), 233 pp.

3. Ibid., 20-21.

4. Ibid., 26-27.

5. Ibid., 32.

6. Ibid., 34.

7. Ibid., 37-38.

8. Ibid., 17-18.

9. Ibid., 18.·

10. Andrew Hacker, *Two Nations: Black and White, Separate, Hostile, Unequal* (New York: Scribners, 1992). He compares this to Gunnar Myrdal, *American Dilemma,* 1944.

11. O. Patterson, 41.

12. Hanna Rosen, "Hiding from a Killer," *Atlanta Journal-Constitution,* July 2, 1995, B1-2.

13. Ellis Cose, *The Rage of the Privileged Class* (New York: HarperCollins, 1993), 5-7.
14. Ibid., 1.
15. Ibid., 6-7, 38.
16. Ibid., 2, 33.
17. O. Patterson, op. cit. , 34.
18. Read Tom Morganthau, "What Color Is Black," and succeeding articles, *Newsweek*, February 13, 1995, 63-72.
19. Sharon M. Collins, *Black Corporate Executives: The Making and Breaking of Black Middle Class* (Philadelphia: Temple University Press, 1997).
20. Joe Klein, "Time to Pull the Plug on Affirmative Action?," *Reader's Digest*, June 1995, 105-106; *Newsweek*, February 13, 1995.
21. Ibid., 106-107.
22. Ibid.
23. Larry Reibstein, "What Color Is an A?," *Newsweek*, December 29, 1997-January 5, 1998, 76-77.
24. Julian E. Barnes, "A Surprising Turn on Minority Enrollments," *U.S. News & World Report*, December 28, 1997-January 5, 1998, 32-34.
25. Ibid., 85, but see the whole of chapter 2 on "Liberal American Advocacy."
26. John Hope Franklin, *The Atlanta Journal*, July 16, 1995, R3.
27. See "The Divided State of Black Leadership," *U.S. News & World Report*, July 18, 1994, 29.
28. John Leo, "A Controversial Choice at Justice," *U.S. News & World Report* May 17, 1993, 19.
29. Tony Brown, 8.
30. Coss, *The Rage*, op. cit., 179.

Chapter 16: Women

1. Leslie Kaufman-Rosen and Claudia Kalb, "Holes in the Glass Ceiling Theory," and Bob Cohn, Bill Turouque and Martha Brant, "What About Women," *Newsweek*, March 27, 1995.
2. See the graphs and figures in chapter 11 (11a-11f); also my description of these changes in the way divorce has been progressively made easier, from rigid divorce laws, to quick divorces, to no-fault divorce, to instantly accessible divorces by mail or in department stores, see *Our Dance*, 119.
3. Joe Maxwell, "Standing in the Gender Gap," *Christianity Today*, June 22, 1992, 69-72.
4. Christina Hoff Sommers, *Who Stole Feminism? How Women Have Betrayed Women* (New York: Simon & Schuster, 1995).
5. Naomi Wolf, *The Beauty Myth: How Images of Beauty Are Used against Women* (New York: Doubleday, 1992), 180-182.

6. Gloria Steinem, *Revolution from Within, A Book of Self-Esteem* (Boston: Little Brown Publishers, 1992), 222.

7. Richard Gelles and Murray Straus, *Physical Violence in American Families* (New Brunswick, NJ: Transaction Publishers, 1990); cf. John Leo, "Is it a war against women?," *U.S. News & World Report*, July 11, 1994, 22.

8. Christina Hoff Sommers exposes this perversion in chapter 7, "The Self-Esteem Study," 137-156.

9. See Cynthia Tucker, columnist for the *Atlanta Journal*, "Dads Can Save Their Daughters from Disaster," November 2, 1997, C7; Nicky Marone, *How to Father a Successful Daughter* (New York: McGraw-Hill, 1988), 240 and following.

10. Sommers, 160-161, but see the whole chapter on "The Wellesley Report," 157 ff.

11. Ellis Cose, *A Man's World: How Real Is Male Privilege and How High Is Its Price?* (New York: HarperCollins, 1995), 132.

12. Chapter 10 on "Rape Research," 209-226.

13. Sylvia Ann Hewlett, "Running Hard Just to Keep Up," *Time,* Special Issue, Women: The Road Ahead, Fall 1990, Vol. 136, No 19.; see her book, *When the Bough Breaks: The Cost of Neglecting Our Children* (New York: Basic Books, 1991).

14. Martha Priddy Patterson and Kerry Hannon, "A Woman's Special Dilemma," *U.S. News & World Report*, June 13, 1994, 93; See also, Linda Kelley, *Two Incomes and Still Broke*, (New York: Random House, 1998).

15. See Wilson, *Our Dance*, 111-113, from a Friedan speech in New York, November 1979

16. Sara Davidson, *Friends of the Opposite Sex* (New York: Doubleday, 1984), 288; Dr. T. Bery Braxelton, "Women Are Literally Splitting Themselves in Two," *Atlanta Journal*, November 27, 1985, 19 and following.

17. Karen Springer and Debra Rosenberg, "The New Providers," *Newsweek*, May 22, 1995, 36.

18. "The Marriage Crunch," *Newsweek*, June 2, 1986, 54-63. While these figures have been challenged, the crunch factor is certainly real.

19. Dr. Matina Horner, *U.S. News & World Report*, November 1, 1981.

20. See "Another World," *Psychology Today*, February 1986, 22-27.

21. Robin Knight, "Gender, Jobs and Economic Survival," *U.S. News & World Report*, September 29, 1994, 63.

22. This is very important but too detailed a matter to fully substantiate here, but I have dealt with it elsewhere and George Guilder has given more extensive explanations. See Wilson, *Our Dance*, 35-37, 62-64, 98-101.

23. Ellis Cose, *A Man's World, A Man's World* (New York: HarperCollins, 1995); see excerpt "Black Men & Black Women," *Newsweek*, June 5, 1995, 66-69.

24. Margaret Mead, in Fairchild's *The Way of Women*, 20.

466 *Endnotes*

25. J. D. Unwin, *Sex and Culture* (London: Oxford University Press, 1934), cf. Pitirim Sorokin, *The American Sex Revolution* (London: Porter Sargent, 1956), 108-113.
26. George Guilder, *Sexual Suicide* (New York: Bantam Books, 1975), 88, 101, 193.
27. See Wilson, *Dark Shadows*, chapter 20 where the whole fraud of modern sex is reviewed.
28. Gertrude Himmelfarb, *The De-Moralization of Society: From Victorian Virtues to Modern Values*, (New York: Alfred A Knopf, 1995), 236; for her source, she quotes Arland Thornton, "Changing Attitudes toward Family Issues in the United States," *Journal of Marriage and the Family*, November 1989, 884.
29. Cheryl Russel, *The Official Guide to the American Marketplace*, 2nd edition, New Strategist Publication; cf. Alan Guttenmacher Institutes, *Family Planning Perspective*, March/April 1993, in which he says men have a *median* number of 7.3 partners.
30. Barbara Defoe Whitehead, "Dan Quayle Was Right," *Atlantic Monthly*, April 1993, 47-84.
31. See Ellen Goodman, "Choosing a Policy Strategy for Child Care," *Atlanta Journal/Constitution*, January 18, 1998, E5.
32. Tammy Joyner, "Parents Often Struggle with Child Care Costs," *The Atlanta Journal/Atlanta Constitution*, January 18, 1998, P3.
33. Tammy Joiner, P3.
34. Ellen Goodman, E5.
35. Margaret Sanger gained the help of wealthy Katharine McCormic, of McCormic manufacturing wealth and an MIT graduate, and working with biologist Grego Pincus at Worchester Foundation for Experimental Biology developed "the pill" in 1960. Planned Parenthood distributed it.
36. Michele Ingrassia, Karen Springen and Debra Rosenberg, "Still Fumbling in the Dark: Contraception . . . ," *Newsweek*, March 13, 1995, 61, cf. 60-62.
37. Ibid., 61.
38. Naomi Wolf, "The Abortion Debate: A Call for Truth," *The Atlanta Journal*, November 5, 1995, Fl.
39. Laura Shapiro, et al., "What Is It with Women and Breasts?," *Newsweek*, January 20, 1992, 57.
40. Mary Cagney, "Good News for Women?", *Christianity Today*, April 6, 1998, 54-59.
41. Toni Grant, *Being A Woman* (New York: Avon Books, 1988), 1.
42. Kay Ebeling, "The Failure of Feminism," *Newsweek*, November 19, 1990, 9.
43. Elizabeth Fox-Genovese, *"Feminism Is NOT the Story of My Life,"* (New York: Doubleday, 1996); also her *Feminism without Illusions*, and others.
44. Midge Yearley, "Early American Women," *Atlanta Journal and Constitution*, October 17, 1976; see my discussions in *Our Dance*, 57-58, 62-64.

45. Linda Kelley, *Two Incomes and Still Broke* (New York: Random House, 1998), 321.

46. Susan Faludi, *Backlash: The Undeclared War against American Women* (New York: Crown, 1991), xxii.

Chapter 17: Men and Children

1. Cose, *A Man's World*, 71.

2. Ibid., read 189 ff.

3. Ibid., see Cose's chapter 4 on "The Rise and Demise of the Sensitive Man," 91 ff.

4. Ibid., 150, see chapter 7 for a lengthy discussion about this.

5. Ibid., 53-54.

6. Cynthia Tucker, "Dads Can Save Their Daughters from Disaster", *Atlanta Journal & Constitution*, November 2, 1997, C7; cf. Nicy Marone, *How to Father a Successful Daughter* (New York: McGraw-Hill, 1988, 240; H. Norman Wright, *Always Daddy's Girl*, (Ventura, CA: Regal, 1984), see chapter 2. This was a number 1 best seller.

7. Ibid., 39-40.

8. Wilson, *Our Dance*, 132.

9. David Blankenhorn, *Fatherless America: Confronting Our Most Urgent Social Problem* (New York: HarperCollins, 1995), 1.

10. Shere Hite, *The Hite Report on the Family: Growing Up under Patriarchy* (Emoryville, CA: Publishers Group West, 1995).

11. Himmelfarb.

12. Wilson, *Our Dance*.

13. David Popenoe, *Life without Father* (New York: The Free Press, 1996), 3.

14. Ibid., 48; see Leibowitz, *This Week*, December 15, 1957 abbreviated and reprinted in *Readers Digest*, March 1958.

15. Himmelfarb. For parallels in the growth of unbelief, divorce, and illegitimacy in Britain and elsewhere; especially her epilogue with graphs of the U.S., England, and Wales where there are parallels in both nations of illegitimacy and crime, 229-232.

16. Mary Cronin, "Gilded Cages," *Time*, May 25, 1992, 52-54.

17. John W. Whitehead, *The Stealing of America* (Westchester, IL: Crossway Books, 1983), 75.

18. Ibid., 80.

19. Thomas Sowell, 176; quoted from Elena Neuman, "Child Welfare or Family Trauma?," *Insight*, May 8, 1994, 6.

20. Hite, *Report on the Family*, 54, 345.

21. Maggie Gallagher, *The Abolition of Marriage* (Washington, DC; Regnery Publishing, 1996), cf. John Leo, "Where Marriage Is a Scary Word," *U.S. News & World Report*, February 5, 1996, 22.

22. Armand M. Nicholi II, 11.
23. Carl Wilson, *Our Dance*, 120, Urie Bronfenbrenner, *Readings in Social Psychology* (New York: Holt Rinehart and Winston, 1958), 424; and *Two Worlds of Childhood: U.S. and U.S.S.R.* (New York: Pocket Books, 1970), 102, 105, 109.
24. Urie Bronfenbrenner, *Two Worlds*, 121-123.
25. Peter G. Peterson, *Will America Grow Up before It Grows Old?*. He is one of the best U.S. economists as director of the Federal Reserve Bank of New York, Chairman of the Council on Foreign Relations, Chairman of the Institute for International Economics, Director of the National Bureau of Economic Research, and has been an advisor to four presidents.
26. Ibid., 25.
27. James Vaupel, "New Views on Lifespans Alter Forecasts on Elderly," *New York Times*, November 16, 1992.
28. Peterson, 34; Robert D. Reischauer, 33.
29. Ibid.
30. Ibid., 35.

Chapter 18: Homosexuality

1. Jeffery Satinover, *Homosexuality and the Politics of Truth* (Grand Rapids: Baker Books, 1996), 250.
2. I have presented much more comprehensive data in my book, *Dark Shadows*, chapters 3 and 20.
3. Aron Krich, ed., *The Sexual Revolution: Pioneer Writings on Sex* (New York: Dell Publishing Company, 1963), 149-256.
4. Margaret Mead, *Sex and Temperament* (New York: Mentor Books, 1950), and *Male and Female* (New York: William Morrow & Company Publishers, 1949).
5. Satinover suggests some of these, 18-20, but I have stated these in my own way.
6. Wray Herbert, "Freud under Fire," *Psychology Today*, April 1984, 12; E. M. Thornton, *The Freudian Fallacy*, (New York: Dial Press, 1984).
7. Paul Johnson, *Modern Times*, 6. Also, I have given an evaluation and documentation of this, *Dark Shadows*, chapter 20.
8. For example, "Freud's Oedipus Complex Challenged," *Science News*, vol. 148, no. 16, October 19, 1991, 248-250; Paula J. Caplan, "Take the Blame Off Mother" *Psychology Today*, vol. 20, no. 18, October 1986, 70-71; Stephen Jay Gould, "Freud's Psycholgenic Fantasy," *Natural History*, vol. 96, no. 12, December 1987, 10-19; James Hillman, et al., "Reexamining Freud," *Psychology Today*, vol. 23, no 9. September 1989, 48-52.
9. See the notes of the *American Advancement of Science*.

10. Judith A. Reisman, ed., *Kinsey, Sex and Fraud* (LaFayette, LA: Lochinvar Huntington House, 1990), 246 pp.; see also David Chillton, "Kinsey Lied," *World*, April 24, 23.
11. Satinover, 32-39.
12. Paul Billings and Jonathan Beckwith, "Born Gay," in the MIT *Technology Review*, July 1993, 60.
13. See K. Lansing, "Homosexuality: Theories of Causation, Reorientation, and the Politics and Ethics Involved," minutes of Annual Scientific Meeting of the National Association for Research and Treatment of Homosexuality, 1993, 50.
14. Dean Hamer, *Science* magazine July 15, 1993.
15. Satinover, 111-112, referring to Risch and others, "Male Sexual Orientation and Genetic Evidence."
16. Ibid., 112.
17. William Byne and Bruce Parsons, "Human Sexual Orientation: the Biological Theories Reappraised," *Columbia University Archives of General Psychiatry*, 228-239 from Satinover, 114.
18. Satinover, 82, 92.
19. See discussion of the work of Gunter Dorner and of Ingeborg Ward in Jo Durden-Smith and Diane de Simone, *Sex and the Brain* (New York: Warner Books, Inc., 1983), 123-126.
20. See the evidence given by the following: Satinover, 93-108; David Gelman, "Born or Bred?", *Newsweek*, February 24, 1992, 53; Sharon Begley and David Gelman, "What Causes People to Be Homosexual?" *Newsweek*, September 9, 1991, 52; Dennis Grady, "The Brains of Gay Men," *Discover*, January 1992, 29; Daniel Cappon, *Toward an Understanding of Homosexuality* (Englewood Cliffs, NJ: Prentice Hall, 1965, 67-117; Peter and Barbara Wyden, *Growing Up Straight* (New York: Stein and Day, 1968); John Leo, "Homosexuality: Tolerance vs. Approval," *Time*, January 8, 1979, 48-51.
21. Satinover, 141.
22. A. Bell et al., *Sexual Preference*, (Bloomington, IN: Indiana University Press, 1981).
23. A. Belland M. S. Weinberg, *Homosexualities: A Study of Diversity among Men and Women* (New York: Simon & Schuster: 1978), 308-309.
24. Satinover, 55-56 (see footnotes for references to each study).
25. Ibid., 168-169.
26. See Satinover's review of the statistics on this, Ibid., 168-169.
27. Ibid., 169.
28. Ibid., 174 ff.
29. Ibid., 181, 203.

30. Ibid., W. Odets, in a report to the American Association of Physicians for Human Rights, cited in E. L. Goldman, "Psychological Factors Generate HIV Resurgence in Young Gay Men," *Clinical Psychiatry News*, October 1994, 5.
31. Satinover, 56-57.
32. L. S. Doll et al., "Self-Reported Childhood and Adolescent Sexual Abuse among Adult Homosexual/Bisexual Men," *Child Abuse and Neglect* 16, no. 6 (1992), 855-864.
33. Satinover, 62-63.
34. For Clinton's two speeches see "Repealing Morality?" November 22, 1997, 19, and "The Diversity Diversion," December 6, 1997, 18 of *World* magazine.

Chapter 19: Terminus in Judgment

1. William J. Bennett, *Devaluing*, 45, 48-49.
2. Ibid., 47.
3. Daniel Dennett, *Darwin's Dangerous Idea* (New York: Simon Schuster and Sons, 1994).
4. Sommers, 118-119. See all of chapter 6, "A Bureaucracy of One's Own."
5. See Gene Edward Veith, Jr., *Postmodern Times: A Christian Guide to Contemporary Thought and Culture* (Wheaton, IL: Crossway Books, 1994), 51-60.
6. George Will, "Our Expanding Menu of Rights," *Newsweek*: December 14, 1992.
7. Robert J. Samuelson, "I Am a Big Lawyer Basher," *Newsweek*, April 27, 1992, 62.
8. Mortimer B. Zuckerman, "Beware the Adversary Culture," *U.S. News & World Report*, June 12, 1995, 94.
9. Daniel Borestein, Parade Magazine, *Atlanta Journal and Constitution*, Sunday.
10. David Gergen, "America's Legal Mess," *U.S. New & World Report*, August 19, 1991, 72.
11. John Leo, "The Worlds Most Litigious Nation," *U.S. News & World Report*, May 22, 1995, 24.
12. Matthew Cooper, et al. "Marching to a New War: Civil Rights Groups Confront a Conservative Challenge, Public Doubts and Fraying Coalition," *U.S. News & World Report*, March 6, 1995, 32-34). There are many articles about individual lawsuits.
13. Robert J. Samuelson, "I Am a Big Lawyer Basher," *Newsweek*, April 27, 1992, 62.
14. Ibid.
15. Robert J. Samuelson, "A Nation of Experts," *Newsweek*, June 5, 1995, 49.
16. Harold J. Rothwax, *Guilty: The Collapse of Criminal Justice* (New York: Random House, 1996).
17. R. Albert Mohler, "Fellow Nonbelievers," *World*, August 8, 1998, 19.

18. Philip K Howard, *The Death of Common Sense: How Law is Suffocating America* (New York: Random House, 1994).
19. John Leo, "Our Hypersensitive Society".
20. Zuckerman, "Beware the Adversarial Culture".
21. Ibid., 94.
22. Robert Samuelson, "The Surplus: An Accident," *Newsweek*, February 16, 1998, 44.
23. Carl Wilson, *Our Dance*, 192-195.
24. Robert J. Samuelson, "Judgment Calls, the Peace Dividend," *Newsweek*, January 26, 1998, 49.
25. Allan Sloan, "The Budget: Books, Cooked D.C. Style," *Newsweek*, February 16, 1998, 42.
26. "About All those Bailouts Now: U.S. Taxpayers Help Support the IMF. Do They Get Their Money's Worth?," *U.S. News & World Report*, December 8, 1997, 31.
27. David Gergen, "Chasing Better Schools," *U.S. News and World Report*, December 8, 1997, 100.
28. Arnold Toynbee, *Civilization on Trial and The World and the West* (New York: Meridian Books, Inc., 1959), 32-33.
29. J. Tinbergen, "Global governance for the 21st century," *Human Development Report 1994* (New York: Published for the United Nations Development Program, Oxford University Press, 1994), 88.
30. Ibid., 99.
31. Zbigniew Brezinski, *Out of Control* (New York: Charles Scribner's Sons, 1993), x.
32. Aleksander Solzhenitsyn, "The Relentless Cult of Novelty and How It Wrecked the Century," *New York Times Book Review*, February 7, 1993, 17.
33. See Moynihan, *Pandaemonium*, xiv.
34. Joel Kotkin, *Tribe* (New York: Random House, 1993), 3-4.
35. Charles Colson, et al., Michael Scott Horton, ed., *Power Religion* (Chicago: The Moody Bible Institute, 1992). Their arguments will be more fully developed in my book, *The Call*, which is the sequel to this emphasis, *Man Is Not Enough*. There the divine answers for God's people are more fully presented.
36. Ralph Reed, "We Stand at a Crossroads," *Newsweek*, May 13, 1996, 28-29.
37. Toynbee, 9-10.

Chapter 20: Conclusions

1. Robert H. Bork, *Slouching Towards Gomorrah: Modern Liberalism and American Decline* (New York: Regan Books of HarperCollins Publishers, 1996).
2. cf. Davidson and Ress-Mogg, *The Sovereign Individual*.

3. A. W. Tozer, *The Waning Authority of Christ in the Churches* (Christian Publications, Inc., Harrisburg, PA). First published in *The Alliance Witness*, May 15, 1963.

4. I am saying that according to the Scriptures, the Spirit promotes repentance and conversion in a person in the following way: A person must first be shown by the Spirit that his values are wrong and destructive, and he should repent. Then the Spirit shows him that Christ offers complete forgiveness through the cross and resurrection, so that the sinner then *wants* to turn back to God. He then is willing to be shown that he has not been logically consistent and he is wrong. In other words, his presuppositions were a deception and led him to interpret the world wrongly. He is then open to being shown the correct interpretation of the data by truth of Scripture. In other words, axiological apologetics must come first (see Edward John Carnell's, *A Philosophy of the Christian Religion*), and seeing the consequences of his sin, he will then be open to want the good news of forgiveness through Christ's atoning death and his justification as seen in the resurrection. After trusting Christ and having his presuppositions changed, (see Presuppositional apologetics in Cornellus Van Til, *The Defense of the Faith*), the repentant sinner can then be shown his inconsistencies in his unbelief (see Carnell's, *An Introduction to Christian Apologetics*) and be led to properly interpret the data about the world so that his faith is strengthened (see my book, *Dark Shadows*, or Wilber Smith's, *Therefore Stand*, or Josh McDowell's, *Evidence that Demands a Verdict*, or *Other Evidence that Demands a Verdict*).

5. See my discussion of these in my book, *Our Dance*, 71-76.

6. Erwin W. Lutzer, *Hitler's Cross* (Chicago: Moody Press, 1995).

7. Write Carl W. Wilson, Andragathia, P.O. Box 642, Fayetteville, GA 30214-0642 about committed men joining the Andragathia order.

Index

Index

-W-

Warren, Earl, 129, 236, 241

Weisman, Michal, 107

Weitzman, Lenore, 334

Wellesley Report, 329

Wesley, Charles, 142

Williams, Jim, 247

Williams, Roger, 132

Wilson, Carl, 56, 57, 137, 138

Wolf, Naomi, 326, 341

women's rights movement, 138, 172, 173, 214, 216

women, role of, 57, 323, 357

Worldwide Discipleship Assoc., 247

-Y-

Y2K problem, 428, 429

youth, 28, 54, 60, 61, 65, 67, 77, 86-88, 141, 164, 208, 218, 229, 232, 235, 239, 244, 247, 249, 277, 286, 308, 310, 328, 337, 361, 362, 368-374, 390, 396, 404, 410, 414

Youth For Christ, 164, 247

-Z-

Zeus, 49-51, 54-60, 66, 67, 71, 76, 113, 120, 122, 430, 440

zigzag pattern, 5, 25, 31-33, 47, 111, 145, 175, 191, 221, 228, 408, 427, 428

Zimmerman, Carl, 59, 60

Zuckerman, Mortimer B., 404, 408, 409